The Russians in Germany

The Russians in Germany

A History of the Soviet Zone of Occupation, 1945–1949

Norman M. Naimark

The Belknap Press of
Harvard University Press

CAMBRIDGE, MASSACHUSETTS
LONDON, ENGLAND / 1995

Library of Congress Cataloging-in-Publication Data
Naimark, Norman M.
    The Russians in Germany : a history of the Soviet Zone of
occupation, 1945–1949 / Norman M. Naimark.
        p.   cm.
    Includes bibliographical references and index.
    ISBN 0-674-78405-7 (alk. paper)
    1. Germany (East)—Politics and government.
2. Communism and culture—Germany (East)   3. Germany
(East)—Economic policy. 4. Sozialistische Einheitspartei
Deutschlands.   5. Germany (East)—Social policy.   I. Title.
DD285.N35   1995
943.087′4—dc20   95-7725

For Lila, Sarah, and Anna

Contents

Illustrations

Acknowledgments

THIS PROJECT HAS BEEN WITH ME in one form or another for my entire adult life. In 1965, as a twenty-year-old Stanford junior, I crossed the Berlin wall and happened to meet a fascinating group of East German young people. The friends I made then are still part of my Berlin circle of friends today. Their stories, and the stories of their families and friends, became part of my own autobiography. Some endured harrowing escapes to reach the West; some were eventually arrested for attempting to flee the republic *(Republikflucht)* and were sent to prison; a few stayed behind and tried to make a life for themselves in the East. That the lives of these good people were penetrated by fear, persecution, and pressure to conform led me to ask how the communist East German state had come into being. This book is intended as an answer to that question. It could never have been completed without the interest and support of these former East Germans—neither "Ossies" nor "Wessies"—and without their ongoing willingness to share their histories with an American friend. In many ways, this book belongs to them: Evelyn and Günter Reiss, Norman Herbst, Renata and Gerd Schubring, Monika Wellenbrook and Dieter Flügge, Heidrun and Rudolf Steiner, Manuela and Lutz Wruck, Ulf König, and Ilse and Rudy Hahn.

I consider myself fortunate in having been associated with institutions of higher learning that have consistently supported my work. The research for this project was started more than a decade ago with the encouragement and financial help of Boston University and of the Russian Research Center at Harvard. With their interest and their comments, my colleagues and friends in Boston University's History Department—John Gagliardo, William Keylor, Fred Leventhal, Arnold Offner, Dietrich Orlow, and

Nancy Roelker—made an important contribution to this book, especially in its European dimensions. The director of the Russian Research Center, Adam Ulam, and a number of Center stalwarts—Walter Connor, William Fuller, Alexander Nekrich, David Powell, and Nina Tumarkin—taught me invaluable lessons about how the Soviet system worked.

The first research trips to Germany for this project were supported by the Alexander von Humboldt foundation, to which I owe a special debt of gratitude. In Germany, I benefited greatly from my association with a number of superb research institutions and their directors: the Osteuropa Institut of the Free University of Berlin (Hans Joachim Torke); Zentral-institut 6 of the Free University (Hartmut Zimmermann); and the Mannheim University Institute for the Study of GDR History and Politics (Hermann Weber and Dietrich Staritz). With the support of the Volkswagen Foundation, I was also fortunate to spend three months at the Bundesinstitut für ostwissenschaftliche Forschung in Cologne (Heinrich Vogel, director). Gerhard Simon and Fred Oldenburg of this institute were particularly helpful in testing my ideas about Soviet-German relations. Altogether, the scholars and staffs of the West German academic and research institutions—including the Bundesarchiv in Koblenz, the Archives of German Social Democracy in Bonn, and the State Archive of Berlin—could not have treated me more kindly nor given my work a more sympathetic hearing.

The National Council for Soviet and East European Research was instrumental in supporting a full year of research and writing in Washington, D.C., at the National Archives and in Palo Alto, California, at the Hoover Institution Archives. In the Military Section of the National Archives, I benefited from the extraordinary knowledge and experience of John Taylor. Visits to Washington archives were also supported by a Short-Term Grant from the Kennan Institute of the Woodrow Wilson Center. From the time I was a graduate student to the present day, Hoover Institution archivists and librarians have been of critical importance to my work. This project in particular owes a great deal to Agnes Peterson, Elena Danielson, and Anne van Camp. Permission has been granted by the Hoover Institution Archives, copyright © Stanford University, for the quotation of excerpts from the David Harris Collection and the Howard Palfrey Jones Collection.

Since my family and I moved permanently to Stanford University in 1988, I have benefited from the splendid intellectual and institutional resources of the Stanford community. Trips to the newly opened archives in East Berlin and in Moscow were funded in part by the Institute of International Studies, the Office of the Dean of Humanities and Sciences, and the Center for Russian and East European Studies, as well as by the International Research and Exchange Corporation (IREX). Through their good questions and consistent interest, colleagues and graduate students in the Stanford History Department too numerous to mention have contributed to this work. I remain deeply grateful to my teachers and now colleagues Terence Emmons and Wayne Vucinich for their ongoing enthusiasm for my research and their unflagging dedication to the historical enterprise.

I spent a blissful year at Stanford's Center for International Security and Arms Control, writing up the largest portion of this book. For intellectual companionship and support during that year, I am especially beholden to the center's codirector, David Holloway, and to its marvelous staff. The dedication of Irina Barnes and Rosemary Schnoor to the university's Center for Russian and East European Studies made it possible for me to take off the necessary chunks of time from my duties as director to finish this book. I would also like to thank Nan Bentley, Monica Wheeler, and the History Department staff for their good-natured assistance at critical junctures.

The SED archives changed hands several times between the summer of 1991, when I first was able to use them, and the summer of 1993, when I last worked there. Through it all, the archivists at Wilhelm Pieck Strasse 1 were consistently welcoming and helpful. For making possible the quick and efficient use of the Stasi archives, I would also like to thank Monika Tantscher and Walter Süss of the Abteilung Bildung und Forschung of the so-called Gauck Behörde, which oversees the documentation of the GDR's Ministry for State Security. In connection with my work with these papers, I gratefully acknowledge the assistance of the Historische Kommission of Berlin and Jürgen Schmädeke.

In my research in the Russian archives, I also repeatedly encountered able and helpful professionals. For the assistance of their staffs, I would like to thank the directors of the three archives where I did most of my research in Moscow: Sergei Mironenko of the State Archives of the Russian Federation (GARF); Kirill Anderson of the Russian Center for the Preservation and Study of Documents of Contemporary History (RTsKhIDNI); and Igor Lebedev of the Foreign Policy Archives of the Russian Federation (AVPRF). Under sometimes enormously difficult circumstances, the *sotrudniki* (archivists) who work in these collections guided me through complex research problems and demonstrated good spirits and great patience, even when I sometimes lost mine.

I consider myself especially fortunate in having friends and colleagues who gave willingly of their time to read and criticize the book manuscript. Recognizing their contributions in no way removes the deep debt of gratitude I feel for their unselfish work and good suggestions for revision. David Holloway read the chapter on science; Jan Foitzik the chapter on Tiul'panov; and John Connelly the chapter on culture. The most difficult chapter for me to come to peace with was that on rape and gender. I sought out criticism on that chapter from several scholars, who willingly engaged its problems and offered opinions. In particular, I would like to thank Laura Engelstein, Susan Gal, Robert Moeller, and my colleague Estelle Freedman for encouraging me to pursue this work and making thoughtful suggestions for revision.

I am deeply indebted to those colleagues and friends who braved the entire draft manuscript and engaged its arguments: Alexander Dallin, Gregory Freeze, David Pike, and James Sheehan. I have also benefited from the wisdom of many scholars who read shorter parts of the manuscript, commented on talks and papers, or answered inquiries through correspondence. In particular, I would like to mention the valuable remarks of Rolf Badstübner and Eve-Marie Badstübner-Peters, Bernd Bonwetsch, Elisabeth Domansky, Aleksei Filitov, Dietrich Geyer, Gert Glaessner, Atina Grossmann, Jeffrey Herf, Mark Kramer, Henry Krisch, Jochen Laufer, Wolfgang Leonhard, A. James McAdams, Lothar Mertens, Gábor Rittersporn, Ronald Suny, and Stefan Troebst. My thanks to Stanford graduate students Katherine Jolluck, Joshua Feinstein, Karin Hall, and Semion Lyandres for their comments and conversations related to the manuscript. I also had a series of fine research assistants, among them Milena Chilla-Markoff, Bruce Lidl, Jonathan Rosenwasser, and Jenny Schmitz.

James Hershberg and the Wilson Center's Cold War International History Project provided a number of lively forums in both Russia and Germany in which I could test my ideas on the Soviet Military Administration. Part of Chapter 7 on the East German police was first published as Working Paper no. 10 (1994) in the Cold War Project's series. Another part of Chapter 7, on the Soviet special camps in Germany, was published in *The Soviet Empire Reconsidered: Essays in Honor of Adam B. Ulam,* edited by Sanford R. Lieberman, et al. (Boulder, Colo.: Westview Press, 1994).

In short, I have been blessed with a group of colleagues, teachers, students, and friends—here and abroad—who take seriously the highest ideals of the community of scholars. But they know, as do I, that the sole responsibility for the content of any book is the writer's.

The final acknowledgment is the hardest, because it can in no way encapsulate the depth of my gratitude or the extent of my debt. My wife, Lila, and my daughters, Sarah and Anna, have remained constant friends through the long and sometimes painful process of researching a book twice, once before the archives in the East opened and once after. For their patience and good cheer through it all, both when going with me and when staying home, I dedicate this book to them with love.

The Russians in Germany

Abbreviations

ACC	Allied Control Council
CDU	Christian Democratic Union of Germany
CPSU(b)	Communist Party of the Soviet Union (bolshevik)
DEFA	German Film Studio, AG
DVV	German Education Administration
DVdI	German Interior Administration
DWK	German Economic Commission
FDGB	Free German Federation of Unions
FDJ	Free German Youth
GDR	German Democratic Republic
GlavPURKKA	Main Political Administration of the Worker-Peasant Red Army (GlavPU after 1946)
KPD	Communist Party of Germany
LDP	Liberal Democratic Party of Germany
MGB	Ministry of State Security
MVD	Ministry of Internal Affairs
NKFD	National Committee for Free Germany
NKGB	People's Commissariat of State Security
NKVD	People's Commissariat of Internal Affairs
OMGUS	Office of Military Government for Germany, United States
ONO	Education Department (of SVAG)
OSS	Office of Strategic Services
SAG	Soviet stock company
SED	Socialist Unity Party of Germany
SMERSH	Death to spies (Soviet Military Counterintelligence)
Sovnarkom	Council of People's Commissars
SBZ	Soviet zone of occupation
SPD	Social Democratic Party of Germany
SVAG	Soviet Military Administration in Germany
VdgB	Association for Mutual Farmers' Help
VEB	People's factory
VOKS	All-Union Society for Cultural Ties with Foreign Countries

Introduction

THE RED ARMY MARCHED into eastern Germany in the spring of 1945, fresh from a series of spectacular victories over the Nazi enemy. Though tattered and war weary, the Soviet officers and men were confident and brash, looking forward to a new era of peace in Europe and an end to isolation and economic want at home. How different the world appeared in the summer of 1994, a half century later, as the last contingents of Russian troops returned home from Germany to an atmosphere of uncertainty and upheaval, of privation, doubts, and pessimism. Behind them, the evacuated soldiers left run-down barracks and old target ranges, rusted vehicles and an environmental catastrophe that will take decades to repair. Of the Germans who watched as the Russians marched off, many from the former German Democratic Republic (GDR) felt twinges of nostalgia and regret. However painful, part of their own history had vanished forever; the Soviet occupation was over.

The Russians also left behind them in Germany a legacy of resentment and anger. The years of the occupation regime, 1945–1949, were harder on the Germans in the Eastern zone than they were on their brethren in the West. In all the zones of occupied Germany there was severe economic privation, and there was widespread bitterness as a result of Germany's total defeat and unconditional surrender. None of the Allies had much affection for the Germans, and the occupation authorities treated local populations with hostility and disdain. The terror, destruction, and mass murder wrought by the Wehrmacht and the SS during the war resulted in the Germans' having few sympathizers in Europe, and even fewer friends.

But the Soviet occupation was especially difficult for the Germans. They were forced to kowtow to the occupation administration of a nation they had been taught to believe was inferior in every way to their own. They had to endure in silence the brutal reality and humiliation of widespread rape and violence on the part of Soviet soldiers. They had to make believe, and in some cases did believe, that the "Bolshevik way" of doing things was good for Germany and for their compatriots. To make matters worse, for almost forty-five years after the beginning of the occupation, Germans in the East were not allowed to dwell on the difficulties of this period. In the cant of the German Democratic Republic, eastern Germany was not "occupied" but "liberated." Until the very end of the GDR, even the best histories that dealt with the Soviet zone said almost nothing of substance about the policies and actions of the Russian occupiers.[1] Forced amnesia is never healthy for a nation, and there will be many difficult moments in the "new Bundesländer" before this past can be grappled with openly and honestly.

The Russians today face problems that differ from those of the East Germans. At this juncture in the post-Soviet era, Russians are far too occupied with issues of survival to cross swords with the dangerous ghosts of history. Besides, historical issues of how Russians treated those outside of the Soviet Union, whether Poles, Germans, or Hungarians, are dwarfed by problematic relations with the non-Russian peoples of the former Soviet Union who reside within the Russian Federation—for instance, the native peoples of Siberia, the Chechens and Ingush of the Northern Caucasus, and the Volga Tatars. Not to mention the serious confrontations with peoples in what is today called the "near abroad"—the Balts, Ukrainians, Georgians, and Central Asians.

The hysterical quality that attends public discussion of relations between Russians and the nationalities of the former Soviet Union is personified by Vladimir Zhirinovsky, with his bellicose rhetoric. Whether or not he succeeds as a political force in the Russian future, his platform epitomizes the extreme vulnerability of Russians to distortions of their historical relations to other peoples. Like the Germans after World War II, the Russians still have to deal with issues that penetrate the very core of their twentieth-century existence: in particular, the Stalin dictatorship and the murder of millions of innocent Russians by their own government. As a result, despite new opportunities for research in the Russian archives, there has been very little improvement in the meager Soviet historiography of the USSR's role in postwar Germany.[2]

Until 1989 the West Germans also demonstrated a remarkable lack of interest in the history of either the Soviet zone of occupation or the German Democratic Republic. Some of the reasons for this were fairly straightforward: primary sources were lacking; memoirs were often unreliable; and, in the eyes of German scholars, the postwar period belonged to the realm of *Zeitgeschichte* (contemporary history), sociology, and political science, not of real history. Other reasons, however, were deeply rooted in the complex, even tortuous, relationship between politics, history, and memory in West Germany. During the cold war, studies of East Germany tended to see little else but the communist takeover and the Soviet exploitation of the region. But in the 1960s and 1970s, such studies were very much discouraged in the academy, where historians were deeply absorbed in trying to understand the Nazi regime and its integral links to structural elements of the German past. In the politically charged atmosphere of the German universities, any emphasis on the harsh realities of the Soviet occupation of the East indicated tacit approval of the anti-Bolshevik program of the Nazis. The new generation of German academics felt morally obliged to convince their elders in politics, government, and the academy of their responsibility for the crimes of the Nazis.[3] In doing so, however, they could not allow the older generation either the real or vicarious status of having been victims of the Soviet occupation. For years, Wolfgang Leonhard's gripping memoir, *Child of the Revolution,* stood in the place of a history of the Soviet occupation of Germany.[4] Gradually, however, a number of West German political scientists interested in the functional aspects of the GDR's social and political system began to explore its historical origins.[5] By the 1980s, West German political scientists felt comfortable enough with the system in the East to begin writing about its history in a comprehensive manner.[6] Taken as a whole, however, this historiography—and its Anglo-American counterpart—did not solve the problem of how to deal with the Russian occupation.[7] Instead, it analyzed the ways in which the German communists acquired and used state power in the East to maintain their political hegemony and transform the society. Only at the end of the 1980s did historians in the Federal Republic begin to work seriously on the history of the Soviet occupation, and the milestone that marked this change was the publication of the massive *SBZ Handbuch,* an encyclopedic compilation of articles about German state institutions and political parties under Soviet occupation.[8]

Since the fall of both the German Democratic Republic and the Soviet Union, many more historians have been working on various aspects of the Soviet presence in Germany. Most of the political constraints on talking honestly and openly about previously ignored issues are gone. For the first time, for example, German scholars have begun to think about the importance of rape in the postwar period: what it meant to German society in the East and, most important, how it affected German women.[9] Questions about the development of the Stasi (the Staatssicherheitsdienst, State Security Service), and the terrifying history of the "special camps," where tens of thousands of Germans died, have quickly been transformed from nonissues into subjects of intense historical and journalistic inquiry.[10] Paradoxically, it took the fall of the GDR for both scholars and politicians to appreciate fully the unique character of the society that had developed out of the marriage of German communist traditions and Soviet occupation politics. The Soviet Military Administration in Germany (SVAG) and the newly established Socialist Unity Party (SED) changed eastern Germany in ways that will not be quickly reversed. To understand how that change came about, a new generation of German historians is at long last turning its attention to the Soviet zone and the origins of the German Democratic Republic.[11] Even former GDR historians, now removed from positions of power and influence, are contributing to a lively debate about the nature of the communist system in the East.[12]

The peculiarities of the historiography of eastern Germany help to explain why this book constitutes the first comprehensive historical work about the Soviet occupation of Germany. They also help to explain how the book was written. In search of the origins of the German Democratic Republic, I looked to the Soviet occupation of the Eastern zone and the ways in which the Russians changed the lives of the Germans in that region. Neither the defeat of the Nazis in May 1945 nor the foundation of the GDR in October 1949—the rough chronological limits of this work—should be thought of as deep notches in the historical periodization of twentieth-century Germany. Still, the four-and-a-half-year history of the Soviet zone of occupation provides a convenient prism through which to examine the changes in East German society and culture in the postwar years.

In making this study, I drew primarily on archival sources from the period itself to survey the history of the Eastern zone from the point of view of the Soviet occupiers and the defeated Germans. I sought to understand how Russians and Germans viewed each other, interacted, and cooperated to build a new society in the East. Questions about Soviet occupation policy led me inevitably to broader issues of Soviet intentions in Germany and the role of Soviet German policy in the development of the cold war, the formation of the Soviet bloc, and the ultimate division of Germany. What did the Soviets hope to gain from their occupation of Germany? How long did they want to stay? Were they looking to divide Germany? What was their role, versus that of the German communists, in the development of institutions in the East? Between 1945 and 1949, the culture, economy, and society of the zone were transformed to such an extent that the foundation of a separate country, the German Democratic Republic, came quite naturally to the leaders in the Eastern zone. What role did the Soviets play in that transition? How much of it was determined by Soviet priorities and how much by the demands of the SED? To what extent did the German people themselves play a role in land reform, school reform, the expropriation of industry, and denazification?

As my research continued and the number of questions multiplied, it became clear to me that a chronological account of the history of the Soviet zone could not do justice to discrete groupings of interrelated questions. Instead I developed eight thematic chapters to represent those groupings. Each chapter covers the whole chronological period and seeks to recreate a set of issues from the perspective of the immediate postwar era, rather than from fifty years later. This explains why I have relied much more on archival records for bringing the postwar world to life than on interviews or memoirs, not to mention secondary sources.[13] History and memory inevitably influence each other, but in dealing with issues that have serious contemporary relevance for both German and Russian society, I have done my level best to let the past tell its own story.

During the first year of the occupation, from May 1945 to April 1946, the Soviets' primary tasks in Germany were defined by the immediate need to administer and rebuild the country. Above all, this meant establishing a functional system of military and civilian government. Chapter 1 of this book examines the ways in which the Soviets established this new administration and fostered the participation of Germans in government institutions. As a counterpoint to the discussion of administration, Chapter 2 examines the question of rape, one of the most serious, yet understudied, problems of the Soviet occupation. Russian-German relations in the zone were influenced as much, if not more, by the everyday interactions of Soviet soldiers and German civilians as they were by formal administrative arrangements. Examining the ways in which both the Soviet command and the German communists dealt with gender issues in the zone can help one understand the dynamics that undermined communist rule in the East. The subjects of discussion in Chapter 3 (reparations and the economic transformation of the zone) and Chapter 4 (the Soviet use of German science, technology, and uranium) suggest, as do the first two chapters, that Moscow's priorities in Germany were often determined by considerations that superceded Stalinist ideological dictums and the political aims of SVAG.

In April 1946 the Soviets stage-managed the union of the Communist Party of Germany (KPD) and the Social Democratic Party of Germany (SPD) into the new Socialist Unity Party of Germany. From that point until the quick escalation of cold war tensions in the spring and summer of 1947, politics occupied the center ring of Soviet concerns in the zone. Chapter 5 tells the story of the formation of the SED and examines the party's role in the creation of the socialist state in the East. Chapter 6 shifts the focus from the Germans to the Soviets, and explores the role of the information officer Colonel Sergei Tiul'panov in the development of communist politics in the zone. With sound documentation from the Soviet Central Committee archives, one can now trace policy arguments about Germany in Moscow and in Karlshorst, headquarters of the Soviet military government in Germany.[14]

From the summer of 1947 until the formation of the GDR in October 1949, the Soviets began to think of the Eastern zone as part and parcel of their empire in Eastern Europe. During this period, Soviet policy sought to consolidate communist rule in the East while trying to prevent the formation of the West German state. That Moscow succeeded in the former while failing in the latter owed a great deal to the development of the "internal security" apparatus and political repression in the zone, the subjects of analysis in Chapter 7. One cannot understand the "success" of the SED and its domination of the government and society without taking into account the activities of the Soviet security organs and their German helpmates. But as Chapter 8—on culture and education—demonstrates, Stalinism was too complex a phenomenon to be reduced to a matter of politics and the mailed fist alone. The ways in which Soviet models were used to alter traditional German educational and cultural norms were key elements of the transformation of society in the East.

These eight chapters do not cover all the groups of issues that one might explore. For instance, I did not examine the importance of the Berlin blockade to the development of the zone, because critical documents on the subject in Russian military archives were inaccessible. Separate studies could be (and have been) written on the "bourgeois" parties in the East—the CDU (Christian Democrats) and the LDP (Liberal Democrats)—as well as on such important topics as denazification in the East, and agrarian and school reform. Even on those questions that are dealt with here, there is a great deal more work to be done. The Soviet occupation of Germany is a complex and newly charted subject in the history of modern Europe. This book should be seen as an initial attempt to make sense of it.

The reader should also know at the beginning that this work is not intended as a comparative study of occupations, though I do make periodic references to Allied occupation policies in the Western zones. Good work has been done on the general period of the occupation, and there are established studies of each of the Western occupation zones of Germany taken individually.[15] In addition, it was not feasible to write a history of the Soviet occupation of Germany that analyzes as well the German occupation of the Soviet Union. There are some excellent studies of the German occupation; historians were long ago able to use the documents of the Nazi administration in Russia.[16] Nor is this book meant as a contribution to the pseudoscience of comparative victimology—who suffered the worst, at whose hands. It is important to be explicit about this subject, because of the understandable sensitivities of German historiography in the wake of the *Historikerstreit.* To suggest that Germans were victims of Soviet transgressions in no way exculpates the Nazis for their crimes in the Soviet Union or elsewhere. Anyone who has read in the historiography of the German occupation of Russia cannot fail to be overwhelmed by the brutality of the Nazi occupiers, the Wehrmacht included.[17] At the same time, the fact that German men and women in the Eastern zone suffered at the hands of their Russian occupiers should not be eliminated from historical analysis because of the justifiable contrition of many Germans for their country's misdeeds in the Soviet Union. Both Germans and Russians have to face squarely a painful and complex episode in the history of German-Soviet relations. In this book I seek no more than to make that common past accessible to all who are interested.

When I began this project more than a decade ago, I could not have dreamed that I would be able to use the archives of the Soviet Military Administration located in Moscow or the SED archives at the Institute of Marxism-Leninism in East Berlin. My intention was to use American and West German archives to write this book. Even during perestroika, the best one could hope for was access to Russian-zone military newspapers at the Lenin Library or restricted doctoral dissertations from the Humboldt University collection. Furtive talks with GDR historians about what they knew (but could not publish), and interviews off the record with veterans of the Soviet Military Administration produced what then seemed to be precious firsthand material.

The fall of the GDR in 1989 and the collapse of the Soviet Union in 1991 changed this situation dramatically. First, the SED archives opened, as did the archives of various ministries of the former East German government. Then Soviet government and party archives from the postwar period became available (the note on sources, at the back of the book, explains some of the problems concerning the use of Russian archives today). However, it is important to state at the outset of this book that, despite the extraordinarily good access I had to Soviet Central Committee and government archives relevant to the Soviet occupation of Germany, I was unable to use archival sources from a number of repositories, the most important being the KGB, Ministry of Defense, and "presidential" (or Kremlin) archives, which would have provided a more comprehensive view of the major institutions that influenced the development of the Soviet zone. It is also worth pointing out that archival evidence itself must be read as carefully and critically as secondary sources, memoirs, or newspapers. Soviet bureaucrats communicated messages in a language sometimes coded with multiple layers of meaning.

Despite these caveats, the materials I was able to use in the archives of the Soviet Military Administration in Germany, the Central Committee of the Communist Party of the Soviet Union, and the Foreign Ministry provided ample opportunity to look behind the ostensibly monolithic edifice of Soviet policy-making in Germany. When combined with the SED archives, the archives of Western intelligence organizations, and the SPD Ostbüro archives, the Soviet sources give us a unique perspective on events, personalities, and society in eastern Germany. This book tells the story of Soviet policy-making in the zone, but it also tries to reveal how the lives of German men and women were changed by the new circumstances of Russian occupation. The dynamic interaction of Soviet soldiers and German civilians in the Eastern zone changed the destiny of Germany for a very long time to come.

From Soviet to German Administration

SOVIET PLANNING FOR POSTWAR GERMANY during the "Great Fatherland War" of 1941–1945 depended on the fortunes of the battlefield and the vicissitudes of relations among the Allies. At the Teheran Conference in November 1943, Stalin advocated dividing up Germany and eliminating forever its ability to function as a single state in the center of Europe. At Yalta in February 1945, the Soviet leader favored the maintenance of German unity, while supporting its division into the Allied occupation zones worked out by the European Advisory Council in 1943 and 1944. Stalin confirmed at Potsdam in July 1945 that until a peace treaty was signed, Germany would be governed as a single economic unit by the Allied Control Authority, while the individual military governments would be given responsibility for administration in their zones.

But the evolution of Soviet thinking on Germany did not follow a clear trajectory. Instead, as Vojtech Mastny has pointed out, the Soviets' "tortuous handling of the German question" during the war (and after) frustrated Western statesmen and diplomats, leaving the impression—correct, as it turned out—that Stalin's views on Germany were subject to sudden and unpredictable shifts of emphasis.[1] Part of the problem was that the Soviet leadership pursued a number of parallel policies for a German settlement that were fundamentally inconsistent.[2] Another problem was that Soviet policy in Germany was, at its core, opportunistic, which left plenty of room for tactics and diplomacy. The boundaries of what was acceptable and unacceptable in Germany were less clear than in Eastern Europe, which fell into the Soviet security zone, at least as Moscow defined it, and in Western Europe, where the immediate interests of the United States and Great Britain were involved.[3] What would happen to Germany was the biggest question mark in wartime Europe. When the war came to an end on May 8, 1945, the Soviets had no ready answers.

At the outset of the occupation, the Soviets' hazy vision of a future German settlement was counterbalanced by a firm set of immediate priorities. Given the devastation of the USSR's industrial potential, Moscow was determined to secure payment of a reparations bill of $10 billion. Access to the Ruhr's coalfields was also considered vital for Soviet economic recovery. This was combined with a determination to acquire as much German scientific knowledge, weaponry, and military technology as possible (and to deny them to the West). While seizing military-industrial assets, Moscow also intended to deprive the Germans of the ability to make war again on the Soviet Union, which meant the demilitarization of the country, the decartelization of industry, and the denazification of German institutions—in education, the government, the economy, and the arts. The Soviet view of German militarism, shared in part by the Western Allies, was that the upper classes—the Junker landowners and the industrial magnates—were responsible for having fostered the Nazi war machine and should be deprived of their property and influence. Therefore, land reform and the expropriation of factories also ranked high on the Soviet list of priorities.

The political goals of Soviet policy in Germany were less critical at the outset of the occupation than the economic and geostrategic ones. In Moscow during the war, the Soviets had set up the National Committee for Free Germany (NKFD) and the Union of German Officers as instruments for use in case the Third Reich looked for a separate peace with Russia or Hitler was overthrown by the army. The Central Committee of the Communist Party of the Soviet Union, the CPSU(b), also fostered the development of the German communists who were in exile in the Soviet Union. Under the watchful eye of Georgi Dimitrov, the senior "foreign communist" in Moscow, experienced German communists like Walter Ulbricht, Wilhelm Pieck, and Anton Ackermann developed an approach to postwar German politics that called for a "bloc of militant democracy," uniting antifascist forces in Germany under the command of the occupation powers.[4] Political parties would not be allowed to be formed, and the occupation was envisioned as lasting for several decades. But once the occupation began, the Soviets abandoned this approach in favor of the creation of separate parties united in an "antifascist democratic bloc," a preemptive move that was intended to seize the political initiative in Germany.

To accomplish their political, economic, and military goals, the Soviets' central task in the first days and months of the occupation was to provide competent administration for their zone. For this purpose, Moscow relied primarily on the Soviet Military Administration in Germany (SVAG in Russian, SMAD in German), which was set up on June 6, 1945. The administration became the main instrument for applying Soviet policy to everyday German life. During the course of the occupation, SVAG officers increasingly turned over control of zonal institutions to their communist German helpmates. This chapter looks at the origins and development of SVAG and traces the transfer of its powers to the Germans. Few who witnessed the chaotic nature of the beginning of the process could have predicted its end, the creation of the German Democratic Republic in the Soviet zone.

THE COMMANDANTS

On April 16, 1945—at 5:00 A.M. Moscow time, soon to become Berlin time as well—the Red Army launched the last great offensive of World War II from its staging area on the Oder. More than 2.5 million soldiers took part in the attack. The Soviets used 42,000 guns and mortars, 6,200 tanks and armored personnel carriers, and 7,500 fighter planes.[5] The largest salient of the offensive was occupied by the First Belorussian Front, commanded by Marshal G. K. Zhukov. His troops drove straight to Berlin, entering the northeastern parts of the city by nightfall on April 21. The Second Belorussian Front, commanded by Colonel General V. I. Chuikov, headed north to Schwerin, Rostock, and the Baltic Sea. The First Ukrainian Front, commanded by Zhukov's archrival, Marshal I. S. Konev, seized Bautzen and Dresden and, on April 25, met up with advance units of the American First Army at Torgau on the Elbe, effectively splitting the German army into northern and southern sectors. By May 1, the Third Reich had been obliterated. Hitler and his entourage committed suicide in their Berlin bunker, and Soviet soldiers raised the Red Flag over the Reichstag. But the victory was enormously costly. The Soviets had suffered huge casualties: 300,000 men killed, wounded, or missing. Altogether in the Battle for Berlin, a half million people were killed, injured, or wounded.[6]

Between May 9, 1945, when the Germans signed the unconditional surrender in a formal ceremony at Karlshorst, and June 6, 1945, when the Council of People's Commissars signed the rescript authorizing the creation of the Soviet Military Administration in Germany, the Soviet military governed Germany through a chaotic and uncoordinated system, in which a multitude of newly created administrative units shared authority without a clear sense of hierarchy.[7] Army units issued orders, as did the political administrations of the fronts. The German-language newspapers, published by the fronts, sometimes contradicted the messages of the local army commanders. General responsibility for the political statements of the fronts fell to the Seventh Section of GlavPURKKA (Main Political Administration of the Worker-Peasant Red Army), which had directed anti-Nazi propaganda among Germans during the war. In the following section, I will examine the role of GlavPURKKA in the occupation. But it is worth pointing out here that political goals often got lost in the day-to-day work of administration. Especially in the first months after the peace, administration meant the work of the commandants, whose local headquarters—the *kommandanturas*—became the functional units of administrative authority in Soviet-occupied Germany. Especially before the establishment of the military government in June, but even after, the commandants created fiefdoms in which their orders constituted local law. Marshal Zhukov repeatedly stressed that the Soviets would impose a "strict regime" on occupied Germany.[8] What he did not say was that this regime would operate according to a variety of different rules.

In the original script for Konrad Wolf's 1958 film, *I Was Nineteen*, the famous East German filmmaker portrayed the story of his own experience as a German-born soldier in a Soviet unit at the end of the war. Because he was a German native and fluent in the language, the young man— "Gregor" in the film—was called upon to serve as commandant in a small town in occupied eastern Germany. His good sense and innate decency served him well in making decisions for the population. The SED's chief film censor, Anton Ackermann, who had also been an important KPD advisor in formulating Moscow's occupation policies, criticized Wolf's treatment of the way commandants were appointed, and insisted that Wolf and his screenwriter, Wolfgang Kohlhaase, revise the filmscript. "These [Soviet] officers," Ackermann protested, "were prepared for their jobs, in no way did their naming occur by happenstance." Ackermann went on to claim that he himself had been informed by Dimitrov in mid-April 1945 about the specific duties of the commandants.[9] While Ackermann's recollections of Dimitrov's remarks may have been accurate, Wolf's portrayal of the haphazard naming of the commandants certainly fits the chaotic character of the first weeks of the peace. No doubt Ackermann conveniently forgot one of his own reports from Dresden written in mid-May 1945, in which he complained about "self-appointed commandants" who seized grain, distributed property, and locked up and even executed alleged Nazis, without consulting higher military authorities, not to mention asking the advice of German antifascists.[10]

In most cases, the political sections of the fronts selected the commandants on the basis of political and military criteria, and gave them instructions to maintain order and set up local administrations as quickly as possible. The Seventh Section of the First Ukrainian Front, for example, gave no more guidance than to urge the newly named commandants to seek out well-known and popular local antifascists and opponents of Hitler and name them, regardless of party affiliation, as the mayors, *Landrats* (county commissioners), and police chiefs.[11] The First Ukrainian Front's newspaper, *Za chest' rodiny* (For the Honor of the Homeland), placed special emphasis on the commandant's responsibilities for protecting German property and factories for eventual Soviet use.[12]

At a meeting of 160 newly named commandants together with security and political officers of the Second Belorussian Front, held in Stettin at the relatively late date of May 18, 1945, instructions to the commandants were somewhat more concrete. Citing the Soviet State Defense Committee's directive of May 2, 1945, the convenor of the meeting, General Lavrenti Tsanava from the People's Commissariat for State Security (NKGB) stated that local German administrators should be named from antifascist circles, especially from those groups repressed by the Nazis, and that they should also be loyally disposed to the Soviet occupation. At the same time, the commandant was to assume complete responsibility for the activities of the Germans. Tsanava also announced that every kommandantura would have a deputy commandant for civilian administration, who would be assigned by the security services. The deputy commandant would command a People's Commissariat of Internal Affairs (NKVD) operations group *(opergruppa)* of twenty-four officers and men. The commandants were responsible for general policy; the deputies would deal with "terrorists, diversionaries, and other fascist elements."[13]

There were numerous cases in which even these vague guidelines for the organization and activity of the kommandaturas were completely ignored. American intelligence officers from the Office of Strategic Services (OSS) noted that, unlike the local branches of the American military government, the kommandanturas often had no specially trained staff and that Soviet officers were assigned to regions and jobs about which they had little or no knowledge. There was no evidence of handbooks, and

Russian maps tended to be cutouts of outdated German originals. The OSS concluded:

> Under such circumstances, much of the actual administration of German territory is left to the German civil administrators. Soviet military interference, in short, is apparently at a minimum, as long as the German administrator [abides by] his general Russian directives. On the other hand, it is obvious that the German officials are not always certain of their own authority and not infrequently find themselves overridden by local Russian commanding officers.[14]

Even after the establishment of the Soviet military government in July 1945, when local kommandanturas were authorized only to carry out SVAG directives and to ensure public order and troop security, commandants routinely interfered in the economic rebuilding of their districts. Part of the problem was that commandants sometimes also commanded local combat units stationed in their localities, and they saw to the soldiers' welfare at the expense of the civilian economy. In other cases, the same districts had a number of commandants whose functions were not sharply delineated from one another. In Dresden, for example, there were four kommandanturas, one for the city, one for the district, one for the headquarters of the provincial military administration, and one for the First Tank Regiment. Reporting functions were confused, and there were problems with those units in the city that carried out strictly military activities.[15]

The primary difficulty with the system was that the commandants' mandate to "observe and report" was interpreted as an injunction to make things work properly in local government, which led to almost constant interference, sometimes from the kommandantura itself, but also from its NKVD apparatus.[16] The kommandanturas generally consisted of five departments—Political, Propaganda, Military Affairs and Security (under the deputy commandant), Economics, and Supply. The security apparatus functioned as an autonomous unit, independently procuring German agents to work on a variety of assignments. The Propaganda Department specialists supplied the names of reliable informants, usually from the ranks of KPD members, and the operations groups then used them for specialized missions.

During the first summer of the occupation, the problems with the commandants were legion. According to a lengthy August 1945 report from a Soviet observer in the zone to Georgi Dimitrov of the Central Committee, there were frequent complaints that commandants in the provinces simply ignored Zhukov's orders about legalizing political parties. Some commandants relied exclusively on German communists for help, bypassing the other parties and nonparty antifascists, which directly contradicted SVAG policy. The commandant in Eisenach, for example, refused to allow the Social Democratic Party of Germany (SPD) to function or the trade unions to organize among the workers. Not infrequently the commandants also treated their regions as "their own patrimonial estate" *(votchina)*, not allowing the removal of any materials or goods, no matter where the orders had originated. There was also a lot of corruption and exploitation, the report continued, which was completely unacceptable, since the kommandantura was the basic unit of Soviet administration in Germany. Only in rare cases were these units organized professionally, and they were especially lacking in their understanding "of the most elementary of political questions."[17] Soviet complaints about the political ineptitude of the commandants was matched by German leftists' irritation with their activities. Repeatedly commandants were accused of "insufficient vigilance," because they relied on former Nazis and Nazi sympathizers to lead local governments and they paid insufficient attention to corrupt practices among German administrators. Many communists were upset that they were systematically excluded from power in the localities; sometimes, if they protested too vigorously, they were banned from meetings or even arrested. Some corrupt mayors, protected by the local commandants, behaved like "small kings," who were able to control the distribution of food and supplies, and therefore were hard to challenge.[18] Ulbricht was so upset with the situation in Friedenau (Berlin), where the commandant had reportedly allowed the local administration to be dominated by ex-Nazis, that he went over the head of the local kommandantura and used his ties to the NKVD leadership in the Soviet zone to "clean up" the local administration.[19]

Even after the replacement of most of the "front" commandants with military administrators in the late summer and fall of 1945, complaints continued to mount about corruption and favoritism in the kommandanturas. On the island of Rügen, the commandant was known to have protected SED members who had been repeatedly censored by central party institutions for corruption and bribery.[20] In Brandenburg, a number of commandants were taken to task by Major General V. M. Sharov for conniving with local farmers to keep threshing and delivery quotas down for the profit of both.[21] The SPD activist Erich Gniffke wrote to SPD chairman Otto Grotewohl in October 1945 that many commandants locked up honest and loyal SPD members in order to clear the decks of local government for KPD cronies. The worst case, Gniffke wrote, was in Apolda, where the commandant and local KPD leaders had such close economic ties that all SPD members were excluded from office.[22] Lieutenant Colonel "K," the commandant of Neustrelitz, was accused of falsifying delivery figures and selling grain on the private market. Nineteen Soviets and Germans were arrested in the case; nine were sentenced to jail terms. According to *Pravda* correspondent Iurii Korol'kov, who reported on the problems to the Central Committee, "there were a whole series of similar cases."[23]

As a result of the first German local elections in the fall of 1946, and the concomitant Soviet policy of placing more responsibility for local government on the German administration, the number of kommandanturas decreased from 507 in April 1946 to 325 in August 1946 and to 157 in June 1947.[24] The Central Committee also tried to professionalize the kommandanturas by getting the Cadres Department of SVAG more involved in the naming of local and regional Soviet officials. Despite these policies, however, complaints continued to pour into the Central Committee about corruption, favoritism, and bribery, as well as about the bullying and scolding of loyal SED members and city administrative personnel.[25] The problem was in part endemic to the situation of occupation. The Soviets were teachers of "democracy" (as were their American counterparts), and the commandants were urged by their superiors to take a greater role in helping to build German democratic institutions.[26] In assuming superior wisdom and experience in regard to democracy, the Soviet schoolmasters naturally offended their German pupils, and if they were in the least inclined to hostility and resentment toward the Germans, as many were, they were not afraid to exploit their positions or to use the stick.

GLAVPURKKA

The primary responsibility for the political education of the Soviet troops in the zone resided with the Main Political Administration of the Red Army (GlavPURKKA or, after 1946, GlavPU). During the war, this training was superficial at best. Soldiers were inducted into the party for bravery and good work; political criteria vanished altogether. Even after the war, political education for the Soviet officers and men of the occupation

army did not begin in a systematic fashion until after a series of demo-
bilizations that reduced the size of the force from somewhere near a million and a half at the end of the war to 700,000 in September 1946, 500,000
in February 1947, and 350,000 in July 1947. From that point to the end
of the GDR in 1989, the number of troops in eastern Germany remained
relatively constant, between 350,000 and 500,000.[27] But even with the stabilization of the size and number of units in the summer of 1947, problems with political education continued. Soviet military newspapers were
filled with glowing descriptions of discipline and cleanliness, hard work
and continuing political education. Photographs of sparkling, well-or-
dered "Red Corners," showing soldiers reading Soviet newspapers and
discussing the latest Sovnarkom decrees, were interspersed in these papers
with calls for heightened vigilance and loyalty to the homeland. Officers
and men were always neatly dressed, even when enjoying a day off in the
woods or at the lake. Soviet soldiers were pictured in full uniform, and
they radiated good health and a positive demeanor. But Soviet newspapers
depicted life as it was supposed to be, not as it was, and the excessively
rosy articles about the high level of political education and discipline
hinted that the problems were as severe as those indicated by émigré
newspapers and reports from deserters.[28]

Especially at the beginning of the occupation, GlavPURKKA was also
responsible for the political education of the Germans. Almost immediately after the Nazi attack on the Soviet Union, GlavPURKKA had set up
the Seventh Section to deal with propaganda and counterpropaganda
among the German troops at the front and in POW camps. German
communists were recruited for this work, as were Soviet political officers
who knew some German and had had advanced political training. Each
army front's Seventh Section ran a network of schools for captured
German soldiers. German communists were brought to the fronts to issue
defeatist leaflets and to man loudspeaker trucks that carried the same
message: German soldiers should mutiny, desert, surrender; the Nazi
cause was hopeless; why should innocent Germans die for the Hitler
clique? According to Soviet political officer Grigorii Patent, the work at
the front was much more successful than the antifascist schools in the
POW camps.[29] True or not, in the POW camps the movement for Free
Germany spread and even won over important officers, such as General
Paulus and General Seydlitz, who also made up the leadership of the
Union of German Officers that was allowed to function in the Soviet
camps. The Free Germany movement expressed a hodgepodge of popular

front–style ideas focused on the need for the Germans to overthrow Hitler in a democratic-socialist coalition. The National Committee on Free Germany, which included communists Anton Ackermann, Willi Bredel, and others, developed a series of radio broadcasts and a newspaper for the purpose of spreading their ideas back to Germany itself. As Ackermann recalled, almost as soon as Hitler attacked the Soviet Union, he began to work intensively with the Seventh Section, writing "texts of leaflets, appeals, exhortations, front newspaper [articles], etc." Ackermann and the National Committee, working in close cooperation with the Seventh Section, hoped that these broadcasts and newspapers would provide a rallying point for Germans who wanted to overthrow Hitler, or at least aid the Soviet advance by promoting domestic resistance.[30]

Until late 1944, the work of the Seventh Section focused exclusively on spreading the message of Free Germany to Wehrmacht soldiers at the front and in POW camps. Once the Soviets actually occupied German territory, Central Committee experts Dimitrov and A. S. Paniushkin recommended to V. M. Molotov and G. M. Malenkov that the "organization and content" of Seventh Section activity be changed to accommodate the new circumstances. Free Germany was no longer an important factor; there had been little German resistance to Nazism and no uprising. Instead Germany was forced to accept unconditional surrender and four-power occupation. GlavPURKKA should take over "the entire leadership of propaganda," Dimitrov and Paniushkin wrote, and the National Committee should be kept separate from these efforts. German communists and antifascists were needed to help publish newspapers by writing articles and editorials. The newspapers should have some kind of "national" title. (In the end *Deutsche Volkszeitung* [German People's Newspaper] and *Neues Deutschland* [New Germany] were used.) But the program of the National Committee was to be deemphasized.[31]

In the first days of the occupation, the Seventh Section conducted oral and written propaganda efforts to convince the Germans to submit to the occupation regime and to remind them that the Soviets had honorable intentions regarding the unity and integrity of Germany. The most difficult part of the Seventh Section's task, one that was abandoned within a year of the occupation, was to make the Germans understand that the death and destruction that surrounded them was the product of their own failings. The Germans tended to blame everyone but themselves for the catastrophe that had engulfed them. Loudspeaker trucks were used for the Seventh Section's propaganda, especially before the first radio broadcasts in mid-May of 1945. The Seventh Section also held a series of open meetings; at the one in Güstrow, thousands of Germans showed up. But despite the high level of interest in what the Russians had to say, the meetings were often punctuated by unpleasant confrontations with German young people. As Major General M. I. Burtsev, Seventh Section chief, reported, "At the meetings they [the German youth] conducted themselves hostilely and in many cases asked provocational questions."[32]

The Seventh Section also put out political "Information Sheets," which were posted on kiosks and drew the attention of sometimes hundreds of curious Germans.[33] For the first five days of the occupation of Berlin, the Soviets instituted a ban on all printing, but after the ban was lifted, on May 3, a newspaper called *Nachrichten für die deutsche Bevölkerung* (News for the German People) appeared for eighteen issues and in larger and larger editions. Then on May 15 a new German-language newspaper appeared, the *Tägliche Rundschau* (Daily View), which was initially produced by the First Belorussian Front's GlavPURKKA and later became SVAG's major newspaper for the civilian population. On May 21, 1945, the Soviet kommandantura in Berlin put out its own newspaper, the *Berliner Zeitung* (Berlin Newspaper), which one month later was turned over to the city government as its own publication.[34]

With all this journalistic activity, GlavPURKKA had to recruit additional cadres to supervise the content of the papers. In May Burtsev ordered 30 additional propaganda officers to Germany, and in June 40 more. As part of the Seventh Section operation, Burtsev also brought back to Germany from the Soviet Union 70 additional German communists, as well as 300 former POWs who had attended antifascist schools. A group of 10 experienced Soviet front school instructors in the Seventh Section were also transfered to the Soviet zone for agitational work among the German population.[35] From this group came many of the future Soviet leaders of German political life in the zone, including S. I. Tiul'panov and G. I. Patent. The tasks of the Seventh Section operatives were not spelled out in detail, but the outline was clear: to set up local governments, to find acceptable city magistrates and village elders, to staff police and court administrations, and to organize antifascists for rebuilding local institutions and economic life. GlavPURKKA's Seventh Section officers were sometimes made deputy commandants for political affairs, and as such they were supposed to conduct discussions with the Germans, both to get them to understand their responsibility for the war and the chaos it had engendered and to engage them in the work of reconstruction. The mayors of towns did not necessarily have to be communists, Burtsev wrote, but it was still an important task of the Seventh Section to get the communists involved in local government, albeit under the "harsh rules of a strict occupation regime."[36]

Although GlavPURKKA was officially a part of the People's Commissariat (later Ministry) of the Army, it operated in good measure as a section of the Central Committee of the Communist Party of the Soviet Union. Indeed the main reporting function of the Seventh Section appeared to be to the various iterations of the International Department of the Central Committee, headed by Dimitrov and Paniushkin, and later by Andrei Zhdanov and Mikhail Suslov.[37] But after the first summer of the occupation and the maturation of the Soviet military government, especially its Propaganda Department, the role of GlavPURKKA and the Seventh Section declined noticeably. An idea was floated in Soviet-zone political circles that the Office of the Political Advisor to the Commander-in-Chief, headed eventually by V. S. Semenov, incorporate all the Seventh Section operatives into its apparat. But Major General F. E. Bokov, senior member of the Military Council of SVAG and therefore formally responsible for political work in Germany, was against this move.[38] Instead Bokov looked to expand the Propaganda and Censorship Department (later, Administration) as the center for Soviet political efforts among the Germans.[39] The Central Committee agreed, and the Propaganda and Censorship Department took control of newspapers and publishing, absorbing with those functions the majority of Seventh Section propagandists in the zone. As the senior Red Army political officers in the zone, Generals M. I. Burtsev and I. V. Shikin (chief of GlavPURKKA) continued to report to their superiors on the Central Committee about political conditions in the zone. But by the fall of 1947, the Seventh Section ceased to exist altogether, and its functions in the zone were completely absorbed by the newly named Information Administration (formerly Propaganda).

SVAG

On June 6, 1945, the Council of People's Commissars of the Soviet Union announced the creation of the Soviet Military Administration of Germany, and named Marshal Zhukov as commander-in-chief and Colonel General V. D. Sokolovskii and Colonel General I. A. Serov as his deputies.[40] Three days later, on June 9, Marshal Zhukov announced the goals of the new organization: (1) to supervise the unconditional surrender of Germany, (2) to administer the Soviet zone of Germany, and (3) to see to the implementation of the most important Allied decisions on military, political, and economic matters.[41] Then, on June 10, the three fronts of the Red Army in Germany (the First and Second Belorussian and the First Ukrainian) were reorganized into the Group of Soviet Occupation Forces in Germany, which was also commanded by Zhukov. Sokolovskii took over day-to-day charge of the Group of Forces, which was headquartered in Potsdam; Serov was given "leadership and control" of the administration of Germans in the zone, which had its headquarters in Karlshorst, a suburb of Berlin.[42] Some 8,000 Soviet troops were stationed at the Potsdam headquarters of the Group of Forces; the rest of the Red Army's troops, some 273,000 altogether, were strategically distributed around the zone. In addition 29,000 Soviet air force and 2,700 Soviet naval troops were stationed in eastern Germany. The Soviet Military Administration itself commanded 20,000 troops attached to the military government, and it had access to the 20,000 security (Ministry of Internal Affairs [MVD] and Ministry for State Security [MGB]) troops stationed in the zone.[43] American intelligence sources suggested that the Red Army (the Group of Forces) was separated from the Soviet administration to protect SVAG from the terrible reputation of the army.[44] But it is more likely that the separation was carried out for security purposes—that is, to keep military government specialists out of military planning issues and to keep military planners isolated from issues of administering Germany.

At the outset SVAG had twenty different departments, each of which was staffed by the cognizant ministry or organization in Moscow. Heads of departments were nominated by the ministries and organizations and confirmed by the Council of People's Commissars. According to Western accounts, which mesh well with evidence from Russian archives, the Soviets organized the divisions of their military government only after the November 10, 1944, creation of the Allied Control mechanism for Germany by the European Advisory Commission. Later the Soviets expressed some concern that the way they organized the military government (and therefore German administrations) had been unduly influenced by the Western Allies.[45] Western sources put it more bluntly: Soviet representatives organized the divisions of their military government according to a plan worked out by the U.S. Group of the Control Commission in London and later developed by the U.S. Military Government in Berlin. In other words, the twelve directorates of the Allied Control Council served as the basic divisions in the Soviet military government.[46]

As people's commissar of the army, Marshal N. A. Bulganin was responsible for building up the staff organization of SVAG. A. I. Mikoyan took charge of the economics departments, and the State Defense Committee's chairman, T. Golikov, staffed the special reparations sections.[47] Most of the line officers of SVAG were recruited from officers already stationed in military units in Germany. The chief of the staff of SVAG, Major General M. I. Dratvin, worked with the Cadres Department to try to find officers who would make good military government officials. In addition, cadres for SVAG's economics departments were recruited from the State Defense Committee's Special Committee on Germany, which in the first months of the occupation assessed and helped remove German industrial "objects" as reparations.[48]

Initially the most important political questions relating to the occupation were resolved by A. A. Sobolev, a representative of the Commissariat of Foreign Affairs and Semenov's predecessor as political advisor to the commander-in-chief. Sobolev was made responsible for both the Political Section of SVAG and the Propaganda and Censorship Section, whose chiefs reported directly to him. The head of the Education Department also reported to him.[49] Censorship proved to be a particularly difficult problem for the Soviet military government. Every kommandantura had its own censorship office, which operated according to its own guidelines. Zhukov finally centralized the system in mid-August 1945, placing all censorship in the zone, including that of the radio, film, and newspapers, under the Office of the Political Advisor. But the attention of Sobolev, Semenov, and their deputies was not on zonal affairs at all; it was on negotiations in the Allied Control Council and drawing up Soviet positions for the council's agenda. The result was that, between August and the beginning of October 1945, political matters internal to the Soviet zone of occupation were increasingly handled by the Propaganda Department of SVAG, commanded by Colonel S. I. Tiul'panov. The Propaganda Department also took charge of a variety of departments that dealt with political concerns, education and censorship among them.[50] Tiul'panov reported directly to the Central Committee of the party through GlavPURKKA and through General Bokov, a member of the Military Council of SVAG (and later through Generals V. E. Makarov and A. G. Russkikh).

It quickly became apparent that the Economics Department of SVAG was severely understaffed and not up to the multiple tasks associated with both rebuilding German industry and removing it. As a result, Zhukov wrote to Mikoyan, Molotov, and Malenkov in November 1945 to request a complete reorganization of the Economics Department. The Germans were not capable of organizing their own reindustrialization, Zhukov claimed. Therefore he requested that General Koval be named as a deputy commander-in-chief and given control of an expanded, unified Economics Administration that would include 786 specialists.[51] Although Koval's rank and status within SVAG helped in establishing a hierarchy among Soviet economic organizations in the zone, he was far from being able to control the many reparations and military technology teams that periodically removed factories, machines, and goods from the eastern zone without even informing SVAG. General I. S. Kolesnichenko from Thüringen was so frustrated by the number of Soviet officials going in and out of factories, laboratories, and plants that he issued a special order in April 1946 "categorically" forbidding entrance to anyone not having his express permission. In addition, no machinery could be removed without his signature on the order.[52] But neither he nor Koval could effectively control the activities of the various special economic organizations, which sometimes had their own military detachments assigned to them by Moscow to enforce their orders.

By the spring of 1946, SVAG consisted of a variety of organs, including the kommandanturas for civilian government and the five provincial Soviet Military Administrations—Brandenburg, the state of Saxony, the province of Saxony (Saxony-Anhalt), Thüringen, and Mecklenburg-Vorpommern (after March 1946, known simply as Mecklenburg). The central SVAG organization, headquartered in Karlshorst, included the apparatus of the political advisor (Semenov), the staff, the Political Administration (responsible for politics in SVAG itself), the Propaganda Administration (responsible for German politics), and twelve other administrations. In September 1945, some 5,000 men and women served in the central apparatus of SVAG, 500 of whom were civilians.[53] According to data from the Central Committee archives, in November and December 1946 there were 49,887 members of the Soviet Military Administration in Germany: 21 generals, 14,552 officers, 7,324 civilians, 27,990 soldiers and sergeants. Although the organizational table *(shtat)* of SVAG called for 65,543 personnel, the Council of Ministers in August 1946 withdrew the remaining vacant positions. By August 1948 the number of SVAG members had been reduced to 31,500, far less than the shtat, which showed 41,378 positions. Of these, 2,619 were supposed to work in the economy and on reparations questions, 503 in politics in the Soviet administration and among Germans, 392 on relations with the Allies, and 1,038 on military questions, command staff, and in the kommandanturas.[54]

During the spring of 1946, SVAG experienced a major shake-up when Stalin removed Marshal Zhukov as commander-in-chief, demoted him to the position of commander of the Odessa Military District, and replaced him with Sokolovskii. While Sokolovskii's appointment ensured continuity in SVAG, the removal of Zhukov was correctly interpreted as part of a government-wide initiative to reduce the prestige and political influence of the Red Army and to build that of the Communist Party.[55] The Main Political Administration of the army became less central to the running of Soviet affairs in Germany, while SVAG's party organization became more important. According to Central Committee data, in September 1948 the SVAG apparatus included some 3,011 communists (out of 8,618 officers and men) organized into basic party cells, all of which were subordinated to the Political Administration of SVAG. Eighty-two percent of the civilian specialists were in the party, a much greater percentage than among military officers, 69 percent of whom were party members or candidate members.[56] According to documents from the spring of 1949, the party organization in SVAG conducted elections to a new presidium, which indicated its growing importance and prestige within the military administration. Individual officers were listed in sequence according to their importance in the party. Sokolovskii was listed first, followed by Dratvin, Russkikh, Russov, Semenov, Koval, and Koval'chuk. Eleventh in importance was the newly promoted Major General Tiul'panov, head of the Information (formerly Propaganda) Administration and the most direct link to the Germans.[57]

INSTITUTIONAL PROBLEMS

Despite increasing party control over SVAG activities, the problems of rivalries within the administration and overlapping competencies were legion. A major source of the rivalries derived from the confusing power structure of the USSR as a whole in the postwar period. Stalinism was hardly a perfectly functioning system of dictatorial hierarchy controlling all aspects of state and society. Stalin was a cruel and omnipotent dictator, to be sure, but one who spoke only rarely in this period, and in deliberately opaque terms, providing ambiguous policy directives that could be interpreted in a variety of ways. Certainly he intervened directly and forcefully when the spirit moved him, and no important decision could be made without his approval. But it was hard to predict when he would intervene and on what issues.

Therefore a great deal of latitude was given to Stalin's administrators, especially those located far from Moscow, who were in the unenviable position of trying to anticipate the Kremlin's wishes. There was little incentive to take any initiative, and there were no clear lines of responsibility. At the same time, Stalin and the system he created perfected local mechanisms for destroying social networks, class and professional associations, labor solidarity, and village community.[58]

If one compares, for example, the American and Soviet military administrations in Germany, it is apparent that General Lucius Clay, head of the U.S. Military Government in Germany (OMGUS), had much more power than did Marshal Zhukov or his replacement, General Sokolovskii. To be sure, Clay spent a great deal of time and energy protecting his freedom to make decisions against the encroachment of a variety of bureaucracies and politicians in Washington. But the Soviet administration had many more checks and balances and had much more difficulty carrying out unified decision making than did Clay. First of all, the interests of the Soviet party and state structures in SVAG were not easy to harmonize. Ultimately SVAG was responsible to the Sovnarkom (Council of People's Commissars, later the Council of Ministers). But the periodic battles over turf and German politics waged between the Office of the Political Advisor (Semenov) and the Propaganda (Information) Administration under Tiul'panov often reflected differences between the Sovnarkom and the Central Committee of the Communist Party on how to run affairs in Germany. Even within the state structure, GlavPURKKA, formally responsible to the People's Commissariat of the Army, articulated a different set of interests than did the Ministry of Foreign Affairs, represented in the zone by the Office of the Political Advisor. To make matters more complicated, the various Soviet ministries responsible for the Soviet forces in Germany underwent a bewildering series of reorganizations after the war.[59]

Under Lavrenti Beria, the People's Commissariat of Internal Affairs (NKVD/MVD) established offices in the Soviet zone that operated independently of the military government, as did, for the most part, the offices of Soviet counterintelligence, SMERSH (an acronym for "Death to spies!"). At least the NKVD operations groups tended to work in tandem with the commandants; in the case of SMERSH, there were few lines of responsibility through the SVAG command, and SMERSH's operatives interfered repeatedly in the business of military government. Without terribly much to do in the way of uncovering fascist plots and sabotage, especially after the summer of 1945, SMERSH increasingly turned its attention to investigating the credentials of SVAG's Soviet civilian employees in Germany—secretaries, translators, and office personnel.[60]

Even more disruptive to the smooth functioning of military government were the reparations teams that operated on the orders of the Interministerial Committee on Reparations, which supervised an operation in the Soviet zone of over 70,000 officials, almost all in uniform and with officer's rank. The departments and administrations of SVAG that dealt with economic questions could do little but defer to the reparations officials' wishes. The hierarchy of economic decision making was particularly complicated during the first year of the occupation, when the Commissariat of Foreign Trade, under Mikoyan, was given unlimited access to German factories, equipment, and products. There were a number of cases in which Marshal Zhukov and General Sokolovsky assured Wilhelm Pieck, head of the German communists, that particular factories would not be subject to dismantling—only to have to renege on their promises when it became clear that the decision was not under the jurisdiction of the commander-in-chief.[61] Wolfgang Leonhard told a story of driving through the Soviet sector of Berlin with an officer of the Main Political Administration. In a residential neighborhood, the officer waved his hands and said, "That's where the enemy lives!" "Who—the Nazis?" asked Leonhard. "No, worse still," the officer replied, "our own reparations gang."[62]

Further problems emerged as a result of the independent initiatives of the commanders of each of the five provincial Soviet military districts, as well as those of the largest city kommandaturas. The Berlin, Dresden, Halle, and Leipzig kommandanturas reported directly to the Kommandantura Department of SVAG rather than to their district or provincial headquarters, and this caused a great deal of confusion, not to mention rivalry.[63] Some provincial commanders, like Thüringen's General Kolesnichenko, did not bother to wait for orders from Karlshorst and inserted their views into local political and economic affairs. Kolesnichenko was well known in the zone as a despot who bullied local "bourgeois" politicians, intimidated opponents of the SED, and ordered the provincial assembly to pass certain laws. On the other hand, Lieutenant General D. G. Dubrovskii of the state of Saxony restrained the communists, encouraged democratic politicians, and protected local manufacturing and administrative institutions from overzealous socialist activists. Meanwhile, each of the province's commanders tended to protect the interests of his own fiefdom both against intrusions from Berlin and in competition with the other provinces. The state of Saxony, for example, reneged on promises of delivering textile goods to Thüringen, because the latter government had not delivered promised agricultural products.

Soviet units in remote localities and small towns had even more autonomy in making decisions and, as a result, engaged in a far greater variety of activities than has often been assumed. In many cases, lines of subordination and reporting were unclear, and coordination among the institutions of military government was weak. In Frankfurt-Oder, for example, the city commandant refused to follow the instructions of the Eberswalde military district, in which Frankfurt was located.[64] There were also serious problems of coordination between SVAG and the Group of Soviet Forces, and this had a negative effect on attempts to contain the growth of crime among Soviet soldiers in the zone. Military unit commanders shielded their soldiers from SVAG organs of justice, a situation that led to hostility and repeated appeals to the commander-in-chief. Finally General Sokolovskii had to issue a set of quite specific orders to enforce cooperation between the military prosecutor's office, the military police, and staff headquarters in Karlshorst.[65]

Within SVAG itself, frequent attempts to coordinate overlapping efforts of different administrations and departments were often a response to German complaints about divergent policy directives. The German labor unions, for example, received one set of instructions from the Manpower Department, another from the Office of the Political Advisor, and a third from the Propaganda Administration.[66] Perhaps even more dysfunctional than overlapping functions were the multiple demands placed on SVAG departments. A good example of the confusion of roles, functions, and demands was seen in the Education Department (ONO), which was overwhelmed by its tasks from the very beginning of the occupation. Its overstrained cadres were badgered by the commander-in-chief to open schools in the fall of 1945, and then harshly criticized for allowing so many former Nazi Party members to teach and so many fascist textbooks to be used.[67] Although ONO was put in charge of curricula for schools throughout the zone, those Soviet officials who could follow through on and enforce the plans, the school inspectors, were placed initially under the local commandants. Much of the problem was that the cognizant organization in Moscow, the Ministry of Education, was utterly uninterested in ONO's work. Consequently the Ministry of Armed Forces made decisions on behalf of education in the zone that confused normal Soviet procedures.[68] The Education Department had the additional problem of being assigned responsibility for setting up Russian schools for the children of the officers and specialists in SVAG and the Group of Forces. After the department had managed to set up the Russian schools, including two boarding schools and a number of kindergartens, the Council of Ministers placed responsibility for the schools on the Political Administration of the Group of Forces, forcing yet another shake-up in the personnel and structure of ONO.[69]

Administratively, ONO had no permanent home. During the first summer and early fall of the occupation, it was placed under the Office of the Political Advisor (Sobolev) and then under the deputy commander-in-chief for civilian affairs (Serov). The department also had a very uncertain relationship with the Propaganda (Information) Administration under Colonel Tiul'panov. Especially because printing and publishing sections were placed under Tiul'panov's control, ONO felt compelled, in the words of its unofficial history, "sometimes to subordinate our activities and plans to the plans of the Information Administration."[70] The school inspectors were also moved from the shtat of the commandants' staffs to that of the Information Administration, even though ONO formally set the policies that they were supposed to enforce.[71]

With almost no support or direction from its cognizant ministry in Moscow, ONO was forced to turn to the Central Committee of the CPSU(b) for its instructions. But the Central Committee was far too occupied with other matters, mostly of the domestic politics sort, to take part in creating policy guidelines for education in the zone. As a result, the party organization within ONO became increasingly important, to the point that party meetings "discussed almost all basic measures" undertaken by the department.[72] Still, without a powerful protector in Moscow, ONO suffered particularly when it came to filling vacant positions, a problem that was endemic to SVAG as a whole. The Education Department had to employ school inspectors who had no experience in the education field at all; even the department's best pedagogues spoke primitive German at best, and therefore had to operate with translators. Department administrators felt fortunate to be able to pick up new personnel from recently demobilized officers who wanted to stay in Germany. But the talent pool was not the best, and repeated criticisms of the qualifications of ONO's cadres from the party organization were well deserved.[73] In this regard, however, ONO was not unique. The Agriculture and Forestry Department of SVAG was filled with "instructors" who had no experience other than having lived on collective farms, and sometimes they had no farm experience at all. Even those Soviets with the appropriate background—doctors from the Health Department and engineers from the administrations dealing with industry—were embarrassed by the injunction to pass on "the most progressive science in the world" to German doctors and engineers, who had far better training and more knowledge.[74]

CADRES

One of SVAG's biggest problems was maintaining a staff of qualified and politically reliable specialists. The military government was rent by corruption and, in the opinion of the party, morally degenerate behavior. Large numbers of officers had to be sent home for a variety of offenses, and it became increasingly difficult to replace them. This was especially the case after the summer of 1947, when Soviet officers in the zone were isolated from the German population and suspicions grew at home about anyone who had spent time abroad. The Soviet Military Administration's worries about personnel dominated much of its internal activities. Because of the great secrecy surrounding it, the role of the Central Committee's Cadres Department has been much underestimated in the historiography of Soviet government and politics; this is especially true for treatments of the Soviet military government and the development of German institutions in the zone. There can be little question that the growing inclination on the part of the Soviet authorities to turn over as much government as possible to the Germans derived in good measure from SVAG's problems with cadres.

During the first six months of the occupation, the Cadres Department of the Central Committee—the chief personnel office of the Soviet government—had little opportunity to check out the officers chosen for duty in one branch or another of SVAG. As of January 1, 1946, only 1,750 out of 12,992 men and women who had been sent to work in SVAG from the Soviet Union passed through the Cadres Department process. Most of the SVAG staff was sent directly by the Ministry of Armed Forces to Germany or was selected from units already stationed there. During the first ten months of 1946, the Cadres Department sent an additional 1,500 specialists to the zone, of whom some 100 were withdrawn because they were compromised in one way or another. For example, General "G" from the Brandenburg SVA was accused of being "degenerate in his life." With a wife and two children at home in the Soviet Union, he lived with a repatriated Soviet woman who was accused of having taken German citizenship when the Nazis occupied her hometown. A Chemnitz general was also removed because his wife was alleged to have collaborated with the Nazis in Bobruisk. General "I" from Berlin was accused of leading an undisciplined life, of excessive drinking, and of being "degenerate" in his personal relations.[75] Eventually some of the leading figures of the military government in Germany were sent home accused of various forms of corruption and thievery. Only in the rarest cases, like that of General Kolesnichenko from Thüringen, were "political mistakes" cited as the cause for removal.[76]

Mounting evidence of corruption and indiscipline among high-ranking SVAG officers led to a Central Committee investigation and the resolution of April 25, 1947, "On the Insufficiencies of Work with Cadres in SVAG." According to the resolution, the Cadres Department of SVAG was ordered to take a more direct role in the review of the work of the military administration. Younger and more competent people were to be promoted, while lazy and corrupt officials, who had no business working abroad, were to be removed.[77] Part of the problem faced by the Cadres Department was that SVAG was already desperately short of personnel. During the year 1946, 5,000 SVAG workers had to be sent home, and many of them had not been replaced.[78] Only 31,411 places out of a designated shtat of 41,379 had been filled, and the ministries were even slower in supplying replacements, a process that was tied up further by the requirement—not always met—that new designates be registered with the Council of Ministers' Bureau on Soviets Living Abroad. By mid-1947, most ministries refused to participate at all in the naming of new cadres for SVAG. As a result the Central Committee was forced to turn to the Moscow and Leningrad city and regional party organizations to recruit new officials.[79] The manpower crisis reached severe proportions in 1947 and the first quarter of 1948. Not counting normal transfers, 6,823 SVAG workers were released from their posts and sent back to the Soviet Union, of whom 3,513 were considered politically or morally compromised. Only 844 arrived in Germany from the Soviet Union to take their place—which, the Central Committee Cadres Department noted, was insufficient to make up for the huge loss of staff.[80] The problem was partly due to a freeze on positions imposed by the Council of Ministers, but the primary shortcoming was that the department was unable to find new cadres to appoint.[81]

The shortage of cadres in the zone, it should be clear, was not caused simply by bureaucratic politics, but rather by the idiosyncracies of the Soviet totalitarian system. From mid-1947 on, a Soviet officer caught living with a German woman was immediately sent back to the Soviet Union. Talking in off-hours with other Allied officers could result in severe punishment. Many SVAG officers of Jewish origin were sent home because the Cadres Department thought that Soviet interests were hurt by so many Jewish officers serving in Germany.[82] Other officers fell victim to excessively rigid standards of appropriate political behavior. There were also cases in which personal rivalries and bureaucratic infighting led to political denunciations that found their way into the Cadres Department's files. Even Vladimir Semenov, political advisor to the commander-in-chief, was not free of the suspicion of the Cadres Department. In August 1948, Deputy Foreign Minister Andrei Vyshinskii suggested that Semenov be promoted to the rank of "ambassador extraordinary and plenipotentiary." But the Central Committee Cadres Department recommended against the promotion, on the grounds that Semenov "often opposed the decisions of SVAG's command" and even countermanded Ministry of Foreign Affairs directives. (One would think that Vyshinskii would know more about this than the Cadres Department.) When Semenov was once confronted with the fact that he did not read all the cables that came in from Moscow, he supposedly responded that it was impossible for him to read "every piece of nonsense" that was sent his way.[83] But the attacks on Semenov pale in comparison to those on Colonel Tiul'panov, head of the Information Administration, who was excoriated for a variety of political errors.[84] If SVAG's leading figures had such troubles with the Cadres Department, it is no wonder that hundreds of lesser figures were removed.

Further complicating the recruitment of new cadres for SVAG were the increasingly unpleasant conditions of service in Germany. From the fall of 1947, officers were forced into isolated settlements, and their contact with the German population was severely restricted. There were fewer and fewer opportunities for wives and children to accompany the men to Germany, and the SVAG schools for Russian children had a reputation for being subpar and poorly staffed. At the outset of the occupation, Russian officers and men had lived in comparatively luxurious circumstances, with access to products and foodstuffs that they could only dream of at home. By the end of 1947, with the devaluation of the ruble and the growth in the relative value of the Reichsmark, it became harder and harder to attract specialists to Germany by offering them financial gain. Given the increasingly strident calls for political vigilance in Moscow and the launching of the anticosmopolitan campaign in 1948, potential recruits for SVAG would certainly have thought twice before accepting a position in Germany. The Cadres Department noted in June 1948 that SVAG was especially in trouble when it came to recruiting technical specialists, who were also highly valued at home.[85]

SOVIET SOLDIERS IN GERMANY

The situation for Soviet officers and men in occupied Germany was nevertheless, especially at the beginning, very favorable. They were paid in both rubles and Reichsmarks and could purchase the kinds of goods—cigarettes, liquor, and sausages—that made them popular and attractive among German civilians. Soldiers and officers took excursions to downtown Berlin and took pictures of the damage, proud of their efforts in destroying fascism. Special military stores were set up to take care of their needs. Soviet officers took over the best villas, houses, and apartments for their living quarters. While large numbers of Germans treated the Russians with suspicion, if not hostility, many cooperated with the conquerors, either out of an honest desire to create a new and orderly society or because only through the Soviets could they gain access to material goods and influence. Officers of SVAG were allowed to bring their families to Germany, and many Soviet families did very well living on the German economy. A few even attended the newly opened Alexander Nevsky Orthodox Church in Potsdam. Many enjoyed the Soviet theaters, movie houses, and music performances supported by SVAG and the Group of Forces to bring familiar Soviet culture to Germany for their officers and men.

However, there was also a darker side to the Soviet occupation. When the Soviet armies marched into Germany in the spring of 1945, large numbers of officers and men engaged in the rape and plunder of the German population. The problem of rape will be considered in full in the next chapter, but it is important to understand here that even after the occupation government was established and the Group of Forces had placed its units in confined bases, the military administration continued to face severe problems with discipline and morale. If reports from deserters are to be believed, relations between officers and men often left a great deal to be desired. The soldiers were subjected to physical beatings and abuse and, especially in the initial period of the occupation, were sometimes confined to barracks while officers cavorted about in the town. But there were enough cases reported of excellent relations between Soviet officers and men to make one wary of generalizations in this regard.[86]

Similarly, relations between Soviet officers and men and the German population ranged from brutal and exploitative to friendly and even intimate. The trumpeting of good relations in the press and on the radio left those who witnessed the bad, like *Pravda* correspondent Iurii Korol'kov, shocked by the cruelty and indifference of some Soviet officers to the plight of the Germans. Korol'kov reported the terrible scenes that took place in September 1947, when Soviet officers, ordered by SVAG to move into discrete sections of the towns and cities, forced Germans out of their apartments without the least regard for their attachment to their homes and belongings.[87] In too many cases, commandants also treated the Germans with brutal indifference. Some commandants were reported to have beaten up German servants; in one case, a commandant struck a seamstress for doing a poor job on his wife's dress.[88] Especially officers and men from units of the Group of Forces tended to treat the local Germans dismissively, if not brutally. In the Luckenwalde region, for example, the commander of an artillery range gave no quarter to neighboring farmers who wanted to plant their fields or work in the woods.[89] Despite many similar cases of indifference to the Germans' needs, however, it is hard to say whether the Soviets were any worse than the other occupying armies in the extent to which their tanks and artillery weapons ruined farmers' fields and destroyed barns and silos.

As the occupation went on, the nature of disciplinary problems changed, but the concern among SVAG leaders about the behavior of their troops far from abated. Drunkenness continued to plague the occupation army and had a great deal to do with the growing incidence of fatalities associated with severe automobile accidents.[90] Also associated with excessive drinking were the large number of drownings of Soviet soldiers, which periodically prompted the military administration to ban swimming in the lakes around Berlin.[91] Reports of accidental shootings and armed robberies also noted the heavy use of alcohol and general rowdiness. Under these conditions, the men paid little attention to their appearance and ignored virtually all the regulations about proper sanitation.[92] A Cadres

Department report on the "political-moral condition of SVAG" for 1946 recorded 2,376 cases of the disruption of military discipline and 1,429 cases of "immoral" activities (living with German women, desertion, degeneracy, veneral disease, habitual drunkenness, and rape). According to the same data, in 1946 there were 41 desertions, 5 cases of treason, 187 armed robberies, 62 suicides, 150 serious automobile accidents, 284 soldiers killed or wounded, and 29 cases of soldiers abandoning their post.[93]

Corruption and thievery seemed as endemic to the occupation as drinking and violence and were prevalent in the ranks from the lowest privates to the top generals. Even Zhukov was accused of outfitting several of his Moscow apartments with furniture and goods from the zone of occupation.[94] The fundamental problem was that Soviet officers and men were often in the position of extorting goods from the Germans and selling them illegally. General V. M. Sharov reported that a number of officers from his Brandenburg military district engaged in a variety of businesses based on just such extortion.[95] In 1947 and 1948, a group of officers in a rich Mecklenburg agricultural district purposely underreported grain and meat production to be sure to meet their quotas, and then sold off the excess in private markets.[96] Two majors in the Angermünde region sold ration cards to the Germans in a scam that depended on artificially reporting a higher number of residents than actually lived in the area.[97] According to correspondent Korol'kov, corruption was especially widespread in Schwerin, where senior officers supported the illegal black market dealings of a German merchant by the name of Benthin. In a well-developed underground operation, Benthin effectively held a monopoly on tobacco sales and was also heavily invested in the textile and dry goods trade. Benthin allegedly covered his operations by joining the SED and paying off the senior officers in Schwerin in goods and services. Korol'kov claimed that the officers had earlier been associated with the "shady machinations and speculation" of Lieutenant General M. A. Skosyrev, who had already been removed, and that they were only continuing his bad habits.[98]

The Cadres Department, in particular, despaired at the large number of officers in SVAG who were supposedly under the influence of "bourgeois" ideology. While the SVAG administration devoted itself more to the tasks of maintaining order, building up the economy, and getting the Germans to participate in production, the Cadres Department focused on the problematic behavior of the officers themselves. Many senior officers of the military administration were accused of being haughty, acquisitive, and imperious with their subordinates. These attitudes developed in conjunction with corruption and bribery at the very highest levels of SVAG. The head of the Fuel and Energy Administration was accused of surrounding himself with German sychophants who constantly saw to his well-being, including his large number of private automobiles. The head of the Finance Administration of SVAG was accused of sending two railway cars full of furniture back to Moscow for his personal use. He also illegally sent the Ministry of Finance nine automobiles, one for his own use.[99] The Cadres Department condemned Colonel "T" of Brandenburg for dissolute behavior and for enriching himself through his position. The cases go on and on—deception, excessive drink, *barakhol'stvo* (disorderly conduct), carrying on with German women, stealing cars and furniture and illegally shipping them back to the Soviet Union.[100] There were even repeated instances of juvenile delinquency among the children of the officers and specialists in the Soviet administration. Things got so bad that a separate order was released in January 1947 for the purpose of restoring discipline among Soviet youth in the zone. Except for special showings in movie houses, they were forbidden to go to "German theaters, cabarets, operettas, or other entertainment institutions."[101]

The Cadres Department also censored Soviet officers at the highest level for political offenses. The commandant of Berlin, Major General A. G. Kotikov, was accused of *chvanstvo* (conceit). Allegedly, he paid no attention to the Communist Party organization, refused to come to party meetings, and did not seem interested in what good communists had to say. The head of SVAG's Transportation Administration was repeatedly cited for ignoring the party organization and refusing to take the Bolshevik practice of self-criticism seriously. He allegedly was also impatient and nasty with subordinates, which—as in the Kotikov case—was considered inappropriate behavior for a party member.[102] The outspoken Thüringian commander, General Kolesnichenko, was criticized for having bullied Communist Party political workers in the province at a June 5, 1947, party meeting. The Cadres Department also attacked the alleged incompetence of SVAG leaders. In particular, the department criticized the supposedly poor work of I. N. Karasev, director of the Justice Department of SVAG, and of P. V. Zolotukhin of the Education Department. Karasev was taken to task for not initiating serious judicial reform projects and for not purging Nazis and other reactionaries from the judicial system. Zolotukhin was accused of being an uninspiring leader with less than desirable ethical standards. The Cadres Department also alleged that Zolotukhin, like Karasev, was not firm enough in finding ways to eliminate reactionaries from positions of importance in the universities.[103]

If the Cadres Department officials had had their way, most of the senior officers they singled out for criticism would have been removed immediately from Germany, as well as thousands of other SVAG and Group of Forces officers and men who failed to meet arbitrary tests of moral and political purity. But the Cadres Department did not have its way, at least in part because there were no ready candidates to replace the many qualified specialists who were deemed unworthy of working for SVAG. In several cases, repeated reprimands and recommendations for removal were not enough to overcome the officers' value as experts to the military government. In the cases of thousands of offending officers of lesser rank, military "honor courts" were convened, either by the commanding officers or on the petition of other officers, to remind the accused of their moral and political duties. Sometimes the officers were punished with a "reprimand" or "severe reprimand," but stronger punishment was seldom applied.[104] In any case, it was difficult to remove an officer from duty on charges of corruption or of leading an immoral life.

POLITICAL EDUCATION

During the summer and fall of 1947, the Soviet military government was faced with a noticeable crisis in troop morale as a result of increasing political demands on the army and the isolation of all soldiers—officers and enlisted men—from the German population. Rates of desertion and suicide rose dramatically as the once highly desirable stationing in Germany turned into hardship service. There were violent arguments between soldiers and military police officers that ended sometimes in knifings and shootings. Officers had to give up their automobiles, or they had to apply for special passes to use them. It was no longer possible to hire German maids or servants.[105]

The soldiers were bored and frustrated, and the SVAG command staff knew they had a problem on their hands. As a result, they instituted a series of programs to get soldiers involved in political education, both to improve their knowledge of Marxism-Leninism and to give them a better sense of the purpose of the occupation of Germany. A Main Political Administration directive of June 17, 1947, introduced the mandatory study of Marxism-Leninism as a regular part of the activities of the kommandaturas.[106] In Thüringen, as a result, the Political Section of the local military government put together a forty-hour course of instruction in Marxism-Leninism that began with a unit entitled "The Bolshevik Party on the Eve of the Revolution."[107] In Saxony-Anhalt, the Political Administration set up evening schools for officers to study Marxism-Leninism— a measure that was repeated all over the zone. At the end of 1947, General Kolesnichenko of Thüringen issued an order that every officer participate in an evening group class on *The History of the Communist Party of the Soviet Union [b]*, known as the "Short Course," the standard Stalinist textbook on the history of the party.[108] It is hard to imagine that these studies did much for morale. But the evening schools required mandatory attendance, and officers were occupied, if nothing else.

The curriculum of study in these Marxist-Leninist schools in late 1947 and early 1948 revealed a curious tendency to reinforce standard party rhetoric while ignoring the growing confrontation between the Soviets and the West over Germany. The form and content of study was that of rote memorization and the incantation of familiar, time-worn formulas, rather than an exploration of the problems of the cold war, an expression the Soviets never used in their public (and even private) discourse, or of the growing tensions in Berlin. By late 1948, however, the reverberations of the Berlin blockade could be felt in the intensification of political studies among the officers and men of SVAG, though this did not, interestingly enough, result in study of the actual Berlin situation.[109] (The Soviets purposely avoided the term "blockade.") Instead, the Soviets focused on the importance of the "anticosmopolitan campaign" for the political health and morale of SVAG. There is a lot of evidence that in fact this campaign was not well understood by Soviet citizens in Germany. In Saxony-Anhalt, for example, the Political Administration of the military government criticized the kommandanturas and local institutions for "poorly organizing work for the explanation of the decisions of the Fifth Plenum of the Supreme Soviet of the USSR and the question of the antipatriotic activity of the bourgeois cosmopolitans in the areas of science, culture, and art." As a result, the political officers suggested the systematic, organized reading of the appropriate texts of the resolutions that explained the criminal activities of the "rootless cosmpolitans," to increase the "vigilance" of Soviet citizens abroad and to activate "the struggle against the remnants of capitalism in the consciousness of Soviet people."[110] While the officers were supposed to devote special sessions to the anticosmopolitan campaign, they were also to continue their Marxist-Leninist studies. They were expected to be fully acquainted with the "Short Course" and with the biographies of Lenin and Stalin. Now they were urged to return to the biography of Stalin and to read and discuss it chapter by chapter.[111]

CULTURE AND LEISURE ACTIVITIES

Political education may have helped some officers hew to the straight and narrow path. But for the vast majority of soldiers in Germany, problems of morale could not be solved by the "Short Course" and the biography of Stalin. The Soviet Military Administration therefore sponsored and promoted a variety of activities that would keep Soviet soldiers occupied and out of trouble. Chess tournaments were often used by local military governments as "one of the forms of sensible and cultured relaxation for Soviet people."[112] Special emphasis was placed on celebrating Soviet holidays and anniversaries while abroad. International Women's Day became a major holiday for SVAG soldiers, as well as for the Germans, who were urged to celebrate it. In connection with the one hundred fiftieth anniversary of Pushkin's birth in 1949, a series of ten lectures on the poet made the rounds of the kommandanturas through the country. "Pushkin the Poet," "Pushkin the Revolutionary," and "The World Significance of Pushkin," were among the subjects that SVAG officers and men were supposed to discuss.[113] According to Soviet newspapers, wide-ranging discussions were held about Pushkin's life and work, accompanied by readings and recitations of selections from his best writings. In all the Red Corners of kommandanturas and SVAG buildings, pictures and busts of Pushkin were supposed to be displayed, along with tributes to his work written by local officers and service men.[114]

Sports activities were also sponsored by SVAG as a way to relieve boredom and promote discipline. In a draft order on sport, Commander-in-Chief V. D. Sokolovskii wrote that sport was important for the general physical development of the individual and also to prepare him for "productive work and the defense of the Fatherland." But even more important to the officers and men of SVAG was Sokolovskii's realization that "mass sport activity is a powerful factor and means for discipline and for deflecting Soviet people from harmful free-time activities."[115] As a consequence, the military government sponsored soccer and basketball tournaments, weight-lifting competitions, and swimming meets. Victorious sportsmen and teams were given special honors, medals, and ribbons. Intraprovince and interservice competitions were encouraged. But by

SVAG's own admission, organized sports in the Soviet zone suffered from a lack of good coaching, poor "sport technique," and a generally low level of competition. Moreover, stadiums, gymnasiums, and swimming pools were poorly maintained and unlikely to inspire enthusiasm among the troops who might want to compete.[116] Matters seemed to improve somewhat in 1948 and 1949, especially with the emphasis on the Ready for Labor and Defense (GTO) military sports program, which attracted large numbers of soldiers to conditioning and weapons-sports exercises. Because the GTO program had such a strong relationship to military preparedness, good coaches, trainers, and equipment were more easily available.[117]

The Soviet military authorities in Germany also emphasized the importance of Soviet musical and artistic performances for the men in maintaining discipline and encouraging healthy free-time activities. Soviet films were brought from Moscow and shown in Soviet theaters. Soviet opera, philharmonic, and ballet companies visited the zone, giving performances for mixed German and Soviet audiences. By the summer of 1949, SVAG even had its own theater with its own producer-director, the Ukrainian playwright G. N. Polezhaev.[118] But there were also serious problems with the program of cultural activities from home. First of all, it was very hard to bring famous companies to Germany, and the visits were few indeed. There was a famous (and enormously successful) tour of the Aleksandrov Company of singers and dancers during the summer of 1948, but even then the company could not get around to most of the kommandanturas and troop posts in the zone. With increasing political restrictions on travel abroad, SVAG turned instead to what was called "artistic self-development," urging the formation of volunteer collectives of Soviet musicians, artists, dancers, and actors already in the service, who could put on amateur shows for their fellow soldiers. Officers' wives often participated, as did civilian employees who had some artistic talent. The productions were often quite sophisticated; the lighting and costumes were sometimes professionally done.[119]

STUDYING GERMAN

Both from a practical point of view and from the perspective of maintaining discipline and order among Soviet officers, SVAG made a major effort from the very beginning to get the officers to learn the German language. But Soviet officers were no more interested in studying German than German secondary school students were interested in studying Russian. In March 1946 SVAG issued an order for the mandatory study of German that cited the abysmally low level of competence in German among officers in the administration and the kommandanturas. Very few attended the available German classes, however, to the point that in many locations instruction had to be terminated altogether.[120] Threats by SVAG to list publicly the names of officers who failed to attend German class did not have any more effect than did the periodic reprimands. During the summer of 1946, out of thirty officers signed up to take German in the Magdeburg district, only seven to ten, on average, attended class. According to a May 1946 order, another Magdeburg group was started in German, but only nine or ten showed up, and by the end of the term only five or six students remained. It was certainly the case, as one report noted, that the officers were often busy with other things, but the basic problem was "the lack of a serious attitude toward the study of German."[121]

Continued threats to send grades and lists of absentees to commanders did not make much difference. Soldiers of the occupation—whether Soviet or American—were simply averse to learning the language and culture of the local population. But since the Central Committee had charged SVAG with teaching German to its officers, it was forced to set up the courses. The job of creating courses for SVAG was handed to P. V. Zolotukhin, head of the already overtasked Education Department. However, the Education Department, in particular, had little leverage in getting officers to attend class. Many officers—like those in the Political Section and the Cadres Department of SVAG—protested that there was no reason for them to learn German, because they had little or no contact with the civilian population. Some commandants, a report to Zolotukhin noted, took no interest themselves in promoting the study of German, which then made it impossible to get their subordinates to attend classes.[122] And in many units with large numbers of men from Central Asia, officers had to worry about whether their soldiers knew enough *Russian* to follow basic orders. Getting the soldiers to study German was the last thing on their minds.[123]

Initially the problems with German study among Soviet officers did not cause any major disruptions in the administration. But in late 1948 the unfolding of the anticosmopolitan campaign focused the Central Committee's attention on the large number of Jews in SVAG, especially in the Information Administration. For a variety of reasons, many of these Soviet Jews spoke German and thus carried a major part of the burden of communicating with German politicians and administrators. The situation was also made serious, especially in the eyes of the Cadres Department, by the fact that so many Information Administration officers had German girlfriends.[124] In other words, just at the time when Soviet politics at home was heating up on the question of Jews and their alleged connections with foreign spies, the Cadres Department experienced a nightmare in which the leading political organ of the military administration included large numbers of German-speaking Soviet Jews who had liaisons with German women. As a result, two processes were initiated simultaneously in the middle of 1948. A disproportionately large number of Jews were sent back to the Soviet Union, and the Cadres Department pursued the SVAG leadership for not taking seriously the matter of teaching German. Even those officers who had worked with Germans for more than three years, since the beginning of the occupation, still did not know the language. Those who ostensibly spoke the language, Cadres officials wrote, did so poorly and made no effort to speak correctly or with proper pronunciation.[125]

The problem of teaching German to occupation officers was never adequately resolved. New programs were introduced at the outset of 1949, using new textbooks and newly trained teachers. But a report from Bitterfeld in May 1949 indicated that the fundamental problem—that officers did not take German study seriously and underestimated its importance—had not been solved. Of the twenty officers originally signed up for the program, only five really attended classes. Even those who attended knew very little of the language, and what they knew was grammatically incorrect.[126]

GERMAN CADRES

The Soviets' lack of preparation for the occupation dictated that they use Germans' help in rebuilding an orderly and peaceful Germany wherever they could. This necessity overlapped directly with the goals of Ulbricht, Ackermann, and the other German communists, who returned to Germany from Moscow in May 1945. "When we arrived in Berlin," Ulbricht wrote to Pieck on May 17, 1945, "we could barely find our way through the rubble because of the smoke."[127] In fact Ulbricht and the others did find their way—with a twofold program for getting the Germans to accept their culpability for the Nazi crimes and building a new antifascist administration. The former task proved elusive and even self-defeating, however. Consequently Ulbricht, in particular, attacked the problem of building an administration with even greater vehemence and intensity. He wrote to Dimitrov that there were all kinds of committees, commissars, and groups around, but he had shut them all down. "We gave. . . orders that all our people should work in the administrative and communal apparatuses."[128] Ulbricht forced the communists to give up their red armbands and Bolshevik slogans and enter the newly emerging regional and local administrations.[129] Despite the fact that so-called communists popped up everywhere to offer their services—Ackermann noted archly that "it turned out that in the Soviet Union there are fewer Bolsheviks than there were in Hitlerite Germany"—Ulbricht understood that he immediately needed help from Moscow.[130] He asked Pieck to send "all appropriate reserves to Berlin, that is also the POWs, who have been delegated for work among the masses."[131]

During June of 1945, some 70 German communists and 300 POWs from the antifascist schools were sent back to Germany for administrative work. But this was still far from adequate, as Ulbricht noted repeatedly in his communications to Moscow in the summer and fall of 1945. While the Soviets pressed for a politically balanced administration and did not seek to impose communist domination, Ulbricht proved an excellent student of Stalin's dictum, "Cadres are everything." Even before the Communist Party was legalized in the zone, Ulbricht urged Pieck to create a Cadres Department of the KPD that would funnel handpicked communists into the administration. It was not that Ulbricht was interested at this juncture in revolutionary activity or a communist takeover. On the contrary, he firmly held to the party's principle, *"We must avoid extremes,"* which was central to German communist planning for postwar reconstruction.[132] At the same time, Ulbricht insisted that the highest value in administration be placed on order and control, and that this could be assured only by communist dominance. As a result, in November 1945 the Germans urged the Soviet Central Committee to help transport German communist exiles who were in Mexico (Merker, Jungmann, Abusch, and others) back to Germany, and to allow the return of antifascist instructors from the POW camps, the most important of whom was the Spanish Civil War commander Wilhelm Zaisser (Gomez).[133] In addition, the Soviets made arrangements for the evacuation of some 8,000 to 10,000 Sudeten German communists from Czechoslovakia to the Soviet zone.[134]

When there were no special internal security considerations involved, the Soviets obliged the many German requests for additional cadres. They also shared the Germans' interest in continuing the so-called antifascist education in the POW camps and sending approved graduates back to the zone to work in the administration.[135] Initially the curriculum in these schools—the largest was in Krasnoiarsk—was supervised by what was known as the Institute 99, a Soviet organization that produced educational materials and supervised the teaching by German communists. At the same time, the internal security police (NKVD) actually ran the camps and engaged in "operational work" among German antifascists. In other words, large numbers of Soviet agents were also recruited from among the POWs slated to return to Germany. At the end of December 1946, Institute 99 was closed down and the camps and schools were transferred to the Political Section of the Main Administration for POWs.[136]

Of the thousands of "antifascist" POWs released to work in the German administration in the zone, many if not most ended up in the police and later in the paramilitary "barracked" police *(kasinierte Volkspolizei)*. But even for the well-treated police, the transfer from antifascist schools to German reality was often difficult and jolting. First the returnees had to face the harsh conditions in the transit camps and deal with the poor organization and preparation of their KPD/SED sponsors. In the POW camps, they had not been presented with a realistic picture of the Soviet occupation, and, as a result of the tough conditions of work, many—up to 30 percent, in Zaisser's estimate—ended up leaving for the West.[137] Returning POWs nevertheless formed a central recruiting base for many of the new German administrations. The Justice Administration, for example, was so hard-pressed to recruit antifascists as judges and prosecutors that it had to compete with other branches of government, especially the party and the security apparatus, for those returning POWs who had not been Nazis or members of the Hitler Youth. As the Justice Administration put it, the most important qualities for good officials were political and moral: "Particular education is not mandatory, only being able to write and speak good German."[138]

Recruitment of KPD veterans of the Spanish Civil War, the Slovak uprising, and the underground in Europe was only marginally more successful than the recruiting of antifascist POWs. As a cadres specialist, Franz Dahlem, who himself had been in exile in France before spending time in Mauthausen, took on the responsibility of placing these veterans in key positions in the administration. But many experienced communists, especially those who had fought in the resistance, were unhappy with Ulbricht's fetish for administration and his apparent indifference to revolutionary politics. One such KPD veteran, Heinrich Fomferra, found it tremendously difficult to deal with the apolitical or even ex-Nazi "slime-people" who had made it to the top of the administration, often with the help of the Soviet Military Administration and the KPD.[139] When Fom-ferra entered the German Interior Administration, he complained to General Mickinn, chief of its Cadres Section, that except for a few communists in charge, "all the rest were, as far as I can tell, former military specialists from the Nazi army." Fomferra added that at that point the advice and recommendations of the "friends" (the Soviets) were decisive in personnel appointments of former Nazis and Wehrmacht members, and this was often hard to stomach for the German communists who had fought the fascists or had been persecuted by them.[140]

Building a New Administration

The leaders of SVAG acknowledged that when they had first come to Germany they had had no clear idea about how to set up a German administration, what its tasks should be, and how it should relate to the Soviet military government.[141] In the first six weeks or so of the occupation, the Soviets encouraged the reconstitution of local "self-governments" to keep fundamental services intact, but otherwise left open questions of the hierarchy of the German administration. At the end of June and the beginning of July 1945, when the Americans and British withdrew their troops from territory in the western parts of the Soviet zone and moved, along with the French, into their designated zones of Berlin, SVAG issued a series of orders that created a Soviet Military Administration in each of the five new provincial units of eastern Germany (Thüringen, the province of Saxony [Saxony-Anhalt], Mecklenburg-Vorpommern, the state of Saxony, and Brandenburg) and authorized the establishment of civilian provincial governments, headed by a collegium comprised of a president and a group of vice presidents. At the same time, SVAG created eleven central German administrations—five more were added in June 1947—to set general policies, while the provincial governments were made responsible for implementation and everyday administration.[142]

This emerging administrative structure had to grapple from the beginning with a number of weaknesses. First of all, the final determination of the relationship between central and provincial German administrations depended on the course of Allied negotiations over the fate of united Germany. Socialist Unity Party leader Otto Grotewohl's notes from his discussions with Stalin and Molotov at the end of January 1947 reflect some of the dimensions of this problem. Stalin apparently told Grotewohl that the German central administrations were only temporary, given the fact that the Americans would oppose a centralized government. This statement prompted Grotewohl to jot down the reminder that the Germans needed to develop a better argument for a centralized government. At the same time, Molotov let Grotewohl know that Stalin endorsed the development of German central administrations and that he had even suggested an expansion of their number to include all areas of government "except for the military and state security." On this point, Grotewohl's notes read: "Unif[ied] Central Administration for all of Germany until the formation of the government, [this is to be] immediately the *platform* as a stage [in the formation] of the government."[143]

Even taking into account Allied indecision on the final nature of the German government, within the Eastern zone itself there was no temporary definition of the relationship between the central and provincial German administrations. Until the middle of 1946, only SVAG was authorized to give orders to the provincial administrations. The German central administrations maintained tenuous links to the provincial governments and had, in the words of a Western report on the situation, "only fragmentary information" about economic events in the provinces, "let alone any power to influence them."[144] This became a particularly serious problem after the fall of 1946, when local, regional, and provincial elections were held for the first time. In January and February 1947, the newly elected Landtags (provincial assemblies) adopted constitutions, elected minister-presidents, and confirmed their nominations for ministers.[145] As elected constitutional leaders, the minister-presidents and their governments were in no mood to follow policies of the central administrations, which were in their view comprised of appointed communist courtiers. The Soviets, who increasingly favored the central institutions, had to intervene repeatedly to settle quarrels of jurisdiction between them. Sometimes special agreements were reached between the central and provincial administrations that defined, on an ad hoc basis, the corresponding powers of each. For example, after tortuous negotiations, the German Education Administration signed an agreement in April 1947 with its principal provincial counterparts that gave the central administration the right to control educational programs in the provinces, but only on the basis of cooperation with the provincial educational ministries.[146]

Another weakness of the administrative arrangement in the zone was the Soviets' unwillingness to let the Germans administer their own affairs, even in the most inocuous of matters. Soviet officers intervened routinely and reversed decisions that sometimes had been long in the making. Especially in the first year of their existence, the German central administrations had to spend most of their energies lobbying the corresponding SVAG administrations in the hope that the Soviets would follow through on German-inspired policies. But the Soviets regularly ignored the administrations when it was useful to do so, and made their lives miserable by dogging their every move and complaining about every misstep.[147] Typical was a Seventh Section (GlavPURRKA) report to Semenov in October 1945 that complained that the Germans were poor administrators and did not understand how to delegate authority or run an apparat. However, the report recognized that Soviet officials were themselves partly to blame, because they disrupted normal adminstative practices and discouraged initiative by constantly ordering the Germans around.[148] The SVAG administrators were the worst offenders. Yet when Deputy Commander-in-Chief Serov invited criticism of SVAG practices at a November 1945 meeting of German provincial and central administration leaders, few Germans—understandably—dared to raised their voices in protest.[149]

Ulbricht's response to the Soviets' interference, inconsistency, and the ingrained habit of blaming others (in this case the Germans) for their own failings—was to focus even harder on the question of getting the right cadres in place for the German administration. By developing reliability and competence, both of which were highly valued by the Soviet leaders in the zone, he was certain that the Germans could eventually assume control over their own affairs. At the same time, Ulbricht was intent on getting rid of political enemies from the German bureaucracy. This meant first of all removing prominent bureaucrats like Dr. Ferdinand Friedensburg, who was a cofounder of the Christian Democratic Union (CDU) in the East and president of the German Central Fuel Industry Administration.[150] Ulbricht was convinced that Friedensburg favored circles of prewar industrialists, discriminated against socialists in his administration, and was tied to reactionary monopolists in the West. But because of Friedensburg's support within the Soviet Military Administration, he was able to hold on until the end of 1947, when, under great pressure from his German opponents and their Soviet sponsors, he fled to the West.

Ulbricht also sought to develop internal KPD/SED policies that would make the German socialists "the party of order" and the party of administrators. Through internal party cadres policies, Ulbricht sought to reduce institutional conflicts and make administrative practices more hierarchical. Here, too, it took Ulbricht until the fall of 1947 to create the kind of *nomenklatura* system—a "unified personnel policy"—that would deliver the appropriate cadres to the administrations. According to that system, the SED's Personnel Policy Department (for the time being, the word "cadres" was not used) had to approve all appointments to leading positions in the party, administration, and public institutions. The Personnel Policy Department was also made responsible for any and all investigations of SED party members in the administration. Any complaints about particular comrades were to be directed to the section, which was authorized to take appropriate action. Like the Cadres Department of the Soviet Central Committee on which it was modeled, the Personnel Policy Department of the SED was to keep complete data on all members of the party. Personnel officials were responsible for the accuracy of the information provided by every party member on his or her biographical questionnaire.[151] Undoubtedly, these files were used by Soviet as well as SED officials.

In 1947, Franz Dahlem took control of the cadres work, and in his appointments he tried to balance the competence of the individual with their party attributes. Dahlem explicitly acknowledged that he was looking for contributions to administrative efficiency, as well as for economic and political leadership abilities.[152] But this balanced approach to *nomenklatura* appointments gave way by 1949 to a more blatantly politicized cadres policy. The signal for this change came from Stalin. In his December 18, 1948, discussions with the SED leadership, the *vozhd'* (leader) made it clear that the Germans should worry less about pure competence and more about politics: "The old state apparatus has been destroyed. In the new state apparatus the working class has decisive influence, but not yet sufficient influence to drive out finally the remainder of the reactionary bureacracy, which hides entrenched behind [the notion of] 'professional competence.' "[153]

In March 1949 Wilhelm Zaisser, at that point head of the Saxon Interior Ministry, put the problem of cadres succinctly: "One can learn specialized skills. To this extent one could say that the most decisive [factor] is democratic convictions." "Really progressive-democratic people," Zaisser continued, must be appointed to the leading positions in the administrations, and he said that each individual must be asked and be able to answer these precise questions: (1) what are his views of the establishment and of the furthering of "our democratic order"? (2) what does he think about the unity of Germany on a democratic foundation? and (3) "what is his attitude toward the only friend [the USSR] that the German people has in its fight for unity?"[154]

PROVINCIAL ADMINISTRATION

The senior American political advisor in Germany, Robert Murphy, wrote to the U.S. secretary of state on September 11, 1945, telling him that the Soviets had just informally advised him of the creation of provincial German administrations, but that this move had nothing to do with creating the core of a new central German government, which "would be years (repeat years) in the making." Murphy's informant, A. A. Sobolev, political advisor to SVAG, had added that one of the purposes of the new structure was to destroy the old Prussian state administration, a goal that had been agreed on by all the Allies.[155] Sobolev had emphasized, as did all the early reports on the German provincial administrations, that the provinces were directly under the orders of the regional Soviet Military Administrations. Germans in the provincial governments were in daily contact with their Soviet counterparts, were responsible for carrying out the provincial SVA's orders, and could engage in no major initatives, especially on the economic front, without the SVA's agreement.[156]

The relations between the German provincial governments and their Soviet counterparts were less problematic than those between the provincial and central German institutions. To create some clarity about these relationships, Marshal Zhukov sponsored a meeting on November 13, 1945, between the presidents of the provincial administrations and the heads of the German central administrations. Dr. Rudolf Paul, Thüringian president, stated the case for the provinces in uncompromising terms. At first, he said, the provincial governments welcomed the formation of central administrations as institutions that would coordinate activities and issue general guidelines that the provincial administrations, the *real* administrations, would implement if they could. But the central administrations were not satisfied with this role and, Paul protested, "independently interfere in the work of the provinces." "That is unacceptable. As president I am responsible for the province and I cannot allow the central administrations [to mix] into all kinds of questions without my knowledge. It simply cannot be [accepted] that the central administrations undertake hirings and firings without my knowledge."[157]

Ferdinand Friedensburg, Ulbricht's nemesis in the Central Fuel Industry Administration, offered a somewhat different perspective from Berlin.

The provincial administrations, Friedensburg claimed, felt themselves to be under siege because they were three or four months behind the central administrations in putting together their staffs. The overlapping of functions was inevitable, Friedensburg added: "A precise delineation of competencies is also hardly possible." Friedensburg stated that the central administrations simply could not restrict themselves to making suggestions without also giving instructions. The central administrations were in a double bind, he said. On the one hand they received orders from the Soviet authorities to get concrete tasks accomplished; on the other, they were not allowed to confer with the presidents of the provincial administrations or even with the other central administrations.[158]

Zhukov contradicted Friedensburg's contention that he was ordered not to consult with other German administrations. But he also upheld Paul's view of the appropriate relationship between the central and provincial administrations. Ultimately the presidents of the provinces were responsible for their administrations, and therefore the central administrations should not involve themselves in bureaucratic or personnel issues. The job of the central administrations, Zhukov reiterated, was to advise SVAG on issues involving the Soviet zone as a whole, and to coordinate zonal operations in three concrete areas: railways, postal service, and supply. Otherwise, their job was simply to advise SVAG on policy guidelines. "The states and provinces are therefore in no way subordinated to the central administrations. In specific, they do not have the right to give the states and provinces instructions or even to place under [their authority] provincial offices, officials, or organs."[159] Zhukov's support for the decentralization of administration derived in good measure from the Potsdam agreement, which stated that there should be no central German governmental institutions before the signing of a peace treaty.

In this situation, the SED found itself struggling to exert some kind of control over the quickly growing admininistrations, both in Berlin and in the provinces. In November 1946, the Central Secretariat of the party sent out instructions to the provincial secretariats, designating those ministries that could be controlled by the middle-class parties—the Liberal Democratic Party (LDP) and the CDU—and those that were to be held by SED members. The Central Secretariat insisted that it be informed about any variations on the pattern. When the designated ministers themselves were not SED members, the rule was that the number-two person, the ministry director, should be from the SED. In addition, according to this party directive, all the higher offices in the economic planning ministries were to be occupied by SED members.[160] The SED also tried to get Soviet officials to pay attention to the party's interest in administrative decision making. Ulbricht wrote to General Makarov about a case in which the SVAG Finance Administration got in touch directly with the finance ministries of the provinces about a legislative proposal regarding taxation that was to be voted on by the provincial Landtags. Not only was the Central Finance Administration not informed, Ulbricht wrote, but also its leaders knew nothing at all about the legislation. Ulbricht suggested that the Central Secretariat's apparat, in this case the Provincial Policy Department, should serve as the coordinating point in such matters.[161]

The Soviets understood that the situation had become more complicated in December 1946 and January 1947 with the election of the minister-presidents and the beginning of constitutional government in the provinces. As a result, at a meeting in February 1947, SVAG urged the elected minister-presidents and the heads of the central administrations to reach a new agreement about dividing competencies. The agreement, codified by Sokolovskii in a subsequent order, gave the central administrations that dealt with industry, fuel and energy, and trade and supply greater responsibility for coordinating provincial efforts than they had previously possessed.[162] But the fundamental problem remained: according to the provincial governments (and their constitutions), their only responsibility was to the duly elected Landtags. The Landtags themselves were downright hostile to any influence from the central administrations and sharply complained at the least perceived incursion.[163] British military observers caught the essence of the problem when they noted that "there was no single ordnance [sic]" that laid down the powers of the central administrations versus the provincial governments, nor any hierarchy established between the elected provincial officials and the appointed German members of the central administrations.[164]

With tensions between East and West on the rise in the middle of 1947, the Soviet military authorities increased the powers of the central administrations above and beyond those of the provincial governments. Certainly the SED encouraged them to do so, warning of the dangers of provincial particularism. The SED worked especially closely with the German Interior Administration, making sure that the internal security apparatus in the zone was firmly centralized. According to an August 1947 report, the Interior Administration was to designate a representative to each of the provinces "who would work in the closest ways with the Ministries of Interior [all SED members anyway] in the five provinces."[165]

Furthermore, the SED insisted that the Interior Ministries in the provinces not use terms like *"Staatsregierung"* or *"Staatsministerium"* (state government or state ministry) and instead refer to the "provincial government" *(Landesregierung)*, so that no one could assert that Germany was being divided into smaller states.[166]

The fear of giving an impression of federalism also influenced Soviet perceptions of the Sokolovskii compromise of February 1947. Soviet officers opposed federalism not just as a practical matter for the administration of the zone, but also because their intense arguments with the Americans in the Allied Control Council about the future of the German government were shaped by the Soviet critique of federalism. With the Allied arguments in mind, Semenov's deputy, M. G. Gribanov, complained that various individually negotiated agreements between the central administrations and the provincial governments smacked of "federalist tendencies." One such agreement, signed in June 1947 between the German Agricultural and Forestry Administration and the provinces included a rider added by the state of Saxony, that only those directives that were approved ahead of time by the provincial governments could be released. For Gribanov, such an agreement carried with it "negative political consequences." Provincial governments, he concluded, needed to receive a firm warning about the evils of federalism.[167]

Certainly in the Eastern zone itself the Soviets worried less that the principles of federalism would take root in the provinces than they worried about their lack of control over the implementation of SVAG orders. In discussing laws related to the rehabilitation of "nominal" Nazis, the Soviets noted that the enforcement of the laws depended on the various provincial ministries, "and not all [the ministries] carry them out with the same initiative." Tough laws had supposedly been enacted against speculation, but the individual justice ministries "did not always take the lead [in implementing] these laws." For the Soviets' tastes, provincial judges and courts were too old-fashioned and not sufficiently geared to the new "democratic" needs of the day. There were even instances in which the Landtags could block legal measures initiated by the Soviets. In one case, for example, the Landtags refused to pass a law authorizing provincial governments to search and inspect postal packages. The Soviets were upset that CDU and LDP deputies could block such a "progressive" measure, and urged that the provincial constitutions be changed to eliminate the need for a two-thirds vote to implement a new law.[168] For convenience and for ideological reasons, the Soviets were ready to support the SED's arguments that the power of the German central administrations should be increased and their cadres systematically politicized. By the beginning of 1948, there was talk of removing the offices of the central administrations from Berlin to Leipzig, both to isolate the growing state bureaucracy from Western influences and to implement greater centralization in zonal affairs.[169]

THE GERMAN ECONOMIC COMMISSION

It would have been very much against the inclinations of Soviet bureaucrats and German communists to resolve the tensions between the provincial governments and the central administrations in favor of the provinces. Among the Germans, Ulbricht, in particular, repeatedly raised the issue of implementing an economic plan that would give the workers confidence in the future. Otherwise, he stated, the only "plan" that operated was the plan for reparations, leaving the German working class despondent and without hope.[170] Within the Soviet administration, the Office of the Political Advisor was the most insistent about avoiding the slightest hint of federalism. In good measure, this came from the Soviets' growing confrontation with the Western powers about the nature of the future German government. However, the crucial initiative for the formation of a new, centralized administrative body—the German Economic Commission (DWK)—came from the Soviet Union. Sokolovskii issued the order authorizing formation of the DWK, Order no. 138 of June 4, 1947, after returning from a trip to Moscow.[171]

The provisions of the order coordinating the economic activities of the various zonal ministries and administrations struck most German and Soviet observers as being quite positive. The commission itself consisted of the presidents of five German administrations: industry, transportation, fuel and energy, agriculture, and trade and supply, who were to be joined by the chief of the Free German Federation of Unions (the FDGB) and the chairman of the Association for Farmers' Mutual Help (the VdgB). Bruno Leuschner served as the temporary head of the DWK, but he was later made chief of the planning section, and Heinrich Rau became official chairman. To deflect Allied criticism of the new body, the Soviets let it be known that "all activity of the DWK was carried out under the control of SVAG." The SED also insisted—somewhat too vigorously—that the convening of the DWK did not constitute the formation of some kind of rump East German state.[172] The Soviets also took concrete measures to ensure the DWK's subordination to SVAG. According to Order no. 0315 of September 9, 1947, Sokolovskii placed the work of the DWK under the supervision of SVAG's director of the Economic Planning Department, M. I. Perelivchenko. Furthermore, the administrations that were included in the DWK were expressly forbidden to publish their own directives without consulting their SVAG counterparts.[173]

Pressure for the further consolidation of decision making in the DWK came from a number of sources. The SED was determined to make the DWK into an exclusive party preserve, but it ran into considerable SVAG resistance on this point. Ulbricht's calls to purge the DWK were mooted by a growing need for competent specialists, though some "objectionable" officials, like the nonparty president of the Industry Administration, Leo Skrzypczynski, were forced to resign.[174] Also, just as the formation of the German Economic Council for the British and American zones had contributed to the initial Soviet decision to create the DWK, so the development of Bizonia, the fusion of the American and British zones, which took place at the end of June 1947, prompted the Soviets to strengthen the powers of the DWK.[175] As a result, Sokolovskii issued an order (Order no. 32 of March 20, 1948) that gave the DWK the right to release instructions and decrees that were binding on all German organs of the eastern zone. Moreover, the DWK was now seen as having "the right and the duty" to make sure that its policies were carried out. From the point of view of Ulbricht and the SED leadership, this meant that the Germans could take over many of the functions of SVAG and resolve once and for all the debilitating conflicts between the provincial governments and the central administrations. Their work would "finally be coordinated," and the backbone of the "democratic economy," the newly sequestered people's factories (VEBs), would be centrally directed.[176]

One reason for the SED's enthusiasm about the reformed DWK was revealed in a document, approved by SVAG, that Pieck and Ulbricht passed on to the Soviet Central Committee for Stalin. Not only would the commission formulate an economic plan for the zone and see to its fulfillment, but also the German administrations and the Soviet authorities would be required to stick to the plan unless both agreed to some changes.[177] In other words, the commission would be able to rein in the Soviet proclivity to engage in irregular and sometimes devastating removals of machinery and goods from German factories.

The Soviet Military Administration was also pleased that the DWK would take more than formal responsibility for the economic well-being of the zone. By the spring of 1948, problems of staffing in SVAG had become severe, and Sokolovskii feared even greater gaps between the personnel he needed to run German affairs and those officers who were actually available to him. For a variety of reasons, some quite trivial, the Cadres Department had removed thousands of officers from the zone. Others had left voluntarily, because their terms were up and conditions for Soviet soldiers had become more difficult. Some schools were closed, and families were forced to return to the Soviet Union. Technical personnel were lured away by better salaries and conditions back home. Sokolovskii let Central Committee secretary A. A. Kuznetsov know in April of 1948 that it would be better if SVAG focused more on planning, reparations, and the supply of troops, while leaving the work of coordination and implementation of economic policies to the Germans.[178]

The Soviet Central Committee agreed with Sokolovskii's assessment and in November 1948 authorized an increase in the number of DWK members from 36 to 101. From that point until the founding of the German Democratic Republic (GDR), the DWK, in the words of the Ministry of Foreign Affairs' internal history of the German question, "was in fact the highest legal, administrative, and executive organ of government in the Soviet zone of occupation."[179] With greater power in the hands of the DWK, the SED looked to strengthen its role in the organization even further. It made sense, Ulbricht and Fechner wrote, to coordinate the work of the state administrations, the provincial governments, and the DWK through "common consultations with the affected leading SED functionaries." Increasing SED influence over the DWK was also intended to head off the growing tensions between the DWK chairman, Heinrich Rau, and his Soviet superiors. The basic argument between the two sides was over the legal structure of the economy, with the Soviets insisting on "innovations" derived from Soviet practice, and the leaders of the DWK anxious to maintain basic German economic laws. The Germans even accused SVAG of providing ammunition for German reactionaries, who protested the Sovietization of the Eastern zone, but the Soviets dismissed these worries as ludicrous.[180] In return, the Soviets chided the DWK and the German administration as a whole for harboring too many ex-Nazis. As of December 1, 1948, stated the Soviets, there were sixteen ex-Nazi Party members and twelve former Wehrmacht officers in the leadership of the DWK, the central administrations, and among the ministers of the provinces. Within the entire bureaucracy of the DWK, the Soviets added, there were 169 former members of the Nazi Party and other Nazi organizations and 148 former Wehrmacht officers. A total of 2,170, or 40 percent of all DWK functionaries, had served in the bureaucracy under the Nazis.[181]

Another reason that SED domination of the DWK was so critical was that, in April 1948, the commission's secretariat had already resolved "to impose order on the economy and administration as well as to establish uniform control measures" by establishing control commissions in the DWK and in their partner ministries in the provinces. These in turn would cooperate with the "people's control commissions" established by the party to guard the economy against alleged saboteurs and reactionaries.[182] By the beginning of September 1948, the SED had established guidelines whereby the Central Control Commission would be attached as an independent organization to the DWK. The commission would have nine appointed members in addition to the president of the German Interior Administration. Similarly, the provinces were to appoint five-member commissions from nominations by the minister-presidents and the ministers of the interior, with the agreement of the chairman of the Central Control Commission. The responsibilities of the commission were multifarious, but they centered on the enforcement of the Two-Year Plan and on the investigating and intercepting of "enemies."[183] In this form, the control commissions combined economic planning and policing functions. Ten months later, judicial functions were added to this mixture to make it possible for the DWK to prosecute its employees or others in the economy who violated the secrecy of the plan or disturbed its implementation. According to DWK directives of July 28 and 29, 1949, "If by any act considerable damage has been done to the antifascist democratic order or the reconstruction of the peaceful economy, the offender is to be punished by imprisonment in a penitentiary [for] not less than two years."[184]

CREATING A NEW STATE

In 1948 and 1949, the DWK increasingly looked and acted like an incipient government bureaucracy. While it continued to carry out concrete Soviet orders in the broad areas of its competency, it also took on the trappings of a German government.[185] Especially when the SED announced the Two-Year Plan in July 1948 (to begin in January 1949), the formation of the German Democratic Republic, one that would ostensibly include the Western zones, was on everyone's mind. Ulbricht was ebullient and confident of victory. In a particularly aggressive March 1949 speech in Dresden, he even dared to threaten the West militarily:

> If the enemy in order to provoke a war carries out warlike aggression
> . . . against the Soviet Union, then as a German people we will do ev-
> erything in our present power to support the Soviet Union . . . That
> means it is in our interests that aggression is defeated as quickly as
> possible, and thus it will not have the possibility to carry out warlike
> measures in the so-called West German areas . . . The gentlemen [of the
> West] should know that the distance from Berlin to the [English] Chan-
> nel is not so far.

For all of his bellicose rhetoric, Ulbricht's speech took on more sober
tones when he spoke about the internal development of the Eastern zone.
Following Soviet prescriptions, he urged his comrades to understand that
it was too early for a people's democracy to be formed in the East, because
"securing the democratic order" was still very much on the agenda and
most likely would be for a long time to come. So long as there was a mixed
economy that included state factories, private enterprise, and artisanry,
one could not really speak of "socialist economic planning," which depended on a socialist state structure. Ulbricht implicitly suggested that it
would be a simple matter to join the economy of the West with that of
the East, and he expressed considerable optimism about the prospects for
this. With the Two-Year Plan in place to guarantee the national future,
he felt, it would be natural for all of Germany to turn to the Eastern zone
for leadership.[186]

Ulbricht's optimism on the national issue represented a new stage in
the development of the SED's national platform. To be sure, as early as
August 1946 he had urged the Soviets to begin the process of building a
government on the basis of a draft constitution derived primarily from
the Weimar Constitution.[187] Shortly afterward the SED's draft, "On the
Formation of an All-German Government," had provoked a storm of
controversy in Soviet diplomatic circles over whether the SED proposal
conformed to the Potsdam decisions as interpreted by Molotov and the
Ministry of Foreign Affairs.[188] The official point of view of the ministry
(and of its Office of the Political Advisor in the zone) was that the Germans themselves should decide what form of government they wanted,
but that the four powers would have to determine whether their plan was
acceptable before it could be confirmed.[189] In taking this stance, the Soviets
gave Ulbricht carte blanche to place the SED at the head of the national
movement. By initiating what it called the People's Congress Movement
for Unity and a Just Peace, the SED and the Soviets had hoped to influence

the London foreign ministers conference in December 1947, and along with it public opinion in western Germany. The head of the CDU in the East, Jakob Kaiser, had resisted the charade of political unity, and as a result had been forced to flee the Soviet zone. The Second People's Congress, held on March 18, 1948, had been intended to ignite a national show of force for the unity of Germany on the centenary of the 1848 revolution. But the hubbub around the People's Congress did little to hinder the growing certainty of the formation of a West German state— although it did a lot to convince Germans, East and West, that the SED controlled bloc politics to the exclusion of the "bourgeois parties."

At the beginning of May 1949, a series of meetings was held in Moscow and Berlin to breathe life into the People's Congress movement and to wave the flag of the National Front. The idea was to disrupt the Paris Conference, at which the Western Allies intended to create the new West German state. In mid-April, Pieck had stopped in Moscow on his way to taking a cure near Sochi on the eastern shore of the Black Sea. After seeing the May Day parade in Moscow, he met with Stalin on May 6. According to Pieck's notes, Stalin wanted the SED to initiate positive steps beyond the People's Congress movement, before the Paris Conference had a chance to convene. Pieck summarized the conversation as follows: "In order to broaden and deepen the resistance [to] and the struggle against the policies of the Western powers, the proposal for building a National Front came up, for which we received the suggestion from St[alin]."[190] On his way back from Sochi, on May 18, Pieck met with the Soviet Politburo (enlarged with the participation of Chuikov, Koval, Semenov, and Tiul'panov) to review the problems of Germany and the Paris Conference. After a meeting with Dimitrov in Moscow, Pieck returned to Berlin on May 21.

Semenov also was in Moscow at the beginning of May 1949 and must have received instructions to inaugurate a National Front campaign, because he had already talked to Grotewohl about it on May 6, just after he returned from the USSR. At SED party headquarters on May 20, Semenov changed the order of business and informed the assembled comrades about the need to create a National Front.[191] On May 27 Grotewohl informed the plenum of the SED Party Executive that the party should take the lead on the national question, and that party activists should not be afraid of making the necessary tactical alliances with bourgeois forces for this purpose. In the view of Grotewohl (and Semenov), the SED should lead the middle classes as well as the workers into the national breach.[192]

Predictably, none of this activity forestalled in the least the Allied preparations for a West German state. But neither the Soviets nor the SED gave up on the National Front tactic. In a series of meetings in late June and early July, following the end of the Paris Conference and the announcement of the new Federal Republic in West Germany, Semenov met repeatedly with SED leaders for the purpose of drafting the manifesto of the National Front. Fred Oelssner was charged with writing the draft; Semenov checked it over.[193] Pieck also noted Semenov's major role: "In long meetings and with the special collaboration of Comrade Semenov we worked out a proposal for a resolution about the National Front and the Socialist Unity Party, which was to serve as the basis for the propaganda of the National Front." On August 23, added Pieck, the Party Executive established a commission to work out the final version of the resolution, which was then submitted to Stalin for his "opinion."[194]

For the leaders of the SED, three interrelated processes were of supreme importance in the spring and summer of 1949. One was the expansion of the People's Congress movement into the National Front, which would allow the SED to pose as the genuine defender of national unity in contrast to the "splitters" in the West. It was also extremely important for the SED leaders to form an East German state that would both guarantee their access to political power and create a powerful magnet that could attract adherents in the West.[195] Finally, the SED was anxious to diminish or at least remove from sight the Soviet occupation regime in Germany, because of what this would mean for their own ability to run affairs in the East. It would also lift the burden of guilt by association—for the rape, plunder, repression, economic exploitation by Soviet forces—that had weighed on the party's shoulders since the beginning of the occupation.

The SED took the first steps toward accomplishing its goals in March 1949, with the acceptance of a draft constitution for the German Democratic Republic by the Volksrat (People's Council), the protoparliament elected by the Second People's Congress. At the end of May 1949, the Third People's Congress met, elected a new Volksrat drawn exclusively from representatives from the Soviet zone, and issued a "Manifesto for the Expansion of the National Front for Unity and a Just Peace." During the summer, the SED intensified its campaign for the National Front while making it clear to the Soviets that it was time to form a government in the East. Pieck stated the problem quite unambiguously: the situation in the West made it imperative that a German government be formed in the Soviet zone. To campaign effectively against the West German govern ment, the people (in point of fact, the SED) needed their own German government. "We therefore ask for the counsel of Comrade St[alin] how we should go about the forming of a German government . . . [and] *as quickly as possible.*"[196]

Of course the SED had a plan worked out with Semenov and counted on the fact that Stalin would approve it. There would be no elections, at least not until the following spring, when the "proper conditions" could be prepared.[197] The bourgeois parties would protest, but they would have to be convinced. Some concessions would also have to be made to them, like allowing CDU leader Georg Dertinger to be the first foreign minister of the German government. Some SED members might not understand how this would be possible, Grotewohl admitted, but it was not anything to worry about: "We will also have our own Anton Ackermann [right] beside him, and Anton Ackermann will give Mr. Dertinger just a little help in making the right decisions in these [foreign policy] questions."[198] On October 5, 1949, the bloc of parties urged the Volksrat to proclaim itself a provisional Volkskammer (People's Assembly) and to form a government according to the provisions of the constitution. Two days later the People's Congress proclaimed the founding of the German Democratic Republic, calling it "a powerful bulwark in the struggle for the accomplishment of the National Front of Democratic Germany." The Volksrat announced that it would henceforth serve as the provisional Volkskammer and charged Grotewohl with forming a government.[199]

On October 8, 1949, the next day, three formal actions confirmed the creation of the German Democratic Republic. Johannes Dieckmann, chairman of the presidium of the provisional Volkskammer, sent a letter to the commander-in-chief of SVAG, asking for recognition of the decisions of the provisional Volkskammer as having the force of law. At the same time, Chuikov and Semenov sent to the Ministry of Foreign Affairs the results of talks that they had held with the SED and other parties, agreeing on the composition of the provisional government of the German Democratic Republic. The Soviet Military Administration itself had approved the list of senior officials and now asked for confirmation from Moscow. Also on October 8, the deputy foreign minister of the Soviet Union, Andrei Gromyko, passed on to the Central Committee of the CPSU(b) his ministry's recommendation that a German government be formed, emphasizing that the SED had a majority of votes in its presidium.[200] On October 11 the newly formed Landkammer (States' Assembly), elected by the five Landtags, met with the Volkskammer in joint session and elected Wilhelm Pieck as the first president of the GDR. On October 12 the provisional Volkskammer then confirmed Otto Grotewohl as prime minister, along with his cabinet.

Pieck and Grotewohl turned immediately to the Soviet Military Administration and expressed their confidence that it would change its basic functions in Germany, withdrawing altogether from the work of administration, while continuing to exercise control over those matters related to carrying out four-power decisions and those responsibilities related to the Potsdam agreement. Pieck assumed, however, that the Soviets would continue to supervise the ministries and maintain their own "organs" for investigative and executive purposes. They would be fewer, Pieck hoped, and therefore would give the new government and the Volkskammer greater authority in the society.[201] The military administration dissolved itself on October 10 and was replaced by a Soviet High Commission, also commanded by Chuikov. The era of the Soviet occupation administration, if not of Soviet control, had come to an end.

SVAG AND THE GERMAN ADMINISTRATION

Up to this point, I have discussed the formal administrative arrangements—both Russian and German—that the Soviets constructed and nurtured to govern their zone of occupation. It is apparent that the Soviets increasingly sought to transfer day-to-day administration to German institutions, even while maintaining ultimate control, through the SED, over the direction of German policies in the East. But some consideration of the nature of the relationship between the Soviet and German administrations is also important, to capture the essence of the new German government that was being formed in the zone. To be sure, the quality of the relationship changed over time, from the beginning of the occupation until its formal end, and it depended a great deal on the personalities of the individual Soviet officers involved. Whether the Soviets were dealing with comrades in the SED or "bourgeois" politicians also made a significant difference. Not that the Soviets necessarily treated SED members any better than other Germans. Certainly the leading party figures who had been in Moscow during the war (like Pieck, Ackermann, and Ulbricht), and former SPD converts like Grotewohl and Fechner, were treated with respect and even deference, but this was based on the supposition that they understood the realities of Soviet control. The attitude of the Soviet administrators even toward the highest-ranking Germans was one of superiority in both knowlege and ability, stemming from their intimate ties to the "great" Soviet culture. Their willingness to order the Germans about, as a result of the higher order of their understanding, was more pronounced at the beginning of the occupation than at the end, but there was never any question who was in charge and whose judgment was preferred. The friends, as the Soviets were called by SED leaders, were friendly so long as the Germans followed the rules of the game.

Soviet officers in the zone also took special pleasure in undermining the Germans' wartime claims of Aryan superiority. The Russians had turned the tables on the Germans; they were now the ones from the superior civilization, which out of its deep humanity was ready to share the benefits of its higher organizational forms and greater efficiency. The Soviets were the teachers and the Germans the pupils, and this cloying Soviet didacticism pervaded the relations between Russians and Germans during the occupation. According to many Soviet officials, the Germans were dirty, disorganized, and lazy. They showed no initiative and relied on the Soviets to take care of them. The attitude of Colonel General I. I. Fediunskii, chief of the Mecklenburg military government, was not atypical. During the first year of the occupation, he periodically assembled the province's local officials and berated them for their poor performance. At one such meeting at the Schwerin city theater in August 1945, Fediunskii stated: "One must ask: where is here the [famous] German efficiency of both the *Bürgermeisters* and *Landrats?* Until now things have been very bad with the registration of cattle, cars and trucks, and horses . . . We have to be done with this lack of efficiency." Fediunskii added that the German officials would be held responsible by the Soviet Military Administration "for the attitude of the population, [and] for their well-being." They would have to answer for "every instance of provocation or sabotage [carried out] by fanatic elements," and it was their job to take appropriate measures to prevent it from happening. Germans too easily remained passive in the face of political threats and economic want, waiting for their commandant to take action instead of doing something themselves, he said. Germans should stop sitting on their hands, Fediunskii insisted. Why was it necessary for the Soviets to send out their military doctors to fight disease and epidemics in the countryside when the Mecklenburg authorities could have taken action themselves? Fediunskii also let his listeners know that Mecklenburg would have to learn to make do with the resources it had; German officials should stop whining about the shortfalls in fuel deliveries from other provinces, he said, and instead find ways to substitute for outside supplies.[202]

Fediunskii's attitude toward the Germans—schoolmasterish, dismissive, and impatient—was shared by other provincial administration commanders as well. But the way they usually dealt with the problem of the lack of initiative on the part of the Germans, which was probably their most common complaint, was to issue a flurry of orders that, along with the orders from SVAG in Karlshorst and the direct orders from local commandants, left German officials reeling from regular waves of insistent Soviet injunctions.[203] Major General Sharov from Brandenburg, for example, issued orders if he wanted a particular *Landrat* arrested for hiding grain production; he issued orders to mobilize workers if an important factory was short of labor; he issued orders that forbade poor-quality textiles from being turned in for reparations payments; he issued orders for instituting hygienic standards to avoid the spread of spotted fever (typhus), and so on.[204] In every instance, he expected an immediate response. In Thüringen the SVA chief, Lieutenant General Kolesnichenko, also issued flurries of orders on everything from setting the date by which trolleybuses in Weimar should be running again to regulating the printing of ration cards.[205]

The Soviets issued thousands of orders, and the Germans scrambled to respond. When German officials were unable to meet the demands, whether they were Communist Party members or not, they often faced anger, disdain, and derision from their Soviet bosses. One of the hardest Soviet commanders to please was Major General P. A. Kvashin, chief of SVAG's Transportation Administration. Kvashin was known to fly into a rage when railway workers frustrated his plans to deliver materials and goods on time. Coal delivery quotas were particularly hard to meet, given the difficult loading procedures. When railway officials suggested that the hungry workers might perform better with higher rations, Kvashin exploded, claiming that the problem was that they were lazy, inefficient, and indifferent, not poorly fed. What was needed, Kvashin insisted, was better leadership among the Germans. "What is absent is the knowledge and the will to take matters in their [own] hands and to organize." The unions and the party were to blame for not taking charge and for leaving malingerers and fascists in positions of responsibility. Kvashin repeated the familiar refrain that the Germans took no initiative and left everything to Soviet officers.[206]

From the point of view of the German communists, Kvashin posed a serious problem. He was not in the least interested in cooperating with the communist vice president for the Transportation Administration, Otto Kühne, and he made personnel decisions without even informing him, much less asking his advice. Kühne's complaints to Ulbricht in December 1945 about Kvashin's lack of responsiveness to problems of thievery at the train stations also went unanswered. In February 1946 Kvashin, again upset with the alleged inefficiency of the Transportation Administration, had his translator call the administration's office and berate Kühne and his colleagues for harboring a bunch of saboteurs. In a note to Ulbricht, Franz Dahlem expressed the party leaders' frustration with Kvashin's attitude: "It is simply impossible that the General passes on to Kühne such a message *through a translator.*"[207]

The German communists faced analogous problems with General I. V. Kurmashev, chief of SVAG's Fuel and Energy Administration. Like Kvashin, Kurmashev was interested in results and not politics. Consequently, he dealt directly with the head of the corresponding German administration, Friedensburg, who was considered a leading authority in the energy field. But as Friedensburg was also a founding member of the CDU, a figure of great stature among the German middle class, and someone who had ties to German industrialists in the West, the KPD/SED leaders took every opportunity to discredit him. Gustav Sobottka, one of the KPD-initiative-group leaders to return to Germany with the Soviet army, was vice president of the administration, and he complained bitterly about being overlooked by Kurmashev: "He [Friedensburg] is the only one responsible and decides all administrative issues in consultation with Kurmashev."[208] The SED had an easier time dealing with Friedensburg than it did taking on Kvashin or Kurmashev. Sobottka took the lead, complaining to Generals Serov (NKVD chief) and Bokov (member of the Military Council of SVAG) that Friedensburg maintained contacts with Nazis in the West and that he conspired to keep communists out of important decision-making positions.[209] Ulbricht's deep hostility to Friedensburg also helped Sobottka's cause, though as a favorite of the Soviets and an example of their declared neutrality in party politics, Friedensburg was not removed until December 1947, when he fled to the West, where he briefly served a term as mayor of West Berlin.

The examples of Kvashin and Kurmashev, Fediunskii and Kolesnichenko, were repeated in various forms at various levels of the Soviet Military Administration, all over the zone of occupation. In an earlier section, I examined the bossy commandants who, in their fiefdoms, caused endless problems for their German vassals. But that same kind of arbitrary behavior went all the way to the top. Orders were issued in no particular pattern and with no clear sense of their provenance. An American intelligence report ably summarized the problems faced in this case by the Germans.

> The Soviet Military Administration at Karlshorst is literally unable to describe the exact pattern of delegation of Soviet power to German administrations because no such pattern exists. There is absolutely no single man or group of men in Karlshorst or elsewhere who at any time can say what the SMAD is delegating, planning or doing throughout the Zone on all subjects. There is no administrative procedure for the delegation of authority, no philosophy, whether direct or implied, which covers all cases, and there is no reason to expect the same policy to apply throughout the entire zone on any one subject. An example of the way business is done is very well illustrated by this little transaction: ten thousand tons of crude oil are shipped to the Soviet Zone from Austria monthly for refining. The German Central Administration and several departments of the SMA in Karlshorst have been unable to find the methods by which these are handled financially and they have been told, in effect, that they should not question such things.[210]

At a November 13, 1945, meeting in Karlshorst called by Marshal Zhukov, the president of the German Industry Administration, Leo Skrzypczynski, expressed satisfaction that orders once issued by the Russians without any discussion with the Germans were by that point at least the subject of periodic consultations. But, he added, "commandants in the factories" disrupted the normal processes of production by imposing arbitrary priorities on the factory administrations. Zhukov protested that there were no commandants in the factories, only "representatives," who did not have the right to make production decisions.[211] But the basic problem was that just about every Soviet officer who was in the position to do so acted like a commandant, ordering Germans about under the assumption that Soviet ways were inherently better and that the Germans were always trying to shirk work and find excuses for why they could not deliver goods and services on time. These attitudes were not terribly different from those of occupation armies anywhere in twentieth-century Europe. Soviet officers confiscated attractive villas in the cities and seized at will vacation houses at the beach or in the mountains. On whims they ordered from the Germans deliveries of fine food and drink, cigarettes, and clothes.[212] The Germans could be prosecuted for wastefulness, but not the Soviets.

The German communists in the KPD/SED were in a peculiar position in all of this. They resented being at the beck and call of the Soviet "friends," and they had to put up with endless complaints, especially from the trade unions, about the Soviets' seizure and abuse of the country's resources. It was particularly difficult for the SED to swallow some of the hard facts of occupation life, like the Soviets' use of grain confiscated from hungry farmers to make vodka for their troops. At the same time, the German communists themselves enjoyed privileges and special amenities in return for their loyalty and hard work. From the very beginning they received special *payoks* (packages of goods) and supplements to their salaries.[213] The Soviets turned over preferred housing to the communists and set up special SVAG schools for their continuing political education that were also supplied by the Soviet army with food and materials.[214] Some of the communists held the highly prized *propusk* (pass) that allowed them in and out of Soviet bases and into special Soviet stores. Given these privileges, it was especially difficult for them either to protest Soviet abuses or to be reminded of their inferior status by Soviet administrators.

Even when the Soviets treated the Germans with respect and tried to work with them in constructing a new German administrative apparatus that would meet Soviet standards, it was apparent who made the final decisions. When Soviet political officers met with German editors, for example, they often simply told them what was good and what was unacceptable about their stories, always using Soviet standards as the measure for what was appropriate or not.[215] At a December 1947 meeting about the provisions of Order no. 201, SVAG's major denazification initiative, Erich Mielke announced to his coworkers that every arrest order had to be confirmed first of all by the local SVAG office. The German police, especially, needed to understand that SVAG's Internal Affairs Department was the "responsible office" for all questions. In every case, the advice of the representatives of SVAG was to be followed, Mielke stated; "no other instructions are valid."[216]

Ulbricht and the German communists submitted a proposal to the head of SVAG's Justice Department, Colonel Karasev, about reorganizing the German judiciary. The tone of Karasev's reply of October 27, 1945, is as striking as its contents in the way it emphasized the Soviets' right to interpret what was in the interests of democratization and what was not. According to Karasev, Ulbricht's suggestions about naming judges and prosecutors from the masses served the interests of democratization, while his idea of setting up special people's courts did not serve "democratic principles" and was therefore rejected out-of-hand.[217] For the Soviets there was no need to explain any further.

The Soviets followed up formal controls on decision making with direct scrutiny of German officials, whether they were in the SED or not. For example, inspectors from the Education Department of SVAG kept the work of schoolteachers, principals, and school councils under close surveillance. A director of the Teachers' Courses, SED member Erich Reich, was described as not consistently following the party line: he was "an individualist, [who] doesn't like criticism of his work [and] doesn't consult with democratic organizations about his work." The Soviet school inspector concluded that Reich could be allowed to stay at his post, but that "his work should be [kept] under constant control."[218] Initially SVAG education inspectors were supposed to play a central role in the universities, as well, picking and choosing faculty members and students, but the severe shortage of cadres had made it necessary to rely on the SED to do it. The job the SED did, however, was not good enough for SVAG, and the Information Administration, under Colonel Tiul'panov, insisted on placing Soviet officers directly in the universities. In February 1948 Tiul'panov noted that the situation of higher education was much better since Soviet officers were directly involved in setting the political agendas of the universities. Experience demonstrated, he wrote, "that it is necessary to have in every university at the very least one [Soviet] political worker, controlling and directing the ideological-political life of the university."[219]

The immediate involvement of the Soviets in German civilian administration also occurred in the court system. Generally the Soviets were unhappy about the Germans' attachment to traditional legal norms. They accused the German courts of not being aggressive enough in pursuing big-time Nazis. At the same time, they complained that the German courts had missed the point of Order no. 201 on denazification, which drew a clear distinction between nominal Nazis, who were needed for the democratic construction of the country and therefore should quickly be given back their political and civil rights, and former active Nazis, militarists, and war criminals, who should immediately be brought to justice.[220] When the German justice system dallied, the Soviets sometimes simply lost patience, took over the trials, and punished the alleged offenders.

Incessant SVAG interference in German civil matters did not help the Soviets in their genuine attempts to win sympathy and friendship from the Germans. In the first days after the end of the war, good deeds—in the form of feeding the German population and rebuilding city infrastructures—quickly evaporated in German memory in the face of continuing rape and plunder, which took place throughout the summer of 1945. The beneficial effects among the population of the Soviet kommandanturas' unexpected generosity during the Christmas and New Year's season of 1945–46, and of the lifting of the curfew in the cities of the zone, also dissipated in the face of the fierce campaign waged by the Soviets to unify the SPD and KPD in the spring of 1946.[221] The Soviets tried to defuse criticism of their interference in German politics by dressing in civilian clothing (which was often hard to obtain) at party and union meetings and otherwise posing as Germans. But this often worked out badly, and the Soviets increasingly sent trusted SED members in their stead. For example, SVAG officers insisted that the Germans take a more active role in the "democratization" of the trade unions by making sure that a representative of the antifascist bloc be present at every trade union meeting in every factory, "to direct the meeting politically, to organize the leadership, not allowing the disruption of democratic procedures and so on."[222]

Anton Ackermann recalled in his unpublished memoirs that he had urged German communists to remember that "the church had to be kept in the village," meaning that the SED should not simply ape every practice of the Soviets.[223] The Soviets also understood that the Germans had to develop their own political profile. In the early fall of 1946, Tiul'panov considered the idea of setting up a "special section" of SVAG to fight the internal enemies of the SED, which would function, however, "without any ties to the NKVD," given the latter's deservedly terrible reputation among the Germans. But even then, Tiul'panov admitted, it would be hard to engage in such activity without compromising the SED as the "hand of Moscow."[224]

The perception of the ubiquitous influence of the hand of Moscow plagued the KPD and SED from the beginning of the occupation of eastern Germany to the end of the GDR's existence. Part of the problem lay with the Germans, who were understandably reticent to protest Soviet incursions into their spheres of activity, even when repeatedly invited by its commanding generals "to criticize the work of SVAG."[225] But the real problem derived from the Soviets' lack of restraint and their intolerance. At the end of December 1946, Sokolovskii, who was perfectly aware of the issue, released an order in an attempt to institute a more circumspect occupation regime when dealing with the Germans. According to the new guidelines, only a limited number of SVAG officers were to communicate with the SED, and then only with a selected group of party leaders, Ulbricht being chief among them. The policies and personnel of SVAG were not supposed to favor the SED, and the function of the military government was to be to "control," and not to interfere in decision making or administration. Sokolovskii urged his comrades to advise the Germans, drawing on the experience of the CPSU(b), rather than to issue orders on the spur of the moment.[226]

That Sokolovskii's initiatives did not signal a major shift in Soviet policy in the zone is evident from a speech about the same issues that he gave to the SVAG party *aktiv* more than three years later, on March 9, 1949. "It is necessary," Sokolovskiii stated, "to put an end decisively to the crude interference in the internal matters of the SED, in trade union matters and [those of the] other mass organizations." Commandants, Sokolovskii noted, interfered far too often in German civilian affairs. Moreover SVAG's eternal nitpicking with SED policies had negative political consequences, Sokolovskii insisted, because it kept the party from learning how to make its own decisions. Sokolovskii also made it clear—in an indirect swipe at Colonel Tiul'panov—that there was no reason for SVAG officers to speak at SED party meetings. (Tiul'panov had given a major policy address at the SED's First Party Conference in January 1949.) From Sokolovskii's point of view, it was time to make friends with the German communists, help them when they asked for help, and bring a halt to the practice of ordering them around.[227]

In the final draft of a July 1, 1949, speech to the Society for the Study of the Culture of the Soviet Union, Wilhelm Pieck made a revealing correction to the original version. Instead of speaking about "good cooperation with the Soviet *Besatzungsmacht*" (occupation power), he substituted "good cooperation with the Soviet *Militärverwaltung*" (military administration).[228] In doing so, Pieck tried to emphasize the formal and impersonal administrative quality of SVAG's activities versus the hard realities of its occupation regime. The highly politicized historiography of the GDR also tried to obliterate the memory of direct control and interference in German affairs. But in this case, as in so many others, memory proved more enduring than history. Attempts to gloss over the realities of the Soviet occupation convinced GDR citizens all the more that Soviet control continued until the very end.

Soviet Soldiers, German Women, and the Problem of Rape

IN EARLY MARCH 1944, the Soviet spring offensive drove the Germans out of the Ukraine and liberated Khar'kov and Kiev. By the end of April, the Red Army was fighting Germans in the foreign territory of northern Romania. The Soviet offensive in Belorussia began in late June: Minsk, Kovno, and Vilnius were liberated in July. By September 1944, the Soviet armies had seized Bucharest and were poised to enter Warsaw on the banks of the Vistula. Some soldiers thought the war was over, or at least that the fighting would slow down. As a result, the Red Army political officers felt compelled to intensify their campaign dedicated to rousting "the fascist beasts from their lair"—"On to Berlin!" and "Destroy the Hitlerites in Their Den" were some of the slogans posted in the Romanian countryside.

Soviet soldiers also ignored the warnings of their newspapers and commissars not to be diverted by the seeming riches of the West. In fact, both officers and regular soldiers were anxious to explore the strange and delicious world of bourgeois decadence. However, fierce German resistance and periodic counterattacks by the still resourceful fascist enemy convinced the soldiers that the war was far from over, that Berlin was indeed the object of their efforts. Some of the most deadly battles—Budapest, Breslau, and, of course, the struggle for Berlin itself—lay before the exhausted Soviet troops.

The combination of the grim realities of continued warfare and "the world of restaurants, wine, gypsy violins, rich clothes, and miraculous shops" described by one veteran of the Romanian campaign may well have intensified the Soviet soldiers' proclivity to take what they could not buy and to rape local women in the anger of incomplete victory.[1] J. Glenn

Gray emphasizes that the "impersonal violence of war itself" breeds rape, as the conquest of females complements or, in some cases, substitutes for the defeat of an enemy.[2] It is instructive in this instance to compare the problems of rape and pillage in Romania and later in Hungary with the generally exemplary behavior of Marshal F. I. Tolbukhin's troops in Bulgaria. The differences may well have to do with superior leadership and discipline in the Bulgarian campaign.[3] On the other hand, a century of friendly relations, similar cultures and languages, and a genuinely open welcome for Soviet troops from the Bulgarian population explains, at least in part, the relative absence of rape. On all counts, the Hungarian case was different. In Hungary there was an alien language and culture and a much higher standard of living, which was a source of much resentment in the victorious Soviet Army. Also, many Hungarians continued to contribute to the Germans' defense. There can be little question, as well, that the bloody siege of Budapest, which cost tens of thousands of Soviet casualties, inflamed the situation and led to the beserk behavior of Soviet soldiers in the defeated city. A terrible rampage of rape and pillage followed the Soviet seizure of the city in February 1945. "It was impossible," wrote Julius Hay, "to spend a day or even an hour in Budapest without hearing of brutalities committed by [Russian] soldiers."[4] Hungarian girls were locked in Soviet quarters on the Buda side of the city, where they were repeatedly raped and sometimes killed.[5] Even the Swedish legation was attacked by rampaging Red Army soldiers, who stole possessions and raped women regardless of their nationality. The Swedish newspaper *Ny Dag* (May 17, 1945) suggested that the Soviet units might have believed they were attacking a Nazi stronghold, since part of the legation had indeed been occupied by Germans.[6] In any case, in this atmosphere of fighting, pillage, and rape, one can understand how Raoul Wallenberg—the Swedish angel of mercy for Hungarian Jews—could have been seized by Soviet troops and taken away without any explanation of why he was taken or where he was going.

Milovan Djilas and the Yugoslav partisans had also had to deal with the issue of rape, when Soviet units crossed into northeastern Yugoslavia in the fall of 1944 to spearhead the liberation of Belgrade. It was particularly traumatic for the partisans to be faced with the evidence that their heroes, the brave soldiers of the Red Army, could engage in such actions. The partisans also worried that the widespread tales of rape of Serbian women by Soviet soldiers would sully their own reputation and weaken their political standing among the Serbs. But their remonstrations with the chief of the Soviet mission, General Korneev, led only to bitter protests against the "insults" directed at the glorious Red Army. Later investigations by the Yugoslav authorities, based on complaints by individual citizens, documented 121 cases of rape, all but 10 of which involved rape and murder. In addition, there were 1,204 cases of looting with assault, figures, as Djilas tells us, "that are hardly insignificant if it is borne in mind that the Red Army crossed only the northeastern corner of Yugoslavia."[7] The Yugoslav protests also got nowhere with Stalin, who took umbrage at Djilas's interference: "Can't he understand it if a soldier who has crossed thousands of kilometers through blood and fire and death has fun with a woman or takes some trifle?" Stalin also kissed Djilas's wife and joked, writes Djilas, "that he made this loving gesture at the risk of being charged with rape." Stalin's lack of sensitivity to this issue, Djilas adds, was also apparent in his attitude toward complaints during the East Prussian campaign. "We lecture our soldiers too much," Djilas reports Stalin as saying, "let them have some initiative."[8]

Stalin's response to Djilas foreshadowed his apparent indifference to similar complaints from communist leaders throughout Soviet-occupied Europe. The behavior of Soviet troops in Slovakia, for example, prompted the Czech communist leader Vlado Klementis to complain to Marshal I. S. Konev in Vienna. Konev reportedly responded that the main culprits were gangs of Soviet deserters.[9] Even so, Marshal Konev's troops were known to be relatively disciplined when compared with Marshal R. Ia. Malinovskii's army, which was reputed to include large numbers of released criminals who left a trail of rape and murder from Budapest to Pilsen.[10] Wolfgang Leonhard recalls that there were several discussions between Socialist Unity Party members and Soviet leaders in Moscow about the issue of rape and plunder in Germany. Stalin answered the concerns of the Germans with a Russian proverb: "In every family there is a black sheep." When a member of the SED delegation tried to give the question a more serious tone and hinted at the profound political consequences for German socialism, he was interrupted by Stalin: "I will not allow anyone to drag the reputation of the Red Army in the mud."[11]

EAST PRUSSIA AND SILESIA

The serious problem of rape by Soviet soldiers in Eastern Europe turned out to be a pale foreshadowing of what was to face the German population when Soviet armies initially marched into Germany territory. Reading the

Soviet hate propaganda could lead one to believe that it was as important for the Soviets to humiliate the German population for what had been done to the Soviet Union as it was to defeat the German army. Front newspapers encouraged soldiers to recite the harm done to themselves and their families and to keep "a book of revenge" that would remind them of the need to repay the Germans for their evil.[12] Ilya Ehrenburg's chants of ritual hatred for the Germans were so often printed and repeated that they became national slogans. "We shall not speak any more. We shall not get excited. We shall kill. If you have not killed at least one German a day, you have wasted that day . . . If you kill one German, kill another—there is nothing funnier for us than a pile of German corpses." Hang them and watch them struggle in their nooses. Burn their homes to the ground and enjoy the flames. These were the messages that permeated the last years of the war.[13] Marshal Zhukov's orders to the First Belorussian Front on the eve of the January 1945 offensive into Poland did little to dampen the Soviet soldier's lust for revenge: "Woe to the land of the murderers," the orders stated. "We will get our terrible revenge for everything."[14] A veteran of the East Prussian campaign described the national hatred that fed the Soviet march. "As the front drew closer to the borders of Germany, the propaganda of hate not only of the German army, not only of the German people, but even of the German land itself took on a more and more monstrous character." The final directive from the Main Political Administration of the Army on the eve of crossing the borders of East Prussia said that "on German soil there is only one master—the Soviet soldier, that he is both the judge and the punisher for the torments of his fathers and mothers, for the destroyed cities and villages . . . 'Remember your friends are not there, there is the next of kin of the killers and oppressors.' "[15]

There is little evidence that Soviet commanders purposely used violence in East Prussia as an example for the rest of Germany, in the hope of inducing an early German surrender. They surely would have been aware that the Wehrmacht could use the East Prussian case to bolster the determination of its own troops. In fact, there seems to be good reason to believe that Soviet officers were surprised by the intensity of the terror that followed the invasion. Despite Nazi propaganda, the German population was also caught unaware.[16] It was not untypical for Soviet troops to rape every female over the age of twelve or thirteen in a village, killing many in the process; to pillage the homes for food, alcohol, and loot; and to leave the village in flames. The reports of women subjected to gang rapes and ghastly nightly rapes are far too numerous to be considered isolated incidents.[17] Lev Kopelev, then a captain in the Soviet Army, tried to stop a group of rampaging soldiers and was accused of having engaged in "bourgeois humanism."[18]

Alexander Solzhenitsyn, who was also an officer in East Prussia, provides a fitting testimonial to what he witnessed in that region in *Prussian Nights,* here in translation by Robert Conquest.

> Zweiundzwanzig, Hörlingstrasse
> It's not been burned, just looted, rifled.
> A moaning, by the walls half muffled:
> The mother's wounded, still alive.
> The little daughter's on the mattress,
> Dead. How many have been on it
> A platoon, a company perhaps?
> A girl's been turned into a woman.
> A woman turned into a corpse
>
> . . . . .
>
> No point in driving on—eh, fellows?
> Unless we leave them some mementos?
> Without orders, as it takes us,
> Here, there, everywhere, look—scores
> Of smoky-red, dark-gleaming fires!
> Well, now we're getting our revenge lads.
> We've hit him good and hard, the foe!
> Everything's aflame—
>
> . . . . .
>
> The whole district sees a dawn
> The like of which it's never known!
> Our columns pour ahead like lava.
> With wild cries, whistling, headlights glare
> —Klein Koslau, Gross Koslau—
> Every village—is now a fire.
> Everything flames . . .[19]

The berserkers in East Prussia hindered military efficiency, and eventually Marshal K. K. Rokossovskii, in charge of the front, restored order. It also became increasingly apparent that the territory of East Prussia would fall to the Soviets and to the Poles. Political and economic officers realized how much was being lost to the Soviet Union through the burning of farms and the pillaging of estates. At the very least, food supplies and material goods could be sent home to the impoverished Soviet cities.[20] As a result, in some cases Soviet supply officers promised protection to German villagers (and even landowners) if they would continue to work the land and supply food for the home front.

Yet these promises were often broken, and protection proved illusory. Continued rape and plunder drove the Germans to desperate actions. As a state security officer in East Prussia cooly reported back to Moscow: "The suicides of Germans, especially women, have become more and more common."[21] Even after German troops were thoroughly defeated and East Prussia was under occupation, the threat of rape continued to plague German women. Hermann Matzkowski, a veteran German communist and a newly appointed local mayor of a district of Königsberg, reported that one of the only sources of food in town after its fall in early April 1945 was horsemeat from the veterinary hospital on the outskirts of the city. Of those women who went to fetch the meat, barely one-half returned unscathed. Many were raped; some did not return home at all. The only Germans in Königsberg who were well fed, Mayor Matzkowski continued, "are women who have become pregnant by Russian soldiers." On November 6 and 7, 1945, Red Army Day, the mayor wrote, Russian soldiers actually seemed to have permission for every kind of transgression against the Germans. "Men were beaten, most women were raped, including my seventy-one-year-old mother, who died by Christmas."[22]

The dreadful disorder resulting from the East Prussian campaign did not make enough of an impact on the Red Army hierarchy to institute the kinds of punishment that might have prevented further rape as Soviet armies pushed beyond the Vistula into Silesia and Pomerania, what was to become western Poland. Once again, the road signs urged Soviet soldiers to hurt the Germans: "Soldier: you are in Germany, take revenge on the Hitlerites."[23] The German social democrat August Sander collected eyewitness accounts of the Soviet takeover of this region that document the fate of countless German women.[24] Soviet soldiers again took out their revenge on helpless women and girls, often—as in East Prussia—while under the influence of alcohol. One German village captured on February 26, 1945, was systematically plundered, and virtually all of the women were raped. "The screams of help from the tortured could be heard day and night." Twenty-five to thirty were left pregnant; some one hundred females contracted some form of sexual disease.[25] Polish women were not spared the horrors of the Silesian campaign either. Sometimes Soviet soldiers did not believe their protestations that they were Poles and not Germans; sometimes it didn't matter to the rampaging soldiers.[26]

Typically, one finds reports of the most brutal rapes interspersed with examples of the kindness of Soviet soldiers. In one case a family prepared to commit suicide after the mass rape of their neighbors and friends, but they were stopped by a sympathetic Soviet officer who promised them protection. In another case two Soviet soldiers risked their own lives to prevent the attack by a group of Soviet marauders on a young girl in the presence of her father.[27] A local mayor (Bezirksbürgermeister) from Breslau (Wrocław) wrote: "One has to have experienced how a Russian soldier could give his last piece of bread to German children, or how a Russian truck driver on the road could voluntarily give an old mother with her broken-down wagon a ride home. One also has to have experienced how these same people could lie in ambush, perhaps in a cemetery waiting to attack unaccompanied women or girls to rob them and to rape them."[28] The papers of the German antifascist group in Breslau reflect a similarly bifurcated view of Russian activity. On the one hand, the antifascists praised the Soviets for protecting them from vengeful Poles. On the other, they bemoaned the violence of drunken Russian soldiers: "One heard during the day, but especially at night, the screams of women in the streets. Houses were burned and people were robbed."[29]

The desperate situation for German women in Silesia was in general exacerbated by the Poles, whose "desire for retribution" was often as intense—for very understandable reasons—as that of the Russians.[30] More often than not, the incoming Polish authorities were even less concerned about the safety of German women than were the Russian officers, to whom the German population turned for protection. After all, the Silesian territories had been turned over by the Allies to Polish occupation, but not yet to incorporation into the new Poland. Orders went out from the Polish communists to expel Germans by whatever means necessary, to ensure incorporation as well as occupation.[31] As a result, the Polish administration of the new territories made little effort to protect local Germans from the depredations of Polish or Russian rapists and thieves.[32] In a city like Breslau, the Germans' fear of the Russians was quickly replaced by fear of the Poles. In fact, it was almost too much for the Germans to survive the Russian attacks only to have the Poles persecute them once again. "The Germans in Breslau," wrote the city's antifascist group, "are steadily being spiritually driven into the ground [*gehen langsam seelisch zu Grunde*]."[33] Even the Soviets expressed shock at the Poles' behavior.

Polish soldiers, stated one report, "relate to German women as to free booty."[34]

INTO THE SOVIET OCCUPATION ZONE

The fierce fighting in the Ardennes in January 1945 and the conclusion of the Yalta Conference in February convinced Stalin and the Soviets that there would be no separate peace between the Western Allies and the Germans. It became apparent that the occupation of Germany would proceed as called for in the Allied meetings of 1943 and 1944. Now the Soviets' priorities shifted from the short-term question of the morale of their soldiers and civilian population to long-term Soviet objectives in Central Europe, from a war of elimination against the Germans to an attempt to establish ties with German antifascists and other elements in German society willing to break with the Hitlerites. As a result, there was also a radical shift in official Soviet attitudes toward Germans. This was clearly reflected in the April 14, 1945, *Pravda* article by G. F. Aleksandrov, head of the Propaganda Department of the Central Committee. Apparently speaking for the Communist Party and for Stalin, Aleksandrov attacked Ilya Ehrenburg's well-known view that the war was a struggle of extermination against the Germans. "If one would agree with Ehrenburg's views," Aleksandrov wrote, then "one would have to conclude that the entire population of Germany must share the fate of the Hitlerite clique." Aleksandrov concluded by restating Stalin's order of February 23, 1942, which became the slogan of slogans in Soviet-occupied Germany: "It would be laughable to identify Hitler's cliques with the German people, with the German state. *Historical experience shows that Hitlers come and go; the German people, the German state, remain.*"[35]

The Soviet government's attitude—that it had allies in the German people and German state—was never far from the surface of Soviet foreign policy during the war, even during the periods of the most bitter anti-German rhetoric. The creation and maintenance of the National Committee for Free Germany during the summer of 1943 and the periodic initatives of the Soviet government to conclude a separate peace attest to this fact.[36] Aleksandrov's article was published and broadcast to the front two days before the last great Soviet offensive that would carry the Soviet army from the Oder to Berlin. Stalin's command to his troops reinforced the Soviet desire to find supporters among the German population. In conquering the capital of Germany, Stalin ordered, Soviet soldiers should demonstrate the highest discipline, proving the high level of Soviet morale to the world as a whole. According to Stalin's order, the soldiers were to carry with them the great idea of communism, which was not to be compromised by the least indiscipline.[37]

In typically self-contradictory fashion, Stalin insisted that undisciplined behavior was not the fault of the troops, while at the same time providing them reasons for engaging yet again in violence and pillage. In his message to the Oder front, Stalin wrote that the rampaging and marauding had been caused by penal battalions, enemy agents, and pure malcontents, who had been relieved of duty. Passing over his own role in encouraging the earlier depredations, Stalin then stated that "the cruel treatment of the German population is not useful for us, because it increases the resistance of the German army."[38] In other words, the Germans deserved the worst, but their mistreatment did not serve Soviet interests. At the same time, Marshal Zhukov warned his troops to pay attention to their military duties during the offensive and occupation: "Soldiers, make sure that in looking at the hemlines of German girls you don't look past the reasons the homeland sent you here."[39]

The admonitions of Zhukov, Aleksandrov, and Stalin about violence against the Germans were easier to publish than to enforce. Even a number of Soviet memoirists wrote that it was far from simple to get the troops to think of Germans as human beings deserving of respect. "Was it so surprising that they [the soldiers] wanted to exact revenge?" noted Lieutenant General F. E. Bokov, later chief of the Military Council of the Soviet Military Administration. "It was a long way from the slogan 'Death to the German Occupiers' to a differentiated attitude toward each individual of the German population."[40] The great Soviet military hero, later commander of the Soviet army in Germany, V. I. Chuikov, also noted that when his army crossed into Germany it was still impossible for the Soviet soldier "to distinguish the [German] people from fascism and its leader, Hitler."[41] Besides, many of the slogans posted by Soviet soldiers countered the official message emanating from Moscow. "Here it is, accursed Germania," read the Soviet signs on the border of Poland and Pomerania.[42] "*Here* it is, the fascist lair—Berlin!"[43]

In fact, the wartime Soviet propaganda had been very effective in exposing Russian soldiers to the worst crimes of the Nazi occupiers. Vivid pictures of Majdanek published in the press and the horrors of the concentration camps discussed in agitational meetings were very much on the minds of Soviet soldiers as they marched into Germany. (However, only rarely were these mass killings associated with Jews; usually, the victims were identified simply as Soviet citizens.[44]) Even without the press, Soviet soldiers learned plenty about German atrocities in their march through territory decimated by the Nazis. This is not to mention the intense personal losses they themselves often had suffered. Despite the best efforts of the Main Political Administration of the Red Army, GlavPURKKA, there was simply not enough time to convince Soviet soldiers that what had been a brutal war of elimination between Germans and Russians was now to be a class war. The political instructors themselves had difficulty absorbing the new lesson that fascism was an alliance of Junkers, big industrialists, and bourgeois politicians rather than the clearest expression of German national traits. Instead, the words of Ehrenburg continued to ring in the ears of Soviet soldiers: "Don't count days, don't count versts, count only the number of Germans you have killed."[45]

Hatred of the Germans was fed by anger and resentment about their wealth. One Russian sentry told the American journalist Alexander Werth in Berlin, "They lived well, the parasites. Great big farms in East Prussia, and pretty posh houses in the towns that hadn't been burned out or bombed to hell. And look at these datchas here! Why did these people who were living so well have to invade us?"[46] This anger about German wealth is reflected as well in the diaries of Dmitrii Shchegolev, an officer and Military Council representative of the First Belorussian Front:

> April 28, 1945 [in the village of Jansfeld, outside of Berlin]. We are now billeted in a small block of flats previously occupied by railway clerks. Each small flat is comfortably furnished. The larders are stocked with home-cured meat, preserved fruit, strawberry jam. The deeper we penetrate into Germany the more we are disgusted by the plenty we find everywhere . . . I'd just love to smash my fist into all those neat rows of tins and bottles.[47]

THE TAKING OF BERLIN

After more than two weeks of fierce fighting in which up to half a million people were killed, wounded, or injured, Berlin finally fell, and the Nazi state lay in ruins. On the third of May—the first day of the peace—some Berliners made their way out of the bunkers onto the streets. The scene, described by Soviet veterans, was one of people wandering and stumbling about, of machines, tanks, and jeeps, and of burned out, smoldering buildings. Public transportation was not functioning, so the Germans made their way by foot, sometimes with families loaded in wagons or carts, trying to find a roof to put over their heads.[48] As for the Soviet soldiers, writes Roman Karmen, a veteran of the taking of Berlin, they all made an obligatory visit to the Reichstag, celebrating briefly before their tanks and jeeps kept rolling, through Berlin and on to the suburbs.[49]

The problem of rape in the period of the taking of Berlin, until the formal surrender on May 9 and the creation of the Soviet Military Administration on June 9, was every bit as severe as it had been in Silesia. "Of course . . . a lot of nasty things have happened," commented Lieutenant General (later Marshal) V. D. Sokolovskii to Alexander Werth in a June 5 interview. "But what do you expect? . . . In the first flush of victory our fellows no doubt derived a certain satisfaction from making it hot for those Herrenvolk women. However, that stage is over . . . Our main worry," he grinned, "is the awful spread of clap among our troops."[50] But Sokolovskii was wrong to give the impression that the raping would cease after the establishment of the military government. At least until the end of June and the beginning of July, when many military and civilian administrations were removed from the hands of battle-worn officers, hundreds of local commandants, each with his own policies and preferences, set the tone for the treatment of the German population. The commandants treated the regions as personal fiefdoms, complained one Soviet report, and they simply didn't bother reporting the "excesses" of their troops.[51] Sometimes rape and pillage were severely punished, by death or a severe whipping. But too often local commandants sympathized with their soldiers' anger and frustration and ignored their nightly rampages, which were now almost always exacerbated by the influence of alcohol. Adding to the problem in the first few weeks of the occupation were the terrifying attacks by released Russian POWs and forced laborers, who also engaged in rape and pillage. As one Soviet eyewitness stated, the "responsible organs" (meaning the NKVD, GlavPURKKA, and military police) did very little to control the activities of these Soviet marauders.[52] It was not until Soviet troops were confined to strictly guarded posts and camps during the winter of 1947–48 that German women were freed from the persistent threat of rape.

The taking of Berlin was accompanied by an unrestrained explosion of sexual violence by Soviet soldiers. Ambassador Robert Murphy concluded in a memorandum of July 19, 1945, that "according to trustworthy estimates . . . the majority of the eligible female population" was reported to have been violated.[53] Murphy's estimate is probably exaggerated; some intelligence reports indicated, for example, that although rape was quite common in those days, "it was not as widespread as some sources would have made it."[54] In any case, there are so many reports that indicate a systematic carrying out of violence against Berlin's women that it is hard to dismiss the seriousness of the problem. Even as they entered bunkers and cellars where Germans hid from the fierce fighting, Soviet soldiers brandished weapons and raped women in the presence of children and men. In some cases, soldiers divided up women according to their tastes. In others, women were gang-raped.[55] Generally, the soldiers raped indiscriminately, not excluding old women in their seventies or young girls. The first antifascist mayor of Charlottenburg wrote: "In the beginning, the Russians looted on a grand scale; they stole from individuals, warehouses, stores, homes. Innumerable cases of rape occurred daily. A woman could not escape being raped unless she kept in hiding . . . It is difficult to grasp the full extent to which rape is practiced."[56]

Rape in the bunkers was followed by restless pillaging and rape in apartments and homes throughout Berlin. Countless reports were filed by Germans complaining to their local government. Typical was the following police report sent to Rathaus Spandau and passed on to the Soviet commandant of Spandau. (The names are blacked out in the archive files.)

On the night of May 6, 1945, at 2:30 in the morning, three Russian soldiers broke through the window in the hallway. A tenant was hauled out to open the door. At this point, all of the apartments of the house were to be searched by soldiers, supposedly on the orders of the kommandantura, and the three soldiers searched the house. They got as far as the second floor when they returned to where two young women were sleeping with a baby. The two soldiers then sat down on the bed with Frau [A] and Frau [B], both twenty-four years old, with a child of six months on the bed, smoking cigarettes and demanding then that they should sleep with them. At the moment the two women wanted to scream [the soldiers] threatened them with a pistol. Frau [A] called her mother, and the third soldier stood guard when she came and forced her into another room where he held her back with a machine gun. There he went through all the suitcases, from which he took just a pen holder. In the meanwhile, the other two soldiers raped the two young women. Shortly after a quarter to four in the morning, they left the apartment. In addition they took an accordian from the apartment of family [C]. (Signed by the petitioner and four witnesses).[57]

Sometimes, the cases were more violent, as in a June 28, 1945, petition from Berlin-Reinickendorf.

> In the night of the 4th to 5th of May of this year, the married couple [A] and Frau [B] were attacked by two drunken Russians in our apartment. During this [attack], I—a 62-year-old wife—was violated by both [soldiers] and my husband, 66 years old, was shot [to death] without reason. Then in a half an hour a third Russian also came, after the others were gone, and I was abused again, and this act in the apartment of a renter who had in the meantime taken me in . . . As a note: my husband belonged to no Nazi organizations and I ask the Herr Commandant for a hearing. (Signed by petitioner and four witnesses).[58]

The garden-house settlements on the outskirts of Berlin were frequently the targets of nightly raids, plundering, and rape. At one of them, Mächeritzwiesen in Tegel-South, local Communist Party activists tried to get weapons to protect themselves against the marauders. In their appeals to the KPD central, they noted: "The occupation by the Red Army has unfolded into a real plague on the land. No day or night goes by that the bandits in Red Army uniform, even in attack formation, engage in plunder and rape against the garden colony settlers."[59]

Monsignor G. B. Montini, the Vatican representative in Berlin, also reported the ubiquitous nature of rape, though one suspects—as in the case of Robert Murphy—that he may be exaggerating the extent of the terror. Still, his report of October 1945 is chilling:

> Women from 10 to 70 and 75 years of age have been ravished; consequently, there have been pregnancies, abortions, and 80% of the women have become infected by venereal disease . . . The worst crimes have been committed in the district of the Kurfürstendamm in the presence of their parties (husbands, fathers, mothers, brothers). Nuns were raped in the Franziskus Sanatorium, even though they were wearing their religious habits . . . Professor Schüler of the Rutberg-Krankenhaus in Lichterfelde killed his wife and daughters and then himself not to have to bear the anguish [of their rape]. Many women lived on rooftops for weeks to escape Russian violence.[60]

The Swiss journalist Max Schnetzer notes in his diaries that one could not condemn all the Russian soldiers for rape; still, in his collection of eyewitness accounts of the first days of the Russian occupation of Berlin, he made clear the extent of the violence. How did the Russians behave, Schnetzer asked a journalist colleague, who described the fighting in Wannsee: "In part like pigs, in part like angels . . . In single apartments it often came to wild scenes with women and girls. One woman died from being misused by the soldiers. In other houses, the Russians acted more like friends . . . They are like a hailstorm that only destroys part of the harvest." The situation in Dahlem seemed, from Schnetzer's reports, to have been more serious:

> In one case, a father tries to protect his child, a young girl. The Mongols [the generic term for Soviet Central Asians] stick a three-edged bayonet in his gut. The Russians stand in lines of dozens in front of lone women. In their eagerness, they don't even notice that they [the women] are dying, perhaps because they swallowed poison or from internal bleeding of the organs. Many women bite and scratch to defend themselves, but they are hit over the head with gun butts. Men throw themselves at the soldiers but are dispatched in no time with a shot. Women and girls are chased in gardens and through the streets, followed on top of roofs, and the pursued jump [for their lives]. The women are herded together into rooms. Soldiers pry open their mouths and force them to drink.[61]

Ellen Gräfin Poninski kept a diary of the first weeks and months of the Russian occupation, from the vantage point of her family home in Potsdam. Like Schnetzer, she emphasized the extremes in the behavior of Russian soldiers toward the defeated Germans, from the most brutal and inhuman to the unbelievably generous and kind. Still, she wrote:

> Almost no evening went by, no night, in which we did not hear the pitiful cries for help from women who were attacked on the streets or in the always open houses. All of these abominations are well known. Perhaps in the more lucky zones [of occupation] one thought that the descriptions were exaggerated. But unfortunately the reality was actually even much worse, and I don't have to repeat here the tortures that women and girls, from 10 to 80 years of age, were forced to endure.[62]

Like a number of other diarists and memoirists of the period, Poninski compared the behavior of Soviet soldiers to that of primitive children, who could be extremely kind, especially to children, and also viciously brutal. Peter Bloch, who lived through the first weeks of the occupation in Kleinmachnow, outside Berlin, wrote about the Russians: "They were unpredictable, brutal as Huns and innocent as children. One never knew where one stood. They could calmly shoot down people and rape women; [they could] give children chocolate, and stand before a stall of young rabbits and carry on laughingly and wonderingly."[63] Even American intelligence officers had trouble reconciling the stories of "raping, looting, and assault" with the numerous reports of kind and correct behavior.[64]

The Soviets certainly knew that the Germans were afraid of them in Berlin. Major General I. V. Shikin, commander of GlavPURKKA, noted that when German women met up with Soviet soldiers, they would "raise their hands, cry and shake all over from fear." According to Shikin, though, once the women realized that nothing would happen to them and that the Nazis had lied about the true nature of the Soviet soldiers, everything was fine.[65] In a post-perestroika interview, Shikin's deputy, Major General M. I. Burtsev, former head of the Seventh Section of Glav-PURKKA, claimed that stories of rape had been much overdone. Besides, he chuckled, most of the cases of rape were like the woman who had complained to him about having been raped on the floor instead of in the bedroom.[66]

RAPE IN THE ZONE

Although Greater Berlin seems to have absorbed the brunt of the rape and pillage by Soviet soldiers, the rest of the zone occupied by Soviet troops did not avoid similar horrors. One report from Rostock noted that during the first two or three days of the occupation, Soviet soldiers were too busy chasing after the retreating German troops to cause much damage among the civilian population. In fact the civilians took few precautions as they looted food storage centers and foraged for fuel. "But from the fourth day this was interrupted. After the entry of new troops, an unbroken chain of plunder and rape began. Men, like Prof. Büchsel, who wanted to protect their women were murdered; women and girls were raped in the presence of their children and parents." Even after the normal work of the occupation began, continued the Rostock report, rape and pillage went on unabated.[67] Despite complaints from the German authorities in Rostock to the SVA-Mecklenburg headquarters in Schwerin, incidents of Soviet criminal violence in Rostock continued to be reported in great numbers, at least through the summer of 1946. This was due in good measure to the indiscipline of Soviet naval units stationed close by in Warnemünde.[68]

The Russian commandant in Magdeburg was known to be very hard on soldiers who raped, sometimes executing those caught in the act. In the Magdeburg district, rape was most often attributed to recently released Russian POWs or those who had been in forced labor.[69] Small towns sometimes suffered the worst problems from Soviet troops. A Social Democratic Party informant in one such town outside of Dresden wrote: "To be sure, I found my hometown on the surface completely untouched, but I noticed how the Soviet troops had plundered everything that came into their hands. I saw how German women and girls, sometimes just children, were raped."[70] In Gernerode, the German police chief could not control marauding drunken soldiers and had to ask for help from the local commandant two or three times every night.[71] In Bitterfeld, the incidence of rape reached shocking proportions.[72]

There was very little that the German police could do about the situation. In the first months of the occupation, they were armed only with billy clubs and intervened at their own risk. Meanwhile Soviet soldiers usually carried their weapons with them on their rampages—pistols and machine guns—and did not hesitate to turn them on the police. Even after the German police began carrying sidearms at the beginning of 1946, they were not allowed to use their weapons against Allied soldiers. The police archives are filled with complaints about their inability to protect German women from rapists "in the uniform of the Red Army."[73] Even when the police were able to seize the culprits, they had to turn them over to the local commandants, who sometimes were uninterested in prosecuting the criminals. There were even a number of cases in which German police and civilians tried to stop the rapes by seizing the offending soldiers, only to be attacked by other soldiers. In some instances, German police officers and civilians found themselves arrested by NKVD operations groups for abusing Soviet soldiers.[74] The NKVD personnel were also known to brutalize the population and even engage in rape themselves, which made the problem of controlling Soviet troops all the more complicated.[75]

Even in those areas initially occupied by the American and British troops and turned over to the Soviets in late June and early July 1945—in exchange, according to Allied agreements, for the Western zones of Berlin—rape became a severe problem for the German population. The later mayor of Zerbst, a communist since 1926, had waited with high expectations, he reported, for the Americans to leave and the Soviets to march in, a feeling shared by a large number of leftists in Thüringen and parts of the province of Saxony (later Saxony-Anhalt) in late June 1945. He and his comrades had heard rumors of rape in the East but had considered them typical Nazi propaganda. After the arrival of the Russians, however, "the first women came to us who had been raped and raised a great fuss. We yelled at each other. I was affected the worst ... Rapes, assaults, murders, one after the other. Over a hundred raped women were cared for just in the local school. These women had been manhandled by the Russians in the most horrible, animal-like manner."[76] Reports from Halle and Weimar also emphasized the lack of discipline among the Soviet troops pulling into former American-occupied territory.[77] A description of an incident in Weimar is not untypical of this aspect of daily life in the newly acquired territories of the Soviet zone.

> In Weimar on the Marktstrasse, a Russian first lieutenant came into a barbershop at the beginning of October [1945]. He was drunk and although the waiting room next to the salon was full of people, he grabbed the good-looking 21-year-old cashier and raped her on the sales table. None of the men present dared to interfere with the officer. Only when the proprietress of the store asked help from two Russian officers on the street, could this animal be overpowered.[78]

In the Weimar case, as in many others, "a great number of highly educated and cultivated Russian officers were terribly ashamed of the behavior of their compatriots."[79] Yet today, when interviewing veterans of the Soviet Military Administration and veterans of the East Prussian campaign, one gets the overwhelming sense that former Soviet officers are anxious to forget the behavior of their fellow soldiers (and their own indifference to it at the time). Neither in memoirs nor in histories of the period is the issue of rape treated as a proper subject of discussion.

The attempt by Soviet authorities to push along the social revolution in the zone was also accompanied by rape and pillage. Junkers and large-scale farmers, especially, became the objects of retribution for Soviet soldiers, partly in response to the ideological presuppositions and campaigns about the role of the Junkers (portrayed as *pomeshchiki*, or noble landowners, and kulaks) in Nazism, partly as a result of the intense land reform program carried out by the Soviet Military Administration and its German allies. The process of dispossessing large landowners was not infrequently accompanied by rampages by Soviet soldiers, first when they entered the local agricultural regions in April and May 1945 and then again in September 1945, when the Soviets took the initiative—along with the German authorities—in carrying out far-reaching land reforms. More than 8,000 families were affected by the expropriation of landholdings of more than 100 hectares. In addition, approximately 4,000 other farms were expropriated as part of the campaign against alleged former Nazis and war criminals.

In Vorpommern, Brandenburg, and Mecklenburg, areas of larger landholding, German Junkers and farmers sometimes fled for their lives to the West. Those unlucky enough to be caught on their estates during the initial Soviet advance received some of the harshest treatment from the invading soldiers. Rape, death, destruction, and pillage were characteristic of the fate of German "Junkertum." Suicides were also not uncommon when families faced the invading army and the threat of rape and humiliation. But even after "order" was established, the families of large landowners had little or no protection from German or Soviet authorities against the whims of local soldiers. In a recent collection of some 150 cases describing the situation of landowners in the East, few of the reporters were anxious to talk about the problem of rape; as for many memoirists, it was hard for them to recall the trauma and shame of that period. Still, dozens of these cases explicitly described terrible instances of rape and violence, and even more implied the same.[80]

Even after the expropriations and arrests of the Junkers, the rural nature of Mecklenburg and the constant movement of refugees and troops in the countryside made rape a constant occurrence. Erich Gniffke wrote to Pieck and Grotewohl in June 1946 that all of Mecklenburg, but especially the counties of Neubrandenburg and Rostock were "deeply troubled" by the incessant violence: rapes, beatings, shootings, and the like. People who refused to turn over goods to the Soviets or who resisted rape attempts were shot and sometimes killed. Isolated farm houses were broken into and the women raped. During the first three weeks of May (1946), Gniffke wrote to the party leaders, there were twenty-four incidents of breaking and entering combined with rape.[81]

According to records kept at the German refugee camp in Hof/Moschendorf and translated by American military intelligence, incidents of rape continued to plague the lives of German women in the Soviet zone at least until the beginning of 1947. It is probably inevitable that refugees from the Soviet zone exaggerated the harshness of conditions they left behind. Still, a brief digest of a small section of these reports provides shocking evidence that the problem of rape continued long after the initial occupation and the setting up of the military administration.

—8 June '46. Mistreatment, rape of a 14-year-old child, pregnant and with VD. Shooting, even of a Frenchman who stood up for a German. Rape and impregnation of the daughter of the man who had been shot . . . Daughter died 19 Sept. '46 from the consequences of mistreatment. —14 June '46 . . . Rapes, one woman 5 times within 2 hours. —15 June '46. Rapes up to 80 years, escape of women; jumps out of windows, breaking feet and legs. Raping in presence of husbands. Looting . . . Mistreatments, shootings, looting, rapes, mistreatment of women (on bare behind, in spite of being sick) with whips . . . —22 June '46. Attempt of rape with threat. Spared because of pollution [menstruation] . . . —22 June '46. Looting, rapes; herself raped three times in succession; once more the same day. The next day raped three times . . . —25 June '46. Rapes; herself raped twice, once, and four times; age 16 years. March to [from?] East Prussia. Mistreatments. Mother presumably shot.[82]

Other evidence also indicates that despite the improvement in administration and law enforcement by the fall of 1945, poor discipline of Russian troops continued to create problems for an otherwise generally competent administration in the Soviet zone. The Potsdam kommandantura compiled a list of crimes carried out by Russians against Germans in July and the first half of August 1946, in which rape and attempted rape figured prominently along with thefts, beatings, and illegal expropriations.[83] On similar lists of Soviet crimes compiled in Brandenburg, Saxony, and Mecklenburg, the incidence of rape was comparable with that of armed assaults, beatings, and thievery.[84] In the district of Brandenburg, for example, the local information officer reported to his superiors that in May 1946 alone there were seven cases of rape by Soviet soldiers, forty-two of "marauding," and twenty-one others. These did not include frequent instances of thievery from gardens and orchards, drunken debauchery, or attempted rape. The Soviet officer added that all of this crime gave ammunition to those who claimed that "indiscipline and lack of respect for the law is a general characteristic of Russians, and that, as long as the Russians are in Germany, Germans cannot feel safe . . ."[85]

In fact, American military intelligence noticed that more and more

German letters from the Soviet zone (perlustrated by American authorities) compared "favorably [the] conditions in the Soviet Zone with conditions in the American and British Zones." But if food rations were superior in the East and denazification less chaotic and inconsistent, the letters continued to complain about rape.[86] The dismantling troops in the Soviet zone, often comprised of former POWs, caused particular problems, as did the dangerous labor battalions, whose members had already committed disciplinary infractions. In terms of personal security for women in the Soviet zone, matters seemed to get only worse again during the summer and fall of 1946, but they improved by the beginning of 1947, at least according to SPD observers in the West.[87] Still, according to the same sources, garrison towns, like Frankfurt-Oder, remained severe trouble spots long into 1947. After dark, German women in Frankfurt were forced to barricade themselves in their homes. Even the Soviet commandant was hesitant to discipline the large contingents of Soviet troops gathered there to return to the Soviet Union. Periodically in Frankfurt, when the raping and pillaging threatened to turn into drunken riots, the Soviet authorities called in tanks and reinforcements from nearby Fürstenwalde.[88]

When considering the problem of rape in 1946 and 1947, regional variations play a very important role. In border towns like Frankfurt-Oder, for example, and in naval centers like Rostock and Warnemünde, rape was an endemic problem. The readiness of local commandants to deal with the problem similarly affected the incidence of rape. Sometimes outbreaks of rape and violence accompanied the movement of troops, or the stationing of large numbers of new arrivals, as was in the case in Neubrandenburg (Mecklenburg). If the incidence of rape was brought under control for the most part in Berlin, some other large cities, like Chemnitz, experienced periodic outbreaks of violence. In March 1946, just within a couple of days, numerous cases of group and individual rape were reported, some of which resulted in the murder of German women. Chemnitz SED leaders wrote several letters to the city's commandant asking that something be done to stop the violence. Most Germans could understand the problems of discipline immediately following the capitulation, wrote the German communists: "that—is a function of war." But it was completely unwarranted eight months later. After noting the "systematic" and "planned" character of the violence, the local Soviet political officer noted: "the behavior of the troops in the city of Chemnitz is unacceptable; it arouses the dissatisfaction of the population and aggravates their relationship to the Red Army."[89] But Chemnitz was not alone as a trouble spot among the large cities of zone. According to the kommandantura in Leipzig, every day Soviet soldiers were reported to have committed five or six cases of thievery, assault, beating, and rape.[90]

Transportation centers and railway crossroads also proved particularly dangerous for German women in the zone. The Lehrter Bahnhof in Berlin was a notorious hangout for Russian soldiers, who got drunk and molested passengers. The SED Women's Committee reported that drunken Russians climbed on the trains, stole food and belongings, and, almost as an afterthought, raped the women. Railway officials who attempted to intervene were threatened and beaten up.[91] Rank-and-file antifascist women complained at a Berlin meeting that they could not go outside of town to organize village women because they would be attacked by soldiers on the trains. Besides, they stated, the conditions for women in the villages themselves were exceedingly dangerous: "outside of town soldiers knock on doors all night long, enter homes, and demand whatever they want, threatening with weapons." The chief of labor recruitment for the Berlin magistrate, Hans Jendretzki, put the problem unambiguously. It was important to send women out of the towns to help with agricultural work and with bringing in the harvest, "but to send them outside of town means to doom them to rape."[92] An SED report correctly noted that: "These facts hurt our movement, because the village inhabitants unfortunately think that we are in the position to help them." The "general outrage" was great, people were angry about the stories of brutal rape, and many now felt that Nazi propaganda had been right all along about the Russians.[93]

Although the Soviets did the best they could to bring their troops under control, it is important to understand that incidents of rape continued up to (and no doubt after) the founding of the German Democratic Republic. Throughout the period, the port towns of Mecklenburg remained dangerous for German women. One Soviet report noted that in Schwerin a Free German Youth (FDJ) functionary's wife was raped by two Soviet officers and that a city official was kidnapped by Russian soldiers, driven out of town, repeatedly raped, and left for dead. The same report, from February 1948, also noted that in Wismar, workers refused to go out at night because of attacks by Russian soldiers, and in Rostock things were quiet only until a new ship arrived, when assaults and rapes multiplied again.[94] Some towns labeled the roads between the garrisons and towns as "streets of death," and German women learned to avoid going on the roads at night. The local Frauenbund (Women's League) in Klausdorf complained to the Soviet commandant in April *1949* that "men in Russian uniform" harassed and attacked so many women that it was impossible to hold any meetings after dark. No woman in her right mind would venture onto the streets.[95]

THE SOVIET RESPONSE

Soviet authorities understood perfectly well how much political damage they suffered as a result of the behavior of their soldiers.[96] In Moscow, Dimitrov received a report from the zone in November 1945 that the bourgeois parties in particular were having a field day exploiting the terrible behavior of Red Army soldiers: " 'So, you'd like to become a Communist?' they said to the workers. 'Here, look at what the Red Army men are doing. And who are these Red Army men? They are the Communists. Do you really want to be like that?' "[97] Even K. Gofman, who was a special correspondent in Germany for the Red Army newspaper *Krasnaia zvezda*, complained to Dimitrov that Soviet soldiers were completely out of control, and that orders against rape and pillage did little good. He suggested that the propaganda organs of SVAG and GlavPURKKA deal with the soldiers on an everyday level to eliminate "this evil, which carries such a huge cost for our political prestige in Germany."[98]

It was not until the replacement of pure military commanders with more experienced administrators in late June 1945 that a concerted effort was made to stop the waves of rape and pillage in the zone, but even then some commandants simply ignored the problem. The fact that many local troops were not under their command in any case made the situation even more difficult. Some German and Soviet observers noted that frontline troops tended to be more disciplined that those who followed. But what became apparent as the occupation progressed was that each successive set of replacements began their encounter with Germany with rape and plunder, whether they were the very first troops in Berlin, or those who came in 1946 and 1947.[99] In other words, the problem was not one particular cohort of troops or another; it was, rather, the ignitable combination of aggressiveness and defensiveness that was associated with first-time occupation duty. In addition, virtually any time troops were moved, or shifted from summer camps to winter barracks, the moves were accompanied by outbreaks of violence, rape included.[100]

A serious setback to discipline in the ranks was caused by the demobilization order of June 23, 1945, which released from duty older soldiers among the enlisted men and noncommissioned officers.[101] Younger soldiers from Ukraine and Belorussia, areas that had experienced the brunt of Nazi occupation, are known to have been more prone to rape than the older soldiers who were demobilized. Those demobilized also included soldiers who had a higher or secondary agricultural education, former teachers and professors, and soldiers who had been wounded three or more times or who had been in the army seven or more years. Soldiers who had started their higher education before the war could return to finish. It was probably also important to the new wave of rapes that all women who had been sergeants or in regular formations—except those specialists who wanted to stay in the army—were immediately demobilized by the June 23 order.[102]

In a recent interview, the SVAG veteran I. S. Drabkin suggested that it was not the soldiers who caused most of the problems with rape in the occupation administration, but former Soviet POWs and Soviet citizens working for SVAG, who often wore uniforms like any other Soviet soldiers. They were the ones who harbored the deepest resentments against the Germans, Drabkin noted, feelings that periodically erupted in rape and looting.[103]

Perhaps even more important for the incidence of rape was the fact that local commandants, subject to the orders and influence of SVAG headquarters in Berlin, had little control over the combat units stationed near their towns, which were often commanded by officers who had superior rank and who were indifferent to the political goals of the Soviet occupation. The case of Merseburg was typical in this regard. The police chief there complained to the commandant about the growing reports of "murder, robbery, and rape." In his view, the ability of the perpetrators to withdraw to their barracks and camps without being arrested by the police made crime too easy for them. The commandants tried to help, he stated, but they, too, were frustrated by having no control of local units. This was especially the case when Red Army men committed repeated crimes during the May Day holiday:

> Even on the eve of May Day, a number of women returning home from the torch-light parade were trampled on purpose by a group of soldiers on horseback and were beaten . . . After the plundering [of their homes], the women residents regardless of their age were severely abused and then raped. (Apparently, one of the occupants was shot first and then

raped.) During the day as well in the city parks the story was the same, where women walking alone had their clothes torn off them by several soldiers and were raped five or six times by several soldiers.[104]

The Merseburg police chief reported, in conclusion, that from January 1, 1946, to May 3, 1946, serious crimes carried out by "persons in Soviet uniform" in the region of Halle-Merseburg included: 34 murders, 345 robberies after breaking and entering, 328 robberies on the street, 60 train robberies, 123 stolen cows, 212 assaults and injuries (10 ending in death), and 162 rapes.[105]

After the summer of 1945, Soviet soldiers caught in the act of rape were generally punished, though the harshness of the punishment varied. In some cases the offender was severely punished (even executed, in the case of rape and murder) in front of his entire battalion, to get the point across to other soldiers.[106] For "debauchery," including attempted rape, public drunkenness, and disturbing the peace, one group of Soviet soldiers received ten days in detention. In a violent assault and rape case, the soldier had hit a superior officer who tried to take him in for the crime. In that case, the soldier was sentenced to four years in a labor camp, with the loss of his civil rights.[107] But far too often there seemed to be no punishment at all. At the same time, it was difficult if not impossible for a German woman to bring a Soviet soldier to justice.[108] In the cases where the German police were able to seize the perpetrators before they disappeared back into their units, the soldiers were always turned over to the Soviet military authorities, and the Germans had no control over the further course of the investigations.

After a period of great laxness about relations between Russians and Germans that lasted until the spring and summer of 1947, the Soviet authorities tried to deal with a variety of problems—rape included—that had strained Soviet-German relations by increasingly isolating their troops from the German population. Unlike the Americans or British, the Soviets had initially had no rules against fraternization with Germans, something that had worried American analysts who saw it as giving the Soviets an advantage with the German population.[109] (Not a little jealousy about the successes of Soviet soldiers with German women was also at play here.) Soviet officers were often billeted with German families, usually with excellent results. As Alexander Werth observed, "There was more mateyness between the Russians and Germans than one would have expected."[110] "In many German families," wrote an SPD observer, "single Russians have acclimated well and act like sons in the house."[111] Much as in the other zones of Germany once the nonfraternization rules were abandoned, liaisons were formed between German women, whose husbands had died or were still in POW camps, and Soviet soldiers, especially Soviet officers, large numbers of whom had "occupation wives."[112] The Soviets had the same advantages as their Western counterparts: they could supply decent food, fuel in the winter, and something to drink and smoke.[113] The fate of these "families" varied. A few escaped to the West, others fell apart when the Soviet officers were recalled home, and still others were broken up by jealous wives who intervened with superiors in Moscow.[114]

There were also very nasty cases of the brutal exploitation of German women servants by Soviet officers. Those women who were forced to take care of the bachelor officers' quarters had a particularly hard time of it. Sometimes the women were repeatedly raped; other times they were beaten. The head of the Information Administration in Zittau, a Senior Lieutenant "R," lived with a German women, but constantly drank and caroused with other Germans from the town. A truly debauched character, at least according to reports from his superiors, "R" invited a group of local German industrialists and their wives to his birthday party, where he raped one of the women in front of the rest. The reports on the lieutenant indicate only that he was given a leave of absence as a result.[115]

A number of issues contributed to the first sporadic orders banning fraternization in the Soviet zone during the summer of 1946. Certainly the spread of venereal disease was a factor, as was the continuing indiscipline of Soviet troops and the growing number of mixed German-Russian households. Increasing manifestations of the cold war also made Soviet-German contacts more suspect. In Magdeburg in July 1946 an order was issued requiring Soviets to obtain written authorization from the city commandant to visit German apartments; Germans and Soviets who did not comply with the order were to be "severely punished."[116] By June 1947 the Soviets had adopted a State Secrets Act that assessed harsh punishment for passing on almost any kind of information to foreigners, and in January 1948 unofficial contact with foreigners was outlawed altogether.[117] These laws had an immediate effect on the still relatively loose relations of Soviets with Germans in the zone. Commanding officers were pressured to enforce the ban on cohabitation, which called for the removal of any officer caught fraternizing with a German woman; this kind of "immoral behavior" on the part of Soviet officers would not be tolerated. General Kolesnichenko from Thüringen complained about the order, which he claimed would compel him to send more than a third of his officers back to the Soviet Union. These were healthy men with normal sex drives, he wrote indignantly to the Central Committee. They found themselves "in a situation of constant temptation," since German women sought the material benefits of liaisons with Soviet officers. Kolesnichenko warned the Soviet party leaders that unless they made sure that no bachelors were stationed in Germany and that families were sent along with married officers, the order could not be enforced.[118]

During the spring and summer of 1947, the Cadres Department of the Soviet Central Committee increased its influence on personnel policies within SVAG, insisting that officers who associated with German women be sent back home. Of a group of 223 officers sent to the Thüringen kommandantura in 1947, 48 were relieved of their duties because of "immoral" behavior and 30 more because of "moral turpitude." Some had exploited their positions to gain favors from German women. The others were accused of drunkenness, debauchery and rape, living with German women, and armed assaults.[119] Typically the Soviets explained these transgressions to themselves as the consequences of insufficient propaganda among officers and men in Germany about their occupation mission. As a result, within the Group of Forces there was a noticeable upswing in mandatory classes, Komsomol meetings, and general propaganda and information sessions during the summer of 1947.

According to a secret CPSU(b) communication of July 16, 1947, all communists in the Soviet zone were called on to make concerted efforts to improve "the honor and dignity" of Red Army officers and SVAG employees in Germany by enforcing the orders on cohabitation and fraternization.[120] At the same time, Marshal Sokolovskii issued the command to move Soviet soldiers out of entire villages and city sections in order to avoid any regular contacts with the German population.[121] Germans were moved out of areas where the Soviet troops were to be concentrated. According to Iurii Korol'kov, special correspondent for *Pravda* in the zone, this order increased rather than decreased the level of violence and disturbances in the zone, once again discrediting the Soviet occupation authorities and creating an "unhealthy mood among the German population." The Germans were understandably panicked by the order to move; many committed suicide, and even "antifascist" politicians complained about Soviet methods. In Stralsund, 480 families were forced to move within a few days, and 162 of them had been refugees in the first place. Usually they were given no time to pack, and the evictees' personal belongings were simply dumped into the steets. Carefully nurtured gardens were destroyed and abandoned. New housing was hard, if not impossible, to find. The Soviet officers, unhappy about the action in the first place, treated the Germans very badly. In the end, Korol'kov asked, what was the sense of such an operation, especially in view of the fact that the SED would be lucky to get the support of 10 percent of the population in the areas of forced evacuation.[122] In Potsdam, Magdeburg, Leipzig, and many other cities, large apartment houses were sequestered by the Soviet authorities for their personnel, and whole streets of large cities were taken over by the army, their German residents expelled. "In the cities, barbed wire was erected around these 'Military Districts.' In the countryside, whole villages were transformed into Russian settlements."[123]

The motivations behind these actions are made clearer in the text of a comparable top-secret order—Order no. 009 of May 23, 1947—for the Soviet forces in Austria, signed by Major General Kurasov, that was later published by an émigré newspaper: "Recently it has been noticed that many Soviet officers have been yielding to bourgeois ideology thanks to their relations with the local population. This produces in them an anti-Soviet disposition and [even can turn them into] actual traitors to their country." Russians were supposed to defend the peace and "demonstrate the superiority of Soviet life through conduct befitting the Soviet soldier," the order said. Sometimes, however, Soviet officers too easily forgot that they were "raised in the highest intellectual culture on earth—Marxism-Leninism-Stalinism." Too many lived among the civilian population and with German women. Kurasov's order brought an end to all of this: "Not a single officer is allowed to carry on a relationship with the local population, under threat of the strictest punishment." All Soviet officers and soldiers were ordered to reside in their barracks and quarters, a strict system of special passes for non-official travel was instituted, and the absolute ban on relations with the local population was reiterated. The order also was intended to eliminate indiscipline among the troops. It called for the severe punishment of drunkenness and made officers responsible for their soldiers' behavior *day or night*.[124] At the same time, similar pressure was put on Soviet officers by SVAG and the Group of Soviet Occupation Forces in Germany to step up their efforts to fight criminality and defend "social order" among their troops.[125]

Despite the apparent strictness of the orders, the initial attempts in the summer of 1947 to eliminate contacts between Soviet soldiers and German civilians were often subverted by illegal fraternization. As one of the subjects in the Harvard Interview Project reports, officers "hid German girls in their room. One chief of command hid his girlfriend in a safe"; those who were sent to check on the illegal presence of German girls in officers' billets were sometimes beaten up and even murdered by the suspected offenders.[126] Still, many officers were caught and punished, and others were sent home. Captain Shulin, senior officer in the Quedlinburg kommandantura and secretary of the local party committee, was repeatedly chastised for living with a German girl, but he refused to mend his ways. As a result, he was transferred at the end of 1948 to another post. There he decided to escape to the West with his girlfriend. As General Russov reported to the SVAG party aktiv, the new kommandantura had not been informed of Shulin's problems: "Only thanks to the vigilance of a border guard was he caught up with, and [then he] committed suicide."[127]

Despite their official actions, the Soviets were not yet ready to admit to a nonfraternization policy. At a public forum in January 1949, a German communist, Helene Berner, claimed that there was no formal ban on fraternization: "Of course members of the Red Army and Soviet citizens in general can discuss with Germans, can invite them as guests, and can visit them."[128] But even these kinds of "visits" were made impossible in the summer of 1949, when stricter rules were introduced that totally isolated Russian troops from German citizens. Under no circumstances could Soviet army officers be permitted "to have their own apartments, or to employ German servants or to live in dwellings where Germans lived," all of which were methods used to avoid the nonfraternization rules.[129] An SPD reporter observed the strict rules in Scharfheide in July 1949; the Russians, he wrote, "were not allowed to visit any locales nor could they speak with any Germans, and were completely cut off from the world."[130]

The clearest message to the troops about the unacceptability of rape did not come until March 1949, when the Presidium of the Supreme Soviet issued a directive increasing the punishment for the crime. The directive was sent by SVAG to every kommandantura in the zone, for distribution to all soldiers, sergeants, and officers. The communication pointedly stated that the new directive would be applied to all Soviet citizens in Germany. The new punishment for rape, according to the law of January 4, 1949, was considered Draconian in comparison to early Soviet laws: now conviction for rape carried a mandatory sentence of ten to fifteen years in a labor camp; rape of minors, group rape, and rape resulting in severe injury carried sentences of ten to twenty years.[131] Only through strict enforcement of this law could the Soviets eliminate what Tiul'panov called "the unpleasant impression" left by the behavior of the Red Army soldiers and address the constant lament of the Germans, that women could not "walk on the streets at night."[132]

VENEREAL DISEASE

The primary reasons for separating Russian soldiers from the German population were political and ideological. But certainly the persistence and spread of venereal disease in the ranks provided another motivating factor for the new strictness about relations with Germans. At the outbreak of the war, in both the Soviet Union and Germany, the incidence of venereal disease had been remarkably low. The war accelerated the spread of the affliction, but the occupation of Germany turned venereal disease into a "plague on the population" *(Volksseuchen)*.[133] Part of the problem was that syphillis was initially branded by Soviet authorities as a "bourgeois" disease, as symbolic of the moral inferiority of the West, to be treated with punishment and isolation rather than with medicine.[134] Moreover, until late 1945 and early 1946 there was almost no penicillin available to Soviet military doctors, and earlier, more primitive methods of combatting venereal disease—including the use of sulpha drugs—took a long time and were much less effective. The German press in the East complained that the West purposely withheld the technology for the mass production of penicillin from the Soviets.[135] In fact most of what the Soviets knew about penicillin they learned from the German health industry technicians and laboratories that they seized in the Eastern zone.[136] Even after Soviets and Germans in the zone began producing penicillin, however, there was still a severe shortage, and it was available only in the most extreme cases.[137]

Soviet soldiers who committed rape were a major cause of the rapid spread of the disease in the zone. Especially in the more isolated villages in Saxony and Mecklenburg, far from any medical help, rape victims of all ages suffered from venereal disease.[138] In the Soviet Third Attack Army in Magdeburg, a special battalion had been formed of troops infected by venereal disease. They were kept isolated from the German population as well as from other Soviet military units.[139] Unfortunately for the German population, the isolation practices did not always have the desired effect. A senior instructor for propaganda in Luckenwalde, Lieutenant Gusenko, reported to his superiors a particularly horrendous series of events. Preparations for the May holidays (1946) were going as planned, but the mood in the town, Gusenko wrote, was awful.

> This can be explained by the fact that in the first days of April of this year, a military unit (a camp of those sick with venereal disease—syphilis) moved near the town. The venereal disease camp was strictly guarded, [and] enclosed by wire. But individuals managed to break through to the town, to populated areas, and did great damage to the population of the region. They raped women, vandalized apartments, beat up Germans who opposed them ... Ten to fifteen such incidents were registered by the kommandantura every day. On April 15, two soldiers beat up a secretary of the Socialist Unity Party, "A," because he wouldn't give them anything to smoke or drink ... In a forest on April 17, two soldiers raped a sixty-year-old woman from Luckenwalde.

The report continued with a long list of robberies and rapes by diseased soldiers, including the rape of several children. The culprits were sometimes caught and returned to their camp, only to break out again. Lieutenant Gusenko's complaint was sent up the line, first to his Propaganda Administration superior, Major Mil'khiker, and then (in much abbreviated form), to Major General Sharov, commander of the Brandenburg SVA. Sharov then sent a report (May 7, 1947) to Lieutenant General Makarov, a member of the SVAG Military Council. From all of these reports, it is apparent that the venereal disease unit number 12202 had a history of this kind of behavior, and that is why it had been moved to Luckenwalde in the first place. While the reports circulated, the attacks in the village continued. On May 5, a group of soldiers from the camp forced their way into a restaurant, stabbed a customer, and raped three women. On May 6, a sixteen-year-old girl was raped and found dead. Patrols were strengthened in the town, but the problems continued until special measures were instituted by the Brandenburg command and the local citizenry.[140]

The prevalence of prostitution or semiprostitution, including the exchange of sex for a meal or cigarettes, also contributed to the rapid spread of venereal disease. During a series of raids on bars in Saxony in 1946, it was found that some 60 percent of the women carried some form of sexually transmitted disease.[141] Like many of the other problems that plagued Soviet-occupied Germany in the first days after the peace, preventing the spread of venereal disease was the responsibility of local commandants, some of whom reacted immediately, others of whom ignored the problem. The Soviet commandant in Tempelhof (Berlin) released Russian doctors from their normal rounds and hired German assistants to examine German rape victims who feared they had been infected by sexually transmitted diseases.[142] On June 1, 1945, the commandant and the local mayor of Reinickendorf (Berlin) already agreed that "immediately all women who have been visited several times by soldiers of the Red Army should register themselves at the local mayor's offices. Due to the fact that many of these women will not register of their own free will, all neighbors are obligated to get them to register." Both the women and the neighbors could be punished for lack of compliance.[143] However, many commandants did little to attack the problem until August 1945, when the Soviet military government finally issued a formal edict, Order no. 25 of the Supreme Command, "On Measures to Combat Sexual Diseases in the Soviet Occupied Zone in Germany."

Order no. 25 provided medical personnel for newly funded clinics devoted to stemming the spread of venereal disease. The order also mandated that women working in all food industries, as well as in hotels, restaurants, bakeries, canteens, grocery stores, and similar institutions, have a monthly medical examination. While measures against prostitution and semiprostitution remained erratic and inconsequential, the order did insist in a general sense that "one must carry on a determined struggle against prostitution. Those women who have been prostitutes and have venereal disease must be taken care of, even if by force. Those women who have no means to live must be given work in industry or in agriculture."[144]

That Order no. 25 did little to contain the serious spread of venereal disease is apparent from the language accompanying Order no. 030 of February 12, 1946. According to Order no. 030, civilians suffering from venereal disease were not being treated in hospitals and clinics: "The battle against prostitution, the main cause of [the spread] of venereal diseases, is not being carried out." Although the new order made little progress in establishing methods for controlling prostitution, it did specify guidelines for the German health administration and responsible Soviet medical officers on treating sick women. It also made available a specific sum of money to pay for medicines, provided some raw materials to make them, and layed out a plan to increase the manufacture of penicillin in the zone.

Unfortunately, the attitude of Soviet authorities to the disease in their own ranks was not very enlightened. Even though Soviet soldiers obviously feared retribution if they were diagnosed with venereal disease by their own doctors, Order no. 030 forbade German doctors, under the threat of severe penalities, to treat Soviet soldiers suffering from the disease.[145] The Soviet authorities responded to the increase of infection among their soldiers by launching a "decisive struggle" against the lack of discipline and "sexual licentiousness" in the ranks of SVAG and the occupation forces. "Strong disciplinary measures" were to be taken against the offenders.[146] In responding to these orders, the Brandenburg deputy commander insisted that every soldier and sergeant (though not officer) who returned from a leave in town had to be given a clean bill of health before he could return to the barracks.[147]

The medical authorities of the German administration in the zone tried to respond to the Soviet orders by instituting a series of measures against the spread of venereal disease. The city government of Berlin, for example, called for all waiters, waitresses, cooks, and musicians, as well as all personnel in dance halls, bars, and the like, to be examined by medical doctors. The German authorities also issued much stricter regulations regarding prostitutes, first by insisting that they be examined weekly, and second by defining prostitution broadly enough to include semiprostitutes and dance-hall girls.[148] The German authorities followed up Order no. 030 by establishing a widespread educational program that included films, traveling exhibitions, and lectures. The women's antifascist committees also got involved in the "fight against venereal disease," by sponsoring a series of lectures and informational brochures.[149] Other useful measures included the founding of "homes for wayward girls" and the institution of a number of "night clinics" that were available for diagnosis and treatment of venereal disease twenty-four hours a day.[150]

But it was simply beyond the resources of either the Germans or the Soviets to handle the spread of the disease. In Potsdam, for example, sexually diseased women and girls (many no older than fifteen or sixteen) were confined to an isolation camp of some eighty primitive barracks buildings. Some of the girls were not infected at all, but were placed in the camp for "licentious behavior and the frequent changing of partners." With the filthy conditions and the absence of even the most basic facilities for washing and cleaning, the women caught all kinds of other diseases as well.[151] Some progress was made in the struggle against the disease when the Allies in Berlin introduced measures that made it possible to prosecute and punish women with fines or forced labor who infected Allied soldiers, but there was of course no recourse for German women who were infected by Allied soldiers. The kommandantura in Berlin passed a series of measures in the fall of 1946 that forced doctors to devote part of their practice to the newly established night clinics, to treat sexually diseased Germans. At the same time, the Allies ordered that all female employees of restaurants, hotels, bars, and nightclubs be subjected to monthly health examinations.[152] In May 1947 the Coordinating Committee of the Allied Control Council itself finally got involved in the attempt to contain venereal disease, by instituting a number of measures intended to share information about each zone's problems with prostitution and venereal disease.[153] But the generally absymal state of the health and nutrition of young people in the Soviet zone and elsewhere in Germany made these measures seem hollow.

SOLDIERS AND BANDITS

The march into Germany was accompanied by an elaborate education program directed at Soviet occupation troops. In military newspapers, in the local Red Corners, and in schools for officers and soldiers, Soviet political officers repeatedly pointed to the superior discipline and behavior of Soviet troops, in the hope that the ideal would become reality. In a typical campaign of this sort, the newspaper *Krasnaia zvezda* (Red Star) published in June 1945 a story about a heroic regiment of guards that had been instrumental in the taking of Berlin: "In their quarters—there was ideal cleanliness. Everywhere was exceptionally good order . . . Everyone is engaged in study, from the oldest officers to the last regular soldier." According to the article, the soldiers carried out tactical exercises, practiced sharpshooting, and listened attentively as veterans described the great campaigns of the war. In the evening, to raise the level of "vigilance," local agitators from the ranks led political discussions on a wide variety of subjects.[154] All the major military newspapers in the Soviet zone and at home painted the same picture of the exactness of Soviet discipline and the high level of political and military preparedness. Nowhere was there any indication of soldiers' incorrect behavior regarding the German population.

If the Red Army was not dominated by the depraved and thuggish creatures pictured in the émigré newspapers *Za svobodu Rossii* (For the Freedom of Russia) and *Rossiia i emigratsiia* (Russia and the Emigration), it was also certainly not the disciplined, highly principled formation depicted by the Soviet military newspapers. In fact, the lack of open recognition by Soviet authorities of the problem of rape unquestionably contributed to its persistence. Certainly attempts were made to convince Soviet soldiers that not all Germans were fascist beasts. The Seventh Section of GlavPURKKA, which had been in charge of propaganda among Nazi troops during the war, turned its resources in occupied Germany to promoting the attributes of progressive Germany. Above the entrance of Humboldt University in Berlin, the Seventh Section raised a banner in Russian that read: "At this University studied the founder of scientific communism, Karl Marx." On the royal Prussian library, the Seventh Section put up another sign, again in Russian for Soviet troops: "Here, in 1895, worked the leader of the Great October Revolution and the Founder of the CPSU(b), Vladimir Il'ich Lenin."[155] In Russian-language newspapers and lectures, Soviet troops were likewise told of the martyrdom of Ernst Thälmann and the close ties between the Bolsheviks and German communism.[156] Russian troops were even told stories of the lives of famous German artists, such as Goethe, Schiller, and Beethoven, to develop their appreciation of German cultural achievements.[157]

The growing insistence in the Soviet press during the summer of 1945 on the exemplary behavior of Soviet troops indicates the extent to which Soviet authorities were actually worried about indiscipline and acts of revenge. Foreign reports about Soviet brutality during the war and after were denounced as "idle chatter," "ignorant slander," and "baseless lies." The following explanation of depredations, still a total denial of their having taken place, is not atypical of the military press's approach to the problem.

> After everything we've suffered at the hands of the Germans, the desire to pay them back for the tears of suffering of the Soviet people is a genuine human emotion. But the soldiers of the Red Army are better and more noble than [to allow] the blind feeling of revenge.
>
> We occupied Germany as victors . . . Soldiers of the Red Army take pride in our great victory, in the power and glory of the Soviet fatherland, and would not for anything undermine their authority as victors. The most thoroughgoing execution of all the laws and codes, iron discipline, high organization, the strictest order—this is the unbreakable law for all Soviet soldiers, and especially for those abroad. They are distinguished by their irreproachable correctness, collectivity, and by their smart appearance, both individually and as a group, inspiring the respect of those around them.

There were those who would try to undermine the morale of Soviet soldiers abroad, the article continued. But proper vigilance would help Soviet soldiers persevere in their duties in Germany. In all of his activities, the Soviet soldier "over and over again confirms the honor and dignity of his socialist fatherland."[158]

Only these excessively positive articles about the behavior of Soviet troops in the occupation give one any sense that there were problems between the Soviet soldiers and German civilians. By the beginning of 1947, critical articles did appear in the military press about Soviet troops in Germany, but they condemned the poor political work carried out on the army, as a part of the Communist Party's reassertion of authority over the Red Army.[159] Similarly, *Sovetskoe slovo,* the newspaper of the Soviet occupation administration in Germany, gives a great deal of attention to the problems of political education, focusing especially on the shortcomings of Komsomol instruction.[160] But in these cases, too, the criticisms are couched in the language of effusive praise for new Komsomol agitators and methods of political indoctrination.

In addition the Soviets tried to convince the Germans that the Russian occupation was, in any case, much more lenient than the American. Especially in late 1947 and early 1948, when Allied cooperation broke down on a number of levels, *Tägliche Rundschau,* the Soviet occupation newspaper for Germans, carried a series of articles describing the sad condition of Germans in the Western zones. What is more, the Americans were described in much the same terms that Germans would have used for the Russians—as marauders and brutes. Exposés from those areas of Germany occupied by the Americans before they were turned over to the Russians served as especially poignant material for comparing the brutal Americans with the cultured and magnanimous Russian occupiers. For example, *Tägliche Rundschau* reprinted portions of a diary written during the American occupation of Magdeburg, which described the plunder of the city by U.S. troops. Nazis were allegedly reinstated in important posts, and the people were treated maliciously by the occupying GIs. Naturally, the newspaper concluded, when the Soviets came, the city breathed a collective sigh of relief. The diary ended, "We could be human again."[161]

The Soviets also let the German authorities know that they would not tolerate any public or private discourse that conceded the fact that Red Army soldiers raped German women. Even in the detailed reports of the first German secret police force in the zone, K-5, which listed the rapes of German women, the perpetrators were always referred to as "a man in

Red Army uniform," "people in Russian uniforms," or "a person in the uniform of a Red Army soldier." This was also the case when it was reported that the rapists were caught and turned over to the local commandant, when every indication was that they were Red Army troops.[162] This sort of language was also adopted by SED members and state bureaucrats.

The primary public response to the problem of rape was left to the German authorities in the East. The Soviets tended to stay out of the polemics carried on between the Western radio and newspapers and the media in eastern Germany, which created a counterpropaganda campaign designed to blame rape, murder, and looting on German bandits in Soviet uniform. Gordon Schaffer, an English journalist sympathetic to the Soviet administration in Germany, reported that Walter Jarich, the police president of Leipzig, told him, "It is only necessary for a bandit to put on a fur hat and speak broken German for the word to go around that there has been a crime committed by the Russians. Girls who want to explain an awkward pregnancy always find it easy to blame a Russian."[163] The German press in the Eastern zone was filled with reports of German criminals in Russian uniform carrying out crimes with a modus operandi associated in the public mind with Soviet soldiers. The "bandits" would dress in Soviet uniform and pound on doors, demanding entrance in broken German (or using a few Russian words). They would rob and murder, killing with unusual brutality, and rape old women and young girls. Some of the criminals were former Hitler Youth members (the so-called Werewolves), who purposely schemed to undermine Soviet authority among Germans; others were simply bandits.[164]

The Communist Party's newspaper *Deutsche Volkszeitung* wrote about one group of alleged bandits in Eberswalde: "In criminal fashion, they tried to create the impression that these misdeeds [robbery, rape] were committed by soldiers of the Red Army. They even used Russian words to strengthen the impression among the victims that they were faced by Russians. The accused have in this fashion not just severely branded the German people, but in the most mean way they have tried to undermine the prestige of the Red Army."[165] The Eberswalde bandits served an important propaganda function throughout the zone. With Soviet blessings, the German authorities conducted a major public trial of the group in January 1946. Some six hundred onlookers were invited into a huge theater to observe the proceedings. Again and again the reporting emphasized the fact that over a long period of time these Germans had successfully masked themselves as Russians when committing rape.[166]

It is of course impossible to know just how much of the violent crime attributed to Russians can be explained by the activities of these alleged German bandits. Given their lack of motive, it is unlikely that they were responsible for any but the smallest percentage of rapes in the Soviet zone. On the other hand, the German and Soviet newspapers do not mention that there were other sources of "Russian crimes" in the zone except for the German bandits and Soviet troops. For example, there were a number of reports that gangs of Russian occupation youth—sons of officers and officials—sometimes armed themselves and engaged in robbery and mayhem in the region around their Karlshorst headquarters.[167] There is also evidence that Russians already in detention camps for one infraction or another regularly escaped and wreaked havoc in the surrounding German villages and towns.[168]

More serious were the gangs of Soviet deserters, displaced persons, liberated POWs, and Russians who had served as forced laborers in Germany. Out of a variety of motivations, these bandits feared service in the Soviet occupation army and were disinclined to return home. Some tried to get to the Western zones; others joined huge illegal gangs in the Carpathian Mountains, especially in eastern Slovakia, and carried out guerilla warfare against regular Soviet army troops. With nearly two million Russian deserters and former POWs at large in Soviet-occupied Europe, it is no wonder that banditry on their part became a serious problem for the occupation.[169] That acts of banditry and rape were committed by these kinds of groups in the Soviet zone is a distinct possibility, though there is simply not enough data to determine much about it. There are reports from as late as 1947 and 1948 of the activity of Russian bandits, presumably deserters, in the woods outside of Berlin.[170]

CAUSES OF RAPE

A few weeks after returning to Germany from the United States, Bertolt Brecht wrote in his journal (October 23, 1948):

> still, after these three years, the workers are shaking, I hear it all over, the panic, caused by the plundering and after the rape, that followed the taking of Berlin, in the workers' quarters the people had awaited the

liberator with desperate joy, arms were outstretched, but the encounter became an attack, which did not spare the seventeen-year-old or the twelve-year-old and took place completely in the open, it is reported that the Russian soldiers still as they fought from house to house, bloody, exhausted, embittered, held their fire so that women could fetch water, led the hungry out of the cellars to the bakeries, helped dig the buried out of the ruins, but after the battle drunken hordes marched through apartments, grabbed the women, shot down the men and women who tried to resist, raped in front of the eyes of children, stood in lines in front of houses and so on, kuckhahn saw a seventeen-year-old shot after the rape, and he saw a commissar shot down by two soldiers who had plundered and attacked him when he tried to talk to them.

Brecht tried to make sense out of the reasons for the violence, especially given all the reports of the generosity and decency of many Soviet soldiers and men. In the end, all he could do was cite the argument made by Major Alexander Dymshits, the chief Soviet cultural officer in Germany.

> d[ymshits] reminds us that the particular tragedy lay in the following: it was hard for the Soviets to get their troops to move on the offensive, socialist slogans and the building of a new economy without competitive struggle had made the masses peaceful. now attacked killing had to be taught; the old instincts had to be called forth, especially so in the [more] backward Soviet peoples—the regiments that committed excesses were mostly peasant regiments from beyond the Urals.[171]

Dymshits's explanation does not go very far toward helping us understand one of the most difficult questions involving the rape of German women by Soviet soldiers, and that is, why it happened. Earlier sections of this discussion have tried to demonstrate that the rape of German women was different in quantity and in its level of violence than similar Soviet activities in the taking of Budapest or the occupation of northeastern Yugoslavia. Similarly, even the surprisingly high incidence of rape and violent crime committed by American soldiers can be compared only superficially with the Soviet case.[172] The poor discipline and rapacity of Soviet soldiers was matched in the Western zones only by French Moroccan troops; especially during the initial occupation of Baden and Württemburg, German women were subject to the same indiscriminate rampaging that they faced in the Eastern zone.[173]

Despite these caveats, rape became a part of the social history of the

Soviet zone in ways unknown to the Western zones. (One could not say the same about prostitution and semiprostitution, which seemed to thrive in all the zones, though in the Western zones much more so than in the East.[174]) It is important to establish the fact that women in the Eastern zone—both refugees from further east and inhabitants of the towns, villages, and cities of the Soviet zone—shared an experience for the most part unknown in the West, the ubiquitous threat and the reality of rape, over a prolonged period of time.

Why did Soviet soldiers commit rape against German women in such large numbers? (There are remarkably few instances reported of the rape of men and boys.[175]) The reasons are many and complex, even reaching beyond the eternal patriarchal threat of rape that recent studies claim is an integral part of men's domination of women.[176] Nonetheless this recent work is correct to emphasize the idea that rape is not fundamentally motivated by sexual needs, as some studies suggest, but rather that it is a crime of violence.[177] The literature on rape is dominated by examinations of the legal ramifications of rape that provide little help here, given the extralegal nature of war and occupation, at least in its initial stages. But it is not enough to say that war breeds rape. Of course, war does artificially separate the sexes. It also has "an uprooting character," disturbing as it does the normal social and communal instruments of control. J. Glenn Gray makes the important observation that "the impersonal violence of war" that comes from routinely killing strangers carries with it the ability to make "copulation . . . an act of aggression." In Gray's scheme, "The girl is the victim and her conquest the victor's triumph."[178] Susan Brownmiller, who wrote a pioneering study of rape and provided an overview of the problem of rape by Soviet soldiers in eastern Germany, notes that armies of liberation tend to have a different attitude and subsequently demonstrate more respect for local women than armies of conquest and subjugation.[179] This observation helps us understand why, for example, Soviet soldiers only sporadically engaged in rape against Polish women, while German women were prime targets. In general, it is also the case that Slavic women (Poles, Czechs, Slovaks, Bulgarians, Serbs) were not subject to the same depredations by Soviets as non-Slavs—Germans and Hungarians.

Brownmiller also aptly notes that as the Allies drove deeper into Germany, "retaliation and revenge" increasingly motivated their soldiers, and rape became a convenient outlet for those emotions. Indeed, the reprehensible behavior of Nazi troops on Soviet soil—including extensive rape and pillage—was often used to explain the behavior of Soviet troops. The famous Soviet commandant of Berlin in the first days after the fall of the German capital, General N. E. Berzarin, indirectly excused the "excesses" of Soviet troops in the following fashion: "During my whole life I have seen nothing like the bestial way German officers and soldiers pursued the peaceful population [of Russia]. All of the destruction you have here in Germany is nothing in comparison."[180]

The Soviets attempted (and in personal interviews *still* attempt) to explain the extent and intensity of their rape incidents compared with the other zones by the straightforward fact that they had a great deal more to retaliate for and more reason for revenge. The journalist Iurii Zhukov writes, for example, that the celebrated Soviet war correspondents Konstantin Simonov (in *Krasnaia zvezda*) and Boris Gorbatov (in *Pravda*) purposely used the graphic horrors of Majdanek near Lublin to motivate Soviet soldiers once they were out of Soviet territory. Gory pictures of Nazi atrocities accompanied the Soviet armies into Poland and across the Oder. Zhukov writes: "Who could have doubted at that time that the people who were responsible for these grisly deeds would soon pay."[181]

The images of German women conveyed in the Soviet media certainly did not hinder notions that they should be the objects of Soviet revenge. The caricaturists in the humor magazine *Krokodil* quite justifiably portrayed German women as equally avid supporters of Nazism as the men. But they tended to misrepresent reality by showing fat and spoiled German wives living the good life behind the front. In fact, the war had already taken a severe toll on German women even before the occupation by the Soviets. In one caricature, a prosperous-looking woman, her daughter, and her maid, surrounded by all manner of goods stolen from the Russians, desperately look for material to hang out the window as a white flag.[182] In another cartoon, a plump bourgeois German Hausfrau is confronted by a strong, lean Russian woman who had worked for her as forced labor. "Now you'll see, Frau," she says sternly, "I've come to collect."[183] Throughout the Soviet press, the idea was widespread that the Germans—women on the homefront included—would have to "pay" for their evil deeds. When the occupation took place, German women were shown as having changed colors too quickly. For example, Leonid Leonov wrote, "Our patrols now stride through Berlin, and German ladies gaze in their eyes invitingly, ready to begin payment of 'reparations' at once. It won't work!"[184]

With the combination of hate propaganda, personal experiences of suffering at home, and a fully demeaning picture of German women in the press, not to mention among the soldiers themselves, Soviet officers and men easily turned on the "Frau" as their victim. The anger of Soviet soldiers seemed to grow as German resistance became more fierce, first in the campaign to reach the Oder, and then in the door-to-door battle to take Berlin.[185] The huge casualties taken by the Soviets in the Battle for Berlin added more fuel to their desire for retribution. But it is apparent that even the seizure of Berlin and the defeat of Nazi Germany did not carry with it a cathartic sense of revenge exacted. It was hard to rejoice over the victory, recalled the journalist and writer Vsevolod Vishnevskii in his diary: "How simple it all is . . . Such a strange feeling that the war is all over and done with. There is *none* of that special atmosphere of triumph that we expected from the capture of Berlin, from victory. The war was too long and hard."[186]

Psychologically, the Soviet occupation of Germany was a continuation of the war. Colonel Sergei Tiul'panov remembered that many officers simply hated the Germans too much to carry out the regular duties of occupation officers. These officers were relieved of duty, he added, and the staff "granted their wishes to return home."[187] Colonel General V. I. Chuikov, one of the great heroes of the final drive into Germany, also wrote about the deep hatred for the Germans, though, like Tiul'panov, he denied any wrongdoing by Soviet soldiers. At the opening of Jena University, Chuikov—then commander of Soviet troops in Thüringen—gave the welcoming address: "I should admit, ladies and gentlemen, that back then at Stalingrad I had such a strong antipathy toward Germany and the German people precisely because the German army carried on its banner only contempt, hatred, and barbarism. After the winning of victory . . . our hatred evaporated . . . One does not beat the vanquished."[188]

Clearly not all the Soviet soldiers who bitterly hated the Germans were sent home or—like Chuikov—changed their minds. Many took out their hatred on innocent German women and girls. Indeed, to borrow from Chuikov's phrase (and the Russian proverb) the vanquished were beaten and beaten again. German police reports from the zone document an atmosphere of violence only barely distinguishable from war itself.[189] The important liberal politician Ernst Lemmer, who otherwise tried to play down the importance of rape in his memoirs, reported a horrible scene during the occupation in the house of the famous actor Friedrich Kayssler. The actor himself was shot and killed, while two young actresses were raped and slit open by Russian marauders.[190] The hatred that produced such crimes was ubiquitous, not just of Germans by Russians, but of Russians by Germans. Soviet soldiers could read the hatred and fear in the faces of their victims, and that probably made it easier for them to attack.

Nazi *Gruelpropaganda* during the war—stories of Soviet atrocities that often had rape as their centerpiece—had been intended to bolster the fighting morale of Germans on the eastern front. The stories of Soviet barbarism had become more grisly as the front got closer and closer to Berlin. A captured Nazi document from the propaganda department (February 16, 1945) read: "Everyone must throw themselves into the last defense with the conviction of what will happen to wife, child, and family members if they fall into the hands of the Bolsheviks."[191] While German Wehrmacht officers and even Nazi propagandists had raised serious questions about the effectiveness of such propaganda on military and civilian morale, there can be little question that by the end of the war most Germans—with the rare exception of those on the Left—had an uncommon fear and hatred of the Soviets.[192]

For the Germans, too, more than a decade of Nazi anti-Soviet propaganda and an even longer exposure to racial stereotypes had created an irrational fear, especially of "Asiatic Russians"—not just a fear of Uzbeks, Kalmyks, or Tadzhiks, but of Russians as a mixed Asian and European stock. Just as race is never far from the surface when discussing the history of rape in the United States, so race played a major role in the German images of the Soviet invaders. It took little more than the appearance of Asiatic troops to send the local population into paroxysms of fear. At the end of May 1945, Ulbricht wrote to Zhukov that rumors had spread through the city warning of the coming of the "Mongols," as a result of which women and children went into hiding.[193] The Swiss journalist Max Schnetzer noted a not atypical case in his diaries. Three Russians forced their way into a cellar occupied by half a dozen men and three very frightened women.

> One sits with her mouth wide open, another holds tight with both hands onto the handgrips of the couch, with her knuckles white and pointed. The youngest instinctively grabs her knees which are firmly pressed together. So they sit almost without movement and barely allow themselves a breath ... After a half an hour a new troop arrived. It's the Mongols, and now the women let out a scream. The simple look of these

yellow mugs brought shudders of fear. They shivered and shook out of unrestrained fright. "My God," whispered one, "what terrible faces!" The mother of the doctor glanced at the soldiers and murmured: "Can it be that something like that exists. They must really have come from far away." She looks now at her daughter, who apparently cold-blood-edly looks at the stranger, though she shakes inside and thinks: "No dear God, not that—please, only not that!" ... The Mongols can easily see that the others had already been here. They don't spend much time with their searches. They scarcely pay attention to the old men. One steps up to the couch and grabs a girl. The other follows his example, and now everything goes very quickly ... One grabs the doctor by her elbow, shoves her chin up and looks at her [showing his] yellow, pointed teeth. The old pensioner turns bright red out of anger at the reprehensible scene, and his wife, who fears he may jump up in anger, holds him around the arm and whispers emphatically: "Leave it, leave it, what would that help?" The Mongol forces the doctor into a corner and she feels limp. "Now it's come." But then a thought comes to her ... "He smells like an animal, this fellow, sharp and also a little rancid."

This particular case ended fortunately. A well-intentioned young officer with a machine gun happened into the cellar and drove off the soldiers.[194] But one can see how a scene like this could end differently, given the mutual hatred and anxieties built into the situation.

Of course, it would be absurd to blame rape on the fear of the victims. Still, the behavior of women could sometimes rescue them from threatening situations. There is something to the report by an elderly couple in Dahlem, who said that they owed their lives to Russian help: "A Russian is kind and generous. But you have to know how to handle them. Most Germans are afraid."[195] Knowing the Russian language helped—though not always—as did being firm, dignified, and unafraid.[196] During the occupation, noted an American intelligence report from Berlin, Russian soldiers, simple peasant lads, would "stop unescorted German girls on the street, and when they are unable to express their wishes in German, sometimes turn violent."[197]

Along with many observers, Schnetzer noted that, on the whole, morale and discipline were higher among the officers of the Red Army than among the soldiers, who tended to be the worst rampagers. In fact, the most cultivated and educated officers also exhibited considerable embarrassment at the behavior of their compatriots.[198] Still, especially at the start of the occupation, Soviet officers only sporadically interfered in the activities of their soldiers, especially staying aloof when the latter were intoxicated. The chaotic organization of the Soviet Military Administration in the first days and months after the peace did little to hinder the continuing inclination of Soviet soldiers to avenge themselves on German women. Moreover, the generally high level of brutality among the Soviet forces— a public beating with the *nagaika* (a kind of whip) was still a common form of punishment in the ranks—reinforced a violent atmosphere that spread to the treatment of the civil population.[199]

Schnetzer also underlined the general observation that the influence of alcohol played an extremely important role in the tendency of Soviet soldiers to rape. He wrote (echoing many others): "The drunken Russian is a wholly different person than the sober one. He loses all perspective, falls into a fully wild mood, is covetous, brutal, bloodthirsty."[200] The frequently reported rape-murders, especially, seemed often to be the work of drunken soldiers. In some cases the drunken melees would get so out of control Russian soldiers would end up shooting each other. As late as 1946 in some cities, such as Weimar, periodic drunken rampages by Russian soldiers left the local populations "with a feeling of deep uncertainty."[201] One Russian pilot recalled later in emigration that he had decided to return to Breslau (Wrocław) after the taking of Berlin, to see what was left of the city: "It would have been better not to go. The city had been burned and appeared to have nothing left of it but ruins. On the streets, filled with our soldiers, something indescribable was going on. Shooting and general drunkenness. Somewhere from beneath the ruins were pulled out kegs of wine, beer. They were rolled out in the street. Pistols were fired and [alcohol] flowed in pots and pails. At every step there was the staggering body of a drunk." Later in the same day, the Soviet officer and his compatriot experienced the worst of the outrages when a drunken Soviet tank officer grabbed a German child and threw him into a burning building, instantly killing the boy.

—"Why did you do that? Of what was the child guilty?" [his friend asked]

—"You just shut up captain!! Do you have children?"

—"Yes ..."

—"Well, they killed mine . . ."—he turned around and continued his drunken roaming.[202]

It would not be an exaggeration to say that German women of any age who found themselves in the proximity of these drunken melees would have been hard-pressed to escape harrassment and rape.

Soviet soldiers sometimes got so drunk they left their weapons behind. On June 15, 1946, one such group of thoroughly intoxicated officers in the Auerbach region of Zwickau attacked women at a concert in a restaurant and threatened a major when he tried to call in the commandant. The drinking and the rape lasted until three in the morning. Back again the next day to pick up their weapons, still on a binge, the officers shot the restaurant owner when he tried to close the door on them. "Completely out of control," the Soviets could not be reined in by their division headquarters located outside of town, because there they were "out of petrol."[203]

Certainly Allied soldiers in occupied Germany drank to excess in every zone. It was not the amount that Soviet soldiers drank that proved so disastrous for German women—in comparison, for example, to how much American soldiers drank—but rather the way they drank. As scholars of Russian drinking habits have repeatedly noted, Russians drink in binges, reaching a stage of intense intoxification over a period of several days, and then they are sober for a period before the next binge.[204] The availability and high quality of alcohol in Germany did not help the situation. One SPD informant recorded a hard and fast rule for dealing with the Soviet troops: "So long as he [the Russian soldier] is sober, one has almost never anything to fear. Only under the influence of alcohol and also when several are drunk together do the excesses begin."[205]

The problem of rape in the Soviet zone, then, was influenced by a series of factors unique to the Russian occupation of German territory. The way Russians drink was significant for the problem of rape, as was the widespread Soviet desire for revenge and their hatred of Germans. The fears and prejudices of the German population did not help the situation, nor did the fierce anti-German propaganda that accompanied the Soviet counteroffensive, which drove the Nazis out of the Soviet Union and back into German territory. At the same time, it should be clear that we are also dealing with a form of violence intimately connected with the soldier's psychology in war and occupation. Moreover, as a social act, rape in the Soviet zone had a meaning particular to the nature of the Russian and German societies as they experienced World War II in relation to each other. Gerda Lerner aids the understanding of this phenomenon in a general way by insisting that in traditional society, rape is directed against the men of a society as much as against the women: "The impact on the conquered of the rape of conquered women was two-fold: it dishonored the women and by implication served as a symbolic castration of their men. Men in patriarchal societies who cannot protect the purity of their wives, sisters, and children are truly impotent and dishonored."[206]

Russian culture—and many of the Asian ones associated with it in the Soviet Union—still carries with it many of the characteristics of patriarchal society characterized by Lerner. Rape, especially, has played an important role in the concepts of honor and dishonor that permeate Russian culture. Eve Levin writes, for example, that it was customary in medieval Russia to carry out "vengeance against an enemy by raping his womenfolk." Secular society, Levin adds, understood rape as a crime of violence, "the ultimate insult against a woman and her family in a society which valued honor highly."[207] In her studies of legal penalities for sexual crimes in late Imperial Russia, Laura Engelstein notes that in nineteenth-century Russian legal codes, rape was included in a special section on "crimes against female honor and chastity." It was the men's obligation to defend the chastity of their women; rape, then, constituted a personal insult to the man, as well as violence against the woman.[208]

Combining the ideas of Lerner, Levin, and Engelstein with the vast array of data available on the rape of German women by Soviet soldiers, it is not unreasonable to suggest that rape in the Soviet zone became the final repayment for the German invasion and mauling of the Soviet Union. Russians themselves had been dishonored by a nation so arrogant that it not only invaded, occupied, and destroyed the land and defiled its inhabitants, but it also relegated to itself superior racial attributes. Soviets—the alleged *Untermenschen*—were humiliated by their defeat and retreat, and even more so by the Germans' exploitation and rape. The Germans had turned their attack on the Soviet Union into a race war as well as a war between rival nations. The defeat of Nazi Germany by the Soviet Union did not restore the honor of Soviet men. Only by the total humiliation of the enemy, one might hypothesize—in this case, by completely dishonoring him with the rape of his women—could the deeply dishonored Russian nation win the war, with what Lerner calls "the final act of male domination."[209]

German claims of superiority during the war drove the Russians to rape, but their continued arrogance—despite their fear of the occupiers—made the Soviets' need to dishonor Germans all the greater. Numerous commentators noted the persistent arrogance of the Germans in face of "the backward Russian, whose cultural level was supposed to be so much lower."[210] In some sense, the superior attitude of Germans was less important than the realities of German life. As so many interviewed Soviet deserters after the war made clear, Russian soldiers were stunned by the wealth and prosperity of the Germans. Germans were well dressed and lived in well-built homes and apartments. Everything was clean and orderly. They had running water and indoor toilets. Despite the destruction in German cities, few victorious Soviet soldiers could compare their own hometowns or villages favorably with the Germans', even those that might have survived Wehrmacht shelling or the Nazi torch.[211] The German occupation of the Soviet Union may well have contributed to a national inferiority complex among Russians, and—*Krasnaia zvezda* wrote in its famous September 9, 1945 piece—the men of the Red Army were not "above the blind emotion of revenge."[212] The resulting combination of an inferiority complex, a desire for revenge, and the occupation of Germany was humiliating if not deadly for German women. The Russian soldier's desire for revenge was fed by his desire to restore his honor and manhood, to erase doubts about inferiority that were exacerbated by German well-being and self-satisfaction. Perhaps this is the reason there were so many cases in which a German woman was purposely raped in front of her husband, after which both husband and wife were killed.[213] This may also account for the unusually high number of complaints by Germans that the rapes were carried out in public.[214]

The often inchoate intent of the rapists can perhaps best be understood in the laments of their victims, as in the poem "Thoughts of a Mother" by Erika Trackehnen.

> At home and still not at home,
> The Russians come every night—
> Dear God I beg you
> Let me sleep and forget
> Forget . . .
> Shamed, humiliated, and besmirched
> I get up again with new wounds—
> Forget . . .
> Is a woman there only to be stepped on—enslaved?
> Doesn't anyone ask about simple rights?
> Forget . . .
>
> . . . . .

I beg you God, let me sleep and forget
And don't measure my life by what happens here.[215]

GERMANS AND RAPE

As many of the cases of rape discussed here indicate, there was not a great deal Germans could do to prevent the violence against women. On the other hand, it would be inaccurate to leave the impression that there was no resistance. Women themselves, as we know from the documents, often fought their attackers and sometimes were brutally beaten or killed as a result. In most cases, onlookers stood by out of fear of getting shot; in some cases—especially if the attacker was alone—Germans dared to intervene, with violence if necessary. In one such instance, a group of young people who beat up a Russian soldier attempting to rape a German girl were arrested by the police for being alleged Werewolves—members of the underground Nazi youth.[216] In another, a German policeman was shot and killed while trying to stop the rape of a woman. In a third, the Ministry of Internal Affairs operations group arrested a German policeman who had seized the Russian rapists.[217]

Other Germans found more inventive ways to deal with rapists, since violent resistance by men or women was extremely dangerous. One town managed to hide most of its women in attics, conceal the ladders, and convince the Russians that all the women had fled.[218] Peter Bloch reported the following technique for protecting girls in his town:

> The approach of the Russian marauders was usually easy to notice. If someone saw any Russian approaching, they would open a window to the street, grab two ready kettle tops and bang them together. Everyone who heard this signal would open a window themselves and commence with the kettle-top alarm. The noise would continue its way up the street; in all the windows stood inhabitants banging kettle tops. It was a hellish show [*Höllenspektakel*]. And nothing bothered the Russians more during their raids than noise. At this point, then, most of them quickly left town.[219]

Gerhard Simon, a West German scholar of the Soviet Union, recalled from his youth a similar technique used by the townspeople in a village in Saxony-Anhalt. A lookout with a trumpet kept watch for Russian trucks. At the sounding of the trumpet, all the townspeople gathered in the central square of the town and created a great commotion. With so many witnesses and so great a commotion, the soldiers showed little inclination to engage in mayhem.[220] A variety of sometimes contradictory techniques were used to avoid rape. Usually German women and girls went out of their homes only in baggy, filthy clothes; but in other cases, women dressed in their finest outfits, thinking that their important bearing would deter potential rapists.[221] In a situation of societal breakdown and the fragmentation of the German sense of community and even of family, the threat of rape paradoxically provided an important impetus to rebuild village and town organization and to maintain community unity.

In both towns described by Bloch and Simon, the arrival of a Soviet commandant and formal Soviet administrative offices dramatically cut back the number of problems with Russian soldiers. In some towns, the kommandantura helped the local civilians organize resistance against rapists. Frustrated by the persistence of rape under his command in Gernrode, the Russian commandant Velisov distributed inkwells to the women of the town and promised swift action against soldiers found with ink-stained uniforms. Since each Soviet soldier had only one uniform, eventually a number were caught wearing uniforms marked in this fashion; Velisov had the violators sent back to the Soviet Union.[222]

Many Germans tried to find protection from Russian soldiers through the intercession of local communists or social democrats who worked with the Soviets. (Although in East Prussia and Silesia, the party affiliation or former underground status of a German helped little if at all in preventing rape.[223]) Antifascists often found themselves on the defensive. They had tried to dispel the Nazi "myths" of atrocities committed by Soviet troops, only to find themselves under attack as deceivers and apologists for rape.[224] On top of that, in the last days of the war and the beginning of the peace, Heinz Brandt wrote, members of the antifascist committees sometimes had to conceal their own wives, daughters, and even mothers from those same Soviet officers and men with whom they worked.[225] Reports from all over the zone indicate that FDJ and KPD/SED functionaries, Women's Section members, and women's factory group leaders were just as susceptible to being raped as other women.[226] A Soviet report noted that the Schwerin SED activist "W" admitted flat out that he hated the Russians because soldiers had repeatedly raped his wife.[227]

Although they had been long-time communist resistance fighters, the members of Robert Bialek's family—Bialek was later police chief of Dresden—were not spared from the Soviet marauders. Bialek's wife was raped, and his sister was subject to attempted rape. Later, when Bialek's credentials were established and his worth to SVAG fully proved, his wife was able to make a special arrangement with the Soviet military police, especially since Bialek was frequently out of town on SVAG business.

> So that whenever a drunken intruder appeared, one shout was enough to summon the Military Police. Their method of dealing with the unwelcome guest was unorthodox but effective. They would stop at the cellar door, fire two volleys from their tommy guns into the ceiling and bellow something in Russian. The offender then emerged with his hands up and allowed himself to be marched off without protest. On only one or two occasions did the culprit attempt to put up any resistance or to escape. He was immediately shot.[228]

Only slowly in the Soviet zone of occupation did party or former underground status confer the privilege of having one's house or apartment guarded by Soviet sentries against rampaging soldiers. As a close coworker with SVAG, Erich Gniffke had his house guarded by Soviet troops, ostensibly to protect his family against Werewolves. In fact, many local women took refuge from Soviet soldiers in his house. His place, he wrote, became a kind of neighborhood safe house.[229]

The Moscow German communists, with Walter Ulbricht at their head, were especially reluctant to bring up the question of rape, out of deference to their Soviet "friends" in general and to Stalin in particular. Ulbricht and Pieck apparently did speak to Zhukov on July 12, 1945, about the "increasing rumors" of attacks by occupation troops on German civilians, and Zhukov promised to look into the problem.[230] Pieck also complained to Suslov about the "undignified" behavior of some of the Soviet troops in Germany, and even wrote an article for a special October 1945 edition of *Der Funktionär* (The Functionary), in which he assured his comrades that the CPSU(b) and SVAG were taking resolute measures to keep Red Army troops under control.[231] But KPD/SED leaders on the whole were more upset about the Germans' complaints about rape than about the actions of the soldiers. Fred Oelssner urged his comrades to keep the attacks in perspective: "People have already talked about the attacks of the Russians, they happen and hurt us. [But] what happened in Germany after the occupation and still is happening, this cannot in any way be compared with what happened in the S[oviet] U[nion]."[232]

Even if Ulbricht and other KPD members did not want to bring up the question of rape, some rank-and-file communists were ready to speak out on the issue. Wolfgang Leonhard recalls a meeting of Berlin communists in Charlottenburg, where one comrade in particular spoke out about the terrible things he had witnessed and about the damage that German communism had suffered as a result of the behavior of Soviet troops. "And I tell you," Leonhard reports him as saying, "we've got to establish socialism in Germany without the Red Army and, if necessary, even against the Red Army."[233] In general, however, communist activists turned their backs on the problem of rape. When KPD leaders tried to minimize the problem of rape around Berlin by describing it as "isolated incidents," local party leaders urged them to come out to the countryside themselves and see what was happening.[234] Some communists were so mad that they suggested that bordellos be set up for Soviet soldiers, staffed by fascist and middle-class women, who were "prostitutes anyway."[235]

The SPD was less shy than the KPD in bringing up the issue of rape, though there were also differences among members of the Central Secretariat about just how emphatically one could protest to the Soviets. Erich Gniffke claimed that rape was a standing issue for the SPD, and that "already at the first reception given by Marshal Zhukov in June 1945, we spoke out thoroughly about [the issue]."[236] Otto Grotewohl told a group of Leipzig SPD activists that the SPD leaders had protested to the Soviets about marauders who thought "they have the right to violate our women wherever and in any manner they wish." Supposedly Zhukov promised them, "Things will get better . . . I'll have them shot and hanged when I find them."[237] Otto Meier was active in approaching the Soviets about the question of rape, as was Max Fechner, who—also as a member of the SED—encouraged his comrades to bring up the problem with local commandants. In July 1946, he stated at a plenum of the party leadership: "We cannot be always scared and only look on, but we must say it completely openly to the Russian comrades (absolutely right!) and we should have no hesitancy [*kein Blatt vor den Mund nehmen*]. It hurts us, matters have to be clearly presented, and the Russian comrades are ready to do everything in their power to do away with it."[238] Despite Fechner's bravado, his inability even to mention the word "rape" was indicative of the fact that the SPD and its leaders were also unwilling to make rape a point of contention with the Soviets. At SED party schools, the question constantly came up about what the party was doing to bring the problem of rape to an end.[239] The right answer—though not the one that was given—was not very much at all.

There can be little question that the communists suffered an almost immediate loss of prestige and popularity as a result of the behavior of the Red Army before and after the capitulation. Even Red Army political officers like General Burtsev were forced to report back to Moscow the worsening mood of the Germans as a result of the marauding and assaults.[240] Bernt von Kügelgen, a National Committee for Free Germany member who returned to Berlin from Moscow in August 1945, noted that it would have been better for the German Communist Party "if the war had ended before Red Army troops had entered Germany." (Von Kügelgen, an editorial writer for the communist paper *Berliner Zeitung,* perspicaciously added that it would also have been better for the Soviets, given the deleterious effects on Soviet soldiers of the shockingly higher living standards of German farmers and workers.) "The behavior of Soviet troops has had an adverse effect upon the communist cause in Germany," Kügelgen admitted, and if elections were held in the fall of 1945, he said, the KPD would suffer seriously.[241] The American observer Gabriel Almond wrote from Berlin in October 1945 that any number of socialists agreed that if elections had been held in April 1945, before the occupation by the Soviets, "the communists of Berlin would have won by an overwhelming majority."[242] In an interview with American intelligence officers, Walter Killian—another German leftist journalist—also noted that the Soviets had undermined their own position in Germany by not controlling their troops better. "In the coming elections," he said, "the German Communist Party would have achieved great success if the Russian soldier had behaved differently." Killian added that he doubted seriously whether very many women could be convinced to join the Communist Party, given the problems with Soviet troops.[243]

The Soviets also understood that their KPD clients were in a very bad electoral position as a result of the behavior of the Red Army troops. One Soviet report quoted a barber as stating that Russian culture was epitomized by the horrendous treatment of German women by local soldiers. In the region occupied by the Forty-fourth Tank Battalion, the barber added, not a single women had escaped being victimized by Soviet soldiers.[244] When it came time for elections, as Hermann Matern noted after the communists' abysmal showing in Berlin in October 1946, "we could not, despite all of our efforts in this direction, win over the women."[245] Even Ulbricht admitted that the accusations of rape had hurt the party's political work in Berlin.[246] The same was true all over the zone. Bruno Böttge insisted that the poor election results in Halle were attributable to the stationing of troops in the northern part of the city. "As a result, you simply would not be able to imagine the sense of insecurity that has emerged there."[247] After the elections, party work continued to suffer as a result of attacks by Soviet soldiers. In Weimar, SED leaders Heinrich Hoffmann and Werner Eggerath wrote General Kolesnichenko (January 6, 1947) that it was simply impossible to hold party meetings after dark. The "growing insecurity" among the people translated into less support for the SED: "We sold 2,300 admissions tickets to the celebration of the [Russian] revolution in Weimar, but only 600 people showed up, because the word went around among the people: On the revolution holiday, the Russians would be out of control [*unberechenbar*]."[248]

In those local elections for which there are reasonably good data, it is quite clear that German women gave a consistently higher percentage of their vote to non-communist parties than did the men.[249] In the Thüringian elections of the fall of 1946, for example, women were estimated to have voted three to one for the Christian Democratic Union (CDU) or the Liberal Democratic Party (LDP) against the SED.[250] It would have been hard to find a woman in Mecklenburg, Gniffke wrote to Pieck and Grotewohl, who was ready to vote for the SED.[251] One could argue that the Germans resisted rape in this way by turning it back against the Soviets. So long as Russians ruled in the Eastern zone, there could be no legitimacy for the Communist Party of Germany, which initially might have been counted on to be one of the most promising in Europe. There would always be women like Maria Reuss, who—when asked about the huge Treptow statues memorializing the Soviet liberators of Germany from fascism—was unwilling to "look at the Russians so quickly as friends and liberators; one doesn't forget something like that so quickly."[252]

ABORTION

The victims of rape in the Soviet zone in particular and German women under occupation in general reacted to their situation in somewhat paradoxical fashion. On the one hand they suffered extensive demoralization and depression, but on the other they increasingly found ways to express their independence. The demoralization of German women was a process that spread throughout occupied Germany, but it was more intense in the Soviet zone because of the high incidence of rape. In October 1945, Gabriel Almond observed the problems of women in the American zone, which can be explained, he wrote, "by the complete lack of entertainment, the hunger for chocolate, cigarettes, and so on, the lack of sexual satisfaction as a result of the absence of so many German men, and the complete demoralization that the defeat as such brought with it. It seems to be the same everywhere and goes further than the half-compulsory prostitution—in order to have something to eat—and in the coming winter will certainly spread."[253] The Berlin press was full of cartoons, spoofs, and bitter criticisms of these women. One illustrated newspaper scoffed at the "Frauleins" who "look for parties and amusements" and lead such an apparently "effortless life." They were not interested in "genuine feelings and lasting happiness," it said; they ignored German boyfriends "who have nothing to 'offer' them."[254]

German women sought support and comfort wherever they could find them, and that sometimes meant crossing established lines of social behavior and cultural norms.[255] They were forced to work, cleaning up the debris (the famous *Trümmerfrauen*), rebuilding the cities, getting factories going again, and even digging and hauling in the mines. Those who became infected by venereal disease were forced to endure humiliating examinations and undergo primitive treatments. And in cases where rape led to pregnancy, German women also faced very limited access to abortions. The German legal code's long-standing paragraph 218 severely restricted the possibilities for legal abortions. In fact, in 1943 the Nazis had stiffened the restrictions of paragraph 218 to the point that it was illegal to handle the drugs used for aborting a fetus. Even after the war, the provisions of paragraph 218 continued to be in force, and the Catholic Church remained an implacable opponent of abortion as well. Nevertheless, especially during the first six months of the occupation, German doctors often put aside paragraph 218, performing abortions for thousands of pregnant German rape victims.[256]

The doctors' work was made more difficult by the fact that leading German communists opposed the lifting of paragraph 218. As *Neues Deutschland* put it, abortion meant "the dying out of our German future already in the mother's body."[257] Ulbricht, in particular, was strongly opposed to terminating pregnancies by abortion and opposed a number of attempts by many rank-and-file German communists and social democrats to ease its accessibility.[258] Ulbricht distributed a circular to local administrations indicating that abortions were not to be tolerated, even in the case of rape:

I have been told that the head of the Department of Health has brought in the women who have been raped in order to organize abortions for them. Some comrades share this point of view. We would like to make it clear that examinations of women are necessary in cases of sexual diseases, but otherwise we are against abortions; after a while we will state our reasons openly. The Herr Doctors must be made aware that they should exercise more restraint in this question.[259]

By all reports, the results of Ulbricht's antiabortion policies were disastrous. Even with hospital supervision, the conditions for abortions were very primitive indeed. Disinfectants were hard to come by and, especially early on, anesthesia was nonexistent. Medicines and even hospital instruments were lacking.[260] With typhoid and typhus raging through the zone, a hospital operation often meant death. Then there was the huge number of cases, noted by chief SED health official, Maxim Zetkin (son of the famous German communist, Clara Zetkin), in which women were brought to the hospital in various stages of miscarriage, caused by their own attempts at home to be rid of the fetus. So many of them died, Zetkin stated, that it would be well to rethink the strict interpretation of paragraph 218.[261] Despite the dangers and the cost (roughly 1,000 Reichsmarks), illegal abortions remained quite common. In Berlin alone, there were some 6,000 deaths a year as a result of illegal abortion attempts. Extreme poverty in postwar Germany made illegal abortions a serious problem in all four occupation zones. Altogether it was estimated that among the 20 million or so women of child-bearing age in Germany, approximately 2 million a year had abortions, the vast majority of them illegal.[262]

Initially every province was responsible for formulating its own version of paragraph 218. In Saxony, for example, the SED supported a law of June 1947 that changed paragraph 218 to allow for abortion in cases of endangerment to the woman's life "for social or hygienic reasons." This law, noted one Soviet observer, "conforms in a number of instances to the laws of the Soviet Union."[263] The question of rape was left out of the Saxon law, but it was central to the discussion of paragraph 218 in Brandenburg, where, despite the opposition of the CDU, rape was sufficient cause for obtaining a legal abortion, "because the sexual intercourse from which the fetus resulted represented ... a punishable offense."[264] The problem with the Brandenburg law was that rape victims had to report the crime within two weeks of its occurrence, and the rape had to be confirmed by the police. Especially in the case of rape by a Russian soldier, it would have been nearly impossible to meet these conditions, meaning the pregnant rape victim could not get an abortion under the law.

The Women's Section of the SED issued a revised draft of paragraph 218 that urged the provincial governments and the SED in Berlin to suspend the existing penalties against doctors for performing abortions until a final version of the law was approved. Some SED women, like Grete Wendt, wanted a much more liberal paragraph 218. But a "compromise" version written by Hilde Benjamin prevailed, which emphasized the importance of "social conditions" in considering the woman's need for an abortion but also made medical exceptions to the ban, as well as exceptions for sexual crimes *(Sittlichkeitsverbrechen)*, including rape and incest. Paragraph 218 was suspended at least in the Soviet zone, though it reappeared in a somewhat different guise in the GDR, in a January 1950 law that recriminalized abortion. As the new law was implemented in the provinces of the Soviet zone in early 1948, exceptions were left in the hands of commissions primarily made up of physicians, who would decide whether a woman had good enough reasons for an abortion. But doctors were very hesitant to serve on these commissions, and consequently it remained difficult for women to get an abortion for social reasons or after having been raped. In Berlin, paragraph 218a of the Allied Control Council regulated the conditions for abortion. Social reasons were not included in the law, but abortions were allowed in cases of rape.[265]

Many women, of course, chose to go ahead and have their babies. Many took the infants to relatives, orphan homes, or Catholic charities, like the famous home in Wilmersdorf (Berlin), that welcomed "occupation babies" or "Russian babies" as they were called. There were many cases, however, in which the victims of rape became attached to their babies and raised them themselves, despite the hardships of the early postwar years. In small towns and villages, it was clear to everyone who was a "Russian" child, but everyone understood the circumstances, and the question of fatherhood was quickly forgotten.[266] There are no data available on the number of occupation babies born in the Soviet zone. Certainly in 1945 and 1946, the number was much higher than in the Western zones, where in 1946 approximately one-sixth of births outside of wedlock have been estimated to have been occupation babies.[267] In all likelihood the situation reversed itself in 1947 and 1948, when rape gradually ceased to be a problem in the Eastern zone and Soviet military authorities made it increasingly difficult for Russian soldiers to have liaisons with German women. (As I have noted, Soviet troops were forced into compounds and isolated from the German population.) In the Western zones, on the other hand, the initial strict nonfraternization rules of 1945 and 1946 eased markedly in 1947 and 1948, when it became quite common for Western soldiers to appear in public with German girlfriends.

GERMAN MEN AND WOMEN

Data about divorce in the Western zones and Berlin demonstrate that the experiences of women throughout Germany led to a short-term restructuring of German family life.[268] The divorce rate doubled in the postwar period compared with that before the war, the greatest cause being the long periods of separation for husbands and wives. Wartime marriages, in which the men and women had known each other for only a short period of time before they got married, were especially susceptible to divorce. Particularly in the Soviet zone, the working lives of women also became a source of marital strain. Women became more independent as their work became more central to the rebuilding of towns, factories, and administrations. Their social status also grew, especially since ration cards in the East were allocated according to categories of work as well as political criteria. Rules in the Soviet zone about equal pay for men and women in the same jobs also raised the status of women in society.[269] Marriages suffered especially when the husband's status had depended on his military rank or involvement in Nazi Party activities and professional organizations. During the occupation, more often than not the husband was humiliated by the loss of the war, unable to find work in his former capacity, and dependent on his wife for survival.[270] German men were often described in this period as "fawning and insecure" when faced with Soviet authority, or as hunched and "servile."[271] For them, the occupation by the Russians was a personal as well as national catastrophe.

Robert Moeller has written about the way German women in the West were forced back into the home after the war, despite having acquired the requisite skills to assume a dominant place in the labor force. The politics of restoration in the West reinforced traditional patterns of gender and work, helping the men regain their jobs and social dominance.[272] Women in the East enjoyed the advantage of an occupation power and political leadership that called for "equal pay for equal work" and sought to create equality between men and women in the workplace. But so far as retaining jobs claimed by returning POWs, German women in the East had similar problems to those in the West. The veteran German communist Elli Schmidt wrote that the SED women protested against this practice, but to no avail: "Women worked at the Post Office [for example] during the entire war. Now the men come back and the women are thrown out of the counters, the men take their jobs, and they have to go carry stones. This cannot go on." In public transportation, said Schmidt, the situation was the same; the men "sat in the booths punching tickets while above, the women were standing and clearing the streets of stones and rubble."[273] Even if the "reactionaries" wanted women to return to the hearth, they couldn't, noted a Templin SED activist. Men of marriagable age were few and far between when compared with women of the same cohort. The women simply had to work to support themselves and their family.[274]

The active involvement of women in the workplace during and after the war was accompanied by freer sexual practices, which also put strains on traditional marriages, especially those subject to the double standards of the returning German soldiers. Rape in the Soviet zone unquestionably played an important role in this process. In some cases, the women themselves became disoriented sexually after the experience of rape. Often, through no fault of their own, they were infected by venereal disease and unable to get decent treatment.[275] Meanwhile roughly 40 percent of returning POWs were unable to work, and through injury, trauma, or malnutrition, large numbers were sexually dysfunctional themselves. Husbands were often unable to prevent the rape of their wives; returning soldiers had difficulty empathizing with the trauma suffered by their loved ones; pregnant women or those who bore children as the result of rape were rejected by returning husbands; the experience of mass rape was seen by men "as reducing all [the women] to whores"—all of these factors exacerbated the stresses on marriage in the Soviet zone.[276]

During the prewar period (and after 1955) approximately two-thirds of the divorce petitions in Germany came from women, and in half of all the divorces, the man was judged to be fully responsible for the ending of the marriage. In the immediate postwar period, on the other hand, half of the petitions for divorce came from men, and in only one-third of the divorces was the man judged fully responsible. In other words, women were taking more initiative outside of marriage and providing more "reasons" for men to sue for divorce. Of course the high ratio of women to men in the postwar period also made German men less hesitant about petitioning for divorce. Especially in 1945 and early 1946, before the return of prisoners of war, ratios of women to men in the large cities of Germany contributed to altered social and sexual practices. In the fall of 1945, Berlin was 37 percent men and 63 percent women; Dresden 39 percent men and 61 percent women. In the age group from fifteen to fifty, there were often two or three times as many women as men.[277] In these circumstances, "getting a man" became a common theme for cartoonists and story writers in the Soviet zone's popular press. The subject of rape seemed to have been completely forgotten—censored, self-censored, or at the least repressed—in the frequently jocular portrayals of flirtatious German girls on the hunt for a man, German or Allied.[278]

Some scholars suggest that rape became just another serious obstacle for German women to overcome, like the absence of a roof over their heads, or lack of food for their hungry children. For the sake of survival, they developed personal psychological strategies to put the "incident" behind them as quickly as possible.[279] But even those women in the postwar period who had the courage to protest against their rape received little solace or sympathy from either their men or the occupying forces. According to Allied Control Council guidelines, if bodily harm could be proved, German women who were victims of rape could press charges only after September 20, 1945, and then only for "maltreatment" and "force applied outside the scope of official duties." German women had no right to receive support payments for their occupation children, nor were there specific provisions in Allied law for prosecuting rapists. This meant that each case was treated separately and claims could "be admitted or rejected on the instructions of the Zone commander."[280]

Victims of rape could also expect little solace from the returning POWs. In one of the few serious articles on the problem of the sexes published in the Soviet zone, Helmut Vögt wrote that German men appeared "at a loss" *(ratlos)* in face of the reality of their transformed women, "helpless before the flood of divorces." Many women had forgotten how to laugh after enduring the various hells to which German men had condemned them, and only "patience and forbearance" could produce a cure for all that bitterness. The men could hardly provide consumer goods, much less luxuries. But they could provide "perspective" and support for their women by aiding them in their work and helping to heal the emotional wounds of the war. Of course, Vögt admitted, it often seemed much easier for the men to find a new young mistress with an undestroyed apartment than to rebuild a broken family life. There was no mention of the word "rape" in Vögt's article, nor would it have gotten past the censors. But the piece strongly suggested that unless the men exhibited some emotional understanding of the pain of the women, unless they adjusted to their wives' new role in the working world, then a "pitiless and loveless" generation of selfish women would dominate society, one that "knows only mistrust."[281]

The Soviet Military Administration did very little to acknowledge the problem of rape. In fact, German women were held responsible for the rapid spread of venereal disease among occupation troops. German women were also the focus of resentment on the part of Russian women, both in the zone and at home in the Soviet Union. "Occupation wives" were viewed with loathing and resentment, and rape victims were seen as "asking for it." Returning German POWs and German men in general also showed very little understanding of the problems faced by German women. Many of the men were broken and inward-looking, unable to recover from the shock of total defeat. In the end it was from the German administration that women in the Soviet zone found the most support, and this was out of the administration's recognition that German women would have to be counted on to rebuild the country and shape the "democratic" future of Germany, if there was to be one. The quick formation of the antifascist Women's Committees in October 1945 and the Frauenbund (Women's Union) in 1947 were only a few of the many initiatives intended to keep women active in both the economy and child rearing.[282] In the absence of their men—killed, missing at the front, or waiting in POW camps for return—German women suppressed their physical and spiritual suffering and entered the labor market to provide support for their families, if for no other reason. In its cultural and propaganda activity, the German administration played on these motives to involve German women in the workforce. Though they offered little solace to victims of rape, poems like "You Mothers," by Werner Stern, called on German women to forget their woes in the name of the next generation.

> You Mothers
> You have nothing yourselves that's left to take away from you,
> Crimes, Fires, and War have left you empty.
> You are wounded and affected to the depths.
> For you only hurt, quiet mourning, and pain remain.
> And yet the plea enters your heart
> The Kindergarten mutely implores for hope
> The silent accusation: "Help us"—and erase

From yourselves the guilt that burns in your Hearts!
Don't stand there whimpering, complaining, whining.
We are not interested in your feelings of blame.
We don't need your tears of atonement
Nor your damp eyes full of guilt.
We need deeds, they alone can touch us.
A firm grip of the hand carries more weight
Than any tears that cool the cheeks.
And everything you give us brings us closer.
You women who love your children,
Understand also the misery of other children! Give.[283]

WOMEN'S POLITICS

The threat and reality of rape made many German women fiercely resistant to the appeals of communists on behalf of friendship with the Russians. In an August 3, 1945, meeting of some 600 German women in Berlin Hermsdorf—the first open women's meeting of its kind after the war—the local KPD chief, a Herr Koch, opened the discussion by citing all the material help the Soviets had provided the Germans in the first weeks after the liberation. "At this point [a KPD report noted], a roar went up in the hall, with loud interruptions, insults to the Red Army, for example: 'and then they stole everything from us,' '[Just] stop with your talk about Russians,' etc. With further weak attempts to point to the merits of the Red Army or to justify its behavior as victors, an uproarious, biting laughter arose in the hall." The KPD reporter ruefully noted that the women's meeting quickly turned into an anticommunist and anti-Soviet demonstration: "In the concluding open discussion, the almost fascist mood reached its highest point. The statements of the individual speakers were accusatory and provocational, without any understanding for the actual situation and the limiting difficulties." It was true, he added, that there was little to eat in Hermsdorf and that the women had to stand in "endless lines." But their behavior demonstrated that they were unwilling to accept responsibility for their own situation. In any case, gatherings of this sort were hopeless, he concluded. "We won nothing at this meeting, and lost a great deal."[284]

Rape itself never became an issue of open contention between German women and the party or within the party itself. It was not something people talked about or wanted to admit. Given the defiant stance of the

Soviet Military Administration, there also seemed to be nothing one could do about it except to appeal privately to Soviet leaders in the zone. But on the issue of food, German women were ready and willing to confront the occupation administration and the KPD and SED. As primary providers for their children, their parents (their own and their in-laws), and sometimes their incapacitated husbands, the women demonstrated and engaged in hunger strikes rather than watching passively as their families went hungry.

In preparation for the elections throughout the zone in the fall of 1946, the Soviets signed an order of "equal pay for equal work," to improve the mood of working women.[285] While this helped the Soviets' situation among working women, it accentuated the poverty of housewives, especially those without working husbands, who had to live off of what were called "graveyard [ration] cards."[286] But even working women were crushed under the burden of supporting families and taking care of households on their own. Attempts by the German provincial governments to introduce legislation that gave working women one paid day off a month to deal with household responsibilities were applauded by all concerned. But the Soviets insisted that the measure be financed by enterprises and the unions, and consequently it was never funded.[287]

There were also other issues that perturbed German women in the zone. High on the list was their inability to communicate with their husbands, sons, and relatives in Soviet POW camps. No form of correspondence was allowed, not even a postcard. Unlike the situation in western Germany, in the East there were no bureaus set up to identify the whereabouts of the POWs; German women whose husbands or sons had fought on the eastern front did not even know whether their loved ones were alive or dead.[288] As a result of complaints by both Soviet political officers and German communist leaders, the situation was improved to the extent that some postcards could be sent and received. But these and other efforts to make concessions to the needs of German women—designed to gain their support at the ballot box for the KPD and SED—proved fruitless. The reason had nothing to do with the occupation itself; rather, it was partly owing to the general indifference to politics among German women of all generations. Older women, if they showed any interest in politics, were inclined toward supporting the Church, meaning the CDU. Young women and girls, like their counterparts in the West, seemed most interested in chocolate, dancing, cigarettes, and nylons. Erich Honecker, then chief of the FDJ, could not get very far with this group, given his notion that "We have to overcome their *Drang nach Lebensfreude* [desire for the happy life]."[289]

Women's politics in the zone also suffered from narrow views within the KPD and SED of the role of women in society and the party. Grotewohl complained that many SED members had very "retarded views" of the place of women in the party and relegated them only to "women's issues."[290] There was also a strong current in the party, inherited from the Weimar KPD, that insisted that there be no separate Women's Section of the SED, no separate women's party magazine, even no "women's pages" in party publications. Any efforts to build distinct groups of female activists was "decisively rejected" by the party leadership as "dangerous" for party unity, though the party leadership did finally endorse a Women's Section to operate as part of the SED Party Executive.[291] Even leading women's activists, like Elli Schmidt (Anton Ackermann's wife) and Käthe Kern (who had a long-term relationship with Grotewohl) were unable to do much to change bigoted SED attitudes toward women.

It was precisely on this point that the Soviets were extremely critical of the SED's work among women. They complained, for example, that as late as December 1948 only 3 percent of the leading cadres in the party were female. Even more indicative of the problems of the SED among women, the Soviets wrote, was the inexcusable fact that only a handful of women were studying in higher party schools.[292] Even in the big factories in Berlin, the Soviets noted, the party had made little headway among women. Out of 1,447 women who worked at Siemens, only 2 were party members; out of 800 women at Vogel, only 1 belonged to the party.[293] There was no one to lecture to female factory workers. Female activists themselves were far too few and "severely overburdened." Even those women who joined the SED rarely could be considered members of the party aktiv.[294] According to Major A. Vatnik's reports from Leipzig: "Men refuse to lecture to women, who they think don't know anything, and they [the men] don't understand women's questions." Leipzig party leaders said the right things about women, Vatnik added, but they often didn't allow their own wives out of the house and kept them completely isolated from politics.[295]

The history of women's organizations in the zone reflects both the general antipathy of German women to communist politics and the ambivalence of the KPD and SED toward the women's question. During the summer of 1945, German women from a variety of backgrounds joined together to set up "women's rooms" to provide counseling, a little food, and used clothing for the many desperate women whose homes and livelihoods had been destroyed by the war. The centers sometimes managed to find sewing machines and used them to repair clothes for bombed-out women and children. During the summer of 1945, the antifascist bloc urged these women's groups to reconstitute themselves into antifascist Women's Committees, and in October 1945 Marshal Zhukov registered the committees as legal social organizations in the zone. With expanded resources, some provided by the Soviet military government, the Women's Committees got involved in health and education issues, as well as maintaining the hundreds of women's sewing and clothes exchanges. During the fierce winter of 1945–46, the committees supervised a "save the children" campaign, which provided warm clothes and hot food for needy boys and girls.[296]

By the fall of 1946, there were some 6,000 of these antifascist Women's Committees, many of which performed state functions having to do with family welfare. Although Käthe Kern was nominally in charge of the committees, SVAG was very unhappy about the extensive influence of "bourgeois" CDU women on the committees' day-to-day work. As a way to finesse this problem, the Soviets urged the SED to form a new women's organization, the Democratic Women's Union (DFB), which was confirmed by the military government in May 1947.[297] From the very beginning, however, the DFB was caught in a double bind. Because it was so closely identified with the SED, women were not terribly anxious to join its ranks, and the SED itself offered little help to the DFB, because of its traditional antipathy to separate women's organizations and also because its resources were already severely strained.[298] Gradually, like other societal organizations in the zone—whether trade unions, organizations for the victims of fascism, or associations of farmers—the Women's Committees lost their autonomy and were subjected to state and party domination. In November 1947, the antifascist Women's Committees were disbanded and their state functions turned over to the Frauenreferate (women's advisories) in the ministries themselves, ostensibly to increase women's influence on administrative and public life, but in fact to eliminate the independent agendas of the antifascist committees.[299]

"ABOUT 'THE RUSSIANS' AND ABOUT US"

It is highly unlikely that historians will ever know how many German women were raped by Soviet soldiers in the months before and years after the capitulation. It may have been tens of thousands or more likely in the hundreds of thousands. It is even possible that up to 2 million women and girls suffered this crime of violence, most while being uprooted from their homes in East Prussia, Silesia, or the Sudetenland, others while living in the Soviet zone of occupation.[300] In any case, just as each rape survivor carried the effects of the crime with her until the end of her life, so was the collective anguish nearly unbearable. The social psychology of women and men in the Soviet zone of occupation was marked by the crime of rape from the first days of the Russian occupation, through the founding of the GDR in the fall of 1949, until—one could argue—the present. One Weimar woman, writing her husband in the West (December 17, 1945) speaks for a generation:

> Dear Otto!
>   Please come here as quickly as possible. I can't hold out much longer, because I have such terrible fear. Oh, Otto, I have no peaceful moments any more. If I only hear a Russian or see one, I get so nervous and my heart hurts me from extreme fear ... Can you imagine, Otto, on Saturday evening I was raped by a drunken Russian. [She was abused and manhandled for more than two hours.] You can't imagine how broken I am—inside and out—and what bodily pains I suffer ... I am altogether amazed that after what I experienced on Saturday I am alive at all. But I can tell you, an experience such as that does not leave one unaffected ...
> Hildegard.[301]

The German women's fear of Russians and the association of Soviet troops with rape and looting became the central German argument against closer ties with the Soviet Union. In the West, it became a topos for propaganda against making concessions to the Russians. In the Soviet zone itself, it became a severe handicap for the KPD and SED leadership's efforts to build support for a communist future. The handicap was all the more severe because the issue of rape could not be discussed in public without offending the sensibilities of the Soviet authorities (and therefore of their closest German communist "friends"). Equally important were the social taboos on the subject of rape. The defensiveness of German men on the one hand, and the sometimes repressed, though unjustifiable, sense of guilt among German women on the other, magnified the social-psychological dimensions of rape—that is, the ways it affected the masses of people in their dealings with the Soviets and with each other. Sexual relations between Allied soldiers and German civilians in the Western zones sometimes led to illegal protests by Germans—the German girls' heads would be shaved, or threats would be posted at night against the offending Allied soldiers (especially those of color). But the fear of severe punishment by Soviet authorities muted even these deleterious forms of German protest in the Eastern zone.

Despite the initial leftist upsurge at the end of the war in Germany, the events of the Soviet occupation—not least because of the problems of rape—undermined the efforts of German communists. No amount of positive propaganda about the Soviet Union and Soviet accomplishments seemed to be able to dent the deep, if sometimes inchoate and unarticulated, hatred and fear of the Russians. In fact, many German communists began to complain more strenuously about the negative impact of the Soviet occupation on the development of German socialism. The SED worried that the stepped-up propaganda assaults from the West were having a deep effect not just on Germans in general, but within the party itself. Ulbricht was incensed by the growing sniping against the Russians within the SED: "Whoever carries on or supports anti-Soviet agitation," he stated, "has nothing to seek in the circles of our party members." Local party leaders were so worried about Ulbricht's injunction against even the murmuring of anti-Soviet statements that they tended not to hold party meetings at all, or at least they cut out general discussions altogether.[302]

While it was a relatively simple task to discipline central party organs, addressing the situation in the population as a whole was much more difficult. The SED had become a mass party, and there was simply no way to stop the nasty talk about the Soviets among its 2 million members. According to the GDR historian Wolfgang Schneider, the SED was especially upset about the "still passive attitude toward the Soviet Union" in the working class. As a result, at the end of 1948 the SED leadership decided to "take the offensive" against these "anti-Soviet" attitudes among the masses by confronting them publicly.[303] The political motivations for this offensive must also be seen against the background of events in the communist world as a whole: the beginnings of communist-bloc "discipline" in the Cominform (September 1947), the Czechoslovak coup (February 1948), the Cominform resolution against Tito (June 1948), and the simultaneous acceleration of cold war tensions and of Stalinization in Eastern Europe. The Soviets themselves agreed that holding such discussions was important and "progressive."[304]

The discussions were inaugurated on November 18, 1948, by the editor of *Neues Deutschland,* Rudolph Herrnstadt, in his article, "About 'the Russians' and about Us." The main Soviet occupation newspaper, *Tägliche Rundschau,* reprinted the article "because it deals with the decisive questions of the fate of the German people."[305] The intense passions and debates aroused by Herrnstadt's article led the Berlin branch of the Society for the Study of the Culture of the Soviet Union (later, the Soviet-German Friendship Society) to schedule an open discussion of the article on December 10, 1948, in the large hall in the society's House of Culture of the Soviet Union. An overflow crowd of some 700 people packed the auditorium. The discussions lasted for more than four hours in one of the most lively—and, until the fall of 1989, one of the last—open forums of its kind in the history of the Eastern zone. The intense interest in the subject led the society to schedule a second session in an even larger hall on January 7, 1949, and to publish stenographic reports of both sessions.[306]

Herrnstadt opened the first public discussion with a lengthy restatement of his original argument from the article in *Neues Deutschland.* Because of the influence of the class enemy inside the party of the working class, the SED, he said, "a large portion of our party members" have an incorrect view that the Soviet Union is a "burden" on the development of the party program, rather than recognizing its true role, "namely [that of] an inexhaustible source of strength to the workers' movement at every level of its struggle." These party members, said Herrnstadt, do not understand that one cannot simply pick and chose from the various attributes of socialism and of the Soviet Union. One must "either confirm the process [of revolution] as a whole, or deny it as a whole, parts of it cannot be cut out." Of course, Herrnstadt acknowledged, there are problems in the Soviet Union; nevertheless, "the person who accepts the Soviet Union can only do so as a totality." If a person is critical here or there, he essentially denies the Soviet Union, "whether he understands that or not."[307]

Herrnstadt complained about those comrades he encountered who said, "Yes, if the Russians had only behaved differently in 1945! Then they could have won the entire people for themselves." Rather than speaking about rape directly, Herrnstadt chose to talk about the case of a German communist who was hit over the head and had his bicycle stolen by a Russian, which "determined his [negative] attitude toward the communists for the rest of his life." According to Herrnstadt, this crime by a Soviet soldier— and indeed all crimes, including, by implication, rape—must be seen in the context of the Soviet struggle against fascism. The German working class did nothing, not even at the end, to help the struggle against Nazism.

German workers even carried the Hitlerites' bags to their cars as they fled! "How should the Soviet army have interpreted this attitude of the German people? . . . An active, capable working class did not exist." So far as the comrade who lost his bicycle (or, metaphorically, whose wife was raped, or who was herself raped) is concerned, he (or she) is no progressive at all. These persons have interpreted their individual fate as a defeat, Herrnstadt said, when in fact the victory of the Soviet army was "a world historical victory of the working class—also of the German [working class], if they would only understand how to use it."[308]

Certainly, Herrnstadt admitted, the Red Army that marched determinedly into Germany was inflamed and raw, "but war makes people raw." Still, he said, Germans had no right to complain, because they did nothing to prevent the war. "He [the comrade] saw nothing, he asked himself nothing, he saw only one thing: that his bicycle was taken." If only this man and tens of thousands like him had fought Hitler, everything would have been different Herrnstadt claimed. "The Soviet Army would have had a fundamentally different attitude toward the German people." There might have been some isolated assaults *(Übergriffe)*, he said; one shouldn't make light of the problem. But "a four-year-long gigantic struggle does not ebb in a day."[309] The only answer for the Germans, Herrnstadt concluded, was to throw themselves into the class struggle, see the Two-Year Plan to fruition, and stop the incessant bellyaching about the Russians, which served only the interests of the imperialists.

Professor Peter Steiniger picked up the discussion where Herrnstadt left off, criticizing the Germans for complaining about the terrible behavior of the Soviet troops. (Again, it was clear that he was really talking about rape, not about stolen bicycles or watches.) It was the German war that had turned the good Soviet man into the wild soldier, he said. Those people who forced the Soviets into the whirlwind of war cannot now say "shame on the wild ones." Besides, Steiniger emphasized, whether the Russian soldiers' "boots are clean or not" (whether they raped or not), had nothing to do with the duties of communists.[310] Steiniger repeated Herrnstadt's admonition that a communist is either for the Russians or against, either for progress or against. But he concluded his statement with the first direct reference to rape: those who objected to progress by carelessly repeating the stereotype of Russians demanding "Watches, watches" and "Woman, come!" he said (implicitly equating the two) cannot interfere with "the ongoing process, that one has to see . . . as a whole . . . One can only say yes or no to this process."[311]

Alexander Abusch, editor of the Marxist journal *Aufbau,* also took the podium, but he added little to the discussion. Like the other communist leaders, he publicly demanded that German men and women forget the rapes—which he too trivialized by equating them with stolen watches or bicycles—and get on with the class struggle, which meant the unadulterated, uncritical affirmation of the Soviet experience. Abusch explained the "rawness" of Soviet troops by claiming that the best Soviet socialists had been lost in the first years of the fighting. (And, he might have added, in the Great Purges.) Severe Russian losses in the first year of the war had derived not only from the success of the German war machine, Abusch noted. The Soviets had also expected that their German class brothers would either change sides or overthrow Hitler. When neither happened, the bitterness of Soviet soldiers against the Germans only became more deeply engrained.[312]

At this point in the discussion, a young woman—clearly a socialist and a member of the SED—rose from the audience to ask a question. Although she did not speak directly about being raped, her question clearly and unpolemically stated the problem of East German women.

> Many of us have experienced things that have made it personally difficult for our individual relations in a person-to-person meeting with members of the Soviet Army. My question is this: What can help us overcome this disturbed relationship of one person to another—in my view, peace begins only with the meeting of people with each other. What can help us [overcome] this disturbed relationship, that is, this fear and this mistrust that comes beyond our control—from the emotions—every time we come across a person in a certain uniform?[313]

That everyone understood precisely what she was saying is evident from the way the discussion shifted dramatically from the metaphor of stealing a bicycle to an attempt to explain away rape, because it was a serious impediment to improved Soviet-German relations. Professor Wolfgang Steinitz, one of the founders of the Society for the Study of the Culture of the Soviet Union, again tried to place the responsibility for rape on the Germans rather than the Russians. Whose fault was it that the Soviets had marched into Germany? Hadn't Germans themselves contributed to the problem by believing the horror stories of Nazi propagandists and then greeting the Russians with nothing but hatred and terror?[314] The philosopher Wolfgang Harich showed at least some understanding of the woman's dilemma when he talked about finding ways to overcome "this trauma, this deeply penetrating psychological shock that many people suffered at that time." However, Harich indicated that the trauma was purposely kept alive by the enemies of socialism and that the sufferer could be rejuvenated by participating in the process of rebuilding the country.[315] Here and elsewhere, Harich demonstrated his insensitivity to the specific problems of the rape survivors: "Why is there only one kind of trauma in the world? Didn't tens of thousands and hundreds of thousands of women suffer trauma and a shock during all the terrible nights of fire as the American and English bombs fell on them and on their children? . . . Why does one speak only of the trauma of the meeting with Russian soldiers?"[316]

None of the answers to the woman's question seemed quite satisfactory; as a result, the discussion focused even more exclusively on the important issue she had broached. One speaker asserted that there had been no rape in the Soviet Union in the 1930s, though the war may since have introduced a certain rawness in relations. A second expressed empathy for the woman but pointed to the terrible actions of Germans in the Soviet Union, and talked about the depths of love and hatred in the "Slavic soul." With considerable irritation, a Herr Steidle pointed out that everyone had forgotten what the French colonial troops had done in southern Germany. (He was referring to the mass rapes in Stuttgart.) "One only emphasizes now the not particularly satisfactory [*nicht besonders erfreuliche*] behavior [!] of some Russian soldiers." He added that he had spoken with a young woman who had had one of these "unhappy experiences." He had lectured her (as he was lecturing the young woman in the crowd who had brought up the issue in the first place) about refusing to forget what was done to her but easily forgetting what was done to the Russians.[317] A different question from another young woman in the crowd—why German women were not allowed to marry Soviet citizens—provided Professor Steiniger the opportunity to bring the discussion of rape to an end: "It [the discussion] began with a young friend, who touched all of us the most, who wanted to know how she could put an end to fear and mistrust, and [it] ended with another question of a friend, who wants to know why she can't marry a Russian. To a certain extent, we have walked the path from trauma to dreams."[318]

The second, expanded meeting held on January 7, 1949, had none of the spontaneous qualities of the first, and the issue of rape was totally submerged in a sea of rhetoric. Here the talk was of "the anti-Soviet agitation" that had insinuated itself into the discussion of "the Russians and us." This time a speaker from the Soviet Military Administration, Captain Tregubov, took the podium. He refused to talk about rape and returned to the trivializing examples of a stolen watch or bicycle.

> Can one equate the great, historical, human, and noble deeds of the Soviet Army with a watch taken or a bicycle stolen? (Shouts: No!) A watch taken away is nothing in comparison to the freedom that was brought. Today, one can easily say: Tell me how you relate to the Russians and I will tell you who you are. (Stormy applause.) There can be no honest democrats and freedom-loving people who are against the Soviet Union and go around telling anti-Soviet jokes or stories.[319]

Tregubov's remarks were followed by a chorus of affirmation by a variety of speakers who dutifully criticized those Germans who carried with them "the bacillus of anti-Bolshevism" and held a false sense of their superiority over the Russians.[320]

It was apparent from this second discussion that the fleeting public consideration of the question of rape was finished. The Soviets wouldn't tolerate it, and leading German communists could not have been happy about the public airing of the problem. But one of the participants at the second discussion made it clear that not talking about the problem would not make it go away. Leo Klinger reminded the audience that the battle of opinion would go on, but not in the large halls of the Society for the Study of the Culture of the Soviet Union. "Where does anti-Soviet agitation find its expression?—In daily life, in the streetcars, especially from Potsdamer Platz to Bülowstrasse, at the workplace, in the family, in the doorways, everywhere, day after day . . ." Good democrats and socialists, he concluded from this, needed to speak up more and counter the defamations against the Russians, the liberators of Germany.[321] But with complete power in the hands of those "good democrats and socialists," the issue of rape could no longer be discussed and dealt with.

Although the open discussions in Berlin were halted, the Society for the Study of the Culture of the Soviet Union held continuing discussions on the topic "About 'the Russians' and about Us" throughout the rest of the zone in January, February, and March of 1949. In April, two additional sessions were held in Potsdam, away from the four-power control of Berlin. Thousands of Germans attended these sessions, and the German and Soviet convenors, though completely in control of the proceedings, were still forced to confront sharp questions from their audiences: (1) Why was there so little contact between Soviet soldiers and the population? (2) If the Soviet Union is such a paradise, why are the Soviets' clothes so poor, and why do they have to take our best factories? (3) What kind of culture can they have, given all the assaults and stealing? (4) Where are our POWs? (5) If there is freedom of religion in the USSR, why do they close churches? The questions were answered correctly and thoroughly, wrote a Soviet observer, but apparently the problem of rape did not come up.[322] Yet when reading the German accounts of the same meetings, it is clear that rape was never far from the minds of the questioners: "Why did the soldiers act like they did in 1945?" (Demmin, February 18); "Why did the Russians not act differently toward us when they marched in?" (Güstrow, March 2); "Why didn't the Russians act better in 1945?" (Parchim, February 22); "How can one explain the hatred for and aversion to the USSR?" (Schwerin, January 1).[323] The one issue that needed an open hearing more than any other never got one.

Unfurling the Red Flag from the Reichstag. A staged photograph from
May 1, 1945, the morning after the building was seized.

Bicycles were routinely taken from the Germans after the war.
Berlin street scene, 1945.

A day of rest after the victory, Brandenburg Gate, May 1945.

Black market in the Berlin Tiergarten, 1945.

Russian soldiers were noted for their indulgent behavior toward
German children.

Lieutenant Colonel Ugriumov receives petitioners, Berlin, Summer 1945.

Soviet soldiers in Weimar remove wartime protection around the
Goethe-Schiller statue in preparation for turning it over to the Germans.

Women at the Wriezener train station in Berlin, going out of town to find food for their families, 1946.

The German poet Johannes R. Becher (second from left) and Soviet cultural officer Alexander Dymshits (right) visit the writer Gerhard Hauptmann (center) in October 1945.

Russian soldier in a "victory pose," 1945. Note the watches; Soviet troops considered them prize possessions and often took them from the Germans.

A flea market in Berlin-Lichterfeld, 1946.

Reparations, Removals, and the Economic Transformation of the Zone

THE POLITICAL AND MILITARY GOALS of the Soviet occupation of Germany were complicated by the understandable desire on the part of Stalin and his lieutenants to seek recompense from the Germans for the huge losses of Soviet industrial potential and material during World War II. As a result, during the four and a half years of Soviet occupation the material wealth of eastern Germany was removed in a variety of ways, from looting and trophy collection to the seizure of factories and goods by dismantling teams to the collection of reparations in kind. The Soviet zone was deeply affected by these removals. Soviet actions in the zone after the war altered the economy and society of eastern Germany in ways that still influence the regions involved.[1] In the first instance, the economic restructuring introduced by the Soviets and German communists altered property relations in the countryside, expropriating the so-called Junkers and large landowners and turning over their land to the "new farmers." But restructuring also meant the expropriation of large factory owners, which was confirmed by Saxony's referendum of July 1946, and the subsequent creation of people's factories, the VEBs, all over the zone.

This chapter surveys the problems of the recasting of the economy in the Soviet zone, first from the perspective of agriculture and then from that of industry. On the land and in the factories, the expropriation of former elites marked the first act of the transformation, which was carried out against the background of the removal of tractors and grain, machinery and equipment—indeed of a huge inventory of valuable material ranging from coal to artwork. The second act of the transformation consisted of empowering the farmers and workers to take control of their own economic destiny, a process that was paradoxically linked to the formation of state-supported economic institutions and the state-sponsored workers' emulation movement. The Soviets and the German Left maintained that it was not enough to dispossess the upper classes to create a true antifascist democratic order. The spirit of the working class had to be liberated from its capitalist inclinations by introducing a new culture of work and new structures in the factories. In 1948 and 1949, the Hennecke movement, the final subject of this chapter, sought to capture the allegiance of the German workers through methods adopted from the Stakhanovite movement in the Soviet Union.

THE LAND QUESTION

Throughout Soviet-occupied Europe, land reform was a major objective of the new political elites. In eastern Germany, the consensus between communists, social democrats, liberals, and Christian democrats about the need for land reform was reinforced by a number of factors common to the German situation. Land reform had been delayed in interwar Germany; large, inefficient estates farmed by landless agricultural laborers were characteristic of the eastern provinces in both the Weimar and Nazi periods. The victorious Allies were also determined advocates of land reform, and they were especially fixated on the Prussian Junkers as being the major social bulwark of German militarism. Therefore they insisted that Prussia be eliminated as an administrative unit and that the Junkers be deprived of their estates.[2]

The Allies need not have been quite so distracted by the image of resurgent Junker militarism, however. The war itself had begun the process of the destruction of the Junkers as a class. East Prussia, the traditional source of Junker power, had been turned into a living hell for Germans by the Soviet counterattack in 1944. Junkers and their families were on the run; their estates were burned to the ground; and the partition of the region between the Soviets and the Poles guaranteed the end of Junker domination. Polish occupation and eventual incorporation of German lands east of the Oder-Neisse line—Pomerania, Silesia, and the Neumark—deprived the Junkers of important landholdings. Of 8,827 members of the German nobility listed in one study, 4,948 were killed in the fighting, most on the eastern front, while another 1,500 or so died in air-raid attacks, in detention camps, or while in flight. Hitler also contributed to the process by ordering the execution of fifty-eight Junkers involved in the July 20, 1944, conspiracy; many of the conspirators also lost their estates in the process.[3]

The end of the war did not stop the killing of Junkers. Several hundred were murdered by newly released foreign nationals—POWs, farmworkers, transients—and by Soviet troops. Another 500 or so died in detention. About the same number, including whole families, committed suicide.[4] The East Elbian aristocracy also witnessed the destruction of their estates both during the fierce fighting at the end of the war and in the months following the peace. Estate buildings were burned to the ground, animals were driven off and killed, and fields were rendered useless. There was not much left on the land in those provinces of the Soviet zone of Germany—Vorpommern, eastern Mecklenburg, and eastern Brandenburg—where the Junkers still held substantial property. Often those nobles who remained, afraid of the Soviets, fled to the West. Polish forced laborers who had worked the estates also had gone, taking with them as much farm property as they could. In short, even without Soviet orders or German legislation, significant changes were under way in the countryside.

In comparison to the impact of the war on eastern Germany, the German communists' intense campaign of denouncing the Junkers seemed insignificant indeed. Yet the Junkers played a central role in the communist demonology of the Nazi regime. The Moscow German communists, especially—Walter Ulbricht, Wilhelm Pieck, and Anton Ackermann, among others—conflated Junkers, large landowners *(Grossgrundbesitzer)*, and Nazi bosses into a single category of devils of the Third Reich. Small farmers, landless farm workers, and tenant farmers were also seen as members of a single class, one whose goal in postwar Germany would be to make a revolution by spontaneously seizing Junker estates and driving the reactionaries off the land. But it was clear from the beginning of the occupation that this was to be a limited revolution, with the emphasis on "limited." The Soviets insisted, in fact, that the KPD leaders write into their June 11, 1945, program that only Junkers and war criminals were to be expropriated. Georgi Dimitrov authored the precise language: "It is understood that these measures in no way affect the ownership of property and agricultural production of the large farmers [*Grossbauern*]."[5]

Theoretically, then, the problem of land reform in the Soviet zone of occupation was one of turning over the Junkers' land into farmers' hands, to cite Wilhelm Pieck's famous slogan, *"Junkerland in Bauerhand."* But land reform had very little to do with the Junkers; the war had taken care of that. It had even less to do with the farmers, who, on the whole, had enough land—if too little livestock, equipment, and seed. Land reform was also not a solution to the economic development of the countryside. Virtually every agricultural expert agreed that breaking up the large estates would hurt rather than help production. The war itself had produced an important impetus for land reform: the desperate need to find homes and occupations for the flood of refugees, numbering in the millions, that enveloped eastern Germany, mostly from Poland and Czechoslovakia. But even more important was the communists' firm intention to seize political control of the countryside by "rooting out" the reactionaries. Fritz Lange of the SED's Party Control Commission put the issue succinctly: "The land reform for us was not only a problem of the settlers [*Umsiedler*], but was above all a political problem, and with it [the need] to destroy the strongest underpinnings of the reaction, the land and the manors."[6]

SUMMER 1945

The chaotic conditions in the eastern German countryside at the end of the war did not abate with the coming of the peace. Part of the problem was the fact that the new Soviet military masters pursued contradictory policies. First and foremost, the Soviets insisted that their troops be fed and provisioned by German agriculture in the Eastern zone. Local commandants supplied their troops through requisitioning, sometimes by demanding the delivery of a fixed percentage of production, but more often than not simply by seizing production in the nearest farmsteads. In the latter case, procurement officers frequently took more than they needed, causing a great deal of unnecessary damage both to what was taken and what was left.[7] At the same time, the Soviets were supposed to leave the structure of farming intact, save for the confiscation of large estates owned by Junkers, war criminals, and Nazi organizations. But the very process of breaking up these estates made the process of food requisitioning much more difficult, especially since the larger estates had already been organized for turning over production to the Nazi state.

To make matters worse, the chaos on the land in the last months of the war and the first months of the peace made it nearly impossible to regulate quotas and deliveries. Especially in the heavily agricultural regions of Mecklenburg and Vorpommern (the part of Pomerania that fell under Soviet occupation administration), the wartime agricultural economy had been maintained with forced labor from abroad, most often Poles and

Russian POWs, and supervised by large landowners and their agents. According to Gustav Sobottka's June 1945 report to the Soviet Central Committee, 60 percent of the land in this region was farmed in estates larger than 1,000 hectares (1 hectare equals 2.471 acres). Most small and middle-level farmers had been drafted into the German army.[8] In other words, expropriating the Junkers and their agents meant destroying the basic economic unit of agricultural production.

Things became even more chaotic once the Polish and Russian forced laborers realized the war was over. Not infrequently, they attacked their former landlords and supervisors, ransacked estates, and headed home with whatever they could take in the way of horses, cattle, and pigs. They even took farm machines and household goods. During the most severe fighting in the spring, the fields were not planted, and even those that were planted had been severely damaged during the fighting. After the peace, the fields were ravaged by horses that were allowed to graze freely and by Red Army agents, whose looting included the ripening grain and corn being grown for fodder.[9] Edwin Hoernle, the first head of the German Agricultural Administration in the Russian zone, reported that the number of cattle in the East was down to 40 to 50 percent of the prewar figure; the number of pigs was down to 25 percent, and the number of horses down to 50 percent.[10] The situation was especially serious east of the Elbe, where large gangs of freed Poles, Ukrainians, Russians, Balts, and others looted German villages as they moved back to their home territories. "We have some regions," reported Hermann Matern about Saxony, "where in the villages, in fact in several hundreds of villages, there is not a single cow left. There the Polish returnees have gone through, and not even a single chicken remains as a result."[11] In Mecklenburg and Vorpommern, according to Sobottka, many villages escaped the gangs but nevertheless had no one left to work the farms. There were houses, barns, animals, and chickens, and grain growing in the fields, but no people: "You would run into only one or two old men."[12]

VERTREIBUNG (EXPULSION)

The chaos on the land was made worse by the stream, and then flood, of German refugees coming from the East. The flow of Germans back and forth between the central industrial regions and the eastern periphery had varied according to the fortunes of war. Several hundred thousand Germans had moved to the East as settlers and colonists, following the successful Wehrmacht as it drove across Poland and into the Soviet Union. These followed on some 900,000 Germans from the distant East, who, after the Nazi-Soviet Pact and before the German invasion of Russia, had been called "home to the Reich" *("Heim ins Reich")* to settle the new, expanded Third Reich. In 1944, as the Allied bombing of central German cities intensified, another 2 million Germans had temporarily left for the East to seek refuge from the increasingly devastating air raids. But during 1944, the Soviets drastically altered the fortunes of war, counterattacking on every front and driving the German armies out of Soviet territory and into Eastern Europe.

During the terrifying winter of 1944–45, German civilians in East Prussia, the Neumark, Pomerania, and Silesia had realized their precarious position. They had gathered their families and goods on horseback and in wagons and fled the Russian advance, moving westward in long and difficult treks back to middle Germany. Junkers and large landowners in the East were among the first to leave, in many cases seeking refuge with their relatives and friends in what they thought were the relatively safe havens of Pomerania, Mecklenburg, and Thüringen. But not all were so lucky; 660 Junkers (including family members) died while trying to flee, 249 were murdered (in some cases by the Russians, in others by the Poles), and 453 died in detention camps.[13]

It quickly became apparent from the example of the fearsome Soviet behavior in East Prussia that it was not only the German ruling class that had to fear the invading Red Army. And even after the unconditional surrender of Germany at the beginning of May, Russians, Poles, and others attacked defeated Germans of all classes and forced them to flee their homes in the East. On entering the heart of the Czech lands, for example, even hardened Soviet tank commanders expressed their shock at the cruel punishments they witnessed being meted out to the Germans by vengeful Czechs.[14] The Potsdam conference at the beginning of July exacerbated matters by concluding in Article 17 that the Germans who had been "left behind" in Poland, Czechoslovakia, and Hungary were to be transferred to Germany, though of course in an "orderly and humane fashion." The Poles understood this clause to mean that those Germans inhabiting territories that were given over to Polish administration by Yalta and Potsdam should be expelled. Even before Potsdam, the Polish communist leader Władysław Gomułka had succinctly expressed the Polish case to his comrades: "We must expel all the Germans because countries are built on national lines and not on multinational ones."[15]

Where Germans did not leave voluntarily, they were forced out, beaten, or starved, and their homes were sometimes burned to the ground. In some towns, Germans were required to wear white armbands and to engage in forced labor. Not infrequently, the Poles turned the tables on their former German persecutors, treating them as second-class citizens and denying them the right to use their language in public or to attend schools and public ceremonies. The Germans were in desperate straits; large numbers committed suicide; most hid behind bolted doors, hoping for some relief. The Poles' physical attacks on the Germans—beatings and whippings—also produced the anomalous situation in which the Germans turned to the Russians for help. The case of the heavily German city of Stettin (Szczecin) was typical. At the beginning of July, the Soviet commander let the Germans know that the city would be handed over to the Poles. When the Poles arrived, a KPD informant wrote, they "brought with them an unbounded hatred of everything having to do with Germany." They denied the Germans food supplies and forced them out of their apartments within a few hours, and appeals to the local Soviet commander went unheeded.[16]

It made little difference to the Poles whether the Germans they dealt with were long-time residents of the area or colonists, whether they were Protestants or fellow Catholics. In towns and villages of Silesia, where German Catholics had lived for centuries, "radical, brutal Polonization" appeared to be the order of the day. One local German Catholic official from Waldenburg (Wałbrzych) complained to the bishop of Berlin that it did no good to appeal to the Polish Catholic hierarchy on behalf of the Germans:

> Under the leadership of the Polish militia in our region, the inhabitants of whole streets and sections of town are driven within a few minutes (ten to twenty minutes) out of their homes with severe mistreatment (beaten with clubs, slashed with whips and so on), without being allowed to take with them the most basic of clothes and foods. They had to find themselves a place to live. Officially, every German family was allowed only a barracks room ... Those who do not escape are placed in a internment camp ... the Poles in their merciless retaliatory measures make no distinctions between the guilty and the innocent.[17]

It also made no difference to the Poles (or to the Czechs, for that matter) whether the Germans were communists, social democrats, or members of an antifascist group. To their dismay and surprise, the Breslau (Wrocław) antifascist committee, dominated by communists, found out that the Poles wanted them out of town, plain and simple, and were not interested in the Germans' help in rebuilding an antifascist Poland.[18] The antifascist centers in Schweidnitz (Świdnica) were plundered by the Poles; books, machines, radios, and food items were taken. When Russian troops showed up, the Poles disappeared, but they reappeared, sometimes supported by the Polish police, as soon as the troops left.[19] Similarly, in Hirschberg (Jelenia Góra) in Silesia, the German antifascists tried to set up special soup kitchens for the hungry but were frustrated by the opposition of the Poles, who advised them: "Go to Germany, you can work there." Willi Stengel, who had spent most of the war in a concentration camp, wrote to the KPD in Berlin from Hirschberg on November 20, 1945: "Daily and hourly Germans are being forcibly removed from their homes, beaten along with that, and some are dragged off to the police. Every comrade therefore stays at home in order to defend his family and property from these attacks."[20]

Fortunately for the Sudeten German communists, the Czech and German parties reached an agreement to transport roughly ten thousand German communists and their families from Czechoslovakia to Thüringen and the province of Saxony (Saxony-Anhalt) in the Soviet zone.[21] To their chagrin, the Breslau antifascists were forced to suffer through a much more difficult and humiliating transfer. After enduring a long trek under Soviet guard from Breslau to Dresden, they were confined in a former transient camp without decent sanitation, heating, or food. After bitter quarrels with local party officials and subsequent confinement in the former Buchenwald concentration camp, 600 members of the Breslau group finally found places to live and work in Weimar and Halle.[22]

During the late summer and fall of 1945, the flood of refugees—fascists and antifascists, city and country dwellers, Catholics and Protestants, Junkers and poor farmers—overwhelmed the Soviet zone. By November 1945, there were already at least a million refugees from the East.[23] By the end, some 3.2 million Germans settled in the Soviet zone from the East; another 3 million or so lived in the Eastern zone for a period before going on to the West. (Of course, these were the lucky ones. Gerhard Ziemer estimates that 2,280,000 noncombatant Germans out of a total of 11.5 million refugees died as a result of the transfer from the East.[24]) Periodically the Soviets would close the border crossings just to gain some control over population movement. But the thousands of Germans who then camped out at the borders posed even greater dangers for public health and order.[25] Of those who crossed the border, tens of thousands settled in barns and shacks in the Mecklenburg and Pomeranian countryside, looking for food and work. They were hungry and shelterless. Worst of all, perhaps, their experiences had left them in a state of psychological trauma. Hermann Brill described their situation as a form of infantilization: "They have fully lost the ground from under them. That which is taken for granted by us, a sense of security from life experience, a certain personal feeling for their individual freedom and human worth, that is all gone."[26] The mood of the refugees in the cities was no better. A July 1946 Soviet report on politics in Leipzig described the 28,000 or so refugees in the city as "deeply depressed." They were not able to adjust to their new circumstances; they were "the most indifferent to politics of any group of the Leipzig population"; and they did little else but dream of returning to their birthplace.[27]

The summer of 1946 saw the first of the organized transfers from the East. In June some 586,000 people arrived in the Soviet zone, mostly in boxcars, from Czechoslovakia; a month later, the first of 240 transports of a total of 405,401 people started arriving from Poland.[28] Refugees continued to come to the Eastern zone as late as 1948 and 1949 (though the transfers by that point were much better organized). For example, 3,750 East Prussian Germans, including some 286 orphans, were sent by Russian authorities to the Soviet zone in 1948. As late as 1950, 1,329 Germans, who had worked in the shipyards of Świnoujcie were transferred from Poland to the GDR.[29] In the summer of 1949, Wilhelm Pieck estimated the number of settlers from the East—the SED always used the politically neutral word *"Umsiedler"* (settlers) instead of *"Vertriebene"* (expellees) or *"Flüchtlinge"* (refugees)—at 4.3 million, or nearly 25 percent of the Soviet zone's entire population. He frequently expressed his worries that these settlers were not providing the kind of political participation the SED had hoped for. Instead, they were constantly looking to return to their homes in the East, and this undermined the political and economic stability of the zone: "As much as we [the SED] in the deepest way deplore with the settler families the loss of their old homeland [*Heimat*] and have full understanding of their love for their homeland, our sense of responsibility for the millions of settlers compels us just as much to say frankly to them that they should not fall victim to the mass agitation about return to their old homeland."[30] People must understand, Pieck concluded, that this tragedy was Hitler's fault, not the fault of the Russians. Despite Pieck's worries, the refugees sometimes helped the SED at the polls, especially in agricultural (and normally conservative) Mecklenburg.

LAND REFORM

In May and June of 1945, the initial policy of the Soviet authorities (and the KPD and SPD) was to expropriate Junkers, Nazi war criminals, and large landowners with Nazi ties. But this was more easily said than done. Requisitions officers often preferred to keep the estates together and their managers in place, to ensure a steady flow of agricultural produce to their troop units. Some German communists opposed parcelization, hoping instead to turn estates into collective farms and thereby keep production units intact; SPD activists also favored nationalizing the estates and turning them into large-scale farms. Five-hectare plots, they argued, had little chance of becoming economically viable. Unlike the communists, the social democrats wanted to expropriate Church and monastery lands as well. The relationship of the CDU to land reform was more complicated. On the one hand, the party agreed that it was fair and "Christian" to expropriate Nazi war criminals and supporters of the Hitler regime to provide land to the needy refugees. On the other hand, CDU officials (the LDP followed much the same logic) worried aloud that non-Nazis and even anti-Nazis might be swept up in the process and illegitimately deprived of their lands. Unlike the communists, the CDU and LDP did not support the argument that all Germans shared the guilt for Nazism, and they were therefore unwilling to see good antifascists punished with the loss of their estates. Both "bourgeois" parties also insisted that, at the very least, landowners should be compensated for their property, especially if it had been in the hands of the family before the Nazi ascent to power.[31]

Even many of the local farmers were wary of the land reform. They were sometimes frightened by the notion of expropriation, in many cases wondering whether they might not be next. Walter Ulbricht remembered a July 1945 visit with hesitant farmers in the Bitterfeld region:

> "This is very simple," we advised them ... "You take the land away from the estate landowners, that is already the first step to take on the way to a democratic order." A farmer said: "But we have no law for this, here is no law." "A law?" I asked him. "If the farmers here decide to confiscate the estate owner's land, that is their democratic right." The

farmers responded, "Yes, you are surely right, but a law would be good." We comforted them: "All right, fine, if you want a law, we will make a law so that you can carry it out in a completely orderly fashion."[32]

Sometimes, even if the farmers favored expropriation, they were hesitant about dividing up the estates. A Central Committee report noted that farm workers, landless farmers and refugees were not anxious to become small farmers: "They explain that such small parcels of land are unprofitable, [would] take enormous efforts [to farm] and [that] cooperative farming would be better."[33] The NKVD worried that these small farmers would easily fall prey to agitators working on behalf of the Junkers.[34]

By the middle of August 1945, the German communists had worked out with the Soviets a draft of the land reform edict that was finally passed on to the district party organizations at the end of the month. The idea was to start the campaign in the province of Saxony (Saxony-Anhalt) on August 28 and then to launch similar campaigns in Mecklenburg on September 5, Brandenburg on September 6, Thüringen on September 10, and the state of Saxony (Land Sachsen) on September 11. In the discussions of the "antifascist bloc," in which the CDU and LDP were forced to seek common policies with the KPD and SPD, the liberal parties tried to delay the start of the campaigns until "experts" could assess the economic and legal ramifications of the reform. The CDU was especially wary of proceeding. But the Soviets and the KPD leaders (the SPD acted more or less with indifference) agreed that it would be preferable to move quickly to get land into the hands of the waiting refugees, small and landless farmers, and farm workers as soon as possible. Precise property delineations and legal questions could be settled later. In their assessment, the fears of the bourgeois parties would be overcome by the spontaneous actions of the local and district land reform committees, which would rally the masses to seize the Junkers' land.[35]

The provisions of the land reform were announced on September 2, 1945, in Wilhelm Pieck's speech *"Junkerland in Bauernhand,"* which was published almost immediately as a pamphlet. The actual expropriations began on September 3, accompanied by the appropriate order from the Soviet Military Administration. Pieck did not hide the political content of the reform: "All of these war guilty and war criminals must be made harmless forever," he wrote, "the bases of their power, their lands and their possessions, must be taken from them." This was no more than just, Pieck continued, since these estates had been illegally wrested from the hands of the masses in the first place. The landless and deprived should seize the opportunity "to help" the Junkers and large landowners on their way out, take charge of their own localities and districts, and turn the expropriated lands into strong and prosperous farmsteads. Without referring to the social democrats by name, Pieck also excoriated those who wanted to keep the estates intact for the ostensible reason that small farms would be less profitable and efficient; in his view, this argument constituted nothing more than the "infamous slandering of the farmer."[36]

According to the Soviet order governing land reform, the confiscation of all estates of more than 100 hectares was mandated without compensation. The estates would be turned over to the "new farmers" *(Neubauern)* in 5- to 10-hectare parcels, depending on the quality of the land. Former agricultural laborers as well as settlers from the East qualified as new farmers. Even workers from the city, whose factories had been bombed out or marked for dismantling, looked to support their families as new farmers. The order formally exempted Church estates from expropriation. In addition, a number of estates that had been under Nazi Party or state supervision were made into model or experimental farms. The primary source of the new land, then, was the property of 2,000 or so "plunderers of the people" *(Volksausplundern)*, Junkers, Nazis, and large landholders; the distinctions between them were not sharply drawn.[37] They were deprived altogether of approximately 770,000 hectares of land by the land reform legislation.

In the summer of 1945, many estate holders, especially in Mecklenburg and Pomerania, had already been driven off their lands. Sometimes they were murdered by rampaging Soviet soldiers or by former forced laborers. In some cases, whole families engaged in mass suicide; according to Walter Görlitz, there were 30 such cases in Mecklenburg alone.[38] For those who remained on the land, the confiscations sometimes took brutal and demeaning forms, as local communists and Soviet commandants incited the settlers and new farmers to take over the estates and evict their inhabitants without allowing them time to take their personal effects with them. Those evicted were given no legal documents authorizing the expropriation. Andreas Hermes, the head of the CDU in the East, stated his objection to the land reform less in terms of the principle of reform than in terms of the way it was carried out. We cannot stand by, he stated in an October 1945 Dresden speech, while "completely innocent people" are deprived of their property in a brutal fashion, without even 30 minutes to collect their things.[39]

The actual fate of the property owners in the land reform varied widely, depending on regional conditions. Sometimes former estate owners, supported by local farmers and friends, moved off their property and into neighboring houses. As a result of this practice, Soviet officials intervened and insisted that evicted landowners were not allowed to live within 30 kilometers of their former estates, or they were forced to move out of the district altogether and to learn, as one SED memoir put it, "to work for a living."[40] In Thüringen, land reform legislation contained provisions that allowed those landowners who were proven antifascists to retain up to 100 hectares of their previous estate, together with their inventory and buildings. However, the few Junker families in Thüringen, no matter what their political background, still ended up losing everything.[41] The NKVD reported that it took "appropriate measures" to keep alleged "reactionaries" from disrupting the reform.[42] Any landowners who seriously resisted the land reforms were "locked up . . . as counterrevolutionaries."[43] More often than not this meant they were transported by freight or cattle cars to Stralsund and then forced to trek along a narrow spit of land connecting the Mecklenburg mainland to the island of Rügen in the Baltic Sea. There, thousands of Junker and landholding families were detained briefly before they were distributed among the various communities on the island. They were forbidden to leave the island and were ordered to report regularly to the Soviet commandant. Some were decently cared for, but most lived under abysmal conditions of hunger and cold. Thousands escaped to the West; an unknown number died.[44] Especially landowners from the state of Saxony faced this forbidding and precarious fate during the harsh winter of 1945–46. One pathetic November 1945 letter, which made it to the Saxon authorities from the island and was passed on to the Russians, spoke about the fierce cold and the absence of warm clothing, about hunger and rampant disease. It ended: "Help us please, please . . . we are dying."[45]

It proved easier to drive off and incarcerate the landowners than it was to put Junker land in the hands of the needy refugees. In Thüringen, according to agricultural official Edwin Hoernle, in November 1945 some 100 estates, or 25 percent of the available large holdings, had still not been divided up.[46] In Grimma (near Dresden) as late as January 1946, local communist authorities, opposed to parcelization, had allowed the division of only 3 out of 27 estates. Legalistic chairmen of rural district councils (the *Landrats*) also delayed the creation of new farms. Some estates were kept together because the bulk of the land had been traditionally leased to small and middle-level farmers who would have been deprived of their land if the reform had been implemented.[47] Also during the winter of 1945–46, there were numerous cases reported in which the former landowners and estate supervisors were able to drift back to their estates and hire their former employees to work the fields, to the satisfaction of both parties.[48]

Soviet commandants felt compelled periodically to intervene in the parcelization process, forcing reluctant communists and *Landrats* to move more quickly than they would have liked. The Russians were particularly upset by the maintenance of large estates where no one was at work; sometimes the land laid fallow and the estate buildings remained empty. But equally frustrating were the cases in which a "trustee" had been assigned to the estate and lived on the premises simply for the purposes of defending it against alleged "sabotage" attempts by the previous owners, who were accused of slaughtering livestock, destroying farm equipment, and removing inventory.[49] Periodically the Soviets also tried to restrain the "revolutionary fervor" of their German communist allies on the land. In some cases, KPD activists abused the land distribution system by taking for themselves farms of twenty-five to thirty hectares, which they could work only with the help of hired labor. In other cases the Soviets tried to intervene on behalf of proven antifascists to counteract measures taken by *Landrats*, whose antifascist credentials were much less convincing than those of the former landowners. In fact, Lieutenant General F. E. Bokov and the Soviet military authorities advocated returning some of these lands to their original owners. But Ulbricht protested—successfully as it turned out—that this measure would only increase the confusion that enveloped the countryside over the terms of the land reform.[50]

New Farmers

Even when the estates were successfully divided, the problems of the new farmers were legion. There were no houses, stalls, or farm machines. There was very little seed, and the shortage of livestock meant that farmers could not properly fertilize their fields with manure. Meanwhile, what chemical fertilizer and farm machinery there was in the countryside was hauled off by the Soviet trophy and reparations brigades. Established farmers resented the newcomers and were of little help. The tension between locals and the settlers did not abate with the foundation in October and November 1945 of the Association for Mutual Farmers' Help (*Vereinigung der gegenseitigen Bauernhilfe,* or VdgB). Usually the established farmers simply took over the local VdgBs and manipulated their resources for their own benefit.[51] The established cooperative movement, the so-called Raffeisen cooperatives, named after a nineteenth-century farm innovator, were held in deep suspicion by the communists, who felt they protected established interests in the countryside. As a result, the cooperatives were not allowed to help organize the new farmers.[52]

The outcome was predictable: hunger and want, misery and despair *(Mutlosigkeit).* The archives are filled with countless reports of the "desolate" appearance of the new settlements.[53] Some new farmers left their plots untilled and engaged in petty black market activities. With few healthy young men to work the farms and no draft animals available, women were often seen pulling farm machinery and plows.[54] The new farmers often had only dry bread and potatoes to eat, and as a result they suffered a variety of diseases due to the lack of fats and fresh vegetables.[55] Some 10,000 new farmers, according to Soviet reports, abandoned the land altogether and sought work in the towns and cities or congregated in a variety of makeshift settlements.[56] In the worst case, Mecklenburg, nearly 20 percent of the new farmers left their settlements between 1945 and 1949.[57] Even those who could make some progress on the land suffered severe hardships. As late as February 1948, Mecklenburg agricultural minister Karl Moltmann wrote that 35,000 new farmers in his province still did not have a proper roof over their heads. They often slept piled next to one another in lice-ridden barracks and barns. This meant, he added, that they could not address their farming tasks correctly.[58] They did better, however, than the settlers from the East, who remained in what the Soviets called "quarantine camps," known in the West as "displaced persons" (DP) camps. By the fall of 1947, some 80,000 settler families had received land as new farmers. But this left more than 600,000 settlers still in the quarantine camps or living in temporary, substandard housing. The situation was particularly bad in Mecklenburg, where more than half of the settlers did not have permanent quarters.[59]

As conceived of by the Soviets and the German communists, the revolution in the countryside was to be a controlled and moderate one, fitting the needs of the antifascist democratic transformation, securing agricultural supplies for the Soviet troops, and avoiding any "class warfare" in the villages. For the Soviet officers, in particular, the democratic revolution in eastern Germany was to parallel that of 1917 in Russia, when the *pomeshchiki* (Junkers) were disenfranchised and expropriated, but the kulaks (the *Grossbauern*) remained to feed the Soviet cities during the New Economic Program of the 1920s. All talk of collectivization in the Soviet zone was quashed, and those who wanted to confiscate the big farms—defined as those with 50 to 100 hectares of land—were quickly disabused of that notion. As I have noted, Dimitrov himself had made it clear in June 1945 that the kulaks should not be touched; nevertheless, Pieck was constantly forced to remind his comrades of the folly, at least for the moment, of inciting the class struggle in the countryside. However, as an indication of what was to come, he added: "In the course of further developments many possibilities will manifest themselves for undertaking corrections in this question."[60] For the time being, there was plenty of political work to be done among small and middle-level farmers, many of whom had been ardent Nazis. Some villages, in fact, had been completely Nazi; those who had not joined the Nazis were farmers of such poor reputation and ability that they "commanded no respect in the village."[61] The communists had to compete with the recently created CDU to win over former Nazi small farmers to the cause of the new Germany.

REQUISITIONS

The expropriation of land had very little to do, therefore, with who was a Nazi and who was not. An SPD report from the Schwarzenberg district made it clear that whether or not someone had a Nazi past was not a decisive factor in determining if that person would be expropriated; rather, it was the size of the landholding and the social background of the owner that were critical. Of the total 2,093 hectares of estate land available for redistribution in Schwarzenberg, one estate belonged to a war criminal, three to former Nazi activists, two to fascist organizations, and six to Junkers and nobles *(adlige)* who had not been Nazis.[62]

There were a number of cases in which large landowners appealed their expropriation edicts based on technicalities having to do with the size of their holding or the number of property owners. In one such case, the Brandenburg Ministry of the Interior was tempted to reverse the expropriation of a Herr Hoffmann on the basis of the fact "that Hoffmann is politically clean, has always shown himself to be a good antifascist, and today belongs to the SED." Local Soviet officials insisted, however, that the Brandenburg ministry stand by the letter of the law. The case reached Paul Merker, SED secretary in charge of agriculture, who in turn wrote to Ulbricht with the recommendation that disputes like these should be resolved politically. In this case, the SED argument prevailed and Hoffmann was able to reclaim his land.[63] But other cases did not turn out so well for the former large landowners, even if they were proven antifascists. The Saxony-Anhalt minister of the interior, Robert Siewert, sent out the following directive: "A loyal attitude toward the land reform, proven antifascists, active participation in the carrying out of the land reform, and so on, none of these are grounds for not expelling [former large landowners]." Siewert made no exceptions, even for aged former landowners who wanted to die near their old estates. They, too, would have to be expelled, explained Siewert, because their children would come around and disturb the progress of the land reform.[64] The pathological insistence that former landowners be completely removed from their home districts indicated just how precarious the SED felt its rule to be in the countryside.

On the whole, the confiscation and redistribution of large landholdings was greeted with approval by the majority of farmers. Those who gained most from it, the new farmers, were particularly pleased with the results of the land reform. According to the final SED statistics on the land reform, compiled in the summer of 1948, 2,743,306 hectares of land were distributed: 398,080 to poor farmers, 740,704 to landless farmers and farm workers, and 567,366 to settlers (refugees). Other categories of recipients included urban workers and tenant farmers. About one-third of the land was turned over to the localities and districts for communal purposes: for research institutions, schools, model farms, and the like.[65]

Those driven from their homes in the East especially looked at the land reform as a great boon. One of these refugees, Otto Reinhardt from Günterdorf near Crossen, recalled his feelings in September 1945: "I wanted to settle down. I very much wanted to settle. Nothing brought me more joy than the news of the land reform. I am a refugee, and before me there was always the specter of uncertainty, I didn't know where I would begin, particularly since there were nine members of my family . . . My dream became reality."[66]

Yet almost as soon as the distribution of landholdings took place, the good feelings about it dissipated. The economic dislocations caused by social upheaval in the countryside certainly played an important role, but there was not much that could be done about that. More significant, the continuing needs of the Soviet authorities for agricultural machinery, livestock, and food meant that new farmers started out with fearsome handicaps. Without horses and carts, for example, they were unable to bring in the first harvest. Forced requisitioning of grain and animal products compounded the difficult situation, to the point that, especially in Mecklenburg, Pomerania, and parts of Brandenburg, the established farms, not to mention the new ones, faced severe shortages and privation.

Requisitioning was supposed to depend on a finely calibrated system of local assessments of quotas, based on the size of farms, the fertility of the land, and the ability of the farmer to produce grain or animal products. The quotas were supposed to be set in such a way that surplus production could be sold on the open market. (The temptation to sell surpluses on the black market induced the authorities to create a system whereby the farmers voluntarily turned their surpluses over to the state through controlled channels, and in return the farmers received credits entitling them to priority purchases of industrial goods that were in short supply.[67]) But the problems with the requisitioning system were legion. First of all, quotas were often set for regions. This meant that a region containing less efficient small farms, including the new farms, had to deliver as much as a region with larger landholdings. This embittered the small farmers and favored the *Grossbauern* or "kulaks."[68] German farmers also had trouble adjusting to the quota system. During the Nazi times, they had been forced to turn over fixed surpluses to the state, but the new quotas meant that they often arbitrarily had to plant or harvest crops, and sometimes they were denied any of the product themselves. Abuses by local commandants seemed to be the rule rather than the exception. Complaints were rife, and protests against excessively high quotas met stiff rebuffs from the Russians, who had used the system in their own country during the war and were greatly annoyed by the Germans' foot-dragging.

Under the quota system, every egg was counted and every gram of butter weighed; when the farmers were short, they were subject to stiff penalties as well as sharp rebukes.[69] For the Soviet officers, the immediate needs of their troops or reparations officials outweighed the interests of the farmers. As one SED agricultural specialist stated the problem: "For example, now we have to put aside [harvesting] the turnips and the few potatoes, because [they say] we have to thresh the wheat. We thresh day and night, while outside the potatoes and turnips freeze. But then we already have a new order to bring in the wood. Planned work is no longer possible."[70] Another SED report complained that it was often hard to know which of the many orders to fulfill first: "It was impossible . . . to know which order actually was valid."[71]

The new farmers, in particular, despaired at the policies of mandatory requisitioning, which seemed to take no account of the floods on the Oder in 1946 or the droughts of 1947 and 1948. When the harvest of feed grains was poor, the farmers were forced to turn over valuable bread grains to fulfill their grain quota. An SED report of July 1948 noted that this practice led the new farmers to believe that they could never make their farms economically viable and to look for a way to leave.[72] When the potato harvest did not produce enough to meet the arbitrary quotas, Max Franke, a new farmer, wrote that the villagers were forced to give up their seed potatoes; they then had to purchase more seed potatoes in the planting season and even then often did not receive them on time. Franke continued:

> We have no plow, no yoke, no wagon, no draft animals, not even a spade ... The despair and anger among the settlers know no bounds. We believed the promises and sit today in the deepest misery. We don't even have a decent pair of shoes, not to mention any stockings. Only those who have met their full quota are allowed to slaughter [animals]; now, as before, we eat dry bread and dry potatoes and are supposed to do the same work, even more. We would gladly give up the farm, but no one wants it, because the misery of the settlers is so well known hereabouts that one will take a big detour to stay clear of the settlements. Whole groups of settlers leave the settlements at night and have fled to the West; they've left everything in the lurch and nothing is done to try to come to help them.[73]

It took a full year of harsh confrontations between Soviet commandants and German farmers for the SED to intervene in any substantial way with the Soviet authorities. In a series of discussions in November 1946, the SED urged their Soviet "friends" to take a more reasonable approach to the problem of compulsory deliveries. The SED advised the Soviets to supervise the process, but said that "they should not intervene in individual cases," that there was no sense in treating farmers who could not feed themselves "as criminals" because they could not meet their quotas. The SED also looked for a way to ameliorate the difficult consequences of Order no. 163, which had established Draconian fines for farmers who "engaged in demonstrable sabotage" by not meeting their quotas. Because these fines were levied indiscriminantly against those who did and did not "sabotage" deliveries, the SED suggested that a regular process of appeal be introduced that could revoke unjust fines and adjust excessively high quotas.[74]

The particular problems with meat and dairy products precipitated the most serious confrontations between the Soviet authorities and German farmers. Throughout the period of the Soviet occupation, farmers were faced with soldiers' nighttime raids of their chicken coops, drunken marauders' demands for animals, and the theft of sausages, bacon, and cured meats of all kinds. The smaller and more isolated the village, the more likely the farmers were to be subjected to repeated and habitual attacks.[75] At the same time, because they were forced to give up their rifles and hunting weapons, German farmers were deprived of their partial diet of wild boar and deer, which were now in such overabundance that the animals trampled their fields and destroyed their vegetable gardens. In Mecklenburg, the Soviets suspected the German farmers of underreporting the number of farm animals and, as a result, issued Order no. 121, which penalized farmers who concealed the size of their herds by increasing their delivery quotas by 10 percent. With this order, the big dairy farmers could be taken to court and sentenced to prison for falsifying production figures.[76]

The chief of the Mecklenburg military administration, Colonel General I. I. Fediunskii, repeatedly berated local officials for making excuses for not meeting their delivery quotas. At the same time, he railed at those farmers who slaughtered dairy cattle to sell the meat and thus avoid high delivery quotas for milk and butter. "Those who do not strictly carry out the orders about the slaughtering of cattle," he threatened, "must be held strictly accountable, and if necessary be placed before the courts."[77] But local commandants were as much to blame for the indiscriminate slaughtering of the herds as were the farmers. According to the Mecklenburg SED official Toni Wohlgemuth, when the farmers did not meet their meat quotas, the Soviets responsible would order the slaughtering of even the breeding cattle, which aroused "bitterness and anger."[78]

Complaints continued about requisitions and quotas into 1947 and 1948. Even Otto Grotewohl tried to persuade Ulbricht to intervene with the Soviets to cut back the burden of compulsory deliveries. Especially grating for Grotewohl was the widespread (and accurate) belief among German farmers that the potato harvest was being used by the Russians to produce vodka.[79] The SED was able to reign in the Soviet authorities on some marginal issues relating to the quotas, but the major priorities of Soviet rule in Germany, as restated at the beginning of 1947 by SVAG's chief economic officer, Major General Koval, remained: (1) to ensure the transfer of reparations, and (2) to provide for the maintenance of the occupation army.[80] As a result, the Soviets continued to pressure German farmers for deliveries and only reluctantly lowered quotas.

The summer and fall of 1947 brought no relief to the bleak picture of German agriculture in the Eastern zone. The harvest was poor and a potato bug plague destroyed a portion of the potato harvest. Hunger and malnutrition were widespread. Complaints multiplied about the catastrophic consequences of the land reform for agricultural production. In the villages, SED members were heard to lament the fact that the estates had been broken up.[81] Even among higher SED agricultural functionaries, the belief was widespread that the land reform had been poorly managed.[82] Land had been taken out of the hands of competent farmers and given to incompetent novices. From sympathetic landless farmers and farm workers, the SED had created a hostile group of small farmers. Many let their KPD-SED memberships lapse; others, of course, had joined the party in the first place only to get a plot of land. Dissatisfaction in the villages was rife as a result of uncertain boundaries between properties and frequent revisions of earlier decisions. The conservative *Grossbauern* exerted considerable influence in the villages. As a result, the SED was losing ground in the villages to the CDU; even the new farmers who profitted directly from the communist-sponsored land reform were turning to the CDU.[83]

Not untypically, the Soviets blamed others for the failure of their own policies. Soviet reports accused "enemy elements" of sabotaging agricultural production and illegally reconcentrating wealth in the countryside. "Prosperous farmers" allegedly undermined the economic welfare of the new farmers by holding back the distribution of estate land and interfering with credit and material help for the new farmers. Lieutenant General V. E. Makarov, chief political officer of SVAG, reported back to Moscow: "There were also many cases where the new farmers for one reason or another simply turned their backs on the land [*sgoniali s zemli*]. For a variety of motives, more than 10,000 new farmers left the land ... A portion of the settler population, under the influence of reactionary rumors about a supposedly imminent return to their old lands, turn away from work and permanent arrangements, leaving the land that they received in the reform."[84]

The Soviets appeared to be stymied by the problems in the countryside. On the one hand, the Soviet Central Committee and the chief of the Main Political Administration made it clear in their communications to the zone that there would be no substantial relief in the amount of reparations or the responsibility of political officers in eastern Germany for assuring their collection. On the other hand, the Soviet leadership in the zone could devise no other measures to deal with the crisis on the land except for "strengthening the results of the land reform and the economic arrangements for the new peasants" (Order no. 209) and intensifying the struggle against "enemy elements" who were "sabotaging" land reform and democratization. Order no. 209 did stimulate the building of some new houses for the settlers, but this barely touched the surface of the problem. Newly arrived refugees were ostensibly provided with at least a minimal amount of food and shelter.[85] But the desperate shortages were not alleviated by these palliatives, and agricultural productivity continued to drop. Gangs of new settlers roamed from one part of the Soviet zone to another, looking for available land and constantly being shunted off to another region or province.

COLLECTIVIZATION

From the very beginning of the reorganization of the countryside, the issue of collectivization was on everyone's mind. The left-wing ("sectarian") communists called for the nationalization of all landed property, and in some cases even began to form collective farms in isolated districts. They talked about Marx's ideas on agriculture and about the need to modernize rural life.[86] Some Soviet commandants in the first days of the occupation also initiated the formation of kolkhozes, convinced that this was the only reasonable way to foster agricultural production. But the Soviets, and especially Ulbricht, Pieck, and Ackermann, had to convince their German audiences—communists and noncommunists alike—that collectivization was not in the offing and that private agriculture would continue in the zone, freed, however, from the exploitative manipulation of Junkers and Nazi bosses. This was not easy, especially in face of Western propaganda attacks, which focused on the expropriation of the Junkers as the first step toward "the kolkhoz system." The maintenance of model and experimental farms, the emphasis on peasant cooperation, and the creation of centers for leasing agricultural equipment in the Soviet zone were also attacked in the Western press as proof of imminent collectivization.[87]

While denying any intention to collectivize agriculture, the Soviets and the KPD/SED focused their efforts in the rural areas on the agricultural cooperatives, the VdgBs. These party-influenced organizations were given control of all the heavy farm machinery and combines, as well as more than half the silos and storage space in the countryside. In March 1946, the VdgBs were organized into a zonewide movement, and by the end of 1947 they constituted a "mass organization" with some 477,000 members. As a result, the VdgBs were seen as the primary mechanism for carrying SED social and economic policies into the countryside.[88]

During the crisis on the land in the fall of 1947, the SED reached for solutions from Soviet history. Ulbricht talked about the raising of the class struggle in the countryside, but confined himself in the end to the problem of getting the small farmers involved "in carrying forth the expulsion of the large landowners from their counties."[89] The Soviets also attacked the "big property owners" for undermining the land reform and holding back the progress of the new farmers. They were concerned that most of the big farmers—those who owned between 50 and 100 hectares of land— were supporters of the CDU, and these farmers enjoyed a great deal of authority among the middle-level and small farmers in their villages and regions. But precisely because they were so afraid of losing their land, stated one Soviet report on Thüringian politics, the big farmers offered no serious opposition to SVAG's demands and could be easily manipulated.[90] At the same time, however, they were accused of a variety of nasty intrigues, including trying to dominate the VdgBs and penetrating the newly created farmers' party for the purposes of suppressing the new farmers.[91]

Within the SED, implicit calls for collectivization multiplied during the course of 1948. A Thüringian functionary by the name of Hanusch criticized the timidity of the party's policies toward the kulaks. "In the end," he stated, "the actual proletariat goes hungry and the kulaks and the other bourgeois elements get rich."[92] In August 1948, a *Grossbauer* was expropriated with the explanation that it was "intolerable" in the "new democratic order" that so many new farmers and landless refugees suffered just so the "so-called" rights of "*one Grossbauer* and his heirs" would be honored.[93]

Within the Soviet Military Administration, too, there were signs that agricultural officials looked to collectivization as a way out of the political and economic problems in the countryside. The most significant indication that a change was on the way came from the acting head of the Agriculture and Forestry Administration of SVAG, L. A. Korbut, in a September 17, 1948, memorandum to V. S. Semenov, political advisor to the commander-in-chief. (The memorandum was approved by his superior,

General Koval, deputy commander-in-chief of SVAG in charge of economic affairs.) Citing the Cominform resolution on Yugoslavia and the resolutions of the Polish Central Committee plenum as the inspiration for his reconsideration of agricultural problems in the Eastern zone, Korbut suggested that it was time to resume in earnest the class struggle in the German countryside by using the VdgBs to attack the kulaks. During the period of "the liquidation of the *pomeshchik*-Junker class," it had been justified for the VdgB to be an organization of all farmers. "But isn't it time," Korbut wrote, "to give it a major social thrust as an organization that has as its basic goal the defense of the interests of the poor [*bedniak*] and middle-level [*seredniak*] farmers?" (The terminology, it is important to note, was the same used in discussions about Soviet collectivization in the late 1920s and early 1930s.) To accomplish this goal, Korbut suggested: (1) giving the poor and middle-level farmers priority in the use of VdgB machines, and forcing kulaks to pay much more for available technology; (2) making it impossible for "kulaks and representatives of the bourgeois parties" to control the directorships of the VdgBs; (3) ensuring that the laws forbidding the leasing or selling of the new farmers' land were strictly enforced; and (4) introducing a progressive system of dues in the agricultural cooperatives that would, in effect, eliminate payments by small farmers and greatly increase those of the kulaks.

Korbut also wanted to reduce the number and types of cooperatives, to increase their "democratization." With fewer cooperatives, he argued, the shortage of SED cadres in the countryside would not be as detrimental to the party's political control of German farming. In this way, it would also be possible to introduce a much more sharply progressive taxation policy to reduce what he saw as the unfair advantages enjoyed by the kulaks, especially in meat and dairy production. Finally, Korbut suggested redefining the concept of the new farmer by introducing greater class content. He noted, for example, that in Saxony-Anhalt, there were some fifty kulaks among the new farmers; in the state of Saxony there were eight kulaks among the new farmers. Some of the new farmers in Mecklenburg leased enough additional land to be considered kulaks. (It is interesting that Korbut expanded the category of kulaks to include those farmers who owned between twenty-five and sixty-five hectares of land—in German terms, *Mittelbauern* and *Grossbauern.*) In all of these cases, stated Korbut, kulaks should not be allowed to enjoy the tax breaks and other benefits meant to help the poor new farmers.

Korbut's memorandum fell short of an actual call for collectivization.

But it was clear that he wanted the VdgB to pursue a more aggressive policy in the countryside, based on class. He looked to reduce and consolidate the existing cooperatives and promote their economic operations through greater political control. He also indicated that the 800 or so large estates (262,000 hectares altogether) that had been transferred to the people's domain performed abysmally and had suffered huge losses. There had to be quick action on this problem, he concluded, leaving the question open as to whether transforming these farms into collective farms was the correct answer.[94]

Korbut's argument had political as well as economic sources. The villages were firmly in the hands of the CDU, despite serious efforts by SVAG and the SED to dilute the Christian democrats' influence through the introduction in the spring of 1948 of a SED-dominated Democratic Farmers' Party (DBD). The richer farmers were indeed getting richer, while the general level of agriculture stagnated. Among German and Soviet communists, the idea spread that a "party of the new type" should forge ahead with carrying the class struggle to the countryside, and the Cominform resolutions encouraged the Germans to eliminate kulaks, big farmers, the "parasitical" minority in the countryside.[95]

A number of the German communists took up Korbut's call for class warfare in the countryside with considerable enthusiasm. Paul Merker asked for reports from the provinces about the ways in which the *Grossbauern* sabotaged the land reform. The answer from Thüringen did not please him in the least: "It is completely out of the question that in the whole province of Thüringen there were only two cases of *Grossbauern* sabotage. The report of Comrade Bachmann only demonstrates that neither he nor the district leadership have a realistic view of the circumstances. It is therefore necessary to send several comrades to Thüringen to review the conditions in the villages."[96] Ulbricht's view of the situation was full of contradictions. He urged his comrades to leave the *Grossbauern* alone. Only opponents of the SED, he claimed, could talk about "a second land reform," one that expropriated the *Grossbauern*. But Ulbricht also insisted that the small and middle-level farmers should be helped to protect themselves against the *Grossbauern*. Any big farmers who engaged in speculation, exploited the new farmers, or cheated on their delivery quotas would be severely dealt with.[97]

The first concrete steps toward implementing Korbut's plans were taken in January 1949, when the call went out to the VdgBs to build Machine Tractor Stations (MAS) on the Soviet model. These stations were designed to improve the level of technology in German farming, but more important, they were to serve as a "source of strength" for the alliance between workers and peasants; in other words, the Machine Tractor Stations would see to it that the proletariat (SED) controlled social as well as economic developments in the countryside.

The Machine Tractor Stations provided the impetus for undermining the economies of the big farmers in the countryside. But the fact remained that without an all-out physical attack on the German farmers, of the sort that had occurred during Soviet collectivization, the influence of the *Grossbauern* would continue to be felt. Despite the inclinations of Soviet and German communists, like Korbut and, no doubt, Ulbricht as well, Moscow was not ready for the full socialization of the eastern German economy. The interests of the Soviet Union dictated that the revolutionary transformation in the German countryside go slowly. Soviet leaders were still looking for possible agreements with the Western powers that would avert or delay the creation of a separate West German state. They still sought influence among the West German population; collectivization in the East would have eliminated any chance for support among farmers in the West.

Only in 1952, three years after the founding of the German Democratic Republic, did Ulbricht finally feel secure enough to announce that the GDR would move into socialism. The collectivization campaign, which accompanied this announcement, resulted within a year in the creation of 4,700 collective farms, or *Landproduktionsgenossenschaften* (LPGs). Big and middle-level farmers were attacked, their economies destroyed, and some 20,000 fled to the West. This first stage of collectivization produced LPGs that had some 128,000 members and farmed about 11.6 percent of the GDR's arable land.[98] The second stage, which began in December 1959, eliminated independent agriculture altogether. The German farmer was given three choices: enter the LPGs, go to jail, or flee to the West.

REMOVALS

During the four and a half years of the Soviet occupation, the material wealth of Germany was removed by the Soviets in a variety of ways. In the first stage of the occupation, from the end of April to the end of August 1945, Soviet soldiers engaged in looting and plunder as they moved into and occupied the villages and cities of eastern Germany. Watches were taken, and bicycles; clothes, furs, and jewelry were common objects of looting; German larders were raided for sausages, cheeses, and alcohol. Soviet soldiers even packed up and sent off pianos, wardrobes, and dining room tables. There is no way to know precisely the value of what was taken or destroyed by individual soldiers and groups of soldiers, but by all accounts the amount of looting was staggering.

On the heels of the combat troops, "trophy" battalions moved into Germany, most of which were charged with removing particular items: military machinery, scientific laboratories, printing presses, communications equipment (telephones, cables, even telephone lines), ships and barges. Trainloads of machinery and equipment of all kinds were shipped off to the East. Coal, iron ore, and steel also were loaded into boxcars and sent back to the Soviet Union. Special Sovnarkom (Council of People's Commissars) committees operated in each province, supervising and coordinating the removals as best they could.[99] According to Soviet Foreign Ministry data, until August 2, 1945, the end date of trophy removals by Allied agreement, the Soviets had shipped 1,280,000 tons of "materials" (*materialy*) and 3,600,000 tons of equipment (*oborudovanie*). These figures do not include the vast quantities of agricultural products that were also seized and sent back to the Soviet Union in this period: grain, alcohol, vegetable oil, sugar, and livestock.[100]

The most complex stage of the Soviet removal of material from Germany came after August 1945, especially with the failure of the Potsdam Conference in July to settle the problem of reparations.[101] Without a satisfactory four-power agreement on the collection and distribution of reparations, the Soviets were left with little choice but to take reparations from their own zone. American secretary of state James F. Byrnes suggested as much to V. M. Molotov at the Potsdam Conference. In Moscow, an Interministerial Committee for Reparations was formed under the Sovnarkom to supervise a program for satisfying the Soviets' consistent claim to $10 billion in reparations. Georgii Malenkov was in charge of the committee, and Anastas Mikoyan, the minister of foreign trade, kept track of the transfers of equipment and capital. A July 1946 Foreign Ministry position paper on the question stated that the $10 billion figure was "minimum compensation" for the tremendous losses the Soviets had suffered during the war, and therefore the sum had to be guaranteed by the occupation of Germany. In other words, "the question of how long Germany would be occupied was closely tied to the fulfillment by Germany of its reparations obligations."[102]

In a series of discussions between General V. D. Sokolovskii and General Lucius Clay held in late 1945 and 1946, the Soviets and the Americans tried to reach an accommodation on the reparations issue that would allow the Soviets to receive factories from former leading Nazis and war criminals in the West, clearing the way for a general Allied agreement on the future of Germany.[103] But by the time of the Moscow Foreign Ministers Conference in December 1947, it had become clear to the Soviets that the Western governments were unwilling to allow Soviet reparations demands to be satisfied from the Western zones. The Soviets presented the Moscow conference with the final bill for Nazi-caused destruction in the USSR during World War II: a total of $128 billion. From the Soviet point of view, only hostile intentions could explain the West's refusal to agree to German responsibility for repaying to the USSR a paltry sum of $10 billion.[104] Subsequently, the Soviets looked to extract their $10 billion from the Eastern zone, first in the form of direct transfers of equipment and even whole factories to the Soviet Union, and then, in mid-1946, in the form of the removal of products.

There is no way to know precisely the value of all the German property—machinery, raw materials, products, and so on—that the Soviets removed from the zone between 1945 and 1949. For one thing, there were no centralized accounts kept of the trophy removals, and certainly none were kept of the looting. Soviet data start only with August 2, 1945, when removals were formally charged to the reparations account. The Soviets also continued to remove trophy objects and products that were not part of the reparations account-keeping; long after August 2, for example, they took weapons, rare books, and archives. At the same time, there is no way to track the amount and value of currency, gold, bonds, and other valuable paper removed from the zone. The vaults of some banks and loan houses had simply been emptied into large sacks and shipped off to Moscow. Data from the Russian archives provide some idea of the massive nature of the removal programs, but the totals should be treated as minimum figures.

To get a handle on the amount of reparations extracted from the Eastern zone, the Soviet government formed a special commission in February 1948 that included Anastas Mikoyan (from the Foreign Trade Ministry), A. A. Voznesenskii (from the Central Committee), and Andrei Vyshinskii (from the Foreign Ministry). According to the commission's data, between August 2, 1945, and January 1, 1948, the Soviet Union had received the equivalent of $2.68 billion in reparations. The breakdown of the figures was as follows: $801 million from the East in the form of various materials (factories, goods, and raw materials); $22.3 million from the Western zones; $566 million from the value of the Soviet stock companies in Germany; $603.4 million from current production; $355.4 million in German property outside of Germany (especially in Poland); $127.4 million in forms of transport (railroad cars, ties, tram cars, trucks, and so on); and $200 million in the worth of patents.[105] Using the Soviet numbers as base figures, and considering the fact that removals of current production remained fairly constant through 1950, it seems reasonable to conclude that the Soviets had extracted payment of their bill for $10 billion in reparations by the beginning of the 1950s.[106]

Another way to understand the impact of Soviet reparations extractions from the Eastern zone is to examine the number of enterprises taken. Of some 17,024 "industrial objects" (primarily midsize and large factories) identified by the Soviets, 4,339 were seized for transport in the summer and fall of 1945. In January 1946, the Sovnarkom authorized the removal of 200 more enterprises. If one adds the 50 to 60 Soviet stock companies formed in 1946 to this total, then it is reasonable to conclude that one-third of the productive capacity of industry in the Soviet zone was removed altogether from the hands of the Germans. In addition, according to a different set of figures assembled by the Ministry of Foreign Affairs, the value of the production of eastern German industry and agriculture in 1946 was 5.53 billion marks, of which the Soviet Union took 3.3 billion, or nearly 60 percent of the total. Given the fact that total production was substantially lower than prewar levels because of wartime destruction, Soviet removals of equipment, and a decline in productivity due to postwar disruptions of labor and supply, it should be clear from these figures that the amount of industrial and agricultural goods available to the German population after the war was at a drastically low level, especially when compared with the wartime, not to mention the prewar, situation. According to a frank appraisal by the Soviet Military Administration, this "created a tense situation in the economy and led to the exhaustion of reserves of raw materials."[107]

In short, the Germans suffered a terrible blow to their economy as a result of the Soviet occupation—on top of that caused by the war. But because of the even more desperate straits of Soviet industry and agriculture in 1945 and 1946, the Russian appetite for German factories and goods was insatiable. Shortages in the economy at home prompted Moscow to draw up new lists of factories to be removed. Soviet promises to their German KPD and SED helpmates in the zone that dismantling would come to an end were constantly broken. Not only that, but the lack of clear lines of responsibility for removals and the inconsistent methods used encouraged a kind of feeding frenzy on the part of Soviet officials in the zone. Down to the level of regional and local commandants, Soviets issued orders for the confiscation of all kinds of machinery and products. In no small measure, Ulbricht and the SED's incessant demands for a plan for the eastern German economy were motivated by the desire to have reparations deliveries met on a finite schedule that would get control of Soviets' on-the-spot demands for this or that factory, product, or warehouse full of material.[108] Without such a plan, the periodic seizures of machinery and goods not only hurt the economy but also destroyed the morale of German workers.

SEQUESTERING

From the first days of the occupation, Soviet authorities seized property from Nazis and suspected Nazis. This meant that virtually any property that appealed to them (or to leading German communists) could be taken. The property of non-Nazis and Nazis alike was sequestered, and the variety of things taken was as rich and diverse as German material life could offer: houses and furniture, sewing machines, musical instruments, stores, hotels, automobiles, cows, motorcycles, and bank accounts. Sometimes the articles seized were duly recorded in the actual orders for confiscation, which listed items, locations, and dates of confiscation.[109] Other times, as Vladimir Semenov wrote, sequestering seemed to be little more than "mindless" plundering, especially in the first months of the occupation.[110]

Unpredictable and seemingly arbitrary seizures of German property continued into 1946 and 1947. The SED reported, for example, that a local commandant had seized some 1,800 kilograms of butter in July 1946, but was unable to transport it. As a result, local citizens could only look on in mute anger as the butter spoiled.[111] Fritz Grosse from Saxony recounted a September 1946 incident in which he and a group of party members were stopped by the German police on their way home from a meeting in Dresden. The police sequestered their car with the explanation that the local commandant had ordered them to turn over twelve high-quality automobiles within three hours. None of the local Nazis was still in possession of a car, so others had to be seized.[112]

Next to automobiles, holding on to houses and apartments was the biggest problem for Germans trying to avoid sequestering. By order of local or provincial commanders, beach houses were sequestered, and country villas, manors, palaces, and castles were routinely seized.[113] When Soviet officers were ordered in the summer of 1947 to live only within designated areas of the towns and cities of the zone, a fearful wave of sequestering went on that saw some Germans thrown out of their apartments with only a few hours' notice. Some commandants lived "like little kings," reported Grosse; they simply confiscated what they needed in the way of the best food, the biggest villas, and the fanciest cars.[114] At a party meeting in the spring of 1946, Karl Moltmann, an SED leader from Mecklenburg, called for an end to the seizures of apartments and furniture. He added, "There must [also] be an end to people [Soviets] bursting into a small enterprise and seizing what's left to seize. It should happen according to [regular] procedures through the provincial government and not wildly. (Absolutely correct!)"[115]

But the SED itself was responsible for a big part of the problem. Local SED authorities sometimes sequestered property from alleged Nazis without the permission of the provincial government or even of the local commandant.[116] They seized villas for party houses and cars for party couriers. The local SED authorities were also often much more aggressive in terms of seizing factories, stores, and workshops from alleged Nazis than were the Soviets. In his "farewell letter" of September 13, 1948, the LDP leader and vice president of the Thüringian Landtag, Alphons Gärtner, blamed the SED for the permanent sense of insecurity among the Germans that came from sequestering: "Enterprises were sequestered, the owners of which were only nominal Nazis; however, the turning of these [factories] into state property was desired by the SED and the forces that stood behind the party. The threat of sequestering lies over the whole private sector of the economy and paralyzes any demonstration of free enterprise."[117]

The lack of regular procedures made the problem of sequestering so-called Nazi property even worse. According to Soviet Order no. 124, all property of active Nazis and war criminals was to be seized by the German authorities. The German courts were to decide who indeed had been "active" Nazis and who, as "nominal" Nazis, could hold onto their properties. The antifascist bloc issued guidelines on these distinctions in May 1946.[118] However, on the urging of Ulbricht, the German Committee on Expropriations and Sequestering, which oversaw the implementation of Order no. 124, tried to expand the definition of "war criminals" and "active" Nazis by including large factory owners who had profited from their economic activities during the war.[119] With resistance from the other parties in the bloc, as well as from the factory owners themselves, the process of sequestering through the courts became impossibly complicated and cumbersome.

By the summer of 1947, the Soviets themselves stepped in to break the deadlock. The Political Administration of SVAG complained about the excessive bureaucracy and red tape holding up the sequestering process, noting: "This has extremely negative consequences for the economy of the zone and carries with it undesirable results."[120] The Thüringian military authorities also put pressure on the SED, claiming that some party functionaries tried to stall the process of sequestering in exchange for direct payments and favors from "monopolists" seeking to hold on to their factories.[121] The Soviets also made their dissatisfaction known to Ulbricht, who in turn attacked the Thüringen and Saxony-Anhalt parties for allowing delays and appeals in the denazification of German industry. At a zone-wide conference of ministers of the interior, Ulbricht gave Werner Eggerath, SED chairman in Thüringen, a severe tongue-lashing about the situation in his province. Ulbricht noted that there were still several hundred sequestering cases not resolved, adding, "How long will it take until Thüringen is finished? Karlshorst demands exact data, what do you suggest? . . . Something is politically out of whack with you. It's impossible to explain your loyalty [to the factory owners] in Thüringen. Thüringen is the province where National Socialism ran the deepest, the province where one should have seen the expropriation of the largest number of enterprises. But there the fewest were expropriated."[122]

By the late spring of 1948, the sequestering of factories finally was brought to an end, which the Soviets understood as a positive step both for the new state-run industrial sector and for those private factory owners who were justifiably nervous about the security of their own enterprises. As a way to bring closure to the process, the Soviets returned some of the sequestered properties to their original private owners if they had not been implicated in Nazi activities or profiteering, but they completed the sequestering of other properties when the owners had been so implicated.[123] Most important for the Germans, the Soviets agreed to hand over control of all the sequestered factories to the German Economic Commission to turn into "people's enterprises." Although the sequestered factories amounted to only approximately 8 percent of the total in the zone, Grotewohl pointed out to his comrades that they accounted for 30 percent of all production and therefore would be critical for the successful completion of the Two-Year Plan.[124]

Smaller items sequestered by the Soviet authorities were also given back to the Germans over the period from 1946 to 1948. Printing presses, pieces of land, and some buildings and properties "of commercial character and local significance" were returned.[125] The Soviet Ministry of Finance would have preferred to keep these properties until the Germans had arranged for an orderly payment of reparations and occupation costs, but saner heads prevailed. The return of the properties made it easier for the eastern German government to appear as master of its own economic fate and allowed it to push forward with a unified plan for rebuilding the country while repaying reparations.

ILLEGAL SOVIET ACTIVITY

Throughout occupied Germany, Allied officers and soldiers exploited the defeated Germans for their own economic benefit. From the theft of the rare Quedlinburg Bibles by an American soldier in Thüringen to the exchange of cigarettes for antique watches, Allied soldiers removed goods illegally from their zones of occupation. Sometimes these removals were quite systematic. Small illegal businesses emerged all over occupied Germany that specialized in acquiring German antiques, furs, and artworks for minimal prices, and the Soviet zone of occupation was no exception. To be sure, the Soviet military authorities were on the whole less tolerant of black market activities than the Western occupiers, and they assessed stiff penalties for Germans caught engaging in the illegal economy. Soviet officials frequently complained about the demoralizing effects of the black market on the German working class; a week's wages for a worker just about equaled the cost of a cigarette on the black market. Soviet communications on illegal economic activity, as well as articles in the military press, vigorously denounced black marketeering as a product of reactionary Germans and, in Berlin, of soldiers of the Western armies. Officially, in any case, the Soviets never admitted any culpability for black market activity in their zone.

While it is difficult to capture a complete picture of the extent of Soviet illegal economic activities, it is apparent that a substantial number of Soviet officers were removed from the zone every year because of black marketeering and profiteering.[126] While the vast majority of those sent home were cited for having illegal liaisons with German women, a large number were also involved in a wide variety of exploitative economic activities. Any number of officers accepted bribes from Germans in exchange for economic advantages and favors. As a result, many accumulated large stores of German products from local German businessmen, factory owners, and farmers.[127]

Especially in the first year of the occupation, Soviet officers could ship back to Moscow with relative ease furs, jewelry, furniture, currency, and even automobiles. The great war hero Marshal G. K. Zhukov was known to have outfitted several apartments at home with goods taken from Germany. Unauthorized personal removals became so extensive that the Ministry of the Armed Forces and SVAG staff officers instituted new rules in June 1946 about men and materials crossing back and forth into the Soviet Union. Regular border crossings were established, and officers of the customs service were ordered to observe all the regulations regarding "the import of currency, valuables, and other personal goods."[128] But even then, NKVD reports noted, returning soldiers would sell their German goods before crossing the Soviet frontier, prompting the emergence of thriving pawnshops in border towns like Przemyśl.[129]

Needless to say, the Soviet authorities' measures did not stop the flood of illegal activity, which lasted until the end of the occupation period. Captain "Z," a Berlin propaganda instructor, was sent home for reselling German valuables he had extorted from local German shops. Captain "P," head of a Ministry of Internal Affairs (MVD) operations group in Saxony, was accused of thievery and extortion, along with extreme brutality. For more than a year, he had regularly beaten and tortured German arrestees until they had confessed to crimes they had most certainly not committed. He stole from his victims and shared the loot with his girlfriend, a repatriated Russian, who also periodically abused the German prisoners. When the disgusting pair was finally caught, they were in the possession of some 400 stolen objects, not including 20 gold items he had stashed away and 40 furs and dresses concealed by his accomplice.[130]

A final case from the archives is worth citing for the audacity of the high government official, Deputy Minister "R" from one of the metallurgical ministries. The official used his ministry's airplane and pilot to run a complicated illegal operation in which he would bring into Saxony contraband goods from the USSR and then, using falsified ministerial documents, fly German goods back to the Soviet Union. In both cases, the goods were resold illegally for the profit of Deputy Minister "R" and his gang. He also worked with the Halle regional commandant to confiscate valuables and rare objects from local citizens and resell them in an underground "store" run by German gangsters.[131]

CULTURAL TROPHIES

For the most part, the Soviets' illegal removals from Germany were relatively small, especially when compared with the black market activity of Allied officers and soldiers in the Western zones. On the other hand, the Soviets followed an official policy of claiming German art treasures that was much more systematic than similar policies in the West. The Soviets were naturally interested in recapturing the valuable collections of art and museum treasures that had been seized and stolen by the Germans. These included, for example, the priceless Scythian antiquities from the museum in Kherson, which the Soviets located in Schwerin, as well as the rare archaeological finds from the Novgorod Museum, which were housed in the Prussian secret archives. It was much easier to find these important collections, which had been removed by official German orders, than the huge number of artistic and cultural artifacts that were taken piecemeal by individual German officers. As a result, the Soviets issued orders in the zone to search every possible German institution that might hold their treasures—antique stores, churches, bell towers, museums, art galleries, and so on—and to compare carefully their inventories from 1939 with those from 1945. Unfortunately for the Russians, much of the valuable art and other cultural artifacts were never recovered.[132]

Just as the Soviets sought to recover their own treasures from the Germans, so they also set out from the beginning to seize German art and cultural artifacts as the just trophies of war. The actual collecting of the artwork was done sometimes as chaotically and as destructively as the dismantling of factories. Trophy battalions seized art objects from Nazi storage places on the instructions of a variety of organizations back home, including the Academy of Sciences in Moscow, the Ukrainian Academy of Sciences, and the Committee on Art of the Sovnarkom, headed by M. Khrapchenko. Thousands of paintings and artworks seized from protective storage in salt mines in southern Saxony and the Erzgebirge were transported to Pilsnitz, an estate south of Dresden, where they were sorted and classified by officers of SVAG's Education Department before being flown to the USSR by the various organizations that claimed them.[133]

Soviet art officials were stunned by the richness of the works being sent back to Moscow, which included not just the holdings of German museums but art from all over German-occupied Europe. After seeing Raphael's *Sistine Madonna,* Khrapchenko, the Soviets' leading art official, wrote that it would now be possible to turn Moscow's Pushkin Museum into one of the world's great museums, like the British Museum, the Louvre, or the Hermitage. (Khrapchenko's statement flatly contradicts Soviet claims that the paintings were "heroically" brought back to Moscow just for purposes of preservation.) The Pushkin would need a new building, of course, to match its new importance, Khrapchenko noted, but it would be fitting, he felt, for Moscow's greatness as a world capital to be reinforced by its status as one of the world's great centers of art.[134] His argument no doubt appealed to the growing self-importance of the Kremlin's leaders, Stalin above all, but it helped little with the chaotic organization of art collection in the zone.

Even Soviet documents on the removals indicate that a great deal of damage was done to German art treasures and artifacts. Trophy battalions collected by "various methods," noted one report; "many expositions were plundered," and there was no opportunity to arrange for appropriate transportation. Many paintings and art objects were lost, damaged, or destroyed in the process. Local commandants sometimes obstructed the removals altogether, and the regional offices of SVAG's Education Department were too understaffed to ensure the orderly transferral of museum and art objects.[135] Some estates with valuable art objects were pillaged and burned before cultural officers could get there. Even Pilsnitz itself proved to be a serious problem for the preservation of the German art heritage. In Saxony alone there had been nearly one hundred museums, thirteen of them in Dresden and seven in Leipzig. After the most valuable paintings were shipped to Moscow, the rest were stacked in piles at Pilsnitz, where they were poorly guarded and, given the decrepit state of the building, subjected to the elements. Things were so bad at the end— so much had been damaged or stolen—that Education Department officials in charge of the transfer begged their superiors to be allowed to return the remaining objects and the estate to the Germans.[136]

Some artifacts of cultural and national significance had been returned to the German Education Administration by SVAG. In this manner, the Goethe Museum in Weimar was reconstructed from the returned memorabilia, and a Bach museum was set up from the collection of Bach-era instruments the Soviets found in the basement of the Reichsbank.[137] In addition, as a result of the Pilsnitz problem, SVAG issued Order no. 177 on June 18, 1946, authorizing the return of all confiscated museum objects to the German Education Administration. Although German museum directors had tried to keep track of what was taken and on whose authority, sometimes even risking imprisonment to do so, it was virtually impossible to record all of the paintings, sculptures, artifacts, and the like that had been seized, and it was similarly difficult to complain about the objects that were not returned.[138] To this day, Russian and German officials are still trying to locate thousands of missing museum and art objects taken from the Soviets by the Germans and taken from the Germans by the Soviets.

The situation with books and archives was in many ways analogous to that of art objects. There, too, a number of organizations in Moscow sent special agents into eastern Germany to represent their interests. Lenin Library officials had already arrived in Berlin in June of 1945, and they oversaw the removal of tens of thousand of volumes that were shipped back to Moscow. Many institutions in Moscow (and in the zone) looked to build or rebuild their own libraries from the collections located in Germany. Vladimir Semenov sent his men to search for duplicates of books being shipped to the Lenin Library, for the Ministry of Foreign Affairs library back home as well as for the library of his political advisors group in Karlshorst.[139] Soviet government representatives seized the Prussian secret archives, and the Central Committee's Institute of Marxism-Leninism took the records of the Leipzig trial on the Reichstag fire, as well as books, pamphlets, and collections on German antifascism. Major General L. M. Gaidukov, chief of the Soviet rocket project in Germany, traced the archives of the German rocket industry to a thirty-car train near Prague, and asked Malenkov to transport the whole collection back to the USSR. Meanwhile, the Prague archives of the Russian emigration were also seized by the Soviets and removed to Moscow, where they have only recently become accessible to Western researchers.[140]

At the beginning of the occupation, Lieutenant Colonel Rudomino led a team of experts from the Committee on Culture of the Sovnarkom, which identified libraries and collections to be sent to various repositories in the Soviet Union. The Education Department of SVAG supervised the actual work of packing and shipping. In December 1945, when the initial demands of the Sovnarkom had been met, the Education Department was put in charge of the removal of books and given a number of new staff members to finish the task. Their job was to survey public library collections in the zone for the purpose of rebuilding the many Soviet libraries destroyed by the Nazis. Many of the German collections were still stored in a variety of mines. Between December 1945 and July 1946, the Education Department book specialists gathered up some twenty-five library collections with a total of about 1,300,000 volumes, and transported them to the "A-Z" factory in Berlin, where they were sorted and packed for shipping back to the USSR. The first volumes sent to Moscow were those highest on the priority list: technical books that had been published in Germany during the war. According to SVAG Order no. 012 of March 9, 1946, the Education Department was also given the right to seize private libraries and collections, which then swelled the number of books available for removal.[141]

According to the Education Department's account of its confiscation and shipping of libraries, neither the titles of the books nor the number of crates shipped were recorded by the packers or by any central organization. Rudomino from the Sovnarkom committee removed books without informing the Education Department about the number or titles. Specialized groups from the Academy of Sciences did the same. The best estimate is that 7 million volumes were removed: 1 million from the "A-Z" factory; 1 million by Rudomino; 1 million by the Academy of Sciences; 1 million by a variety of other Soviet organizations; 2 million by SVAG authorities who were specifically charged with gathering all medical books; and another million books went to a variety of specialized libraries back home in the Soviet Union or in the Soviet Military Administration in Germany. The SVAG library, for example, was outfitted with 9,000 volumes from "A-Z," and Berlin's House of Culture of the Soviet Union received 5,000 volumes. By July 1946 the Education Department had finished shipping the books, and in August SVAG issued Order no. 0249, authorizing the return of what remained of the library collections to the German authorities.[142]

DISMANTLING

The Soviets faced a difficult dilemma when dealing with the exaction of reparations from Germany. Unlike the Allies after World War I, who had dealt with a defeated but independent Germany that could bargain for its own future, the Soviets sought to take reparations from a government they had essentially created and planned to support. At the same time, the eastern German leaders—unlike their Weimar predecessors—identified with the Soviets and therefore found it difficult to challenge their demands for reparations. Yet both sides understood how destructive the seizure of factories and goods was for the economy of the zone and, more important, for Moscow's goal of creating a friendly populace and an allied government. Like the problem of rape and plundering, the Soviet seizure of German property to satisfy reparations accounts worked to undermine whatever goodwill the Soviet Union had earned by defeating the Nazis and bringing order to the chaotic conditions of German life in the late spring and early summer of 1945. German communists and the German working class could do little else but look on sadly as the Soviets took away their tools for rebuilding Germany after the war. It is no wonder that despair and disillusionment were so widespread.

The general economic problems of reparations were compounded by the disorder that accompanied the first wave of dismantling in the summer and fall of 1945. A variety of Soviet ministries organized their own dismantling teams, which were not subject to general rules or procedures. The teams pursued their individual objectives according to instructions from the ministries; SVAG itself had very little control over the process. On orders from Moscow, SVAG simply made troops and transportation available to enable the dismantling teams to do their work. Generally, German workers were forced to disassemble and crate the machinery from their own factories, often over their bitter protests.[143] Workers were sometimes pistol-whipped and screamed at by impatient Soviet officers. Even Soviet reports complained about the "tactlessness" and "imperious" behavior of the dismantling teams and of the beating of German workers—including veteran KPD and SPD workers—that took place all over the zone.[144] German workers were so badly treated in one factory in Saxony that they were being forced to dismantle, that they called it a "KZ" (concentration camp) without barbed wire.[145] It should be clear that the gratuitous destruction of factory property was both irksome to the German workers and embarrassing for the higher Soviet authorities, not to mention the KPD/SED. An April 1946 report to the Ministry for State Security (MGB) chief, General Ivan Serov, described the dismantling of the Hazag Works in Chemnitz in the following terms: "In front of the eyes of the German workers, our soldiers under the command of Captain Smotrov broke up and burned furniture from the factory offices, [and] busted the glass in the windows. There were cases where our soldiers assaulted the Germans."[146]

After a substantial number of factories were dismantled in the summer and early fall of 1945, workers painstakingly rebuilt production capacity by using bits and pieces of leftover machinery and warehoused materials.

As often as not, the factories were then dismantled again. In one such case, described by Fritz Grosse of Saxony, the workers tried to protest and were beaten; in another, German workers were forced to work under the supervision of armed guards, who screamed at them—"You German pigs!"—leaving them "angry and confused." In Leipzig, after the dismantling of a factory, the reparations brigade destroyed the factory offices, demonstrably breaking every pane of glass in the place, and this when glass was desperately needed for rebuilding homes and apartments.[147] In Chemnitz, noted one SED member, workers sometimes went "completely out of their heads" after they had first lost work at a dismantled factory and then found another job at a factory theoretically safe from dismantling, only to learn that the new factory had been added to the dismantling list.[148]

German workers were deeply angered by the way the Soviet dismantling teams handled their machinery and equipment. In some cases, the Soviets showed little or no interest in the proper packing of the equipment. Machines were sloppily handled, and the transportation of the equipment was poorly managed. In Plauen, for example, workers protested—"justifiably," according to the Soviet account—when machinery and parts that were not even slated for removal were so badly damaged by the dismantling team that they could not be used again.[149] Sometimes German workers were also forced to see equipment from their factory sit for months on railroad sidings, rusting and deteriorating.[150]

As if these kinds of incidents were not enough to embitter German workers, Soviet dismantling needs were often so pressing that additional workers had to be recruited, usually without pay, to disassemble and transport the factories. In one case, Major Orlov of the Ninth Trophy Brigade (Fourth Battalion) used his troops to surround a soccer stadium, stop the game in midmatch, and haul off workers for the dismantling of a factory. In a similar case, Russian soldiers stopped a movie in the middle (ironically, the Soviet film *Circus*) and seized workers for a dismantling. Dances were stopped to get workers; restaurants and bars were also frequent targets. Even when the Germans went along peaceably with the dismantling teams, they were threatened, cursed, and sometimes pistol-whipped.[151] For German workers, especially those in the KPD/SED or in the zonal trade union (the FDGB), it was hard to understand why the Soviets did not seize former Nazis and government officials for this work. Instead, German workers were forced to labor twelve to fifteen hours a day, seven days a week, sometimes without anything more than vague promises of payment that were seldom fulfilled.[152]

The political fallout from dismantling could not escape even Walter Ulbricht, who rarely demonstrated any sympathy for the hardships that reparations caused workers in the zone. When he spoke to Georgi Dimitrov about dismantling in June 1945, he did so in terms of the distress of "Left" communists, who complained that with the dismantling, the German workers' movement was being undermined by the great workers' state, the Soviet Union.[153] Along similar lines, the Soviets noted the characteristic argument used by the Germans to deter dismantling: "The Russians maintain that they don't want to destroy the German people, but isn't it the case that the dismantling of factories and the transport of raw materials out of Germany will lead to the death of our people?"[154] The political problems of dismantling were even more severe, given the fact that the Soviets periodically promised the SED that the dismantling would be brought to an end. First, the May 1946 unity congress of the SED was supposed to mark the end of dismantling. Then SVAG promised that it would be ended by New Year's Day, 1947, only to have to go back on its word again.[155]

The Soviet Military Administration understood how serious the affect of the removals and dismantling was for their cause, citing a popular ditty from Halle as an example of German feelings:

> Welcome, liberators!
> You take from us eggs, meat, and butter, cattle and feed.
> And also watches, rings, and other things.
> You liberate us from everything, from cars and machines.
> You take along with you train cars and rail installations.
> From all of this rubbish—you've liberated us!
> We cry for joy.
> How good you are to us.
> How terrible it was before—and how nice now.
> You marvellous people![156]

But with so many ministries in the Soviet government able to assert their prerogatives within Germany for their special needs, SVAG was unable either to keep its promises to end dismantling or to control the reprehensible behavior of the dismantling teams. Like other German communists, Anton Ackermann felt that these broken promises—passed on by the SED to the population—were worse than the fact of dismantling itself, and he urged the party to stop making promises about its end; otherwise, he believed, the workers would lose all faith in the SED.[157] There is evidence that Ulbricht periodically tried to get a straight answer about dismantling from the Soviet authorities, but there was very little he could do except gently to remind the Soviet "friends" that these practices in the zone wreaked havoc with the political mood of the working class.[158]

Provincial SED leaders were much less restrained with the Berlin party leadership than Berlin was with Moscow. Heinrich Hoffmann of Thüringen warned the SED Party Executive that workers were so angry about dismantling that they had urged the local SED to ask for Marshall Plan help. "How strong is this mood in Jena?" Ulbricht asked. "Very strong," replied Hoffmann. Werner Eggerath, also from Thüringen, urged Grotewohl to intervene with the Russians before everything was gone from the province, including Thüringen's only cement factory, its roofing manufacturers, and what was left of Zeiss's ability to make eyeglasses. At one point, Eggerath called up Grotewohl and begged him to come to the province to intervene with the local reparations officer, General Dubrovolskii.[159] (Dubrovolskii had apparently refused to see provincial SED leaders.) When approached by Dietz Verlag to intervene with the Russians to stop the dismantling of their last linotype machine, Ackermann answered that there was nothing he could do and recommended that the company work through Ulbricht, who had direct ties to Karlshorst.[160]

German workers also sometimes appealed directly to the Russians for relief. The miners of Niederlausnitz wrote to Sokolovskii in November 1946, describing the situation in the Senftenberg mines. They had been assured by the SED, the miners wrote, that the mines would remain in workers' hands and that after May 1, 1946, there would be no further dismantling. They claimed that the local Soviet authorities had given them the same assurances. Yet reparations teams had showed up in November to dismantle the remaining machinery, without which their mining operation could not function.[161] The SED had explained to the miners that renewed dismantling in the Saxon mines derived from the problems the Soviets were having getting the Donetsk mines back in operation. (In fact, the dismantling of coal briquette–making works ended only in February 1948.[162]) The primary issue in mining, as well as in other areas of the economy, was that Soviet ministries (and the corresponding local ministries in the Soviet republics) were desperately short of basic industrial machinery—turbines, mining equipment, printing machines, rail lines—

and they simply took them from Germany, promises aside.[163] Neither the SED nor SVAG could do much about it.

During the first wave of dismantling in the late summer and early fall of 1945, out of 17,024 major industrial concerns recorded by the Soviets in the zone, 4,339 were dismantled and transported to the Soviet Union, including major targets in the Soviet zone's chemical industry.[164] The second wave, which came in the spring and summer of 1946, was especially embarrassing for the SED, since the party had promised the end of dismantling at the unity congress in May. But after the second wave of dismantling, SVAG was able to take a more active role in protecting Soviet zone industries from a variety of predators at home. For example, with only 60 percent of the original electrical power potential still left in the zone, SVAG issued Order no. 192, which forbade the dismantling of local energy stations without the express permission of SVAG authorities in Karlshorst.[165] In the provinces themselves, commanding generals took a more active role in protecting local industries from dismantling teams. General I. S. Kolesnichenko in Thüringen issued orders that forced dismantling groups to get permission from the SVA headquarters in Weimar before entering any factory in the province. He also tried to help local industries get back on their feet by turning over trophy warehouses, untransported machinery and materials, and ownerless property to local German authorities.[166]

REFERENDUM ON INDUSTRY

Once the Soviets had seized strategic industries and brought factory removals to a halt, there was no reason for German and Soviet socialists to leave German industry in the hands of its previous owners. This was especially the case because German factory owners, like the Junkers, were accused as a group of being responsible for Nazism, whether or not they had actually been Nazis. The generally accommodationist KPD program of June 11, 1945, had left the issue of nationalization in abeyance. But by the spring of 1946, the communists and social democrats decided it was time to expropriate the property of factory owners by means of a "people's movement" initiated by the antifascist bloc of democratic parties.

The most difficult problem with this solution was convincing Jakob Kaiser, the new head of the Christian Democratic Union in the East, to agree with the call for a referendum on expropriation. (His predecessor, Andreas Hermes, had fled the zone for the West as a result of his opposition to the way land reform was carried out.) Kaiser did not oppose the referendum in principle. In the immediate postwar period, the CDU had strong "social" inclinations, and Kaiser himself had come to prominence from the Christian trade union movement. But he felt the referendum should take place only on an all-German basis; if it took place just in the Soviet zone, Kaiser reasoned, a new social and economic system would be erected in the East that would imperil German unity. He agreed, as did the Liberal Democratic Party (LDP), that the real war criminals among the industrialists should be punished with the seizure of their factories. Kaiser was ready to support a strictly defined crime-and-punishment action against Nazi industrialists in the East, but he worried—quite correctly, as it turned out—that the socialist parties had much more in mind. He was unhappy, as well, that the socialist parties were uninterested in the principle of compensating non-Nazi factory owners for seized property that they had legally acquired.[167]

Kaiser fought a losing battle. In some cases the SED went ahead and conducted "spontaneous" seizures of the factories of alleged war criminals without following any regular procedures. Meanwhile, Colonel S. I. Tiul'-panov and the Soviet Military Administration made it clear to both the CDU and the LDP that they would do well to keep to a "democratic" course by supporting the referendum.[168] With the hesitant assent of the CDU and LDP, representatives of SVAG, the Central Secretariat of the SED, and the president of the state of Saxony decided on a course of action. Ulbricht described its outlines in a letter to Bokov: "We draw attention to the fact that this referendum will only be held in Saxony. After the completion of the referendum, in the other provinces of the Soviet occupied zone, [one can] proceed by administrative measures."[169] The idea was to create two lists of factories. List "A" was to be made up of the factories of war criminals and Nazis scheduled for expropriation; list "B" was to contain those factories that were to be returned to their original owners. After considerable wrangling about which factories should be on which list, the final list "A," approved by the Soviets, scheduled 2,341 enterprises for expropriation; 1,900 enterprises on list "B" were to be returned to their owners.[170] There was, of course, no list "C"— factories that had been sequestered by the Soviets and then either dismantled and removed from the zone or turned over to Soviet ownership.

The date for the referendum was set for July 16, 1946, and an intensive campaign about its advantages was conducted by the SED among the Saxon population. The LDP and CDU also participated, as did the Church and a variety of social organizations. It was hard to speak up against the punishment of war criminals, yet there was some resistance to the measures. In some localities, for example, the production committees of the factories themselves came out against sequestering, with the argument that the removal of the established management would endanger their jobs.[171] Soviet referendum observers noticed that workers in smaller factories were especially hesitant to vote for the expropriation of their own enterprises, though they were happy to see other factories expropriated. The Soviets claimed that factory owners employed a number of devices to stay off of list "A." They tried to get workers to intervene for them by handing out rations of potatoes, improving the quality of factory lunches, and distributing textiles and other goods.[172] Ulbricht concluded from the many cases in which "representatives of enterprise workers came to the defense of their factory owners and came out against the confiscations," that fascism had made deep inroads into the consciousness of the German working class.[173]

To make sure that the referendum would go as planned, SVAG called a meeting with the political leadership of Saxony on June 15, 1946. General D. G. Dubrovskii was there from SVA headquarters in Dresden; Bokov and Tiul'panov attended from Karlshorst. Otto Buchwitz and Bernard Koenen represented the Saxon SED, and SED members Rudolph Friedrichs (president) and Kurt Fischer (vice president) represented the Saxon government. (As head of the Ministry of Interior and the highly politicized Saxon police force, Fischer may have been the most important German attendee.[174]) The meeting lasted six and a half hours, and every detail of the referendum was reviewed. The Soviets wanted to know to what extent they would have to be involved to ensure success, but it was clear that the kind of massive interference that had accompanied the KPD-SPD unity campaign in the winter and spring of 1945–46 was not deemed desirable or necessary by the attendees. In fact, those at the meeting concluded that even a negative vote on the referendum would not change much about the fate of expropriated enterprises.[175]

When the referendum was finally held on July 16 with great fanfare and celebration, the voters were asked whether they agreed with handing over "the factories of war criminals and Nazi criminals into the hands of the people." Given the support of the referendum by all the political parties, it is not surprising that it passed by a substantial margin (77.7 percent for and 16.5 percent against). Ninety-four percent of all eligible voters participated; 5.8 percent of the ballots did not count because either nothing was written on them or, as Tiul'panov pointed out, there was everything on them "from pro-Soviet to openly fascist" comments.[176] The actual expropriation law read as follows: "The entire property of the Nazi Party and its affiliates and the factories and enterprises of war criminals, leaders, and active proponents of the Nazi Party and the Nazi state, as well as the factories and enterprises that served [the interests of] war criminals and were handed over to the state government of Saxony, are declared to be expropriated and pass to the ownership of the people." On the basis of the referendum, 1,760 factories and enterprises and parts of 101 others were expropriated without compensation and turned over to the Saxon state.[177] The formula for the expropriations in the other provinces would be the same. As Pieck, Grotewohl, and Semenov agreed, there would be no talk of "socialization," which frightened the middle classes and, in any case, was a "deceptive and empty" concept. Instead, the propaganda would be focused on the fact that the property of fascists and war criminals was to be turned over to the people.[178]

REPARATIONS IN KIND

The referendum in Saxony and the transfer of property into the hands of the provinces was linked logically to a Soviet policy change in the summer of 1946 that mandated the end of dismantling. After the major targets of the dismantling teams had been removed, the Soviets increasingly looked to exact reparations from the Germans in the East by removing products rather than factories. To be sure, reparations in kind had been taken from the zone since the very beginning of the occupation, and highly targeted dismantling occurred even after the shift in reparations policy during the summer of 1946. Still, it was important to the zone (and to the progress of Council of Foreign Ministers' negotiations) that the Soviets now expressed a preference for garnering material support from the Germans through payments in kind. For the Soviets, payments in kind eliminated the costly and enormously wasteful process of removing, transporting, and reinstalling machinery. (There is a fascinating story yet to be told about the successful and unsuccessful rebuilding of German factories in the Soviet Union. Unfortunately for the rebuilding of the country, the success stories were all too rare.) At the same time, the exaction of reparations in kind had the distinct advantage of leaving German workers in place, eliminating much of the source of their dissatisfaction with the

Soviet occupation. Certainly from the SED's perspective, the removal of products was much less galling than the dismantling of factories.

But the new Soviet policy did not eliminate the political problems that derived from the extraction of reparations. In fact, the delivery of reparations in kind brought many of the same hardships that dismantling did, though it allowed the workers to remain at their jobs. Workers had to face a battery of orders issued by Soviet authorities that required a high level of production and overtime work, without consideration of poor factory conditions and without extra pay. Sometimes Soviet orders for the delivery of products carried direct threats of punishment if the quotas were not met or products were of inferior quality. A Brandenburg order, signed by General V. M. Sharov, stated that poor-quality production "will be looked at as opposing the reparations measures of the Soviet occupation authorities and will be punished by criminal procedures."[179] The Soviets refused to accept German enterprises' explanations that they were short of materials or that machines had broken down. Any delays in production were viewed "as a result of their inactivity and [as] sabotage of the measures of the occupation government."[180] General Kvashin of SVAG's Transportation Administration threatened SED factory officials over the phone that if he did not receive 7,000 train cars on time he would treat them all as spies and saboteurs.[181]

Neither the Soviets nor the Germans were happy with the system of delivering reparations in kind. Part of the problem lay with the chaotic and unrealistic demands made by the Russians; part of the problem was that Soviet threats were not combined with sufficient incentives for German workers to perform up to their capabilities. Moreover, dismantling had severely damaged the overall economy of the zone. Some 80 percent of machine-tool productive capacity and 60 percent of light and specialized industrial production had been removed.[182] Spare parts were hard to find and new machines impossible to order. The removal of railway cars and tracks also severely limited the performance of eastern German industry, just as the dismantling of chemical fertilizer plants drastically undermined agricultural productivity. In August 1947, the Soviets reported that only 20 percent of the third-quarter plan of the Industry Administration (and 39.1 percent of plan for the Soviet stock companies, the SAGs) had been fulfilled. The response of the commander-in-chief was resolute. He ordered a complete transformation *("perestroika")* of the work of the Industry Administration, stating that "immediate measures" needed to be taken "for the fulfillment of the reparations plan." Tiul'panov passed on to his SED comrades the bad news that reparations in kind would be pursued "with great decisiveness," which meant that there would be no improvement in the economic conditions in eastern Germany, at least in terms of the availability of goods. "Serious discipline" would be required in both German and Soviet-run factories.[183]

Just when Tiul'panov was calling for greater discipline in the factories, the Economics Department of the SED suggested that the Soviets introduce a three- to six-month moratorium on reparations in the zone, to allow "the entire production in this period [to go to] supplying the needs of the population."[184] As necessary as such a measure was for the economic and psychological well-being of the German population, such fantasies were not to be realized. Instead the Soviets raised demands for this or that product, frustrating the Germans, who were for the most part unaware (and kept unaware by the Soviets) of the desperate economic situation in the Soviet Union itself. All the Germans knew was what they saw in countless films of happy and prosperous Soviet workers and what they experienced in endless demands for their production and labor. Karl Moltmann, an SED leader from Mecklenburg, repeatedly made the point that the party needed to know the real state of the reparations accounts: what the final bill was and how much had already been paid. In the timber industry, he complained, Soviet officers from this office or that made demands for deliveries of wood "on reparations accounts." He explained:

> As political men we need to know very clearly [*klipp und klar*] what Russia now needs and how high the amounts are for what we have to deliver to them ... If I could honestly tell the people out there what is demanded [of them], then they could understand it and I could enlist [help]. But when I myself know nothing about it, and time and again new demands suddenly are dropped on us, and everything that was agreed to no longer holds, we can't work and recruit in this way.[185]

Moltmann's frustration was common to SED leaders concerned about the economy. Ulbricht, too, was anxious to find a way to bring order to the reparations demands, though there can be no question that he saw them as just. Ulbricht's intention was to introduce a plan in the zone as soon as possible, one that included production and reparations totals that would hold the Soviets to concrete demands within the plan's periods. In March 1948 in Moscow, Ulbricht and Pieck handed to Stalin a draft of the SED "Economic Plan for 1948," which gave control of planning the

German economy to the German Economic Commission. The commission's task was to see to the fulfillment of the plan, including the reparations payments in kind to the Soviets. According to the plan, the commission would also be given control of the allocation of raw materials, making it possible to divide supplies fairly between the Soviet- and German-run enterprises (the SAGs and the people's factories, or VEBs). According to Ulbricht's proposal, once the plan was agreed to by the commission and the Economic Planning Department of SVAG, it could not be altered without the agreement of both. At least in theory, then, SVAG would be making a commitment not to place orders for and take production from the German economy outside of the confines of the plan. The SAGs, too, would be subject to the plan, at least to the extent that they would have to report their needs for raw materials, parts, and finished products to the German Economic Commission. According to Grotewohl, the planning process also included a Soviet agreement to regularize the supply of raw materials (coal, cotton, and petroleum) to the zone through trade with the countries of eastern and southeastern Europe.[186]

THE SOVIET STOCK COMPANIES

Until the Two-Year Plan was adopted in late 1948, the primary method of ensuring the delivery of reparations in kind to the Soviet Union was the institution of direct Soviet control over factories, mines, and enterprises in the zone. During the first nine months of the occupation, the Soviets simply took over strategic enterprises that were impossible to remove, turning over the supervision of production to Soviet directors who were responsible to industrial and mining ministries in Moscow. The question of ownership of the factories became more complicated in the fall of 1946, when, following on the referendum in Saxony, large numbers of enterprises were either expropriated by the Soviet authorities and turned over to the provincial governments as people's factories, or allowed for the time being to remain in private hands.

In January 1946, as the removal of strategic factories became increasingly problematic, the Sovnarkom discussed a draft resolution to create Soviet stock companies (*Sowjetische Aktiengesellschaften,* or SAGs), which would conform to German laws and make it possible for enterprises in the zone to be owned completely by foreigners, in this case by Soviet economic organizations. According to the Sovnarkom plan, Mikoyan's Ministry of Foreign Trade would hold 40 percent of the SAGs' stock and the USSR's industrial ministries (or their suborganizations and enterprises) would own 60 percent. The owners would then name the Soviet directors of the enterprises, who would be confirmed by a SAG administration in Germany.[187] After considerable debate about whether the SAGs should operate under Soviet or German law, and once the problems were overcome with the ministries that wanted to dismantle factories designated as SAGs, the Soviet Military Administration issued Order no. 167, which formally transferred German factories to Soviet ownership "as part of the satisfaction of the reparations claims of the USSR."[188]

Two hundred thirteen large enterprises were designated for dismantling and removal to the Soviet Union in April 1946. As a result of the Sovnarkom plan, 50 or 60 of the largest factories that had operated directly under SVAG's direction or that of other Soviet government agencies were instead designated as SAGs and left in the zone. Two hundred smaller firms were similarly transformed into SAGs.[189] By the end of 1946, the Soviets owned close to 30 percent of all production in eastern Germany. After returning a number of factories and mines to German hands, in December 1947 the Soviets owned some 25 percent of production. In Thüringen, for example, the Soviets controlled 88 percent of the potash and rock-salt mines, and 40 percent of the coal mines and the coal-briquette production enterprises.[190] Virtually all of the synthetic fuel and mineral oil production was in Russian hands, as was the entire industrial chemical industry.[191] The SAG system continued to function after the foundation of the GDR as joint Soviet-German stock companies: the East Germans were allowed to keep a portion of the production while the Soviets continued to collect reparations in kind. With very few exceptions—the Wismut uranium mining enterprise chief among them—the Soviets had turned over most of the SAGs to the East German government by the mid-1950s.

Although the SAGs were clearly a better alternative for the Germans than the dismantling and removal of factories, the system nevertheless caused severe dislocations in the economy and aroused considerable resentment among German workers, trade union activists, and SED members. Leaving aside the loss of production to the eastern German economy in the way of spare parts, fuel, and chemicals, not to mention consumer goods, the SAGs demanded and usually received priority in the supply of raw materials. While German-run factories periodically were forced to close down because of a lack of coal or, in the textile industry, because of shortages of raw cotton or wool, the SAGS usually were able to secure their supply needs. As much as the German authorities tried to control the shortage of raw materials through strict planning, the SAGs' demands always came first. In Saxony, to cite Fritz Selbmann's complaint to Ulbricht, this meant that "serious consequences for the rest of the industries of the province . . . cannot be avoided."[192]

The SAGs created a number of problems among German workers. On the one hand, SAG employees were often supplied with consumer articles that were virtually impossible for other workers to obtain: cigarettes, alcohol, extra fats, and butter.[193] Their canteens were superior, and sometimes the pay for the same work was better. On the other hand, depending on the factory, there were widespread reports that Soviet directors abused German workers. The German trade union also complained that the SAGs did little to prevent industrial accidents or to provide workers with sufficient rest periods and time off. Often Soviet managers responded by refusing to talk to union officials and dismissing their complaints. If the factory councils protested too vehemently about conditions in the plants, they could be disbanded or even arrested. A January 1947 SED account from Thüringen noted that in the SAGs, "the trade union representatives are not allowed to meet, they have to hide and work illegally." When regional union officials approached a SAG director about the problem, they reported that "he simply threw us out." The officials concluded from the encounter that the director hated Germans and that the SED had to find a way to do something about the situation. "We must absolutely clearly and unambiguously point to the fact that because of these attacks, the ignoring of laws and rights, the rejection of traditional Marxist demands, and the support of active fascists, the aversion to the Russian occupation authorities is penetrating broad circles of the Thüringian working class."[194]

The Thüringian letter also touched on a serious accusation that permeates both German and Soviet evaluations of the SAGs; the Soviet directors paid little attention to the denazification of their factories. The reports indicate that the SAGs brought back the old Nazi factory directors and chief engineers to run the factories. The Soviet directors trusted their judgment and allowed them to keep their wealth and privileges, which upset SED and FDGB officials and members alike.[195] Under severe pressure themselves to meet production goals, the Russian directors highly valued technical competence and performance, and subsequently worried little, if at all, about who had been a Nazi and who had not. Even in some very "class-conscious" VEBs, where SED workers controlled the Workers' Councils, demands were voiced for the return of Nazi specialists and di-

rectors as a way to improve lagging productivity and overall performance.[196] Soviet directors routinely ignored local SED protests about former Nazis in the factory administrations. However, this became more and
more difficult after the issuance of Order no. 201 in August 1947, which
established procedures for removing remaining former "active" Nazis
from positions of responsibility in the German administration and economy.

In July 1947, a SVAG official complained to V. N. Merkulov, chief of
the Administration for Soviet Property Abroad in Moscow, that the SAG
Synthetic Works at Schwarzenheide had appointed a former Nazi as its
commercial director, "despite the protests of the production council, the
local SED party organization, the factory organization of OSNA [the un-
ion], and the workers of the factory." Merkulov responded that serious
measures were under way "to purge our factories of former Nazis and
elements hostile to the USSR."[197] But even Order no. 201 was not enough
to get the SAG directors to jeopardize the fulfillment of their production
plans. Marshal Sokolovskii was forced to follow up Order no. 201 with a
specific directive (October 9, 1947), insisting that former Nazis be removed from the SAGs and complaining that the directors were doing too
little in this regard: "Many general directors of branches and enterprises
of the Soviet state stock companies do not take decisive measures for
removing former active Nazis from leading positions, but in a number of
cases ... [actually] blocked the implementation of the decisions of the
denazification commissions and, with that, objectively created fertile soil
for earlier Nazis to carry out hostile acts, arousing the dissatisfaction of
workers and democratic organizations."[198]

As a result of Order no. 201 and Sokolovskii's directive, the MGB increasingly turned its attention to the presence of former Nazis in the SAGs.
The MGB chief, Viktor Abakumov, wrote to Molotov in October 1947:
"The Soviet directors of the enterprises [SAGs] do not take sufficient
measures to purge them of Nazis." At the Sachsenwerke in Dresden, Abakumov added, of 1,800 workers and employees, 201 were former Nazis;
41 of those employees were in leading positions at the factory. From the
MGB's point of view, the prominence of so many ex-Nazis in the factory
administrations could clearly be linked to the increasing number of alleged
acts of sabotage in the SAGs: "The organs of the MGB in Germany have
uncovered the attempts of former Nazis and other hostile elements ... to
destroy the work of the factories of the Soviet stock companies." Abakumov ended his letter ominously, with the promise that the MGB organs

in Germany would step up their "Chekist [secret police] work" in the SAGs.[199]

By the beginning of 1947, with dismantling almost completely halted and the bulk of eastern German industry in the hands of state institutions, either Soviet or German, the foundations of a socialist economy was in place. Yet industrial production continued to be plagued by a variety of serious problems. Zonal divisions, especially the growing divide between the Western zones and the Soviet zone in the East, disrupted normal patterns in the supply of raw materials and manufactured parts from West to East. While the Soviets (and, to a lesser extent, the Poles) took up some of the slack, industries in the Eastern zone were crippled throughout the occupation period by supply problems. Some smaller factories had to close down altogether. The catastrophic shortage of coal, especially, forced even large state-run factories to suspend production for weeks at a time.[200]

Increasingly, serious shortages of raw materials also forced individual provinces to develop protectionist economic strategies of their own. Saxony was one of the worst offenders, ignoring at will the directives of the central German administrations with regard to the economy. As a result, a trade war of sorts developed between Thüringen and Saxony, and between Saxony and Saxony-Anhalt. Thüringen SED leader Werner Eggerath told Otto Grotewohl, "The state of Saxony is carrying on an economic war, receiving deliveries from Thüringen without sending [agreed to] deliveries in return." As a result, Eggerath said, Thüringen was determined to withhold further deliveries of agricultural products to Saxony.[201] Fritz Selbmann, the economic "tsar" of Saxony, also complained about the situation: "We ... scream at the top of our lungs about the unity of Germany, but we don't have unity here in our own zone. The central administrations create great difficulties for us. If we want to conclude agreements with other provinces, we have to cross five borders in the zone ... We have laws of SVA, of the Landtags, of the central administrations, which sometimes do not agree with each other."[202] There was plenty of blame to go around. Kurt Fischer singled out the railway administration ("those swine") for hindering interprovince trade.[203] Others blamed black marketeers and reactionaries.

Selbmann, like Ulbricht, felt that the only answer to the shortcomings in the economy was increased planning and control by central German economic organizations.[204] The economy was forced to serve too many masters, and the result was chaos. As early as November 1945, Marshal Zhukov complained about the lack of planning in the eastern German economy, and as a result set up a centralized SVAG Economics Administration under General Koval, who also served simultaneously as deputy commander-in-chief of SVAG. However, despite the fact that Koval assembled a huge staff and asserted his prerogative to run the economy as a whole, planning remained haphazard and inconsistent. Ulbricht constantly urged Moscow to turn over control of the economy to German central organs. But even the creation of the German Economic Commission in 1947 went only part of the way toward solving the economic problems in the zone. For the German communists, who were convinced of the superiority of the planned socialist economy over Western capitalism, continued bottlenecks and underperformance in the zone were both frustrating and unnerving.

To complicate matters, in June 1947 the United States announced the Marshall Plan, which eventually provided generous credits and investment stimuli for European rebuilding. Though the opportunity was in theory left open for the Soviet Union and the "friendly" governments of Eastern Europe to take part in it, the Marshall Plan was clearly meant for Western European reconstruction. Especially in the Eastern zone, the Marshall Plan diverted the strategic planning of enterprises that hoped in vain to take part in its programs. More important for the development of the Soviet zone was the way the apparent generosity of the Marshall Plan highlighted the shortages in the East caused by the Soviets' removals and their continuing demand for reparations in kind.

The initial Soviet reaction to the problems in eastern German industry was to blame reactionaries and saboteurs. During the spring and summer of 1947, SVAG urged the provincial governments to pass laws that carried stiff penalties—in the worst cases, the death penalty—for black marketeering, speculation, and sabotage.[205] But the Soviets understood that the serious drop of 50 to 70 percent in worker productivity in comparison with the prewar level could not be attributed simply to the activities of "enemies." Much of the problem was with the German working class itself. Rates of absenteeism were extremely high—over 20 percent in such basic industries as coal mining, machine building, and metallurgy. According to Soviet data for June and July 1947, absenteeism was 24 percent in factories working for reparations, 14 percent in the SAGs, and 19 percent in factories producing goods for the German population.[206] A Soviet investigative commission concluded in August 1947 that the German workforce was unstable, unreliable, and functioning "at a very low level."[207]

From the German point of view, poor housing conditions, inconsistent wage policies, and the insecure state of management in the enterprises contributed to the problem of workers' morale. But for the Soviets, low productivity was essentially a political problem, and they took the SED leaders to task for not demonstrating leadership in solving this problem and instead leaving it to the unions (particularly, to the Free German Federation of Unions). As for the unions, the Soviets claimed they were rent by "reformism" and "opportunism," and were thoroughly demoralized by the decline of the German work ethic. In some industrial unions, like those in textiles, typography, and leather, the Soviets alleged that the leadership was dominated by "economists," interested only in questions of wages and conditions of work. (Much of this terminology came from Lenin's critique of Russian labor unions in the 1890s!) Moreover, from the Soviet point of view, the unions tended to ignore class differences among the workers; the "labor aristocracy" had no interest, for example, in activating productivity among the unskilled masses of workers, and even stood in its way.[208] As one might expect, Ulbricht agreed with the Soviets' critique. He accused the labor leaders of blocking initiatives to fight "schematicism" and "bureaucratism." All in all, Ulbricht asserted, the unions had stagnated because of their reformism, instead of becoming fighting organizations for the improvement of production.[209]

The primary mechanism the Soviets developed to break through the impasse of low productivity and absenteeism on the part of the workers and formalism and bureaucracy on the part of the unions was Order no. 234, issued by Marshal Sokolovskii on October 9, 1947. The main idea of the order was to provide incentives for workers to produce more by shifting to a piecework system for wages. "The more you produce the better you live!" went the slogan accompanying the issuance of the order. In addition to promising shoes and clothing to workers, as well as a hot meal at lunch, the order initiated an activist movement, one that encouraged workers to fulfill and overfulfill their production goals in the context of labor competitions. Productive workers would be rewarded; widespread leveling (*uravnilovka,* or *Gleichmacherei*) among the workers would be discouraged.

The FDGB dutifully tried to introduce these measures into the factories but met, for the most part, with stony opposition from workers. "Let's eat first, and then we'll produce," responded many workers. "Piecework is death!" protested a number of labor leaders in the zone.[210] But the Soviets and SED leadership responded by urging that workers become model activists; by producing more, each individual activist would contribute to the welfare of German society in the East. They would also earn more. Wage differentials *(Leistungslohn)* and better rations would be the reward for overall productivity, while absentee workers would be penalized. In a "democratic economy," Paul Merker argued, the piecework system and wage differentials were not the same as in a capitalist system, "because the piecework system could no longer be used for the exploitation of the workforce and because the increase in production that is its goal would be used for the benefit of the whole."[211]

The Soviets also argued that Order no. 234 would activate the German people to take an interest in their own economic welfare, in contrast to the western German case, where workers grew apathetic and indifferent while they waited for a mythical flood of dollars from the Marshall Plan.[212] The problem with this logic was that eastern German workers saw the fruits of their production disappearing from view. As far as they were concerned, everything was taken to satisfy reparations accounts. In the shipyards of Rostock and Wismar, workers' quotas were raised by 20 percent along with the introduction of Order no. 234. "Why should we work so much and for whom?" they complained. All the ships they built went for reparations. If just one ship could be used for Germany, the workers protested, then they would be more enthusiastic about their labors.[213] Whether or not this was true, reparations payments unquestionably sapped the German working class of its incentive to produce. Pieck thought that the only way to solve the problem was to improve the material conditions for workers. The needs of the SAGs, of the Red Army, and of reparations must be met, he wrote, but there was also a desperate need to ensure the delivery of German products for domestic consumption.[214]

The food situation was particularly critical, and complaints were rife about the regular removals of trainloads of grain, sugar, and alcohol to the Soviet Union. Some FDGB officials complained that it was wrong to get the workers' hopes up for a hot meal every day when there was so little food available. If Sokolovskii could not procure foodstuffs for this purpose, warned one official, "then we will be shipwrecked."[215] What the FDGB did not know was that there was considerable opposition in Soviet leadership circles to Sokolovskii's promise that more food would go along with the higher work norms. In particular, zonal MGB chief General Serov opposed any attempts to supply the Germans in the zone with more food. He insisted that, as it was, Soviet employees in the zone lived too high off the hog. In Serov's view, the German comrades' pleas for more food were completely unjustified. Stalin agreed with Serov, adding that even after the expected reduction of the number of Soviet troops in the zone by 40 percent, the extra food that they would have consumed should be sent to the Soviet Union rather than left with the Germans.[216]

Consequently, the food situation did not improve as was promised. The unions had little choice in the matter and were forced to adopt the new system of differential wages, higher quotas, and piecework. Even if accepted in principle, the system was applied badly and inconsistently, and it did little to improve productivity or rationality in the factories. Typically, the Soviets blamed the Germans for implementing the measures incorrectly, rather than seeing the shortcomings of the system itself. A senior SVAG economics officer, M. I. Perelivchenko, scolded Heinrich Rau, head of the German Economic Commission: "The *Leistungslohn* [differential wages] have been indiscriminately introduced in most factories in the German national industry, without creating the correct production norms in these factories, and without taking the appropriate organizational measures."[217]

In fact, the introduction of the *Leistungslohn* accomplished little in the factories except for raising overall wages, and productivity remained stagnant. Workers did not like the system, and it remained dubious whether higher productivity would lead to a better living standard. Moreover, the continuation of higher quotas (without improved conditions) and the assessing of new penalties for absenteeism prompted large numbers of workers to pick up and leave for the West—the first of a series of waves of labor migration that plagued the Soviet zone and the GDR until the very end of the "socialist experiment" in the East.[218] It was apparent, Perelivchenko concluded, that without "the greatest possible encouragement" of an activists' movement, the introduction of the *Leistungslohn* would have little impact on the problems of productivity.[219] The only way to make the entire system work, the SED and Soviets agreed, was to invigorate the activists' movement.

The Hennecke Movement

Otto Buchwitz, chief of the SED organization in Saxony, visited the Soviet Union after the war and was enormously impressed by what he took to be the great accomplishments of the Stakhanovite movement.[220] This was very much on his mind when he created the circumstances for the miner Adolf Hennecke to accomplish his "great exploit" of labor heroism— mining a record amount of coal—on October 13, 1948, one year to the day after the issuance of the FDGB proclamation on the need to fulfill Order no. 234. In GDR popular culture and historiography, there was an unbearable romanticization of Hennecke's deeds and the Hennecke movement that followed.[221] To set the record straight, it is useful to quote at length from Buchwitz's report to the SED Party Executive about how he created the Hennecke phenomenon.

> One should not imagine for a moment that this was a chance accomplishment, but we consciously developed the case. I would like to say a few words about this: our goal was to find a way that we would develop an activist movement. We said that for this we needed a central figure, a personality, and I am perfectly happy to admit that we were influenced [by the thought] that we needed someone like Stakhanov here. We looked for a man, and the district leadership helped us . . . We proceeded from the thought that, best of all, we would take him from coal mining, because that is the basic material we need for everything in the economy.
>
> Director Wellershaus looked for a long time, and then found the coal miner Hennecke, whose production already always surpassed that of his colleagues. In the course of the following weeks, he was brought along by Wellershaus.
>
> Therefore, the record was prepared in advance and, to be sure, the goal was set before comrade Hennecke: see that you fulfill your norm by 250%! He hesitated at first and believed that he would be mocked by his comrades at work, perhaps even cursed and insulted. That certainly has happened, and in the next few weeks we must improve ideological training on this question in the mining district. We developed the man in such a way that we sent him first to the district party school [in August 1947] [and we] had him take part in political life until he declared himself that he was ready to take on [the achievement] despite all the resistance he believes it will encounter . . .
>
> That I had the opportunity during my visit to Moscow to observe Stakhanovite workers in a large factory and also to observe their col-

leagues, who stood to the left and right of them. There I understood: that is art—if we can develop an activist movement to which we can attract activists who join their physical powers with their understanding for conquering the materials with which they work.[222]

Buchwitz claimed that his idea of stimulating the activist movement with a Stakhanov-like feat by Hennecke worked extremely well. Hennecke's achievements, he reported, were greeted by "a storm of enthusiasm among the workers." Hennecke and his fellow miners now looked to set new goals and record new deeds of labor heroism. Telegrams poured in from all over Saxony, announcing records in a variety of industries. Younger workers, especially, Buchwitz claimed, were anxious to set higher goals and organize their work to meet them. "We will form an activists' movement using Hennecke's name. We think that the movement should be spread out over the whole zone, so that at last we can move from feats of activists in [discrete] factories and unveil a genuine activists' movement," he declared.[223]

From Buchwitz's report, it is apparent that the Hennecke "record" was planned by the Saxon party and that Hennecke himself was specifically chosen for his ability to work and to learn. His politics were correct (he had been a social democrat before joining the SED), and he bore a resemblance in his simple, straightforward family lifestyle to the great Soviet activist Stakhanov. In autobiographical material, Hennecke stated that he had thought often about Stakhanov before his exploit, that he had devised the attempt at a record himself, and that the Hennecke movement had spread spontaneously to other factories.[224] But Buchwitz stated unambiguously that the Saxon party intentionally transferred the movement to other branches, and that they intended to make a hero of the tall, gaunt, sinewy Hennecke by naming him as the first delegate to the party conference, ahead of other Saxon notables like Max Seydewitz and Buchwitz himself.[225] Historians who study the GDR add the important point that coal was in particularly short supply in the summer of 1948, and that the German Economic Commission, the FDGB, and the SED had agreed that increased productivity on the part of the miners was absolutely critical for the needs of eastern German industry.[226] But in contrast to Buchwitz's optimistic assessment, the spread of the Hennecke movement did not come easily, tied as it was to differential wage rates and the growing prevalence of piecework. Still, there were thousands of letters of congratulations to Hennecke, apparently sent by young workers who saw the Hennecke movement as a genuine opportunity to improve their situation in the factories and to raise their pay outside of the seniority system.[227] By the summer of 1949, according to Paul Wandel, there were 60,000 or so of these Hennecke activists, who had successfully applied "the rich experience of socialist competition in the Stakhanov movement" to the conditions of the Eastern zone.[228]

Certainly the SED and FDGB propaganda and culture departments did everything they could to popularize the activists' deeds. There was a spate of Hennecke songs, poems, and stories, each one more iconographic than the previous. The stanzas of one song ended with the refrain, "We will never forget." In a typical poem, a tractor driver pledged: "I promise you dear Adolf Hennecke, that every day when I go to the fields I will work the way you have demonstrated to us workers." To celebrate the Day of the Activist, Rudolph Hruby wrote the following poem, entitled, not surprisingly, "Adolf Hennecke":

> Du uns ein Vorbild bist!
> Durch dich mancher erst wurde Activist!
> Durch dich stieg nur die Produktion und Norm!
> Du gabst erst er Arbeit Schwung und die richtige Form!
>
> Das ganze Volk dir dafür dankt.
> Du wurdest der Retter in der Not.
> Die Übererfüllung des Zweijahrplans
> Sei unser aller Gelobnis und ein stilles Gebot.
>
> Wir werden auch unsere Feinde besiegen,
> Ohne Krieg, ohne Revolution.
> Wir sehen in dir den Arbeitenhelden,
> Den deutschen Stakhanov, wie ihn besitzt die Sowjetunion.[229]

The miners' greeting, "Glückauf!" (Good luck) became a popular shorthand salute for the activist movement. There were special activist pledges and uniforms, billboards and posters, pins and medals—all of which were attached to Hennecke and his great deed.

The SED's policy on spreading the activist movement was well organized and purposeful. Even before the Hennecke feat, the education system as a whole was ordered to propagandize the benefits of Order no. 234 and labor activism: "In contemporary studies [*Gegenwartskunde*] and in all subjects, Order no. 234 is to be discussed. Work morale is above all to be raised through ethical work education. The ideal of 'The Heroism of Labor' is to be laid out."[230] After the activist movement began in earnest in the fall of 1948, schools and streets were named after Hennecke, mandatory discussions of his feat were introduced into the curriculum, and his face and name were everywhere.

The Soviets took the propagandizing of the Hennecke movement very seriously, seeing it as a confirmation of their own Stakhanovite successes. The December 1948 work plan of the Information Administration in Eisenach began with the task of "daily monitoring the situation of the Hennecke movement in the region, how the SED is propagandizing [the feats] of the Henneckists, what are the measures they take every day." But the Soviets' tasks went much further than simply monitoring. They were to see to the active promotion of the "production activists" within individual factories, and they were to make sure that the Henneckists were properly rewarded for their deeds, if not by the factories themselves, then by the SED or FDGB. Soviet officers were also to ensure that the SED and the FDGB sponsored meetings of Henneckists, with the specific agenda of revamping the old system of production and bringing in the new one with the slogan, "Produce more—live better!" Soviet attention to the activist campaign went so far as not only to instruct local newspapers to popularize the feats of the Henneckists, but also to tell them how to popularize them. The editors were told to run columns entitled, "Keep Up with the Progressivists," in which they were to publish statistics on local heroes of labor to inspire fellow workers to similar heights.[231]

If Buchwitz started the Hennecke movement, the Soviets took it over to make sure that the Germans did it right; that is, to make sure they did it the way it was done in the Soviet Union. Soviet films were shown to demonstrate how real Stakhanovites dealt with problems of production and repelled the inevitable saboteurs.[232] Trade union delegations were sent to the Soviet Union to see how the "new kind of worker," the new kind of human being, had created a revolutionary industrial world.[233] The Soviets allowed Ulbricht to introduce a new Two-Year Plan that would ostensibly allow the Eastern zone to outperform the West in terms of its economy.

Even Stakhanov himself was hauled out and brushed off to help inspire labor activists in the newly friendly countries of Eastern Europe and in the Soviet zone, as well as at home. In the fall of 1945 the Soviet Central Committee provided funds and engaged specialists to get Stakhanov off the streets and out of the night spots he had come to frequent. They painted and fixed up his apartment, bought him books, and tried to get him to be politically active again.[234] Stakhanov's letters to the Henneckists in December 1948 were considered of great importance to the movement—so important, in fact, that the FDGB altered slightly the published version of the correspondence to strengthen some of the language.[235] For Hennecke himself, who became a full-time propagandist for the activist movement, a meeting with Stakhanov in May 1949 was the high point of his visit to the Soviet Union. Two hours with the Soviet activist, Hennecke wrote to him later, had been worth a lifetime of education.[236]

THE WORKERS AND HENNECKE

In his report to the SED Party Executive in October 1948, Buchwitz warned of the possibility of a harsh outcry of workers against Hennecke, attributable to the fact that the workers still held values from the late Weimar period, when they worked for capitalist factory owners and not for themselves.[237] In point of fact, Hennecke's deed did bring out among the workers, in Mathias Kruse's recollection, "the mockers, the envious, and those of little belief." The heroes of labor were "looked at aghast, laughed at, subject to hostility, or at least talked about badly behind their backs."[238] Opposition arose on a variety of levels. Work collectives resented the fact, for example, that individuals from their groups were chosen to receive special benefits. At Max-Hütte, one of the largest factories in the zone, the workers insisted that the National Prize offered one of their members be shared by the workers' collective as a whole; either that or the designee should give it up. In fact, the activist refused the prize.[239] Hennecke himself won a National Prize and wanted to turn over a good portion of the proceeds to a kindergarten or youth home, but Ulbricht scolded him for his naïveté and insisted that he spend most of the money on himself in the true "socialist" spirit of the prizes.[240]

Certainly the German workers in the Eastern zone did not appreciate the way some in their ranks were singled out for effusive praise, extra money, and a variety of perquisites. But their major accusation against Hennecke was that he displayed an apparent acquiescence and even a slavish obeisance to Soviet rule in Germany. This came through loud and clear in the numerous denunciatory letters and postcards sent to Hennecke by his coworkers. Any number of outright death threats were also directed against Hennecke. An August 25, 1949, letter from Erfurt was typical: "You shabby scoundrel, you pimp of Soviet exploitation of German labor, you traitor of German working people, you will not escape your well-deserved punishment. People will tear and scratch [*sich darum reissen*] to kill a disgusting thing like you. It won't be long now!" A post-card sent by the "coalminers" ends: "We won't hang you, we will simply wall you in."[241]

Hennecke took these denunciations and threats very hard. They upset him and made him increasingly determined to help his friends in the mines. Yet the more he was lionized by the press and feted by the party and the trade unions, the more difficult it was for him to make contact with the workers. Those workers who were sympathetic to him and the activist movement tried to get him to pass on their complaints to the party. But there was little he could actually do, and Ulbricht, in particular, was not interested in making Hennecke a force in the fledgling govern-ment. In fact, Ulbricht turned down a suggestion in the summer of 1949 that Hennecke be made the director of the Zwickau mining operation, stating that it was enough for Hennecke to be a labor "instructor," for which he got a secretary and assistant.[242] The former mining hero was kept busy with frequent speeches, and his suggestions for factory work inno-vations were published in the FDGB newspapers.

By the beginning of the 1950s, Hennecke was moved into the mining bureaucracy in the Ministry for Heavy Industry in Berlin, where he was to represent the labor activist movement. But he found himself constantly writing letters and petitions to the party leaders, most of which went unanswered (and barely noticed). There is a deep sadness to Hennecke's notes during this period. He had become a busy, isolated bureaucrat: "I hardly find the time to talk to the miners who work in the industry," he wrote, "and therefore to a certain extent I lose contact with them."[243] Overburdened with complaints and petitions and unable to accomplish much for his fellow workers, Hennecke suffered a series of nervous break-downs and bouts of depression. Still, his fame carried him to the heights of GDR society; he was made a member of the Central Committee of the party in 1954 and served in a number of ministries and as honorary chair-man or vice chairman of a series of organizations until his death in 1974.

Despite the periodic successes of the Henneckists, the activist move-ment fell far short of its goals. Most workers remained wary, if not openly hostile, to the piecework system. The activists seldom had much influence over their fellow workers. In fact, some SED leaders suggested that Hen-necke repeat his famous exploit a year after the original feat as a way to reactivate the movement.[244] Some union officials blamed the stagnation of the labor activist movement on the fact that there was little common agreement about what precisely it was supposed to accomplish, above and beyond the deeds of individual labor heroism. In many discussions it was noted that too often workers simply drove themselves into the ground with their frantic attempts to surpass unrealistic "records." A number of SED officials suggested that the workers alone were not in the position to make great gains in productivity in the factories; that this was an issue of investment, organization, and technology, and depended on the application of the talents of the technical intelligentsia, not the manual laborers.[245] Ulbricht himself was very much of this opinion. He tended to be cool to the labor activists in general and to Hennecke in particular, trusting instead in the planning process and technological improvements to pull the Soviet zone (and later the GDR) out of its production lethargy. With agriculture and industry firmly under state control, it was only a matter of time, in Ulbricht's view, until the beneficial effects of planning would rescue the zone from its economic doldrums.

The Soviet Use of
German Science

THE SOVIETS' ECONOMIC INTERESTS in their zone of occupation were often inseparable from their political calculations about the state of relations with the West and their concerns about the future of Germany. The fate of four-power Germany hinged on the ways in which the Western Allies responded to Soviet demands for reparations. Because the linkage between the reparations issue and the division of Germany was so central to the development of the cold war, scholars in both the East and the West have devoted substantial attention to the problem. Much less developed is the historiography of Soviet and Western rivalry over German scientific and technological accomplishments as it related to the postwar "German question." Part of the problem was (and is) the lack of access to Russian archival sources for the study of Soviet interest in the German armaments, rocketry, and atomic weapons development. The USSR's ambitions regarding German uranium is even less well understood, given the lack of access to serious documentation from the Russian side. So long as the KGB, general staff, and Ministry of Armed Forces archives for the postwar period remain closed to researchers—not to mention the presidential archives—it will be impossible to assess with precision Soviet priorities in Germany for securing technological and scientific "targets." Still, with the help of the archives of American security agencies, newly opened East German archives, and candid memoirs from Soviet participants in scientific acquisition programs, one can begin to make sense of the Soviet occupation of Germany in terms of the attempt to acquire military technology and atomic science.

The importance of German science to the development of *Western* occupation policy in Germany has been most dramatically highlighted by a spate of recent Anglo-American studies about Project Paperclip, the American government's program for the recruitment of German scientists.[1] John Gimbel's important contribution to this literature, *Science, Technology, and Reparations,* demonstrates that the United States engaged in a systematic and wide-ranging program of intellectual reparations, one that justifies the subtitle of his book: *Exploitation and Plunder in Postwar Germany.* Though more tightly argued and exhaustively documented, Gimbel's work resembles the popular histories of Paperclip in one very important respect: his deep sense of moral outrage at the United States' behavior in the postwar world. As a whole, the Paperclip literature is obsessively interested in moral questions regarding the employment of ex-Nazi scientists in U.S. defense-related industries after the war, including the variety of dubious tactics developed by War Department officials to avoid domestic opposition to the program. Gimbel's outrage focuses on the ease with which American officials allowed, and even encouraged, the use of German science and know-how by American industry. According to Gimbel, the "intellectual reparations" reaped by the United States and Great Britain approached the figure of $10 billion dollars. This was the amount that was sought by V. M. Molotov for Soviet reparations at the Council of Foreign Ministers meeting in Moscow in early 1947, a request that was flatly turned down by Secretary of State George C. Marshall.[2]

The American and British programs for recruiting German scientists were linked as much to denying scientific and technical expertise to the Soviet Union as to augmenting their own knowledge in these fields. In fact, Project Paperclip and its related programs can be understood only in the context of the developing rivalry between the Soviet Union and the United States that turned into the cold war. From the Soviet point of view, the occupation of Germany was part and parcel of a larger struggle for military supremacy between the two strongest partners in the alliance against Nazi Germany, as well as an important stage in the development of a possible armed conflict with the American colossus. The Soviet Military Administration in Karlshorst was charged with the task of organizing this struggle in Germany, as were numerous independent organizations in the zone that were answerable to a variety of ministries and interministerial committees in Moscow. Especially after August 1945, when Stalin put Commissar of Internal Affairs Lavrenti Beria in charge of the Soviet atom bomb project, the commissariat's representatives in the Soviet zone, Colonel General I. S. Serov and Colonel General A. P. Zaveniagin, recruited scientists and transported machinery essentially as independent agents of the NKVD/MVD (Peoples Commissariat [later Ministry] of Internal Affairs) within eastern Germany.[3]

ATOMIC SCIENTISTS

From the moment the war ended, indeed even before it ended, all four Allies developed a thoroughly duplicitous set of policies involving the fate of German scientists. They had agreed that German science and technology should serve the purposes of rebuilding destroyed lands and maintaining health and sanitary conditions in Germany, but that all military applications of German science would be banished. This official four-power hypocrisy was written into the Potsdam agreement in July 1945, when the Allies agreed that they would share completely all the past accomplishments and future developments of German science. The Americans went yet a step further in their official occupation directive, JCS 1067: all non-health-related German laboratories would be closed down; no research even vaguely related to military purposes would be allowed.

In the end, Allied agreements and public statements of occupation policy had very little to do with the real fate of German scientists. In the famous case of Wernher von Braun, Walter Dornberger, and their Peenemünde ballistics team, which had developed the feared V-2 rocket, the German scientists took their fate into their own hands. Perhaps with the connivance of the German government, the Peenemünde team fled eastern Germany to Bavaria specifically for the purpose of coming to an agreement with the Americans and to avoid falling into the hands of the feared and despised Russians. The American authorities were unwilling to leave the fate of German nuclear physicists to chance. General Leslie Groves, the chief administrator of the American atomic bomb project, stated the case for finding and holding Werner Heisenberg, the Nobel Prize–winning physicist, in the following terms: "Heisenberg was one of the world's leading physicists, and, at the time of the German break-up, he was worth more to us than *ten divisions* of Germans. Had he fallen into the Russian hands, he would have proven invaluable to them."[4]

As a result the War Department dispatched an intelligence officer, Colonel Boris Pash, on the top-secret Alsos Mission, to contact, capture, and place in "protective custody" the leading scientists, especially atomic physicists, in Germany.[5] The targets included Otto Hahn, the discoverer of uranium fission (he won the Nobel Prize for chemistry in 1944), Nobel Prize–winner Max von Laue, Karl Friedrich von Weizäcker, Werner Heisenberg, Walter Gerlach, and others. Pash recovered laboratory materials, designs, and equipment, as well as one and a half tons of uranium, all of which demonstrated that the Germans were not so far along as the Manhattan Project was in the building of an atomic bomb.[6] Samuel A. Goudsmit, a physicist employed by the Pentagon, traveled to Germany several times in the spring, summer, and fall of 1945 to interrogate the captured scientists and supervise the removal of critical documents. Pash described Goudsmit's work as follows: "Not only were Dr. Goudsmit and his assistants able to gauge German progress but they were able to extract identification of Nazi scientists actively engaged in advanced war research in this field, and their location in the organization."[7] Goudsmit himself reported that "the Alsos Mission located all the centers of uranium research in Germany. The laboratories were investigated and key personnel detained and questioned . . . It is certain that complete research data and all key scientists fell into the hands of the Alsos mission."[8] Goudsmit supervised the removal of ten of the leading German atomic scientists to Farm Hall in England, where they were interrogated and interned until Christmas of 1945, when they were allowed to return to Germany.[9]

The Americans certainly reaped an important harvest when the Peenemünde group surrendered in Bavaria. That they were able to capture the heart of the German atomic physics community as well owed a great deal to sheer luck. The Kaiser Wilhelm Society Institute for Physics—including its leading scientists Werner Heisenberg and Otto Hahn—had been evacuated from Berlin in 1943 and 1944 to a remote location near Hechingen on the eastern edge of the Black Forest, in what eventually became the French zone. Even after the scientists returned from Farm Hall to Germany, Allied intelligence officers justifiably worried that the Russians would try to lure Hahn from Hechingen and Heisenberg from his home in Göttingen in the British zone.[10] At Farm Hall, Heisenberg was recorded as having expressed sympathy for those German scientists who went over to the Russians in exchange for decent living and working conditions.[11] The Soviets were able to seize only those scattered remnants of the Kaiser Wilhelm Society that had not been evacuated and were still available in Berlin, Brandenburg, and other sites in Russian-occupied territory. The laboratories that remained were packed up and transported immediately to the Soviet Union. The Institute for Physical Chemistry and Electrochemistry, the only institute of the Kaiser Wilhelm Society that had not been moved out of Berlin, was also packed up by a team of technicians and officers from Moscow and sent off to the Soviet Union.[12]

The director of the institute and the temporary head of the Kaiser Wilhelm Society was Peter Adolf Thiessen, by most accounts "an ardent Nazi."[13] Nevertheless, after Soviet assurances that they could continue their experiments, Thiessen and a dozen or so of his most important coworkers decided to move with their laboratories to the Soviet Union.

Although most of the Kaiser Wilhelm Society Institute for Physics had moved to Hechingen with Heisenberg, the low-temperature physics section had remained in Berlin under Ludwig Bewilogua, who had been in charge of the exponential uranium pile at the institute. Bewilogua, too, was moved to the Soviet Union, along with his entire institute, its equipment, even its water faucets, doorknobs, and washbowls.[14] While some scientists fled the oncoming Russian armies, most remained with their institutes, many of which were located in Berlin-Dahlem. As a result, what was left of the Institutes for Biology, Biochemistry, Chemistry, Anthropology, and Silicate Research were also transferred helter-skelter to the Soviet Union. The dismantlers showed up at the institutes with vodka and lard: vodka for the local military commandants, whose cooperation was necessary for quickly transporting the labs, lard for the German scientists, to convince them that the Soviets were serious about taking care of them.[15] Haste was critical; the Americans were due to move into the Western sectors of Berlin within a few weeks. As a result, much in the institutes that had not already been destroyed during Allied bombing raids and the fierce ground combat during the Battle of Berlin was mangled during the rushed move. Still, almost all the scientific workers were convinced by the Russians to go with their laboratories to Moscow, where, an American military intelligence informant noted later, "they enjoy all benefits . . . and actively continue their scientific researches. There they exploit all patents and their new discoveries."[16]

While still in Germany, Thiessen was quickly and formalistically denazified by the Soviets—no small task since he had been an official in the Nazi science hierarchy, an "old fighter," and the holder of several Nazi Party awards. He in turn helped the Soviets contact a number of other important scientists.[17] In part through Thiessen's intercession, the Soviets convinced the Nobel Prize–winner Gustav Hertz, scientific head of the Siemens Laboratories, to go to the Soviet Union with his complete laboratory. (Together with James Franck, Hertz had won a Nobel Prize for physics in 1925 for work in the "excitation and ionization of atoms."[18]) Heinz Barwich, his deputy, who also went along, recalled that he and Hertz had talked about working for the Russians even before the war ended.

"Naturally," he added, "at that time we did not count on the fact that all the equipment from the [Siemens] laboratory would be taken to the Soviet Union and we with it, as part of its [the lab's] possessions."[19] In the cases of Hertz and Barwich, the Soviets were interested in their experience with the separation of isotopes. Max Steenbeck, who had worked at Siemens on developing machinery for the separation of isotopes, could not be found immediately. He was eventually picked up in a detention camp near Posen (Poznań), sick and malnourished. The Soviets cleaned him up, cared for him until he was healthy, and transported him to the Soviet Union along with approximately one hundred other German physicists and technicians.[20]

All the evidence indicates that the Soviets had quite specific objectives in mind when they approached German scientists whom they felt could help them with their atomic bomb project. Manfred von Ardenne, who had his own institute in Berlin-Lichterfeld, was approached immediately after the liberation of his region on April 27, by Thiessen and a Soviet major (and chemist) who provided his institute with guards. Within ten days, representatives of the Soviet Academy of Sciences had inspected his laboratory and interrogated him about its contents, which included a special electron microscope that von Ardenne had developed. More important, von Ardenne had succeeded in designing a cyclotron, which Hertz was in the process of finishing at Siemens, but which was not in operation at that point. After lengthy interviews with von Ardenne conducted by Soviet atomic scientists in military uniform—L. A. Artsimovich (who later became a prominent specialist on nuclear fission), G. N. Flerov (a co-founder of spontaneous nuclear fission), and I. K. Kikoin (who worked on isotope separation)—the head of the Soviet delegation and the chief MVD representative on the atomic project, General A. P. Zaveniagin, proposed on May 19 that von Ardenne build a research institute in the Soviet Union. In some ways General Zaveniagin can be considered a "Soviet General Groves." He was an excellent organizer and demonstrated considerable sensitivity to the needs of the atomic scientists.[21] Zaveniagin suggested that von Ardenne could continue his work on the electron microscope in Russia while developing a means to measure radioactive and stable isotopes. Two days later, on May 21, von Ardenne and his wife were on their way to Moscow. As he recalled in his memoirs, "With relatively light hearts, we left the children and everything else behind in Lichterfeld because we had gone for a two week trip to the Soviet Union only 'to conclude a contract.' "[22] Those two weeks turned into ten years. Unbeknownst to him at the time, von Ardenne's family, furniture, and laboratory were being shipped to Sukhumi, where he was to head up a new institute, similar to Hertz's, dedicated to studying specific problems of isotope separation.

Nikolaus Riehl experienced a similar turn of events. He had worked as a leading scientist for the Auer Company in Rheinsberg (Brandenburg), which had been experimenting with uranium and heavy water. In fact, the Auer Company's headquarters in Vienna and its branches in eastern Germany were among the Soviets' most important targets.[23] Like von Ardenne, Riehl was visited by a group of Soviet physicists in colonels' uniforms (he mentions Artsimovich, Flerov, and Iu. B. Khariton), who asked him to brief a group of Soviet colleagues in Berlin for a few days. Those few days also turned into ten years. Under Zaveniagin's orders, the entire Auer Company laboratory was dismantled and sent to the Soviet Union, along with a number of its leading scientists and their families. Although it had been repeatedly bombed by the Western Allies in their attempt to deny the Soviets its contents, the Berlin Auer Company yielded for Zaveniagin several tons of rich uranium oxide as well as some important designs and sketches.[24] On June 9, 1945, the Auer specialists were all flown to Moscow. After a detailed interview with Lavrenti Beria, chief of the Soviet atomic bomb project, Riehl and his group eventually were sent to Elektrostal, near Noginsk (70 kilometers east of Moscow), where they were given labs and equipment to produce pure uranium.[25]

Very few of the one hundred or so scientists who were taken to the Soviet Union by Zaveniagin in the first six weeks of the occupation seriously protested against their fate. Some, like Barwich, were attracted by the material possibilities; after all, Germany was destroyed and was rife with disease and hunger. Others, like von Ardenne and Hertz, seemed most taken with the chance to continue running their laboratories, since opportunities for their kind of scientific work did not exist in postwar Germany. They knew that their colleagues in the Western zones, Hahn, Heisenberg, and von Laue—all Nobel Prize winners—had been forced to endure the indignities of detention in England, and it was unclear whether they would be allowed to continue their work.

Political viewpoints also figured in. Hertz was part Jewish and was considered a virulent anti-Nazi, while Riehl—who had been brought up in St. Petersburg and spoke fluent Russian—had pronounced sympathies for the Soviets.[26] There were also those, like Thiessen, who "had been compromised by high level association with the Nazi regime" and feared that the Western allies might call him to account.[27] Most of the German scientists who wrote memoirs claimed that they were unaware that they were being recruited for the Soviet atomic bomb project when they went to the Soviet Union. Yet one can be certain that when Zaveniagin initially contacted Riehl, von Ardenne, and Hertz in May and June 1945, he had planned on using them for that purpose. The senior Soviet physicist in charge of the atomic bomb project, I. V. Kurchatov, had opposed the plan of recruiting German scientists, arguing that the Soviets could and should build the bomb on their own.[28] But Beria (and presumably Stalin) supported Zaveniagin's recruitment efforts. As a result, a number of additional German scientists were brought to Moscow to work on the atomic project: among them Max Volmer, a physical chemist; Robert Doepel, an atomic physicist from Leipzig; Reinhold Reichmann, another specialist on isotope separation; K. G. Zimmer, an atomic scientist from the Kaiser Wilhelm Society; Wilhelm Eitel, a professor of chemistry from Berlin; and W. Schütze, a specialist in separating isotopes and constructing cyclotrons.[29] Even a number of uranium mining specialists were brought in from Joachimsthal (Jáchymov) in Czechoslovakia to help the Soviets find the scarce and precious metal in the Fergana valley and in Kazakhstan.[30]

The patient, if determined, debriefing of the German scientists in Moscow by Artsimovich and Flerov, as well as by the project director, Kurchatov, was interrupted by the news of the swift advances made in the American atomic bomb project. Though the fundamentals of the research program had been known for months to the Soviets through Klaus Fuchs's espionage, the enormous significance of the new weapon was driven home by the successful test explosion at Alamogordo on July 16, 1945, and even more dramatically by the dropping of the atom bomb at Hiroshima on August 6.[31] The development of a Soviet atomic bomb now became a matter of the highest state priority. Molotov had initially been assigned to supervise the bomb project in 1943, at the same time that the Ninth Section of the NKVD had assumed a prominent role in the development of Kurchatov's small laboratory outside of Moscow. In part because of Kurchatov's complaints about Molotov's indifference to the military potential of atomic energy, in part because Kurchatov's work depended increasingly heavily on Beria's ability to bring the vast resources of the Internal Affairs commissariat to the service of the bomb project, in mid-August 1945 Stalin placed Beria in command of the new, accelerated program and gave him carte blanche to bring it to completion. Contrary to his reputation in the Soviet Union and the West, Beria proved to be an able and practical organizer.[32] Kurchatov was now given all the resources he needed to pursue the building of the bomb.[33]

The Germans also profited from this new accelerated program. By mid-September, Hertz had been set up in a laboratory in Agudzeri near Sukhumi on the Black Sea; von Ardenne's laboratory was constructed nearby in Sinop. The eventual division of labor at the Sukhumi institutes indicated that considerable Soviet forethought was given to the problem of isotope separation. According to an American intelligence report, Reichmann and Barwich worked in Agudzeri on isotope separation by gaseous diffusion, and Hertz worked on isotope separation by countercurrent gaseous diffusion. In Sinop, von Ardenne investigated electromagnetic isotope separation, Steenbeck worked on the ultracentrifuge, and Thiessen dealt with the problems of gaseous diffusion.[34]

Once the Germans began to work on their discrete projects, it was apparent that they had the full support of the combined internal affairs (Zaveniagin and Beria) and scientific (Kurchatov and Artsimovich) communities in the Soviet Union. Although Beria gave up his post as head of the NKVD in January 1946, he continued as deputy minister of the Council of Ministers and in March 1946 was made a full member of the Politburo.[35] In short, his power as head of the bomb project remained unassailable. Moreover, the Germans were also aided by the influential and efficient minister of munitions, B. L. Vannikov, who was put in charge of supplying and organizing the program. M. G. Pervukhin, minister of chemical industries, provided critical chemical technology for a variety of needs, including heavy-water production. Interestingly, the military and the hierarchy of the Ministry of the Armed Forces had almost nothing to do with the project. When the first Soviet bomb was successfully tested in August 1949, the military was little more than an observer.[36] With support from strategic ministries and functionaries, the Germans were able to recruit assistants—sometimes by force, though most often consent—from the Soviet zone and from POW camps in the Soviet Union. They were even able to order special machinery and test equipment from manufacturers known to them at home. Their letters to friends and relatives were dispatched by special NKVD/MVD couriers, and in the Soviet Union itself, they lacked nothing in the way of food and comforts.

The Germans had virtually complete control over the direction of their scientific work, though they had to report periodically to a Scientific-Technical Council in Moscow, which also supervised similar, sometimes parallel, work done by Soviet scientists. Certainly, though, fear was part of their daily lives. Especially when they were summoned to Moscow to appear before the council, they had to endure severe scrutiny and implied threats of punishment. The special committee that supervised the entire project was chaired by Beria, and the Germans were well aware (as were their Soviet counterparts) that the price of failure would be high.[37] Despite periodic bouts of jealousy and rivalry among the German researchers, as well as between the Germans and Soviet scientists, by most accounts the work proceeded smoothly and with a minimum of conflict.[38]

The explosion of the first Soviet atomic bomb on August 23, 1949, owed more to the espionage of Klaus Fuchs than to the work of German researchers. At a critical moment, Nikolaus Riehl's group did produce uranium metal, which might have saved the Soviet project a month or two. But on the whole, as David Holloway has written, "the German contribution to the atomic bomb project was small and limited."[39] More important, perhaps, the Soviet atomic program profited in the long term from a series of German-inspired innovations: Riehl's work on purifying uranium (for which he won the coveted order of Hero of Socialist Labor); Hertz and Thiessen's work on gaseous diffusion; and Konrad Zippe and Steenbeck's improvements of the ultracentrifuge. The Soviets had essentially discontinued their atomic bomb project in 1941 when the war broke out, while the Germans had continued to work, especially on the technical and engineering aspects of harnessing atomic energy. The Germans' experience in wartime laboratories, backed by modern chemical, optics, and electric energy industries, proved to be a welcome addition to the Soviets' theoretical sophistication, espionage successes, and ability to muster the vast resources of the country for building the bomb.

ROCKETS

During the initial stages of the peace, the Western Allies in general and the Americans in particular had by far the best access to German scientists. In May and June 1945, the Soviets engaged in a crash program to remove scientists, equipment, and laboratories from the Kaiser Wilhelm Society's buildings in the Berlin suburbs of Dahlem and Zehlendorf, which by four-power agreement were to be turned over to the Americans at the beginning of July. Meanwhile, the Americans occupied Thüringen, Saxony-Anhalt, and parts of Saxony, which would eventually be turned over to the Russians. As a result, the Americans conducted a similar slash-and-burn policy with regard to German science and scientists in "Middle Germany," the technological heartland of the Nazi military-industrial complex. American Combined Intelligence Objectives Subcommittee (CIOS) teams removed men in large numbers and equipment in staggering quantities from the region. From Nordhausen alone, 1,000 technicians and the parts for 100 V-2 missiles were evacuated to the West. In Jena, Zeiss's patent archives, designs, and special lenses were crated up by the Americans and shipped off to Württemburg, along with hundreds of Zeiss specialists and their families. Altogether, the Americans brought some five thousand German scientists and technicians and their families to western Germany from this region.[40] Apparently, the Americans removed as many people as they did in order to deny them to the Soviets; they did not necessarily intend to use them for American programs. The majority of these specialists remained unemployed and were forced to live in unpleasant compounds and in difficult economic conditions. The situation was not helped any by the fact that the American military government, headed by General Lucius Clay, was generally unsympathetic to the program that had brought the scientists to the West in the first place. Finally, in mid-1948, they were allowed to leave the compounds to go home, if they wished, or to seek employment in other western German industries.

When the Soviets marched into these areas at the beginning of July 1945, they engaged in a program that was much different from their removal of the atomic scientists from Berlin and its environs. The Soviets were now intent on exploiting the German infrastructure and technological know-how to manufacture the German "V" weapons in central Germany itself. Rather than removing the "V" weapons, destroying the plants, and evacuating scientists to the Soviet Union, Soviet rocket and aviation officials tried to restart these plants in the hope of making up some of the ground lost by the evacuation of the first-rank German rocket scientists to the West. They were in fact surprised to find that many armaments-related industries were still operable. On the whole, the Germans in this area had surrendered to the Western Allies with a minimum of fighting, leaving most of the factories intact. The Americans were simply not able to remove all of the region's vast industrial potential. For instance, BMW jet engine factories were intact and in place, as were several large Junkers company airplane manufacturing installations.[41]

We know a great deal about the ambitions of the Soviet rocket and aviation programs in the Soviet zone, because of the defection in 1948 of its leading official in the Soviet military government, Colonel Grigorii Tokaev (Tokady or Tokaty), who later wrote his memoirs while in the

West.[42] Earlier, when working for the Soviet military government, Tokaev had blamed the Western Allies for engaging in precisely the kind of actions undertaken by the Soviets. In an article entitled "On the Question of the Liquidation of the Military Aviation Potential of Germany," he accused the British and the Americans of having kept German aviation scientists at work.[43] While the Soviets claimed to have destroyed all of Germany's war potential when they moved into this region, German V-2 factories were in fact still producing missile parts. German aircraft plants continued to design and in some cases to build a new generation of Soviet fighter planes.[44]

When the Soviets marched into the so-called Mittelwerk in Nordhausen, they found that the leading scientists had been evacuated and that the rockets, the papers of the enterprise, and the sketches and blueprints of the famous V-2s were gone, all taken by the Americans when they left the region in late June. Nevertheless, with the help of some engineers and technicians who had remained and with access to the raw materials that were too cumbersome for the Americans to remove, a group of Soviet specialists from the Ministry of Aviation Industry patiently reconstructed the manufacturing capability of the plant.[45] The Soviets were also able to rebuild the Zentralwerk at Bleicherode, which specialized in the designing of German-guided missile systems. The manufacturing complex was supervised by two Soviet rocket specialists in uniform, B. E. Chertok and A. M. Isaev, who put together the so-called Institute Rabe (Raketenbau und Entwicklung, or Missile Building and Development).[46] The task of the Institute Rabe was to coordinate the various special laboratories necessary to the continuation of the German rocket work. Auxiliary enterprises in Bleicherode, Niedersachswerfen, and Sömmerda were also seized by Soviet military officials.

In the fall of 1945, an interministerial committee chaired by the academics V. I. Kuznetsov, V. P. Mishin, and N. A. Piliugin pushed for an expanded rocket program, as did V. M. Riabikov and D. F. Ustinov from the Munitions Ministry. It was clear that the Institute Rabe could not control the growing tasks of the rocket work in the zone. As a result, a new organization, the Institute Nordhausen, was formed, and Chertok's Rabe became part of a larger system of institutes and bureaus headed up by General L. M. Gaidukov, who had commanded rocket launcher (*katiusha*) units during the war, and by his chief deputy, the famous Soviet rocket engineer S. P. Korolev. Another Soviet rocket specialist, Valentin

Glushko, was placed in charge of the Montania factory, which specialized in the development of jet propulsion engines. V. P. Barmin, who had worked on the *katiusha* emplacements, became chief engineer of the so-called Berlin Institute, which was assigned to develop antiballistic missiles. Korolev, Glushko, Chertok, Barmin, and other leading missile specialists from a variety of civil and military institutions in Moscow organized themselves into a Council of Chief Designers (Sovet glavnykh konstruktorov), which met periodically to solve the plethora of problems that they encountered in Germany. Korolev, wrote Chertok, had already become the informal leader of the group. "He awakened the thought in all of us, that this work—did not consist simply in the restoration of German technology, but [was] the source of a new and more important direction [of work]."[47]

On the German side, Helmut Gröttrup was the leading scientist used by the Soviets to direct the rocket program. Gröttrup was an engineer who had worked as an assistant to the director of the Guidance, Control, and Telemetry Laboratory in Peenemünde. He had collaborated closely with von Braun and was well-versed in the overall design of the German program. In fact, the Americans had approached him to work in the United States, but, like so many other German scientists and engineers, Gröttrup wanted to stay in Germany while continuing his profession.[48] After proving himself to be an able organizer during the rebuilding of the Zentralwerk in Bleicherode, he accepted the Soviets' offer in the spring of 1946 and took charge of the guided-missile development program in the zone.[49] He was visited often by Korolev and Chertok, as well as by a number of Soviet specialists, including Isaev, who had been working on rocket boosters since the early years of the war.[50] During the winter of 1945–46, as many as 5,000 specialists worked with Gröttrup on the rocket project; by the summer of 1946, the high point of rocket production, 7,000 scientists, technicians, and workers were employed. According to an American intelligence report at the time, the German employees received the same pay they had under the Nazis; in addition, they received plentiful fuel and food supplies.[51] Many rocket specialists were attracted back to the Soviet zone of occupation from the West by the attractive *payoks* (packets of food and goods) offered by the Soviet authorities as part of their compensation.[52]

The rocket work was complex and difficult, and it overlapped with Soviet interest in the German aircraft industry. Junkers in Dessau, the

Siebel aircraft factory in Halle, and the Heinkel works in Warnemünde and Oranienburg became an important part of the combined Soviet rocket and aviation program.[53] Askania and Oberspreewerk in Berlin and Siemens in Halle—specializing in electronic control, automatic pilot, and radar systems—were also brought into the network of Soviet-controlled defense industries. Montania in Nordhausen, Rheinmetall-Borsig in Sömmerda, and related factories and laboratories that specialized in producing heat-resistant metal alloys also became critical parts of the rocket and airplane producing industry. V-2s were sent back to the Soviet Union in sections and then assembled for testing in Kazakhstan. Hundreds of Soviet specialists worked side by side with thousands of Germans to rebuild the Nazi rocket program, with the V-2 as its centerpiece. Everyone involved was aware that by applying both German and Soviet technology to improving propulsion and engineering systems it might be possible to create a new super rocket that would be far superior to the V-2 in range and accuracy.

The Soviets' system for garnering German rocket technology was very different from the Americans'. Soviet specialists—Korolev, Glushko, Chertok, Isaev, and others—immersed themselves not just in German technological innovations, but also in the German methods and organization of rocket production. This helped them compensate for the loss of the leading Peenemünde rocket scientists to the United States, not to mention the evacuation by the Western Allies of thousands of technicians from central Germany in Operation Overcast, which had been carried out primarily to deny those technicians to the Russians. It also helped the Soviet rocket engineers make up for blueprints, plans, designs, and patents that had been taken by the Americans and the British. (The Soviets were helped considerably in this regard by their seizure of a trainload of Nazi rocket archives in Prague.[54])

In addition, the Soviets had the distinct advantage in Germany, while continuing to build rockets and airplanes, of supporting the production of the associated aeronautic, electronic, and jet propulsion industries. German scientists and technicians wanted to continue with their work in these industries much as the scientists did in the atomic energy field. And they also wanted to eat. As a result, the Soviets developed a highly differentiated system of payoks to attract German scientists and technicians to work in Soviet-run laboratories and plants. They divided the payoks into twenty-two different categories, ranging from five cigarettes at one end to two cases of food at the other. British observers noted that the Soviets had considerable success in attracting from the Western zones Germans who "had offered their services to one or another of the Western Allies and appear to feel that they have either been completely ignored or fobbed off with vague promises that show no early prospect of materializing."[55]

As German specialists themselves increasingly approached the Soviets for work, British observers complained that Western policies were actually driving competent specialists into the arms of the Russians. "Reparations and de-Nazification policies," wrote N. Reddaway of the British Foreign Office, "have continued to make life impossible for thousands of citizens in our zone," encouraging what both American and British authorities saw as a "flight to the East."[56] The British were particularly irritated that a number of scientists "allocated" to them in agreements with the American and French were "no longer available" because they had signed contracts with the Soviets. These included Ernst Friedrich, an expert on radar and antiradar devices for submarines; P. Kotowski, an electro-acoustic expert who worked on antijamming and other navigational devices; and H. O. Roosenstein, a Telefunken company expert on time modulation and pulse communications.[57]

In the fall of 1945, the German press in the American and British zones was filled with stories about the alleged kidnappings by the Soviets of thousands of German specialists from the Western zones.[58] But it is hard to document these cases, and the actual occurrences appear to have been few and far between.[59] In reality, word had gotten out that the Soviets treated German scientists and technicians with respect, fed them and their families well, and even provided the best housing and ration cards for those who were willing to move from the West. Equally important, as was so often reported by Allied observers, German scientists and technicians were pleasantly surprised by the good conditions of work and by the generally decent relations between themselves and their Soviet supervisors.[60]

The Soviet arms industry in the Eastern zone did not suffer from a shortage of specialists or, in most cases, of material. It encompassed a wide variety of modern weapons production, from airplanes and rockets to chemical weapons, artillery, and tanks. Most of the weapons systems had been developed by German arms manufacturers during the war, and the Soviets saw to their continued production and development after the war.

OSOAVIAKHIM

On October 22, 1946, the very successful system of rocket, airplane, and weapons production in the Soviet zone abruptly came to an end. In a well-planned and neatly executed operation that took place simultaneously in the centers of armaments production throughout the Eastern zone, NKVD and Soviet army units rounded up thousands of German scientists and technicians, with their families and their belongings, and sent them off to the Soviet Union in ninety-two different trains and, in special cases, in airplanes. Some of the scientists and technicians signed contracts; many others did not. In both cases, they were transported to the Soviet Union to continue their work in various branches of the armaments industry there. The operation was commanded by Colonel General Serov, Beria's chief deputy in the zone, and was code-named Osoaviakhim. This was not without some irony on the Soviets' part, for Osoaviakhim was the acronym for the voluntary paramilitary organization of Soviet youth that aided the armed forces (later known as DOSAAF).[61]

The observations of one eyewitness to the October 22 operation in Berlin are characteristic of hundreds of similar reports:

> Since three o'clock this morning, skilled workers, particularly electricians, toolmakers, precision instrument makers and engineers employed in ... EFEM, GEMA, AEG, Kabelwerk Oberspree, Askania, Hermann Grau (and other firms which are now under Russian management) are currently [being] deported from their homes in the Russian sector of Berlin ... Russian military police, reinforced by Russian soldiers, appeared during the night in homes, at public places, bridges and street-crossings and requested that the occupants of dwellings and pedestrians show their labor book [*Arbeitsbuch*]. If they were employees of one of the aforementioned plants, they were *politely* asked to follow. In the dwellings of the families involved, the wardrobes were immediately nailed shut, and guards were posted until a Russian truck with several Russian soldiers arrived who loaded all the inventory and the family (from the grandfather to the baby) and took them to the railway stations of Köpenick or Friedrichshagen ... Everything was carried off, including cabinets, china, carpets, chairs, pianos, bird cages, and I even saw stove pipes. The railway stations ... which had been blocked off already one evening before to all traffic, are overcrowded with railcars as never before ... Russian commando groups and other Russian troops with trucks were posted during the night at streetcrossings in order to nip in the

bud any resistance that might be offered. Deportations were still continuing at 17:00 hours today. Trucks are passing the streets every three or four minutes, each loaded with a family . . . The Russian guards make themselves at home in the furniture loaded on the trucks, sitting in armchairs and on kitchen cabinets, [but they] do not interfere with the lively discussions among groups of Germans on the streets. Apparently, the deportees have been treated politely. From the fifth floor of a house in the Seelenbinder Strasse I had a view of the Köpenick railway station . . . [and] I saw that people were fed a hot meal from an army kitchen. Straw was available in sufficient quantities and it looked from afar as if people had resigned themselves to their fate.[62]

The situation of the deported engineers and technicians is more succinctly encapsulated in a telephone call intercepted by American intelligence:

CALLER: Last night the Russians came with rifles and fixed bayonets; and then there was a furniture van in front of the door. They took Krüger and all their things with them right away. With them were also Engelmann and his family and many other skilled workers. All of them had to go with their families.

ANSWER: How ever is that possible? With furniture and everything else?

CALLER: Yes, just like that, they simply had to [go].[63]

The rocket specialist Gröttrup and his colleagues from Mittelwerk were invited by General Gaidukov to a party on the night of October 21–22, where vodka flowed and caviar and a variety of delicacies were served. At the party they learned that they would meet their families at the train station and be transported to the Soviet Union. Contracts would be signed then and there or while under way. When soldiers showed up at the Gröttrups' apartment in the early hours of the morning to pack up the family, his wife called him to find out what was going on. "Just be calm," Gröttrup told her, "General Godowski [Gaidukov] is in the room; there are lots of officers—you understand. There is nothing I can do."[64] Some two hundred of the leading German scientists, technicians, and their families from Mittelwerk were sent off by special train on the morning of October 22. The Nordhausen and Bleicherode complexes were emptied of their equipment and packed and transported, like their designers, to the East. Once the equipment was removed, a number of the underground facilities at Nordhausen were blown up by Soviet specialists.

The technical personnel in the Jena firms Schott and Zeiss met a similar fate. Some two hundred seventy scientists, technicians, and skilled workers who had worked on specialized optics projects or on self-steering and stabilizing devices—gyroscopes among them—were gathered up at work and at home and sent off to the Soviet Union. (One wonders how Zeiss Jena could have survived at all after the Americans and the Soviets both removed so many specialists and so much in the way of designs and equipment.) The same fate greeted scientists, technicians, and skilled workers throughout the arms industry in the Eastern zone: at BMW Stassfurt (jet propulsion engines), the Leuna Chemical Works in Bitterfeld (jet fuels); Siebel Works in Halle (bombers); and Junkers Dessau (jet fighters). A number of test pilots were also deported from Junkers, along with engineers and technicians.

Berlin, the center of Germany's weapons-related technological research and development in Germany, was particularly hard hit. The city was already buzzing with rumors on Sunday evening, October 20, about the unexpected results of the Greater Berlin elections. The SED had been badly beaten at the polls, finishing third behind the SPD and the CDU. Many citizens looked with renewed hope at the major changes that would be introduced in the Berlin city government (the Magistracy) and perhaps even in Germany as a whole. The deportations of October 21–22 were interpreted very differently, however, and left the Berliners stunned and worried about their future. Warning signs that the deportations were coming became apparent only after the fact; for example, specialists at the Oberspreewerk who had lived in West Berlin had been invited in the early summer and fall to move at very little cost into extremely nice housing in the Hirschgarten district (Köpenick) of the Soviet sector of Berlin. Those Oberspreewerk employees who had earlier worked for AEG and Telefunken on high-frequency equipment, radar for night flying, and a variety of applications for X-ray machinery had also been given extra rations and bonuses. Then, at 3:30 in the morning of October 22, the Hirschgarten district was cordoned off by Soviet army troops, and 200 Oberspreewerk specialists and their families were carted off to waiting trains.[65] Similar group deportations of employees were carried out at GEMA (range finders and sights), EFEM (guidance equipment), AEG–Kabelwerk Oberspree (radio transmitters), the special construction bureau (OKB-4) at Friedrichshagen (automatic piloting systems), and at Askania (radar, automatic piloting systems).[66] Smaller groups of researchers were taken as well, including a team of mathematicians and technicians who worked for a special statistical group at Soviet military government head-quarters in Karlshorst, as well as submarine acoustics and sound special-ists, many of whom were also employed at Karlshorst. Among the smaller groups, specialists in measuring and computation techniques were fre-quently targeted for deportation.[67]

Most German specialists took their families with them when given the choice. But some wives chose to remain behind, which led to hundreds of tearful and wrenching partings. The Soviets were not particular about which women went with which men; as a result, NKVD officers sometimes seized maids thinking they were wives or packed up protesting girlfriends or sisters.[68] There seems to have been no political pattern to those chosen for deportation. SED members were sent off, often to their shock and surprise, as were members of the Free German Federation of Unions.[69] Old and young alike were sent; no one was exempt. Appeals to the Soviet military government were completely useless; SVAG had no control over the operation. The Soviet military authorities in Thüringen, for example, tried to prevent the dismantling of Carl Zeiss AG (optical instruments) and the Schott works (optical glass) and to halt the deportation of so many valuable specialists, but to no avail.[70] American military intelligence reported that the leading Russian economic officer in the zone, General Koval (who was also deputy commander-in-chief of SVAG), did not even know about the operation until it had begun.[71]

Some of the scientists and technicians had signed contracts before they left; some were compelled to sign them on the way to the Soviet Union. But in every case, they seem to have been told that they would be treated exactly the same as Soviet scientists, skilled workers, and technicians of a commensurate level, which after the war was seen by the Germans as a great gain.[72] Some signed up for three years, some for five. Virtually eve-ryone was seized in the middle of the night or early in the morning, but in a number of factories, the specialists were rounded up at work and sent directly to the railway stations, where their families and household goods were already waiting. Families were sometimes shipped off separately, and some were never notified at all. Periodically the Soviets had to resort to the use of outright force to get people to leave. In the Sybel-Werke in Halle, for example, Soviet NKVD units had to chase down workers who tried to resist being deported, and some had to be clubbed into submis-sion.[73] In a few cases, the German police had to be used to reinforce undermanned Soviet contingents.[74]

Violence was only rarely necessary, however. Soviet economic officers, who had close personal contacts with their German counterparts and employees, were systematically recruited to help convince the Germans to sign contracts. Max Rokhlin, who had been involved in reconstructing (and later dismantling) the chemical industry in postwar Germany, recounted the following story that began with a call to appear immediately at NKVD headquarters in Berlin.

> Serov told us [Rokhlin and a colleague] about the operation Osoaviakhim and asked us to contact the Germans on the list [for deportation] that he showed us. We didn't know how he got that list. We asked: "Why, Comrade Colonel General, must they go?" Serov's answer was very simple: "Beria's orders." We were quite shaken; we knew many of the people on the list. These were friends and colleagues. So we asked to go out for a smoke. We smoked and talked. We agreed that we couldn't guarantee these people that they would be happy, even if Serov said that they would move families, furniture, everything. So we went back in and told Serov that our Ministry [of the Chemical Industry] would surely be against such a move, that we didn't think it was a good idea, and that we would like to speak to our minister, Pervukhin. Serov picked up the phone, called Pervukhin and said, "Mikhail Georgevich; your men do not agree with Beria's orders. Yes, I'll give them the telephone." Pervukhin knew me well from the war. He said: "What's wrong with you; follow orders!" That was that.

Rokhlin did as he was told and convinced a number of his German colleagues that they would be able to continue their work in the Soviet Union and that they would be treated well. In several cases, Rokhlin noted, his intervention was crucial in the Germans' decisions to sign up.[75]

In Berlin the Soviet deportation of scientists and technicians went off without a hitch. When complaints were raised by the Germans, Soviet officers are known to have responded in the following manner: "All Berliners are fascists, otherwise they would have voted differently."[76] In fact, the setback for the Soviets in the Berlin elections led some Western observers to conclude that the deportations were undertaken in retaliation for German voting behavior.[77] But the argument holds little weight since, Osoaviakhim had been planned well in advance of the elections. In the early summer of 1946, specialists in a number of factories had already been asked to fill out detailed questionnaires about their training and specialties. It is known, as well, that during the course of the same summer, Soviet authorities gathered names and addresses of employees and, at least at Junkers in Dessau, held these lists in special files.[78] In all like-lihood, the Soviets delayed the deportations until the elections were over—in vain, as it turned out—because they did not wish to jeopardize their chances for a communist victory.

Osoaviakhim may also have been motivated by other factors. Antici-pating poor results in the fall 1946 elections, the Soviets may have thought that they would have to bargain for a four-power withdrawal from Ger-many. Therefore they would have wanted to remove valuable military-technical assets in personnel and material while they still had the chance. The Soviets might also have been worried that renewed British and French interest in German scientists and technicians would give more bargaining power to the Germans, who might have been tempted to "ration" their knowledge.[79] But, as American political advisor Robert Murphy wrote to the secretary of state, the major reason for the dramatic Soviet action was fear of being condemned for noncompliance with Allied Control Council agreements on the liquidation of German war potential.[80] The Soviets themselves were extremely agitated about the alleged maintenance of a German fighting force in the British zone and therefore welcomed the opportunity to inspect factories and units in the West. As a result, new agreements were in the offing about four-power inspections in both East and West. As Murphy wrote, these agreements "doubtless made [the] Soviets realize that [the] activities of these plants [in the East] may shortly come under scrutiny of quadripartite inspection."[81]

At Soviet Military Administration headquarters in Karlshorst, Soviet political officers understood that, as a result of the deportations, their cause in Germany would take a severe beating in the ongoing propaganda war with the West. Although they knew that, strictly speaking, they were within the rights of the occupying powers, they also were worried about the effects of Osoaviakhim throughout Germany.[82] The newspapers in West Berlin, which a few days earlier had carried ecstatic stories about the promises held out by the Berlin elections, now raised specters of further mass deportations and kidnappings. The Soviets tried to control the dam-age by appealing to their Western Allies to censor the "calumnious at-tacks" in the West Berlin press. In fact, Soviet representatives on the Allied Control Council Coordinating Committee intimated that in the name of Allied unity they had restrained their own use of propaganda regarding the earlier removal of German specialists by the Americans and the British. On October 29, the Soviets responded to Western protests about the de-portations by saying that the Soviets had "regarded as quite normal U.S.

and British removal of technicians and had denied wishes of the Soviet press to attack steps taken in this regard."[83] Sokolovskii apparently told Colonel Frank Howley, American commandant for Berlin, "I am not asking the Americans and British at what hour of the day or night they took their technicians. Why are you so concerned about the hour at which I took mine?"[84]

The snide Soviet responses to Allied protests aside, Soviet propaganda officers in the zone felt that they were badly outmaneuvered by the West on this issue. The SVAG Propaganda Administration chief, Colonel Sergei Tiul'panov, sent out an urgent inquiry to his deputies in Thüringen and Saxony to gather information about Western Allies' removal of men and materials from those regions before the Soviet occupation.[85] Although Project Paperclip was well known to the Soviets through American and German newspaper articles, if not through their own espionage sources, they did not, in fact, have a good idea of just how many military-industrial specialists had been evacuated and how much in the way of armaments-related resources had been taken by the British and especially by the Americans.[86] In August 1945, the Soviets had formally complained to President Truman about the removals from their newly occupied territory. Truman in turn had asked Eisenhower for an accounting. According to Eisenhower's response, the Soviet claims of widespread removals were correct, though they substantially underestimated the amount of "equipment, documents, and personnel" that had been evacuated with the American army.[87]

The SED was virtually silent about the deportations. The party could only reprint and restate the arguments in the Soviet-run daily *Tägliche Rundschau* that the specialists had signed favorable contracts to help rebuild the Soviet Union. All the chatter about alleged "kidnappings," the party said, demonstrated the "political shamelessness of the anti-Soviet Goebbelsesque slanders" coming from reactionary circles in the West.[88] The Free German Federation of Unions had no choice but to echo the Soviet explanation that there was nothing unusual about the events of October 22. According to Roman Chwalek, head of the FDGB, it was every good German's duty to help the devastated Soviet economy. The conditions of work in the Soviet Union, added Chwalek, were exemplary: "Many of them [the specialists] went to the Soviet Union with their families. Everyone was given plenty of food. Each one had their own seats in coaches [to counter the rumor that people were sent off in boxcars] and a special freight car for their personal belongings." Chwalek reported that he had asked the Soviet commanders if he might see how the German workers in the USSR were getting along. The answer was that "this possibility is not excluded."[89]

From a political point of view, Osoaviakhim was a disaster. But the Soviets accomplished their primary mission of removing virtually overnight the critical defense industries that they had operated in eastern Germany. The Bleicherode and Nordhausen installations were removed piece by piece, down to the rail tracks and high-tension wires. When everything was taken, the Soviets dynamited the entryways to the underground installations.[90] At Junkers in Dessau and Siebel in Halle, almost every piece of aircraft-building equipment (not to mention the airplanes themselves) was taken, mostly to Kuibyshev, the center of the Soviet airplane industry. Even the four largest wind tunnels were dismantled and removed.[91] Along with the material, the laboratories, the designs, and the machines, the Soviets evacuated a total of some ten to fifteen thousand German scientists, technicians, and skilled workers.[92]

The biggest prizes in this military-industrial complex were the rocket scientists and the laboratories and workshops that supported their research, development, and construction efforts. The most important rocket specialists were assigned to the so-called Scientific Research Institute 88, which was headquartered in Podlipki, some twenty-five kilometers northeast of Moscow.[93] Unlike the atomic bomb project, which was strictly centralized under Beria's leadership, the rocket project was supervised by a number of ministries involved in arms production. But just as Kurchatov played the critical role of chief scientist in the development of the bomb, Korolev played a similar part in making the key decisions on the development of the first generation of Soviet rockets. From the labs in Podlipki, Gröttrup and his team were moved by Korolev to the isolated island of Gorodomlia, located on a large lake in Kalinin province between Leningrad and Moscow, and were charged with building an improved Soviet version of the V-2. With access to the work of Askania, GEMA, and other German technology groups also brought to Russia, and given the Soviets' own substantial accomplishments in the rocket field, Gröttrup's work went quickly and efficiently. On October 27, 1947, just a year after they had been evacuated from Germany, Gröttrup and a number of his colleagues were brought to the Soviet rocket launching site at Kapustin Iar in the Northern Caucasus to test the first Soviet-German product. The launch was an enormous success, and by all accounts the Soviets were ecstatic: "Suddenly, Minister of Defense Armaments Ustinov grabbed Korolev in a bear hug and danced him about. Korolev, in turn, did the same with Gröttrup. There was almost pandemonium in the launch area as word was announced that the rocket had flown almost 175 miles and landed reasonably near target."[94] Irmgard Gröttrup, also at the launch, noted that the Germans were no less thrilled and relieved. Her diary for October 30, the day of the launch, read: "To be sure, last night no one was able to sleep. This was perhaps the most exhilarating, perhaps also the most beautiful night [while we were] in Russia. Who knows? During this night, there were no differences of rank. No professors, no minister, no military. There was only one excited, wild, big family ... As in the Peenemünde times, when the first attempts were successful ... There is here only an uncrowned queen, who is courted by all: the rocket!"[95]

Despite the enthusiasm, there were serious problems with the accuracy and range of the first launches. Among the Germans, Hoch, a specialist on electronic guidance systems, and Magnes, who worked on gyroscope stabilization problems, were assigned the task of improving the rocket's accuracy in striking its target.[96] Meanwhile, Gröttrup and his team were put to work building bigger and more powerful rockets. Between 1947 and October 1951, when for all practical purposes the Germans were withdrawn from participation in rocket production, Gröttrup and his colleagues helped to design twenty different rocket types. In 1949, Gröttrup's R-14 design was completed. The rocket had a range of 1,800 miles and the ability to carry an atomic payload of 6,600 pounds: in Walter McDougall's words "a single-stage finless monster ... [of] the most advanced design in the world."[97]

THE NTOS

It should be clear that the Soviet exploitation of science and technology in the Eastern zone did not end in the fall of 1946 with the deportation of thousands of defense-related specialists to the Soviet Union. However, the Soviets had to act more carefully and subtly thereafter; it was no longer possible to ship off large groups of skilled scientists and technicians. Rumors constantly circulated that new mass deportations would take place, and as a result, the Germans were frightened and wary of the smallest Soviet hint that Osoaviakhim might be repeated.[98] Tokaev reported to Stalin that it was difficult to recruit German aircraft engineers to work on even purely civilian projects after the October action precisely for this reason. "The whole population are afraid of us," he supposedly complained.[99] Osoaviakhim weighed on the Germans in other ways, as well. Many were depressed, even desperate, as a result of the removal of so much of their equipment, as well as their personnel. In Jena, for example, there was a spate of suicides associated with the gutting of the Zeiss plant, despite Soviet and SED promises to rebuild.[100] (Reportedly, of some 10,000 machines only 582 were left.[101])

Still, as needs arose in Moscow for German specialists and the products of their work, they were recruited, with both carrot and stick, to move to the Soviet Union. Sometimes the contracts were signed by the Germans under not very heavily veiled threats. American intelligence reported the case of a Dr. Ludwig, who worked in the Perlon (German nylon) section of AGFA in Wolfen (Saxony). Nylon was a high-priority item for the Russian textile industry. A Soviet recruiter in civilian clothes approached Ludwig on November 1, 1946, with two contracts, and he was told he had to sign one of them. The first read: "The undersigned obligates himself to assist in the reconstruction of the Soviet Union by going to Russia and working for two years in building up the Nylon Works. In return, the undersigned will receive the double allowance of 1,500 rubles, or 3,000 marks per month. Families do not have to go. Quarters with hard and soft furniture will be available." The second contract read: "The undersigned herewith declares his unwillingness to assist in the reconstruction of the Soviet Union."[102] Needless to say, Ludwig was wise to sign the first, and he was not alone. In 1947 and 1948, hundreds of other specialists, engineers, and technicians were "invited" to the Soviet Union to work in a variety of industries—textiles, optics, and television development, just to mention a few.[103]

The Soviets also continued to remove military specialists from eastern Germany, expanding their operation to include pilots and submarine specialists, chemical and biological warfare scientists, and military medical personnel.[104] Most were brought to the Soviet Union by contract; some were dragooned; hundreds were identified by MVD specialists in the isolation camps *(spetslager)* and sent to the Soviet Union to work for a variety of ministries.[105]

The Western Allies were concerned about continued Soviet recruiting in the Western zones. The Soviets offered generous payoks and promises of leading positions in new scientific and technical groups being formed all over the Eastern zone. As a way to avoid increasing Western counterintelligence measures, the Soviets maintained an underground organization in the West, called "U-Bahn," to lure former pilots, officers, and mining and torpedo specialists out of the Western zones and into the East, where they could be transported to the Soviet Union.[106] Werner Heisenberg, himself the object of Soviet recruitment tactics, used the fox and the bear parable to explain to a colleague in the East why so few physicists in the West were ready to accept Soviet offers: "The fox notices that many trails lead into the cave of the bear, but none come out."[107] Until the KGB and Soviet military intelligence archives are opened, it will be hard to know precisely how many specialists were taken from Germany, both East and West, in the post-Osoaviakhim period, and the extent to which they were taken by force, moved as a result of direct and indirect threats, or willingly signed contracts to work in the Soviet Union. But we do know that the MVD was repeatedly charged by Soviet military and military-industrial ministries "to acquire" these specialists and bring them back to the Soviet Union along with their families.[108]

The Soviets removed most of the scientists and technicians important to their armaments industry in the October 22 operation, and they took others periodically by a variety of means from the Western and Eastern zones. They also continued to remove military and defense-related equipment into 1947 and 1948.[109] Henschel bombs were being manufactured in Dessau and transported to the Soviet Union as late as August 1949.[110] But Soviet technical experts understood that they still had a lot to gain in the way of knowledge and expertise from the high level of German technological achievements, industrial infrastructure, and production methods in the Eastern zone. On September 30, 1946, less than a month before Osoaviakhim was put into operation, the Council of Ministers issued an order that addressed this realization. An Administration for the Study of Science and Technology in Germany was attached to SVAG headquarters in Karlshorst. This central administration was to supervise a network of Science and Technology Offices (NTOs) in each of the provinces and many of the large cities in the Eastern zone.[111] The provincial Science and Technology Offices supervised the contracts concluded between the individual industries, technical laboratories, or special scientific groups in the region and the ministries, institutes, or research groups in the Soviet Union. The NTOs also looked after the growing number of Construction Bureaus (OKBs) that were set up by the Soviets—usually with a single Soviet supervisor and a number of German specialists working under him or her—to perform specialized industrial-engineering tasks. German groups and OKBs might sign contracts with agencies of the Soviet military government in Karlshorst or with representatives of the Soviet government from Moscow. (Until October 1947, the latter was the case for the Nordhausen group.)

The contracts were for a mix of military-related and civilian work. A former Wehrmacht officer, General Ludwig, worked on "contemporary fortifications" for the Soviets; Fritz Gabriel finished a study of artillery targeting; as I have mentioned, a Dessau OKB worked on Henschel bombs. The Ministry of the Aviation Industry sponsored dozens of major projects, some of them purely theoretical. But in all defense-related cases, German employees were sworn to silence about their work and threatened with severe punishment if the rules of secrecy were broken.[112] The Soviets also sponsored a series of research projects (themes, or *temy,* as they were called) on polymers and plastics.[113] The Ministry of Textile Industries underwrote some fifteen projects on Perlon that were seen as some of the most important in the zone. Soviet food ministries sponsored a large number of projects related to the meat and dairy products industries. One OKB in Dresden that specialized in the confectionary industry, received a contract to build a chocolate factory in Bukovina.[114] An OKB in Weisenfels worked exclusively for the Petroleum Ministry in Moscow, designing and constructing equipment for drilling and pumping oil.[115] A number of OKBs in Saxony were under contract to Soviet machine-building ministries, through the Saxony NTO, to improve machine-building technology, including the development of mechanical calculating machines.[116]

The Administration for the Study of Science and Technology in Germany, located in Karlshorst, was responsible for the general conditions of contractual work: determining salaries, fees, and payoks. But the individual working groups and OKBs were almost always headed up by a Soviet who maintained contact with the respective contractor in the Soviet Union. "These Russian heads," stated a British report, "are invariably technicians and generally carry the rank of colonel."[117] According to a SVAG report to the Council of Ministers, by the end of 1948 there were thirty-six NTOs in the zone, which supervised the work of ninety-six established installations, ninety-five laboratories, and thirty production complexes. Altogether in the NTOs, 611 Soviet specialists oversaw the work of 6,014 German scientists and technicians, plus 7,067 German workers. Between 1946 and 1948, the NTOs supervised the completion of 7,069 projects, some of which had great practical value for Soviet industry.[118] From German specialists the Soviets learned how to make high-octane gas and carbon fuels. They learned how to produce liquid fuels and build turbines that could be run on liquid fuels. They created a Soviet nylon industry from German accomplishments in that field, and adapted the Buna chemical factories' advancements for the creation of synthetic rubber. Similarly, the technology of the German coal briquette industry was adapted for Soviet use, a technology that was particularly useful later on in the German Democratic Republic, when it was denied traditional sources of hard coal from the Ruhr and Silesia. Other Soviet industries that benefited in particular from German technologies developed by the NTOs included ceramics, metal finishing, film developing, and metal plating. Almost 4,000 prototypes of a variety of machines, production stations, and technologies were transferred to the Soviet Union in this period, through the NTOs.[119]

Although the work of the NTOs should be judged a success, certainly more so than the dismantling that characterized the initial period of Soviet industrial policy in the zone, there were serious problems with them as well. The question of who owned the machines and technologies developed by the Germans for the Soviets constantly plagued NTO administrators. One NTO chief from Thüringen wrote in great frustration: "We need patent laws; we need patent offices." Otherwise, continued the official, it would be impossible to control the spread of their new inventions, not to mention the old.[120] In addition, as more and more local industries were returned to German administration at the end of 1947 and in 1948, it became more difficult for the NTOs to move from the stage of studying a German product or innovation to the important work of creating a prototype and bringing it into serial production, either in the zone, to be duplicated in the Soviet Union, or in the Soviet Union itself. German-run factories were less amenable to subsuming their plans to NTO needs than were those run directly by Russians. Increasingly, the ministries themselves were unwilling to do more than support the development of new processes and products; whether they were actually employed in German or Soviet industry seemed less relevant to them.[121]

The Thüringen report of January 1949 on the problems and accomplishments of the NTOs noted that there were too few Soviet specialists trying to supervise the work of too many German technicians and workers; sometimes one specialist was forced to oversee the work of up to 400 Germans. This led to an inefficient use of resources and an inability to take advantage of German know-how. The Thüringen report went so far as to suggest that the previous methods of work in the NTOs and OKBs no longer made sense, given the problems of controlling the outcome of the contracts. General Koval and his fellow economic experts urged, therefore, that all the ministries that had previously contracted work through the NTOs should gradually begin to deal instead with the Soviet stock companies (SAGs), Soviet-owned companies in which a significant cadre of highly trained Soviet engineers and specialists were still employed.[122]

By the end of 1946 and the beginning of 1947, the SAGs had already become important mechanisms for the transfer of technical knowledge to the Soviet Union. An Administration for Soviet Property Abroad in Karlshorst, subordinated to the Ministry of Soviet Property Abroad in Moscow, was commanded by Colonel General B. G. Kabulov, who ran a small empire of some fifty to sixty of these large Soviet-controlled enterprises.[123] The sole purpose of the SAGs was to fill Soviet orders and provide for Soviet needs, especially for defense-related items. But many civilian products were also needed by the Soviets. Max Rokhlin, a Soviet chemist, recalled that his chemical factory in Niederau, south of Dresden, was transformed into a Soviet-owned enterprise to produce phenols and DDT, both of which were in very short supply back home.[124]

By the middle of 1950, the NTOs and OKBs had been closed down, and the ownership of most of the SAGs had been transferred to the East German state. The most critical industries for the Soviets in the zone were transformed into Soviet-German joint stock companies, a process that continued to ensure that the programs of Moscow's industrial and technical ministries were augmented by German technological gains.

THE ACADEMY OF SCIENCES

Whether it was in atomic physics, rocket science, or industrial technology, the Soviets sought engineering, technical, and organizational skills from the Germans. In terms of theoretical science, the Soviets actually stood at a commensurate level and needed very little assistance from the Germans. Still, it was in the scientific, as well as political, interests of the Russian occupiers to reinvigorate the work of the German academic intelligentsia, which had deteriorated badly in the last years of the war and the first years of the peace. Academics were hungry, mistrustful of Soviet rule and—not surprisingly—very unproductive. The Soviet Military Administration did help reconstruct the Academy of Sciences in Berlin, the heir to the old Prussian academy. Though most of its equipment and property, including invaluable libraries, had been removed, bits and pieces were returned to the newly reconstituted academy.[125] With the Kaiser Wilhelm Society institutes completely dismantled and eliminated, the Berlin Academy served as the only academic research center of note in eastern Germany. It was extremely small (only fifty scientists) and poor; especially without its equipment and libraries, it was little more than an honorary society.

Under the leadership of SVAG's Education Department, this situation began to change, and the academy was able to expand its scientific base. Order no. 309 of October 23, 1946, placed the eastern German astronomy, geodesic, and seismological institutes under the academy's control. By the end of 1947, some eighteen scientific institutes and nineteen journals were under the aegis of the academy. A new SVAG order of April 9, 1947 on the organization of scientific research in the zone clearly differentiated between applied research in both military and civilian sectors, which was placed under the NTO administration in Karlshorst, the so-called Administration for the Study of Science and Technology in Germany, and basic research, which was turned over to the Education Department. The Education Department also tried to bolster the research activities of the university system, especially Berlin University (later Humboldt University). Already distinct in its activities from the newly formed Free University supported by the Western governments, Berlin University quickly grew to include more than 150 scientific research institutes and seminars.[126]

At the beginning of 1949, with the creation of the GDR just around the corner, the Soviets and the SED realized that further investments in German science and technology might serve their long-term goals. The Soviets approved a broad-ranging program to raise the living standards of the intelligentsia as a whole. Academics were to be elevated to a privileged position in society, and the newest Soviet innovations in biology, genetics, and linguistics were to be broadly propagated among the educated elite. The German Economic Commission, which acted as a surrogate central government in the East, reorganized the Academy of Sciences into an active research center, with twice the number of academicians (from 60 to 120) and a number of new buildings placed at the academy's disposal. By April 1, 1949, all of the academicians' salaries were to be doubled, and they were granted generous credits to build new homes.[127]

Similar programs were introduced by SVAG and the German Education Administration to promote the welfare of professors, engineers, and other "workers in science, literature, and art." New apartments were to be built for intellectuals; mortgage credits and coal would be made available, as well as rest homes, vacation retreats, and visits to health spas. A new fund was created to restore Humboldt University in Berlin, the Dresden Higher

Technical School, and the Jena and Leipzig universities. New scholarships were to be made available for exceptionally talented students. (There had been many complaints among the intelligentsia in the Eastern zone that university admissions policies in the East discriminated against their own children.) The German Academy of Sciences was to be made into an institution parallel with the Soviet Academy, to facilitate contact between the two and make it easier for them to share scientific innovations, while ensuring Soviet control of scientific thinking.

The reality of the situation was much different, however; even Soviet sources indicate that the academicians were resistant to the Stalinized science being propagated by Moscow. There were repeated complaints from the Soviet side that German academics had insufficiently absorbed the lessons of Lysenko on biology or Stalin and Marr on linguistics. "Marxism-Leninism still does not occupy its appropriate place in the institutions of higher education," complained the semi-official SVAG history of education in the East; "We very weakly popularize Soviet science."[128] Material incentives were useful in neutralizing the opposition of German professors and academics to Soviet rule. But it was difficult, if not impossible, to get them to give up their attachment to "bourgeois science."

URANIUM

The combined effect of the work of German scientists and technical specialists, the removal of defense-related technologies, and the fulfillment of contract work for Soviet ministries provided an important impetus to the Soviet atomic bomb project, the Soviet rocket program, and to postwar Soviet military and civilian modernization as a whole. Soviet occupation policy in Germany (and German reaction to these policies) was often determined by the need to improve military technology and to meet the demands of industrial ministries at home. No consideration of this Soviet calculus for defense-related gains from Germany would be complete without an examination of the Soviets' interest in German uranium.

General Leslie Groves was convinced that if the Western Allies could corner the world supply of uranium, the Soviets would be unable to build the bomb for ten years, even if they had the know-how. He estimated that the Czech and Russian supplies of uranium constituted no more than 5 percent of the world's supply. As a result, even if the Soviets could produce a bomb in the short run, based on their small stores of uranium, they would never be able to keep up with Western bomb production, given its corner on the uranium market.[129] Even more important than Western control of bomb technology, which, Groves correctly surmised, would be easily attainable through espionage, the West's monopoly on uranium would establish a "Pax Atomica" dominated by the United States.[130] Therefore, Groves's first goal was to seize control of the uranium stores in the Congo, Brazil, Sweden, Canada, and elsewhere. Second, he intended to seize the German supplies, again more to deny them to the Soviets than to use them for the American program. According to Boris Pash, his Alsos Mission under Groves's command identified at least ninety metric tons of sodium uranate, which was removed from Germany and Belgium by U.S. authorities.[131] The Alsos Mission also turned up twenty grams of pure German radium, which, according to the Alsos science advisor, S. A. Goudsmit, was "a significant fraction of the entire world's supply of radium."[132] On Groves's orders, the Alsos Mission located and secured German uranium supplies throughout Western-occupied Germany: in Stadtilm, Thüringen (uranium ore with 43 percent uranium content), in Stassfurt, in the Harz mountains, and in the Bavarian Alps. Almost all of this German uranium, in the Americans' opinion, came exclusively from original Belgian sources.[133] The Joachimsthal (Jáchymov) mines and refinery, which produced some twenty metric tons of refined uranium a year in 1938 and 1939, had ceased production during the war.[134]

The Soviets' worries about uranium were no less severe than the Americans'. They, too, understood that without the precious metal, their bomb project would suffer severely. To their great surprise and delight, Soviet physicists were able to seize more than 100 tons of uranium ore from the Auer Company. The Soviet physicist Iu. B. Khariton said Kurchatov told him this had saved them a full year on the bomb project.[135] Yet the Soviets faced a serious problem replenishing their stocks of uranium. Future mining operations in the Fergana Valley, in Tadzhikistan, and in Estonia had not yet been developed. The Jáchymov mines, which fell under Soviet administration when the Red Army occupied northern Bohemia, could not produce enough uranium-rich pitchblende to satisfy the needs of a full-scale atomic project. A Russian informant reiterated Groves's assessment of the Soviet predicament when he told American intelligence that "the biggest drawback to making a Soviet atom bomb is the terrific lack of pure uranium which is available to the Soviet Union."[136]

With this background in mind, the odd story of the Soviet occupation of the western Erzgebirge (Ore Mountains) in the summer of 1945 becomes even odder. This area, located on the Czech border just across the mountains from the uranium mines of Jáchymov, eventually became one of the richest uranium producing regions in the world. Encompassing some seventeen towns, eighty villages, and roughly 250,000 inhabitants located in the triangle marked by the towns of Aue, Johanngeorgenstadt, and Annaberg, the region was famous for the radium baths of Oberschlema, and it was known that a series of mines in the area had produced pitchblende at the turn of the century. In fact, the entire area was studded with tin, cobalt, and wolfram (tungsten) mines, not to mention deserted silver and zinc mines, some of which were more than 100 years old. Jonathan Helmreich suggests that the Germans had discovered uranium in the region in 1943.[137]

Despite this history, there is no evidence that prior to the end of the war either the Americans or the Soviets understood the potential for uranium mining in the area.[138] At the end of April 1945, American contingents of General Patton's Third Army appeared in the region on their way to Prague.[139] By the beginning of May, the lines between the American and Soviet armies, which had penetrated into southern Saxony, were very unstable. According to Robert Murphy, the Russian commander then asked permission to move troops behind U.S. lines to occupy the territory up to the Mulde River near Zwickau, but his request was denied by the American Twelfth Army Group, and the U.S. Military Mission in Moscow informed the Soviet High Command of the decision.[140] On May 12, the Americans themselves pulled back to the Mulde River, leaving the region of the western Erzgebirge unoccupied by any Allied troops. From mid-May 1945 until the end of June, when the Americans withdrew from all of Saxony, Thüringen, and Saxony-Anhalt according to their agreement with the Soviets and the Soviets moved in to replace them, the region had no military government.[141]

The history of the German population of this region after the defeat of Hitler and before the occupation by the Soviets is a fascinating one in and of itself, and is told elsewhere in this book.[142] When the Soviets moved in, they only gradually became interested in the possibilities of uranium mining, which also indicated that they had no firm notions of the region's potential in this regard. During the summer of 1945, the leading doctors from the radium baths of Oberschlema were taken to Moscow and debriefed on the radium content of the local soil.[143] However, the fact that the Soviets resettled a large number of Saxon miners to Mecklenburg for the purpose of helping with the harvest in the fall of 1945 meant that the Soviets were not yet contemplating large-scale uranium mining.[144]

It took a full year, until the summer of 1946, for the Soviets to begin serious explorations for uranium in the Erzgebirge. In July the radium baths in Oberschlema were reopened for use "without any special authorizations" for the first time since the war, just as the Soviets began the first drilling nearby.[145] But by the beginning of August 1946, the baths were closed down again, with the explanation that they could be used only by Russian officers. At the end of September, the radium baths and the entire surrounding area were cordoned off from the general population with barbed wire and wooden fences, while four to five thousand workers dug below the cure halls and explored old silver-mine shafts.[146] The work gradually expanded to the south and east, toward the Czech border. By the end of 1946, the word had gone out to German labor exchanges that 20,000 additional workers would be needed for the mines. New shafts were dug, and new equipment and specialists were brought in from the brown coal mines in Senftenberg and moved to Johanngeorgenstadt near the Czech border.[147] At the same time, the mines in Jáchymov in Czechoslovakia were reactivated as part of the Soviets' intensified search for uranium.

WISMUT

During the first months of 1947, the entire region of the western Erzgebirge was cordoned off by Soviet military units, while the mining districts themselves were surrounded by three-meter-high fences and guarded by MVD troops who were not subject to normal SVAG orders and operated independently of Karlshorst.[148] It was not an entirely dissimulating response by Major General Lavrent'ev of SVAG when he answered the inquiry of Brigadier General Walter Hess of the U.S. forces on August 1, 1947: "In reply to your letter of July 26, 1947, containing a request for permission for you to visit the region of the uranium mines, Colonel General Malinin has instructed me to inform you that these mines are not under his jurisdiction and nothing is known of their existence."[149]

The mines were placed under a strict regime, and an increasing number of shafts were opened for work in Aue, Schneeberg, Oberschlema, and Johanngeorgenstadt. All local train and truck transportation was rerouted for the purposes of importing labor from the rest of Germany and exporting pitchblende to the Soviet Union. Under the names of Vitriol and Wismut, the Soviets took complete ownership of the mines, thereby trying to avoid problems with the Saxon government and with trade union groups.

But the sheer size of the enterprise and its costliness in terms of men and material made it difficult to avoid the attention of Germans all over the zone. If the uranium industry had been as capital intensive and labor efficient as the airplane or shipbuilding industries, for example, the Soviets clearly would have been successful in their efforts. But this was not the case with the mines. The great majority of the shafts in the Erzgebirge had not been mined for decades, some not even since the end of the nineteenth century. Equipment was short, and there were too few specialists. As a result, the Soviets had to start from scratch. The first step was for assayists to search for radioactive ore with a Soviet version of the Geiger counter.[150] Then the shafts were excavated, usually by hand—that is, by pickax and sometimes pneumatic drill. The ore was packed in wooden crates and carried to the surface, again usually by hand, where it was taken to a pithead, tested again, separated according to grade, and then loaded onto trucks to be taken to the railway station. Sometimes the ore was taken to nearby refining stations; sometimes it was removed directly to the Soviet Union by open or closed freight cars, or even by airplane from Dresden.[151]

The labor-intensive methods of uranium extraction required tens of thousands of workers, but the Soviets were in no mood to improve conditions so that workers would be enticed into the mines. Instead, a German Kolyma of sorts was created in the Erzgebirge, with forced labor brought to the region and subjected to humiliating and unbearable physical circumstances. The mining operation was turned into a death march. In the case of the Erzgebirge, however, news of the conditions in the mines could not be kept from Germans in the East or the West. Still, the Soviets' desperate need for workers in the uranium mines blinded them to both the sharp political problems they engendered by exploiting German men and women in this fashion and to the economic problems they created by forcibly drafting a workforce for their uranium operations from their already labor-scarce zone.[152]

The first drafting of forced laborers took place in the late winter and spring of 1947, producing some twenty-five to thirty thousand workers, predominantly from the Saxon cities of Dresden, Leipzig, Zwickau, and Chemnitz.[153] But the Soviets felt they needed at least 75,000 more workers.

As a result, in June 1947 workers were drafted from Thüringen and Mecklenburg, as well as Saxony-Anhalt.[154] The Soviets presented German labor exchanges with higher and higher quotas, which meant that workers would have to be drafted without regard to their previous profession or even to their state of health. The Soviet commandant of Dresden ordered the German medical inspectors to speed up the processing of recruits for the mines and to exempt fewer workers from hard physical labor.[155] In Thüringen, General Kolesnichenko arrested and fined a number of physicians for conspiring with labor draftees who sought to avoid work in the mines. He set up an entirely new board of medical inspectors to ensure that they would do their job properly.[156] The result was plain to see: tens of thousands of office workers, craftsmen, students, and apprentices with no mining experience and often without the requisite physical stamina were sent to the mines.[157]

By early 1948, the labor exchanges had completely exhausted the supply of "unattached labor"—those who were unemployed or between jobs as a result of dismantling, and young people not yet in the workforce or just out of school. Consequently, the labor offices had to turn to those already employed to fulfill their quotas, by "having each plant submit a certain number of names of men and women between the ages of 18 and 45 years to the local labor offices."[158] In addition, work in the mines was increasingly used as punishment for criminals. To meet labor quotas, local authorities would ship off to Aue black marketeers and thieves, and Germans who had been caught trying to cross illegally the border to the West. Returning POWs from the Soviet Union were also used to feed the seemingly insatiable appetite of the uranium mining enterprise for fresh workers. Those returning POWs without official personal documents or special political credentials, especially, were sent on Soviet orders directly from Frankfurt-Oder, their muster point in the Soviet zone, to the mines in the Erzgebirge.[159] Some returning POWs were unaware of the conditions in the mines and, given the promise of high wages and good living conditions, actually volunteered for the work.[160]

With tens of thousands of workers pouring into the Erzgebirge through the central distribution point of Aue (appropriately named the Gate of Tears), the already difficult conditions of work deteriorated further.[161] The population of the mining towns grew much faster than the region's capacity to house the new workers. Makeshift barracks and tents often became the miners' homes, cots were used in shifts, and it was not unusual for workers to sleep on the ground without any bedding or blankets. The population of Oberschlema grew from 2,400 in 1946 to 5,600 in 1947 to more than 9,500 in 1951; Johanngeorgenstadt grew from 6,000 in 1946 to 13,600 in 1947 to 38,300 in 1951. The county of Aue, like most of the region, doubled its population between 1946 and 1951, from 110,000 to 212,000.[162]

The conditions in the mines themselves were even worse than the housing conditions, and labor leaders in Saxony were aware of the problems from the very beginning. Otto Grotewohl was apprised of the situation by union activists, and his brief notes reflect the depressing situation: the Oberschlema mines were using prison labor; "women are being beaten"; there were outbreaks of skin diseases and no soap; "the doctors are helpless"; and, perhaps most difficult, "the responsible party is *directly* subordinate [only] to Moscow," meaning there was little or nothing he could do about the situation.[163] However, the SED in Saxony continued to push for greater regulation of the mines, as rumors about the harsh mistreatment of the workers spread to all segments of society. A careful March 18, 1947, summary of complaints emanating from the Erzgebirge insisted that the SED act on behalf of the miners: "The conditions of work [in Aue] are pictured in such a way that one might believe these are reports from a penal colony. On the surface or underground, the people stand knee-deep in slime [*Morast*], without rubber boots or water boots. The work places are cold and drafty, so that within a short time, [the people] suffer from colds." The SED summary elaborated a litany of complaints. Unless the miners had a high fever, the doctors refused to excuse them from work. People were jailed or were deprived of their already meager rations for allegedly not working hard enough or missing work.[164]

The SED member Helmut Lehmann—formerly of the SPD and an official in the Labor and Welfare Administration—pushed his comrades in the Party Executive to deal with the problems of the uranium workers. In an August 12, 1947, letter to Grotewohl, he wrote that the conditions in the mines "were extremely bad":

Often, people are drafted into this work whose health and physical condition make them inappropriate [for mining]. Given the strenuous labor, their housing and upkeep is completely inadequate . . . Protection of the workers is less than insufficient, the effects of which are even worse, given the fact that the greatest portion of the workforce are novices. The physicians, who are in charge of health supervision, are urged, against their convictions, to declare workers as fit for work although they are not.[165]

Lehmann also tried to get the SED Central Secretariat to consider the unusual damage being caused to the health of the uranium miners by sending his comrades a series of reports issued by responsible physicians. One, from Dr. Wildführ, a leading Saxon health official, warned of severe health damage that could result from uranium mining. This was a difficult and unknown field, the physician wrote, one in which little data was available on the subject. Also, there were no regulations about uranium mining, because it had not been previously carried out in Germany. Nevertheless, he was certain that severe harm could come to the miners' health from breathing radioactive dust, along with "the effects of rays or emanations from the material of the mine puddles." (Virtually every report of the mines described workers knee-deep in radioactive slime.)

> In addition to these effects [cancerlike lung diseases, even tuberculosis from breathing in silicates], one must take into consideration that extended exposure to radioactive waves can lead to irreparable health damage . . . Radioactive waves attack [body] cells. The harmful effect consists first of all in the damage to the life functions of the cell that finally, with high enough doses, leads to the death of the cell. Tissue damage can take many forms: changes in the skin . . . bones that become decalcified and deformed, or cancerlike deterioration in the blood, for example through the reduction of white corpuscles (Leukemia) . . . in the lungs, [one can develop] in the above-mentioned sense fibrosis. After initial heightened activity, general weakness appears and wasting away of the inner organs [sets in]; sterility accompanies the other symptoms of radioactive damage.[166]

Even if other physicians had less knowledge of the harmful effects of exposure to radioactivity than Wildführ, they nevertheless also decried the standards of health in the mines. Their focus, like Lehmann's, was on the dangerous mining conditions, rather than on the effects of uranium itself. In fact, American intelligence reported a series of terrible accidents that accompanied the primitive conditions of uranium mining in the Erzgebirge.[167]

Lehmann's agitation in inner party circles on behalf of the uranium miners bore some fruit. Grotewohl finally arranged a meeting on May 23,

1947, with Major General A. M. Mal'tsev of the Ministry of State Security, who ran the mining administration for the Erzgebirge. Mal'tsev agreed to improve the salaries and increase the allocations of food to the miners, as well as to institute regular vacations.[168] Grotewohl was also assured that the living and hygienic conditions among miners had improved to the extent that local people were actually volunteering to work in the mines. But from Grotewohl's papers, it is clear that the SED leader would not pursue the issue of the special dangers of uranium mining. It is possible that he believed the allegation that Western Allies were spreading the rumors "that radioactive elements are damaging to their health" to create "dissatisfaction among the miners."[169] Typical of the attitude of SED functionaries on this question was the comment from a Saxon party official, that there were no special dangers from uranium mining because no damage had been reported by the miners.[170]

By the end of 1947 conditions did indeed improve for miners, in part because of the intercession of the SED. And through higher salaries and better ration allocations, the Soviets were able to attract more volunteers.[171] Still, the continuation of old methods of drafting labor and the new tactic of making promises that were often not kept gave the uranium mining enterprise a terrible reputation throughout Germany. The Mecklenburg newspaper *Der Demokrat* wrote somewhat disingenuously in October 1947 about the fact that only 400 men had showed up at muster when the province was supposed to provide 3,000 workers for the mines: "The low number of those who reported no doubt is attributable to the fact that the people of Mecklenburg are unaware of the conditions in the Saxon mines and that there is some hesitancy to engage in work in mining."[172] Of course, the problem was exactly the opposite; the Mecklenburgers knew precisely what to expect.

The incessant lying about what was going on in the Erzgebirge had a negative effect on a wide variety of problems in the zone. Herbert Gessmer, a commentator on Berlin radio, complained that the policy of denying what everyone already knew—that uranium was being mined under strict Soviet supervision in this region—was ridiculous and counterproductive. Gessmer added that the West was able to make great propaganda gains by exposing the obvious lies from the East: "And the only thing we accomplish [by denying the existence of uranium mining] is that people don't believe anything else we say about other areas [of our endeavors.]"[173] Deceptive recruiting practices were also the subject of high-level reports to the SED leaders. As late as August 1949, Pieck suggested to Ulbricht that these reports be discussed in the Small Secretariat of the party. Pieck noted: "As a result of this practice [deceptive recruiting] and the methods that were used in the past to recruit workers for Aue [forced labor], the people—including a broad segment of members of our own party—look at being conscripted to Aue as the worst punishment that an inhabitant of the Eastern zone can face."[174]

Beginning in the summer of 1947, when the Soviets informed the labor boards that 60,000 additional workers were needed for the mines, a stream of potential recruits left for the West. Authorities in the American zone were worried that thousands of these refugees would overburden their already strained food and housing resources. In fact, they were considerably relieved when many of the refugees who were interviewed stated their readiness to return to the East once conscriptions for the mines were over.[175] The conscriptions during the summer of 1947 also led to renewed rumors of war, because they were accompanied by the mandatory registration of all former German military personnel in the Soviet zone.[176] This upset the Soviets, as did the fact that so many of the people who fled to the West because of "rumors of forced labor in the uranium mines" were the natural supporters of socialism in the East—good, solid representatives of the working class and "even members of the SED."[177]

But for the Soviets, the acquisition of the precious uranium metal was more important than placating German society in the Soviet zone. On August 30, 1947, a Wismut official named Iliukhin pressed the case for an additional 20,000 workers from the German Administration of Labor and Social Welfare. He insisted that labor recruitment was going too slowly and that the Germans would have to continue with conscriptions if their propaganda campaigns for additional workers did not succeed in recruiting the targeted number. Iliukhin ordered the Germans to fulfill their obligations to supply labor for the mines; one way to do so, he suggested, was to increase the number of women in the eligible labor pool: "The carrying out of the order must be followed more carefully. You can't simply say there is no more workforce there. You have to make sure that they are there. There is enough money in the Offices for Labor and Social Welfare to use for retraining workers. This [money] should be used to retrain women for certain jobs more than has been done before."[178]

The Soviets were also completely unresponsive to attempts by the FDGB to establish factory councils in the mines. When FDGB mining section officials tried to press their case about union representation with the local commandant in Aue on September 23, 1947, he responded by saying "there will be no more discussion" of the matter. When one of the FDGB officials then explained that they would have to protest the commandant's ruling to Karlshorst, the commandant responded that Wismut did not answer to Karlshorst and that he really did not care to whom the Germans complained.[179]

In early 1948, German newspapers were filled with glowing descriptions of the work in the mines. The *Landes-Zeitung* in Stralsund, for instance, extolled the housing and food allocations provided by the mining administration. If conditions were bad at the beginning, the newspaper stated, they had vastly improved; now miners were living in settlements of one-story houses with basements and gardens. "Everyone has the opportunity to take up work in Aue, in order to enjoy the happy state of very favorable working conditions."[180] It is unlikely that very many Germans were deceived by the descriptions of a workers' Nirvana in the uranium mines. Yet the SED's campaign to recruit volunteers for the mines by appealing to their sense of patriotic duty seemed to have some effect. The story of a group of Güstrow volunteers epitomizes the fate of these groups. The secretary of the Güstrow Committee for Unity and a Just Peace, a young SED member named Fraulein Träder, led a group of women and students to volunteer for work in Aue. The women, mostly in their young twenties, were shocked by what they found. When they arrived there was no place for them to sleep and nothing to eat. At every turn, they were horribly mistreated. There were no separate facilities for men and women, and they were warned that 80 to 90 percent of the workers had some kind of venereal disease. Comrade Träder gathered up her recruits and returned to Güstrow as quickly as she could, where she wrote a bitter complaint to the party's Central Committee.[181] Some of the other volunteers in Aue, who were recruited by the Free German Youth (FDJ), were not so lucky. They were forced to remain in the mines even though many wanted to go home. Not infrequently volunteer work turned into forced labor.[182]

As indicated in Träder's report, as other supplies of labor dried up in 1948, Wismut and the labor exchanges increasingly turned to female recruits for work both above and below ground. In the fourth quarter of 1948, some 10,000 female recruits joined the 10,350 women already there. In many cases, the labor exchanges recruited indigent or transient women by promising high wages and good living conditions. Local doctors reported that more than half of the new female recruits carried some form of sexually transmitted disease when they arrived for work at the mines. It is no wonder that the women who worked in the mines ended up, in the words of one SED report, embittered and "morally and socially depraved."[183] Werner Knop described truly appalling conditions in which the women were sexually exploited by the Russian guards, not to mention completely debased by the general atmosphere among the forced laborers in the mines.[184] One SED report concluded, no doubt correctly: "It is completely irresponsible to recruit further groups of women for the mining operations before a special transit camp is constructed for women and enough homes for women are available."[185]

The recruitment of women to Wismut did not relieve the pressure to find more able-bodied workers for the mines. In June of 1949, Lehmann was charged with recruiting yet another 20,000 workers, and he despaired of being able to find them. Part of the problem was that terrible health and safety conditions in the mines continually depleted the labor resources that were already in Wismut. The SED reported that the number of accidents was growing; "in the first quarter of 1948 there were 574 accidents reported, in which on the average ten or more people died."[186] Part of the problem was also that some fifteen to twenty thousand German workers had been siphoned off from the Wismut projects to work in the mines in Jáchymov in Czechoslovakia, where new shafts were being dug and old ones expanded.[187] There were even rumors in September 1948 that the Czech uranium mines would be incorporated into the Wismut complex, which in turn would be governed autonomously.[188]

Those workers designated by their factories for work in the mines still frequently opted to leave for the West. With some regret, SED officials noted as late as the summer of 1949 that thousands of skilled workers preferred flight to working in the mines.[189] By 1949, Wismut would not accept workers who had been in the West at all. Some workers used this as an excuse to avoid the mines, but it also meant that many competent workers who, for one reason or another, had been in the West and ended up in the mines, were now arrested for spying and sent off to the MVD camps in Buchenwald or Sachsenhausen.[190] Once again, Lehmann tried to convince the Soviets to improve the conditions in the mines to attract free labor rather than relying on the dysfunctional labor drafts. He urged Cherniaev, a Wismut executive, to muster resources to rebuild the entire area, "at least to introduce some changes in the region." Lehmann suggested "radical measures" to attack the continuing, widespread problem of sexually transmitted diseases among the miners, and he brought to the attention of the Wismut leadership the continuing reports about the lack of work clothes, protective gear, and medical supplies.[191]

For the most part, Lehmann's appeals fell on deaf ears. Even after the founding of the German Democratic Republic, the German authorities had no right to interfere in the lives of their citizens in the uranium mining districts of the Erzgebirge. What was worse, they were obligated to hunt down and return workers who escaped, whether they were conscripted workers or volunteers.[192] When the GDR came into existence in the fall of 1949, Ulbricht finally began discussions with the Soviets about spreading German social legislation to the miners in the Erzgebirge and about applying normal administrative rules and practices to the towns and regions of Annaberg, Aue, and Marienburg counties, the centers of the uranium enterprise. Ulbricht even expressed optimism that Wismut would take over responsibility for the recruitment of workers, which would force the enterprise to provide attractive wages and living conditions, while freeing the German labor exchanges from the onerous task of drafting labor for the mines.[193] But the May 1950 report of the Aue Commission, whose task it was to review the needs of Wismut, made it clear that the fundamental problems of uranium mining had not changed. The commission accused the German trade unions of not doing their job and the German mass organizations of "being completely asleep," because Wismut was still short 93,000 workers! Rather than Wismut's taking responsibility for the recruitment of workers, as Ulbricht had suggested, the SED was charged with finding more "volunteers" for the mines. This could be done, the commission suggested, in the agricultural sector, which was undergoing "rapid modernization" (that is, collectivization). The SED's new point of view was that "the recruitment of workers for the Wismut AG must be seen as a national task in fulfilling our economic plans."[194] Throughout the 1950s, conditions in the mines remained poor. The pay was substandard and, as the SED itself wrote, "the housing situation was very bad."[195]

The Soviets' demand for uranium in the Erzgebirge promoted a series of policies that seriously undermined the formal political and economic goals of their occupation of Germany. The populace was perpetually frightened of being sent to the mines. Certainly thousands (if not tens of thousands) of skilled workers left for the West to escape just such a fate. Labor markets in the East—already badly distorted by the effects of the war—were thrown into chaos by the Soviets' insatiable need for uranium miners. The low health standards and primitive working conditions in the mines meant that Wismut's demand for labor was all that much greater, as large numbers of miners had to be hospitalized or released, or died on the job. Unlike the work camps in the Soviet Far East and north, it was impossible to hide the exploitation of labor in the Erzgebirge. Yet the German unions (the FDGB) and the SED could do nothing to aid the uranium miners. The credibility of the German socialists was badly damaged, and their inability to come to the defense of their own workers undermined their sense of purpose and autonomy.

The Western press was filled with the most horrendous tales from the Soviet labor camps in Aue. Clever American military-government propagandists bolstered the veracity of these lurid tales with the publication in German of books like the *History of the Soviet Prison Camp System,* by David Dallin and Boris Nicolaevsky, which implied that eastern Germany had become a part of the Soviet prison camp system. Even after the signing of formal agreements between the Wismut authorities and the GDR in 1953 and 1958, the uranium mines remained a symbol of Soviet coercion in Germany, one that is still not easy to forget.[196]

By early 1949, it was apparent to both the Soviets and the Western Allies that the cold war had divided Germany. There would be a West Germany and an East Germany for some time to come, whatever form the states on either side of the Iron Curtain eventually assumed. As a result of this split, the Soviets were able to take a long-term view of the exploitation of German science and technology, and of the extraction of uranium. On the uranium question, the Soviets allowed the Germans to become increasingly involved in the actual administration of the mines, forming in 1956 a joint stock company, the German-Soviet AG Wismut, which was based on the idea that the mining of uranium "had equal importance for the Soviet Union and the GDR."[197] AG Wismut was one of the last joint stock companies to be formed and one of the last to be disbanded. Health records from the giant enterprise indicate that at least 20,000 miners died of or suffered from lung disease "induced by exposure to radiation and dust."[198] Germans today are still living with the byproducts of Wismut: mounds of radioactive waste are scattered near abandoned shafts all across the once idyllic Erzgebirge.

The creation of the GDR in October 1949 also made possible the return from the Soviet Union of the tens of thousands of German technicians and scientists (and their families), who had worked on the atomic bomb project, on rocket projects, and in other defense-related industries. Some of the first specialists had already returned in the summer of 1949, provoking an argument between the political authorities of SVAG, who were anxious to reinstate German specialists in their jobs, and the MVD, which sought to keep the Germans in isolation for as long as possible. Technicians from the Wolfen factory complained about MVD chicanery in its attempts to prevent their scheduled return from Ukraine, setting off a series of protests by East German public figures.[199] But the Wolfen technicians, most of whom were associated with the photography industry, were lucky. Many of the Askania, BMW, and Junkers specialists, despite their initial five-year "contracts," were not allowed to return to Germany until the late 1950s.[200]

By 1951, the Soviets felt that they had learned what they could from the German atomic and rocket specialists. It had always been their goal to foster as much of a purely native scientific elite as possible. The Germans had helped the Soviets to catch up after their long war-time hiatus in atomic and rocket research, to "put them back on schedule," in Walter McDougall's words, and now it was time to honor their agreements and return the Germans to their native land.[201] The Soviets insisted that the Germans take a three-year "cooling off" period, however, before allowing them to leave the USSR. Most returned to the GDR by the middle of the 1950s. Some departed immediately for the West; others, like von Ardenne, became established figures in the world of GDR science and technology. A few scientists even became Soviet citizens and stayed, as did Baroni, who feared that his background in the Waffen SS might cause him additional problems at home in Austria.[202]

By any number of measures, the Soviet programs in atomic and rocket science, the extraction of uranium, and the adaptation of German technology were a great success. Capable and innovative Soviet atomic scientists, like Kurchatov and Khariton, and rocket specialists, like Korolev, Glushko, and Chertok, used German advances made during the war to keep the Soviets technologically competitive with the Americans at the outset of the cold war. On August 23, 1949, the Soviets exploded their first atomic bomb—to the great surprise, shock, and dismay of their American rivals, who were certain that they had denied the Russians the material and scientific wherewithal to accomplish such a complex task. The Soviets later developed the first intercontinental ballistic missile and put the first satellite in space. Clearly there would have been a Soviet space program without the Germans and a Soviet atom bomb without Wismut and the German physicists. But there is no question that German science, technology, research methods, and material were important, if not indispensable, to these accomplishments.

The political costs of the Soviet exploitation of German achievements were, however, severe. Operation Osoaviakhim branded the Soviets as kidnappers and bullies. As a result, no German technician in the Eastern zone could feel completely safe. Although the operation was conducted peaceably and even politely, its essence was clear to victims and observers alike. The Germans were terrorized in the sense of knowing that opposition meant facing unknown and potentially fearsome punishments. Even the highest ranking scientists, like Steenbeck or Riehl, had to watch their conduct carefully. There was always the possibility that they could be given sentences in labor camps if they voiced too loudly a desire to go home, or if they made serious errors in their work. Terror was also at the core of the Wismut mining enterprise. Factory workers could be requisitioned to the uranium mines just as skilled technicians could be drafted to work in Soviet defense-related industries. Only flight to the West could spare workers the possibility of a hellish fate in the mines.

In short, the Soviet desire to acquire German science, technology, and material, especially uranium, brought the Stalinist terror very close to home for the Germans. Many succumbed, acquiesced, and even joined the system, although many also escaped to the West. Simultaneously, many in the West grew increasingly determined to avoid the fate of their brethren in the East, and some were willing to resort to open resistance in order to do so. The blatantly exploitative Osoaviakhim operation and the horrific conditions of the Wismut enterprise exposed the bald repressiveness of the Stalinist system. As a result, the Soviets seriously undermined their ability to rule the Eastern zone of Germany.

The Soviets and the German Left

THE SOVIETS MARCHED INTO GERMANY with a number of purposes in mind. Certainly the defeat of Hitler and his armies was their highest priority, followed by the determination to eliminate the ability of the Germans to wage war for yet a third time in the century. To achieve these goals, the Soviets felt that they would have to destroy the roots of Nazism and militarism in the country. Land reform and the sequestering of major industries resulted from these intentions. The Soviets also occupied Germany with the idea of securing the payment of reparations for the enormous damage inflicted on them by the Germans. Repayment would take many forms, but the overall policy was unambiguous; German industry, science, technology, labor, natural resources, and knowledge were there for the Soviets' taking. When it became clear at Potsdam in July 1945 that the Western Allies were unwilling to allow the Soviets to extract large sums as reparations from their zones of occupation, the Soviets tightened their economic vise on the Eastern zone, removing whole factories and installations, down to the wiring and plumbing. Only in late 1946 did the Soviets settle into an economically more rational policy of taking large amounts of production in kind as reparations.

The political intentions of the Soviet occupation were less clear. The Soviets were initially committed to the unity of Germany: the German nation and state, as such, would not be destroyed. In their slogans and by their actions, the Soviets also separated those Germans responsible for the Third Reich's institutions from the average citizens. A theoretical argument had been carried on in Moscow during the war, about whether there were any redeemable Germans and how long the occupation would have to last to reeducate the rest. But in practice, Soviet commandants in the occupation zone were urged to reconstitute local government, using whatever human material was at hand.[1] In the spirit of the resolutions of the Seventh Congress of the Comintern in 1935 and the Popular Front, the Soviets looked to support both political forces of the Left and the progressive bourgeoisie, which would complete the "antifascist democratic revolution" in Germany. The KPD's moderate Brussels and Bern programs (1935 and 1939, respectively) also developed these ideas, urging the formation of coalitions in the name of a democratic Germany.

THE INITIATIVE GROUPS

During the war, the German communists in Moscow were very much on the defensive, given the quiescence of the German proletariat in the face of the rise and even the fall of Nazism. For the most part, German communists worked in the shadows of Georgi Dimitrov's larger-than-life figure. As head of a surrogate Comintern, the Committee for International Relations of the Central Committee, Dimitrov consulted with the KPD veterans to develop an ideological approach to the liberation of their homeland, one that would emphasize the uniqueness of the German situation. The KPD veterans also worked closely with the Seventh Section of the Main Political Administration of the Red Army (GlavPURKKA), for whom they wrote pamphlets and leaflets, and conducted defeatist propaganda programs among their conationals at the front and in POW camps. With the approach of the Soviet armies to the Oder River, KPD chief Wilhelm Pieck sent a formal request to Dimitrov, asking to send a group of German communists with the Red Army to liberate Berlin. Dimitrov approved the request, and the Cadres Department of the Central Committee submitted a list of qualified candidates for work in Germany to Dimitrov, V. M. Molotov, and G. M. Malenkov.[2] On Dimitrov's recommendation, the Central Committee decided to send three groups to Germany, one with each of the major armies (fronts) that would partake in the occupation: the First and Second Belorussian Fronts and the First Ukrainian Front. Dimitrov also informed the groups that no political parties would be allowed to function in the newly liberated territories and that their task was to help the Soviets set up a German civilian administration, nothing more. Their slogan was, The Rapid Normalization of the Life of the Population.[3]

As a result of Dimitrov's planning on behalf of the Central Committee, three groups of KPD activists accompanied the Soviet armies into Germany in the spring of 1945. The "Ulbricht Group" joined the First Belorussion Front on April 27 and entered Berlin while the fighting was still going on.[4] Anton Ackermann's group linked up with the First Ukrainian Front on May 1 and moved with the Soviet armies into still-smoldering Dresden. Gustav Sobottka's group was attached to the Second Belorussian Front on May 6 and operated in Mecklenburg and the Baltic towns of Schwerin and Rostock. The KPD supported the creation of an antifascist democratic order, referring for its justification to prewar KPD programs and to the activities of the German communists in Moscow on behalf of the National Committee for Free Germany (NKFD), the antifascist organization of German POWs in the Soviet Union. But the future of the NKFD had depended on hopes for an end to the war through a German popular uprising, an army coup, or a negotiated peace. With the Nazis' unconditional surrender in May 1945, the NKFD was disbanded and its members, depending on their political profiles, were gradually integrated into the state and security apparatus of the Eastern zone. The communists were also asked to become administrators, at least for the short run. Long years in the Soviet Union had convinced the leading members of the KPD that careful attention to the Soviets' political and international needs paid organizational and personal dividends. Few were better schooled in this lesson than Walter Ulbricht, and it was Ulbricht who oversaw the creation of a new German administration.

In the days following the Nazi surrender, local administrations were put in the hands of seventy German communist emigrants from Moscow, as well as some three hundred former German POWs in the USSR, most of whom had been associated with the NKFD and had attended antifascist schools. The Seventh Section of GlavPURKKA was nominally in charge of the operation. It brought in additional Soviet political workers who knew German and could be entrusted to organize propaganda among the population. The Seventh Section sent out German-speaking propagandists on trucks mounted with loudspeakers, to go from town to town announcing the new Soviet policies for Germany. They also published the first German-language newspapers.[5] The Seventh Section and the German antifascists had their work cut out for them. The Germans were in a terrible state: panicked, depressed, and helpless. Only gradually did they emerge from hiding, to find out that the Soviets at least would not let them starve or ship them all off to Siberia, as Nazi propaganda had led many of them to believe. Still, the population was wary and scared, a problem that was exacerbated by continuing assaults on German men and women by Soviet soldiers. In the first six weeks of the occupation, suicides were quite common, sometimes committed by individuals, sometimes by whole families or groups.[6] Even after the incidence of suicides and assaults abated, the Soviets and their German helpmates faced hostility and suspicion among the population. Especially in the villages, but also in the cities, many Germans still pictured the Russians through the lenses of Nazi propaganda. Exhausted, apathetic, and hostile to the Russians, Germans looked to their future with a combination of indifference and fear.

Sectarians and the Socialists

This generally bleak picture of "zero hour" *(Stunde null)*, as the Germans call the first weeks and months of the occupation, would not be complete without an understanding of the tremendous upswing of political activity within the remnants of the German Left in general and among German communists in particular. The end of the war brought significant numbers of German communists into political action who had previously been in jails, concentration camps, and in the underground, hiding from the Nazis. These communists cared no less for the Soviet Union than did their comrades who had spent the war years in Moscow, but they were generally less adept at adjusting to the Kremlin's shifting political demands. Their views at the end of the war were remarkably consistent, given the lack of any central underground communist organization: the collapse of fascism and the victory of the Soviet Union made possible the creation of the socialist Germany for which they had fought so long and sacrificed so much. Many of these communist groups suffered from what their contemporaneous KPD critics (and later GDR historiography) labeled as "sectarianism."[7] In other words, they wanted to set up soviets (workers' councils), fight the counterrevolution, and—with the onset of the Soviet military occupation—begin the process of creating a "Soviet Germany."[8] In this way, there would be no need to ally with other emerging parties, because the combination of a highly centralized KPD, modeled on the Bolsheviks, and the Red Army would suffice to bring about the success of the revolution. Some groups even demanded weapons from the Soviet commandants to begin the process.

Especially during the first few weeks of the occupation, when instructions to the commandants were extremely vague and each commandant acted largely autonomously, the "sectarians" dominated the emerging German political landscape.[9] Even Ulbricht was unable to control the situation and was criticized by his Soviet overlords for being badly out of touch with the situation.[10] Moreover, there was little agreement about tactics within and among the three German initiative groups. As a result of this chaotic approach to politics in the first period of the occupation, the reinvigorated communist Left was allowed to indulge in its fantasies about a new German Bolshevik revolution. Some local communists began the collectivization of agriculture; others, waving red flags and singing "The Internationale," set up Soviets of Workers' and Peasants' Deputies. Streets were renamed after such German communist heroes as Rosa Luxemburg, Ernst Thälmann, and Karl Liebknecht. Pictures of Stalin and Thälmann were carried as religious icons by KPD "revolutionaries."[11] Even when chastized by Soviet commandants and told that they were not allowed to establish "Soviet power" or the "dictatorship of the proletariat," they answered: "OK, fine, we won't call it Soviet power, but it will be Soviet power in any case; it can't be anything else."[12]

Usually, however, the Soviet commandants did not even bother to try to rein in the leftists. In Pirna (Saxony), the communists changed the day of rest from Sunday to Friday and insisted that citizens greet each other with the KPD slogan, Rote Front (Red Front), instead of "good day." In Klausdorf (Brandenburg), the communists posted the following revolutionary poem:

> Wacht auf, hell beginnt's zu tagen
> durch's Licht zur Freiheit
> Vorwärts, ohne zu zagen
> "Rotfront," freie Bahn,
> die Strasse frei,
> das rote Battalion rückt an.
> Jetzt stehen wir zum Kampf bereit,
> der Weg zur Freiheit ist nicht mehr weit.[13]

Until May 17, all of the Soviet zone of Germany was on Moscow time; soon, the leftists argued, Poland and Germany would also be Soviet republics. The first number of the Coswig (Anhalt) newspaper *Rote Fahne,* published on May 8, 1945, recalled the sufferings and death of Ernst Thälmann in Buchenwald and ended with the call for "the building of a Leninist-Marxist state. Hail to Moscow [*Heil Moskau*]." The third number of *Rote Fahne,* published on May 16, indicated that the communists controlled the economic and social life of the town. Schools were reopened by the "workers' state"; the local commandants issued their orders through the communist-dominated soviet.[14] In several other towns, KPD leaders called themselves "commissars," insisted that red flags and banners decorate the towns, and renamed streets and plazas. The first Soviet reports on these activities reflected a kind of patronizing amusement regarding these "Reds." They also indicate that measures were taken to correct these KPD "errors and blunders."[15] More often than not, however, the commandants themselves contributed to the problem, either ignoring the leftists or condoning their activity.

Ulbricht, in particular, had no love for the sectarians, the "ultraradicals" *(Überradikale)*, as he frequently called them. In his view, they got in the way of zone's new administration and unnecessarily scared off the German bourgeoisie.[16] Ulbricht and the German communists who had been in Moscow also were averse to another variety of underground German communists in this period: those who wanted to abandon normal party activity for antifascist fronts, a tactic that many had learned initially from the NKFD broadcasts from the Soviet Union to Germany in 1944 and 1945. Several communist groups called for the establishment of a "bloc of fighting democracy," which would join all antifascist organizations, parties, groups, and individuals in the struggle for a socialist democratic republic.[17] These communists called for the dissolution of the KPD and the formation of new political unions as the way out of the traumatic errors of the past, since, in their view, disunity had made possible the tragic Nazi seizure of power. Often, both KPD and SPD activists in the countryside and the towns—at the grass roots, one can say with some confidence—found a variety of ways to merge their parties and actions, sometimes even joining with local Soviet commandants sympathetic to the general united-front approach.

The antifascist committee of Haselhorst, outside Berlin, issued a proclamation on the liberation of their town:

> Hang your flags! Today is your birthday; the day on which we have the right to demonstrate our political maturity. Let's form *one* large "German Workers' Party." Show the International that you are worthy of the great gift which you have received today—namely the right to express openly your political opinion through the founding of a large strong Workers' Party, [which has been] tested through misery and distress. Prove that we have finally come to the long desired goal—"*Unity*" . . . There can be no more 1918s and no 1933s . . . Long live the International![18]

In Köthen (Saxony), communists and social democrats spontaneously merged their efforts in a Socialist Workers' Party, which NKVD General Serov characterized as suffering from "petit-bourgeois radicalism."[19] Fritz Koehn recalled that after he was liberated from prison in Treptow, he and his comrades thought that within a few months communists and social democrats would form a large workers' party, the dictatorship of the proletariat would be introduced, and "we would not need any more middle-class people."[20] With the Soviet occupation, antifascist groups emerged from the underground, or were newly formed, with the clear agenda of uniting the former enemies on the Left, the communists and social democrats, and repairing the terrible rift that had made possible, from most socialists' point of view, the rise of fascism.

In Moscow

Soviet and German political leaders could look with some sense of accomplishment at the first month of the Soviet occupation. After the capitulation itself, resistance was minimal and Nazism seemed largely quiescent. Units from Soviet Military Counterintelligence (SMERSH), charged with uncovering the last pockets of resistance, had surprisingly little to do. Municipal administrations had been revived, and the infrastructures of the bigger cities had returned, if not to normality, at least to the level where water, electricity, and sewage disposal could be counted on. Food and medical services reached broad cross sections of the population. The first newspapers were being printed by the military authorities, and the first cinema houses and even theaters were being reopened. Though gratified in general by the upsurge in political activity on the part of the German Left, both the Moscow KPD leaders and the Soviets were concerned about the ideological chaos they perceived among German socialists. Serious political work among the German population, in their view, could be undertaken only with a unified approach to the problems of ideology. As a result, the leaders of the initiative groups, Anton Ackermann, Walter Ulbricht, and Gustav Sobottka, were recalled to Moscow at the beginning of June to consult with the Soviet leadership about the formation of political parties and trade unions, as authorized by a Soviet directive of May 26.

The first meeting between the initiative group leaders and the Soviet leadership—Stalin, Molotov, and Zhdanov—took place on June 4, 1945. Wilhelm Pieck was also there, and it is to his sketchy notes that we owe our knowledge of the discussions. The primary issue at hand was the intention of the Soviets to legalize the KPD as "the *party of labor* (workers, farmers, intellectuals)," whose goal would be "the completion of the bourgeois-democratic revolution." In other words, the KPD was to be a mass party, interested in democratic transformations. At this meeting, the Soviets and Germans also named a nine-member Politburo and a five-member Secretariat for the new KPD, and they even named a translator who would report the proceedings of the new party organs to the Soviets. In accord with Ulbricht's inclinations in particular, the Soviets endorsed the elimination of the antifascist groups: in Pieck's notes, "*the formation of antifascist committees* also is not useful, because the danger exists that they will have independent power next to that of the city and local government."[21] In a meeting with Georgi Dimitrov and A. M. Paniushkin of the Central Committee on June 7, Ulbricht also warned of the dangers of "dual power" if the "antifas" (antifascist committees) were allowed to continue.[22]

The most astonishing jottings in the Pieck notes of the June 4 meeting read: "*Perspectives*—there will be two Germanys—despite all the unity among the Allies." But it would be unwise to interpret this statement as indicating that Stalin was already pointing to the future division of Germany. Rather, in the language of the time—that often used by the Soviets' international "theoreticians" Zhdanov, Dimitrov, and Eugen Varga—the "two Germanys" may well have referred to a progressive and a reactionary Germany, which would not necessarily have indicated any geographical divide. Even if one of the Soviet leaders meant the statement literally, it is important to add that in Pieck's notes, Stalin, in particular, expressed his clear opposition to the division of Germany and indicated that the newly formed KPD should be dedicated to maintaining unity.[23] He stated: "The unity of Germany to be ensured by the unified KPD [,] a unified ZK [Central Committee,] a unified party of labor [and] in the middle point a unified party." Moreover, neither Ackermann's KPD party program, prompted by the June 4 meeting and released on June 11, nor the extensive report of the initiative group leaders to Dimitrov and the International Information Department of the Central Committee on June 7 gave the least hint of dividing Germany into two geographical entities. On the contrary, both documents placed the efforts of the newly formed KPD directly in the center of a new, united, antifascist, democratic Germany, one that would be neither Soviet nor capitalist.

During the June 7 meeting, as might be expected, Dimitrov and Paniushkin of the Central Committee expressed a great deal of interest in the mood of the Germans and the possibilities for their reeducation. Both Ackermann and Ulbricht responded that the most difficult problem was to get the Germans to accept "responsibility for the crimes that were committed by the Hitlerites." Given the way the Germans responded to the problem of war guilt, Ackermann added, one would think that 90 percent of them had been in the resistance.[24] Typically, Ulbricht attacked both the social democrats and communists for their problems in accepting responsibility for the past. According to Ulbricht, socialists protested the Soviet dismantling of German factories with the argument that the new democratic Germany could be trusted to embark on a path of friendship with Russia. Ulbricht reported that he rejected these protests in sharp and uncompromising terms, emphasizing that there was no guarantee that fascism would not rear its ugly head again in Germany.[25] Ulbricht was characteristically much more generous toward the social democrats and the bourgeois politicians than he was toward the "sectarians" and "antifascist committees," because the latter interfered with efficient administration. Ulbricht noted, for example, that getting social democrats and "the Catholics" (former Center Party members) to join local administrations increased the authority of the government institutions and the Red Army. Germany did not need any new experiments or foolishness regarding the socialization of property, he concluded. "Red Front" greetings scared away the average citizens. The primary tasks at the moment were to combine patient work in the local administrations with massive reeducation of the population through the newly formed political parties.[26]

The June 4 meeting with Stalin alerted the Germans to the Soviet plan to consolidate the administrations of the three army fronts and the Seventh Section of GlavPURKKA into a single military government. In Order no. 1 of June 9, 1945, Marshal G. K. Zhukov duly announced the creation of the Soviet Military Administration of Germany (SVAG). At the same time, following up on the Moscow consultations, the Soviets and the KPD leadership disbanded at least 200 antifascist committees from all over the Soviet zone. Like Ulbricht, SVAG was more interested at the moment in administration than in politics. There was a shortage of capable and reliable bureaucrats to occupy positions in town and village government. With their diverse political, educational, and cultural initiatives, the antifascist groups disrupted the flow of personnel into the German administrations. Protests by the antifascist committee members, some KPD activists, and even by some Soviet officers against breaking up the "antifas" were answered with the admonition by Zhukov and Ulbricht that the best of the antifascists should leave the work of politics and ideology to the parties and join the administrations and local governments instead.

The Soviet military government also closed down the antifascist groups because it wanted German leftists to participate in the political life of the parties it was about to legalize. According to Order no. 2 (June 10), antifascist political parties, trade unions, and other professional and social organizations were allowed to carry on activities if they registered with and were found acceptable by SVAG. Many of the German antifascist activists, especially the communists, were taken by surprise by the broad range of political options offered by the Soviets; others, however, were upset and disappointed by their banishment. On June 11, the KPD issued its program, the one written by Ackermann in Moscow; the SPD announced its formation and its program on June 15; and the Christian Democrats (CDU) and the Liberal Democrats (LDP) followed soon after. By setting up the SPD and the nonsocialist parties so quickly, and then joining them in an antifascist bloc, SVAG preempted those communists who advocated the establishment of Soviet power and the crushing of the bourgeoisie. The sectarians found as little sympathy within SVAG as they had among the Moscow KPD leadership. In setting up both the KPD and the SPD, SVAG also indicated that there would be no amalgamated workers' party to seize control of the administrations.[27]

BUCHENWALD AND BRILL

The historian can get closer to understanding the diversity of leftist responses to the Soviet occupation and the creation of political parties by looking at several discrete cases. There were significant variations between them, depending on region and town. The inclinations of the local commandants made a huge difference, especially in the first month of the occupation, but also after the founding of SVAG. And the dynamics of Nazi support during the war and of leftist traditions during the Weimar period also influenced the nature of local politics. Parts of the zone were initially occupied by the Americans and British, and that, too, helped shape subsequent events, as did the initiatives of individual local leaders. Altogether, politics in the Eastern zone were much more diverse than has been assumed by scholars in the former GDR and in the West.

By the end of the Second World War, the concentration camp at Buchenwald had turned into a hotbed of underground politics. The Nazi SS controlled security and dealt with Soviet POWs, Poles, and Jews, but the internal administration of the camp—the clinics, the offices, the stores—was largely in the hands of the politicals, most notably the hundred or so communists and the fifty to sixty social democrats who were active in the camp.[28] The communists in Buchenwald were able to listen to NKFD broadcasts during the war and, partly as a result, they developed a hybrid program of leftist KPD slogans combined with the antifascist democratic rhetoric of the Free Germany movement. In an April 22, 1945, conference shortly after liberation, the Buchenwald KPD called for the formation of a "people's republic," based on antifascist democratic principles. The conference noted that the world bourgeoisie still harbored "imperialist goals," but that it was not yet time to introduce the dictatorship of the proletariat. Instead, the people's republic would be an intermediary stage on the road to socialism in Germany. The Buchenwald KPD's program differed most strikingly from the Moscow-based initiative groups in its uncompromising attitude toward former Nazis, who should, it stated, "be driven out of their hiding places, out of their offices, out of the police, and placed in forced labor for the rebuilding [of Germany]." Flying in the face of Ulbricht's tenets, the program also insisted that all large industries should be nationalized and all power in anti-Nazi Germany should be turned over to the antifascist committees.[29]

During the war, the Buchenwald KPD vacillated between maintaining the traditional attitude toward their SPD brethren—calling them "social fascists" and accusing them of having helped Hitler come to power—and cooperating with them in concrete resistance activities.[30] As the war drew to an end, the KPD and SPD organizations formed a common Action Committee, which played an important role in the actual liberation of the camp, and even before the KPD drew up its Buchenwald resolution, the SPD had met on April 12 to consider the unification of the two parties. Hermann Brill, Benedikt Kautsky, and other SPD leaders convinced the assembled social democrats to abandon the policies of the past and to form a new party, the League of Democratic Socialists. Brill, in particular, was dedicated to updating the teachings of Marx and Engels and to founding a movement that would overcome the destructive hostility between social democrats and communists.[31] Brill's ten-point "Buchenwald Manifesto," of which thousands of copies were printed after liberation, called for the immediate formation of a democratic socialist republic, not terribly different in concept from the people's republic called for by the Buchenwald KPD program of April 22. The capitalist system had been destroyed by the war, Brill claimed, and, as a result, the "accomplishment of socialism was not a matter for the future state, but the immediate task of the present."[32]

After the liberation of the camp, the Buchenwald socialists spread out over Thüringen and the rest of the Eastern zone to engage in the task of rebuilding Germany. But before dispersing, Brill and Kautsky urged all social democrats and communists to give up any idea of forming separate parties and instead to join a "people's front" that would create an antifascist militia, nationalize large industry, and build "a socialist and democratic organization."[33] Brill himself managed to convince the American occupation authorities that his League of Democratic Socialists resembled the British Labor Party and, with his impeccable antifascist record, was made minister-president of Thüringen. Most, though not all, of the KPD veterans denounced Brill's participation in the American-sponsored government and operated underground instead. At one point, American soldiers stormed the United Trade Union building in Weimar and burned the red flags that the communists had hung out the windows. The Americans also refused to allow the communists to hold a May 1 celebration.[34] The situation changed dramatically when the Soviets took over Thüringen by prior agreement at the beginning of July. Committed to establishing the KPD and SPD as separate parties in Thüringen, SVAG ordered Brill to disband the League of Democratic Socialists and its associated antifascist committees. The Soviets then insisted that Brill reconstitute the Thüringen Social Democratic Party and take over as its chairman.

Brill's position was a delicate one. He was thoroughly disliked by most of the communists, who insisted that he be removed as minister-president. Because he had worked for the Americans, the Soviets distrusted him as well.[35] By the middle of July, the Soviets had removed Brill as minister-president, and they began putting pressure on him as head of the SPD to renounce the still influential Buchenwald Manifesto. Lieutenant General I. S. Kolesnichenko, head of the Soviet Military Administration in Thüringen, met with Brill in Weimar on July 24 and virulently attacked his program. Kolesnichenko was especially critical of the manifesto's call for the socialization of the economy. When Brill responded that without nationalization the big landowners and industrialists would use their economic power to finance new fascist groups, Kolesnichenko bristled: "The Occupation Army will see to it that fascism will never rise again." The general also criticized the utopianism of the manifesto's political program, which called for a peaceful transition to a people's democracy through

parliamentary elections. Finally, Kolesnichenko attacked Brill for not being a good social democrat—that is, for ignoring the Berlin Central Executive's policy of building a strong, separate SPD organization while cooperating in the antifascist bloc with the communists. The interview ended
badly; the general was clearly upset with Brill's pretensions to understanding the dynamics of socialism in Germany. This did not bode well for
Brill's future.[36]

Brill did not help his cause when he determinedly resisted the Soviet-
and KPD-inspired campaign for unity with the SPD that began in the fall
of 1945. Brill rallied former Buchenwald veterans, mostly social democrats
but also some communists, to resist local pressures for unity. At a Thüringen SPD meeting in Weimar on November 11, 1945, Brill reportedly
went into a tirade against the Russians: "If you want to know what Soviet
culture is, you just have to look outside your window and see the Ivans
in their filthy uniforms. And *they* want to teach us how to build socialism
in Germany!"[37] With the support of Karlshorst and the encouragement
of the local KPD, Kolesnichenko kept the pressure up on Brill, attacking
him and his policies as stubbornly reactionary. Finally Brill could no
longer hold out. Bullied by Kolesnichenko and threatened with arrest, Brill
fled to the West during a Christmas 1945 trip to Berlin.[38] Brill's "heresy"
was carried on, however, during the resistance in Thüringen to SED policies in 1947 and 1948.

THE MANSFELD REGION

The Soviet occupation authorities were not the only ones who had to cope
with the obstinate independence of the antifascist committees. The Americans and the British also faced conflict with radical circles and programs
in Munich, Cologne, Bremen, and Leipzig, among other large cities. In
the Mansfeld region of Saxony-Anhalt, the KPD had a particularly strong
record of underground activities at the end of the war. One communist-
organized circle called the Antifascist Work Group of Central Germany
(Antifaschistische Arbeitsgruppe Mitteldeutschlands, or AAM) issued a
leaflet in March 1945 demanding that workers form armed groups to stop
the war.[39] Led by the KPD activist Robert Büchner, who had attended the
Comintern's "Lenin school" in the early 1930s, the antifascist movement
in the Mansfeld town of Eisleben was one of the strongest in all of Germany. It was known in GDR hagiography for having hidden away and
preserved during the war a Lenin statue, which had initially been brought

from the Russian front to be melted down.[40] At the end of the war, the AAM was certain that Eisleben and the rest of the district would be occupied by the Soviets. As a result, Büchner and his fellow communists issued leaflets predicting the intensification of the struggle between "reaction and revolution, between imperialism and socialism." The Soviet march into Europe had made possible the great victories of the Greek and Yugoslav revolutions. Now, they thought that the time for revolution in Central Europe had arrived.[41]

The Eisleben communists adjusted quickly, however, to the news of the impending American occupation. Büchner renamed his group the Antifascist Citizens' Committee and formed a police force of 120 antifascist workers to seize control of the Rathaus just as the American forces moved into the town. At the onset of the occupation, the Americans were happy to have Büchner and his committee do their work for them. Büchner was made mayor *(Oberbürgermeister)* and another communist and member of the committee, Otto Gotsche, was appointed *Landrat*. Together they cleaned out the local government of the most obnoxious Nazis and began to restore order in the town. But the Americans soon wearied of the communists' activities, and they showed no interest in having the Lenin statue erected in the center of town, as Büchner and Gotsche had planned.

Büchner, Gotsche, and the antifascist committee also tried to take over Mansfeld AG, the largest manufacturing enterprise in the region, seeking to place the administration of the factory under the city government. Büchner explained in his unpublished memoirs: "We seized control of the factory with the help of our factory councils; our police also conducted house searches in the apartments of the Mansfeld directors. We collected material about the war crime activities of the Mansfeld enterprise bosses and organized a broadly based movement among the population for [their] . . . removal as war criminals."[42] When it became clear that the Americans would leave the region, Büchner, Gotsche, and their committee put up posters forbidding the removal of machines and material, trucks and cars. They organized meetings to convince the local citizenry that Soviet occupation would not produce the horrors predicted by the Nazis. But when local workers refused to help the Americans load up their trucks with expropriated machines and goods, the American authorities had enough of Büchner and Gotsche and removed both of them from their offices for "communist agitation" and "superpatriotism."[43] At this point, the AAM went underground, issued a few leaflets, and prepared for the long hoped-for Soviet occupation. The Americans withdrew from Eisleben on July 2, and the AAM emerged for the second time from the underground. Within a few hours, they had erected the three-ton Lenin statue in the center of town and turned the marketplace into "a sea of red flags."[44]

It took some time for the Eisleben communists to adjust to their new circumstances under the Soviets. In Büchner's view, a new Workers' Party *(Partei der Werktätigen)* should be formed to lead the revolution in Germany. Given antifascist unity in Eisleben, it seemed "greatly surprising," even anachronistic, for the Soviets to insist on the formation of two parties of the Left, one communist and one social democratic.[45] Some of the AAM members expressed great unhappiness with the policies of the Soviet military authorities and the KPD central in Berlin. For example, they wanted to expand the site of the Lenin memorial in town while tearing down the town's Luther statue, but they were forbidden to do so by the Soviets.[46] Even though the Eisleben sectarians continued to be a source of problems during the unity campaign later in the fall, Büchner himself submitted to party discipline and was again made mayor of Eisleben, while other local communists were also convinced by Eisleben's Soviet commandant to abandon their "revolutionary illusions."[47]

MEISSEN

Meissen, the home of the famous porcelain factory, also harbored the most fiercely sectarian communist movement in Saxony. Led by an elderly KPD veteran by the name of Mücke, the local communists had organized four regional party organizations and four communist youth organizations by the time of the liberation. Like their Eisleben comrades, the Meissen communists seized control of the Rathaus before the Soviets entered town. As a result, Mücke was made mayor, and he proceeded to appoint commissars for every branch of civilian administration. As Anton Ackermann reported to the Central Committee in Moscow: "The mayor was the first commissar of the city, his deputy was a commissar for industry—for supplies [there was] a commissar, for trade a commissar, for finances a commissar, for the rebuilding of the destroyed city a commissar, for the socialization of industries a commissar, as head of a factory a commissar. In general, Soviet power in anarchist light [*osveshchenii*]."[48] The communists confiscated one of the nicest buildings in town, named it the Ernst Thälmann House, and made it headquarters of what they called the Communist Party, Unity. They put out nine issues of a party newspaper, *Die Volksstimme,* which advocated the establishment of the "dictatorship of the proletariat." So far as Mücke was concerned, the Meissen communists were beginning the process of establishing a Soviet Germany. All city government measures were countersigned by the party organization. Five-pointed Soviet stars could be seen all over town.

The Meissen communists, at least at the outset, had the complete support of the local Soviet commandant. With the latter's approval, wealthy families were turned out of their apartments and workers' families moved in. Factories that had belonged to Nazis and "Nazi collaborators" were transformed into "socialist property," which usually meant they were placed under the control of party commissars rather than being turned over to local government, which was the case in most of eastern Germany. The distribution of goods followed "the principles of socialist justice." In Meissen, according to General M. I. Burtsev, chief of the Seventh Section of GlavPURKKA, this meant preferential treatment for antifascists as well as a "leveling" *(uravnilovka)* of the sort that took place in the Soviet Union before the early 1930s, when Stalin put a stop to it. Burtsev added that while the Meissen communists were to be commended for exposing Nazis and turning them over to the Soviet authorities, the commissars often went too far, especially when they arrested prominent members of the intelligentsia who had only been minor figures in the Nazi Party.[49]

For nearly a month, then, Meissen had a communist government, which took with utter seriousness all the revolutionary rhetoric about a Soviet Germany and a government of commissars.[50] GlavPURKKA was, however, worried. The Soviet officers understood, of course, that these communists were decent, upright socialists and not "secret Nazi agents," as claimed by some of their opponents. They were deeply concerned, though, that "the people's commissars" were turning the German population against the Soviet occupation. As a result, officers of GlavPURKKA remonstrated with the local commandant and convinced him that he was pursuing incorrect policies. They then arranged for a meeting between Ackermann, Mücke, and thirty of the leading citizens of Meissen, to redirect local politics along the antifascist democratic lines pursued in other parts of eastern Germany. But it was harder to convince Mücke of the incorrectness of his ways than it had been to change the commandant's policies. Ackermann felt that Mücke understood the new communist line; the Meissen commissar simply felt that conciliatory KPD policies were no longer necessary, given the fact that the Soviet army controlled all of eastern Germany. Ackermann described his discussions with Mücke as "difficult and complicated."[51] In his June 7 report to the Central Committee, he summarized the Meissen experience by noting that the communists promised to mend their "sectarian" ways, but he added, as well, that Mücke and others continued to pursue their "old politics"—that is, revolution—behind the backs of the Soviet military authorities.[52] The Seventh Section of GlavPURKKA recommended taking firmer action against the Meissen group; Burtsev suggested that they not be allowed to form any political parties or groups until they were completely freed "from deeply engrained and dangerous sectarianism, until they are convinced of the correctness of our policies."[53]

Needless to say, the Communist Party, Unity was closed down. The Ernst Thälmann House disappeared from Meissen, as did the Soviet star as a German communist symbol. *Die Volksstimme* ceased publishing, and city government returned to regular administrative procedures. The Meissen revolution was brought to an end by the Soviet occupation power. General I. V. Shikin, commanding officer of GlavPURKKA, succinctly summarized the Soviet action in a letter to G. Aleksandrov, head of Agitprop at the Central Committee: "Responsible officials of the political administration [GlavPURKKA] went to the place [Meissen] and disbanded all party and communist youth organizations in the city, shut down the newspaper, and formed a city administration on the same principles as are followed by the municipal governments in all the cities of Germany occupied by units of the Red Army."[54]

SCHWARZENBERG

One of the most fascinating cases of antifascist activity in postwar Germany took place in the district of Schwarzenberg in the western Erzgebirge, near the border of Czechoslovakia.[55] Known for the uranium mines that the Soviets developed in the area, the region *(Landkreis)* of Schwarzenberg—including the districts of Aue, Schneeberg, Schwarzenberg, and Johanngeorgenstadt—experienced only partial occupation from the third week of April 1945, when the Americans appeared briefly at various points in the region, to mid-May, when they withdrew completely to the west bank of the Mulde River near Zwickau. From the middle of May to June 21, when the Soviets began their occupation of the region, this relatively large mountainous area, containing seventeen towns and cities and about eighty villages with a total population of more than 250,000, was not occupied by any of the victorious powers. For reasons that are still not clear, the Soviet commandant in Chemnitz (Karl Marx Stadt during the

GDR period) appeared unaware that the region fell into the Soviet territory of Saxony by prior Allied agreement.[56] The Americans showed some interest in occupying the city of Aue, but withdrew on May 9. As a result, even after Germany's unconditional surrender, a number of Nazi and SS groups continued to operate in the mountains. Martin Mutschmann, former gauleiter of Saxony, hid out in hunting cabins until he was seized by armed antifascist police on May 16.[57] In fact, antifascist groups took over the entire region during the seven-week period in which there was no occupation.

Anton Ackermann reported to Moscow that the antifascist committees of Schwarzenberg were dominated by "progressive workers" from the socialist parties, but that they appropriately accepted "petit-bourgeois elements" from the towns, including intelligentsia and artisans.[58] In Stollberg district, which included the towns of Stollberg, Zwönitz, and Thalheim, the antifascist committees had sixty-seven members during the war, nineteen of whom had belonged to the KPD before 1933, twenty-five to the SPD, and twenty-three to no particular party.[59] In Meinersdorf on May 9, an armed antifascist group, comprising primarily workers, seized the Rathaus and arrested the Nazi mayor and other functionaries. In Schwarzenberg, the antifascist committee decided to take over the police force first, and on May 12 it drove off the Nazi mayor with an armed detachment of twelve workers.[60] The Schwarzenberg antifascist committee appointed a new mayor, the communist Willy Irmisch, and formed an Action Committee to take care of the most important tasks of the moment—most significantly, seizing control of the supplies and the distribution of food and goods.

Generally, communists and social democrats cooperated well and joined forces effortlessly, though in some towns, such as Johanngeorgenstadt, the social democrats refused to let communists join the local administration.[61] In Auerbach, Gablenz, Hormersdorf, and Jahnsdorf, there were social democratic mayors; in Leukersdorf, Lugau, Meinersdorf, Oelsnitz, and Thalheim, communists occupied the head positions.[62] In Stollberg district, an antifascist organization called the Notgemeinschaft (Emergency Organization) devoted much of its energy to trying to alleviate what the mayor of Stollberg called a "catastrophic" food situation.[63] Thousands of miners in the region participated in electing representatives to factory councils, which in turn simply took over the two largest mines, those called Germany and God's Blessing. By May 9 and 10, they had the mines working again. The Schwarzenberg region "antifa" consisted of some six thousand dues-paying members; in the town of Schwarzenberg alone, some six hundred members were divided into local committees that met regularly and held broad-ranging public discussions about the crimes of the Nazi regime and the horrors of the concentration camps.[64]

In his novel *Schwarzenberg,* in which Stefan Heym paints a romantic picture of antifascist activity in the Erzgebirge, he appends a fictionalized "Constitution" that ostensibly unites progressive Germans in a socialist democracy. There was no such constitution in reality, and the citizens of the region needed the help of the neighboring occupying powers to control the Nazi bandits in the mountains and to ensure food supplies. Local churchmen turned to the Americans in the hope that they would occupy the region. In Annaberg, the communists sought aid and advice from the Soviets in dealing with the problems of food procurement and security. Still, it is worth underscoring the fact that Germans were able to throw the Nazis out of local government on their own and to reconstitute administration and society on an antifascist and democratic basis. They published newspapers, held meetings, took control of factories and public works, and reopened schools and churches—all without Allied guidance. There was relatively little sectarianism or exclusionary policy on the part of the antifascist committees. Of course, when the Soviets marched into the region at the end of June, everything changed. But it is interesting to note that the Schwarzenberg experience continued to have an impact on the region. The antifascists expressed their displeasure at being forced to divide into individual parties.[65] In the first year of the Soviet occupation of Schwarzenberg, the communists dominated politics, as they did in most of the Eastern zone.[66] But by the fall of 1946, politics became moot with the discovery of uranium. Schwarzenberg, cordoned off by NKVD/MVD troops, became unrecognizable, though its experiment with antifascism became part of the mythology of democratic socialist resistance in the GDR.

BERLIN

The former capital of the Third Reich was the scene of a wide variety of KPD and antifascist responses at the end of the war. Especially for the first few weeks he was in Berlin, Ulbricht continuously fulminated against the ultraradicals and sectarians whom he estimated made up the majority of the five thousand or so pre-1933 KPD members still active in the city. "The committees, the commissars, and so on" annoyed him endlessly, with their red armbands and their red-painted automobiles, which were also adorned with hammers and sickles and red stars. The newly liberated communists established KPD offices and hung out red flags and KPD signs. Some were armed; many were ready to set up revolutionary barricades to defend the revolution against the bourgeoisie.[67]

The ultraleftists set up the International Militia in Spandau, the Workers' and Soldiers' Soviet in Wittenau, and the Wilmersdorf International Communist Party. In Charlottenburg, the KPD bureau called for the immediate establishment of Soviet power in Berlin. In Kreuzberg, the sectarian Left joined with the NKFD antifascist committee to begin the process of rebuilding the infrastructure of the district.[68] In Neukölln, many communists refused to leave the underground until the beginning of the revolution. Their KPD chairman, Gertrud Rosenmeyer, later recalled that "a great majority of our comrades thought that the destruction of fascism would bring socialism . . . Not even the regular cadres understood at the beginning the orientation of the party [the KPD] regarding the completion of the bourgeois-democratic revolution, the construction of an antifascist democratic order, and cooperation with bourgeois forces." When Ulbricht approached them to give up their socialist activities, abandon their intentions to construct a Soviet Germany, and join the local government, many communists refused, arguing, "We don't want to be bosses."[69] But Ulbricht was uncompromising. He wrote to Dimitrov on May 9 that he had closed down their communist bureaus, removed their signs and flags, and "made it clear to the comrades that all energy must be concentrated in the city administration."[70]

Wolfgang Leonhard, one of the original members of Ulbricht's initiative group, described a different variety of antifascist activity in his memoirs. Soon after arriving in Berlin with Ulbricht in early May, Leonhard visited an antifascist committee that had established its headquarters on the Kurfürstendamm in Berlin-Charlottenburg. Under the banner of the NKFD, whose broadcasts they had listened to in the last days of the war, Charlottenburg antifascists from a variety of parties and backgrounds had helped the Soviet troops take control of the city, organizing food and health services as well as rebuilding housing and sanitation facilities. But the Kurfürstendamm committee was no more acceptable to Ulbricht than were the KPD radicals, and he ordered Leonhard to close it down. Leonhard hesitated, but to no avail. Ulbricht insisted that the antifascist committees were nothing more than cover organizations to frustrate the development of real democracy in Germany. In any case, Ulbricht told Leonhard, "We cannot allow errors of the Greek Party to be repeated here in Berlin. In Greece, members of the party collaborate in committees like these while their enemies set about establishing control of the government."[71] Ulbricht vented his frustration with the committees in a May 9 letter to Dimitrov: "I've had just about enough of fooling around with these antifas."[72]

In the end, Ulbricht and the Soviet administration closed down the antifascist committees and the KPD bureaus because they could not control them. The Stalinist distrust of spontaneous institutions permeated SVAG's attitude toward these relatively free-floating leftist committees. The NKFD had called for the formation of antifascist committees to ease the entry of the Red Army into the towns and villages of Germany and to prevent the looting of factories, the mining of bridges, and the senseless and bloody resistance of young boys and old men in militia detachments. So far as the Soviets were concerned, these tasks were no longer relevant. From Ulbricht's point of view, the sooner the sectarian KPD of the Weimar period was renewed with an influx of new, more pliable young Germans, the better.[73] It was time to get on with the job of rebuilding Germany on SVAG's orders. In some cases, antifascist committees had chased off bourgeois specialists whom the Soviets wanted reinstated in the factories. Sectarian workers' committees had expelled from the factories valuable skilled workers because they had been Nazis.[74]

Ulbricht had much less control over this activity than either he would have liked or the Soviets would have wanted. On the one hand, Ulbricht bragged to Dimitrov that he had told German communists in no uncertain terms that they would have to give up their dreams of a Soviet Germany.[75] On the other hand, Soviet reports from the spring and early summer of 1945 were critical of Ulbricht for not being able to communicate the new Soviet line to the KPD subgroups and antifascist committees. They also took him to task for not communicating with the local commandants; even the "security organs" were unaware of his activities, they complained.[76] But the real problem was not Ulbricht. It was the fact that tens of thousands of active leftists who had survived the Nazi dictatorship had different needs, pursued different goals, and used different methods than the Soviet occupiers and their Moscow German friends.

UNITY OF ACTION

Soviet and East German historical literature notes with great satisfaction that by issuing Order no. 2, the Soviets became the first of the Allied occupiers to allow political activity in their zone. But for large numbers of German antifascists, the beginning of the political parties and the operation of the antifascist democratic bloc meant the end of active politics. For instance, substantial numbers of former KPD and SPD activists who had joined Brill's League of Democratic Socialists in Thüringen refused to enter the reconstituted political parties after the league's banishment, convinced that these were a lower form of socialist development. Many of Rosenmeyer's Neukölln comrades refused to join the reconstituted KPD because they considered its program a step backward from the prewar program. East German memoir literature by "activists of the first hour" underlines the fact that the first months of liberation and occupation, April through June, were the most exciting and fruitful periods in these SED veterans' political lives.[77] Order no. 2 did not simply create political parties; it gave the Soviets the opportunity to monitor, check, and control all political activities in their zone of occupation. Very quickly, the excitement and the initiatives of the first weeks after liberation faded into the mandates of bureaucratic politics.

In disbanding the antifascist committees and KPD bureaus, the Soviets counted on the centralized socialist and bourgeois parties' joining in a single bloc to redirect the political energies of the German people. Mass organizations—such as the Free German Federation of Unions (FDGB), the Free German Youth (FDJ), and the Democratic Womens' Association (DFG)—also played an important role in bloc politics and were used by the Soviets to channel and control political activity in their zone. Certainly within the antifascist bloc, SVAG made every effort to support the KPD and its recruitment campaigns, publication efforts, and attempts to control the local administrations. But at the same time, Soviet commandants carefully nurtured the other parties and involved them in local government. They aided the SPD, in particular, more scrupulously than the KPD would have liked, creating the impression among some social-democratic leaders that the Soviets actually preferred working with SPD politicians. For example, KPD activists in Kotzsche (Saxony) tried to bully the town's SPD by arresting and imprisoning the local SPD leader. When the Soviet commandant learned of these events, he released the social democrat from detention and turned over the town's administration to him and his comrades, much to the chagrin of the communists.[78]

SVAG had specific goals in mind with this temporary support of the SPD. First, it wanted to dissuade social democrats from pursuing their immediate postwar desire of forming a united party of the Left. Second, the Soviets looked to temper the SPD's radical social program. At least on paper, the SPD was by far the more extreme of the two socialist parties, calling for the immediate nationalization of industry and the land, a strategy markedly different from that of the communists. The SPD slogan was, "Democracy in the state and the governments, socialism in the economy and society."[79] The KPD program of June 11, on the other hand, did not mention Marxism, much less Leninism, and talked exclusively about the need to complete the bourgeois revolution of 1848. As a result, while the SPD advocated turning over expropriated land in Saxony to the state, the communists followed the SVAG policy of turning over land to small and landless farmers.

From the Soviet point of view, neither the communists nor the social democrats were ready for political unity. Not only were the social democrats too strong, but their politics were also too uncertain for SVAG's purposes.[80] If a socialist unity party were to be formed, then SVAG wanted a more compliant and predictable SPD as one of its partners. For the moment, the Soviets rejected those proposals from within both the SPD and KPD for immediate unity and encouraged instead the platform of "unity of action." Formally, this SPD-KPD alliance was intended to develop the ability of the two parties to work together. But for the Soviets, it was more important that the "unity of action" help establish discipline in the SPD and bring it into conformity with Soviet ideas of social democratic politics. In addition, by reconstituting the SPD in the East, the Soviets could test the SPD's relationship to Kurt Schumacher, the emerging leader of social democracy in the West, who was already proving to be an obstinate foe of the Soviets and their occupation policies.

Despite these Soviet policies, both social democrats and communists continued to pursue their own ideas of united socialist politics. Left-wing SPD members protested the creation of the two parties and signed petitions urging the building of a single powerful workers' party.[81] Similarly, KPD members often did not understand the need for two parties. Sometimes they suggested simply absorbing the SPD into the KPD, which had actually taken place in a number of localities; in some cases, they just refused to let the SPD form at all.[82] In Forst (Brandenburg), 200 SPD members and 200 KPD members signed a resolution of the "United Socialist Parties" that read, "There is nothing more in the way of our political goals or our strategic paths that can separate us. We have now only one goal, that is true democracy of the German people under the leadership of the united working class."[83] Hermann Matern noted how difficult it was to convince his Saxon comrades that two parties were necessary:

"Why two parties?" they often asked him. "This is all nonsense—from the beginning [we should have] one party!"[84]

A number of scholars have suggested that SVAG's primary motivation for delaying unification was its desire to strengthen the KPD in size and ideological quality before allowing its merger with the SPD.[85] In fact, in the first months after the Nazi capitulation, the KPD grew at an extraordinary pace, in part due to Soviet encouragement but also in part due to the persistence of the KPD leadership and the Germans' attraction to the conciliatory KPD program. From approximately 100,000 members in 1932 in what was to be the territory of the Soviet zone, the KPD grew to 150,000 members at the end of August 1945 and to 375,000 in December 1945. The SPD had some 375,000 members at the end of August 1945 in the East, and 681,000 by March 1946, roughly duplicating its 1932 membership of 581,000 in what was to be the territory of the Soviet zone.[86] Large numbers of left-wing SPD members also joined the KPD out of a spontaneous desire for unity, though where possible the Soviets and Ulbricht tried to discourage this, even to the point of insisting that former SPD members rejoin their SPD comrades in their own party.

The fact remains, in any case, that the KPD could take great satisfaction in its new status as a mass political party, even if the ideological level of the new recruits remained questionable. Most of the new members of the KPD were workers with non-Nazi backgrounds, recruited initially by SVAG and the KPD leadership to take leading positions in the administrations and local governments, as well as to assume important new posts as people's judges, police officers, and schoolteachers. Many of them were exuberant, hard working, and dedicated to the new Germany. Some KPD reports indicate that the recruits were useful to the party for outflanking the numerous inflexible sectarians from the pre-1933 party. But other reports suggest that the new recruits created more problems than they solved. There were too many dishonest "adventurers," admitted Franz Dahlem, including "criminals [and] lawbreakers." Hermann Matern put the problem even more strongly: "Many dirty elements have placed themselves at the head of our ranks."[87]

Still, the KPD leadership complained much more about continuing sectarian tendencies in the party than about problems with careerists and criminals. Primary among these tendencies was the idea that socialism was imminent and that the Red Army guaranteed its establishment in Germany. Talking to a group of former Breslau antifascists in Dresden at the end of July 1945, Hermann Matern expressed the frustration of the

KPD leaders on this issue: "To talk of the dictatorship of the proletariat today is utterly absurd and anyone who comes to us with such nonsense has either not understood the situation or is an enemy. I think that we understand each other. It is imperative that one says this in such a hard and sober way, because we live in hard times."[88] Maria Rentmeister, a leading KPD women's activist, reported that in mid-July in Halle many party members had not even bothered to read the June 11 KPD program, believing it to be nothing but a smokescreen; instead, she said, "sectarian tendencies were everywhere."[89] In Weimar, Georg Schneider tried to rein in the KPD leftists by arguing that they were only helping the fascists with their communist extremism: "Every word about socialization in Germany is [pure] radicalism, is . . . petit-bourgeois chatter."[90] Berlin remained a severe problem in this regard, where report after report on local KPD groups spoke of the ubiquitous "sectarians." In Wedding and a number of other "red" districts, the KPD leaders could think of no other solution to the dominance of the sectarians than changing the local leadership.[91]

In addition to continuing to bring up the problems of rape and dismantling—subjects that drove the leadership to distraction—the KPD "ultraradicals" simply did not accept the party's line on how to deal with former Nazis. The KPD leadership advocated working with the "small Nazis," the so-called Pgs (nominal party members), while at the same time strenuously insisting that the entire German nation was responsible for the Nazi crimes. The issue of general German guilt was often met with "icy silence" by KPD audiences, especially KPD workers, while attacks on Nazis, all Nazis, roused great enthusiasm.[92] In Bernau, the local party group cut rations to former Nazis, demanding that they "should work more and eat less." In Oranienburg, former Nazis and even family members of former Nazis were not allowed to stay in their houses and apartments.[93] The Soviet political officers noted, however, that the KPD leadership was getting nowhere with the issue of general German guilt and recommended that the KPD follow the successful example of the SPD and worry more about the future instead of dwelling on the past.[94]

The SED

The story of the eventual unification of the SPD and KPD into the Socialist Unity Party (SED) has been told often enough and well enough to require only the briefest recounting here.[95] By the early fall of 1945, it became clear to the German communists and to the Soviets that the strengthening of the KPD had not given it a dominant place in society. On the contrary, the KPD leaders were increasingly seen as bullies and stooges whom the Soviet authorities manipulated for their own ends. The radicals in the KPD—the "Radikalinskis," as one report called them—had thoroughly alienated the SPD rank and file by repeatedly violating the principles of the antifascist bloc, arrogating to themselves the best jobs, not to mention superior rations, cars, and apartments.[96]

Neither the KPD in the Western zones nor the SPD in the Soviet zone was able to counter the growing influence of Kurt Schumacher on the development of German social democracy. In elections in Hungary (November 4) and in Austria (November 25), the communists did very poorly, demonstrating the vulnerability of Central European communist parties and their growing isolation from the interests of the masses of workers and farmers. Colonel Sergei Tiul'panov, chief of the Propaganda (later, Information) Administration of SVAG, said that he understood in the fall of 1945 that the KPD could not win at the polls alone, and therefore he devised the strategy of unification between the KPD and the SPD as a way to win an eventual election in Germany.[97] Pieck felt the same way. It was crucial in any election, he noted, that "the two parties not stand against each other but rather with each other in a common electoral program."[98]

The West German scholar Hermann Weber argues that cadre problems also encouraged the KPD to seek immediate unification with the social democrats. The KPD, he suggests, found itself short of experienced and capable working-class activists to fill the administrations, local governments, and economic institutions of the zone; the new recruits from the cities and villages simply had too little education and administrative experience to carry out the required tasks. At the same time, the SPD enjoyed much more continuity with prewar labor organizations and represented a valuable source of administrative talent for the KPD leadership.[99] But the main impetus toward unity was the Soviet desire (and Ulbricht's, as well) to crush the SPD as an active force in the politics of the Eastern zone. By the end of 1945, the SPD represented the most serious domestic threat to Soviet control of the zone. Political officers of SVAG—despite early "comradely" relations with SPD leaders—never lost their deeply held prejudices against the German SPD. Perhaps even more important, Schumacher's intransigent and bellicose anti-Soviet socialism posed a particularly sharp threat to Soviet authority in Germany. From SVAG's point of view, the longer the Soviets remained in Germany, the greater the danger that the SPD would pursue an anti-Russian program.

During the early fall of 1945, the first indications that SVAG and the KPD were considering unification of the two parties came from speeches made by Ulbricht and Pieck. In the long-term perspective, they argued, the "unity of the working class"—that is, the joining of the KPD and the SPD—would serve the cause of the "antifascist democratic transformation." It would also conform to developing ideas of the "German road to socialism," which had been broached by the KPD in its June 11 program (this was more fully articulated in the famous February 1946 article in *Einheit* by Anton Ackermann). The problem was that while the KPD (and SVAG) became increasingly convinced of the necessity of unity, Otto Grotewohl and the other leaders of the Central Executive of the SPD grew increasingly wary.

In mid-September 1945, Grotewohl stated that the "preconditions" for unity of the socialist parties were not yet present; by November, the SPD leader appeared to be even more hesitant.[100] "One day," when the problems and tensions between the two parties were overcome, he stated, a unified working-class movement could be created. Only when "the last and simplest class comrade" understood the need for unity could it be accomplished.[101] At the end of November, Grotewohl gave a speech in Dessau that was decidedly lukewarm about unity. Altogether, Grotewohl's behavior in the fall of 1945 concerned the Soviets greatly; it was increasingly apparent to them that the SPD leadership was dragging its heals on unification.[102] Also, for Grotewohl, Schumacher's unequivocal opposition to the new joint party meant that the chances for a four-zone approach to German politics were in jeopardy. As the strength and prestige of the SPD grew in the East, its leaders became more and more concerned about losing their advantages by filing joint electoral lists. And, as Pieck pointed out, the SPD also did not want to merge with the KPD because then the social democrats, too, would be held responsible for the many "unpleasantries" of the Soviet occupation, in particular at this point, the continuing dismantling and removal of goods from Germany.[103] The case against unification was also made by senior KPD members, who had participated in the struggles of the pre-1933 period and questioned the wisdom of joining with their former enemies.

By the beginning of December 1945, SVAG increased the pressure on the SPD Central Executive to speed up the unification process. At the local level, officers from the regional branches of the Propaganda Administration met constantly with SPD groups, urging them to demonstrate to Berlin their wish for unity. (It should be clear that there was still considerable sentiment among the SPD and KPD in the provinces for the kind of unified party of the Left that was championed by the antifascist committees.) At the same time, Marshal Zhukov, General Bokov, and Colonel Tiul'panov worked hard to align the leaders of the SPD, especially Grotewohl, on the side of the unity campaign. Tiul'panov entertained and flattered the SPD leader. Grotewohl was a serious amateur sketch artist and painter, and Bokov indulged him with art books and paint supplies.[104] Zhukov helped get Grotewohl's son, Hans Günter Grotewohl, out of a British POW camp, for which Grotewohl was deeply grateful.[105] But this kind of solicitude on the part of the Soviet authorities did not alleviate growing suspicions among the SPD that the KPD was not capable of engaging in a genuine merger. Erich Gniffke documented a series of KPD violations of previous agreements to work together.[106] Grotewohl himself noted that SPD members might simply refuse to join a unified party, even if the Central Executive agreed to terms: "The fault lies with the deep bitterness that the Communist Party has fostered in our ranks over the last six months through the repeated uncomradely attitude toward lower officials, through the pressure exerted [on the SPD members], and through the one-sided preferential treatment of the Communist Party by the officials of the Soviet Military Administration."[107]

Given the increasing pressure for unity from the KPD and from SVAG, Grotewohl, Gniffke, Max Fechner, and the other leaders of the Central Executive agreed to meet with KPD leaders at the so-called Conference of Sixty (thirty from the SPD and thirty from the KPD) on December 20 and 21, 1945. At the conference, the SPD leadership restated its position that no union should take place without the participation of parties from all the zones of occupation in Germany. Grotewohl expressed the fear that unity might add to the threat of the division of Germany. Further, the SPD representatives complained to their KPD interlocuters about the inequality of their treatment by the Soviet commandants and about the KPD control of many local administrations.[108] But once the SPD had had a chance to air its complaints and receive assurances from the KPD that these transgressions would not occur in a unified party, the party appeared to concede to the plan for unity by accepting—to the surprise of Pieck—the KPD's version of a final resolution.[109] In fact, as soon as the meeting was over, the KPD leaders sent Lotte Ulbricht to Moscow with materials to prepare for a late January or early February meeting with the Soviet leadership, to review the details of the unification program.

Attempts to attract the Central Executive to the benefits of unity coincided with an apparent order from SVAG headquarters in Karlshorst for local commandants throughout the Soviet zone to begin the actual unification campaign. At this point, as Tiul'panov put it, "a tenacious struggle emerged with the enemies of unity throughout the Soviet zone of occupation."[110] Soviet officers pressured local SPD politicians to begin the process of unification at the local level and to insist that their Central Executive in Berlin do the same. Lieutenant Colonel A. Vatnik, who was in charge of the Propaganda Administration in Saxony, wrote to Tiul'panov in mid-January that it was necessary to begin "open struggle" against those "right-wing" SPD members who resisted unification.[111] Some prominent SPD politicians, such as Friedrich Ebert of Brandenburg, who were notably unsympathetic to unity, were browbeaten and tongue-lashed by local Soviet officers, who then closely monitored their activities. Some social democrats who openly resisted unification, like Brethorst of Leipzig, were turned over to Russian military tribunals for a variety of crimes allegedly committed against the occupation administration.[112] In Thüringen, General Kolesnichenko attempted to speed up the merger in mid-January 1946. He summoned August Fröhlich of the SPD and KPD district leader Werner Eggerath to his office and told them it was high time that the parties unified. Even if the Central Executive was not ready for the merger, the local parties, Kolesnichenko noted, should lead by example. Fröhlich reported that the general had insisted that unity "should come from below, where it is ripe, that is where there is the least hesitation. One should begin with the factories; joint [SPD and KPD] assemblies of workers should elect a united leadership."[113] Kolesnichenko's vigorous involvement in the unity process paid dividends; Thüringen was the first province in the Soviet zone to announce the union of the two parties, on April 6, 1946.

Soviet pressure on local SPD organizations sometimes amounted to outright intimidation and threats. Cases were reported of SPD leaders' being arrested and sent to prison as counterrevolutionaries for resisting the unity campaign. Usually, however, it was enough to threaten SPD functionaries with the loss of their administrative or party posts, which would mean the reduction of their rations and the loss of other privileges. A February 1, 1946, report from the Magdeburg district SPD to the Central Executive complained about SVAG's interference in the SPD's successful election campaign in the trade unions: "They don't even shrink from threats and arrests. Two of our most qualified functionaries were taken off by order of the SVA to Magdeburg, so that they would not appear at the conference. In addition, our party secretaries are subject to constant surveillance, and every speech is written down by stenographers and sent off to General Kotikov in Halle."[114] Even the KPD's Wilhelm Pieck admitted at the second Conference of Sixty, in February 1946, that the Soviets had pressured local SPD politicians. But he claimed that the KPD leaders intervened on behalf of their social democratic comrades:

> Much has been made of the fact that here in the Soviet zone the process of union has been preceded by a campaign of force and pressure carried out by the Soviet occupation authorities. Comrades, in general one doesn't need in the least to regret this fact, if as a result the unity of the working class is accomplished, so that one can firmly hold the reins in hand on the reaction . . . But, comrades, I tell you with complete candor: Where we heard that overzealous commandants have tried to speed up the understanding between the two parties through any kind of special influence, we protested to the supreme military government with absolute decisiveness, because we understood that the interference of the military commandants was completely unnecessary.[115]

The speech by Pieck made it clear that Western complaints of a "forced union" (*Zwangsvereinigung*) had some basis in fact. At the same time, as a number of German historians have pointed out, it would be a mistake to assume from this that there was no sympathy, especially at the local level, for the union of the two parties.[116]

To accomplish the merger of the KPD and the SPD, SVAG used persuasion as well as coercion. In his memoirs, Erich Gniffke asserts that Marshal Zhukov went so far as to assure Grotewohl that the military authorities would remove Ulbricht from the KPD leadership to smooth the SPD's entrance into the new party. Gniffke added that others besides the members of the SPD Central Executive would have been pleased by Ulbricht's political demise. Numerous KPD leaders, among them Franz Dahlem and Anton Ackermann, resented Ulbricht's increasing control of the administrative apparatus, as well as his tendency to present the KPD party leadership with accomplished facts rather than political options.[117] Yet Ulbricht had powerful allies in the occupation government and presumably in Moscow as well. Colonel Tiul'panov, who can be considered one of them, repeatedly visited Central Executive members to coddle, bully, and tempt them into the union. In late January 1946, he informed the group as a whole that they must make a decision immediately; Karlshorst would not tolerate further delay. Roughly at the same time, Zhukov seemingly lost any remaining confidence in achieving a short-term solution for the unity of Germany with the "parliamentary democratic republic" that he reportedly favored. As a result, in Zhukov's last interview with Grotewohl at the beginning of February 1945, he told the SPD leader to go ahead and unite with the communists and that SVAG would see to it that conditions in the Soviet zone would improve and that Soviet troop levels would even be reduced.[118] At the same time, Zhukov let Grotewohl know that he had little choice. Tiul'panov wrote: "I remember how he [Grotewohl] hesitated, before he arrived [at the decision to unify.] I remember up to the last conversation with the marshal [Zhukov], when there was only he and no one else, and the marshal directly put the question—whether you like it or not, this is the political situation."[119]

Grotewohl's role in the SPD's final decision to unite with the KPD is a matter of considerable historical speculation. There is simply not enough evidence to explain with complete assurance why he shifted from rejecting the immediate need for (if not the principle of) unity in December 1945 to insisting in February 1946 that the Central Executive vote for unity. Certainly Grotewohl had grown fond of his privileged position in the Soviet zone, and he understood that it would only get better if he joined the unity movement. But he also felt the pressure from the local organizations, and he sensed that the SPD faced a genuine dilemma. Meetings with Schumacher had produced no agreement with the SPD in the West and no commitment from the Western comrades to aid the Central Executive in its struggle to remain independent. Schumacher rejected Grotewohl's idea that Russian security interests would be fully satisfied by a strong German social democratic regime.[120] During his visit to Berlin in February 1946, Schumacher ridiculed Grotewohl and his comrades for cooperating in any way with the Soviets, especially in a unity campaign, leaving Grotewohl no alternative but to support the unity campaign or join the Western SPD.[121] Isolated from the SPD in the West, Grotewohl must have worried that the Eastern SPD would become isolated as well from politics in the Soviet zone. As a result he argued, as did the SPD committee in Chemnitz, that to resist Soviet demands for unity would mean giving up any further influence on the political development of the zone: "Therefore there is nothing else for the SPD to do than to seize the initiative."[122] In reading Gustav Klingelhöfer's reasoned argument that the SPD should unify with the KPD only if it were done on an all-German basis, Grotewohl noted in the margins that this would mean putting unity off forever.[123] Gniffke reported from his travels around the provinces:

"Everywhere I heard the same thing: Conclude a unity resolution in the Central [Executive]; otherwise we'll do it ourselves on the spot. We want finally to be left in peace. [*Wir wollen endlich Ruhe haben*]."[124]

On February 11, 1946, the Central Executive endorsed unity by a vote of eight to three; the chairmen of the five provincial organizations affirmed the Central Executive's decision. The Soviets prevented attempts by some SPD leaders to hold referenda on the unification question in various areas of the Eastern zone. But in Berlin, the problem of preventing a referendum was complicated by the existence of the three other sectors run by the Western powers. In addition, both the KPD leadership and Grotewohl had overestimated the support for unity among the SPD rank and file. The Soviets were furious when Pieck gave his approval for a Berlin referendum without consulting SVAG beforehand. The KPD and SPD could not very well come out *against* a referendum, so they devised a strategy whereby the parties would agree at their March 5 joint meeting to endorse a referendum to be held on March 31—with no intention, however, of actually holding it. The idea was, in the meantime, to call a city-wide SPD conference on February 21, at which a resolution for unity would be adopted, thus mooting the need for the referendum.[125] To ensure that the SPD would vote for unity and to avoid fulfilling the promise of a referendum, Ulbricht interceded with the Soviet Central Committee to take some action to halt the dismantling and to relieve the Germans' distress about unaccounted-for POWs.[126] But all of this maneuvering did not prevent the February 21 meeting from calling for a referendum in those districts of Berlin that asked for one. In East Berlin, the Soviets in the end resorted to force, closing down the voting stations half an hour after the polls had opened. But in West Berlin, the referendum was held. With the majority of SPD members voting, 2,937 (12 percent) voted for unification; 19,526 (82 percent) voted against. Equally suggestive was the polling that demonstrated the continued strength of the sentiment among SPD members for unified activities. To the question of whether SPD members favored "an alliance [between the SPD and KPD] which will guarantee cooperation and exclude fraternal strife" 14,883 (62 percent) voted yes and 5,559 (23 percent) voted no.[127]

Even before the Berlin vote, the decision had been made in Moscow to form a unity party; the KPD and SPD leadership in the East concurred. Ulbricht reported back to his comrades from the Moscow meeting of February 6 that "there's agreement on unification—the line is correct . . .

Socialist Unity Party Germany." Ulbricht also emphasized that the program of the new unity party would be different from that of the Soviet party—"on the democ[ratic] road to workers' power, not dictatorship."[128]

Despite Ulbricht's optimism, the Socialist Unity Party was born with serious defects. Not only did it preempt developments in the West and therefore undermine, as many predicted, any program for the unity of Germany, but it also created an enormous problem in Berlin. The majority of the Berlin SPD did not join the SED, which the Soviets understood would be a serious problem for the party. The Soviets were annoyed, as well, that some 10 percent of Berlin's KPD—even in the traditionally communist districts of Wedding and Neukölln—did not join the SED, complaining that the new party was deviationist and "opportunistic."[129]

The actual unification congress of the new Socialist Unity Party was held in Berlin on April 21 and 22, 1946, amid great celebration and hope. The new party cochairmen—Wilhelm Pieck from the KPD and Otto Grotewohl from the SPD—dramatically strode to the center of the stage and shook hands to mark the compromise between the two parties. The union joined some 600,000 communists and 680,000 social democrats in what would clearly be the most powerful and influential political party in the Soviet zone. The program of the new SED reflected both Moscow's insistence on a gradual transition and the KPD's efforts to develop a peaceful and democratic "German road to socialism": "The Socialist Unity Party of Germany fights as an independent party in its country for the true national interests of its people. As the German socialist party, it represents the most progressive and best national forces."[130]

No doubt many KPD members took this national, democratic rhetoric seriously. After all, SVAG and the KPD leadership had spent the better part of a year disabusing the KPD rank and file of the not uncommon idea of establishing a Soviet republic in Germany. Still, the leading cadres of the KPD, along with the political leadership of SVAG, Sokolovskii and Tiul'panov, thought of the creation of the SED as a continuation of the KPD. While the SED formally announced that it was a Marxist party, Ulbricht, Pieck, Matern, Bernard Koenen, and others did not give up their adherence to Leninism or their dedication to the Soviet style of government. Even their Soviet "friends" gently chided the former KPD chiefs for continuing to meet separately from the former SPD leaders, and for talking and thinking about the SED's history in terms of the KPD.[131] This division was felt on the level of everyday activities as well. The situation in Schwerin, described by one SED member, was probably not atypical: "The SPD and KPD live under one roof—in a legal marriage, but inside [the house] they prefer to live separately."[132]

THE SOVIETS AND THE SED

Despite protests to the contrary, Soviet sponsorship of the SED meant that the German party would have a distinctly Russian tint. Fresh from victory in a war of stupendous proportions, Soviet communists were supremely confident, at least on the surface, about the way they did things at home. By force of habit as well as conviction, Soviet political officers encouraged their charges in the fledgling SED to follow similar patterns of organization and behavior. They were the schoolmasters of the SED, and the headmaster, Colonel Sergei Tiul'panov, set the tone for the development of the new party. It is important to understand, above all, that unlike Semenov and some comrades in Moscow, Tiul'panov expressed considerable unease about the SED's attempts to pose as a national German party. For Tiul'panov, all the SED's talk about "special German culture" and "special paths to socialism" smelled of creeping nationalism and a lack of appreciation for the teachings of Lenin and Stalin. Tiul'panov warned of "very severe inadequacies" in the SED that could endanger its Marxist, working-class, and pro-Soviet character.[133] As a result, from the very outset Tiul'panov and his lieutenants in the zone subjected the SED to a barrage of ideological lessons. The SED, in their view, was excessively antifarmer and insufficiently sensitive to the dynamics of the worker-farmer alliance. They believed the SED's leaders took an incorrect view of the SPD in the West, not differentiating enough between the reactionary leadership and the salvageable SPD rank and file on the Left.[134] The Berlin party organization was accused of both excessive sectarianism and of making too many concessions to reformism.[135] The protocols of SED Central Secretariat meetings from May to July 1946 reveal that Soviet Communist Party officials excoriated their German comrades for ignoring major issues of ideological training and for paying far too much attention to small questions, like ordering furniture for the party school, changing place and street names, and issuing stamps and official portraits.[136]

The irony of this incessant Soviet harping about the ideological weaknesses of the SED was the fact that Soviet officers often directly controlled SED organizations. In August 1946, the Berlin Propaganda Administration took direct control over the unity newspaper, *Vorwärts,* to strengthen its ties to the Soviet political authorities.[137] The head of the SVAG Culture Department, Alexander Dymshits, stated that the Mecklenburg SED party organization "is under our strongest tutelage. Even more than that, we very often do the party's work." Dymshits understood that in this regard, the Soviets' close control of the SED deprived it of its initiative and its "spirit of struggle."[138] The deep involvement of Soviet political officers in day-to-day SED affairs was criticized by Germans and Russians alike. In Erfurt, the political officer, Lieutenant Colonel Sherstinskii played such an important role in SED politics that the locals joked that it was called the Sherstinskii Party not the Socialist Unity Party.[139] Friedrich Ebert asked whether the Soviet officers who constantly attended their SED meetings could at least dress in civilian clothes so as not to be so conspicuous. Ebert suggested as well that SVAG should circulate an order to Soviet officers "not to mix into every and all affairs, and also not in our inner-party matters."[140] Ulbricht had expressed the hope that the creation of the SED would reduce the role of SVAG from "commanding" to "controlling."[141] But very little had changed; control continued to mean command.

Soviet commands reached down to the smallest details; in fact, the smaller the details, the more important they seemed to the local officers. Meetings and celebrations had to have banners and flowers, triumphal music, and full attendance. Virtually every report by Propaganda (Information) Administration officers on local SED meetings commented on the appropriateness of the decorations and ceremonies. For example, Lieutenant Colonel Vatnik from Saxony wrote to Tiul'panov on June 11, 1946, about a recent united trade union (FDGB) meeting: "In the hall were flowers, banners, many red cloth panels, a portrait of Bebel in the center, photographs. The conference was started with choral music, which was taken from old mining workers' songs."[142] Each of these details was extremely important to the Soviets, and if the flowers were absent or the songs were politically inappropriate, the local SED was told about it in no uncertain terms. When new SED party cards were issued to KPD and SPD members in Berlin, the Soviets expressed considerable irritation that the Germans thought of this as only a "technical" matter, not as a chance to stage a party ceremony, as had been held in the USSR. To make sure the SED did its job correctly, with the appropriate pomp and circumstance, the Berlin Propaganda Administration sent its officers to every district to issue the new cards. The Soviets also were annoyed that that SED did not understand how to carry out an electoral campaign in proper style—that is, in the way it was done in the USSR. They had to push the SED to get its famous intelligentsia members involved in the campaign. Soviet political officers also told the SED to set up People's Houses, where electoral meetings could be held, and encouraged them to think of the elections as a mass propaganda event, focused on triumphant celebration and 100 percent voter turnout.[143]

To say the least, the constant tutelage of the Soviets did not help the SED develop a sense of independence and confidence. The self-image of the SED was also poorly served by the need for its leaders to petition repeatedly to the Soviets on a wide variety of material and personal issues. The triumphant founding congress of the SED was barely over when Pieck had to ask for additional allotments of payoks for the new functionaries from the ranks of the social democrats.[144] Pieck constantly found himself in the position of asking the Soviets to return one German POW or another, who might have been a relative of a party member or a promising recruit for the bureaucracy. Pieck also episodically petitioned the Soviets for the return of leftist Germans still "living" in the USSR.[145] For example, he intervened with Mikhail Suslov to return Kurt Liebknecht, grandson of the famous German communist Wilhelm Liebknecht, to his parents in Berlin, so long as there were no "special reasons" this could not be done.[146] Pieck also found himself in the position of interceding in Moscow for German comrades who needed special medical operations, pharmaceuticals, visits to health spas, or even divorces. For instance, Fred Oelssner desperately wanted a divorce from his Russian wife, with whom he had no contact. Pieck urged Suslov to help take care of the divorce so that the SED would not suffer negative publicity about Oelssner's second, German "wife" in Berlin.[147]

Ulbricht, too, repeatedly asked the Soviets for special help for the SED: for gas, cars, payoks, paper, and even printing presses. He had to ask the Soviets' permission to start a newspaper or to have certain comrades transferred from one position to another. He had to turn to the Soviets to get food for the Ernst Thälmann party school or to stop the Soviet military's appropriation of buildings or machines used by the party. He was even reduced to asking SVAG for help in getting materials for SED party badges![148] Ulbricht also had to turn to the Soviet "friends" for political favors, whether it was to exert control over the Association for the Victims of the Nazi Regime (VVN), which at times demonstrated considerable hostility to the SED leadership, or to resolve a squabble between himself, the SVAG Trade Union Department, and Roman Chwalek, head of the FDGB.[149]

Ulbricht often felt it was necesssary to explain his requests to Bokov and, in particular, to Tiul'panov. Tiul'panov in turn treated Ulbricht like he treated all members of the SED leadership, with critical distance, which Ulbricht surely noticed. In his reports to Moscow, Tiul'panov paternalistically "forgave" Ulbricht his "sectarian" past, which was always brought up. At the same time, he and his Moscow colleagues repeatedly noted how unpleasant and rigid Ulbricht was, how he was given to "stubbornness and ambition," qualities, one Central Committee report added, that had also been ascribed to Ulbricht in reprimands from the Comintern.[150] In CPSU(b) practice, nothing was forgotten and nothing was forgiven. At the same time, leaders of both parties were perfectly aware that Ulbricht was the contact man between the Soviets and the SED. Lieutenant Colonel P. F. Nazarov, Tiul'panov's deputy in the Propaganda (Information) Administration, was Ulbricht's "protector" in the Soviet Military Administration and his contact man with the Soviet party organization.[151] In most policy issues, Ulbricht turned to Bokov and Tiul'panov for help; in the major questions, like the establishment of the People's Council or the promulgation of a new economic plan, Ulbricht directly approached the Central Committee in Moscow for advice.

In July 1946, Ulbricht sent Peter Florin to Moscow with a letter to the Central Committee reporting on the referendum in Saxony and requesting help on several important questions.[152] First of all, Ulbricht wanted to send a delegation of notables from the Eastern zone to the most destroyed areas of the Soviet Union, to convince skeptical Germans that their complaints about dismantling were petty and mean-spirited. But the leaders of the Soviet Central Committee were not inclined to show Germans the horrible conditions still extant in their land, and they suggested that the SED use films and photo exhibits instead. Ulbricht also asked that German POWs in the USSR be allowed to correspond with their families at home; the absence of any contact had become an important propaganda issue that was exploited by the Western press. In this case, the Central Committee promised some relief by initiating an interagency program to improve communications between those in the camps and their relatives at home, at the very least to find out who had died and who was really still in the camps. Ulbricht requested help in spreading Soviet culture in the Eastern zone, and Central Committee functionaries responded that they would set up a Soviet House of Culture in Berlin. Moscow turned down Ulbricht's request, however, to start a judicial process against Mutschmann, the former gauleiter of Saxony, to publicize the horrors of fascism to doubting Germans. The Soviets argued that Mutschmann was too old and sick to be tried. But the real reason was that the Soviets did not think it would be good politics in the zone to stage show trials against former Nazis. Finally, Ulbricht gently informed the Central Committee that the German workers suffered severe economic deprivation. It would give them hope, he wrote, if the Soviets would engage in greater economic planning in the zone, and it would improve their mood during the upcoming municipal elections if SVAG would increase their rations.[153] Ulbricht often judiciously urged the Soviets to take particular actions, and they took his suggestions seriously, accepting or turning them down as they saw fit. On the other hand, Soviet communications to Ulbricht were seen as orders. Primarily, he was used to pass on ideological directives and to discipline particular SED members.[154]

It should be understood that Ulbricht was not the only one who turned to the Soviets for help. Elli Schmidt begged Bokov to provide her with a car, pointedly noting that, as head of the Women's Department, she was the only member of the Central Secretariat not to have one. Pieck also asked Bokov for a car, for Max Fechner. According to Pieck's letter, Fechner had been held up and robbed by "bandits in Russian uniform" (Soviet soldiers, no doubt!), who stole his Opel as well as his money.[155] Otto Grotewohl probably had the most complex relationship with the Soviets. He was courted by the Russians from the very beginning and shamelessly flattered.[156] He was sent special goods and materials and was praised for his dedication to socialism. In return, Grotewohl expressed what was undoubtedly genuine appreciation for the Soviets' solicitude. He used similar phrases in responding to both Bokov and Kotikov: "I often feel with you that your understanding [*Verständnis*] comes from the deepest socialist openness." Grotewohl also was attached to the metaphor of "the sun rising from the East" to shed its light on the West, which he used as a way to praise Marxism-Leninism and Soviet life.[157] Despite the Soviets' genuine admiration for Grotewohl's gifts as a politician, especially in comparison with Ulbricht, Pieck, and the others, they also made sure that he understood, even long after his "conversion," that he had come from the SPD, that he had "wavered" before joining the unity campaign, and that with this background he could never quite match up to the Soviets' understanding of German affairs. Along these lines, the Soviets dismissed Grotewohl's resistance to accepting the finality of the Oder-Neisse border with Poland as a sign of his petit bourgeois past.[158] Still, as late as the summer of 1948, Major G. I. Patent, a Soviet cultural officer, went so far as to suggest that Grotewohl's background was little different from that of the vilified SPD renegades Kurt Schumacher, Franz Neumann, and Kurt Swolinsky. Grotewohl was angry and irritated by Patent's statements, calling them "tasteless" and "more than surprising."[159] But, like the other members of the SED who had an SPD background, Grotewohl had to live with the persistent Soviet attitude that the Germans lagged far behind in their understanding of the postwar world.

The Soviets' interference in SED affairs, their attitude toward the party's leaders, and the need of Ulbricht, Pieck, Grotewohl, and others to turn to the Soviets for help, gave credence to the accusation that the SED had become a Soviet-run party. When Tiul'panov spoke at the Second Party Congress of the SED in September 1947, some party members complained that this demonstrated to all their enemies the SED's dependence on the Soviets and Pieck's confused response to the complaints did not help matters any. Just because Tiul'panov shared their views, Pieck stated, it did not mean that the SED was dependent on the occupying power. "But, on the other hand," he said, "we are not independent, that is correct." Nevertheless, added Pieck, the SED was "completely independent" in its political formulations and conclusions. Pieck went on to say that the party leaders shared their opinions with the Soviets in private, and that more often than not, they got what they wanted.[160]

Given Soviet attitudes, it is not at all surprising that the leaders of the SED grew more and more impatient with their dependence on the military government. Ulbricht, Pieck, and others had a terrible time getting SVAG to act on even the most pressing issues. General Bokov especially frustrated the Germans by sitting on documents for months on end without acting on them.[161] But even after Bokov was removed in the fall of 1946, it was hard to get SVAG to act on matters of significance. Paul Merker wrote to Grotewohl in July 1947 that he had submitted important draft child labor laws to SVAG months earlier, but no one was willing to sign off on them. Merker suggested that Tiul'panov be enlisted to get the appropriate SVAG bureaucracy to do its job.[162] Fritz Grosse from Saxony noted that the SED made numerous recommendations for removing particular *Landrats,* mayors, or school principals, only to have the Saxon military government ignore the recommendations for six to eight months. Grosse ended his report with a very relevant question: How much authority could the SED have if it could not even get a local Nazi removed from his post?[163] The situation in Thüringen was even worse. The president of the administration, Rudolf Paul, dealt only with the Soviet commander, General Kolesnichenko, who personally approved or turned down almost every measure proposed in his province. Local SED party groups had virtually no influence on matters of policy or personnel; everything was handled between Kolesnichenko and Paul.[164]

THE SOVIETS AND SED POLICIES

To understand the way Russian officers operated in the zone, one would do well to consider several concrete cases of Soviet involvement in German policymaking. As was discussed in chapter 1, in October 1945 the Soviet justice officer Ia. Karasev rejected out of hand as undemocratic Ulbricht's suggestions to set up people's courts. Three years later, in the fall of 1948, SVAG's Education Department faced a crisis in the German universities, prompted by a perceived lack of SED influence on the German Education Administration. (Only 54 percent of the employees of the administration were members of the SED.) Even within SED ranks, "party discipline" was completely lacking, as noted in the unofficial SVAG history of education in the zone; officials carried out policies regardless of the SED's wishes. In this atmosphere, it was particularly hard to get the universities to introduce mandatory courses on Marxism-Leninism. As a result, the Soviets directly intervened in setting up the courses; "only thanks to the firm recommendations and sometimes even demands" of SVAG's Education Department was any action taken. Even at that, the Soviets felt they had to supervise directly the party committees in the German Education Administration and insisted that they, in turn, monitor the courses on Marxism-Leninism, otherwise nothing substantial would be accomplished.[165]

The other cases are worth quoting in full from a Central Committee investigative report in the Russian archives, because they give a good sense of the complex interaction between Soviet and SED needs and policies. In the case of the question of religion, policy documents originated in SVAG and were adopted by the SED; in the case of communal constitutions, the documents originated in the SED and were revised and approved by SVAG.

> Question:—What does the Department on Parties [of the Information Administration] do in terms of directing the parties; what place do you have in the preparation of political documents [and] of political actions?

Com[rade] Nazarov [chief of the Department]: All documents, which come from the SED, almost all are prepared by us here. If they prepare the draft, then we look at it here and introduce all our comments. There are no documents that would not be formulated by us and which would not be fully affirmed by them; such documents do not exist. A concrete example would be with religion. Among ourselves in the department we discussed what kind of document would be necessary to prepare in order that in the electoral campaign . . . the Churches not be given a chance to act on behalf of the CDU. We outlined a whole series of questions. These questions were approved by the Comrade Colonel [Tiul'panov]. I went to Pieck and said that we had this point of view. It would be good, if the SED would adopt a document in which the point of view of the SED in relation to the church and religion would be articulated. Pieck said—that's correct. I've already talked about it.—Now, but maybe you have some questions, which you would like to ask?—I said that we have conceptions, these are not our orders, but we have conceptions. I have a preliminary document for the next meeting of the Secretariat. In order not to hold up Pieck, we went to Ackermann and discussed this question more thoroughly. The next day I arrived and said: so, is the document ready? He said—ready. I gave instructions. And took the document. In this document Meier wrote: that . . . I [Meier] spoke today with Major Nazarov, who expressed his point of view that it is necessary now for us to outline [policies] in relation to religion.—I [Nazarov] said that it was not appropriate for comrade Meier to refer to my name in the document, in case the document should land somewhere or other. So, Meier said—I will go to the secretary now, he will bring the document. The document was brought in and it was destroyed at once. After this, they prepared all of these instructions in a commission, and this commission worked out this question [of religion].

Moreover, it is possible to take the question of . . . the communal constitutions, which were affirmed. The TsK [Central Secretariat] charged Grotewohl with this matter, inasmuch as he prepared this constitution already in 1923. They sent this draft here [to us]; Lt. Col. Zdorov worked on it and, in my offices, Major Shishliannikov. They [the SED] adopted a communal constitution, the constitution of the Weimar Republic, included our remarks, and after this the constitution was reported to the Colonel or to Zdorov. Afterwards, our man went to the TsK and settled things there. They took all of our suggestions.[166]

These examples demonstrate good, collegial relations between SVAG and the SED in working out specific policy recommendations. But it is also clear that the SED was subordinate to SVAG. Sometimes, SED leaders were able to put pressure on the military government and to encourage Soviet officers close to them to take action when others in the administration were dragging their feet. But on the whole, SED leaders were forced to ask or encourage rather than demand or insist. These documents also demonstrate Soviet sensitivity to the appearance of directing the SED's work. At one point, Tiul'panov sharply criticized Pieck for publicly letting on that Moscow had approved an adumbration of an SED proclamation.[167] At the same time, Tiul'panov was willing to interfere in the most minute details of SED life. For example, Tiul'panov approved of Hermann Schlimme's report to the SED Party Executive of a trip he took to the Soviet Union. But the published version, Tiul'panov insisted, should "have rather less [of a tone] of rapturousness, especially on the question of the situation of the POWs in the Soviet Union, for this would place in doubt the correctness of the remaining impressions."[168]

Soviets and Germans

The Soviets were in charge in postwar eastern Germany, not the Germans, though sometimes the distinction was not so easy to make. There were hundreds of Germans with Soviet citizenship employed in the administration of the occupied zone. Markus Wolf and Peter Florin were among them, as were Frieda Rubiner and Fred Oelssner. Most of these Soviet citizens of German origin were members of the SED and occupied prominent positions in state institutions; they hid their Soviet citizenship from their fellow workers and comrades for political reasons. In January 1949, the Soviet Central Committee recognized that this was a terribly difficult situation for the 165 Germans who were still in this position. Unless there were "special circumstances," the Central Committee recommended that they all give up their Soviet citizenship.[169]

Many German communists—with or without Soviet citizenship—had lived in the Soviet Union, survived the period of the purges, and been fully inculcated with the same values and habits that infused their Soviet partners in the military government.[170] Any number would have fit Cultural Officer Alexander Dymshits's description of Hans Klering, head of DEFA, the Soviet-run film company in the Eastern zone. Klering had been in the KPD and then joined the SED. He had lived in the Soviet Union for fourteen years. "He is in actuality a Soviet actor," Dymshits wrote. He had Soviet medals, a Russian wife, and a Soviet passport. "*He works for us here as a German.*"[171] Others, like Richard Gyptner, might as well have been Soviet citizens. In a letter to Suslov of March 8, 1948, Gyptner stated that Soviet medicine had saved his life, for which he was eternally grateful. "My strength was preserved," he wrote, "for the service of *our* party."[172]

If the Soviets were careful not to create a Soviet Germany, they were perfectly willing to accept the Sovietization of individual SED members. It made the Germans more pliable and flexible, less bound to doctrine and more attuned to the subtle shifts in Stalinist policy. It also created a culture of mutual acceptance and understanding between Soviets and Germans. There was no need to explain certain things having to do with what was politically acceptable and what was not. Certain kinds of questions were not asked; certain subjects were not broached. Many of these Germans' children had gone to Russian schools, first in the Soviet Union and then in the "commandants' schools" for Russian youth in the occupied zone. Russian and Soviet culture, language, and habits became second nature to these children, as well as to many of their parents. However, when a special German-Russian school was set up for these youths, a number of problems arose that exemplified the negative consequences surrounding the emergence of a new Sovietized German elite. Following the example of the adults, the children not only separated themselves from other young Germans but also thought of themselves as better and more deserving, because of their attachment to the superior Russian culture. They often spoke only Russian among themselves and looked down on their German teachers. The arrogance of the students grew so pervasive at the German-Russian school that the school had to be closed down altogether.[173] But the problems remained; a new Sovietized German elite had been placed in charge of the Eastern zone. Until the very end of the GDR, they were open to charges of doing the Russians' bidding.

Finally, it is important to mention in this regard that Soviet officers on the whole demonstrated considerable ability in winning German officials and public figures over to the Soviet cause. A combination of intense social interaction and flattery went a long way toward recruiting skeptical Germans. Grotewohl was of course the prize recruit, and most of the credit for him goes to Kotikov, Bokov, and Zhukov. Tiul'panov played a rather more Machiavellian role in the Grotewohl case, though he claims to have reeled in the line on Grotewohl. But Tiul'panov could also be charming and ingratiating, as demonstrated by his subtle handling of Thomas

Mann's visit to Weimar in August 1949. Tiul'panov and his wife met with Mann, showed him around, talked politics, literature, and peace with him, altogether making a very favorable impression on the circumspect and well-informed writer.[174]

General Sharov and his wife in Brandenburg were well known for their hospitality and convincing charm. Carl Steinhoff, an SED member out of the SPD ranks who was president of the Brandenburg administration, was a frequent guest in Sharov's home. The wives of the SED leaders were also invited, and Willy Sägebrecht remembered spending "beautiful hours" filled with conviviality and good food at the Sharovs'. Eventually even Friedrich Ebert, whom the Soviets considered a problem child, spent many evenings with his wife at the Brandenburg general's home. Sägebrecht also recalled, however, that Sharov "repeatedly pointed out to us the shortcomings and insufficiencies in the work of German local government organs." The general was a real Brandenburger, Sägebrecht concluded, because he cared for the people of his province "as a good father cares for his family."[175]

THE SED IN POWER

The Soviets clearly enjoyed their patriarchal role in Germany. It fit them well. If Sharov and Kotikov were seen as beneficent father figures, other generals, like Kolesnichenko from Thüringen, were rather more capricious and autocratic. The SED, like a schoolboy with too many lessons to learn, lurched forward uneasily under the tutelage of these Russian father figures, called "friends." The party had grown remarkably quickly in size and diversity, reaching 1.3 million members in the fall of 1946 and 1.8 million in the fall of 1947. Its leaders—Ulbricht, Pieck, Grotewohl, Fechner, et al.—had reputations as Soviet stooges who were close to the Russians yet unable to deliver on important popular demands, such as bringing an end to the dismantling and revising the Oder-Neisse border. Popular dissatisfaction became manifest in the fall of 1946, when in a series of communal, county, and regional elections, the SED received less support than expected. The Greater Berlin elections of October 1946, in particular, demonstrated that the SED had very little drawing power outside the strict confines of the Soviet zone.

At the local, county, and provincial levels, parity between former SPD and KPD members in the SED more often than not meant a severe split in party organizations. Sometimes, as in the case of the Mecklenburg provincial SED organization, former social democrats dominated and former communists were on the defensive.[176] Usually, however, the communists were firmly in control, leaving the former SPD members angry, frustrated, and, in some cases, ready to engage in underground opposition.[177] In Halle the communists controlled the SED organization to the point that former SPD members were totally excluded. In Magdeburg, on the other hand, where the social democrats were traditionally strong, the SED provincial organization felt constantly under attack from the local Magdeburg party. In some towns, like Frankenhausen, where there was a fairly even split between former SPD and former KPD members, all the former members of the SPD sat on one side of the room and all the former KPD members sat on the other. One Frankenhausen veteran, Werner Bruschke, recalled that for a long time afterward, "one could say those are the leftists and those the Right."[178] Purges seemed out of the question at this point. Otto Buchwitz, SED leader in Saxony, noted that he was hesitant to purge "right-wing" social democrats because one would not know where to stop; with the Right and the Left intermingled, a serious purge would be like trying to grab hold of quicksand.[179]

The party also continued to suffer from divisions on the Left—what was called in the early days sectarianism, but was increasingly branded with the more dangerous appellation of Trotskyism. Berlin remained a serious problem in this regard. In fact, Hermann Matern told a visiting Soviet commission that "ultraleftists" in Berlin were more dangerous to the Berlin SED than the Schumacherite Right. Many of the ultraleftists did not want to join the SED in the first place, and those who did quickly sank into apathy and indifference. Those who did not join, some 10 percent of the total Berlin KPD, gravitated to "Left factional groups of a Trotskyist sort." According to Matern, they existed in ten of the twelve districts of Berlin and concentrated their efforts on denouncing the Soviet Union as an imperialist power.[180] "Trotskyist" groups were also reported to have influence in Leipzig and Dresden, though in Saxony as a whole, the SED leadership seemed most concerned with the so-called Brandlerists, followers of August Brandler, the communist dissident from the Weimar period. In fact, the large and influential Saxon SED was rent by all kinds of divisions. According to Fritz Grosse, there were "Muscovites, Spaniards, Buchenwalders, Sachsenhauseners, Mauthauseners, Waldheimers, and Auschwitzers—[there were] groups of the National Committee [NKFD], front school veterans, and old underground [activists], and also English emigrants."[181] Whatever group it came from, the criticism from the Left was mostly the same: the Soviet Union was not a socialist country but represented state capitalism; rather than liberating the German proletariat, the Soviets enslaved German workers anew by removing factories and equipment and, through their opposition to the Marshall Plan, condemning the German masses to hunger and unemployment.[182]

The unique problems of Berlin aside, the most formidable challenge to the SED leadership was the integration of the huge number of reticent recruits from the SPD, many of whom, at least according to Soviet political officers, had agreed to join the SED only as an interim tactic, in anticipation of the end of zonal boundaries and their reentry into an all-German SPD.[183] Rumors—accurate ones, as it turned out—that the Soviets were considering exchanging recognition of the SED in the West for legalization of the SPD in the East did not help matters any. Schumacherites were said to be everywhere, trying to undermine the legitimacy of the SED by arguing that the unification of the KPD and the SPD had been "prematurely" undertaken.[184] Former SPD members complained that the new communist tyranny was in many ways worse than the Nazi dictatorship. "At least under the Nazis," reported a former SPD activist from Schwerin, "we were not forced to work [with them]."[185] SED meetings were repeatedly interrupted by complaints against the Soviet occupiers that were instigated, alleged hundreds of Soviet reports, by Schumacher supporters. (In point of fact, all one had to do to be labeled a Schumacherite was to criticize the Soviet Union.) The situation was serious; complaints multiplied about dismantling, about the SED's lack of a stand on the Oder-Neisse border, about the absence of news from German POWs, about the lack of fuel and the shortage of food. In a report on political conditions in Saxony, Tiul'panov wrote, "Direct anti-Soviet speeches at SED party organization meetings have become almost constant occurrences. At 209 party meetings of production and district groups taking place in Dresden, there were constant provocational speeches."[186]

The challenges to the SED from the Left and the Right were all the more serious because of the shortage of experienced political leaders in the party. Otto Meier stated at a plenum of the Party Executive, "In spite of everything, we still have to face the fact that at least a half, even maybe as many as two-thirds of our members are fully new to the movement and know absolutely nothing about what it is we actually want (very good!), for whom the word 'Socialism' is basically a concept with which they don't even know where to begin."[187] Bernard Koenen from Saxony voiced similar complaints about local and district SED leaders. When confronted with "anti-Soviet" criticisms, he said, even in the best cases they could think of no other response but to warn that "this can lead to no good." They had no answers to the complaints from the SED rank and file; they were unable to turn the "Schumacherite lies" back on their perpetrators. Reflecting their confusion and lack of backbone, all that the SED leaders seemed capable of doing, concluded Koenen, was to set up a special party committee "for the struggle against Schumacherites."[188] There is a remarkable consistency to the Soviet reports from the first year of the SED's existence. Party meetings were characterized as being of low quality, dominated by social democratic rhetoric, and punctuated by frequent "provocational anti-Soviet speeches."[189]

The crisis in the SED was deep and widespread. Tiul'panov noted that few party members read the SED's theoretical journal, *Einheit,* and even those who did were not helped much by it, because of its frequent mistakes. The fundamental problem, in his view, was that the average party member simply did not understand the difference between "formalistic democracy" and real socialist struggle.[190] This confusion led to a mood of "depression and pessimism," in Franz Dahlem's words, that "expressed itself in doubts about the ability of the party to deal with the difficulties it was going through."[191] To make matters worse, the SED was pervaded by apathy, defeatism, and hopelessness, characterizations frequently used by a variety of Soviet commentators. These attitudes, in turn, spawned hypocrisy and venality among ordinary party members. Sometimes they simply didn't attend meetings. In Zwickau, for example, only 25 to 30 percent of the members attended meetings, while in Aue, attendance was somewhat better, up to 50 percent. Given Soviet boasts about 100 percent attendance at party meetings, SVAG political officers found these figures particularly galling, and they regularly insisted that local leaders take a greater interest in attendance figures.

There were cases in which SED members were expelled for not attending any meetings, for avoiding the party altogether, or for expressing dissatisfaction with the occupation authorities. But the party leaders already had their hands full trying to cope with criminality among SED members: more often than not, SED members were expelled for theft, speculation, or prostitution.[192] According to Soviet figures, in the last six months of 1947, some 2,500 SED members were expelled for "all kinds of criminal violations": corruption, extortion, bribery, and the like. Of the other

12,500 who left the SED in this period, most were party members who went over to the West.[193]

MOSCOW PILGRIMAGES

An integral part of the SED's maturation were the periodic meetings between its leaders and its Soviet sponsors in Moscow. While there is no question that Pieck, Ulbricht, Grotewohl, and others received important instructions and picked up useful hints from Stalin and their Soviet comrades, equally important were the ritualistic qualities of these visits. The Germans gained a sense of stature from being received in the Kremlin, at the same time imbibing the power and prestige of the Soviet capital. They were excited and flattered by being feted and taken seriously by what they perceived as being the strongest nation in the world. For these "Red Germans," their guilt about what the Nazis had done in Russia was combined with their pride in being associated with the accomplishments of the Soviet Communist Party. For Pieck, Ulbricht, Oelssner, Ackermann, and others who had survived the harsh period of purges and war, visits to Moscow were especially important to reestablish their place in the communist hierarchy and to escape, at least temporarily, the unpleasant realities of occupied Germany, including the sometimes overbearing interference of the Soviet political officers.

The first visit of the initiative group leaders—Ackermann, Ulbricht, and Sobottka—to Moscow in June 1945 laid the groundwork for the legalization of the KPD. The second visit of KPD leaders took place in January and February 1946, and it cemented the procedures for the formation of the SED. The third visit, which took place at the end of January and the beginning of February 1947, was in many ways the most important.[194] The SED leadership was faced with a somber mood in the population and deep pessimism in the party. The electoral setbacks in the zone and in Berlin the previous fall had highlighted the growing inroads that the SPD was making in eastern German society and politics. Pieck, Ulbricht, Grotewohl, and Fechner (with Oelssner as translator) stayed in a dacha outside Moscow and were inundated, as was the custom, with Soviet films, rich food and drink, and sight-seeing. Pieck was clearly happy to be in Moscow again and by all accounts seemed to enjoy his time there, while Ulbricht was quickly bored with the mandatory trappings of Soviet hospitality. This was Grotewohl's first visit to Moscow, and according to Soviet accounts of his reactions, he was thrilled with everything. After seeing the Moscow subway system, Grotewohl was reported to have said: "Yes! This is real civilization. And this is possible only here, in a socialist state." Grotewohl was also entranced by the films, the theaters, and the museums. "He expressed his delight," the Soviet report continued, "that the broad masses in our country like and value art so much, [all of which] is accessible to them." The Soviets were clearly still uneasy about Grotewohl's SPD past and his unwillingness, from their point of view, to accept general German responsiblity for the war and the finality of the Oder-Neisse border. Still, they were delighted by his effusive praise of everything he saw and everyone he met. Coming out of his meeting with Stalin, Grotewohl reportedly said: "Comrade Stalin is the greatest socialist in the world, Comrade Stalin is the father of the world." Whenever he or Pieck had a chance, they raised a toast to Stalin and the Soviet Union, which pleased their Soviet hosts to no end. On the other hand, the Soviets made special mention of the fact that Fechner was very quiet and did not play the acolyte, which made them uncomfortable and suspicious.

The most crucial of the winter 1947 meetings in Moscow took place on January 31 in the Kremlin, with Stalin, Molotov, Suslov, and Semenov.[195] Typical of Stalin's work hours, the meeting was held from 9:00 P.M. until midnight. The format for the meeting was also typical: Grotewohl read his report on the situation in Germany, and during the translation that followed Stalin and Molotov replied to specific points. It was clear to the SED chiefs that the Soviet leadership was interested in how the SED could help avoid federalism in Germany, which, in the Soviet view, would institutionalize Western domination of a new German state. Stalin told the Germans, in no uncertain terms, "Your position for the unity of Germany, against federalism, is the correct one." During this meeting, the Soviets also looked to develop political strategies toward the Germans in the West that would prevent the reestablishment of the Weimar coalition between the social democrats and the bourgeois parties. This meant intensifying, above all, "the struggle for the unity of the working class."

Grotewohl wanted to talk to his Soviet sponsors about problems in the SED and weaknesses in the KPD in the West. After sufficient preparation, he noted, it would be possible to establish the SED in the Western zones. But both Stalin and Molotov were more interested in talking about the SPD, especially about finding ways to split Schumacher's ranks immediately by appealing to left-wing SPD members. One of the critical points in the discussion had to do with the Soviets' desire to legalize the SPD in the Eastern zone in exchange for the legalization of the SED in the West.

But this bargain, broached for the first time by the Soviets, constituted one of the SED's worst nightmares.

> [Grotewohl] We think that our demand to allow the SED in the Western zones will raise the question of allowing the SPD in the Soviet zone. Our position is—there is no need to allow the SPD in the Soviet zone.
>
> Response ———[196] "It is necessary to allow it."
>
> "What are you afraid of? Of criticism to allow it [the SPD in the East] within confined limits."
>
> "There is no need to be afraid."
>
> "Conduct counterpropaganda."
>
> "You gain nothing from the path of banning [the SPD] by the occupying power."
>
> "If you can't stand up to Schumacher without the occupying power, then you're weak."

The exchange about legalizing the SPD ended inconclusively, though with a clever twist on the part of the SED. Grotewohl stated how difficult it had been for the SED to work under the conditions of dismantling, reparations, and economic hardship in the Eastern zone. "Response ——— 'Yes it's been hard for the party.' "

Pieck's notes about the important issue of allowing the SPD in the Eastern zone say only: "Allowing of the SPD in the Sov[iet] Occupation Zone, whether the SED is afraid of SPD—one has to defeat them politically."[197] But from the Soviet account of the visit, it is clear that Ulbricht was not at all happy about the prospect of legalizing the SPD. It was critical, he stated, "first of all to strengthen our ranks." He also thought it would be dangerous in the extreme to allow Schumacher the ability to carry out his propaganda against the SED from Berlin, where the new SPD would surely establish its headquarters.

Molotov was given the last word at the January 31 meeting. The foreign minister of the USSR reaffirmed the Soviet commitment to reviving the German economy and helping the country gain access to international markets. "The sooner a general German government is formed," he stated, "the more quickly Germany will be reestablished" and a peace treaty will be signed. Molotov added three points that surely pleased his German listeners. First, he said that if it proved impossible to form a central government in the near future, then the "worst case" would take place; that is, a unified government in the Soviet zone. Second, Molotov stated that "we have no further claims to dismantling. The army will be reduced. The need to feed and supply it [will be] less." Finally, added Molotov, reparations payments could be deferred to a later date; there was no need "to force" them, and there should therefore be no reason that the conditions of the German workers could not be improved. Might there be "small corrections" in the eastern borders? the SED leaders asked (with regard to the Oder-Neisse line). The answer was firmly no. In addition, Molotov responded to German concerns about POWs in Soviet camps only by promising the return of several hundred POWs who had distinguished themselves in the antifascist schools.

According to Pieck's notes, on the evening of February 2, Molotov and Semenov spoke with the Germans to elucidate further Stalin's intentions. Molotov reiterated Stalin's thoughts about the West's trying to deny Germany its rightful place in the world market. He also indicated that Stalin looked to the formation of central administrations in the Eastern zone, covering all areas of state functioning except for defense and internal security.[198] Then, on February 4, Suslov met for about two hours with Grotewohl and Pieck, at the request of the Germans, to explain the organizational structure of the Soviet party and the way the apparatus of the party functioned, especially the Central Committee. During this discussion, Suslov explained to the Germans that for communists (meaning the SED) to constitute a "*government party*," there had to be "socialist society—where the class enemy is liquidated and the *means of prod*[uction] are in the hands of the workers." In an effort to get the SED leaders to improve their propaganda efforts, which were seen as the weakest point in their endeavors, Suslov spent a lot of time explaining the significance of the Central Committee's propaganda and agitation apparatus to the overall work of the CPSU(b).[199]

THE SED AND THE COLD WAR

The January-February 1947 discussions in Moscow indicate that Stalin and his lieutenants seriously considered an "all-German" formula for solving both their problems in Central Europe and the SED's problems in the zone. At the same time, the SED leaders returned home from Moscow with no concessions on the issue of the finality of the Oder-Neisse border, no promises to cancel reparations, and no hopes of the mass return of POWs. On all three issues, the SED had been taking a terrible propaganda beating in Berlin and the rest of the zone. Even more disturbing, the SED faced the haunting specter of having to compete with a legalized SPD for the allegiance of eastern German workers. Just the prospect of the SPD's legalization threatened to split the party between those who saw this as a way to save the unity of Germany and those who predicted dire consequences for the SED.[200] But cold war tensions between the Soviets and the Americans heated up so quickly in the spring of 1947 that any agreement about allowing the SPD in the East or the SED in the West became extremely unlikely. At the Moscow Foreign Ministers Conference in March and April, 1947, the Soviets accused the West of dividing Germany by creating Bizonia. On March 12, the United States enunciated the principles of the Truman Doctrine and began preparations for the economic reconstruction of Europe, which was announced by Secretary of State George C. Marshall at Harvard University's commencement in June. By the time of the Paris meeting of the Foreign Ministers Conference (June 27 to July 3, 1947), cold war tension had reached the critical point. Molotov vituperatively attacked the Americans for conspiring to deny reparations to the Soviets and insisted on Soviet participation in the control of the Ruhr. Meanwhile, in June, the attempt by a number of German minister-presidents to salvage the unity of the country in the face of increasingly divisive East-West tensions had foundered because of the Soviets' and the SED's opposition to federal solutions.[201]

Within the SED leadership itself, there were essentially two kinds of responses to the challenges presented by the cold war. Ulbricht, backed by Pieck and Dahlem, among others, articulated one set of responses, which focused on managing the backbreaking economic problems of the Eastern zone and worried less about issues involving West Germany and unification. Ulbricht argued that while socialism was unquestionably the goal of the SED, economic planning should occupy the "action plan of the day." As noted earlier, in 1945 and early 1946 Ulbricht had demanded that his fellow KPD members abandon revolution for administration; in 1947, he urged socialist politicians to become economic managers and the SED to become "the party of order."[202] The second kind of response came from SED members like Anton Ackermann, Max Fechner, and Otto Meier, who, unlike Ulbricht and Pieck, were greatly perturbed by the prospective division of Germany that they saw emerging from the failed Moscow conference.[203] The "central political question" of German unity, Ackermann correctly sensed, was being pushed into the background by a series of other concerns, whose outcome actually depended on the unity question. It was the premier task of the SED, he stated, to mobilize the masses on behalf of unity, to show them "that there was no other way out of the misery and out of the distress [in Germany]" than through the unity of the country. Ulbricht, Pieck, and their followers concentrated their efforts on strengthening the party in the Soviet zone; Ackermann (and, to a somewhat lesser extent, Grotewohl), insisted that the SED become a real German party that addressed all-German questions, not just issues that emerged in the Soviet zone.[204]

Ackermann first developed his theoretical ideas about unity and the German path to socialism in his article, "Is There a Special Road to Socialism?" printed in *Einheit* in February 1946. In it, Ackermann asserted that the Germans did not need to follow the Soviet model, and that Germany, given its special conditions, could follow a peaceful path to socialism with an antifascist democratic program.[205] In practice, Ackermann shared Moscow's view that the foundation of the SED in the West could serve as the basis for a national German revolution. But the Soviet ranks were no more united on this question than were the German. Tiul'panov, in particular, encouraged Ulbricht and Pieck's suspicions that excessive attention was being paid to Ackermann's "German road." Its appeal to German audiences, Tiul'panov noted, smacked too much of residual nationalism and chauvinism.[206]

But Ackermann persisted, even going so far in pursuit of the "German road" as to complain about the number of foreign words contained in party resolutions.[207] Grotewohl no doubt sympathized with Ackermann's approach and with his national rhetoric, but he had neither the ties to the Soviets nor the confidence of Moscow to pursue this line. Instead, he spoke about an SED that was neither SPD or KPD, but a new type of Marxist party, "built on the soil of the specific social, economic, and political relations of our time."[208] (He did not say *of our country*.) Until the middle of 1947, Ackermann's ideas fit the general theory of separate roads to socialism that was current in Soviet-occupied Europe and fostered by other Eastern European leaders like Władysław Gomułka and Georgi Dimitrov. However, the growing tensions of the cold war and the Soviets' problems with the Yugoslavs, which exploded into the expulsion of the Yugoslav Communist Party from the Cominform in June 1948, quickly made themselves felt in the Soviet zone. By September, Ackermann was forced to recant his "mistaken" theories, saying they had been concessions to anti-Soviet sentiments among the Germans. Ackermann "confessed": "The theory of a special German road to socialism allows room for anti-Bolshevism, instead of determinedly fighting against it with all [our] might."[209]

The cold war and the conflict with the Yugoslavs brought an end to the German road to socialism. But unlike the cases of the people's democracies in the East—Poland, Czechoslovakia, Hungary, and others—no ideological constructs had been developed to take the place of the national road to socialism. This was particularly noticeable in the preparations for the Second Congress of the SED, to be held in Berlin from September 20 to 24, 1947. During the month of July, SED members were to meet, hear speeches, and elect delegates to the Congress. But reports from local political officers all over the zone made it clear that the meetings were poorly prepared and even more poorly attended. In Saxony, all anyone wanted to talk about was the allocation of the third *Zentner* (fifty kilograms) of potatoes, which had been promised by the Soviets but had not been delivered. Major General Dubrovskii of Saxony was so upset by the situation that he insisted that local officers from the Information Administration become directly involved in the electoral campaign. They should "direct and control" the electoral meetings for the Congress, he said, making sure that SED leaders pushed for full attendance and getting the German working class involved.[210] In Saxony and elsewhere, SVAG had to make sure that SED orders from Berlin were followed in the provinces.

But for all their direction and control, Soviet political officers could not overcome the depressingly harsh economic conditions of the summer and fall of 1947 that made the German working class utterly indifferent to the appeals from the SED. Even the party's rank and file blamed these conditions on the Russians and, by extension, on the SED leadership. Pieck and Grotewohl conveyed their sentiments on this point to Stalin on September 3, 1947: "We have not succeeded, therefore, in avoiding the fact that the great economic difficulties . . . and the political poisoning of the masses by Nazi ideology have produced serious doubts in the ranks of our party." The worst problem of all, the SED leaders continued, was that the economic situation did not provide any hope of a "substantial improvement in the position of the working people." There was no food or coal for the upcoming winter, there were no shoes, household goods, or textiles. The situation was so bad, Pieck and Grotewohl wrote, that the party was in "very serious" danger, especially given the heightened attacks from "the reaction." They noted that while there was no chance to meet with Stalin before the Second Congress about the economic situation, they expressed their hope that he would send to the Congress one or two delegates who could brief them about Soviet plans for the Eastern zone economy. Grotewohl and Pieck concluded: "Dear Comrade Stalin! We very much need your counsel and your help."[211]

The Soviet Central Committee responded by sending Suslov and P. N. Pospelov to the Congress as unofficial visitors, rather than as official delegates. Tiul'panov was already scheduled to speak at the Congress, and SVAG was to be represented by an official delegation. Even Suslov's greetings to the Congress, which Stalin had approved, were indifferent in the extreme. The Soviet party wished the SED "success and fruitful work in the matter of completely rooting out the remnants of fascism and building a unified democratic and peaceful Germany." Yet, at least according to Tiul'panov's report, the spirits of those at the Congress were greatly lifted by the presence of Central Committee secretaries. When Suslov's greeting was read: "the delegates stormily applauded, rose to their feet, turned to the boxes where the Central Committee of the CPSU(b) delegation was sitting and sang 'The Internationale.' "[212]

The nervousness and insecurity of the SED leaders in the face of the economic misery in the Eastern zone and the implied threat posed by the introduction of the Marshall Plan in the Western zones reinforced the inclinations of the speakers at the Congress to align themselves even more with the policies of the Soviet Union and with Soviet-style socialism. In his address, Grotewohl advocated the study and application of Marxism-Leninism to the situation in Germany. This led Tiul'panov to note with considerable satisfaction that the attitude of many leading functionaries of the SED regarding the Soviet Union had been transformed from "a tendency toward a certain distance" to one of "decisive defense of the policies of the USSR" and the recognition of "the need to study the experience of the CPSU(b)." Tiul'panov was also pleased with Grotewohl's nuanced attacks on the SPD in the West, as they separated the SPD's reactionary leadership from the social democratic rank and file.

Tiul'panov was much less happy with Pieck's overly radical formulations, which, he felt, unduly demonized the entire SPD. The Soviets were also displeased with Pieck's excessively presumptious declarations about the international implications of the Congress itself, especially when he suggested that it "served as the basis for the reemergence of the new socialist international."[213] It is noteworthy that Pieck's statements about a new international took place almost precisely at the time (September 1947) of the first Cominform meeting at Szklarska Poręba in Poland. The SED leaders had not been invited to the meeting, nor had they been informed of its occurrence. The best they could do was to state their firm support for a development they poorly understood. As Grotewohl noted on October 7 about the Cominform meeting, "So far the SED has not been involved in the various efforts to form a new international organization. [But] it agrees with and supports every effort that serves the interests of peace."[214]

The combination of severe economic problems and worsening East-West relations during the winter of 1947–48 drove the SED deeper into the camp of the Soviets. In December 1947, the London Foreign Ministers Conference, the last meeting of its kind in the postwar world, fell apart because of the intractable differences between the former Allies. The Czech coup in February 1948 worsened the situation. Then, in March, the London Conference of the Western Allies signaled the creation of the West German state and left the Soviets sputtering about blatant and intentional violations of the four-power control agreement in Germany. As a result, on March 20, the Soviets withdrew their representation from the Allied Control Council. Between March and mid-June, when monetary reform was introduced into the Western zones and preparations were under way to do the same in West Berlin, the Soviets gradually reduced access to West Berlin and began what was known in the West as the Berlin blockade. (Soviet documents never refer to a blockade except when describing Western propaganda.)

It is worth adding that Pieck's obsessive complaints about the escalation of Western anti-Soviet and anti-SED propaganda in this period, and his comments about its effectiveness, were not without foundation. Attacks from the West *were* mounting and, unfortunately for the SED, there was a great deal to attack—from the forced labor in the uranium mines and the arrests of former SPD members to the continued Soviet removal of production in kind. Of course the Soviets and the SED also mounted attacks on the West, especially in conjuction with the waves of strikes that enveloped western Germany in the winter of 1947–48. In February 1948, the British ratcheted up the propaganda war with a "Draft Basic Directive on Combatting Communist Propaganda," which developed "more vigorous" techniques of "counterpropaganda" to defend the West's interests in Germany. Among the new guidelines were these:

> You should represent communism and the foreign policy of communist countries as a hindrance to international cooperation and world peace. You should ensure that the immoral, militant, and destructive nature of communist foreign policy in European countries be exposed, and that

its effects in dividing and impoverishing Europe are stressed. You should expose the myth that the Russians never break treaties and you should show up communism as the stalking horse of Russian imperialism. The available evidence on the creation of police satellite states in Eastern Europe dependent on the Soviet Union, and now in the Soviet Zone of Occupation, should be utilized. In this connection, all available facts and verified information discrediting the SED and the communist-dominated governments in the Soviet zone should be used.[215]

In the shadow of the escalating cold war, Pieck, Grotewohl, and Oelssner went secretly to Moscow at the end of March 1948 to consult with the Soviet leadership. On March 26, they met with Stalin, on March 29 with Suslov, and on March 31 with A. I. Mikoyan, returning to Berlin on April 1. As in their previous consultations in January and February 1947, the March 1948 visit was filled with official tourism—movies, galleries, banquets, and flattery. Grotewohl was apparently overwhelmed by Stalin's attention to their needs; he never expected, he reportedly said, that "comrade Stalin would ask them about whether they were well settled in Moscow and whether they needed anything." Grotewohl was also predictably awed by his visit to the Lenin Mausoleum and impressed by how well informed local party leaders were. At a mandatory kolkhoz visit, Grotewohl toasted his hosts using his favorite metaphor for the Soviet Union: "We have a saying that the sun always rises from the East. Today I became convinced that this is indeed true. I am pleased that I have been to the country from which the sun rises. May it shine brighter and brighter."[216]

Pieck's notes of the March 1948 Moscow meetings focus almost exclusively on the SED's political problems in the new, highly charged atmosphere of East-West threats and counterthreats. Anti-Soviet agitation from the West, said Pieck, was the basic source of the SED's weaknesses, and this was made all the worse by the fact that the German masses were beset by "great confusion" and were easily influenced by the enemy. The party still suffered from numerous problems in its cadres, but, Pieck added, there was a greater "inner determination" than there had been a year earlier. Pieck ended his presentation to the Soviets on a positive note, speaking in glowing terms about the new obligatory courses on "scientific socialism" that would be introduced during the summer into the universities and higher schools.[217] G. I. Korotkevich of the Central Committee noted, however, that Grotewohl was markedly unenthusiastic about Pieck's plan.[218] Suslov, too, tried to put a damper on Pieck's effusive readiness to march into the socialist future. During the March 29 meeting, he asked Pieck how many workers and peasants were enrolled in the university, and the SED leader answered only 28 percent. Suslov suggested that the SED would do better at that point to increase the number of workers in the higher schools by developing special workers' faculties rather than by trying to teach Marxism-Leninism to unwilling class enemies. "At this point, he [Suslov] described in detail the experience of the Soviet Union in preparing cadres of the Soviet intelligentsia from workers and peasants through the workers' faculties."[219]

Pieck and Grotewohl also asked Suslov's "opinion" about (that is, permission for) forming a unified sports organization under the SED. Again Suslov demonstrated considerable wariness. Although he approved of the creation of a sports organization in principle, he felt that his German colleagues relied too exclusively on the party for every type of initiative. It would be better, he stated, if the trade union organizations supervised the centralization of the sports movement in the zone.

One further remark by the German guests made a deeply negative impression on the Soviets. The SED leaders had enough courage to express their discomfort with the military display that infused so much of Soviet life in the postwar period. In what has to be considered a mild rebuke of the Soviets, Pieck pointed out the fact that the portraits of Marshal Voroshilov, resplendent with military medals and orders, did not appeal to the Germans. Pieck remarked, "That is the kind of thing that couldn't be done in Germany at all. If the regular, average German sees a portrait of a Soviet person with a number of orders, he has to think about parallels with Göring, who, as is well known, wore many orders. One has to say that Soviet comrades, working in Germany, don't always understand this."[220] In the Eastern zone, for some of the same reasons, SED propagandists repeatedly asked for the withdrawal of Soviet films that glorified the lives of Russian generals like Kutuzov and Suvorov. But to the Soviets, of course, the SED complaints were nothing more than a demonstration of their ignorance of the difference between a socialist army of the people and a capitalist army of the upper classes.

THE PARTY OF THE NEW TYPE

At the Second Congress of the SED, in September 1947, the party reiterated its commitment to Marxism. Grotewohl added that the "accomplishments of Leninism" should also be closely studied, but in no way mechanically applied to the conditions of Germany. In the months following the Congress, which had coincided with the inaugural meeting of the Cominform at Szklarska Poręba, the tone of SED and SVAG pronouncements hardened noticeably. In December 1947, for example, Tiul'panov expressed his displeasure with the flaccid qualities of the SED's ideological production. The party leaders needed, he said, to adopt a clear, unambiguous Marxist-Leninist stance and accept the necessity of establishing the dictatorship of the proletariat in Germany. Still, Tiul'panov hedged, as did Grotewohl at the Second Congress; the dictatorship could take different forms in different countries, the Soviet colonel stated, leaving room for continuing rhetoric about the "German road to socialism."[221] But from the Soviet point of view, the SED did not act resolutely enough to bring its ranks into line with a pro-Soviet program. The party tolerated too many opponents on the Left, mostly sectarians from the former ranks of the KPD, and on the Right, the so-called Schumacherites, unreconstructed former social democrats. The SED was particularly vulnerable to attacks on the USSR from the Left using "falsified Marxism-Leninism." "Only after our intervention," reported Lieutenant Colonel Blestkin, did the SED "begin to take measures to exclude several of them ["opponents of unity"] from the party."[222]

SVAG political officers were particularly disturbed by the situation in Thüringen, where they feared that the leftist and rightist criticisms of the Soviet Union would merge into a common anti-Soviet program, one that asserted that Lenin's policies followed Marxist traditions but that Stalin's had created an imperialist USSR. There, complained General Kolesnichenko, a small group of "leftists" led by the union leader Karl Schmidt, sought to "invigorate" socialism by "reviving" Lenin's policies. Schmidt and his comrades argued that the Soviets had abandoned Leninism through their policies regarding the Oder-Neisse (a clear violation of Lenin's "peace without indemnities") and dismantling, which had left the working class in such terrible straits. The Soviets were upset that Schmidt, while he had been removed as head of the food-processing union, continued to hold his position in the party apparatus.[223] In the opinion of Soviet officers, the SED was also too tolerant of the Schumacherites. They charged that Heinrich Hoffmann, the Thüringian SED leader and former social democrat, refused to expel them and therefore had plunged the party into a crisis. There was a "social-democratic style of leadership," the Soviets claimed, characterized by a false tolerance that in turn left the party without discipline and fighting spirit. All of this indicated, they asserted, that the party needed to take serious measures to remove opponents and tighten discipline. Hoffmann could be left as chairman of the Thüringian party until the next Congress, they concluded, but then he should be removed.[224] However, his deputy, Karl Eckstein, was accused of being "disloyal to the USSR" *(neloial'no nastroen v otnoshenii SSSR)*. As a result, he was removed from his government posts and relieved of his position in the secretariat of the party.[225]

The announcement of the Marshall Plan in June 1947 and its gradual implementation in 1948 and 1949 served as another impetus for the Soviets and the SED to tighten ideological reins on the party. The appeal to the SED rank and file of easy credits from the United States could only be countered by intensified efforts at party schooling and Marxist-Leninist indoctrination.[226] At the June 30, 1948, meeting of the Party Executive, the SED passed a resolution, "The Strengthening and Improvement of Party Schooling," that ended with the words: "We can only fulfill the great tasks in front of us in the political, economic, and cultural fields when we turn our Socialist Unity Party into a fighting party of Marxism-Leninism, into a real party of the new type."[227]

During the course of 1948 and early 1949, SED leaders and their Soviet mentors increasingly called for a tightening of the ranks. Dissident socialists within the SED became the primary targets for party discipline. Ernst Braun, head of the Weimar city party committee, was chided both for being the captive of "social democratic traditions" *and* for being "not free of leftist [*levatskii*] tendencies"—and this for criticizing the existence of many former Nazis in the antifascist bloc and in city government.[228] The SED education specialist Elchlepp was disciplined by Ulbricht when he suggested that all school policies in the Eastern zone should be based on the Marxist-Leninist principles of dialectical materialism.[229] Indeed, one of the fundamental characteristics of the so-called party of the new type was that no one could get things quite right except for the leadership. If local leaders talked about peace, unity, and democracy, they were accused of "hushing up the essential class nature of the party," thus encouraging the ultraleftist KPO (Communist Party, Opposition), "opportunists," and sectarians to accuse the SED of "reformism." If they spoke too much about the class struggle or dialectical materialism, attacked Nazis or the special stores (HOs) developed for the elite, or impugned the special privileges introduced for intelligentsia recruits, they were accused of ultraleftism and even Trotskyism.[230]

In a speech to the higher police school in Berlin (August 1948), Ulbricht emphasized that the party of the new type above all meant recognizing that the Soviet experience served as a model for the working class in every country of the world, Germany included. This model already dominated a sixth of the world, and more was to come. "The close relationship with the Soviet Union is the basic precondition for the victory of the working class in Germany, and without the Soviet Union behind us, without the comradely, brotherly help of the Soviet Union, we cannot win, we cannot come to power," he said. Ulbricht added, as well, that every institution in the zone needed to search the Soviet experience for lessons on how to organize and develop. For the police, for example, this meant establishing close relations with the officers and soldiers of the Soviet occupation army. From the Russians, the German police could learn the important lessons of how to win, how to beat the reactionaries.[231]

Within the SED, the struggle against the Right—the former SPD members, the alleged "Schumacherites," and Ostbüro "agents"—was in many ways easier than the struggle against the Left, because it was more clearly defined. In July 1948, the Party Executive called for the dismissal of SED members who refused to take part in normal party activities. Former SPD members suspected of anti-Soviet or antiparty attitudes were to be singled out and excluded from the party. Walter Ulbricht demanded that the SED no longer tolerate critical distance from the Soviet experience: "Whosoever conducts or supports anti-Soviet agitation has no place in the circles of our party members. (Interpolation: They must be released from their state duties!) That is correct."[232]

At this point Erich Gniffke, the number-two former SPD member in the SED behind Grotewohl, feared party action and even arrest and internment. As a result he fled for the West in October 1948.[233] In his "farewell letter," Gniffke linked the new level of persecution against former SPD members with the transformation of the SED into a totalitarian party.[234] One of the mechanisms for this process was institutionalized in mid-September 1948, when the SED Party Executive set up a Party Control Commission, whose task was to chase down SPD "agents" and expel them from the party. Corruption and careerism in the SED were also targeted by the Control Commission, but only as an afterthought to the primary task of Bolshevizing the party.[235] In fact, a new wave of expulsions and arrests in the fall of 1948 could only lead to the conclusion that the SED was already well on the way to being the party of the new type called for by Tiul'panov, Pieck, and others during the previous summer. The intensification of the class struggle within the SED also prompted party leaders to push forward their ambitions to transform society in eastern Germany. The "special path" to German socialism was abandoned as a "nationalist" deviation, while the experience of the Bolshevik party became the central focus for SED discourse about political and social development. The SED would become a "revolutionary party," like all the others in Eastern Europe.

In anticipation of the First Party Conference, to be held in January 1949, Pieck, Grotewohl, Ulbricht, and Oelssner went to Moscow from December 12 to 24, 1948, to discuss their accomplishments and ideas with Stalin and his lieutenants. Pieck's minutes of the meetings on December 18, the formal Soviet answer to the Germans' questions, and Pieck's notes of the further meetings with Gosplan and with the Central Committee Secretariat indicate that the Soviets were not at all pleased with the SED's drive to turn eastern Germany into a people's democracy like the other socialist states in Eastern Europe. In response to the Germans' request to join the Cominform, the Soviets answered that the SED was not yet "ripe enough." State power in the East had to be strengthened, the Soviets maintained, before the SED could act resolutely to transform society. Also, "it was still too early" for the Germans to engage in the nationalization of all industry, an important step on the road to socialism in the East. In a tactical sense, too, Stalin and the Soviet comrades suggested that the SED not be so blunt about its Leninist program for German society. The party should duck and feint more and engage in a "back and forth," more "opportunistic" program, one that accommodated society rather than constantly battering it over the head. As an example, the Soviets told the SED to have the KPD in the West issue a public statement denying any ties with the SED, while simultaneously strengthening those ties underground.[236] "You Germans are like your ancestors, the Teutons," Stalin reportedly told the SED leaders, in reference to their lack of subtlety and their excessive combativeness. "That is brave perhaps, but very stupid."[237]

While the Soviets recommended that the SED leaders think tactically and move more slowly in their desire to reach the exalted stage of a people's democracy, they simultaneously supported the SED's intention to eliminate parity between former SPD and KPD members and to realize the goal of creating the party of the new type. The plan approved at the Moscow meetings was straightforward. Ideological work, which had been largely ignored up until that time, would be strengthened and improved in order to build a mass party in the image of the CPSU(b). As elsewhere in Eastern Europe, Stalin's "Short Course," *The History of the CPSU(b)*, would serve as the primer for this ideological work, and the Cominform resolutions about the Yugoslav heresy would instruct the SED members in the lessons of contemporary internationalism. In addition, a Politburo would be introduced into the SED to lead the increasingly unwieldy Party Executive, a Small Secretariat would be formed to control the activities of the party departments, and party candidacy would be introduced to test prospective SED members.[238]

With the go-ahead from the Soviets to mobilize the party on a new basis, if not to create a new socialist society in eastern Germany, the SED held the First Party Conference on January 25 through 29, 1949. With great fanfare, the SED institutionalized the party of the new type, which had been in the making, at the latest, since the early fall of 1948. Parity between the SPD and KPD, which had been a fiction for at least a year if not longer, was now formally abandoned, and the percentage of former SPD leaders in the SED hierarchy rapidly diminished in the months that followed.[239] The Sovietization of the party was also institutionalized at the party conference. In addition to the various changes approved in Moscow—the creation of the Politburo, the Small Secretariat, party candidacy, and so on—the SED introduced democratic centralism as the reigning principle of party organization. Factions or groups within the SED were strictly forbidden; there would be no opportunity from the Left or Right to challenge Politburo orthodoxy. The SED also invigorated the Personnel Policy Department of the party, which, like its powerful cousin in Moscow, the Cadres Department of the Central Committee, would be at the heart of creating the emerging East German *nomenklatura.*[240] In sum, the First Party Congress marked the end of the unity party in practice and in theory. The new SED, already in the making by late 1948, became a mass German Communist Party of the Soviet type. Erich Gniffke put it well when he noted in his farewell letter that it was easier for him to leave the party in October 1948 than it would have been a year earlier: "Then I would have had to leave the SED, today I leave the 'Party of the New Type,' or better, I leave the Ulbricht KPD of 1932."[241]

But even this "Ulbricht KPD of 1932" could not simply proclaim an end to criticism from the Right and Left and go about its agenda of communizing the zone. The SED, like the CPSU(b) of the 1920s to which the Soviets often compared it, developed its totalitarian style in contests with the opposition. Even the greater attachment to Marxism-Leninism fostered by the SED did not harness the leftist enthusiasms of many party members. In 1949, especially, a number of Left SED members simply could not understand the perpetuation of the myth that a deal could be made to unify bourgeois West Germany with the socialist East. As Bernard Koenen of Saxony stated the problem: "A part of the earlier members of the KPD see in our contemporary policies a rejection of internationalism. They would like to cease the struggle for the unity of Germany, the success of which, in their opinion, is impossible in any case, and, together with the Russians, carry on a clear Soviet line!"[242] While Koenen did not call his opponents on the unity question sectarians, Colonel General A. G. Russkikh of the Soviet Military Administration did, and he urged the SED to fight against these opponents of the "National Front" policy. But the resistance in the party was determined; numerous local SED groups felt deeply that "the National Front of Germany had already once led to fascism and they would not go along with 'such nonsense' [*solchen Quatsch*]."[243]

Despite the continuing pressure on its critics from the Left, the SED unremittingly complained in 1949 about the ubiquitous opposition of "sectarians," "ultraleftists," and "Trotskyists"—in the unions, the city administrations, and the evening schools. The party felt so vulnerable to leftist attacks that it charged the Higher Party School with formulating a "systematic argument" against the Trotskyists.[244] KPO sympathizers in Weimar continued to cause the party trouble by applying Leninism to the conditions of Stalinist Soviet Russia. Party Control Commmission reports hammered at the "sectarian" and "opportunistic" tendencies that infused the Thüringian party, and accused the leadership of being as guilty in this respect as the rank and file.[245] Even more critical was the situation in Berlin, where KPD groups in the Western sectors, out of reach of Soviet and East German agents, influenced their SED cousins in the Russian zone. If anything, the ideological struggle for the hearts and minds of communists in Berlin intensified in the late 1940s. At a Party Executive meeting of October 4, 1949, Ernst Hoffmann from Berlin denounced the persistent influence of "pure sectarian phenomena" on the life of the party. The Trotskyists, he added, posed a growing threat. For the first time since the founding of the SED, Hoffmann stated, the party leaders had to engage in fierce arguments against internal opponents, "where every comrade, who took part in them, was shaken to the core, and left the meetings upset and deeply shocked."[246]

Proclaiming itself a party of the new type in the Soviet mold did not spare the SED comrades the unrelenting advice of their Soviet "friends." If anything, Soviet officers took the new party line as an open invitation to instruct the Germans on being proper Marxist-Leninists. Not surprisingly, the Soviets found the SED lacking in many respects. They criticized the German party for not understanding the meaning of the dictatorship of the proletariat and for underestimating the importance of the struggle against revisionism, in the form of attacking Schumacherites still in the party.[247] The Soviets chastised the SED for not sufficiently publicizing and discussing the Cominform resolutions on Yugoslavia, and for not understanding their meaning for the German party—no doubt an accurate claim. Soviet political officers seemed intent on getting local SED groups to proclaim out loud their fealty to the Soviet Union as well as to the teachings of Marx and Lenin. The less ambiguous and more ritualistic the SED's proclamations in praise of Soviet communism, the more satisfied the Soviet observers were.[248] Local Soviet political officers also intervened more directly in the work of the party of the new type, rewriting "imprecise" resolutions, showing the SED committee where to hang portraits of Clara Zetkin and Rosa Luxemburg for International Women's Day, and formulating the appropriate proclamations to be adopted by the SED for bringing in the harvest.[249]

At the zonal level, Tiul'panov kept a careful eye on SED work, intervening in a variety of party campaigns and activities. Typical of his schoolmasterish tone and pettiness was his critique of the "serious deficiencies" of the SED in supervising the work of summer Pioneer camps. The camps themselves, Tiul'panov complained, were poorly provisioned and laid out; there were far too few musical instruments, library materials, and sports facilities. Small deficiencies mattered a lot to Tiul'panov, especially when they demonstrated a lack of attention to the way the Soviets did things. "In many camps there are no friendship banners, which are necessary for raising the flag during the celebration of triumphant measures; the overwhelming majority of Pioneers don't have Pioneer scarves." Ignoring the palpable reticence many SED members felt when dealing with summer camp rituals, which had been part of the attraction of Hitler Youth groups, Tiul'panov went on to criticize the lack of organization and discipline in the camps and the inattention to hygiene and health issues. Social organizations like the trade unions (FDGB) and the Free German Youth (FDJ) took too little interest, in his view, in the educational and political activities of the Pioneers.[250] An instructive sidelight to Tiul'panov's scathing criticism of the SED's handling of Pioneer camps was the problem SVAG and the SED had in bringing German and Soviet youth together during these summer activities. Despite efforts of the German children to impress their counterparts with their recitation of Soviet Pioneer oaths and their singing of Russian songs, the Soviet youths remained aloof.[251] This was another case in which the Germans were criticized for not loving and mimicking the Soviet Union enough, and even when they did their level best, they were still treated with indifference, if not disdain.

THE LAST STAGE

The tasks of the SED at the beginning of 1949 were delicate ones, and the persistent criticism from the Left did not make things any easier. The party leaders at once had to Bolshevize the German party while also appealing to Germans in the West to join the accommodationist National Front. They had to purge and discipline masses of party workers while coopting the LDP and CDU at home into continuing cooperation in the People's Congress movement. They had to satisfy the Soviets and earn entry into the Cominform while, at the same time, leading the movement for a united Germany. Wilhelm Pieck had these contradictions in mind when he stopped in Moscow for the May 1, 1949, celebrations while on his way to a health resort near Sochi on the Black Sea. Pieck's notes from this visit indicate that the "Leonhard Affair" was very much on his mind at the time. Wolfgang Leonhard, a member of the Ulbricht initiative group, had fled "head over heels" *(Hals über Kopf)* from the Eastern zone to Yugoslavia in March 1949.[252] Like other party veterans who used Marxism-Leninism as a tool for criticizing Soviet reality, Leonhard was condemned as a Trotskyite.[253] The fact that Leonhard had taught at the Karl Marx Higher Party School before his defection created special problems for the SED, since Leonhard had such widespread contacts among both the old and new generations of party leaders. The Party Control Commission was charged with reviewing the credentials of 4,000 leading SED officials, to ferret out others who might have shared Leonhard's "Titoist-Trotskyite" heresy.[254]

The primary issue on Pieck's mind was how the SED could fulfill the Soviets' mandate that it play the dominant role in the national movement. The People's Congress, with its SED-dominated People's Council, had been put together by the Soviets and the SED leaders in June 1948. But, as Pieck reported back after his trip to Moscow, Stalin felt that the movement had fallen short of its original goals. Many of the communists in the SED itself were repelled by the rhetoric of national unity. More important, the CDU and LDP resisted lining up behind an SED-led National Front movement. At this point, Vladimir Semenov, in particular, as political advisor to SVAG and a representative of the Foreign Ministry in

Germany, seized the initiative to push forward the National Front issue. As a result, in mid-May 1949, the Third People's Congress was called, and the voters were asked to affirm the following statement: "I am for the unity of Germany and a just peace treaty."[255] But even the results of this plebescite were mixed, and, to make matters worse, the Soviets lifted the blockade of Berlin just when the SED had been forced to deal with the negative consequences of the Berlin rail strike.[256]

In sum, the SED's position continued to suffer from its association with the Soviet occupation. All of the activity on behalf of the People's Congress amounted to very little. The initiative neither gave the SED control of the national movement nor prevented elections to the West German Bundestag on August 9, 1949. The poor showing of the KPD in these West German elections convinced the SED that the KPD had been too circumspect about its links to the Soviet Union. The best way to pursue truly national politics, the SED concluded, was to make absolutely clear to the people in the West "that in the world there exist two camps: the camp of imperialism, at the head of which is the USA, and the camp of democracy and socialism, at the head of which is the USSR."[257] With the SED firmly in the camp of the USSR, there still remained the question of what to do with the Eastern zone, now that the West Germans had clearly opted for their own government. To answer the question, the SED leaders, Pieck, Grotewohl, Ulbricht, and Oelssner went to Moscow once more, in September 1949, to confirm arrangements for the foundations of an East German government.

In Pieck's view, the West German elections of August 1949 demonstrated the success of the massive anti-Soviet and anti-SED propaganda campaign conducted by the centers of Western imperialism. But they also indicated that the time had come for the Eastern zone to have its own German government.[258] There was no sense in putting off the critical step any longer. With Semenov's help, the proper documents were prepared that would join the National Front to the People's Council and the other political parties. Problems in the SED—the party of the new type—were far from resolved in the zone, especially in Berlin. In the SED's view, sectarians continued to misunderstand and misstate the dimensions of the national question. But, as Pieck's notes affirmed, "Comrade St[alin]" provided the people of the Eastern zone with wise advice on how to go about forming a German government by affirming the plan presented by the SED leaders.[259] Conflicts within the German Left were submerged in the efforts to build a new state.

The Tiul'panov Question
and Soviet Policy-making
in the Zone

WHEN HISTORIANS OF AMERICAN FOREIGN policy want to understand U.S. policy in Germany after the war, they can draw on a rich array of documents ranging from the papers of presidents and their advisors to the reports of State Department and U.S. Army representatives in Germany. They are able to reconstruct the arguments between the State Department and the War Department about the future of Germany and examine the mechanisms by which these arguments were resolved in practice. They also can demonstrate the ways in which fears of Soviet encroachment influenced the Truman administration's determination to create a West German state within the American sphere of influence.

By comparison, historians of Soviet policy in Germany have been at a decided disadvantage. Until very recently they had to rely on scattered memoirs and published documents for their sources, and they had to conduct detailed analyses of the Soviet press and foreign policy journals in order to reconstruct Soviet motivations and intentions in Germany. To be sure, there was no lack of work on Soviet views *about* Germany, which culled information from Molotov's speeches, Stalin's terse interviews, and seminal Soviet articles about international affairs, published after the war.[1] But the internal workings of Soviet policy—the motivations and intentions of its authors and the dynamics of its implementation—were much harder to establish. Historians could map out the possible alternatives for Soviet German policy, and they could trace the concrete actions taken by the Soviets in their zone of occupation.[2] However, it has been next to impossible to follow the connections between the two.

To finesse the inaccessibility of internal Soviet documents, scholars of Soviet policy used the methods of historical Kremlinology to analyze the fragmentary evidence of Soviet German policy after the war. William McCagg, Jerry Hough, and Werner Hahn looked at the "German question" in the context of Soviet domestic rivalries between Stalin's lieutenants, principally A. A. Zhdanov, G. M. Malenkov, and Lavrenti Beria.[3] More recently, Bernd Bonwetsch somewhat more successfully linked postwar Kremlinology to concrete Soviet policies in the Eastern zone. But at critical points he, too, was forced to rely heavily on a few selected memoirs to prove the connections between Kremlin politics and Soviet actions in Germany in general and in the Eastern zone in particular.[4] Gavriel Ra'anan's book, *International Policy Formation,* took this analysis the furthest, and in this sense his argument represents that of a generation of historical Kremlinologists.[5]

Ra'anan's thinking on the German question focuses on the role of Colonel Sergei Tiul'panov in the Soviet Military Administration in Germany and on Tiul'panov's alleged links with Andrei Zhdanov and the Leningrad group in the Soviet leadership. According to Ra'anan, this group, later purged in the famous "Leningrad affair," supported a more "radical" solution to the German problem—that is, the creation of a Sovietized Eastern zone, which conformed to Zhdanov's own emphasis on the "two-camp" interpretation of the postwar world and anticipated the division of Europe (and Germany) into socialist and capitalist spheres. In Ra'anan's view, Zhdanov—CPSU(b) Central Committee secretary for foreign communist parties—was convinced, as was Tiul'panov, that Walter Ulbricht was the right man to Stalinize the eastern German party for this purpose. As a result of their interest in creating a permanent communist Germany, Zhdanov, Tiul'panov, and Ulbricht opposed the removal of industry in the zone as resolutely as they could.

In this scheme, the Soviet commander-in-chief, Marshal G. K. Zhukov, his political advisor, Vladimir Semenov (who also represented the Ministry of Foreign Affairs in the zone), and Zhdanov's Moscow opponents, Malenkov and Beria, formed an opposing camp that was more committed than the Zhdanov-Tiul'panov group to a neutralized, antifascist, and united Germany. Initially, at least, they opposed the two-camp theory in favor of the more nuanced interpretations of Evgenii Varga, the Hungarian-born communist theoretician who predicted that a "third way" would develop in Europe, neither strictly capitalist nor socialist. Semenov, who was the chief Soviet representative in the Allied Control Council, adopted this more conciliatory approach as a strategy for the Ministry of Foreign Affairs to get the Western powers out of Germany. This group's position on the German question therefore anticipated the withdrawal of all Allied forces from Germany, which complemented their desire to seize and transport German assets from the zone to the USSR while it was still possible. Beria wanted to remove men and material for the purposes of bolstering his high-priority atomic bomb project. As chairman of the Sovnarkom commission on the rebuilding of destroyed Soviet lands, Malenkov was also ready to exploit German industrial and technological potential for Russia's benefit.[6]

Ra'anan and others like him also draw an interesting connection from the rivalry between the Zhdanov and Malenkov-Beria camps to the development of socialist party politics in the zone. Ostensibly Zhukov and Semenov (representing the Malenkov-Beria camp) were initially much less enthusiastic about the formation of the SED in the East, which—given the fierce opposition of the SPD in the West—everyone understood would be a significant impediment to the unification of the four zones. At the same time, Tiul'panov (representing the Zhdanov camp) sought to strengthen the communists in the zone by creating a Unity Party that would defuse the growing popularity of the SPD in the East. Tiul'panov was one of the first advocates for the Unity Party in the fall of 1945 and one of those most determined to bring it about by the spring of 1946. In this scenario, the growth of Tiul'panov's influence in April 1946 at the time of the foundation of the SED was related to Zhukov's removal and replacement in March by his deputy, V. D. Sokolovskii. Tiul'panov's increased stature in the zone also established his long-term rivalry in the Soviet Military Administration (as head of the Propaganda/Information Administration) with Semenov, who liked to think of himself as the Soviet "Gauleiter of Germany."[7] The rivalry was resolved only in the fall of 1949, when Tiul'panov was censored by the Central Committee and removed from Germany in disgrace, and Semenov was made Soviet High Commissioner after the founding of the German Democratic Republic.

While these Kremlinological interpretations include some documentable facts and provide some sense of the political context in which Soviet German policy was made, there is simply not enough good evidence to consider them as anything more than an educated form of historical speculation. Some of the recent German work on Soviet policy in Germany is less willing than Ra'anan and the historical Kremlinologists to draw conclusions about Tiul'panov's role in the Russian zone of occupation.[8]

At the same time, German historians disagree on the most fundamental questions regarding Soviet rule in Germany. Jan Foitzik, for example, thinks that Tiul'panov was not a critical figure in the military adminis- tration and that his importance has been much overstated in both Western and communist historiography. Based on careful consideration of the available sources, Foitzik does not believe that Tiul'panov was able to make policy in Germany, nor does he believe he was head of the SVAG party organization, which would have given Tuil'panov undue influence in SVAG and contacts in Moscow that would have gone beyond his mil- itary rank and his position in the administration. If Foitzik is right, Ra- 'anan's intricate argument linking the rise and fall of Tiul'panov to the fortunes of Zhdanov and the Leningrad group falls to pieces, not to men- tion the countless other assertions that Tiul'panov "was the leading ex- ponent of the position which favored rapid Sovietization" and could do something about it.[9] This leaves the historiography of Soviet intentions for and methods in eastern Germany pretty much where it started, with the reports of Robert Murphy from Berlin and George Kennan from Mos- cow.[10]

The recent *selective* opening of the Russian archives has provided his- torians with the opportunity, at long last, to see behind the facade of Soviet military headquarters in Karlshorst, to trace connections between the So- viet military government and Moscow, and to attempt to solve the Tiul'- panov riddle. In particular the archives of the Central Committee of the CPSU(b)'s International Department(s) have helped answer a variety of questions about Soviet intentions, motivations, and methods.[11] One can also gain important perspectives on the politics of the German question by examining the archives of the Soviet Foreign Ministry, especially the documents on Germany Semenov collected in the zone and sent back to Moscow.[12]

Without access to a whole series of archival collections relevant to So- viet policy-making in Germany, not the least of which are the Presidential Archives, this chapter cannot answer with assurance why particular pol- icies were pursued in Germany and how orders from Moscow were im- plemented by Karlshorst.[13] But new evidence can shed light on the Soviet administration of the Eastern zone by tracing the communications be- tween Moscow and Karlshorst and following the ways in which policies were articulated and implemented. Tiul'panov's role is indeed critical to resolving the questions: Who made policy for Germany, and who carried out policy in the Eastern zone?

THE PROPAGANDA ADMINISTRATION

In the context of the conflicting missions and chaotic lines of administrative responsibility in the Soviet military government, it is no wonder that the political demands of the Soviet occupation received minimal attention during the summer of 1945. Soviet soldiers were still hard to control, they committed repeated offenses against Germans and German property, and they were in constant need of supervision. In sometimes frantic sweeps throughout their zone of occupation, Soviet authorities seized German economic and technical resources to help restore their badly mangled economy at home. At the same time, SVAG was committed, albeit with limited resources, to rebuilding the German economy and administration and maintaining at least a minimal standard of living for the German population. But politics could not long be ignored, and in August 1945 the Propaganda and Censorship Department was created, later to be officially confirmed as an administration by the Council of People's Commissars (Sovnarkom) on October 5, 1945. Paraphrasing a draft of a Central Committee report to Stalin, the purpose of the new administration was to supervise, organize, and conduct propaganda among the German population via print media, radio, and film. It was to encourage the German antifascist parties and organizations to spread the word about their goals, as well as to censor what they produced. But as the same report made clear, the Propaganda Administration also quickly filled a vacuum in the activities of the Soviet military government, arrogating political tasks that had belonged to the commander-in-chief or to the Military Council.[14] Indeed, by the spring of 1946 the Propaganda Administration was running politics in the Soviet zone. Major General I. S. Kolesnichenko from Thüringen summarized the situation as follows: in practice, the officers of the Propaganda Administration "direct [*rukovodiat*] all questions having to do with the democratization of Germany, questions of running the parties, societal organizations, labor unions, and in general all political work among the German population."[15]

From the beginning, the head of SVAG's Propaganda (later Information) Administration was Sergei Ivanovich Tiul'panov.[16] Before the outbreak of the war, Tiul'panov had completed his economic studies at Leningrad University and taught political economy in the Central Committee's "Lenin course" in Leningrad. After the war broke out, he became a prominent figure in the Seventh Section of the Main Political Administration of the Red Army (GlavPURKKA) and operated on both the Stalingrad and Leningrad fronts. The Seventh Section was responsible for counterpropaganda among German soldiers, and it played an important role in recruiting captured German soldiers for the National Committee for Free Germany. By all reports, Tiul'panov had a solid knowledge of the German language and German culture; indeed, he was rumored to have studied for a year at Heidelberg University.[17] In any case, he was linked to circles of leading Soviet propagandists and German communists who initially discussed Soviet occupation policy in Moscow in late 1944. At the end of the war, Tiul'panov found himself in Prague, and in June 1945 he was brought to Dresden as Soviet editor of the *Dresdener Zeitung*. Then, at the end of June, he was called to Berlin to work on the staff of the Office of the Political Advisor.[18] His earlier established ties to communist activists and his German experience in general brought Tiul'panov to the attention of Zhukov and Lieutenant General F. E. Bokov, who nominated him in August for the post of head of the new Propaganda and Censorship Department. During the summer and fall of 1945, Tiul'panov reported to Bokov, a member of SVAG's Military Council, who had titular responsibility for political developments in the zone.

Among German communists and friendly social democrats, Tiul'panov was known simply as "the Colonel." With broad shoulders and a shaved head, Tiul'panov was as physically distinct from most other Soviet officers as he was unusual in his readiness to engage in open political argument. He could be engaging and charming, and he could be blunt to the point of bullying. He and his wife often entertained friendly German politicians, and his office eventually became the hub for the development of relations between the Soviet Military Administration and the emerging eastern German elite. Western intelligence officers were shocked by the chuminess between Tiul'panov and prominent Germans in the Eastern zone. A British officer by the name of Reginald Colby wondered at the sight of Tiul'panov and Paul Wandel (president of the Education Administration) walking out of an East Berlin theater arm in arm. This kind of familiarity, Colby noted, was unthinkable between a Western occupation officer and a German.[19]

In the winter and spring of 1945–46, Tiul'panov's Propaganda Administration grew to include ten departments *(otdel)* and 1,500 Soviet employees—the single largest administration in SVAG. At the time, Tiul'panov was considered by the Germans to be the inside man, the officer who supervised the sometimes violent campaign to unify the KPD and SPD and who forced Andreas Hermes out of his position as leader of the CDU in the East. However, Bokov was still considered the link to Zhukov and Moscow. "He [Tiul'panov] belonged to Lieutenant General Bokov's staff," noted one German report.[20] For matters like getting payoks for party members, or obtaining cars, newsprint for party newspapers, and permission for special cultural programs, SED leaders still went to Bokov as late as November 1946.[21]

In a March 1946 report to G. F. Aleksandrov, the powerful chief of the Agitprop Administration of the Central Committee, Colonel General I. V. Shikin, chief of GlavPURKKA, expressed considerable satisfaction with the work of the Propaganda Administration. "The formation of the Propaganda Administration has fully justified itself," wrote Shikin. "The commanders of the Soviet Military Administration in Germany now have in the form of the Propaganda Administration a powerful political apparatus through which they can control and direct [*kontroliruet i napravliaet*] the social-political life of the Soviet zone of Germany."[22] Shikin went on to praise the administration for its strong leadership of antifascist democratic propaganda, for its successful direction of censorship, and for its dissemination of a positive message about the Soviet Union. He also expressed satisfaction with the administration's role in the major judicial, school, and agrarian reforms that transformed the Soviet zone in the fall of 1945.

Writing at the height of the unity campaign, Shikin noted that he was also pleased that the administration had taken the lead in shaping the bloc of antifascist parties and "in creating the basis for the formation of the unified socialist party."[23] The Propaganda Administration strengthened the democratic forces in Germany, Shikin concluded, and successfully introduced "deep socioeconomic transformations" in the zone.[24] In fact the Propaganda Administration had involved itself to such an extent in the control *(kontrol')* of political life in the Soviet zone that Shikin suggested its name be changed to the Political Control Administration of SVAG. Among other suggestions for improvements, Shikin advised that the Propaganda Administration be allocated at least 500 more soldiers, and he offered cadres from GlavPURKKA to fill the places. Moreover, he suggested that the administration could successfully use an additional 2,000 German POWs—those who had finished antifascist schools in the USSR—to work in local governments and democratic organizations.[25]

Soviet bureaucratic discourse also required some critical remarks about the Propaganda Administration, and Shikin obliged. But when he pointed to a number of "serious weaknesses" in the work of the administration, he opined that they could be solved only by increasing the size (and therefore the power) of Tiul'panov's group. There was not enough propaganda work, he stated, among the peasants, the petit bourgeoisie of the towns and cities, and the intelligentsia. The administration did not pay sufficient attention to young people and women, he believed, not to mention the CDU, the church, or the evening universities, and local Soviet propagandists were of low quality and sometimes made frightful mistakes in their work. Shikin wrote that the administration also needed to engage in "systematic counterpropaganda" in the face of the increasing level of "active measures" taken by Western Allied administrations to keep "democratic ideas and the influence of the Soviet Union" from penetrating into the Western zones, "to weaken Soviet influence in Berlin," and even "to capture the German population of the Soviet zone of occupation for their political purposes."[26]

The issue of counterpropaganda was central, as well, to a more barbed critique of Tiul'panov's activities sent by the Office of the Political Advisor to the commander-in-chief to the Foreign Ministry in Moscow. This May 1946 report expressed considerable worry about Allied (meaning Western Allied) attacks on the Soviet position in Germany: "Allied propaganda actively interferes in all political questions having to do with German life and attempts to resolve them in opposition to our interests."[27] The report went on to complain that there was no real propaganda center in SVAG that could launch a successful counterpropaganda campaign. As for Tiul'-panov's Propaganda Administration, it engaged—according to the report—in all kinds of political activities, "only not in propaganda in the full sense of the word." The Office of the Political Advisor was also upset by what it felt was the Propaganda Administration's excessively close ties with the newly formed SED: "The ties between the SED and SVAG are obvious for everyone to see. In the eyes of the masses, the SED often appears to be some kind of middleman between average Germans and the occupation forces . . . This lowers the authority of the SED as a national party and provides reactionary elements with material for spreading all kinds of slander against the SED as 'an agent of Moscow' and so on."[28] In short, Semenov's office attacked Tiul'panov for manipulating the SED for his own purposes instead of paying attention to the rivalry between the Allies over Germany as a whole.

The Propaganda Administration's increasing involvement with the SED was also the subject of a second report by Shikin, head of GlavPURKKA, to the Central Committee in early August 1946. During this period,

GlavPURKKA occupied a key bureaucratic position, reporting both to the General Staff and to the Central Committee. Though formally a branch of the armed services, it increasingly acted as an agency of the Central Committee and was charged with overseeing the political development of the Soviet zone of occupation. As a result Shikin's opinions carried a lot of weight, and though his August 1946 report was quite positive, he expressed some worries about the upcoming local elections in the Soviet zone and in Berlin. Shikin did not share the political advisor's negative views about the administration's involvement in German politics. Instead, he praised Tiul'panov's operation for taking appropriate measures to ensure victory in the elections, such as formulating the election platform of the SED and rewriting the joint documents of the antifascist bloc. The Propaganda Administration had even succeeded, noted Shikin, in convincing the Christian Democrats and the Liberal Democrats "to change significantly their electoral platforms, throwing out those positions and slogans that were unacceptable to us."[29] The Central Committee, through Shikin, approved of the way the Propaganda Administration manipulated eastern German politics for Soviet ends, and was much less concerned about reactions in the West than was the Office of the Political Advisor.

If Shikin was critical of any aspect of the work of the administration, it was that the Propaganda Administration was not involved enough in politics, especially at the local level. The SED local leadership was lazy and disorganized, he complained. Some SED mayors thoroughly discredited themselves among their constituencies with their inattention to the needs of the populace. Other SED politicians reflected a "backward-looking, nonparty mood." He claimed that many of them did not understand the politics of the party and that they were ill-informed about its program.[30] Given this situation, Shikin concluded, there might be problems at the polls. He continued to maintain that one of the major obstacles to the success of Soviet policies in Germany was the fact that the Propaganda Administration was overburdened and could not handle all of its responsibilities. Therefore Shikin suggested that the Central Committee send to Germany, temporarily, a group of leading political and media specialists to prepare for the elections. He also encouraged Moscow to send musical groups, symphonies, opera companies, and theater troupes, to demonstrate the superior qualities of Russian culture to voters in the zone. Shikin's report was permeated with the accurate perception that the Germans did not fully appreciate the good deeds and intentions of the Soviet occupiers. For officials like Shikin, the only answer was to step up propaganda efforts that would properly inform the Germans of the truth.

THE CENTRAL COMMITTEE AND THE ELECTIONS OF FALL 1946

In the bizarre world of Stalinist Russia, elections played a curiously significant role in the Soviets' evaluations of their policies, both domestically and abroad. Despite the obvious manipulations and rituals attached to elections within the USSR, the political system depended on full participation and the complete confirmation of CPSU(b) "candidates." Similarly, the Soviets took the postwar elections in Eastern Europe and in the Soviet zone in Germany very seriously indeed. Like the elections at home, the results were seen as confirmation of the greatness of Stalin's leadership and the inherent correctness of party policies. Important electoral setbacks in Hungary and Austria in the fall of 1945 were very difficult for the Soviets to absorb, and they played a crucial role in the development of a more aggressive policy in their area of influence.

Shikin's communications to the Central Committee aroused the Secretariat's anxieties about the upcoming elections in Germany. Zhdanov and A. A. Kuznetsov decided to send a commission made up of M. I. Burtsev, A. S. Paniushkin, and K. S. Kuzakov to Germany, to evaluate Shikin's suggestions and to represent their interests as Central Committee secretaries.[31] Even before the commission departed from Moscow, however, the Central Committee received communications that the elections could prove disastrous. Lieutenant Colonel G. Konstantinovskii of the Seventh Section of GlavPURKKA, sent by Burtsev to Berlin to investigate the preparations for the elections, reported back that the Propaganda Administration had all but ignored the needs of the Berlin electorate. Certainly part of the problem, Konstantinovskii noted, was the four-power status of Berlin, which meant that many of the "popular measures" taken elsewhere in the Soviet zone—land reform, factory expropriations, denazification, and the like—could not be applied in Berlin. For this reason, Konstantinovskii suggested, the Berlin SED was weaker and the CDU and LDP were stronger than in the Soviet zone proper. But there were also serious failings on the part of the Propaganda Administration and the Berlin SED leaders, who, in their "pessimism" about the chances for electoral success in the city, had paid little attention to preelection agitation.

The population of Berlin was "indifferent" to the program of the SED, Konstantinovskii correctly reported, and the Berlin SED leadership took a passive approach to the party's lack of popularity. The SED was especially incapable of making gains among Berlin's female population, and the party seemed alienated even from the city's working class. Konstantinovskii's litany of criticisms of the Propaganda Administration and the Berlin SED leadership went on and on: "Ideological-educational work with members of the SED is very weak. SED members are increasingly inactive, and attendance at meetings falls. There are absolutely no theoretical articles in the SED newspapers ... In many lower party organizations in Berlin there is no authentic unity at all, but rather two factions [former KPD and former SPD] opposed to one another."[32] From Konstantinovskii's point of view, the Soviets faced a potentially humiliating electoral defeat in Berlin if they did not take prompt action.

Despite the sharper tone of his criticisms, Konstantinovskii's suggestions for improving the work of the Propaganda Administration were not much different from Shikin's. He urged the Central Committee to send 200 German antifascists to work in the electoral campaigns in Berlin and in the provinces, especially among the intelligentsia. He suggested that experienced female Soviet propagandists and party veterans be sent to Berlin to help deal with the deep antipathy toward the SED among German women. Finally, he urged SVAG (and therefore the Propaganda Administration) to follow a much more determined policy for splitting the Berlin SPD, which posed the most serious political problem for the SED in the city. He felt that there was much to be gained by accelerating the consolidation of the left wing of the SPD to the point of forming a new party, the Left SPD. In this way, Konstantinovskii suggested, the SPD would be rent by such chaos and disorder that the position of the SED would dramatically improve.[33] This was a tactic to which the Soviets would return repeatedly in Western-occupied Germany and Berlin.

Warnings about the elections and the decision to send a Central Committee commission came too late to alter the initial results. The first local elections were held on September 1, 1945, in Saxony, supposedly an SED stronghold. Its provincial government had taken the most determined steps toward implementing a Soviet-style program. The Soviets and the SED leadership saw its police and judicial authorities as the best organized and most "progressive" in the zone. Yet despite the numerous instances of outright discrimination by the Soviet authorities against the CDU and the LDP—in some cases their candidates were stricken from local voting lists altogether—and despite significant material help for the SED, the "bourgeois" parties were able to garner substantial voter support: the LDP, 671,000 votes (22 percent of the total); the CDU, 655,000 (21 percent); and the SED, 1.6 million (53 percent). (The remainder of the votes went to a variety of SED-sponsored social organizations, like the FDGB and the FDJ.) But the big shock for the Soviet administation, not to mention the SED, was the fact that in the big cities of Saxony—Leipzig, Dresden, Zwickau, Plauen, and Bautzen—with their large concentrations of workers, the SED received fewer voters than the LDP and CDU combined.[34] A similar pattern of voting emerged in Thüringen, but the SED did somewhat better in Brandenburg and Mecklenburg (receiving 60 percent and 69 percent of the vote, respectively), where there were fewer local CDU and LDP organizations, often a direct result of the intrigues of the provincial Propaganda Administrations.[35]

The October 20 Kreis and Landtag (district and provincial assembly) elections produced equally discouraging results for the Soviets. In those elections, the SED was not able to obtain a majority of voters, indicating the population's growing reservations about the SED and its program. The Unity Party's popularity was decreasing rather than increasing, and the elections drove this fact home. Perhaps most shocking for SVAG's political officers and the Central Committee observers were the results of the elections in Greater Berlin, which were also held on October 20. Even the pessimists in the Propaganda Admininistration and the Berlin SED leadership would have been hard pressed to predict the electoral catastrophe, in which the SED finished in third place behind the SPD and the CDU: SPD, 1,015,609 votes (48.7 percent of the total); CDU, 462,425 (22.2 percent); SED, 412,582 (19.8 percent); and LDP, 194,722 (9.3 percent). The German historian Hermann Weber writes about how difficult it was for the SED to accept the results in districts like "Red" Wedding, where in 1929 the KPD had received 45 percent of the vote and in 1932, 60 percent of the vote, but in 1946 the SED could manage only 29 percent.[36] (Wedding, it should be clear, was in the British zone.)

TIUL'PANOV AND THE GERMAN PARTIES

The Central Committee commission (Paniushkin, Burtsev, and Kuzakov) that visited the Soviet zone from September 14 to September 30, 1945, took as its primary task investigating the electoral problems faced by the Soviets in eastern Germany. Their first order of business was to attend a

Propaganda Administration conference organized by Tiul'panov to review the results of the local elections and to organize the administration's efforts for the district and provincial campaigns. Tiul'panov dominated the session, downplaying the negative impact of election results as "only the first stage of this great task that we carry on in order to form a new state political apparatus for a democratic Germany."[37] At the same time, he understood that the elections also marked an important stage in the "democratization" of Germany, and as a result, he knew that the Propaganda Administration was obliged to analyze them in depth. When Tiul'panov's introduction was finished, the section leaders from the Propaganda Administration rose one after another to describe the problems in their sections (labor unions, culture, women's groups, and so on). They were sometimes interrupted by questions from their Central Committee guests and often by interpellations from Tiul'panov, who loomed over the two-day session.

The head of the Labor Union Department, A. A. Voskresenskii, was the first to speak, and he set the tone for the rest of the meeting by blaming the failures in the zone on the SED. The leaders of the Unity Party ignored work among the labor unions, he maintained, and therefore they had lost votes in the large working-class cities of Saxony. The SED also made very poor use of Marshal Sokolovskii's order regarding "equal pay for equal work," added Tiul'panov, indicating that otherwise the SED would have been able to garner much more support among women workers.[38] Young workers also had been ignored, and Voskresenskii said that in future elections the Free German Youth should be utilized to a much greater extent to recruit members from the urban workforce. When he suggested that the advocacy of uniform social insurance, like that proposed by the Berlin SPD (but opposed by SVAG), would have attracted considerable support among Berlin workers, Tiul'panov interrupted: "It is categorically forbidden to raise this question. There will be no discussions [about it] with members of the SED or former communists or social democrats. It is forbidden to speak about it."[39] Some methods of electioneering, especially those that would make concessions to "SPD-ism", were unacceptable to Tiul'panov and the political authorities of SVAG.

The head of the Party Section of the Propaganda Administration, P. F. Nazarov, noted that many of the SED's internal weaknesses derived from the fact that a large cohort of former SPD members had entered the party for no other reason than to hide their true politics and wait for the appropriate time to leave. Tiul'panov added that the constant rumors implying that the Soviet Union might withdraw from Germany in the near future bred this kind of wait-and-see attitude among former SPD members in the SED. Tiul'panov insisted, in fact, that the SED and the German population needed to be told in no uncertain terms that the Soviet Union had the strength and durability to carry out its mission in Germany on a sustained basis.[40] In his view, this would have a positive effect on the upcoming elections, convincing especially those who wavered that the future belonged "to those who carry on a firmly expressed, pro-Soviet progressive orientation, or, as is said, an orientation toward the East."[41] Therefore Tiul'panov concluded that the Propaganda Administration should be expanded with additional cadres from the Seventh Section of GlavPURKKA, for the purpose of carrying out propaganda among the Germans about the determination, the moral strength, the military might, and the social accomplishments of the Soviet Union.

Tiul'panov also admitted that the SED suffered serious shortcomings. But he reminded his listeners that in November 1945 he had reported to the Military Council of SVAG that if the Soviets were not able to unite the KPD and the SPD, the communists would suffer severe defeat in the fall 1946 elections. This report, he immodestly added, was one of the "the most important documents" sent on to Stalin in the name of the Military Council to back up the need for the unity campaign. Indeed, all the efforts of his administration had been subsumed to that campaign; there was time for little else. But now, Tiul'panov stated, it was time for the Soviets to reshape the party and to transform it into an effective instrument of Soviet policy, though he explicitly rejected the possibility of conducting a "purge."[42]

Tiul'panov's characterization of the SED leadership does not sustain the assumption in Western historiography that he had a special relationship with Ulbricht. In fact, he talked mostly about Otto Grotewohl, who enjoyed, he stated, "great authority, not just among social democrats but also among communists." Tiul'panov noted with some satisfaction that he was still "specially working with Otto Grotewohl" and expected even better performance from the former SPD leader in the future.[43] The winning over of Grotewohl was particularly important, added Tiul'panov, because if the Soviets were to leave Germany—no wonder the rumors abounded, if Tiul'panov himself was planning for that contingency—Grotewohl was the only figure of stature in the SED leadership.[44] Wilhelm Pieck, in Tiul'panov's estimation, was a likable character, friendly and warm, but he talked too much and too loosely. As for Walter Ulbricht,

Tiul'panov did not share the view of those who thought that Ulbricht was too much of a "sectarian" and an ultraleftist. At the same time, Tiul'panov stated, Ulbricht was excessively sharp with his comrades and he too easily alienated those around him. Still, Tiul'panov admired Ulbricht: "Conspiratorially, he can carry out any kind of political machination and keep it to himself."[45] No doubt these machinations provided a powerful link between Tiul'panov and Ulbricht.

Though hard on the SED, Tiul'panov was much more critical of the so-called bourgeois parties, the CDU and the LDP. In fact, he thought that SVAG had been altogether too tolerant of the parties' leaders, who did not hesitate, in his view, to besmirch the honor of the Soviet Union. To deal effectively with the bourgeois parties, he believed, one had to give them orders and take appropriate "administrative measures." The Germans needed rules to follow, he stated, and they would abide by them as a people who love order: "It is necessary to forbid categorically even the slightest degree of disrespect toward the Soviet Union and Soviet occupation authorities. Once and for all, this is not preelectoral terror, but only quite normal order." The Soviets were not going to let them "spit in our face," Tiul'panov continued. Perhaps there was nothing that could be done about this in Berlin, he said, but anti-Soviet statements could certainly be controlled "in our zone, where in this regard we are the bosses" (*v nashei zone my po etoi linii khoziaeva*).[46]

Tiul'panov's hard line toward the CDU and LDP matched his growing attraction to the two-camp view of the international situation advocated by Andrei Zhdanov. It was important, he stated, to underline the contrast between U.S. secretary of state James F. Byrnes's "plan to enslave Germany" and Soviet foreign minister V. M. Molotov's contributions to German unity and economic development. But he believed it would be a "terrible political mistake" to bring up the possibility of changes to the Oder-Neisse boundary. Tiul'panov insisted, in fact, that, "from this moment on, there will be no discussion at all of the eastern borders, we will not permit any party [to discuss it], and if the bourgeois parties—the CDU and the LDP—start to speak [about the borders], then we will close down these meetings. We'll pick them up on the same day."[47] In the internal deliberations of the Soviet military government, Tiul'panov represented a highly politicized and uncompromising voice for communizing (if not Sovietizing) the zone. There would be no concessions to the bourgeois parties in the zone or to the SPD in Berlin. Tiul'panov also made it clear that Soviet policy would and should be backed up by the use of force and the threat of imprisonment. That would give the Germans a firm understanding of who was in control and what their own limits were.

At the September meeting, Tiul'panov also went into great detail about how the Propaganda Administration needed to help the SED become a genuine mass Marxist party, without, at the same time, mixing into internal party squabbles. The task of the Soviet officers was to instruct, but they were also enjoined to allow their pupils to grow and develop themselves. The SED should be touted not just as a Marxist party, Tiul'panov recommended, but even more widely as a "party of order." (Again, like Ulbricht, Tiul'panov was impressed by how attracted Germans were to law and order.) Many bourgeois professionals and small businessmen who voted for the LDP were worried about their jobs and the possibility that their earlier involvement with the Third Reich might be used against them. Could they not be won over to the SED, Tiul'panov asked, by appeals to their desire for consistency and stability? Drawing from the observation that people had already begun to talk about two zones—one in the East and one in the West—Tiul'panov also suggested that the SED could take greater advantage of the fact that many of the new bureaucrats and office workers in the East owed their livelihood to the Soviet administration and the maintenance of the status quo. These new state workers, Tiul'panov asserted, should be easily induced to join the ranks of the SED.[48]

Tiul'panov's practical—one might say cynical—approach to garnering votes knew few limits. For example, he advocated using American secretary of state Brynes's Stuttgart speech of September 6, 1946, as an example of how the monopoly capitalists were again ready to envelope Germany in war. This could easily be contrasted, he stated, with the slogan, A vote for the SED was a vote for peace: "[How about] a poster, with a woman standing with a child? This would strike at the sentimental feelings of women. This is well-known sentimental propaganda, tied to the danger of dragging Germany into war. And this can be used as a very powerful argument."[49] Tiul'panov also unabashedly advocated using Soviet control of food and heating resources to encourage votes for the SED. "It is necessary to organize the supply situation in such a way that if in Chemnitz the SED wins, then coal is all set to be distributed; there the administration succeeded in improving supplies."[50] He added that it could be made known in Dresden, where the mayor was not a member of the SED, that it would be harder to get heating materials if the SED were not successful. It was even possible, Tiul'panov noted, for trusted SED members to plant rumors that dismantling would take place in those cities where "monopoly capitalism" was strong and the SED was weak (that is, where citizens voted for the bourgeois parties).[51]

Whether the problem was the Church or the CDU, women's organizations or the Free German Youth, Tiul'panov expressed his willingness to cajole and bully, to threaten and bribe in order to win the elections. Even in the Soviet-initiated organization of the cultural and artistic intelligentsia, the Kulturbund, Tiul'panov's only answer to the organization's stagnation was to recommend the removal of Johannes R. Becher, the famous German communist poet, as its chairman. "[He] can no longer be tolerated" *(Bol'she terpet' nel'zia)*, Tiul'panov made clear. In his view, Becher was insufficiently tied to the SED, was not enough of a Marxist, and was basically useless as an organizer of the intelligentsia.[52] Indeed, Tiul'panov was wont to place blame for the weak electoral showing of the SED on just about everyone except for himself. He indicated that Semenov, for example, did not anticipate maneuvers by the Western powers in the Berlin kommandantura and as a result caused problems for the SED in the city. He even criticized his protégé, Otto Grotewohl, for making serious mistakes in his dealings with the Berlin SPD, which presented the SED with a much more serious electoral challenge in Berlin than was necessary.[53]

The members of the Central Committee commission in attendance at Tiul'panov's two-day conference interjected questions and cautiously stated their opinions. They were especially interested in the organization of propaganda and political work in SVAG, and pressed Tiul'panov on his relationship to Lieutenant General Bokov, who was a member of the Military Council and was therefore responsible for political work in the zone. General Burtsev of the Seventh Section got Tiul'panov to admit that he often did not follow Bokov's instructions and sometimes—in order to follow the correct political line—actually countermanded his superior's wishes.[54] According to Tiul'panov, Marshal Sokolovskii supported him in his efforts to pursue appropriate policies in the zone despite Bokov, who often made "serious political errors." Also, Tiul'panov reminded the commission, Bokov often was known to hold up important documents, refusing to act on them and thus delaying time-sensitive actions and impeding the healthy political development of the zone.[55] Burtsev went the furthest of his colleagues in criticizing the Propaganda Administration's lack of interest in bloc politics and its fetish for control when it came to its relations with the bourgeois parties. Burtsev summarized his views: "The impression that has been left with me is that in relations with the bourgeois parties we are people of control and we exert very little influence on the content of their work, [and] along with that, [we don't] exert influence on them as a way of fostering their democratization but as a way of checking on them."[56]

THE COMMISSION REPORT

The Central Committee commission remained in the zone until September 30, 1946, interviewing staff members in Tiul'panov's administration and Bokov's office, as well as other political figures in SVAG. The commission also met with a number of SED politicians, soliciting their views on the party's political problems among the German population. For example, the commission conducted a long interview with Hermann Matern, head of the Berlin SED organization, along with Major General A. G. Kotikov, commandant of the Soviet sector of Berlin. At the end of the interview, Matern predicted that the party would do well in the Berlin elections: "I already said that the largest portion of the population [of Berlin] had not yet made up its mind for whom they will vote. If we avoid committing any major stupid mistakes [*gluposti*] and continue the political approach that we have begun, then we don't look bad at all in Berlin."[57] Neither Matern nor Kotikov seemed to understand the depth of the opposition in the city to continued Soviet occupation and therefore to the SED.

During their inspection visit to the Soviet zone, the commission members mostly kept their opinions to themselves. However, their October 11 report to the Central Committee sharply attacked the work of the Propaganda Administration for its "serious deficiencies" even before the results of the district, regional, and Berlin elections were known.[58] The commission accused the administration of spending too much time worrying about the CDU, especially in the provinces, while it ignored the growing power of the LDP. In the opinion of the commission, the Propaganda Administration had waited until the last minute to focus its attention on Berlin's critically important electoral campaign. Even when Tiul'panov's officers had gotten involved in the campaigns, the report charged, they had caused as many problems as they had solved by removing local SED leaders and engaging in a variety of intrigues involving the leadership of the unions (the FDGB), the youth organizations (the FDJ), and the women's organizations (the DFB), among others.

According to the commission's report, the Propaganda Administration had seriously underestimated the potential danger posed by the Berlin SPD organization, and this was exemplified by the inattention of Soviet political officers to the needs of the Berlin press. Radio, theater, and film went untapped, the report continued, as important sources for propaganda about the Soviet Union. In sum, the Soviet Union's propaganda in the Eastern zone was poorly organized, insufficiently coordinated, and haphazardly carried out.[59] Like virtually all other Soviet officials in the zone and in Moscow, the commission members blamed the growing unpopularity of the Soviet presence in Germany not on the Soviet Union's actions as an occupying power, but on its representatives' inability to communicate SVAG's accomplishments to the German population.

The commission's report also attacked personalities. Bokov did not do his job properly, the report stated, and as a result the Military Council played no significant role in propaganda issues: "Comrade Bokov does not pass judgment on many important questions regarding the organization and content of propaganda, and partly [these problems] go right by him."[60] The commission subjected Tiul'panov to similarly harsh assessments. In terms of his organizational abilities, Tiul'panov was judged to be "helpless and incapable" to lead the Propaganda Administration. He made "serious errors," the commission pointed out; he was "insufficiently disciplined"; and he was "inclined toward intrigues."[61] Tiul'panov's deputy, A. S. Zdorov, was no better in their view; moreover, he lacked sufficient theoretical sophistication, not to mention the ability, to make decisions on his own. Perhaps the most damning criticisms of the Propaganda Administration were that its work lacked any unifying concept and that its theoretical underpinnings were weak and poorly articulated.[62]

As a result of its findings, the commission recommended that Tiul'panov, Zdorov, and virtually all the heads of sections be removed from the Propaganda Administration, and that they be replaced with competent political functionaries. The commission suggested as well that Glav-PURKKA be charged with sending a new cadre of experienced political workers to Germany to lead the Propaganda Administration in the provinces, where everyone recognized there were extremely serious problems. In addition, the report recommended that Bokov be replaced as a member of the Military Council for his failure to provide direction to the Propaganda Administration.[63]

At the same time, the Central Committee commission asked Bokov to analyze the results of the Berlin elections as a way of responding to the report's criticisms of his work. Bokov's report demonstrated not only personal and institutional rivalries with Tiul'panov, but also a different strategy for dealing with German problems, one that was more closely tied to Semenov, his former boss Marshal Zhukov, and the Foreign Ministry. To be sure, he criticized the Propaganda Administration's "political intriguing" *(politikanstvo)*, which followed, he said, the doubtful principle that "in the [name of] the struggle all means are justified."[64] He insisted that a halt be put to "the harmful practice of ordering about [*komandovanie*], of crude interference [*vmeshatel'stvo*], and of tutelage [*opekunstvo*] from the side of the propaganda organs, all the more so since they themselves often adopt completely incorrect and harmful positions."[65]

But Bokov also criticized the Propaganda Administration for ignoring the principles behind the formation of the antifascist bloc and for encouraging "sectarianism" in the leadership of the SED. He suggested that deeper ties should have been developed with the progressive elements of the bourgeois parties and with the "pro-Soviet-inclined part of the SPD."[66] The Propaganda Adminstration should have been more flexible on the German question, Bokov added, and it should not have forced the SED into the position of having to appear as "the Russian party."[67] As for the zone itself, Bokov recommended that censorship be relaxed, that labor conditions be improved, and that the SED learn to deal openly and frankly with the burning issues on the minds of every German: the eastern borders, the continued dismantling of industries, and the return of German POWs from Russia. In short, Bokov recommended a broader, more all-German approach to the problems of the Eastern zone, one that unquestionably conflicted with Tiul'panov's understanding of Soviet priorities in Germany.

Bokov's more compromising salve for the festering sore of demonstrable Soviet unpopularity in the zone and especially in Berlin might have appealed to some of his superiors in Moscow, but it did not save his position. He was removed from the Military Council in November of 1946.[68] However, the problem of what to do with the Propaganda Administration proved to be more intractable. Central Committee secretary A. A. Kuznetsov, to whom the commission report was submitted, turned to the Cadres Administration of the Central Committee for an additional report on the formation and development of the Propaganda Administration of SVAG. This report, dated November 12, 1946, claimed that the staffing of the Soviet Military Administration had to be accomplished so quickly that very few personnel out of the original total of 13,000 assigned to work in Germany had been checked out by the Central Committee, as should have been the case. Most had been passed through the Ministry of Armed Forces, as well as other ministries in Moscow. In addition to the original 13,000 men and women assigned to SVAG, some 1,500 specialists were sent to Germany during the first nine months of 1946. Altogether, some 5,000 people were in the administrations and departments of the central apparatus of SVAG, which—according to the Cadres Department report—should have been sufficient for the military administration to do its business.[69] According to the commission report, originally there were 489 officials in the Propaganda Administration and its local organs, 85 of whom worked in headquarters itself.[70]

Even more than the commission, the Cadres Department was very disturbed by the relatively large number of Jews in the Propaganda Administration. According to its figures, 180 members (37 percent) of the staff of the administration were Jews. The percentage of Jews working on the German-language SVAG newspaper, *Tägliche Rundschau,* was even greater: 38 out of 65, or 58 percent of its employees.[71] This was the first indication of a growing obsession in the Central Committee apparatus with the number of Jews in the military administration in Germany.

THE CREATION OF THE INFORMATION ADMINISTRATION

Several important documents in the Central Committee archives demonstrate how difficult it was for the secretaries to deal with the disturbing problems that had emerged in the Propaganda Administration. Two draft documents intended for Stalin (the first, "To Comrade Stalin, I. V."; the second, "To Comrade Stalin") took different approaches to resolving these problems. The first emphasized the accomplishments of the Propaganda Administration in the transformation of the Soviet zone. The second presented only the failures of Tiul'panov and his operation: the drubbing taken by the SED in the Berlin election, the poor use of antifascist parties and organizations, the absence of forceful counterpropaganda, the SED's reputation in Germany as a "Russian agent," and the lack of ideological and political sophistication of the administration's members.[72] Although both drafts suggested that the heads of the various sections of the Propaganda Administration be removed, they left the issue of Tiul'panov's fate in Stalin's hands; however, they stated unambiguously that Tiul'panov "is helpless in organizational affairs and does not exert leadership over the work of the apparatus."[73]

The letters to Stalin did recommend that the name of the organization be changed to Information Administration, because the name Propaganda Administration was "discredited" in the eyes of Germans as a result of its use by the Nazis.[74] The suggestion derived from a number of letters from Soviet communists in the zone noting the German democrats' misunderstanding of and aversion to the concept of "propaganda." In addition, a number of suggestions were made to improve Central Committee oversight of German affairs, including sending M. A. Suslov and Shikin to Germany for a month to help the reconstituted Military Council of SVAG organize political work in the zone.

Further draft documents that date from December and January 1946–47 explored a variety of ways to reorganize the political work in Germany. A draft entitled "On the Work of the Propaganda Administration of SVAG" suggested making the new Military Council member V. E. Makarov head of the Information Administration and keeping on Tiul'panov as his deputy.[75] But another draft of the same document, dated December 10, 1946, simply left blank the replacement for the head of the Information Administration while making clear that Tiul'panov was to be removed.[76] This document in general sympathized with an approach that focused on the antifascist democratic bloc to resolve the problems of political work in the zone, not unlike that represented by Bokov's critique of the Propaganda Administration.

The determination to remove Tiul'panov that infused this set of documents from the Central Committee indicated that his hard-line approach to politics in the zone was being seriously reconsidered. The second draft document, "On the Organization of a Military-Political Council in SVAG," aimed to correct the tendency at Karlshorst to leave local German politics to the Propaganda (now Information) Administration. In fact, the document specifically forbade "giving general political recommendations to the German parties and societal organizations without the permission of the Military-Political Council." According to this draft document, Sokolovskii would head up the new Military-Political Council and his deputy would be Makarov, who had taken Bokov's place in SVAG. Seventh Section chief M. I. Burtsev would be made head of the new Information Administration and would also serve on the council.[77] Tiul'panov was clearly meant to be demoted or removed altogether from the zone.

The result of this whirl of activity in January 1947 around the reorganization of the Information Administration temporarily altered the leadership of political affairs in the zone. In recognition of the fact that Marshal Sokolovskii was unlikely to be able to exert the necessary control over political matters in Germany, Lieutenant General Makarov was given the new position of deputy commander-in-chief of SVAG for political affairs. In addition, the Secretariat assumed the responsibility of reviewing "all questions having to do with contemporary politics in Germany."[78] By the spring of 1947, Mikhail Suslov apparently took charge of German affairs.[79] (He had already been involved in the international departments since his transfer to the Central Committee in the spring of 1946.[80])

As we know, by the end of 1946 Bokov had been officially removed from his position. Despite the fact that in every draft document on the reorganization of the Information Administration Tiul'panov was slated for removal or demotion, he managed to survive as chief of the new administration. Periodically during 1947 and 1948, documents would appear that were signed by an acting chief of the administration, usually Colonel A. Abramov. By all accounts, however, Tiul'panov remained in the thick of the political struggle that was transforming the Eastern zone, and, by his actions at least, he appeared neither humbled nor reformed by his experiences. On the contrary, Tiul'panov seemed emboldened by the fact that he was not removed, and he continued to push his vision of Soviet-zone affairs from his Information Administration post. In December 1947 he bullied Jakob Kaiser into leaving his position as head of the CDU in the East and forced him to leave for the West. In the spring and summer of 1948, Tiul'panov oversaw the shift of the SED from a mass antifascist party into a "party of the new type." These and other actions indicated his continuing willingness to follow a radical vision of affairs in the Soviet zone.

As chief information officer of SVAG, Tiul'panov also remained active in the Information Committee of the Allied Control Council's Political Directorate. He communicated with American General John McClure about the problems of making the Nuremburg Trial film, and with Colonel Gordon Textor about issues involving the entry of American and Soviet newspapers into the other's zones.[81] He was also the subject of considerable debate (and even embarrassment for Sokolovskii) in the Allied Control Council, when General Lucius Clay complained sharply about Tiul'panov's insulting "anti-American" speech at the Second Congress of the SED on September 20, 1947. Sokolovskii tried to assure the offended Americans that Tiul'panov's speech was directed only against "the reactionary intrigues of American monopolies," not against the Americans. At the same time, he assured his interlocutors that members of the military administration "would not permit themselves any action which might be interpreted as being directed against the Allies."[82]

THE RENEWED ATTACK, SUMMER AND FALL 1948

The reshuffling of political responsibilities in SVAG that centered around the creation of the new post of deputy commander-in-chief for political affairs, held by Bokov's replacement on the Military Council, General V. E. Makarov, did not substantially reduce Tiul'panov's influence on the course of political life in the zone. In fact, throughout 1947 he was as usual in the middle of the fray, advising the SED on how to deal with the minister-presidents' conference in Munich in June, giving his rousing address at the Second Congress of the SED in September, and forcing Kaiser and his deputy, Ernst Lemmer, out of the CDU leadership in December. Makarov was sick during much of this time and made no serious effort to keep Tiul'panov in line. The Central Committee understood that Marshal Sokolovskii was so overwhelmed with the general problems of leading SVAG, resolving economic questions, and working with the troops stationed in Germany that he "paid little attention to the work of the Information Administration."[83] (By the spring and summer of 1948, Sokolovskii also had to be occupied with growing military tensions surrounding the Berlin blockade.)

The Central Committee was deeply concerned about the heightened political tension in the zone. The terrible showing of the SED and the Soviet-supported Free German Federation of Unions in the March 1948 union and factory council elections in Berlin also disturbed Central Committee observers.[84] As a result, the Secretariat set up yet another commission in late March 1948 to review the work of the Information Administration. Once again Tiul'panov and his cohort were taken to task for their lack of political success among the Germans. Once again the commission's report consisted, in essence, of the accusation that Tiul'panov was excessively harsh and premature in his attempts to introduce socialism into the Eastern zone. As in the past, he was criticized for attacking the bourgeois parties and for manhandling bourgeois politicians, while paying too little attention to the needs of shopkeepers, small-time entrepreneurs, and traders. The Information Administration looked at the CDU and the LDP as enemies, the report noted, instead of working with the parties to isolate right-wing opponents and support progressive elements.[85] When the administration did deal with the bourgeois parties, the report stated, it indulged in crude administrative measures, "carrying out one 'palace revolution' after another."[86]

The new commission also accused the Information Administration of continuing to interfere inappropriately in the day-to-day affairs of the SED. At the same time, Soviet officers were condemned for paying insufficient attention to larger ideological and political issues in the German party, such as the continuing problems of "SPD-ism," the lack of criticism and self-criticism among party leaders and rank and file, and the "dangerous tendencies toward a leader fetish" *(vozhdizm)*—a clear reference to the fact that Pieck, Grotewohl, and Ulbricht had an excessive amount of power concentrated in their hands.[87] The SED leaders, the report complained, had become isolated from the masses, and the Information Administration did nothing about it: "No one [neither the SED nor SVAG] is conducting political discussions with peasants and workers; lectures and talks are given only in exceptional cases."[88] Work among the intelligentsia also lagged badly, the commission wrote, and counterpropaganda remained poorly developed and was insufficiently thought through. Finally, the report focused on the catastrophic situation of the Soviet administration and the SED at the local level. No one seemed to be able to do anything about the extremely low standard of political and ideological development among the local commandants, many of whom were accused of being "absolutely incapable" of solving the most straightforward economic and political tasks.[89]

The members of the Central Committee commission expressed utter frustration with Tiul'panov's intriguing, and they seemed to have lost all hope that he would improve:

Colonel Tiul'panov does not understand the historical perspectives on the development of Germany, [he] doesn't understand the distribution of class forces in the zone, [he] is attracted to petty scheming [*melkim kombinatorstvom*]. He lacks the necessary diplomatic flexibility, political tact, and the ability to maneuver. [He] does not have the necessary organizational qualities, and he cannot lead political work in Germany.

His crude meddling in the affairs of the parties and his attempts at self-advertisement make it impossible for him to continue as head of the administration.[90]

The commission concluded its report by suggesting, as well, that local commandants be replaced by more competent officials, preferably with the career profiles of Soviet *raikom* (regional committee) party secretaries. It also recommended that the Central Committee convene a special meeting to discuss the pressing issues of political work in Germany.

The commission report was accompanied by a draft Central Committee resolution that chastised the Information Administration for not accomplishing its basic (though no doubt impossible) mission of convincing the Germans in the Eastern zone that a Soviet-inspired "democratic" transformation was in their interests and those of their countrymen in the West. This failing was particularly critical in light of the serious international situation, the resolution concluded. Moreover, with tensions rising in Germany, the lack of support among the population in the East fostered the growing "influence of the reaction on some sections of the German population in the Soviet zone."[91]

Given the direct attacks on Tiul'panov in the commission report, it is astonishing that he was not removed as head of the Information Administration and that he continued to operate as if nothing had happened. One might speculate that Tiul'panov was protected by Kuznetsov (in charge of cadres), Suslov (in charge of German policy), or Stalin, with whom Suslov in particular was in regular contact. The commission report was addressed to Zhdanov, who by the spring of 1948 was in political eclipse. (He died in the summer of 1948). Makarov *was* replaced as deputy commander-in-chief for political affairs in July 1948 by Lieutenant General A. G. Russkikh.[92] But General Shikin of GlavPU continued to worry about whether Tiul'panov had followed up on the Central Committee's resolutions of the previous spring. He sent his trusted deputy, Colonel Konstantinovskii—who had also been a member of the commission—back to Berlin from mid-June to mid-July 1948, to see that resolutions were being carried out. Konstantinovskii asserted in his August 1948 report to the Central Committee that in a number of areas the Information Administration had markedly improved its work.[93] He noted particularly that the ideological and educational activities among the SED had reached a higher level. He was especially satisfied that "special attention is paid to the study of the Leninist-Stalinist stage in the development of Marxism."[94]

He also expressed satisfaction with the work to date of Russkikh in co-ordinating Soviet political activities among the Germans, one of SVAG's persistent weaknesses in the Eastern zone.

But, stated Konstantinovskii, Tiul'panov continued to make the same "serious political mistakes," especially in dealing with the "nonproletar-ian" elements of the German population—the intelligentsia and the lower middle class. Konstantinovskii also accused Tiul'panov of flaunting the Central Committee commission's explicit orders to develop more fully the coalition (bloc) approach to politics in the zone.[95] Ostensibly citing the statements of Political Advisor Semenov, Konstantinovskii reported that Tiul'panov "openly and repeatedly" told his workers that the Central Committee commission's recommendations about working together with the bourgeois parties could be ignored.[96] The result, in Konstantinovskii's view, was that "leftist mistakes" *(levatskie oshibki)* were allowed to pervade the work of information officers, many of whom were never properly briefed about the Central Committee commission report and therefore worked under a series of mistaken assumptions. Chief among these as-sumptions were that the building of a "socialist republic" in the Soviet zone was already under way, that the phase of the bloc of antifascist dem-ocratic parties had already passed, and consequently that the time had come to move from the politics of the bloc to a "people's front." Typical of Soviet propaganda problems in the zone, in Konstantinovskii's view, was the statement of General Kolesnichenko of Thüringen at a meeting of commandants, that "in Germany we are not building in general a peace-loving democratic republic, but a socialist republic." In the same speech, Kolesnichenko went on to say that the SED should stop worrying about placating the bourgeois parties in the bloc and instead "heat up the class struggle."[97]

Konstantinovskii also accused Tiul'panov of having continued his prac-tice of threatening the rank and file of the bourgeois parties while forcing their leaders to do his bidding. Tiul'panov forgot, he stated, that "in the ranks of the CDU and the LDP are tens of thousands of sincerely misled workers and farmers of Germany, who need to be liberated from the prison of bourgeois ideology."[98] At the same time, Tiul'panov's false at-titude toward the bourgeois parties helped to create in the SED the pre-tensions of being the single "ruling" *(praviashchaia)* party in the zone. In a period in which the SED still needed to free itself from its sectarian ways, this kind of thinking, Konstantinovskii complained, easily fostered the SED's isolation in the bloc and led to the weakness of bloc politics in the

Soviet zone. In Konstantinovskii's view, the Information Administration was correct to recommend that the SED concentrate its political forces against the main dangers of the "Schumacherites" in its ranks. But, he added, in the conditions of a divided Germany, the SED and the Information Administration should also concern itself with the growth of sectarian ideas within the party.

Konstantinovskii's complaints about the organizational work of the Information Administration resembled those of other commissions and reporters dating back to the early fall of 1946. He said that there was insufficient coordination of political propaganda with the major administrative, economic, and political measures taken by the various sections of SVAG. For example, the "democratic monetary reform" in the Soviet zone was not accompanied by a major campaign contrasting it to the "antinational, separatist" monetary reform in the West.[99] The magnanimous release of prisoners and internees by the Soviet state security services announced in April 1948 was also not marked by any serious propaganda campaign. Even if General Russkikh had helped to improve coordination among SVAG branches, Marshal Sokolovskii still was not sufficiently concerned with this problem, which was demonstrated, Konstantinovskii asserted, by the commander-in-chief's refusal to create a "Soviet propaganda council" of SVAG.[100]

Given Konstantinovskii's critique of the Information Administration, it was hardly surprising that he advocated the removal of Tiul'panov and his replacement with the commandant of Berlin, Major General A. G. Kotikov. If this new appointment were impossible because of "international circumstances" (that is, the Berlin blockade) then Konstantinovskii suggested Major General V. M. Sharov of the Brandenburg administration for the information post.[101]

There can be little question that Konstantinovskii represented a very strong current of opinion in the Central Committee—one that persisted even during the Berlin crisis—that the ongoing Sovietization of the zone imperiled long-term Soviet interests in Germany. The secretaries of the Central Committee and their GlavPU representatives in Germany believed that the Soviet zone of occupation should not follow the patterns established by communist parties in Eastern Europe. The SED was not invited to Cominform meetings, nor was it allowed to assume the real or rhetorical status of the leading party in a people's democracy. Even Tiul'panov constantly made it clear to the SED leaders that they were not to think of themselves as being at the same level of historical development as the other Eastern European parties. In April 1948, shortly before the Yugoslavs were attacked by the Cominform, Tiul'panov put the Germans in their place with the following metaphor: "Yugoslavia has already reached the other bank [a socialist state]; Bulgaria is taking the last few strokes to reach it; Poland and Czechoslovakia are about in the middle of the river, followed by Romania and Hungary, which have gone about a third of the way, while the Soviet Occupation Zone has just taken the first few strokes away from the bourgeois bank."[102] Still, Tiul'panov wanted the Germans in the East to follow the path of the newly bolshevized parties of the other countries of Eastern Europe, and it was on this point that his views clashed with those of his superiors on the Central Committee.

THE LAST STAGE

Despite the massive amount of documentation demonstrating that Tiul'-panov was under attack from the Soviet Central Committee, it is still easier to trace his rise to power in eastern Germany than it is to understand why he fell when he did. There is evidence that in the autumn of 1948, the Central Committee once again sought a full-scale review of the work of the Information Administration.[103] This occurred just at the point when Tiul'panov had led the SED to renounce its "German road to socialism" and embark on creating "a party of a new type." It has also been reported that Tiul'panov was recalled from Germany in 1948 for an official inquiry conducted by the minister of the armed forces, Marshal N. A. Bulganin.[104] Documents recently released by the Tiul'panov family indicate that in December 1948, the Colonel faced accusations in Moscow that he had concealed facts relating to the arrests of his father and mother in the 1930s.[105]

One can only speculate about why Tiul'panov was allowed to return to his post after these severe attacks in late 1948, much as he had survived similar criticisms in the fall of 1946 and again at the beginning of 1947. First of all, General Russkikh played a much more active role as deputy commander-in-chief for political affairs than did General Makarov or, for that matter, General Bokov, who were—de facto if not de jure—responsible for political affairs in the zone. Russkikh took over some of the communications functions to the Central Committee, though Tiul'panov continued to file reports on selective issues.[106] Presumably Russkikh also helped to supervise Tiul'panov's activities, while protecting him from the continued scrutiny of the Main Political Administration and the Central

Committee. It is also possible that Tiul'panov was protected in late 1948 and 1949 by his gradually diminishing role in zonal affairs. According to Jan Foitzik, during this period Tiul'panov's administration was reduced in size from 150 officers and ten sections to only 80 officers and five sections.[107] Semenov's steadily rising star might also have indirectly helped Tiul'panov avoid the attention of the Central Committee. In January 1949, Semenov was finally named to the rank of ambassador, and after the founding of the GDR in October 1949, he was appointed political advisor to the Soviet Control Commission.[108]

It is also possible that after a second serious attack on his position, Tiul'panov learned to control himself better and fit the less dangerous model of the faceless, unemotional Soviet bureaucrat who was indistinguishable from any other. Certainly he ruffled many fewer feathers with his work in setting up the German Democratic Farmers' Party (DBD) in April and the National Democratic Party of Germany (NDPD) in May of 1948, though Soviet and SED control in these cases was nearly complete at the parties' inceptions. At a congress of the Thüringen CDU in December 1948, Tiul'panov gave a notably conciliatory speech that responded almost directly to the Central Committee commission's and Konstantinovskii's criticisms, though of course this came a year after he had chased Kaiser and Lemmer from the party leadership. In any case, Tiul'panov reportedly encouraged the CDU to pursue its unused possibilities for development. The Soviet military government, he stated, could not base its hopes just on the SED; it was time for greater activity on the part of the CDU.[109]

Tiul'panov also oversaw the transformation of the SED into a party of the new type in the summer of 1948, and he played an important role at the SED's First Party Conference in Berlin in January 1949, an evolution of SED affairs that reflected his concept of the party more than it did Konstantinovskii's. Nevertheless, he got into trouble again when he made a virulently anti-Western speech at the conference, emphasizing—presumably without Moscow's permission—the fact that Germany was already divided into two parts and that the Soviet Union fully supported the SED. Tiul'panov had overstepped his bounds again; SVAG interrupted the speech's radio transmission a few minutes after its airing and ordered that its text not be printed.[110]

The paradoxes in the Tiul'panov story continue until the very end. Despite all the criticisms of his work, Tiul'panov was promoted to major general in May 1949, soon after Marshal Sokolovskii was replaced as commander-in-chief by Colonel General V. I. Chuikov. At the same time, there is evidence that Tiul'panov had been nervously making inquiries about attitudes toward him in Moscow.[111] Tiul'panov's anxiety was well-founded. At the end of 1948, the Ministry for State Security arrested his driver, Lukin, for harboring anti-Soviet attitudes and for thinking about desertion to the West. Under interrogation the driver allegedly testified that Tiul'panov himself demonstrated some "negative attitudes."[112] Moreover, many of Tiul'panov's most trusted deputies in the Information Administration had been forced to return to Moscow because of their alleged "lack of political dependability."[113]

In fact, many of the recalled officers were Jewish and had been caught up in accusations surrounding the anticosmopolitan campaign at home. The most serious of these cases was that of Senior Lieutenant I. E. Fel'd-man, who had been in charge of the Press Department of the Information Administration. Fel'dman was accused by MGB chief V. S. Abakumov of anti-Soviet attitudes, which were demonstrated by his statement to an English journalist in 1947: "I admire the fact that citizens of Great Britain are able to express their feelings freely on any subject." During his interrogation, Fel'dman confessed that he also sometimes defamed the Soviet Union by suggesting that the country was run by a small clique in the Politburo and by denying "the democratic character" of the USSR. Abakumov accused Fel'dman of organized extortion, as well, which took the form of allowing German newspapers and magazines to continue publication in exchange for large payoffs. In his interrogations, Fel'dman allegedly implicated Tiul'panov in a series of extortion schemes dating back to early 1946.[114] To make matters worse, Tiul'panov was again charged with "concealing from the [Soviet] party" the facts that both of his parents had been convicted of spying (his father in 1938 and his mother in 1940); that his sister-in-law, with whom he had good relations, had been tried for her connections with British intelligence; and that his sister-in-law's father had been shot for belonging to the "right-wing Trotskyite counterrevolutionary organization," the alleged conspiracy in which Bukharin was said to have played a prominent role.[115]

Of course, none of this was new in the fall of 1949, and one can only assume that an unassailable case was being prepared for the purpose of removing Tiul'panov from the zone. At this point, there was no way Tiul'panov could evade the mounting attack on his position. GlavPU and the Central Committee Cadres Department called for Tiul'panov's removal, and Commander-in-Chief Chuikov and his deputy, A. M. Vasilevskii, agreed. As best we know, Tiul'panov was forced to return to Moscow at the end of September 1949, shortly before the creation of the German Democratic Republic. The Secretariat of the Central Committee confirmed the proposed removal on October 18.[116] In November 1949, the much-reduced apparatus of the Information Administration was absorbed into the newly created Soviet Control Commission.

Later, as a professor of political economy at Leningrad State University, Tiul'panov attributed the turn of events in September 1949 to the intervention of the Ministry of Internal Affairs, which he claimed had manufactured the case against him because of his complaints about MVD interference in the political affairs of the zone.[117] Whatever the real source of Tiul'panov's troubles, they stayed with him throughout most of his career as a scholar and as chairman of the Leningrad section of the Society for German-Soviet Friendship. The Central Committee would not give him permission to travel abroad, and he found himself in the humiliating position of not being able to accept the countless invitations from grateful GDR institutions to visit the land he had helped to create.[118] Finally in 1965, after several petitions, Tiul'panov was allowed to return to Germany for a visit. He retired from the university in 1979 and died in 1984.

Until historians have complete access to documents of the postwar Soviet party and government, and especially to those documents that link Stalin to his ministers, the Central Committee secretaries, and his commanders in Germany (like Zhukov and Sokolovskii), it will be impossible to answer in any more than proximate fashion the question, Who made policy? The documents reviewed in this chapter indicate that policy-making for the Soviet zone of Germany was carried out in the Secretariat of the Central Committee, on the advice and with the contributions of the secretaries responsible for international issues, Zhdanov and then Suslov, as well as of the Main Political Administration of the Army, its commander General Shikin, and General Burtsev, head of the Seventh Section. The Main Political Administration acted as part of, and yet distinct from, the Central Committee apparatus. The documents from the Central Committee archives also indicate that policy was made primarily in reaction to concrete events in Germany. The investigative commissions spawned policy directives that in turn were communicated to Karlshorst through the Military Council in the person of General Bokov and later through the deputy commanders-in-chief for political affairs, Makarov and Russkikh.

But as Central Committee documents make clear, Tiul'panov also made policy, in the sense of developing and articulating goals for German society that were to be followed by his staff and by the German parties and government agencies with which he dealt. He also made policy, one could argue, by ignoring the various commissions' injunctions to act differently. As a policy-maker, Tiul'panov had the distinct advantage of supervising a sizable (certainly by SVAG standards) staff, which—though heavily criticized, and often justifiably so—was able to exert power in the countryside of Mecklenburg or the mountains of southern Saxony. Many of Tiul'panov's officers knew German, followed his orders, and were able to mobilize local politicians and social leaders to accomplish his goals. American intelligence assessments that Tiul'panov was the "director of Communist activity in Germany" may not be so far off the mark after all.[119]

These Central Committee documents indicate, as well, that communications between Moscow and Karlshorst were not particularly good. Here and elsewhere, one reads of the general indifference of Moscow to the difficulties of the Soviet administration in Germany. Moreover, the commissions' criticisms often reflect a deep ignorance of the situation on the ground in Germany. Tiul'panov was able to take the initiative not just because Sokolovskii and Semenov were happy to leave day-to-day politics to him, but also because the Central Committee secretaries had their hands full too, more often than not with relatively trivial questions having to do with arcane cultural, ideological, or scientific struggles in the capital. Zhdanov and Malenkov were locked in a bitter struggle; the Leningrad affair was brewing. It is no wonder that a silent, dour presence like Suslov was charged with taking over German affairs. To be sure, Suslov, Beria, Shikin, Burtsev, Paniushkin, and a host of other important government figures traveled to Berlin and met with Tiul'panov and other SVAG leaders. The Germans—Grotewohl, Ulbricht, Pieck, and others—also regularly traipsed off to Moscow to meet with Soviet leaders, even with Stalin. This gave the SED leaders some leverage with Tiul'panov, but they really did not need any. Tiul'panov took advice from them as easily as he gave them orders. Though this is a different story, in Tiul'panov's world of decision making, the SED's leaders played an extremely important role.[120]

How did Colonel Tiul'panov make the kinds of decisions that his superiors—Bokov, Makarov, Russkikh, Semenov, and even Sokolovskii—were unwilling to make? Part of the answer has already been suggested: the others did not want to make decisions. The Russian archives provide no evidence that Tiul'panov occupied a leading position in the SVAG party organization, though they do indicate that he was an important party functionary. In the protocol of a SVAG party meeting on March 9, 1949, Tiul'panov was listed only eleventh; General Russov presided.[121] There is also no available evidence that Tiul'panov had influential protectors. To be sure, he had ties to the city of Leningrad and had been a student (an adoring student one might add) of A. A. Voznesenskii, the rector of Leningrad State University, minister of education, and one of the major figures in the Leningrad affair along with his brother, N. A. Voznesensky, and A. A. Kuznetsov, both Central Committee secretaries.[122] But there is no archival evidence now available that demonstrates that Zhdanov protected Tiul'panov, as is so often asserted in the historiography, or that Tiul'panov's "fall" in 1949 had anything to do with Zhdanov's political problems or his death.

It is more likely the case that Tiul'panov was able to make policy in the Soviet zone of Germany for many of the same reasons that General Lucius Clay was able to run the American zone. While Clay was unquestionably the superior administrator of the two, Tiul'panov—like Clay—knew the Germans and German institutions extremely well, certainly better than any other senior official in the zonal administration. Clay used the threat of resignation to maintain his policy prerogatives versus the U.S. Department of the Army and especially the State Department. Tiul'panov instinctively used the threat of removal in much the same way. In the face of unambiguous and repeated recommendations that Tiul'panov be dismissed, the secretaries of the Central Committee could not envision a successful Soviet policy in Germany without him, and therefore they kept him on. The frequent recommendation that Tiul'panov instead be demoted to deputy head of the administration support the argument that there were no senior officials who could operate in the German environment with the ease that he did.

Finally, as few others, Tiul'panov anticipated developments in Germany before they actually occurred. He was a "Sovietizer" in a situation that did not call for Sovietization; in fact, in the Eastern zone the Soviet Union had different intents and purposes than it did in Poland, Romania, or even Czechoslovakia and Hungary. In Germany, the Soviets were interested in maintaining maximum flexibility to accommodate to a four-power agreement on the unification, demilitarization, and neutralization of the country. The Soviets were too desperate for a share of West German coal and mineral resources and too worried about the integration of West German industrial power into an American-dominated Western condominium to give up easily on hopes for a neutral Germany. There can be little question that, as a result, the formal Soviet policy in the Eastern zone was to go slowly, show patience, and encourage the development of "antifascist democratic" forces.

Tiul'panov, on the other hand, instinctively, almost by force of habit—as well as through personal conviction—led the drive in the Eastern zone to eliminate independent bourgeois groups and politicians, to undermine German socialist traditions, especially those associated with the SPD, and to introduce the "Bolshevik way" of organizing society. He was ahead of his time, and therefore he provoked the constant complaints of his superiors in Moscow. Unlike many of his colleagues (and like Clay in the American zone), Tiul'panov anticipated the division of Germany, and he acted in the Eastern zone to secure Soviet interests. More than anything else, the fact that Tiul'panov was not removed from his post indicates that Stalin himself shared many of the Colonel's instincts. The Soviet dictator stood above the fray and allowed a variety of Soviet policies to be followed. There can be no doubt that he was kept fully informed of events in the zone. Now and again he even intervened directly and forcefully, but never to the extent that his subordinates could establish a clear framework for action in Germany. With Tiul'panov in the zone, Stalin kept his options open.

Soviet soldiers with Mecklenburg "new farmers."

The famous *Trümmerfrauen* (literally, the rubble women) clean away the debris in Berlin (Behrenstrasse), 1946.

Young German women at the corner of Unter den Linden and
Friedrichstrasse, Berlin, 1948.

The famous handshake between Wilhelm Pieck (left, under the portrait of Engels) and Otto Grotewohl (right, under that of Bebel) at the Unity Party Congress, where the KPD and SPD were joined as the SED, April 21–22, 1946.

Colonel S. I. Tiul'panov speaks at the conference of the Berlin Women's Committee, July 13–14, 1946. On the podium are (from left to right) Arthur Werner, Käthe Kern, Magda Sendhoff, Otto Grotewohl, and Helene Beer. The slogan behind them reads, "Through peace, work, and construction; For democracy and equal rights."

School reform in the countryside. The textbook title is,
We Learn Russian.

Parade on May 1, 1947, Berlin Lustgarten. With members of the
Free German Youth marching at the front.

Marshal V. D. Sokolovskii (second from left) at meeting of the
Allied Control Council.

Massive union poster on the front of the Leipzig Opera House. It reads: "German reconstruction plan to counter Marshall [Plan] slavery: The growth of production is decisive for a better life."

Wilhelm Pieck (left) and Vladimir Semenov (right) at a reception at the House of Culture of the Soviet Union in Berlin, November 8, 1948.

The first meeting in Moscow of the labor activists Alexander Stakhanov
(left) from the Soviet Union and Adolf Hennecke (right) from the
Soviet zone of occupation, May 1949.

Soviet Central Committee secretary Mikhail Suslov enjoying his reception
at the First Party Conference of the SED, January 25, 1949. Behind him
are (from left to right) Wilhelm Pieck, Otto Grotewohl, and
Walter Ulbricht.

Building the East German
Police State

FEW HISTORICAL SUBJECTS HAVE ATTRACTED more attention in Germany recently than the East German police regime and the "Stasi," or Staatssicherheitsdienst (State Security Service). Exposés of Stasi activity repeatedly show up in German newspapers and weeklies and on television. A special German government commission has been set up to investigate the totalitarian system in the East.[1] A new federal office was created, the so-called Gauck Behörde, which is specifically charged with making Stasi documents available both to its victims and to its historians.[2] However, despite the public's fascination with the Stasi, scholars have written relatively little of substance about its past. The reason for this is partly historiographical; before the fall of the Berlin wall and the unification of the two Germanys, it was considered politically inappropriate for West German scholars, in particular, to dwell on the totalitarianism of the East and the mechanisms of repression that East German citizens were forced to endure.[3] The reason also partly relates to the unavailability of good documentation on the Stasi during the pre-1990 period, though those scholars who wanted to write about the subject were able to do so through access to first-hand testimonies and even some archival collections, like the papers of the SPD Ostbüro, which closely followed the Stalinization of East German life.[4] With the opening of the archives of the former GDR Ministry for State Security, an important step has been taken toward developing resources for the study of the Stasi.[5]

Despite these new sources of information, significant impediments to studying the origins of the East German police state still exist. First, the extent to which the history of the Stasi remains a political issue in the new German state has undermined the ability of scholars to survey the past calmly and with detachment. Second, problems with documentation persist. The archives of the Soviet Committee for State Security (KGB) and Ministry of Internal Affairs (NKVD until 1946, then MVD) remain closed to researchers of the postwar era, though some NKVD documents from the postwar period have recently been made available.[6] Without access to documents from the Soviet security services, only part of the story of the origin of the East German police state can be told. Soon, however, new joint projects between German scholars and the Russian state archives should provide a fuller picture of police repression in eastern Germany.[7] In addition, American military intelligence reports are helpful in filling in some of the "blank spots," as are other documents from American, British, SPD, and SED archives. It is a worthwhile lesson in Soviet history to note that the archives of those institutions that had so much to do with Soviet policies in the Eastern zone (the Central Committee, the Ministry of Foreign Affairs, and the Soviet Military Government itself) scarcely mention the question of East German internal security, leaving that to the security organs themselves, about whom very little is said.

As a result of this situation, the first part of this chapter on the building of the police system in eastern Germany should be seen as exploratory in nature. It focuses on two German organizations that eventually merged into the Stasi: K-5 of the Criminal Police, and the Intelligence and Information Department of the German Interior Administration (DVdI). It also looks at the beginnings of several other police organizations in the zone, including the Alert Police (Bereitschaften), which served as the foundation of the National People's Army (NVA). The second part of the chapter examines the role of Soviet intelligence organizations in eastern Germany, in particular the NKVD/MVD operations groups. It also analyzes the development of the Soviet special camps *(spetslager)* in the zone, which became such important symbols for the nature of repressive Soviet policies in Germany.

This kind of investigation is useful for two purposes. First of all, it makes it clear that the Stasi formed the backbone of the German Democratic Republic and permeated the country's every aspect, and that it did so as an integral part of the historical emergence of the country. In other words, the Soviets and the SED did not create the Stasi as an afterthought for securing the East German state structure and protecting its accomplishments. Rather, from the very beginning, security concerns within the

German party and the Soviet military government helped to create an East German state that was inseparable from its internal police functions. Second, it is worth thinking about general Soviet policy considerations in light of the systematic attempt by the Soviet Military Administration to build up secret police and paramilitary police units. There is no reason to doubt the sincerity of Soviet statements (and actions) intended to foster the unity of Germany and the end to four-power occupation in the immediate postwar period. At the same time, the way in which Soviets and the KPD/SED constructed the police structure in eastern Germany corroborates the argument that plans were in the making for the permanent Sovietization of the zone.

STUNDE NULL—ZERO HOUR

From the perspective of the Soviets, no single administrative task was more important in May 1945 than the reorganization of the German police. For the German communists and in particular for Walter Ulbricht, getting police into the streets was also a critical first step toward reestablishing order. Therefore it is no wonder that neither the Soviets nor the German communists looked too closely at the antifascist credentials of the newly recruited police officers in the Soviet zone of occupation. Not only were Nazi and Wehrmacht veterans able to join up, but significant numbers of former Nazi storm troopers and SS members also found their way into the police.[8] Certainly the communists sought to control the leadership of the police from the very beginning. In Berlin, three KPD veterans who had been in Brandenburg prison were placed in strategic posts in the Berlin Police Presidium. One was Walter Mickinn, who became an important contributor to the development of the postwar communist police. Mickinn was soon joined by Erich Mielke, who had spent much of the Nazi era in the Soviet Union. Accused of having been a member of a communist gang that killed two German policemen in 1931 (he was sentenced to a prison term for the crime in 1994), Mielke attended the Lenin School in the Soviet Union before participating in the Spanish Civil War, going underground in France, and fighting with the Red Army during World War II.[9]

If, as the German communists later complained, "hundreds of fascists, criminals, and unworthy elements" found their way into the police after the war, it was also the case that a combination of new communist police experts—some who had suffered at the hands of the Gestapo (like Mickinn), and some who had direct experience with the NKVD and Soviet military intelligence (like Mielke)—immediately began transforming the police into the central fighting instrument of the antifascist democratic order.[10] In the new Soviet socialist state established after the Bolshevik Revolution, victims of the tsarist police had become the commissars of the police. Felix Dzierzynski, head of the Cheka, was only the most well known. Similarly, after 1945, police matters were placed principally in the hands of victims of fascism, like Mickinn and Erich Reschke, the first president of the German Interior Administration. Similarly, police schools were often run by communists who had been interned in Nazi prisons, many of whom were also members of the Association for the Victims of the Nazi Regime (the VVN). But always in the background were loyal servants of Moscow like Mielke and Kurt Fischer, who was minister of the interior in Saxony before taking over for Reschke in the summer of 1948.

During the first months of the occupation, however, there could be no talk of a communist police force. If any party held sway in the police bureaucracy, it was the SPD, many of whose members had worked for the police before, and sometimes after, 1933. The biggest problem in the police force at the outset of the Soviet occupation was not political; rather it was the fact that police units were disorganized and sometimes engaged in illegal activities.[11] Formally, they were under the command of the local Soviet commandants, who used them for specific tasks ranging from guard duty and patrols to raids on local red-light establishments. But without provincial, not to mention zonal, oversight, the police were easily susceptible to corruption and extortion.[12] The police initiated their own investigations, confiscating materials and goods without reporting them to higher authorities; in many cases, police officers simply resold the goods that they seized. Sometimes they kept regular hours; sometimes they did not. The Soviets were particularly frustrated by the numerous cases in which the police walked away from guard duty whenever they got tired of it.[13] The police were also not averse to abusing their connections with the NKVD operations groups and settling personal grudges through denunciations and arrests.[14]

These excesses reportedly reached their worst extreme in Mecklenburg and Brandenburg. There, the police engaged in a wide variety of criminal activities that the Soviets had no way to curtail. In Saxony, on the other hand, police matters were put under the control of Kurt Fischer, who was able to centralize the provincial police administration almost from the first days of his arrival in Dresden as a member of Anton Ackermann's "initiative group." When the Americans pulled out of Thüringen and the province of Saxony (Saxony-Anhalt) at the end of June 1945, the Soviets already had two months of experience in organizing police activities. In Saxony-Anhalt, for example, they brought in the communist Robert Siewert, a former Buchenwald internee and VVN member, to run the police as vice president of the province. Siewert recalled that opponents of the Soviet occupation called the new police "Vice President Siewert's Billy-Club Guard."[15]

At first, Allied agreement prohibited German police officers from carrying firearms. They rarely had uniforms and were identifiable only by their armbands, their billy clubs, or sometimes their hats. They took a terrific beating at the hands of armed "bandits," who were sometimes Germans but more often than not Soviet soldiers or deserters. Gangs of drunken soldiers frequently terrorized urban and rural populations in the summer of 1945 and the fall and winter of 1945–46. Sometimes attempts by German police to intervene in the activities of these bandits resulted in tragedy. Not only did the police take their lives in their hands if they tried to seize Soviet soldiers for their misdeeds, but also, even if the police were able to catch the culprits, they had to turn the soldiers over to their Russian commanders, who routinely took no action against them.[16] In fact, large numbers of German policemen lost their lives in the struggle against bandits during the fall and winter of 1945–46.[17] No issue frustrated the new police officers throughout the zone more than the fact that they were forbidden to carry weapons. A Criminal Police report of January 21, 1946, made the point that they would continue to be paralyzed in the struggle with bandits and gangs unless they were allowed to use firearms.[18]

The position on arming the police changed after January 1, 1946, when the Allied Control Council lifted the ban on the use of weapons by the German police forces.[19] The Soviets then supplied some pistols and guns to selected police detachments, but, as Mickinn told Ulbricht, in "absolutely insufficent" quantities. Ulbricht responded: "There must be forthwith a complete arming [of the police]. Where are there more weapons?"[20] But Ulbricht should have known that weapons themselves were not the answer, at least not in the case of dealing with crimes by Soviet soldiers. German police forces were not allowed to use weapons against Allied soldiers, even if they were caught in the act of a crime. In fact, German police sometimes found themselves in the embarrassing position of being disarmed by Soviet bandits.[21] By the late spring of 1946, however, armed German police detachments fought with Soviet soldiers and MVD operations groups to subdue gangs of criminals, some German and some Russian. Even heavy weapons were used on both sides, recalled Walter Besenbuch, a communist police veteran, and many police officers lost their lives.[22]

According to SVAG Order no. 112 of May 1946, which sought to eliminate deficiencies in police work in the zone, the problem with the police was not the absence of weapons but rather the lack of organization and discipline. Despite the increase of resources directed to police work, crime was on the rise. Only 40 percent of crimes were solved, which the Soviets attributed primarily to poor coordination between the Criminal Police (Kripo) and the Civil Police (Schutzpolizei, or Schupo), between judicial and police organs, and between police organizations within the different provinces, not to mention between the provinces.[23] Some relief in this situation was expected from the formal creation—long kept secret—of the German Interior Administration on June 30, 1946.[24] But so long as the local and regional police bodies were responsible to the provincial governments, the DVdI would not be able to develop the level of control and coordination that the KPD (and later the SED) insisted was critical. The MVD was also interested in having the DVdI develop into an effective security organization that would eventually join "the future [all-German] Ministry of Internal Affairs," after the appropriate training and indoctrination.[25]

Subsequently, in December 1946, Ulbricht and Fechner of the SED met with Fischer, Warnke, Bechler, and Siewert—representing a variety of communist police interests—as well as with the presidents of the Interior Ministries, to straighten out the problem of reporting. The SED's priorities were transparent. They wanted the DVdI to assume responsibility for police activity throughout the zone, while the budgets of the police would still be formally under the provinces. All laws on the police passed by the provincial legislatures would have to be agreed to beforehand by the DVdI. All police appointments, transfers, and firings also had to be approved both by the provincial Soviet Military Administrations, as well as by the president of the DVdI. The SED also sought to assert special prerogatives when it came to Interior Ministry matters. "All important questions that have to do with the activities of the Ministries of the Interior, should be agreed to by both party chairmen of the lands and provinces and the SED comrades who are ministers of the interior."[26]

Until the opening of the archives of the KGB and the Ministry of Internal Affairs of the Soviet Union, it will be difficult to describe with precision the nature of reporting between the German police and the Soviet officials in Karlshorst. Certainly the president of the DVdI, Erich Reschke (and later, Kurt Fischer) reported directly to the Internal Affairs Administration of SVAG. It is known, for example, that the MVD directly supervised the purging of Nazis and "anti-Soviet elements" from the police.[27] One can also assume that, informally, many DVdI leaders and those in the rank and file reported directly to the Soviets, whether in the Ministry of Internal Affairs, the Ministry for State Security (MGB), Military Intelligence (GRU), or in a variety of other Soviet intelligence organizations in the zone. One can be almost sure that this included Erich Mielke, who seemed to be the Soviets' man in the DVdI. It is known, for example, that he had a direct cable telephone hookup with Karlshorst.[28] There is also considerable evidence that Mielke upheld the interests of the Soviets even when the SED might have been compromised by doing so.

Throughout the period of the Soviet occupation, Mielke's overt role seemed to be to try to increase the political content of police work. In one of his speeches to the police, for example, he argued that there was nothing wrong with politically tendentious police activity. In his view, it was their duty to be tendentious. The hypothetical example he used made a mockery of the severe fate met by opponents of communist control in the East. Still, Mielke made his point. In his example, two drivers of cars were detained because of moving violations for which they could have been fined fifty marks or more apiece: "In one case we are dealing with an honored worker or workers' functionary, and the other person is known to us as an archreactionary. It would be idiotic and would show nothing about democratic consciousness if we were to treat both cases democratically 'the same.' It is clear that we take care of the case with the worker through a few friendly words and [that] we jack up the fine as high as possible for the other enemy of the democratic development."[29] Of course, Mielke very much joined company with Soviet officers in his attitude toward "bourgeois objectivity." A SVAG justice official, Major Nikolai, stated the case even more clearly at a meeting of German Justice Department functionaries in March 1948. Too much attention was paid to so-called "personal freedom," he told them. One cannot guarantee personal freedom for "Nazi activists, black marketeers, or racketeers, but only for the democratic strata of the population."[30]

K-5

The fifth department *(Dezernat)* of the Criminal Police, K-5, was the first German political police force to operate in the Eastern zone after the war. The organization was first formed in Saxony in the late summer of 1945, evolving out of the surveillance department of the Dresden city government's personnel administration. Under Kurt Fischer, Saxony had become the model for police organization in the zone. (The communists often recognized Saxony's tradition as an independent princedom by giving it pride of place over the other provinces in the zone.) By September 1945, Saxony had a provincial criminal police administration with five departments, including K-5, whose function was initially to check out police officials in the administration and eventually to keep tabs on the police force as a whole.[31] The department also took responsibility for providing surveillance of officials in the Judicial Department, preparing dossiers on every judge and prosecutor and forwarding them to the MVD and MGB in the zone.[32] By the beginning of 1947, K-5 already had 160 employees in Saxony and had spread its network to the other provinces of the zone.

From the very beginning, K-5 was seen by the communists as being different from other branches of the police. No one from the pre-1945 cadres of the police was allowed to join the new watchdog of the administration, and previous models for the German political police were explicitly rejected. Yet almost by osmosis K-5 began to take on some of the characteristics of the Gestapo, to the point that even the SED complained that the criminal police were getting a terrible reputation in the zone for their brutal methods and were "as feared as the Gestapo was."[33] Some police officials even spoke positively about the "exactness and cleanness" with which the Nazi police had done their job. They knew how to strike quickly without waiting, noted one Schwerin official, while the police chief of Rügen suggested that a lot could be learned about police work by studying the archives of the previous system.[34]

Once the DVdI was formed, its K-5 department put together a central information file that contained detailed biographical information on Interior Ministry employees, including the police, from all over the zone. Along with biographical and political information, the files contained anti-

SED or anti-Soviet statements made by the "targets," which could be used at any time by the MVD and MGB for recruiting or punishing Interior Ministry police employees.[35] The DVdI was also able to take strong measures in Mecklenburg and Saxony-Anhalt, where the police had resisted K-5's influence, removing the chiefs of the criminal police in the two provinces on the grounds that "they were not real democrats." By March 1947, the DVdI had successfully centralized criminal police activity under its Section K in Berlin.[36] The power of K-5 within the Interior Administration was evident from the fact that its provincial chiefs were automatically made deputy chiefs of the provincial police offices. American intelligence reported that "if the Chief of the Provincial police office was not considered politically reliable, his Deputy had the authority to prevent him from learning all details about the 'K-5' sections."[37]

The development of K-5 and the political police in the zone received a powerful impetus from Order no. 201 of August 1947 on denazification. With this order, the Soviets gave K-5 primary responsibility for eliminating all former active Nazis from the state administration and leadership in the economy and society. To carry out the task, K-5 was given authorization to recruit large numbers of new cadres from the "working class," and to set up special schools to train the recruits in the fine points of enforcing the order. Specialists in K-5 were trained for the "penetration and investigation" (*Durchdringung und Durcharbeitung*) of the growing state and provincial apparatus in the Soviet zone. This meant undercover work, as well as learning the specialized methods of police investigations.[38]

Order no. 201 also served as an important weapon for politicizing the police. For example, the provincial police chief in Saxony took his K-5 section to task for processing too many workers, small business owners, and middle-level employees for Nazi activities (50 percent of the 5,000 cases). He exhorted his men to turn their attention to the *real* Nazis, "who were able to gain personal advantages and secure material and financial support under fascism as a result of their economic situation."[39] Ulbricht, too, repeatedly emphasized the importance of arresting those former Nazis who had been (and sometimes still were) economically powerful and leaving the workers and everyday employees alone, unless they had committed war crimes.[40] Ulbricht even wanted major show trials of Nazi capitalists, but the Soviets vetoed his idea, arguing that show trials would cause unnecessary turmoil among the Germans. In fact, given the upheaval caused by Order no. 201, both the Soviets and the SED wanted to finish with denazification as soon as possible.

Meanwhile, K-5 had become the central organ for the political activities of police authorities in the zone. According to its organizational chart of January 8, 1948, K-5 was an all-purpose unit that was divided into five sections: the first was responsible for investigating political crimes, including violations of SVAG orders; the second oversaw violations of Control Council orders; the third dealt with sabotage of the rebuilding; the fourth with antidemocratic activity; and the fifth was an all-purpose technical group.[41] The last section dealt with surveillance methods, data collection, and postal interference; the first four sections focused on the prevention of a variety of political crimes. Those most often mentioned included assassinations, sabotage, public demonstrations, and underground resistance, and any profascist or anti-Soviet activity, including the tearing down of posters or the destruction of "democratic" literature. At the same time, as an SPD Ostbüro report noted, "all the leading personages in public life [in the Eastern zone] are subject to constant surveillance"—a huge job, given the rest of K-5's responsibilities.[42]

Not surprisingly, Erich Mielke looked at K-5 as an incipient office of state security. Its job, he stated, was "to defend democratic institutions, their further development, and the economic rebuilding of the SBZ from attempts to undermine them [*Störversuche*]." "Enemies" had made their way into the political parties and mass organizations, Mielke continued. "Schumacher agents" were everywhere, trying to undermine the democratic rebuilding. The task of K-5 was to uncover their plans and disrupt their activities.[43] But K-5 was also an office of state security that operated on the Soviet model, meaning it carried out its mandate on behalf of a ruling political party, in this case the SED. As a K-5 veteran reported: "Members of the SED who were expelled [from the party] would in any case be processed by K-5. If the SED had a political enemy whom it was difficult to compromise, K-5 would receive orders to 'construct' a case. Those who left the SED on their own volition were also watched by K-5. SED politicians are the confidants [*Vertrauensleute*] of the K-5. They had to work with us whether they wanted to or not."[44] In some cases SED officials even took part directly in the K-5 interrogations of political opponents.[45]

Despite the SED's growing influence in K-5 affairs, it was clear to everyone that the Soviet authorities, in particular the MVD and MGB offices in the zone, were directly responsible for the activities of K-5. Not only that, but from the very beginning K-5 was charged with carrying out specific missions for the Soviet military government. Officers of K-5 vied with one another to bring the best information or the most outstanding German operatives to the attention of the Soviets. Soviet intelligence officers directed and advised their K-5 subordinates on every level. The most important interrogations were supervised by the Russians. In fact, German K-5 police officials could undertake no serious investigation without the prior approval of the responsible SVAG office.[46]

Even the resolution of cases was expressly in the hands of the Soviets. In the thousands of cases from the immediate postwar period contained in the archives of the Ministry for State Security concerning every kind of political issue from the spread of illegal posters and pamphlets to the seizure of underground weapons, K-5 routinely turned over its completed investigations to the Soviets for resolution. This often meant perfunctory prosecution by Soviet military tribunals and detention of the offenders in camps and prisons.[47] Sometimes no judicial procedures were necessary at all, and alleged criminals were placed in the special camps on the administrative order of the MVD or MGB. It was also the case that K-5 could not countermand Soviet orders. One former K-5 operative in Kyritz reported that his group would often have to simply sign forms given them by the MVD, stating that a particular individual had fled to the West. "These are people who disappear, and we don't know what the circumstances are and [we] must—without asking—sign."[48]

In the spring of 1949, K-5 achieved complete independence from the German provincial authorities and worked exclusively with the Soviets and with the DVdI in Berlin. Even the small amount of control exerted by the provincial ministers of the interior was removed. By this point, K-5 papers were kept completely separate from the rest of the police files and no non-K-5 members were allowed to interfere (or even to ask questions about) the section's activities.[49] In 1948 and 1949, as more and more Soviet intelligence activity in the zone was taken over by the MGB, K-5 became a specialized MGB task force working among the German population. (In May 1946, the Third Directorate of the MGB had already taken over most of the Soviet Military Counterintelligence (SMERSH) operations in the zone, which focused on the Soviet military and civilian population.) The K-5 offices routinely carried out Soviet orders for investigations—though the arrests were often left to the MGB and MVD—because, from the Soviet point of view, arrests made by German institutions might disturb the work of "other agencies."[50] Of the 51,236 cases processed by K-5 in Saxony in 1948 (which, significantly, was twice as many as in 1947), 14,137 were assigned to them by the Soviets and 1,318 by the German authorities. The rest resulted from normal investigations and surveillance worked out by both Soviet and German authorities.[51]

INFORMATION SERVICE

Evaluators of K-5 activity in 1948 and 1949 often came to the conclusion that the police section had too few operatives, and that the ones they did have were not adequately trained. Reports that K-5 police officers were being lost to other branches of the police and civil service also lead one to suspect that the Soviets were siphoning off the best agents to serve directly in their intelligence services. (By late 1948, the Soviets were drastically shorthanded in the zone.) As a result, K-5 was badly overworked and understaffed, and it was apparent that it could not report the kind of information about the mood of eastern German society that the SED felt was necessary for its political control of the zone.

Initially the information offices in the provinces had concentrated primarily on collecting materials from newspapers and the media and distributing press releases for journalistic consumption. Each provincial office did something slightly different. In Thüringen, the information office simply distributed press releases, while in Saxony and Saxony-Anhalt, the offices collected material and produced analyses of the public mood. In these latter cases, the information office reported to the Ministry of Interior; in the case of Thüringen to the Press Ministry.[52] While the information offices worked on spreading SED propaganda, as early as the summer of 1946 the police were warning private citizens that receiving "reactionary" mail, meaning subscriptions to Western newspapers like *Der Tagesspiegel* or *Telegraf* from Berlin, could result in punishment.[53]

By the summer of 1947, sentiments were expressed in the DVdI for the creation of a zonewide information service, an idea that seemed to reverberate positively in the Soviet Military Administration. At a conference of ministers of the interior in October 1947, Ulbricht suggested that after consultations with the appropriate SVAG authorities, an information service should be set up under Mielke's supervision in the DVdI.[54] (Mielke at this point was a vice minister and controlled several branches of police work, including K-5.) The Soviets gave their approval, and on November 11, 1947, Mielke set up a new Intelligence and Information Department *(Nachrichten und Information)* in the DVdI.

According to Mielke, the justification for the new department was self-evident: it was needed to counter the nefarious activities of the reactionaries, who did not hesitate to exploit all kinds of "subjective or objective" difficulties in order to slander and disrupt the development of democracy in the zone. In Mielke's view, these agents of reaction had sowed rumors and spread illegal propaganda, permeated the zone with sabotage and spying, and even carried out their first successful assassination attempts. As a result, a two-fisted information policy needed to be carried out. On the one hand, the public needed to be better informed about the political and administrative measures undertaken by the German government in the East. On the other, the government needed "to be constantly informed about the positive as well as the negative occurrences in the country, to be able to undertake when appropriate the necessary decisions and measures."[55]

Strikingly, many of the prescribed activities of Mielke's new department in late 1947 presaged the disinformation, spying, and intrigue that would characterize the Stasi operations supervised by the GDR's Ministry for State Security, of which Mielke was the last and most influential chief. Like the Stasi, the department was created to influence public opinion by sponsoring the writing and planting of articles, reports, news, and photographs in the press that would get the population to think positively about the government and the SED. The press itself was to be under the firm hand of the new department; one of its goals was "to influence the attitude and reporting of the press through the closest personal dealings with reporters and editors, [carrying out] individual and group discussions with them about the . . . important questions of the day."

But also like the Stasi, the Intelligence and Information Department sought much more than simply to control the press. It was mandated to collect information about any body or group working against "democratic developments"—in short, "about any intentional or unintentional activities that are designed to hurt us"—including gathering information about reactionary intentions from the Western zones. The agency's founding document states that "to secure the quickest possible communication of such ongoing information, it is necessary to form a comprehensive and as seamless as possible *network of confidants and informants,* who, with the single goal of serving the democracy, rationally formulate their reports with great objectivity and without consideration of their personal or other views." A number of permanent and occasional informants had already been turning over material to the police. Now the idea was to turn them and other recruits into a permanent network of information sources in all branches of the economy, society, mass organizations, and political parties. There would be informants, as well, in the German government at all its levels, in Berlin and in the provinces. The task of the provincial information offices, to use Mielke's inimitable language, was *"to know everything and to report everything worth knowing."*[56]

The information agencies in the provinces that had formerly dealt with press releases and newspaper policy were now ordered to call themselves "press agencies," and in fact the task of monitoring and guiding the press was given over to them. Some of the information offices that had been maintained by the DVdI, like N-2 (Political Information) and N-2b (Observation of Countercurrents and Underground Movements), were melded into the new Intelligence and Information Department.[57]

Mielke's attitude toward the new organization was duplicitous in the extreme. In a public speech, he told his listeners that it made no sense in an antifascist state "to build up a huge police and spy apparatus," because every decent German citizen "could sing a song" about such organizations from the Hitler times. Yet he insisted that reporting to the police about what one's fellow citizens were doing should not be considered denunciation, but rather "antifascist vigilance."[58]

POLITKULTUR

By the middle of 1948, the Soviets and the SED leaders saw the People's Police as much more than an institution for maintaining order and suppressing real and potential political opposition to the communist domination of the zone. Mielke wrote: "The police . . . are the sharpest political military fighting weapon of the working class." He believed that, as the "heartbeat of the democratic order," the police force should increase its awareness of the political tasks of fighting secret agents, provocateurs, and Schumacherites, and worry less about normal crime, which had been brought under control.[59] Also indicative of changes in police practices was the appointment of Kurt Fischer, the communist police specialist from Saxony, to become the new president of the DVdI in September 1948. Fischer, a trusted Moscow communist, replaced Erich Reschke, who had developed his antifascism in Buchenwald but was now relegated to the post of commander of the Bautzen prison complex.

New political tasks required new personnel policies. According to Mielke's instructions of June 28, 1948, all employees of the DVdI who had been members of the Nazi Party or its allied organizations (not including the Nazi youth groups) were to be released from the police. Typically, though, there was a clause that made it possible for highly desirable ex-Nazis to continue their work in the police force. Those "who have demonstrated their antifascism by putting their lives on the line" were exempted from Mielke's new order, for example. At the same time, no one who maintained "ties to the enemies of the democratic order" could remain on the force.[60] These instructions led to a widespread purge in the police. In August and September 1948, approximately 20 percent of those in the police organizations in the provinces were purged, 10 percent of those in the police force in the Soviet zone of Berlin, and 5 percent of those in the DVdI. Several senior police officers were purged, some of whom were tied to Reschke. The personnel in a number of police districts in the zone that had been run by non-SED members were completely replaced.[61] Every police officer who had been in a Western POW camp or who had relatives in or contacts with the West was to be checked out carefully and placed under special surveillance. Mielke also insisted that all former members of the National Committee for Free Germany, of whom there were substantial numbers in the police force, were also to be kept under surveillance.[62]

Mielke simultaneously sought to raise the political consciousness of the police through intense schooling. His idea was to create "in every police force member a conscious enemy [crossed out was the word 'hater'] of [crossed out 'international'] imperialism and reaction."[63] Ulbricht, Mielke, and the Soviets were determined to raise both the ideological content of police work and the fighting spirit of the police force. As a result, they introduced into every police unit a political-cultural *(Politkultur)* officer, whose job—like the political officers in the Red Army—was to ensure a high level of readiness and political watchfulness. Under the supervision of Major General S. F. Gorokhov and Colonel A. M. Kropychev from SVAG's Internal Affairs Administration, the DVdI set up a special institute to train the Politkultur officers for their tasks: to make sure that every officer learned devotion to the working class and "pitiless opposition [*Feindschaft*] to the forces of reaction . . . to teach the members of the police to recognize the enemy, to provide the People's Police with concrete examples of the activity of the enemy, to explain the methods of activity of the enemy counterintelligence and counter-counterintelligence [*Gegenabwehr*]."[64] The Politkultur officers were also given an intensive course on nineteenth- and twentieth-century Russian history, as well as on the tenets of Marxism-Leninism-Stalinism.

From Mielke's point of view, it was extremely important that the Politkultur officers, like the police as a whole, be chosen only from "the best and most reliable sons of the working class."[65] Mielke himself was put in charge of the Politkultur Department, and the leading positions in the department's bureaucracy had to be confirmed by the Central Secretariat of the SED. By mid-July 1948 there were 720 Politkultur officers in the DVdI, one for every 100 to 110 police officers in the zone. The creation of this new department, designed to exert political leadership among the police, gave Mielke just the chance he was looking for to get rid of the Workers' Councils (Betriebsräte) in the police force. Initially the councils had served the positive functions of helping to politicize and denazify the police and, even more important, increasing the role of the central German authorities versus the provincial and local governments in police matters. But by the summer of 1948, the Workers' Councils acted as a brake on the executive power of the DVdI. As vice president of the DVdI in charge of the Main Politkultur Directorate, Mielke was able to use the support of the Central Secretariat of the party to force officials of the zone's labor union, the FDGB, to give up "as superfluous" its organizations within the police.[66]

DEFENSE OF THE ECONOMY

It should be apparent that in the case of the Politkultur Department of the DVdI, as well as in the police force as a whole, the Soviets exerted total political control by the summer of 1948. Also, virtually all the materials, land, buildings, and weapons for police schools were supplied by the Soviets. Even the regular police force budget came in good measure from direct Soviet sources.[67] It is hardly surprising, then, that the SED leaders regularly informed the Soviet leaders in Moscow about the development of their police work. During one of their trips to the Soviet capital, from December 12 to 14, 1948, Pieck, Grotewohl, Ulbricht, and Oelssner reported to Stalin great successes with the program of political-cultural education among the police. They also called attention to another important change in the organization of police activity in the zone. To purge the Criminal Police and to improve its ideological quality, the SED reported that the K-5 section as it had earlier existed would be dissolved, to be replaced by a Main Directorate for the Defense of the Economy and the Democratic Order.[68] This new DVdI directorate took both cadres and methods from a similar body that had been formed in the German Economic Commission (DWK) in May 1948.[69]

In theory, then, the Main Directorate for the Defense of the Economy and the Democratic Order succeeded K-5 as the political branch of the

Criminal Police. In fact, however, K-5 continued to exist as a specialized organ of the DVdI for personnel issues in the German government apparatus as a whole. Since both organizations were under Mielke's direct control, there appeared to be no difficulty transferring earlier K-5 functions and operatives to the new directorate.[70] The SED explained to its Soviet comrades: "Among its [the new Main Directorate's] tasks [are included] the defense against sabotage . . . assassinations, and other endeavors, explosives and weapons violations, the struggle against illegal organizations, as well as the fight against antidemocratic activity. Bureaucratically, this Main Directorate belongs to the Criminal Police. But in fact it works independently under the direction of the Soviet occupation authorities, as well as the president of the DVdI and the provincial chiefs of police."[71] Mielke himself interpreted the activities of the "class enemy" so broadly that the mandate of the new directorate was virtually unlimited. Enemy activities could be clandestine or out in the open, Mielke asserted. Every factory fire and explosion needed to be investigated as the work of saboteurs. At the same time, he said, the enemy could conceal its counterrevolutionary activities behind the promotion of "lazy work habits" and "undisciplined attitudes," all of which also needed to be countered by the police.[72]

With the foundation of the German Democratic Republic in October 1949, the Main Directorate, still commanded by Mielke, was included in the new Ministry of the Interior, headed initially by the former social democrat Carl Steinhoff. But such a situation could not last long. After a virulent campaign of exposing spies and saboteurs in the GDR, the Soviets, Mielke, and the SED created in February 1950 a Ministry for State Security, headed by Wilhelm Zaisser. The new ministry came primarily from Mielke's Main Directorate for the Protection of the Economy, but it also absorbed the personnel and functions of K-5, the Intelligence and Information Department, and the Politkultur Department. After the June 1953 uprising, the Ministry for State Security was reincorporated into the Ministry of the Interior, but it again became an independent ministry in 1955, and it continued to exist as such until the end of the German Democratic Republic.

ALERT POLICE (BEREITSCHAFTEN)

Two sets of state functions were performed by the police in the Eastern zone. One had to do with the "security" needs that characterized communist systems wherever they emerged: fighting internal enemies, collecting information, ferreting out alleged saboteurs, and smashing clandestine political opposition, whether real or imagined. The second set of functions performed initially by the police in the Eastern zone had to do with organizing the armed force of the state on behalf of its preservation, against both internal and external foes. In fact, almost from the moment the Allies agreed that the police forces could be armed, at the beginning of 1946, the Soviet military government tried to form disciplined and hierarchically organized paramilitary brigades out of the ragtag police units that had been assembled in the provinces and Berlin. During the summer of 1946, the Soviets helped provide the police officers with new uniforms and regular weapons. They took "a stronger hand" in the organization of the police by introducing a rigid system of ranks, as well as the duty to salute. Soviet officers also sometimes taught the police close-order drills and techniques for handling their weapons.[73]

In the fall of 1946, according to Order no. 0155, the Soviets turned over the functions of border control to local German Civil Police units. But, under orders from five different provincial governments, the units lacked coordination and a consistent set of guidelines for their activities. In August 1947, SVAG issued orders to its provincial Soviet counterparts to unify the border police into a single service, outfitting them with distinct green uniforms and providing them with pistols, rifles, and machine guns. However, they were still under the command of local Soviet army detachments and provincial police officials.[74] With the concurrence of its Soviet advisors, the DVdI took the initiative to centralize the Border Police both organizationally and budgetarily under the Interior Administration. At the same time, the Border Police increasingly recruited young unmarried workers from all over the zone to its ranks. The recruits were placed in barracks and garrisons and given specialized military training. Although within the organizational structure of the DVdI, the Border Police were under operational orders from local Soviet military authorities and could be used any time by the Soviets as special police commandos. This became especially important during the Berlin blockade, when brigades from the Border Police, reinforced by a substantial number of civil police units, played an important role in encircling West Berlin.[75]

The formation of the DVdI in the fall of 1946 also accelerated the development of centralized Alert Police units. Willi Seifert, who had been interned as a communist in Buchenwald, played a very important role in the efforts to create a centrally directed force, as did Erich Mielke and

Wilhelm Zaisser, who was a veteran of the Spanish Civil War and a former chief of the German section of the antifascist schools in the Soviet Union. The leaders of the Berlin police force, Paul Markgraf and Richard Gyptner, defiantly rebuffed protests from within the Interior Administration about the militarization of the police: "It is obvious that pacifist ideas within the People's Police cannot be tolerated . . . The uproar about a supposed 'Militarism' from among imperialists and warmongers in and outside [the zone] means we are doing things right."[76] It was not until the spring and summer of 1948 that a series of changes in the organization of the police prepared the way for the formation of a paramilitary force. First, the president of the DVdI, Erich Reschke, was forced to resign his post. Though known for his blind loyalty to the Soviets, Reschke's lack of Moscow experience clearly made it difficult for him to anticipate the Soviets' needs as Mielke and his eventual replacement, Kurt Fischer, could.[77] Fischer had undergone military training in the Soviet Union and fought in the Spanish Civil War, qualifications that were more to the point than Reschke's experiences as a "victim of the Nazi regime." Zaisser, who had also fought in the Spanish Civil War, under the name of "Gomez," was made deputy minister of the DVdI.

With this new team in place by July 1948—Mielke, significantly, was the only holdover—the Soviets could go ahead with their plans to establish the Alert Police, a force of armed units that were housed in barracks and trained in a military fashion. Later known as the Barracked People's Police, these units became the basis of the East German National People's Army, formed in 1955. Like the NVA, the Alert Police were originally part of the general Soviet effort to bolster the combat readiness of its own forces in the zone by developing a German auxilliary.[78] At the time of their formation, each of the forty units of the Alert Police in the zone consisted of 250 men, making a combined force of roughly 10,000 "soldiers." Many of the officers and men were recruited from among German POWs in the Soviet Union. In some cases, POWs already on their way home at the transfer station in Frankfurt-Oder were offered a choice of working in the mines in the Erzgebirge or joining the Alert Police. In other cases, the POWs were recruited after being interrogated in the Soviet Union itself. It was reported, for example, that some 1,000 Germans who worked in the mines in Stalino were selected to serve in these new units.[79]

Even the commanders of the Alert Police were selected from the graduates of antifascist courses in the POW camps. Lieutenant Hermann Rentzsch of the Reichswehr, who had served on the Stalingrad front, became the chief inspector (police general) of the Department of Border and Alert Police. The former Luftwaffe major general Hans von Weech was made chief of supply for the new armed police units. Former Reichswehr lieutenant general Vincenz Müller helped the DVdI (and later the NVA) to organize its military staff operations.[80] The Soviets had not been satisfied with the first commanders of the Alert Police, who had the appropriate political credentials as victims of fascism but did not know how to conduct proper drills. At the same time, Walter Mickinn, who as chief of the Personnel Department of the DVdI played such an important role in the denazification of the police apparatus, apparently argued with Fischer about the wisdom of appointing former Wehrmacht officers to such important posts. Mickinn was removed in October 1948 and sent to the Karl Marx Higher Party School for a six-month course, no doubt to improve his understanding of the dialectics of using the talents of those who had fought for the Third Reich to build socialism in the zone. For similar reasons, Robert Bialek was forced out of his position as head of the police section of the Central Secretariat of the SED.[81]

At a meeting on September 11, 1948, attended by Ulbricht and Fischer, as well as by Colonel Sergei Tiul'panov, chief of the Information Administration of SVAG, Fischer reportedly told the former Wehrmacht officers: "You, dear sirs, now have to turn your attention to restoring military discipline among the police."[82] In the fall and winter of 1948–49, German factories and SED officials turned over weapons to the new paramilitary units in a series of ceremonies marked by militaristic speeches that emphasized the aggressive intentions of the West and by effusive thanks to the Soviet military authorities for showing such confidence in the new German democracy.[83] Between the fall of 1948 and the summer of 1949, reports poured in to Washington from American military intelligence sources that the Alert Police regularly engaged in field exercises, target practice, and close-order drills of the sort characteristic of standing military formations. In Mecklenburg, the Alert Police were reported to have engaged in military training with various infantry weapons, as well as with automobiles requisitioned from the civilian economy. In some exercises, the Americans noted, police were trained in the use of mortars, machine guns, and antitank weapons. Reports came in from Cottbus that German and Soviet medium and heavy tanks were used in police training, and that Soviet officers were taking a prominent role in the exercises.[84]

All of these reports indicate that the Alert Police was not a police force at all, but rather a paramilitary formation that was armed for special missions. Eventually the troops received excellent rations and a special allocation of ten cigarettes per day. At the outset, there were serious problems with desertion, but the improvement of the conditions of service and the introduction of strict military regulations by the former Wehrmacht officers stabilized the Alert Police force, at least to the extent that it could be considered a reliable ally of the Soviet occupation army. The gradual centralization of the Alert Police also contributed to its usefulness to the Soviet authorities. In November 1948, the DVdI took over full responsibility from the provincial authorities for the Alert Police (and the Border Police).

In July 1949, the German Interior Administration recognized that the Alert and Border police performed essentially different functions than the other police forces, and it joined them in the so-called Administration for Schooling, a cover name for the paramilitary section of the DVdI commanded by Zaisser. The budget for the new administration was handled strictly within the DVdI, unlike other branches of the police, which were funded at least formally through the provinces. In contrast to the regular police, units of the new administration were also to be under "strict military discipline" and their training was to differ substantially from that of the regular police. Reportedly, the Alert Police took an oath to fight together with the troops of the people's democracies to repel attacks by the reaction.[85] American intelligence materials observed that some of the Alert Police units on parade marched in goose-step, sometimes "bringing cheers from the crowd." Roughly 200 of the Alert Police's leading officers, including Rentzsch, Markgraf (chief of the Berlin police), and Richard Staimer (Pieck's son-in-law), were sent for a year to Soviet military academies for further schooling. All of these changes in the Alert Police were correctly interpreted in the West as the beginning of the development "of a cadre communist army," complete with tanks and armored vehicles.[86]

The Soviets also reorganized the way they dealt with police units in the zone. Initially Major General P. M. Mal'kov, head of SVAG's Administration for Internal Affairs, commanded the police, and he was succeeded in 1948 by Major General S. F. Gorokhov, who initiated the formation of the Alert Police in the summer of 1948. (It is perhaps indicative of the importance of the change that Mal'kov was a specialist in internal security and Gorokhov had worked in SVAG's kommandantura organization.) But in August 1949, reflecting the changes in the DVdI, a new Department for Military Affairs was formed in SVAG, commanded by Major General Petrakovskii. Zaisser then reported directly to Petrakovskii, who treated the Alert and Border Police as subordinate military units of the Soviet forces in the zone. In fact, with twenty tanks, large trucks, armored personnel carriers, and 20-millimeter artillery pieces, Zaisser's Alert Police units began looking more and more like miniature army divisions.[87]

Despite the impressive growth of the paramilitary police in the East, U.S. State Department analysts were correct in their fall 1949 assessment of the military balance, that the Alert Police's "military value is still insignificant and its political reliability untested."[88] Plans to expand the size of the individual units were frustrated by a severe shortage of committed personnel; many candidates preferred to serve in the burgeoning state apparatus. In fact, Alert Police inductees were frequently recruited by the other branches of state service. The serious security problems that resulted from desertions also meant that long and painstaking procedures were required before new members could be recruited. Vice President Seifert of the DVdI admitted to Lieutenant Colonel Solov'ev of SVAG's Internal Affairs Department that the Germans were "encountering great difficulty in finding the appropriate number of personnel for the police service."[89] Nevertheless, the Alert Police served a valuable function in the occupation period by helping the SED maintain order in the Soviet zone without having to rely on a demonstrable show of force from Soviet troops. Like the Barracked People's Police, and the National People's Army after it, the Alert Police fulfilled important internal security functions and provided a defense force for the zone, as well. At least until the uprising of June 1953, when the internal security function of the Soviet Army was demonstrated with brutal clarity, the Alert Police also ostensibly served as a manifestation of the independent power of the leading political force, the SED, in guiding the destiny of Germans in the zone.

THE POLICE STATE

Despite a high rate of turnover and constant problems recruiting enough members, especially for its barracked units of Alert Police and Border Police, the Soviets constructed an impressive police system in the zone in a very short time indeed. Each province maintained five police groups: Administrative Police, Criminal Police, Civil Police, Railway Police, and Alert Police—a total of some 80,971 men and women as of September 1948 if one also includes 6,700 Border Police and 800 special DVdI police that were used to protect the Interior Administration's buildings and installations. That number also includes K-5 and the special Intelligence and

Information Department, whose existence was supposed to be kept secret from the West, because of Allied Control Council regulations abolishing "all German police agencies and bureaus which have as their purpose the supervision or control of the political activities of persons within Germany."[90]

The Soviets understood that they had created a potential military strike force on German soil, and therefore control of the Alert Police, in particular, was "of paramount importance." Colonel General Serov's successor as head of the MGB in the zone, N. K. Koval'chuk, warned fellow SVAG officials that enemies had "wormed their way" into units of the police force. A reparations official and important CPSU(b) apparatchik in the zone by the name of Lebedev used the analogy of the barbarian invasions of Rome to remind his comrades of the dangers of not paying sufficient attention to the armed police: "We cannot allow the kind of situation like the one used by the Teutons against the Romans, when they stabbed them in the back. We should not be like the Romans, and [we] should not forget that we are in the country of the Teutons. We have to keep our eyes wide open. We give weapons to the police, and [we] must deal with them strictly and watch [them] carefully."[91]

The SED leadership also realized the importance of having armed forces under their command. At the First Party Conference in 1949, Erich Mielke let his comrades know, in no uncertain terms, that these forces were critical to the party's calculus for building its influence in East German society. The People's Police was "an essential part" of the state apparatus, Mielke noted, and "the instrument of the dominant [working] class."[92] Everything the police did was in the name of the working class, and every effort had to be made to convince the workers of this fact.

In preparation for the May Day holiday in 1949, Mielke made sure that the police units sang the right fighting songs and gave the right speeches. He wanted police officers to appear sober, correct, disciplined, and in full uniform to celebrate the holiday with workers in the factories and mass organizations. They were to march in unbroken ranks and leave the impression of complete control.[93] That they were well on their way to this control was certainly the case. But in the occupation period, just as later, there were chinks in the armor of the "German Chekists." Despite good pay and generally good working conditions, the morale of rank-and-file police officers was often low. The constant political education did not go over well.[94] It seemed that there was a steady flow of officers who defected to the West. In the end, the police could not control the masses and the

SED leaders could not control the police, and Mielke lost his war to create an infallible police state and a new communist 1,000-year Reich. But many would suffer and die before the last battle.

THE CAMPS AND THEIR VICTIMS

On September 24, 1992, German newspapers reported that fifty mass graves had been found near the earlier Nazi concentration camp of Sachsenhausen. The evidence was unambiguous that these graves dated not from the Nazi period but from the postwar Soviet administration of the camp. Buried in layers, sometimes sixteen feet deep, the thousands of decomposed bodies represented only a portion of the 12,500 Germans who died—primarily of hunger and disease—while imprisoned in Sachsenhausen's Special Camp *(Spetslager)* no. 7 of the Soviet Commissariat (later, Ministry) of Internal Affairs.[95] The grisly discoveries continued. In Berlin-Hohenschönhausen, near what had been Special Camp no. 3, some 3,000 bodies were discovered, while explorations near the Ketschendorf (Fürstenwalde) camp turned up some 6,000 bodies.[96] In Bautzen, a few meters from the walls of the prison that was part of Special Camp no. 4, more mass graves were found that contained many of the camp's 18,000 dead.[97]

Although the newspapers reported the official number of dead in the camps, these figures have to be treated with extreme caution. According to Soviet documents released by the Brandenburg Ministry of the Interior just before the collapse of the GDR, some 122,671 Germans passed through the camps, of whom 42,889 died "as a result of sickness."[98] These figures generally agree with MVD documents that will soon be published by the Russians (see Table 1). The official Soviet statistics confirm, for example, the fact that more than a third of the internees died in the camps. The data also make it clear that only a small fraction were actually tried by Soviet military tribunals. But it is also important to note that the official statistics may well vastly underestimate the true number of dead. American military intelligence units and SPD groups in the late 1940s and 1950s assessed the total number of prisoners and the number of dead at nearly twice the official Soviet number (see Table 2). Karl Wilhelm Fricke's investigations of the number dead, noted in Table 2 in parentheses, also support the higher estimates. On the whole, the higher death counts in Table 2 are also confirmed by the recent discoveries from the mass graves. Since the *Wende* (turning point) of 1989–90, a number of groups made

Table 1. Fate of prisoners in the NKVD/MVD special camps

	Germans	Soviets	Others	Total
Arrested	119,743	33,641	569	153,953
Of these:				
Sentenced to USSR	1,148	26,592	18	27,758
Sent in special contingents to USSR	5,035	5,403	0	10,438
Sent to Poland	0	0	86	86
Assigned to POW camps	6,680	0	0	6,680
Assigned to repatriation camps	0	21	1	22
Assigned to disciplinary battalions	0	89	0	89
Turned over to MGB and tribunals	5,297	801	33	6,131
Released	30,519	204	17	30,740
Died	41,907	64	73	42,022
Shot	756	28	2	786
Ran away (22 caught)	109	16	0	125

Source: "Spravka o nalichii i dvizhenii zakliuchennykh, soderzhashchikhsia v spetslageriakh MVD SSSR," A. N. Dugin, "Neizvestnyi Gulag: Dokumenty i fakty" (unpublished manuscript), pp. 50–51. The document is a copy of the original signed by Capt. Skvortsev of the MVD's special camps section.

up of camp survivors and their families, such as the Bautzen Committee and the Working Group of the Mühlberg Camp, have published specialized studies indicating that the higher numbers may be more realistic.[99]

The camps were labeled "special" because the Soviet authorities insisted that the internees be cut off completely from the civilian population.[100] One could also call them death camps to the extent that, like the camps of the Gulag, little effort was made to ensure the physical—not to mention spiritual—well-being of the internees. In Sachsenhausen, for example, daily rations were normally one and three-fourths liters of the thinnest soup and 450 grams of bread daily, just enough, remembered one survivor, to keep internees alive enough to be truly hungry.[101] As a result of the hunger and the cold, thousands of prisoners suffered from tuberculosis. In Sachsenhausen, 10 to 20 internees died every day from the dreaded disease, forcing the camp to build special barracks to hold the overflow of tuberculosis patients. Internees also suffered from a wide array of other diseases, the most common being dysentery and malnutrition.

Table 2. Number of inmates and dead in the special camps

Camp	Number interned	Number dead
Bautzen	30,000	16,700 (12,000)*
Buchenwald	30,600	13,200 (13,000)
Hohenschönhausen	12,000	3,500 (3,000)
Jamlitz	14,200	5,200 (5,000)
Ketschendorf	19,850	7,200 (6,000)
Landsberg	9,800	3,800 (2,500)
Mühlberg	21,750	8,800 (7,000)
Neubrandenburg (Meck.)	17,200	6,700 (6,500)
Sachsenhausen	60,000	26,143 (20,000)
Weesow	13,750	1,400 (1,500)
Torgau	11,050	3,000 (2,000)
Total	240,000	95,643 (78,500)

Source: Sopade Informationsdienst, Denkschriften 55, "Die Straflager und Zuchthäuser der Sowjetzone: Gesundheitszustand und Lebensbedingungen politischen Gefangenen," HIA, Grabe, box 1; "Supplement to 'Germany: Weekly Background Notes No. 109,' " September 25, 1949, NA, RG 260, box 75, pp. 5–6; "Penal Camps and Prisons in the Soviet Zone," NA, RG 84, TSGC, box 3.

*Figures in parenthesis are from Karl Wilhelm Fricke, *Politik und Justiz in der DDR: Zur Geschichte der politischen Verfolgung 1945–1968* (Cologne: Verlag Wissenschaft und Politik, 1979), pp. 73–79, and are similar to those in the pamphlet, Memorial Library to Honor the Victims of Stalinism, "Sowjetische Internierungslager in der SBZ/DDR 1945–1950."

After a few months in the camps, it was not unusual to see formerly strapping prisoners weighing less than 100 pounds. In Bautzen during the hard winter of 1946–47, 50 to 60 internees died every day. Tuberculosis again took a terrible toll. In one Bautzen compound, more than 400 prisoners lay sick with the disease; on one day in the barracks, it was reported that 14 young people died.[102]

INTERNAL AFFAIRS

Milovan Djilas recalled that Stalin once said to him during the war that the victors' armies would bring their social systems with them to the territories they occupied.[103] Stalin might have added that wherever the Soviet armies went, NKVD operatives would go as well, and with them, the brutal system of secret police interrogations and judicial repression. (In 1946, both the NKVD and the NKGB were renamed. The NKVD, the People's Commissariat of Internal Affairs, became the MVD, the Ministry of Internal Affairs, and the NKGB, the People's Commissariat for State Security, became the MGB, the Ministry for State Security.) From the very beginning of the occupation of Germany, Lieutenant General Ivan Serov, an experienced NKVD officer and deputy commander-in-chief for civilian affairs of the Soviet Military Administration in Germany, led an almost completely independent Soviet secret police operation in the zone. Serov was responsible only to his NKVD/MVD superiors in Moscow, and he himself was appointed deputy minister of internal affairs in 1946, while he still served in Germany. Serov's powers in Germany were virtually unlimited, and his experience as a "Sovietizer" in the Baltics and in eastern Poland from 1939 to 1941 served him well in eastern Germany. The mission of the NKVD in Germany was defined by its leaders in the following terms: "The planning, arrest, and investigation of cases against spies and diversionaries; the dispersal of agents for intelligence purposes in the [Western] Allied zones of occupation; the investigations of agents of previous intelligence services in Germany; the processing of émigrés; and so on."[104]

Serov quickly built a pervasive network of so-called operations groups (*opergruppy,* or sometimes *opersektory*) that were attached to every Soviet administrative unit in the zone, from the local command posts, the kommandanturas, to the central Soviet military headquarters in Karlshorst. Local operations groups consisted of 4 to 8 officers with 6 interpreters and 10 NKVD/MVD soldiers. Provincial headquarters had 30 to 40 officers with 25 interpreters and 150 to 200 NKVD/MVD troops. Serov's empire also included a number of specialized operations in Germany, including the huge uranium mining enterprise in the Erzgebirge on the Czech border, as well as a series of weapons, rocketry, and aviation "bureaus" that provided products and specialists for Lavrenti Beria's special projects in the USSR. But the operations groups served as the core of the NKVD/MVD work in Germany, and they were charged with ferreting out and arresting former fascist activists and helping to promote Soviet policies in Germany. Local Soviet political officers routinely called on the operations groups whenever they suspected resistance to Soviet political aims, whether it involved breaking up opposition student groups and defiant circles of union activists or preventing the formation of Silesian interest groups.[105]

The operations groups also recruited local Germans to serve as informants and provocateurs. Especially in the first months of the occupation, former Nazis, who were afraid for their lives, served this function quite admirably. Over time, however, mainly loyal German communists worked for the NKVD/MVD as spies and informants. One of them, Rudolf Bühring, recalled that when he was recruited in the fall of 1945, he was a partisan of a "Soviet Germany" ("German Democratic Republic or Soviet Germany, then there was not such a big difference"). He said, "I also received from the NKVD very direct and purposeful questions that I was to investigate. Yes, and this began with an assessment of persons, of comrades in my own party. I had to report what I thought about functionaries of the KPD, how I assessed [them]."[106] Despite occasional doubts about what he was doing, and the fear that these doubts would cause his own arrest, Bühring—like countless other informants—provided the operations groups with important intelligence for their activities. For example, when an operations group in Halle tried to recruit teachers' union leader and SED functionary Seidel to report on union activities, Seidel protested that it would limit his effectiveness as an SED leader. After unsuccessfully seeking to get the local commandant to intervene on his behalf with the insistent operations group, Seidel escaped to the West.[107] Spying for the NKVD operations groups was often a test of a German's loyalty to the Soviet Union, as well as a source of valuable information.

Particularly during the first year of the occupation, Soviet intelligence agencies often worked at cross-purposes and even in competition with each other. The NKGB/MGB had its own agents working on its own projects, as did the NKVD/MVD. The MVD and its operations groups usually concentrated on internal security issues, operating openly and in uniform, while the smaller MGB focused on undercover work and spying.[108] Then there was the special wartime Soviet counterintelligence agency SMERSH—an acronym for "Death to spies"—which continued to function in occupied Germany until the spring of 1946. For the most part, SMERSH worked among the local population only to the extent that it checked out German employees of the Soviet Military Administration. Otherwise, it was charged primarily with the surveillance of Soviet personnel in Germany, both civilian and military. It assessed the mood of Soviet soldiers and officers and reported on potentially disloyal cadres.[109] According to American intelligence reports, Soviet security operations underwent a major shift in late 1946, when the MGB absorbed SMERSH's tasks and increasingly exerted control over the local MVD operations groups. Agents of the MGB then were able to order uniformed MVD units to engage in specialized operations. As the profile of the enemy underwent a transmogrification from that of underground Nazis and so-called Were-

wolves to SPD opponents of unification and groups of secret "reactionaries" and then again to saboteurs, terrorists, and agents in the employ of
Schumacher and the West, the MGB assumed greater overall responsiblity
for intelligence operations in the zone.[110]

During the first summer and fall of the occupation, operations groups
arrested Germans on the slightest suspicion of harboring Nazi or anti-
Soviet views.[111] Youth clubs, social groups, and industrialists' circles were
raided and members indiscriminately seized. For example, the twelve leading sugar manufacturers in the East were arrested in 1945 and placed in
detention. (Reportedly, only one survived.)[112] For alleged or even potential
opposition to land reform, large landowners—the Junkers—and large
farmers *(Grossbauern)* were arrested in sweeps of the countryside and
interned on the island of Rügen, located off the Baltic coast.[113]

Unsubstantiated denunciations from Soviets or Germans also often
ended in arrest and detention. An SED functionary reported that the district commandant of Schöneberg (Berlin) was infatuated with a local
butcher's daughter but that the proper butcher refused to let her see the
officer. As a result, the butcher was arrested, much to the dismay of the
local citizenry.[114] In a second case, a Christian Democratic Union official
was reported to have campaigned against his own election because the
local commandant had threatened him with arrest if he were elected.[115]
More often than not, the Soviet security services targeted particular political opponents. The "investigative methods" used by the NKVD and
later the MGB in Germany were depressingly similar to those the Soviets
used at home.[116] The security officers developed informants with the idea
of gathering compromising materials on their enemies, which led inevitably to denunciations, interrogations, and imprisonment.

The operations groups oversaw a growing network of spies and informants in the West as well. Sometimes Soviet intelligence services recruited
German spies in the POW camps and then sent them to the West either
to perform concrete tasks or simply to restart their lives as civilians and
wait for further instructions. The Soviets also recruited Germans from
among the prisoners in the special isolation camps in the zone. In these
cases, the recruits underwent brief surreptitious training and then "fled"
to the West as informants and spies. (Some had already performed these
functions in the camps.[117]) According to General Sergei Kondrashev of
the KGB, who worked for the MVD in Germany after the war, by the time
of the Berlin blockade, Soviet agents in the West had established underground communicatons networks and even stores of arms in case of war

between the Soviets and the West.[118] Mielke later outlined the tasks of those agents who reported to the German authorities in the East: "to sow panic, demoralization, strife; to arouse a lack of trust; to send letters back to the GDR about the poor conditions [of their lives]; and to keep Western agents occupied." At the same time, the agents were periodically recalled to the Eastern zone to provide political evaluations of the situation in the West for East German security agencies.[119]

Much as they did in the zone, Soviet operations groups recruited KPD members in the West to report on both friends and enemies. In some ways the entire KPD hierarchy in the West was used as an "information organization." The party was charged, for example, with keeping track of all businessmen and traders who traveled back and forth across the East-West interzonal borders. In one case, the KPD in Düsseldorf passed on information through the SED that one such businessman, who carried Russian documents, was a dangerous ex-Nazi and "unquestionably [should] be made harmless."[120]

THE TARGETS

The operations groups made a special point of intimidating and arresting German young people, who by all accounts were the most resistant to Soviet rule in the East. According to the Soviet authorities, thousands of these mostly fifteen- to seventeen-year-olds, former members of the Hitler Youth and the Association of German Girls, were organized as the Werewolves—underground armed bands whose intention was to carry out acts of sabotage and resistance against the occupying forces, most notably the Soviet Union.[121] There is very little evidence that such highly organized, underground groups actually existed, however, except in the fertile minds of the NKVD. Instead, the young people who were arrested as Werewolves were usually caught posting anti-Soviet or anti-KPD/SED leaflets, singing old Hitler Youth songs, or simply loitering and engaging in small-time black market activity.[122] There were also cases, like that of the Alona Group in Chemnitz-Hellersdorf, in which young "reactionaries" allegedly set out to disrupt Free German Youth meetings by asking embarrassing questions. Six of the group's members were arrested and turned over to the Soviet military authorities.[123] In 1947, the special police unit K-5 reported that there were twenty-eight suspected fascist groups operating in the underground, but that none of them posed a serious threat. They were mostly made up of local youths, K-5 added, and these groups had no ties with similiar groups in other parts of Germany.[124]

Otto Buchwitz, SED leader from Saxony, reported to the Party Executive about a group of young "rogues" *(Lausejungen),* who hooted and hissed at a Dresden movie theater when a film short was shown of Soviet ships delivering grain to Germany. Buchwitz had the theater emptied to check whether the young people worked as "paid agents."[125] In many such cases, the ringleaders would be arrested as Werewolves. In Leipzig, film showings became a central battleground for the struggle between German young people and the authorities. A Leipzig SED circular condemned the fact that Soviet films "are being sabotaged by the public, which in itself is a victory for the enemy ..." These same enemies used the films, the Leipzig SED alleged, as "ideological attack points against the SU [Soviet Union], SVAG, and our party and democracy." The strongly worded circular urged party members to take "active measures" in all the theaters of the city to make sure that screening of Soviet films and newsreels were not disturbed by "reactionary" youth.[126]

There were a number of serious cases in which gangs of German youths attacked and beat up Soviet soldiers.[127] Young people were also caught with weapons. Sometimes German police officers were attacked by young workers involved in strikes or threats of strikes. There were also cases in which swastikas were painted or chalked on SED buildings and campaign posters or on Soviet graves and memorials. "Victims of fascism" commemorations were periodically marred by the appearance of Nazi flags and shouts of "Heil Hitler!" There were also numerous instances of suspected sabotage: explosions in factories were attributed to underground Nazi groups, and bombs were exploded in SED party houses and FDJ meeting places. In 1948, for example, the police reported that in the factories there were 51 explosions and 300 cases of other kinds of sabotage, including unexplained fires and equipment damage. In fact, in that year the police asked for reinforcements as the result of an increase in bombings, shootings, and sabotage that they associated with a concerted attempt to disrupt the Two-Year Plan.[128] While such incidents of anti-Soviet and anti-SED resistance and Nazi activity clearly did take place, historians have so far not turned up fully documented cases of serious conspiracies, either on the part of Werewolves in the first years after the war or "counterrevolutionary" and "Schumacherite" underground operations in the period from 1947 through 1949.

Much more common (and frustrating for the police) than periodic incidents of resistance were the frequent cases of young people painting and chalking anti-SED and anti-Soviet graffiti all over the zone. In one instance, K-5 organized a major effort in December 1947 to chase down the youths responsible for defacing the Hoyerswerde Ratskeller with the rhyme: *"Der Winter ohne Kohlen, die Schuhe ohne Sohlen, die Lehrer ohne ABC"* (Winter without coal, shoes without soles, teachers who don't know the ABCs).[129] There were also numerous instances in which the graffiti artists creatively played on the letters of the SED, writing: "Satanic Elements—Dismantling" or "Soviet Property of Germany" *(Sowjetisches Eigentum Deutschland)*. None of this activity was overlooked by the police, and thousands of German young people were arrested for relatively minor infractions.

The high incidence of arrests of young people alarmed German society, especially given the fact that no formal procedures governed their detention. The West German press and radio constantly reported tales of the kidnapping and political reeducation of children in the Soviet zone, many of whom were accused of being Werewolves.[130] These charges were bred by the fact that suspected Werewolves were known to have simply disappeared, and no officials could account for their whereabouts to frantic parents and relatives. The SED leadership also was upset by this problem. In December 1947, Wilhelm Pieck sent along a letter from a "loyal comrade" to the Central Committee of the Soviet party, protesting that many of the alleged Werewolves were innocent young people, some even sons and daughters of SED members, who disappeared as the result of unfounded denunciations. In the letter, Pieck assumed that the youths were deported to the Soviet Union, and he begged to know where and under what conditions they were being held: "When will orderly procedures be introduced regarding these youths that will provide the innocent with an opportunity to contact their families and to return to their homes?"[131]

Although the operations groups were faced with a generally depressed and passive German population, there was enough resistance in the society to create a climate in which NKVD/MVD agents could think of themselves as being deeply involved in the class struggle. May Day celebrations often provoked social resistance. In Annaberg and Radebeul, for example, on May 1, 1946, posters were torn down, decorations defaced, and SED slogans rewritten.[132] Tensions between the Germans and Russians were so high in some towns that Soviet security troops regularly patrolled the towns day and night during Soviet holidays, watching for any demonstration of anti-Soviet behavior.[133] The operations groups, responsible for arresting the culprits, used the most brutal threats and torture in the NKVD/MVD investigative cells to ferret out the "guilty." Soviet authorities had a rather more difficult time controlling the many anonymous letters written to editors denouncing SED and Soviet rule in Germany, not to mention the many rumors that circulated, ranging from reports of an impending withdrawal of Soviet troops from Germany to the incorporation of the Eastern zone into the USSR.[134] Soviet political officers also requested that the operations groups turn their attention to the growing problem of hunger demonstrations, led mostly by women in various parts of the zone.[135] However, the spontaneity of these demonstrations stymied the operations groups' attempts to deal with the organizers. During the harsh winter of 1946–47, there were twelve different hunger demonstrations, many of which involved hundreds of women and children; in addition, thirty-three posters and leaflets turned up protesting against the shortage of food.[136] Workers, too, caused problems for the NKVD/MVD in a number of situations in the zone. For example, in anticipation of Stalin's seventieth birthday in November 1949, miners were supposed to pledge an extra hour of uncompensated work, but it took a number of votes and revotes, plus threats and intimidation, for a successful pledge vote finally to be tallied.[137]

In addition, operations groups arrested and detained German POWs who had been processed in Western POW camps and cleared to return to their homes in the East. According to British intelligence sources, some groups of returning POWs had their documents confiscated and were sent to Erfurt for five weeks of quarantine and political reeducation. The vast majority were then interned in Sachsenhausen. Often the healthiest among them were deported to forced labor camps in the Soviet Union. In one June 1947 case documented by the British authorities, a trainload of 774 German POWs sent back from England to their places of residence in eastern Germany was not even allowed to disembark but was instead sent on to Frankfurt-Oder, where the POWs were deported to the Soviet Union.[138]

THE POLITICALS

Until the Russian government makes complete arrest lists from the KGB archives available to researchers, it will be impossible to know precisely how many Germans were deported to the Soviet Union in the postwar

period and how many arrests were attributable to the alleged Nazi background, social position, politics, or some other characteristic of the individual German detainee. What is known for certain is that by the winter
and spring of 1946, the NKVD special prisons and camps, eleven in all,
were bursting with inmates. Order no. 201, which authorized the arrests
of a variety of categories of Nazi offenders, made the situation even
worse.[139] Prisons were so crowded in Thüringen and Saxony-Anhalt that
the German authorities stated that they simply could not fulfill all of the
conditions of the order.[140] But the operations groups' most serious targets
were not ex-Nazis or even the pre-1945 German economic elite, who were
held responsible for Nazi crimes whether they had been in the Nazi Party
or not. Even members of the bourgeois parties, the Christian Democratic
Union and the Liberal Democratic Party, though subject to NKVD/MVD
harassment, intimidation, and sometimes arrest, were not considered serious problems by the Soviet authorities.[141] Rather, the parties of the Left
were considered the greatest enemies of Soviet power, and therefore they
consumed the energies of the operations groups.

As noted earlier, when the Soviets first marched into Germany in April
and May of 1945, the "sectarian" Left was one of their greatest concerns.
The KPD leadership, Walter Ulbricht in particular, and NKVD operatives
cooperated in disarming sectarian groups, bringing them under administrative control, and making it clear to them that it was ideologically
incorrect and that it played into the hands of the reactionaries to work
for a Soviet Germany. Many disgruntled communists left politics altogether; a number fled to the West, and some were arrested for their stubbornness. But by far the majority conformed to the Moscow line. While
the Soviets continued to complain about sectarian elements in the SED,
they understood that the SPD, the social democrats, presented a far more
serious challenge to the military government.[142]

When the Soviets legalized both the KPD and the SPD in June 1945,
they harbored visions of the communists' outpolling the social democrats
in future elections and, as a result, dominating the antifascist democratic
bloc of parties. The operations groups were used to intimidate the SPD
in the hope that the party would accept its Soviet-designed role as junior
partner to the communists. In August 1945, Otto Grotewohl, then leader
of the SPD in the East, noted that any time the SPD protested about
problems with the occupation authorities, they did so "under threat of
their own personal security." In one case, wrote Grotewohl, "I thought
we would not come home from these discussions."[143] When it became

apparent by the fall of 1945 that the communists were actually losing ground to the social democrats in the working class as well as elsewhere in society, and that an embarrassing election in which the communists lost to the social democrats would be a serious setback for Soviet goals in Germany, the Soviets decided the time was right to unify the two parties. Pressure for unification increased in the winter of 1945 and 1946, culminating in the Unity Congress of April 1946. At least formally, the new Socialist Unity Party operated on the basis of parity between former communists and former social democrats. But in July of 1948 even the formal principle of parity was abandoned in favor of a "party of the new type," based on the "scientific" principles of Marxism-Leninism.

The Soviets increasingly saw the social democrats, both inside and outside the SED, as the principle enemies of Soviet influence in Germany. All social democrats were potential "Schumacherites," followers of the hated Kurt Schumacher, leader of the SPD in the West. Unlike his SPD heirs Willy Brandt, Egon Bahr, and Helmut Schmidt, Schumacher was openly anti-Soviet, nationalistic, and deeply commited to socialism. Out of reach of the Soviets in Hannover (and prudently accompanied by British soldiers whenever he visited Berlin), Schumacher was seen by the Soviet security services as the chief figure in the conspiracy of monopolistic capitalism to undermine Soviet rule in eastern Germany. That the SPD in the West set up an Ostbüro at the beginning of 1946 to collect information about and maintain contacts with social democrats in the East only added fuel to Soviet accusations that the SPD—in the language of the cold war— was directed by Washington and Wall Street to deprive the Soviet Union of its rightful gains in Germany.[144]

While the political officers of the Soviet Military Administration carried out an open ideological campaign against the so-called right-wing SPD, the operations groups became specialists in terrorizing SPD members and sympathizers through more forceful means.[145] Members of the SPD who resisted the unity campaign—appropriately labeled in German the *Zwangsvereinigung* (forced unification)—were bullied, cajoled, and, in thousands of cases, arrested and interned.[146] Typical in a number of ways was the situation of Brethorst, secretary of the Leipzig region SPD. On January 14, 1946, the Grimma city commandant ordered leading members of the KPD and SPD to appear at Soviet headquarters. According to Brethorst's account of the meeting, the Soviets bullied and berated the SPD members, even using weapons to threaten them if they would not agree to join the Unity Party. Brethorst's mistake was in publicly exposing the

Soviets' threats. He was charged with attempting to compromise the authority of the Soviet occupation, arrested, and turned over to the Soviet military tribunal for "provocational activities."[147] Even after the party unification had been completed in April, the struggle went on against those SPD members who refused to join the SED. Many, like Hermann Brill of Thüringen, simply fled to the West, fearing arrest and incarceration. Those who joined the SED but defended too insistently the rights of parity, or who criticized Soviet influence on the policies of the SED, were also subject to intimidation and arrest. Even the most "loyal" former SPD members, the Soviets' prize pupil Otto Grotewohl or the Saxon SED leader Otto Buchwitz, for example, constantly had to prove that they had shed the evil path of "SPD-ism."

The situation for former SPD members became particularly difficult in the spring and summer of 1947, as cold war tensions increased and the communist leadership of the SED felt increasingly confident of their control in the Eastern zone. For example, both the Soviets and the German communists especially resented the influence of former SPD members on the trade unions. New waves of arrests resulted, as an increasing number of SED members were accused of being Schumacherites and were interned. According to SPD reports of September 1947, there were 400 social democrats in the Zwickau prison, 900 in the Dresden prison, and 800 in Buchenwald.[148] Like the former Nazis immediately after the war, former social democrats were arrested for no reason other than their earlier party affiliation and lack of interest in the SED.[149] Part of the campaign against the SPD included closing down the more than 100 private detective bureaus all over the zone, which were allegedly involved in spying for the Ostbüro.[150] By the beginning of 1948, the situation had degenerated even further. Former social democrats, especially those who maintained any contacts with the West, were routinely accused of being agents of the Ostbüro and "carrying on espionage activities at the behest of American intelligence." According to one Soviet military government report, the "organs of the MVD" arrested sixty-nine members of the SED, presumably all earlier SPD members, for working for the Ostbüro and the Americans.[151] The German police unit K-5 broke up a large number of alleged underground SPD groups and turned over their members to the Soviets. The police reports noted, however, that the groups often were made up of no more than a half dozen members and that conspiratorial ties between them could not be firmly established.[152] Some areas proved more resistant to MVD and German police penetration than others. The city of Leipzig, for example, was the source of more than half of the 700 cases of illegal leaflets uncovered by the police in Saxony in 1946 and 1947. Of thirty-three illegal organizations, fifteen were in Leipzig.[153]

The history of the Ostbüro's activities and especially of the SPD's ties with American intelligence is still to be written.[154] But much as was the case with the so-called Werewolves, it is extremely unlikely that underground SPD organizations in the East engaged in the kinds of sabotage and espionage that the Soviets accused them of. Most of their activities consisted of printing and distributing anti-SED (notably *not* anti-Soviet) material and maintaining contacts in the hope of reestablishing their party in the East. (And Soviet archival documents indicate that this was not at all an impossibility in 1946 and 1947.) The following spoof on the "Deutschlandlied"—many copies of which showed up all over the zone— was characteristic of the kinds of leaflets distributed by the underground SPD groups.

> Deutschland, Deutschland ohne alles
> ohne Butter, ohne Fett
> und das bisschen Marmelade
> frisst uns die Verwaltung weg.
> Hände falten, Köpfe sinken,
> immer an die Einheit denken.
>
> Die Preise hoch
> die Läden dicht geschlossen
> die Not marschiert mit ruhig festem Schritt.
> Es hungern nur die kleinen Volksgenossen
> die grossen hungern nur im Geiste mit.
> Komm, Wilhelm Pieck, sei unser Gast
> und gib, was Du uns versprochen hast.
> Nicht nur Rüben, Kraut und Kohl,
> sondern was Du isst und Herr Grotewohl.
>
> Zu Kaisers Zeiten wars fein
> da hatten wir unserer Schwein
> Als wir den alten Hindenburg hatten,
> gabs ab und zu auch Braten
> Bei Hitler und bei Göring,

hatten wir mindestens noch 'nen Hering,
aber bei der jetzigen Leitung
steht alles in der Zeitung.[155]

But it was not just the SPD, of course, that was accused of oppositional activities in the zone. The authorities identified the " 'right-wings' of the bourgeois parties" as the allies of the illegal SPD organizations. The police hounded dissident religious groups, especially the Jehovah's Witnesses, as inimical to the antifascist democratic order in the zone. The Soviets and K-5 also maintained surveillance on Protestant churchmen. At a meeting of the ministers of the interior in February 1948, for example, Ulbricht urged that the police keep a close watch on the transport of Western CARE packages sent over the border to churchmen, because the pastors were responsible, in all likelihood, for passing on these packages to agents.[156] In fact, Western intelligence sources mention underground groups in Thüringen that were run by churches and clergy in the East and were funded by churches in the West.[157]

PROBLEMS FOR THE SED

The NKVD/MVD's arrests, interrogations, and internment of German civilians were well known throughout the Eastern zone. Even when the rumor networks and informal information sources did not inform the Germans about the arrests, there was simply no way for the Soviets to keep Western-licensed newspapers and radio broadcasts out of the East. The SED found itself in the uncomfortable position of having to defend the Soviet police system, while sharing many Germans' concerns about the "disappearance" of so many citizens. Otto Buchwitz of Saxony constantly brought up the issue of the arrested youths with the SED Party Executive. Through personal influence with the military government, he was able to secure the release of four hundred to five hundred young people. But as a result, he claimed, he was besieged by petitions and personal inquiries from worried families about their relatives' whereabouts. "We have to try yet once again to deal with Karlshorst on this question," he concluded.[158] Erich Lübbe from Berlin noted, as did many others, that the main problem for family members was not knowing where those arrested were interned, and even when they knew, they were not allowed any contact with them. "Now that we have an SED," he stated, "it has got to be possible to reach an agreement with the Russians" to keep track of the arrested through a central office in Karlshorst or elsewhere. Lübbe, a former social democrat, claimed that some twenty of his comrades from Berlin were still missing without a trace.[159] Heinrich Hoffmann, SED chief in Thüringen, wrote to Pieck and Grotewohl in a similar spirit. He claimed that the quality of relations between the military government and the German population had noticeably declined as a result of so many young people having been arrested for "security reasons." Surely, he stated, many of them could be released, since they had never been proven guilty and they could pose no danger to "our democratic development." At the very least, he said, it should be possible to arrange for communications between family members and their relatives. Hoffmann concluded: "In general, it would be a good thing if the security organs of the occupation power would operate less crudely and rather more delicately."[160]

The complaints of SED leaders clearly had an impact on Pieck and Grotewohl. Many of the SED's leaders were deeply concerned about the party's serious loss of legitimacy as a result of the NKVD/MVD's actions. In his notes in preparation for a March–April 1948 meeting with M. A. Suslov, A. I. Mikoyan, and V. N. Merkulov in Moscow, Pieck emphasized that the Western powers were trying to incite the German masses in the East against the Soviet Union and had achieved "a measure of success." Initially Western propagandists had focused on the alleged "violence carried out by [Red Army] troops" (rapes and assaults) after the war. Later, their campaign against the Soviet Union targeted the "security measures" (arrests and internments) and the "alleged disappearances" in the Eastern zone.[161] Grotewohl succinctly stated the SED's growing problem at a meeting of the Party Executive: Western propaganda about "the supposed wave of arrests and lack of freedom" seriously undermined the SED's authority in the zone and in Germany as a whole. This propaganda created a "political psychological burden" for the SED that could be removed only by the Russians.[162]

SOVIET CONCERNS

The SED was not the only group that understood the serious price the communists had to pay because of the arrests and internment of Germans in the zone. Russian archival documents demonstrate as well, that Soviet political officers in the provinces also periodically complained to Karlshorst about the activities of the NKVD/MVD. In an unsigned report about the work of the operations group in the Cottbus region, an officer criticized the many excesses of the NKVD, its bullying and threats, its obvious intimidation of German politicians and its exploitation of the population: "The members of the operations groups of a number of the districts in the region carry on extremely undesirable work among the German population through their tactless activity, their crudeness, and in many cases their [inappropriate] exploitation of their positions."[163] In another instance, a political officer complained directly to the head of the operations group of Brandenburg province that the ubiquitous arrests and investigations made his own work with trade unions and political parties impossibly difficult. Since the NKVD actions affected so many family members of the political and union leaders in the region, the officer asked for an explanation for the arrests.[164]

The repeated entreaties of SED members and the complaints by local Soviet political officers had an effect. The political leaders of the Soviet Military Administration approached the Central Committee in Moscow with the problem, albeit very delicately. In a report to Suslov of August 31, 1946, Colonel Tiul'panov attacked Western allegations about the kidnappings of thousands of German children, who were then supposedly sent to reeducation camps. All of the Western complaints, Tiul'panov noted, boiled down to nothing more than "a small number of Nazi criminals from the youth, who were arrested for their participation in underground terrorist and diversionary groups." But more propaganda attacks of this sort could be expected, Tiul'panov warned, because "the parents of those young Nazis arrested by the Soviet authorities receive no news from them [their children]."[165] The Soviets understood that they were taking a severe propaganda pounding in the zone, and in 1948 they created the position of deputy commander-in-chief for political affairs, in part to deal with this problem. Lieutenant General A. G. Russkikh, who held the position, also attributed the Soviets' problems with the Germans to the slowness and inconsistency of the MVD's returning of young prisoners from the Soviet Union to the zone.[166]

The most striking Central Committee document complaining about the activities of the operations groups in the zone was written by Major General I. S. Kolesnichenko, chief of the Soviet Military Administration in Thüringen.[167] Kolesnichenko had always been something of a maverick, as well as an unusually outspoken and determined political activist in his advocacy of the unification of the SPD and KPD into the SED. He was also well known for his blunt confrontations with the SPD and CDU leaders in Thüringen.[168] In other words, Kolesnichenko could hardly be considered to be a liberal, or to be "soft" on the opponents of the SED. Yet he was angry and upset about NKVD/MVD actions in Thüringen that he felt undermined the Soviet cause in Germany. (Kolesnichenko, like many other Soviet and German leaders, continued to refer to the renamed MVD as the NKVD). In a December 1947 letter to the leadership of the military government, Kolesnichenko noted that loyal CDU and LDP politicians consistently reported that the main sources of hostility toward the Soviets in the East were "the activities of the NKVD." The SED leaders were of the same opinion, Kolesnichenko added, even if they were hesitant to say so openly. Instead, the SED was forced to operate on the level of appealing to Kolesnichenko or Sokolovskii for the release of individual internees. The alleged "lack of freedom" in the East, Kolesnichenko wrote, was one of the most powerful weapons in the hands of the American-inspired "campaign against communism," and this had a powerful effect, even on members of the SED who were supposed to be the supporters of Soviet occupation policy in Germany.

Kolesnichenko's strategy in his letter to the SVAG leadership was an interesting one. He expressed his confidence that the NKVD arrested only the guilty and that the arrests were carried out only after thorough investigations. Therefore, he asked, why were the arrests kept secret and the indictments not released to the public? Of course enemies of the Soviet Union would always complain about NKVD methods. But, Kolesnichenko claimed, the Soviets were also in danger of losing their friends, all because of the secrecy surrounding the arrests and imprisonment of genuine criminals. Arrests and indictments should be made public, he said; family members should be able to correspond with their arrested relatives; and the Church should be allowed "to tend to the souls" of the interned. He suggested that if his recommendations were accepted, the NKVD would not be looked at by the Germans as a frightening specter, as it so obviously was at that moment, but rather as a "state organ, guaranteeing the interests of the new developing democracy in Germany": "This would also serve to passify the members of the SED and their leadership, as well as other progressive Germans, and would remove the soil from under the feet of the 'brave' Americans, who attack socialism with the goal of protecting 'the freedom of the individual,' which has supposedly been liquidated in our zone by the organs of the NKVD."

Kolesnichenko's entreaty was answered by Lieutenant General V. E. Makarov, at that point a member of the Military Council of SVAG. Makarov said that he had raised the problem with Molotov, who had stopped in Berlin on his way to the Foreign Ministers Conference in Paris. Supposedly, Molotov talked about changing "the system" of arrest and incarceration in the zone. But according to Kolesnichenko, there were no changes for the better. As a result, he decided to turn directly to the Central Committee in Moscow, which was the only body that might have some influence on NKVD practices. In a December 1948 letter to the party chiefs, a year after his appeal to the SVAG leaders, Kolesnichenko sent along his previous letter and repeated his fundamental point that "the greatest source of dissatisfaction" among the German population was caused by the " 'disappearance' of people with the help of our operations groups." Western propaganda had been devastatingly successful, and the most widespread view of the Soviet zone among Germans in both the West and East was that there was no "freedom of the individual." "I would venture to assert," Kolesnichenko wrote, "that these activities of our security organs encourage the most severe anti-Soviet propaganda, as well as hate for us from the side of the Germans." He was convinced that only the Central Committee could deal with this problem, and that it had to be dealt with "if we want to get better results from our activities and our politics in Germany."[169]

THE LAST STAGE, 1948–1950

The complaints from Soviet officers had no appreciable effect on the conduct of the operations groups. Within the Soviet political system, exaggerated, even psychotic, concerns about security and control gave the NKVD/MVD an extraordinary ability to maintain its investigative and internment practices in the zone. Yet the Soviet authorities understood that the continuing arrests and incarcerations were undermining their position and that of their SED allies. The military government therefore undertook a number of measures in 1948 and early 1949 to improve the situation. It was clear, for example, that the Soviets had little to gain from continuing to arrest and isolate former Nazis from the population. As a result, the denazification commissions were formally disbanded in the spring of 1948 and in May and June of 1948, the military authorities gave their blessing to the new National Democratic Party, which was intended to attract "nominal [Nazi] party members" to the SED-run coalition.

On March 18, 1948, Marshal Sokolovskii also announced an amnesty on the occasion of the centennial of the German revolution of 1848. The amnesty provided for the release of those Germans serving prison terms of less than a year, as well as those who were accused of minor crimes but had not yet been indicted.[170] For the most part, the prisoners affected were precisely the "nominal party members" whom the Soviets were trying to integrate into the political and economic structure of the zone. In mid-April, Sokolovskii also agreed to expand the amnesty to include a large number of youths who had been arrested for minor crimes and to provide Germans who had been arrested for more serious crimes with the opportunity to appeal their cases to SVAG judicial boards. At the April 14 and 15 plenum of the SED Party Executive, Grotewohl took credit for the mass release of "political prisoners and youth."[171] The Soviet-licensed newspaper, *Tägliche Rundschau,* also willingly gave credit for the releases to the "repeated representations" of SED leaders Pieck and Grotewohl to Sokolovskii.[172]

In preparation for the release of large numbers of prisoners, conditions in the internment camps improved dramatically. There was finally an increase in the prisoners' starvation-level rations; the ghastly tuberculosis barracks were cleaned up; medicines were made available; and the death rates substantially declined. Before their actual release, inmates were moved into quarantined barracks and provided with new clothes and a higher level of rations. The Soviets later announced that some 28,000 prisoners had been released in the summer of 1948; the total number for the spring and summer may have been as high as 46,000.[173] Some prisoners were released right away; some, inexplicably, were detained and quarantined for a longer period of time.[174] To avoid releasing particular categories of political opponents, the military authorities deported thousands of prisoners to the Soviet Union; it is impossible to know how many.[175] By the fall of 1948, enough prisoners had been either released or deported to the USSR that the Soviets could close down eight of the hated special camps; only Buchenwald, Bautzen, and Sachsenhausen remained open, holding, respectively (on May 5, 1949), 6,481, 10,110, and 11,901 prisoners.[176]

When Wilhelm Pieck went to Moscow in September 1949 to ask "the advice of Comrade St.[Stalin] how we should proceed with the formation of the [East] German government," he also brought with him a plan for closing down the remaining three MVD camps. "Criminals" sentenced by Soviet organs should be transferred to the USSR, he said, and the remainder of the prisoners should be turned over to the German authorities for detention if they had already been sentenced, or if not, they should be prosecuted.[177] For Pieck, as for Kolesnichenko, the issue was much less the welfare of the prisoners themselves than the desire to get "some substantial relief from the campaign carried out against us from the West."[178]

For the most part, Pieck's suggestions were followed. On the orders of General Chuikov, Sokolovskii's successor as commander-in-chief, the Soviets finally closed down the special camps of Bautzen, Sachsenhausen, and Buchenwald in January and February of 1950. Of the prisoners still in Bautzen at this point, 5,400 were turned over to the German police, 700 were sent to Waldheim to face trial by the German authorities, and an unknown number were deported to the Soviet Union, among them members of the burial battalion, who otherwise might have exposed the existence and even location of the mass graves.[179] Buchenwald and Sachsenhausen were turned over to Soviet military authorities for their own use. The Bautzen prison was given to the German authorities, who treated the inmates, many of whom were angry and frustrated at not being included in the amnesties, no better than their NKVD/MVD warders had. In March 1950 the prisoners staged a series of protests against conditions in Bautzen and subsequently negotiated with both the Soviet and the German authorities about improving them. On March 31, 1950, the prisoners instigated one more protest, but this time the People's Police was ready; hundreds of prisoners were badly beaten, and the string of Bautzen demonstrations ended.[180]

Soviet judicial and police repression in the Eastern zone set the tone for the arbitrary and brutal treatment of prisoners during the years of the German Democratic Republic. But even the East German police authorities were shocked by the complete absence of proper judicial procedures governing the disposition of the German prisoners during the four and half years of the Soviet occupation regime. This became even more apparent when a commission comprised of Erich Mielke, Hilde Benjamin, and Karl Maron reviewed many of the 11,000 or so cases of Germans who had been interned on the orders of Soviet military tribunals and, after the founding of the GDR, were in the hands of the German authorities. The SED leaders wanted to amnesty many of the prisoners as part of the third-anniversary celebration of the GDR in 1952. The problem was that there were no judicial documents attached to the prisoners' records. There were no depositions or testimonies; no indictments or justifications for sentencing; and no summary statements from the prosecution or the courts. The only materials attached to the cases were the name of the perpetrator, the date of sentencing, and the general category of the crime: "spying," "anti-Soviet agitation," "distribution of pamphlets," "theft from Soviet citizens," "possession of weapons," and so on.[181] In the end, the commission decided to include in the general amnesty and immediately release most of those who were eighteen or younger at the time of their alleged crimes. Those who had committed severe crimes against Soviet citizens during the war—such as rape and mass murder—received sentences of twenty-five years in prison or in some cases, life.[182] The rest were soon released. But, as Mielke put it: "Our state power and state order is so assured that the release of a part of those sentenced . . . is no danger [to us]."[183]

By the beginning of the 1950s, the GDR's police and judicial agencies took over the responsibility for political repression in East Germany, though the Soviets—the MVD and the MGB (later, KGB)—remained very much a part of the picture until the very end. The history of the East German regime's repression of its own people is a different story, even though it begins with the Soviet occupation of the country. And in their current ardor to expose and prosecute former Stasi agents and SED leaders, German government figures tend to obfuscate the crucial historical role of the Soviet occupation authorities in constructing totalitarian institutions in the East. The Germans need to ask difficult and complex questions about the extent of Soviet influence on the SED regime and about the level of Soviet secret police involvement in judicial repression in the Soviet zone and the GDR. To deal with those questions, the Russians themselves need to care about the answers and open the KGB files from the postwar period. Only then will both nations be able to clear the air about a difficult and tragic episode in their common past.

The Politics of Culture and Education

IN THE SOVIET SCHEME OF THINGS, culture was the most visible demonstration of the superiority of Marxism-Leninism and the higher stage of socialism into which the USSR had entered. This concept of culture included classic ideas of culture (theater, music, and literature) as well as popular culture (folk dance, film, and public ceremony). From the point of view of the Soviets, the traditional conflict between high and low culture had been theoretically resolved by the Bolsheviks when they turned over all production of culture to the masses.

According to its proponents, Soviet culture operated at an inherently higher level than other, bourgeois cultures. It combined the highest standards of the classics—Pushkin, Chekhov, Tchaikovsky—with the progressive accomplishments of Soviet society—Mayakovsky, Simonov, and Shostakovich. Much like the political system of the Soviet Union, the greatness of Soviet culture was seen as having been confirmed by the Russian victory over the Germans in the "Great Patriotic War." Those who represented this culture in Germany, the officers and men of the Soviet occupation army and the military government, were supposed to serve as examples of its superiority. This was particularly important in Germany, since for more than a decade the Nazis had denigrated Soviet culture as the low-grade product of the inferior Judeo-Bolshevik civilization.

The Soviet occupation authorities therefore had an important cultural mission to accomplish in Germany. They had to reeducate the Germans and force—in the words of Johannes R. Becher, the chief German cultural leader in the East—a "radical break with the reactionary past." This meant, above all, a "national liberation and rebuilding effort in the ideological-moral sphere of the most significant sort."[1] The Soviets were intent on liberating the Germans from what they felt were the horrible prejudices about culture instilled in them by the Nazi fiends. They also had to rebuild the cultural foundation of the new Germany by getting the Germans to understand the superiority of the humanistic and progressive core of the "victorious" Soviet culture. This was a more daunting and challenging task than that of the Western occupiers, concluded Lieutenant General I. S. Kolesnichenko, commander of the Soviet Military Administration in Thüringen. In the East, a new and progressive ideology had to be installed by the Soviet occupiers, while in the West, the Americans, British, and French could simply allow a return to the old bourgeois culture of the Weimar period.[2] Western political officers saw things differently. In the Soviet zone, the British complained, the Soviets' deep commitment to their cultural mission produced an atmosphere of excitement and accomplishment: "Theatrical, book-publishing, art, and musical activities are conducted with a hustle which conveys the impression that something new and lively is going on." As supporters of "free and personal culture," Western officers were poorly equipped to counter the "politicized culture" of the Soviets.[3]

The Problem of the Intelligentsia

While it is certainly the case that Western cultural officials envied the energy and success of their Soviet counterparts in a variety of cultural fields, the Soviet military government had an extremely difficult task in trying to win over to its side the German cultural intelligentsia, not to mention the population as a whole. Most cultural figures remained skeptical of Soviet claims to a superior culture and indifferent to politics in general. The declaratory nature of Soviet political culture alienated even those intellectuals and artists who were initially sympathetic to socialism and to alternatives to restoring Weimar norms. The KPD/SED cultural specialist Klaus Gysi tried to convince the Soviets that the intelligentsia had to be treated differently than the rest of the German population. "The members of the intelligentsia demand that their own point of view be respected, that things they don't understand be explained to them, that they be allowed the opportunity to discuss freely," he said. Gysi added that the intelligentsia was particularly sensitive to the "freedom of the word" and therefore gravitated toward Western newspapers, which would publish just about anything, instead of to Soviet-sponsored newspapers, which censored almost everything.[4] Becher noted that the problem for the German intelligentsia was not so much Soviet policies and prescriptions as it was the German Communist Party itself, which demonstrated little subtlety in translating those policies into German reality. In fact, in his view, most thinking people regarded the party as nothing more than "a party of Quislings, a party of the Soviet occupying forces."[5] This ultimately made it more difficult for the Soviets to appeal to the progressives throughout Germany.

Despite his Moscow and KPD background, which was not without its Stalinist loyalties, Becher was insistent that the narrow dogmatism of the KPD and SED carried much of the blame for the intelligentsia's resistance to the natural superiority of Soviet culture. He felt that the party was too small-minded and dependent on every word the Soviets wrote in their occupation newspaper, *Tägliche Rundschau*. In Becher's view, the SED too easily sacrificed its appeal to the German intelligentsia and gave over control of culture to narrow-minded "party functionaries."[6] The Soviets also criticized the SED's approach to the intelligentsia and, like Becher, blamed their lack of success on the German party's indifference to questions of culture. Especially in the provinces, the Soviets complained, the SED ignored the intelligentsia, whose leadership it left to the clergy. Armed only with the most primitive understanding of Marxism and events occurring in the world around them, local SED functionaries made little headway in bringing the cultural intelligentsia under the party's leadership.[7] The situation was just as bad with the technical intelligentsia, the doctors, agronomists, engineers, and scientific workers. One SVAG report concluded that "a significant portion of the German intelligentsia knows literally nothing about the Soviet Union and lives with the notions of Hitler times."[8] For the Soviets, then, the struggle for the allegiance of the German intelligentsia became an integral part of their occupation goals in Germany. Only through the German intelligenstia could the cultural attributes of Soviet civilization be spread in the eastern zone. But from the point of view of Soviet internal documents, they were fighting a losing battle because of the indifference and obtuseness of the German communists.[9]

THE KULTURBUND

The responsibility of progressive German intellectuals for the moral renewal of the German people was an idea already deeply ingrained in the activities of German writers and cultural figures in the Soviet Union during the war. Becher, a poet and writer, stood out in this group for his passionate commitment to getting Germans to admit their collective guilt for the war and forge a new Germany through a combination of repentance and reeducation. Becher had worked closely in Moscow with Walter Ulbricht and the KPD leadership on a number of projects, including the editing of Georgi Dimitrov's book on the Reichstag fire, and as a result he had good ties to the German party leadership.[10] Ulbricht was already anxious to get Becher involved in propaganda among the German intelligentsia in May 1945. But Becher was returned to Germany only on June 10, after the KPD initiative groups met with Stalin and the Central Committee.[11] Becher was therefore the perfect choice to head up the new Kulturbund zur Demokratischen Erneuerung Deutschlands (Cultural Union for the Democratic Renewal of Germany), formed by the Soviets and the German communists on July 3, 1945.

Initially Becher's goals meshed nicely with those of the Soviets and the KPD, and with Ulbricht's in particular. The Kulturbund would be an organization of the intelligentsia and would stay clear of partisan party politics, while organizing intellectuals and cultural figures on behalf of the "antifascist democratic" transformation of Germany. For Becher, the German historical spirit contained the material for the renewal of the German people on new and "progressive" bases, and the intelligentsia could serve as the standard bearers for this national renewal. The ultimate "Germanness" of his goals, which bordered on the kind of socialist nationalism that later characterized the GDR, was apparent in his writings and speeches in this period. The following speech of August 19, 1945, commemorating nineteen German writers and poets who died during the war, is a perfect example.

> We commemorate the dead Germans, [who are German] not just in name, in origin or speech, but Germans who had maintained in themselves the best of German tradition, and who in the most difficult, distressful time of our history held steadfast to these traditions, remained true to them and placed a seal on them with their death. Every one of our dead lived, worked, suffered, and went to their deaths for the *human* empire of the German nation. German poets, the true Germans that they were, could and would not be silenced as Hitler brought ruin to Germany.[12]

However, from the very beginning there was a tension in the Kulturbund between the organization's formal desire to avoid partisanship and to appeal to the national sentiments of all the German intelligentsia, and the Communist Party's determination to control the Kulturbund for its own immediate purposes.[13] Becher recognized, of course, that the Kulturbund was not intended simply for the cultivation of the arts; rather, it was designed for the "high political task" of "the democratic regeneration of Germany."[14] But he understood that the KPD/SED was not adept at reaching out to the intelligentsia, indeed that it was rent by *Kulturfeindlichkeit* (aversion to culture).[15] Therefore, while he was perfectly comfortable with running the affairs of the Kulturbund with a four-man working committee of communists (himself, Alexander Abusch, Heinz Willmann, and Gysi), Becher was determined that it remain independent of the party, with an identity that was national in character and open to all democratic forces in society, including the Christian Democrats and nonparty intellectuals.

The initial reports on the Kulturbund's work in the summer of 1945 were very positive.[16] The Soviets helped considerably by providing a canteen for artists, writers, and dramaturges, and by quickly getting theaters and concert halls back into use. The Soviets set up a club in Berlin for cultural figures, called the Seagull (Möwe), which enjoyed some popularity among the city's artists, providing them with a decent meal and a bit of rest and comfort during very hard times.[17] Similar clubs and canteens were opened in other cities of the zone. By the end of the occupation, the Soviets had also provided rest homes, vacation colonies, and health spas for the use of the "democratic" German intelligentsia. The Soviets' attention to the needs of the cultural intelligentsia derived in part from lessons learned at home: a well-fed, well-treated intelligentsia wrote, produced, and acted in the kinds of artistic productions that the state was interested in fostering. But it also came from a cynical view of the Germans' respect for the intelligentsia, especially those who held the title of doctor. Colonel Tiul'panov, in particular, was anxious to win over the intellectuals by giving them "greater chances" in society.[18]

Despite the auspicious beginnnings of the Kulturbund, which won the praises even of Western political observers, the Soviets very quickly became disgruntled with its work. In a November 1945 report on the Potsdam section, the Soviet officer in charge complained about excessive tolerance for "bourgeois tendencies in art and literature; futurism, impressionism, etc."[19] In the province of Brandenburg, as elsewhere, the intelligentsia demonstrated little allegiance to the Kulturbund. This was sometimes attributed to the heavy concentration of former Nazi Party members in some localities. But mostly the problem was that the intelligentsia was either indifferent to the Kulturbund or deeply suspicious of its ties to the Communist Party. In the town of Brandenburg, fifty leading members of the intelligentsia were invited to a meeting for the purpose of forming a Kulturbund section; only twenty-three showed up. All of those who were elected to the presidium of the Brandenburg group tried to resign the next day.[20] Lieutenant Colonel Vatnik, the chief propaganda officer in Saxony, wrote in January 1946: "With the Kulturbund, things are simply very bad." Becher's worst fears had come true. The organization had become a party organization filled with functionaries who had little or nothing to do with the cultural intelligentsia. In fact, before his removal as the secretary of the Saxon organization, a man named Hanstein, "a writer of very low qualifications," bragged about his connections with the NKVD and threatened even Russian propaganda officers with punishment by his "friends."[21]

The Soviets were particularly irritated by the Kulturbund's inability to organize the intelligentsia to support "democratic" changes going on in the zone. The attitude of Russian cultural officers was typical, in the sense that the Germans in the Kulturbund could never do anything up to Soviet standards. There were complaints that the organization was too political and that it left out of its purview large segments of the cultural intelligentsia. There were almost no major figures from the intelligentsia in its ranks, Tiul'panov pointedly noted. Only a few cultural activists, like the writer Willi Bredel, who ran the journal *Demokratische Erneuerung* (Democractic Renewal), and Hermann Henselmann, a left-wing architect who set up a school for architecture and art in Weimar, were doing much for the democratization of the zone.

Unlike Becher, Tiul'panov wanted the SED itself to get more involved in the organization and devote more of its resources to intelligentsia recruitment. He complained that "the SED [did] not carry the banner of the intelligentsia" and that it was not interested in fostering the growth of the Kulturbund.[22] The Kulturbund itself, from Tiul'panov's point of view, misunderstood its role as a supraparty organization. With 120,000 members, 20 percent of whom were SED, 15 percent CDU and LDP, and 65 percent without party affiliation, the Kulturbund had adopted a nonparty stance, abdicating its responsibility to advance Marxist goals. The Berlin section of the Kulturbund fit Tiul'panov's model better. According to Hermann Matern, the SED was the de facto head of that organization and recruited members from the theater, the arts, and higher education.[23] At the same time, the clear SED connection was one of the reasons the

Kulturbund was banned in the American and British sectors of Berlin on November 1, 1947.[24]

Tiul'panov was deeply disturbed by the general development of the Kulturbund; he was critical of Becher's approach to the problem of the intelligentsia, and he communicated his objections to the Secretariat of the KPD, which in turn passed a resolution on the work of the Kulturbund (February 14, 1946): "The numerical weakness of the communists in comparison to the other forces has led to [the fact] that . . . a [whole] line of cultural-political questions of the highest importance has been ignored. In particular, up to this point the Kulturbund has not assumed a clear position on the democratic school reforms." The struggle against "reactionary influences and tendencies" should be sharpened, the resolution continued, though the KPD had to proceed carefully, given the real array of class forces. In line with the KPD's continued emphasis on the "German road to socialism," the resolution concluded with the rather mild admonition that the Kulturbund (KB) should publish more German classics. "The communists in the KB should bring to the fore more resolutely than to this point everything that was freedom-loving and progressive in the history and culture of our people, and nurture all the progressive traditions in our history."[25]

This weak reprimand only made Tiul'panov more upset with the Kulturbund's work. As the chief Soviet officer in the zone in charge of German political and cultural life, he found the organization's stance unacceptable, and he attributed its stubbornness to Becher's good relations with both Ulbricht and with General F. E. Bokov, a member of SVAG's Military Council and nominally in charge of political developments in the zone. Despite Becher's strong support within SVAG, during the new phase of zonal politics after the creation of the SED in the spring of 1946 and the heightening of political tensions surrounding the elections of September and October 1946, Tiul'panov insisted that the head of the Kulturbund stood in the way of political progress. He said that the Kulturbund could no longer serve simply as a collection of intelligentsia, as Becher would have it, and that it should be led by SED cadres. "Without this, only negative results can come . . . and Becher cannot and will not take care of this. . . . In his entire intellectual efforts, not only is Becher not a Marxist, but he also directly orients himself not on England or America, but on Western European democracy. He is ashamed to say that he is a member of the Central Committee of the SED. He won't even let us call him comrade—just Herr Becher." Becher refused to lead the intelligentsia,

Tiul'panov's vitriolic complaint continued; he simply adapted to what they wanted. As a result, he said, "We [the Propaganda Administration *and* the Party Executive of the SED] have come to the firm conclusion that Becher needs to be replaced. There is no way to tolerate him any longer."[26]

In the case of Becher, however, Tiul'panov did not get his way, and he was forced by his superiors to back off from his demand for the German poet's removal. The reasons for this were complex and had to do with Tiul'panov's own troubles (see Chapter 5). Nevertheless, Tiul'panov's prodding did increase the SED's pressure on Becher to politicize the Kulturbund's activities. In May 1947, for example, Wilhelm Pieck and Otto Grotewohl sent official greetings to the first meeting of the new Secretariat of the Kulturbund, emphasizing the need for the organization to take political stances: "Regardless of its neutrality vis-a-vis the political parties, the Kulturbund takes a critical and open position on all contemporary problems that affect the fate of Germany."[27] Tiul'panov himself and the officers from his administration met repeatedly with Kulturbund figures to encourage their participation in the political struggle. Tiul'panov even took his family to the Kulturbund summer retreat on the Baltic Sea in Ahrenshoop, where he joined the discussions and inserted his point of view.[28]

As a result of the clash over the role of the Kulturbund in politics, personal relations between Becher and Pieck deteriorated badly. They argued on the phone; Becher threatened to resign as head of the Kulturbund, as he had done repeatedly almost from the moment he had become its president; Pieck called him a "political ignoramus."[29] Pieck was also upset that Becher did not take his party duties seriously. Becher refused to attend meetings of the Party Executive, of which he was a member, and he was unwilling to engage himself in the work of the Cultural Committee of the SED, which had been sharply criticized for its lack of activity.[30] At the December 8, 1947, plenum of the SED Party Executive, the leadership's attacks on Becher reached a crescendo. Interestingly enough, Tiul'panov's report on the meeting reflected his own chastening on the Becher issue: "The pointed attacks of W. Pieck against the leadership of the 'Kulturbund,' especially against Becher, before the plenum, and his unnecessarily sharp skirmishes with Otto Meier to the point that Meier intended to walk out of the meeting, created a tense situation. In the 'Kulturbund' there is the threat that Becher will resign his post as chairman, which at the present time is fraught with serious consequences for us."[31]

In the end, Becher's concept of the Kulturbund's program more nearly reflected that of Moscow than did Pieck's or Tiul'panov's. That Becher won the battle over the thrust of the Kulturbund's role with the intelligentsia was manifested by the granting of one of Becher's most cherished wishes—a Kulturbund delegation was at long last received in Moscow during the spring of 1948. Two important factors must be kept in mind when thinking about the delegation's trip. For Becher, Ulbricht, and others who had spent time in Moscow, the enormity of the Soviet accomplishment and the greatness of the Russian people were hard to communicate to skeptical Germans. Therefore they saw delegations' visits to the Soviet Union as the most effective form of pro-Soviet propaganda. On the other side, the Soviets, while certainly sharing this point of view, were extremely reluctant hosts. At this point there was no such thing as a simple visit to the Soviet Union. A delegation from abroad meant a huge amount of preparation and planning. Nothing could be left to chance; no effort was spared to accomplish the goal of winning friends for the motherland of socialism. As a result, few of the German proposals to send delegations were accepted, and then only after the most careful consideration.

All such delegations had to be very carefully chosen, and the one from the Kulturbund was no exception. Together with Major Alexander Dymshits, chief of the cultural section of SVAG's Information Administration, Becher put together a list of prospective delegates and sent it on to Pieck and Grotewohl, who forwarded the formal request through Dymshits to M. A. Suslov on the Central Committee. Finally, in April 1948, the delegation, which included, among others, Anna Seghers, Günter Weisenborn, Jürgen Kuczynski, and Becher himself, visited Moscow. The names of the delegates reveal that the goal of the visit had changed from one of "winning over the German intelligentsia," as Becher had originally stated the issue, to exposing "progressive" intelligentsia figures, who were already firmly in the SED camp, to the accomplishments of the Soviet Union. Soviet reporters noted that the task was a formidable one, given the fact that many of the visitors, though thoroughgoing German Marxists, expressed an annoying and unacceptable sense of superiority to the "backward" USSR. By lavishly entertaining the delegation, the Soviets hoped to convince the Germans that true culture and civilization were at their zenith in Soviet Russia. They would then return home and spread the word to their countrymen.

One widely reported "experience" of the Germans demonstrates the extent to which the Soviets were willing to go to impress their guests. The delegation was taken on an obligatory tour of the Moscow Metro (subway), which was indeed a magnificent engineering and construction achievement in the postwar world. At one Metro station, the story went, a group of Muscovites—soldiers and workers—overheard the delegates speaking German and asked who they were. When the crowd was told their names, the Russians broke into applause and demonstrated their intimate knowledge of the Germans' work and antifascist background. The Soviet reporters and the Kulturbund delegates did indeed take this incident as a sign of the superiority of Soviet culture. Back in Germany, however, though there seemed to be a great deal of interest in the delegates' reports about what they saw, one can assume that listeners treated the story of the Metro with justifiable skepticism.[32]

While Becher managed to keep the Kulturbund focused on the needs of the German intelligentsia—at least as he defined them—he could not avoid the politicization of the organization under what the SED called "the new conditions of the class struggle" in 1948 and 1949. The tasks of the Kulturbund had changed, the SED Small Secretariat noted in April 1949. The struggle against the remnants of Nazism was now considerably less important than the fight against the warmongers in the West and their lackeys in the East. The Kulturbund, in other words, had to join in the cultural and ideological class war as it was unfolding in Germany. In the view of the SED leadership, the Kulturbund needed to transform itself from a club for progressive intellectuals into a mass organization for political struggle, and it could only do this by undertaking two simultaneous programs. First, in the spirit of the Two-Year Plan, the Kulturbund needed to include more scientists, engineers, and other members of the technical intelligentsia in its ranks. Second, the leaders of the Kulturbund were prompted to get over their sectarian tendency to isolate themselves from the working class.[33] The SED wanted Kulturbund leaders to stop talking about abstract issues regarding the ties between the intelligentsia and the masses and to provide instead concrete tasks for artists and writers to perform in the factories and villages of the zone.[34]

The Kulturbund was also charged by the SED to be more explicit in its charter about the links between being a "progressive intellectual" and having "a positive view of the Soviet Union." When the organization returned a draft charter that still did not satisfy the party on the "Russian question," the SED proposed more concrete language itself: "The stance toward the Soviet Union must be more positively and clearly defined in the sense that the Kulturbund not only recognizes the great cultural achievements of the Soviet Union, but that it also views the Soviet Union as the most solid and secure guarantor of the peace, because of its high culture and its progressive social development."[35] Despite acquiescing on this issue, Becher and the Kulturbund found it hard to be quite as sychophantic about the Soviet Union as many of the other mass organizations that were more directly run by the SED. As a result, the Kulturbund was deliberately snubbed when a delegation to the Soviet Union was assembled for Stalin's birthday celebrations in December 1949, a slight that deeply bothered and frustrated the always ambitious Becher.[36] In any case, Becher later made up for his lack of ardor by writing a series of poems celebrating the greatness of Stalin, for which he was awarded a Stalin Peace Prize in 1952.

THE SOCIETY FOR THE STUDY OF THE CULTURE OF THE SOVIET UNION

The primary impetus behind the formation of the Kulturbund was the desire on the part of the Soviet and German communists to organize the German intelligenstia in support of the so-called democratic renewal of the country. Becher's sensitivity to the problem of appearing to be nothing more than an appendage of SVAG or the SED provided the Kulturbund with some autonomy to carry out its own programs and refine its commitment to the promulgation of a progressive German culture. Consequently, however, the Kulturbund was not enough of a help to the SED and SVAG with the task of spreading the word about the superiority of Russian and Soviet cultural achievements. Therefore, in May 1947, the Soviets decided to create a new German organization to oversee a variety of efforts already under way to make Soviet culture accessible to the population of the Eastern zone. The Soviets had set up a well-appointed House of the Culture of the Soviet Union in Berlin, which showed films, put on exhibits, and held guest lectures. Western cultural officers, as well as German visitors from both East and West, were deeply impressed by the energetic Soviet representatives and the interesting programs at the House of Culture.[37] In addition, in Weimar and Leipzig, and in other towns and cities in the zone, there were a number of local "friendship" organizations that were formed after the occupation to play Russian music and discuss Russian novels, sometimes inviting Soviet officers to serve as lecturers or discussion leaders. Some of these organizations owed their initiation to enthusiastic Germans, some to the local Russian authorities. For example, in Dresden the newly formed Cultural Friendship Society was clearly the product of the Political Department of the Dresden city kommandantura, which had ordered the local German education officials to establish such a society based on the pre-1933 model of the Society for Friends of the Soviet Union in Germany.[38]

The first formal Societies for the Study of the Culture of the Soviet Union, into which all these organizations merged, were founded in Brandenburg and Saxony-Anhalt in early June 1947. But the work was difficult and the vast majority of Germans were far from ready to seek any benefit from association with the culture of their occupiers. "We often felt like we were 'Callers in the Desert,' " wrote Heinrich Hoffmann, an SED leader who helped to organize the society in Thüringen. Everyone was afraid of the Russians, Hoffmann added, both among the intelligentsia and the working class. Only the most tried and true SED members would show up for the society's meetings.[39] Many SED loyalists did not want to participate in the society's activities for fear of appearing as members of a "Russian party." But this fear became less relevant once the SED declared itself the "party of the new type" in the summer of 1948; by that point devotion to the Soviet way had become an explicit part of SED ideology. Yet even then, society meetings sometimes were little more than informal gatherings of local notables from the intelligentsia, who drank vodka together and discussed Russian literature and music.[40]

The outright antipathy of significant sections of the population to the work of the society was evident in the discussions at the founding meeting of the zonal organization, on June 30, 1947. Jürgen Kuczynski, the society's first president, noted in his address that there were indeed Germans who had already begun studying the culture of the Soviet Union: "But the greatest majority of our people—we have to state this clearly—is still negatively disposed to the Soviet Union. And also one should harbor no illusions: there are also in the Eastern zone still many people who are under the influence of the reaction and think badly of the Soviet Union." In his speech at the founding meeting, Colonel Tiul'panov also was willing to admit that German friendship for the Russians was a goal rather than a reality. The Soviet Union was interested in building friendship societies with all peoples, he stated. But in Germany, he said, "We are not ready yet to found such a society," because it was still hard to predict whether the Germans would become "a real democratic people." Nevertheless the Soviet government had determined that it was important to start the process of building cultural bridges, Tiul'panov noted, and he pledged financial support from the profits of the occupation newspaper, *Tägliche Rund-schau.* Ever the radical, Tiul'panov also insisted that the Germans should understand that Russian culture was not just splendid art, music, and literature. In fact, from his point of view, the Germans spent far too much time reading and discussing Dostoyevsky and Chekhov, while forgetting altogether about the Bolsheviks. Russian and Soviet culture was above all about socialism, he stated, and it was important for the Society to teach Germans about its characteristics. Tiul'panov ended his speech by promising that SVAG would help the Germans set up a house of Soviet culture in every town in the zone and a room for Soviet culture in villages, factories, and schools.[41]

The founding meeting of the zonal society concluded with a common project to develop lectures, meetings, and exhibitions on the topic of thirty years of the Soviet Union. The lesson of these programs was to be twofold. First, Germans would learn about the ways in which the peoples of the Soviet Union overcame "unbelievable difficulties," making Germany's problems of postwar construction seem less daunting and overwhelming. Second, lecturers were instructed to demonstrate that the Soviets had overcome all of their inherent problems of development, indeed had reached the pinnacle of modern civilization by the first half of 1941, when the Germans attacked. In other words, any problems with Soviet soldiers in the zone or deficiencies in the organization of the military government were to be attributed not to some weaknesses in the Soviet system itself but to the devastation caused by the German-incited war.[42]

Ulbricht further elaborated on the general program of the society in a letter to Pieck and Grotewohl of October 30, 1947. He suggested that Soviet scientists be recruited as guest lecturers in German universities and that Soviet scientific works be translated into German and published in the zone. Ulbricht wanted to intensify a program of guest performances by Soviet artistic groups, like the enormously popular Alexandrov Ensemble, which had been such a major success in the zone. Ulbricht also repeated his suggestion—one that he made frequently, usually without success—that the number of German delegations to the Soviet Union be greatly increased.[43] In his view, the way to put a stop to the Germans' incessant complaining about reparations was to have delegations visit the destroyed parts of the Soviet Union, a suggestion the Soviets repeatedly turned down.

In theory, the program of exchanges, publications, lectures, films, and exhibitions was comprehensive and intense, and it was supported, as well, by the most important political figures in the zone, Ulbricht and Tiul'pa-nov. Yet the society ran into formidable obstacles to its goal of bringing the achievements of Soviet culture to the attention of the German population. The Germans themselves were still very resistant to the ostensible accomplishments of Soviet culture. In the House of Soviet Culture, visitors recorded their impressions in a guest book, and at the outset, at least, the remarks seem to have been candid and open. Obviously the visitors were receptive to the exhibitions; otherwise, most would have not come in the first place. Marianne Ebeling, a seventeen-year-old schoolgirl, showed that she had learned her lessons well when she commented on an exhibition of Soviet art: "In these rooms I saw that we have a lot to learn from the Soviet people, not just in the realm of ideology but also we could learn very much about culture, and it is a great duty of the German youth to learn from the USSR so that the errors of the past years not be repeated." But the negative comments in the book reflected the depth of hostility felt by even those who chose to visit the House of Culture. Three men signed the following: "How is it possible that the fighters and carriers of the culture shown here (the Red Army, etc.) could behave in the way we were forced to endure during the invasion of these liberators?!!"[44] A Soviet political officer in Brandenburg, Major Martem'ianov, similarly reported to Tiul'panov that there was deep skepticism among the population about the work of the society. A number of Germans thought "that there was nothing to learn from the Soviet Union because its culture was of a lower sort." Martem'ianov added the familiar refrain that the bourgeois parties ignored the society because they saw it as propagandizing communism, and that the SED stayed away from it because it was afraid to be identified as the Russian party.[45] But Tiul'panov was unremitting in his dedication to the principles of the organization: "The study of Soviet culture—this is a great and important [task], not just a cultural task in the narrow sense of the word, but also a moral [one]; I would say, not just a task, but an obligation."[46]

VOKS

Many of the problems of the Society for the Study of the Culture of the Soviet Union were due less to German hesitancy than to inefficiency and indifference on the Russian side, particularly on the part of the organizations in Moscow responsible for disseminating Soviet cultural accomplishments abroad. In particular, the All-Union Society for Cultural Ties with Foreign Countries, or VOKS, was in charge of fostering Soviet cultural ties abroad and providing the necessary materials—books, posters, exhibitions, phonograph records, and so on—for the promulgation of Soviet culture. It was supposed to arrange for lecturers and traveling exhibitions as well as serve as the conduit for contacts between cultural groups in the Soviet Union and abroad. Certainly VOKS played an important role in Germany and helped to foster Soviet-German cultural ties. At the same time, however, like many other Soviet organizations, VOKS was not nearly as committed to winning over the Germans as was the Soviet Military Administration. Nor did VOKS have the resources or manpower to fill the many requests for personnel and material pouring in from the zone.

Even before the foundation of the Society for the Study of the Culture of the Soviet Union, SVAG cultural officers in the zone—Alexander Dymshits (head of the Cultural Department), Il'ia Fradkin (head of the theater group), Grigorii Patent (head of cultural relations), and Tiul'panov himself—made repeated requests for materials from VOKS that would show off the accomplishments of the Soviet Union. They asked for exhibits, cultural journals, and Soviet books published in Western languages. Dymshits complained to VOKS that not only had SVAG not received the materials after repeated requests, but that VOKS had also not even bothered to answer his letters.[47] In turn, VOKS was irritated with the volume of requests from the zone, especially from the Information Administration. It claimed that it had its own plan to meet and could not deal with the volume of additional requests or the immediacy with which materials were needed. If Tiul'panov wanted additional materials, VOKS advised him, he should contact his own superiors in Moscow to take on the extra work.[48]

Tiul'panov did indeed turn to Suslov and the Central Committee for help arranging visiting lecturers and getting VOKS to be more responsive. With the backing of the Central Committee, Tiul'panov was able to arrange through VOKS the much heralded visit in October 1947 of three Soviet writers to the zone—Valentin Kataev, Boris Gorbatov, and Vsevolod Vishnevskii—to attend the all-German Writers' Congress held in Berlin.[49] The All-Union Society for Cultural Ties also became a more reliable source for a wide variety of materials seen as critical for developing a taste for Soviet culture in the zone.[50] It sent folk, classical, and popular sheet music for the music library set up by SVAG in Berlin, and copies of the choreographies of popular Soviet ballets, such as Prokofiev's *Romeo and Juliet*. For the German productions of Rimsky-Korsakov's *Sadko* or

Tchaikovsky's *Queen of Spades,* VOKS sent librettos and detailed photographs of the Soviet stagings. Dymshits diplomatically sent back to VOKS the rave reviews in the zonal and Berlin press of the productions. Soviet cultural officers were right to note that these Soviet operas and ballets, in particular, helped break through negative German stereotypes of Russian culture.

The German intelligentsia also had a particular liking for Soviet poster art, and, as a result, VOKS sent several exhibitions of posters. (SVAG sometimes complained, however, that VOKS sent inappropriate posters, either in content or in quality.) VOKS also supplied photographs for countless exhibitions on Soviet life, which ranged from "The Soviet Arctic" to "Labor and the Experience of the Kolkhoz." After the establishment of the Society for the Study of the Culture of the Soviet Union in June 1947, and the spread of its branches all over the country, the demands on VOKS's resources were even greater. According to the VOKS plan for 1948, the organization sent material for an exhibit entitled "Fifty Years of the Moscow Art Theater," as well as photographic materials on a plethora of subjects—including Buryat Mongols, Moscow at night, and Soviet sport. It sent sixteen articles and 1,840 books to each of the society's fifty libraries, and 482 books for the libraries of the Houses of Culture of the Soviet Union. It also responded to requests from the House of Culture in Berlin and its director V. A. Poltavtsev for a range of materials, from piano music for the play *Optimistic Tragedy* to scientific articles on Soviet ophthamology. Poltavtsev urged VOKS to send more up-to-date material: "The greatest demand is for literature that portrays the contemporary life of the Soviet Union. [People are] especially interested in literature on the geography and history of the USSR, on Soviet painting, theater, film, music, architecture, sport."[51]

The Soviet Houses of Culture operated independently of the society. They showed films, ran children's programs, gave Russian language courses, put on exhibits and plays, and even put out their own German-language journal, *Die neue Gesellschaft* (The New Society). But the houses were run strictly by the Soviets and, as a result, their problems with the bureacracy of VOKS in Moscow had little direct impact on the Germans. This was not the case for the society, whose chairman in the zone, Kuczynski, was angry and frustrated by Moscow's apparent indifference to his enterprise. Kuczynski's situation, in some ways similar to Johannes R. Becher's, resembled that of the unrequited lover. His appeals to Moscow were frequent and ardent, but at the same time they had a tinge of anger at having been encouraged in the first place and then let down. His letters (and those of Anna Seghers, the deputy chairman) to prominent Soviet cultural figures for help and support went unanswered.[52] His appeals to VOKS for concrete materials about everyday Soviet life—school curricula, kolkhoz plans, Siberian local newspapers—also went unheeded. The society could not even get busts of Lenin and Stalin, though this made more sense in some ways, since the handling of such busts was encumbered by complex regulations that required a huge amount of paperwork.

When Kuczynski went to Moscow in April 1948 with the Kulturbund delegation, he tried to present to VOKS the society's needs, especially for contemporary Soviet literature, and he pointedly compared the meager Soviet efforts with those of the West. But he came away from Moscow bitterly disappointed, which was reflected in a letter to the deputy director of VOKS, Kislova.

> Please see to it that we get some concrete help from VOKS at least in the form of the acknowledgment of our letters and parcels, and of literature being sent to us. Otherwise things will get really difficult for us here with all who, in the right spirit, really desire some kind of contact with the Soviet Union. Please never forget that every fascist or semifascist has every contact with the "Western Powers" that he desires and that French, American, and English literature is coming freely to Germany and so are writers, artists, etc.[53]

Kuczynski's frustrations boiled over in a report he sent to VOKS in December 1948, reviewing the development of the society, which at that point had some 60,000 members. Once again he asked for materials that documented the daily life of Soviet citizens, adding, "But I have expressed these wishes so often and in so many places that I bring them forward once more only out of a sense of duty and not from any hope that they would be fulfilled." He also complained again about "the complete one-sidedness of the communications from the Germans with the Soviet Union, between our society and VOKS."

> With the exception of a series of letters sent to me personally, we have never received a single answer to the numerous letters that were sent . . . whether they were letters of schoolchildren or from factory workers or from scholars, who sent along to Soviet colleagues copies of their own works and publications or gave them some information or asked for some advice or for books. It is clear that this one-sidedness of com-

munications is for us more harmful than the complete lack of ties that was common before my trip to the Soviet Union.

Kuczynski noted that the situation was even more hurtful because the Soviets had encouraged these communications in the first place. He had no complaints about SVAG; the cultural officers, he felt, did their work well. But he could not understand why, after frequent requests, the society had not been allowed to send a delegation of its own to the USSR. (It sent some of its members along with the Kulturbund delegation in 1948). Nor had the Soviets responded to numerous requests from the society for the appearance of Soviet delegations—students, Stakhanovites, or scholars— at the society's cultural celebrations in the zone.[54] Even Tiul'panov was disappointed when no Soviet delegations showed up for the First Congress of the society in May 1948.[55]

Kuczynski's problems with VOKS derived from its relative imperviousness to pressure from German organizations and the society's most solicitous Soviet patrons. Of course without SVAG's backing, the society would have received only the "planned" assortment of propaganda materials. With this backing, it could make specific requests and sometimes get what it wanted. But even direct Central Committee pressure did not always increase the number of lecturers or guest performances. Sometimes, in the Soviet system, it was better to appeal directly to high-ranking Soviet personages for help than to work through the normal institutions. The deputy chairman of the society, Anna Seghers, wanted to vacation with her children in the Soviet Union. Dymshits told her to write directly to Konstantin Simonov, the famous Russian journalist and writer, who might be able arrange the vacation through the Writers' Union. Dymshits handled the exchange of the correspondence, and Seghers, with Simonov's help, got her vacation.[56]

Leading East German cultural figures were on the whole much more interested in contact with their Soviet counterparts than the Soviets were interested in the Germans, and this fact continued to nettle the East Germans until the very end of both polities in the late 1980s. This was part of the reason that Kuczynski and the society incessantly complained about the inattention of VOKS. But Kuczynski also should have realized that Soviet intellectuals, especially in 1948 and 1949, had a great deal to lose from contacts with Westerners, any Westerners. In late 1946, A. A. Zhdanov had already initated a campaign against bourgeois influences in the arts in his attacks on Mikhail Zoshchenko and Anna Akhmatova. The anticosmopolitan campaign, directed against Jews and other "Westernizers," seriously constrained Soviet intellectual life in 1948 and 1949. No wonder the scores of letters Kuczynski brought with him to the Soviet Union during his 1948 visit remained unanswered. He should not have been terribly surprised that so many Soviet academics and public figures declined the opportunity to travel to the zone. At a time when scientists in the Soviet Academy were being criticized for "toadying" to the West because of an excessive number of citations to Western publications in their work, no one should have questioned why Soviet scientists rarely asked for scientific material from their German colleagues. Ironically, neither Kuczynski nor Dymshits showed any signs of understanding what was going on around them, and both were removed from their positions in 1949–50 because of their Jewish origins.

THE SOCIETY FOR GERMAN-SOVIET FRIENDSHIP

Against this background of increasingly militant and closed-minded Soviet cultural policies, Tiul'panov and SVAG decided to go ahead with the renaming and expansion of the Society for the Study of the Culture of the Soviet Union into the Society for German-Soviet Friendship (GDSF). To accomplish this, Tiul'panov entered into negotiations with the antifascist school in Krasnogorsk to recruit GDSF leaders, the first group of which arrived in the zone in July 1949. Some three hundred graduates had been trained to work in the GDSF, and sixteen of them were sent early to Germany to participate in the Second Congress of the Society for the Study of the Culture of the Soviet Union, when the organization was formally elevated to the Friendship Society and its new program was adopted.[57] While the program of the Society for the Study of Culture spoke mostly of exchanges, exhibitions, publications, theater, and Russian language courses, that of the Friendship Society had a much more political edge to it. "The Society for German-Soviet Friendship sets for itself the task of spreading the truth about the Soviet Union, of fighting every kind of slander and opposition [to the USSR] and through this to secure and deepen the friendship of the German people with the people of the Soviet Union."[58]

The most important impetus for the growth and development of the Friendship Society came from the Soviet military government. On August 13, 1949, General V. I. Chuikov (who had replaced Sokolovskii as commander-in-chief) and Tiul'panov sent out a report about the Congress of the GSDF to local military commandants, stating that the plan was for the Friendship Society to grow quickly into a mass organization of more than 140,000 members. Because there were such serious problems establishing contact between German "friendship" activists and Soviet citizens back home, the military government urged all Soviet officials in the zone, whether political and cultural officers or factory directors and engineers, to take an active role in the GDSF.

The local Information Administration offices were especially encouraged to organize "collective meetings of Soviet people with members of the society," whether they were women, youths, technical specialists, or scientists. The Information Administrations were also told to make sure that the SED and other German organizations gave the GDSF a high priority in their daily activities. This included setting up new GDSF branches in industrial enterprises and reminding the labor unions about their obligations to "German-Soviet friendship"—no simple task, since the only organizations that had previously been permitted to have factory branches were the party and the labor unions.[59] The Soviet military government saw to it that the GDSF's poor financial situation was shored up through direct transfers of funds. The Soviets also put considerable pressure on the managers of the SAGs (Soviet stock companies) to recruit Russian and German members for the society from their workforces and to join the Friendship Society themselves.[60]

The rapid growth of the GDSF as a mass organization in the fall of 1949 could not mask the essential inequality of relations between Germans, even "progressive" Germans, and their Soviet tutors. The inherent problems of a Friendship Society with the Soviets, not to mention the nature of the occupation, or any occupation, ensured that such a friendship would be imbalanced. Behind the scenes, in its communications with Dymshits and his successors, VOKS repeatedly scolded the Germans for their poor understanding of Russian culture. The Soviets did not like the Germans to express their point of view about anything dear to Russian culture, whether it was the sainted Pushkin or the more problematic Dostoyevsky. For the celebration of 150 years of Pushkin's birth, the Germans were instructed by VOKS that there would be no articles about Pushkin and German literature, because it was not a legitimate theme for the anniversary.[61] One-sided ideas of "friendship" also pervaded the Soviets' responses to the Germans' best efforts to develop a repertoire of resistance songs from the war and "activist songs" from the postwar period. In the comradely advice it offered in September 1949, the Union of Composers of the USSR displayed a decidedly cool attitude. The resistance songs, wrote V. Belyi, were not completely satisfactory, because "in them there is no direct unmasking of the politically reactionary essence of fascism; their idea is limited by pacifist propaganda, exposing the hopelessness and the catastrophe for the German people of a war with Bolshevik Russia."[62]

The Germans could never do anything quite right, no matter how hard they tried. At the same time, the Soviets made sure that Soviet cultural products elicited the right responses from their German charges by ordering those responses through the Information Administration. For example, the director of VOKS wrote to Tiul'panov that it would be useful for the "progressive peoples of all countries, all those to whom authentic art is dear, art of the highest ideals and of the greatest living truths"—presumably including Germans in the zone—to celebrate 125 years of Moscow's Maly (Little) Theater. The word went out, as a result, that the Germans and the GDSF should organize the appropriate exhibitions, radio programs, and discussions. Tiul'panov was also supposed to arrange for a congratulatory telegram from German theater activists to their Moscow colleagues, commemorating the occasion.[63]

The Soviet lecturers who were delegated by the military government to the GDSF shared VOKS's sense of superiority and the manipulative essence of its dealings with the Germans, though they generally had greater sympathy for the efforts of their listeners than did bureaucrats in Moscow. All over the zone, they lectured about the advantages of Makarenko's system of pedagogy (and the weaknesses of the German), about Pavlov's brilliant experiments (and nothing of Freud), and about the innovations of Marr's linguistics (and the reactionary nature of Western studies). In the land of Volkswagen, BMW, and Mercedes, Junkers, Messerschmitt, and Siebel, they lauded exclusively the Soviet automobile and aircraft industries. (This was particularly ironic, given the extent to which the Soviets dismantled and sent home a very large segment of these industries.) The Soviets also repeatedly urged that their listeners read the "great" *History of the CPSU(b)*, the key intellectual document of the era.

Among the Germans, there was a great deal of both curiosity and skepticism, and the Soviet officers were generally well trained in satisfying the former and deflecting the latter. The subjects for the lectures were endless—Soviet schools, the kolkhoz system, the Soviet budget, the Five-Year Plan—and the lecturers, especially by 1948–49, skillfully handled even the most hostile questions. Indeed the complaints, if any, were that there were far too few lecturers available for the German audiences. According to most reports, the lecture halls were filled, and tens of thousands of people throughout the zone regularly attended.[64]

Soviet lecturers from the military government were bolstered in the GDSF by returning German POWs assigned to the organization. They repeatedly "testified" to how humanely the Soviets treated the German prisoners and how unfair anti-Soviet propaganda was to the high standards of civilization in Russia. At the main Heimkehrer (returning POW) Conference in Berlin on October 29, 1949, the POWs, one after another, addressed the chief theme of the conference, "Why we are friends of the Soviet Union and [why we] will remain so," by lauding their Soviet friends and educators and condemning Western enemies of peace who blasphemed the great homeland of international understanding and friendship. With the founding of the GDR in October 1949, these POWS became the backbone of the GDSF, which itself was turned into one of the constituent mass organizations represented both in the antifascist bloc and in parliament.

FILM

Soviet cultural officers were not satisfied with controlling the major zonal institutions intended to shape German responses to Soviet culture, the Kulturbund and the Society for the Study of the Culture of the Soviet Union, later the GDSF. They also looked to utilize the very media of cultural production—film, theater, and the arts—to spread the word of Soviet accomplishments. Film, in particular, was of critical importance to the Soviets. In the early 1920s, film was already understood by the Bolsheviks to be a powerful weapon for portraying the past and the future as it was supposed to look rather than as it actually was or was likely to be. The reshaping of the images of historical reality lay at the heart of propaganda, which itself was consumed with configuring public discourse according to ideological precepts. As no other medium, film could transform the masses' view of reality, and it therefore occupied a central place in Soviet cultural life.

In occupied Germany, the Soviets worked expeditiously from the beginning to reopen movie theaters and to exert control over their repertoires. The propaganda officers in SVAG were convinced that by showing Soviet films they could transform German images of the Soviet Union and redirect German ideas about culture. The Soviets were not at all interested in showing Germans the hard realities of life in the USSR: the poverty, the destruction of the war, the hunger, and the primitive factories, much less the palpable fear, tyranny, and police intimidation that existed below the surface. As noted earlier, the Soviet leaders were loath to let all but the most trusted Moscow-trained communists come to the Soviet Union at all, and certainly none were allowed to visit the backward provinces. The half dozen or so formal delegations that did go to the Soviet Union in the years 1945 to 1950 visited only Moscow, and even there their itineraries were strictly controlled. At the same time, the Soviets wanted all Germans to see Soviet films. Even visiting SED politicians in Moscow were inundated with mandatory film screenings. The reasons for this are clear: film could transform reality, presenting precisely the visions and memories desired by the authorities. Film was more resistant to questioning than was reality; it left no room for skepticism.

Still, Soviet propaganda officers in the zone learned by trial and error that it was not enough just to show films. To elicit the desired response on the part of the Germans, they had to chose the right films, and the films had to be screened under the appropriate circumstances. For example, many of the younger antifascists and new party members harbored pacifist inclinations and were repelled by the display of militarism present in many Soviet films.[65] Based on an outpouring of complaints, Anton Ackermann wrote to Tiul'panov in January 1946, "We urgently request that the film *Suvorov* be removed as soon as possible from the repertoire of the film theaters of the Soviet zone. . . . It makes our ideological work in the elimination of militarism harder."[66] But neither *Suvorov* nor similar films, like *Admiral Nakhimov* and *The Cruiser Variag,* which struck the German intelligentsia as excessively militaristic, were completely removed from the film program. Though these films were deemphasized, the Soviets simply did not accept the Germans' evaluations of them as militaristic. From the point of view of the occupation authorities, the films needed to be better presented to the German audiences, so that the Germans would "understand" the Soviet obligation to defend the motherland.[67]

The Soviets also did not make many friends by showing documentary and semidocumentary films about the war. Often there would be tears and wailing in the audience when pictures of bedraggled German soldiers and prisoners were shown. In Aue, for example, the film *Parade of Victors,* which showed Soviet soldiers tossing German army insignia in a heap in front of the Lenin Mausoleum, produced sobs and tears among the Germans.[68] An engineer from Nordhausen by the name of Piltz reported after seeing a Soviet war film, "Russian war movies portray Germans as the eternal enemies. Fathers and mothers, sons and daughters, seeing on screen the death of German soldiers, sometimes leave the hall, because these pictures appear to them as pictures of the death and destruction of their children and brothers."[69] It was also clear that films with a heavy-handed socialist-realist message were utterly repugnant to many Germans and even offended the sensibilities of the German intelligentsia. As a result, Becher and his friends in the Kulturbund almost completely ignored contemporary Soviet film and concentrated on theater instead.[70] Major Dymshits found himself in the delicate position of suggesting to his superiors that films like the primitive collective-farm saga *The Tractor Driver (Traktorist),* not be shown in the zone.[71]

When they went to the movies, Germans wanted to escape the grim realities of the war and the occupation, and Soviet cinema had little to offer them in this regard. Even the Soviet films of nineteenth-century Russian classics, which the Germans liked best of any Soviet movies, were still too serious for most filmgoers.[72] The few Soviet entertainment films that were shown in the zone, like *Happy Fellows (Veselyi Rebiata),* did quite well, as did German entertainment films from the Weimar period. A Soviet cultural officer from Brandenburg reported that the Germans liked only films about romance and adventure; they wanted nothing whatsoever to do with films about war, revolution, or poverty.[73] Routine questioning of Germans after the films turned up the same answers: Soviet films were "too heavy" and did not provide a chance "to relax" and "to enjoy one's self."[74]

Poor-quality copies of films and inaccurate and clumsy dubbing also gave Soviet films a bad reputation in the zone. To make matters worse, the movie theaters were poorly maintained and often unpleasant to sit in. During the fierce winters of 1945–46 and 1946–47, many stage theaters and music halls were closed down because of the lack of fuel, but the movie theaters stayed open, wrote a Potsdam cultural officer, as "the main sources of cultural entertainment and relaxation for the population."[75] Even so, the theaters were cold and drafty, making moviegoing, especially to Soviet-made movies, an unpleasant affair.

Colonel Tiul'panov and his Propaganda (Information) Administration also insisted that the reason Soviet films had so much trouble attracting German audiences derived from the way they were chosen and shown, not from problems with the films themselves. Until the end of 1945, all films were distributed in the zone by Soiuzintorgkino, the Soviet film distributor (called Sovexportfilm by the Germans). However, the local commandants could, on their own initiative, approve or forbid the showing of any film, Russian or German.[76] In mid-December 1945, Tiul'panov moved to take the entire process of showing films under the wings of the Propaganda Administration, as "the political organ, capable of understanding the specific circumstances and goals of Soviet policy in Germany." He let it be known that only his administration and its Performances Department had the right to authorize the showing of films and the preparation of their dubbing. He insisted that all Soviet films shown in Germany be censored by his administration: first in their Russian and then in their German version.

Tiul'panov also wanted the showing of every Soviet film to be overseen by a representative of a Soviet organization in the zone, whether it was someone from Soiuzintorgkino or the local commandant, to make sure that the theater managers did not allow lazy mistakes or even intentional "sabotage." In addition, he demanded that every film be presented to the German audiences with a "libretto" that explained its significance: "Not a single Soviet film should be shown at a single theater for a single day without a sufficient number of librettos for sale. The libretto should have a propagandistic-explanatory character and make clear the historical events and social occurrences in the Soviet Union that lay at the base of the particular film. Moreover, every film should be preceded by explanatory captions following the same goal as the libretto." Finally, Tiul'panov wanted to introduce a system of regular special previews for every new film shown in the zone. Local notables, reviewers, and politicians would be invited to attend and comment on the film. Then the actual opening of each film would be accompanied by a flurry of announcements, press reviews, and public discussions, which would help German viewers understand the real accomplishments of Soviet filmmakers.[77]

Tiul'panov's views on the control of film in the zone were amplified in a conference of the heads of the Performance Department in Berlin, held on December 25 and 26, 1945, and were issued as a Propaganda Administration directive. Tiul'panov ordered that more Soviet films be shown in the zone and that they be advertised and presented in the most attractive ways possible. Sound tracks were to be checked before the film was shown and previews were to take on the trappings of a cultural celebration. There would be flowers, posters, decorations, and banners. Before particularly important films, like *Chkalov, Lenin in October,* or *Lenin in 1918,* Soviet cultural officers were to present short lectures, highlighting the importance of the events portrayed in the films.[78] Tiul'panov also made sure that all films in the zone—German and Soviet—went through the process of censorship by his organization. Three times a week films were screened by the censors and then discussed. If they were permitted to be shown, they were issued a special "passport," which had to accompany the film at every stage of its handling. Commandants could no longer approve films for showing if they did not have this official military government document.[79]

Soiuzintorgkino used its monopolistic position as the sole film distributor to favor Soviet movies over German ones, rereleasing the former and withholding the latter, much to the irritation of German film audiences.[80] Since almost all of the movie theaters had been turned over to the states and provinces in 1946, with the justification that movie-house owners had "cooperated" with Hitler by screening Nazi films, the movie houses of the Eastern zone could do little more than accept Soiuzintorgkino's offerings.[81] At the beginning of the occupation, movie theaters typically showed 60 to 70 percent Soviet films and 30 to 40 percent German films, with a couple of English, American, or French films thrown in for the sake of variety. This proportion changed in 1947–48, as the increasing number of films made in the Soviet zone brought the showings of German films to slightly more than 50 percent and the percentage of Soviet films to slightly under.[82] However, for the taste of the German public, there were still far too many Soviet films in their theaters. In Mecklenburg, for example, military government officials complained that the Germans were boycotting Soviet films, but that every time a German film was shown the theaters were filled.[83] Even the low-budget films produced by DEFA, the new eastern German film studio founded in May 1946, were better received than the Soviet films.[84] Cultural officers tried to get the SED interested in using Soviet films for ideological work, but the SED dragged its heels on this issue, preferring to contract for new films with DEFA.[85] (DEFA was sponsored and even partly owned by the Soviets.) Only Anton Ackermann seemed to share SVAG's conviction that Soviet film was integral to the revolutionary process taking place in the Eastern zone, but even he repeatedly urged the Soviets to be more careful to select only the most interesting Russian films to be shown to the German audiences, so that they would get to know "real Soviet art."[86]

THEATER

Just as with film, Soviet cultural officers saw theater as a powerful medium for the democratic transformation of Germany. In the case of film, Tiul'-panov and his colleagues were able to provide a conducive environment for screening technically advanced and politically engaging Soviet films, while making sure that the nascent eastern German film industry followed the basic patterns of Soviet filmmaking. Theater was more complicated, in that the Soviets could not bring Moscow's best drama to the zone, as they could bring the best films. No matter how much the Soviets directed, instructed, criticized, and interfered, the Germans themselves had to present Soviet theater to German audiences in a way that would entice them back for more.

As a result, Soviet cultural officers, such as Il'ia Fradkin, who was in charge of theater in Alexander Dymshits's Cultural Department, had to coddle and encourage "progressive" theater directors and actors to return to work under the extremely trying postwar conditions. Fradkin saw it as his job, first and foremost, to feed and house theatrical artists, to find an extra payok or two for them, and to procure a piece of furniture or a book to help keep up their spirits and get them to join the new theatrical life in Berlin.[87] Fradkin's efforts in Berlin were duplicated by A. N. Kol'shetov in Dresden, whose task was made even more difficult by the fact that not a single theater had been left standing in that city after the war.[88] Throughout the zone, Soviet cultural officers, many of whom had personal past ties to the theater, worked with German notables, such as Max Valentin, Inge Wangenheim, Wolfgang Langhoff, and Herbert Ihering, to reassemble the personnel and rebuild the repertoires of the German theater.[89]

By April 1946 more than 100 theaters were operating in the Soviet zone, most of which were run directly by provincial or municipal authorities. The provincial German Ministries of Education were responsible for the operation of the theaters, while the Propaganda (Information) Administration of SVAG assumed overall control of the theaters from the Soviet side. Theater in the zone was also reorganized so that repertoires were determined regionally and within the larger cities, to avoid "unhealthy competition in the area of repertoires" while making the theaters easier to control.[90] "Control" meant several things at once. The Soviets, for example, set the general guidelines for plays that were to be produced. These fell into four categories: German and European "progressive" classics, like Schiller's *Natan der Weise*, Molière's *Tartuffe*, and Offenbach's operettas;

German antifascist plays, like Friedrich Wolf's *Professor Mamlock* and Günther Weisenborn's *The Resisters;* Russian classics by Chekhov, Gogol, and Ostrovsky; and Soviet plays, especially contemporary Soviet plays, like Rakhmanov's *Uneasy Old Age (Bespokoinaia starost')* and *Mashenka* by A. Afinogenov.

If theater managers were not "progressive enough" to change their repertoires to accommodate the Soviets, the Propaganda (Information) Administration recommended to the local German Ministry of Education that they be replaced.[91] This usually took care of the problem. Lieutenant Colonel Vatnik in Saxony reported that his Propaganda Administration office had reviewed the work of all the theaters in February 1946. Those that would be allowed to continue functioning had to have "demonstrated over the past months a sufficiently high artistic level of work, the political trustworthiness of their leadership, [and] a democratic direction in their repertoires."[92] But it was not at all easy to satisfy the Soviets on the last count, especially since it was difficult to obtain the scripts of Soviet plays, and even those that were available sometimes could not be put on, given the shifting sands of ideological acceptability in postwar Soviet culture. For example, against the background of Zhdanov's denunciation of the poetry of Akhmatova and the satire of Zoshchenko in 1946, Dymshits informed the Brandenburg Information Administration that Mayakovsky's classic, *The Bedbug*, was no longer to be performed. There was no good translation available, he wrote, "not to mention the fact that the play is not well timed," meaning that the biting criticism of Soviet bureaucracy was not appropriate for German theatergoers. Other plays had to be removed from repertoires because of official condemnation by the Soviets—for example, *The Plane Was Late by a Day*, which was criticized as being "without ideals" and "banal." Plays that were acceptable in 1945 and early 1946 could no longer be performed in 1947 and 1948. Ibsen's *Peer Gynt* was removed from the repertoires of the zone's theaters; and Friedrich Wolf's *The Gypsies* was withdrawn for being "out of date."[93]

Dymshits understood that there were too few Soviet plays available for the Germans to fulfill their mandate to stage more of them. Moreover, most of the "acceptable" plays were completely unknown to German producers, not to mention German audiences. Dymshits tried to solve the problem by getting VOKS to send photograph collections about the productions in Moscow. Translations were less of a problem. A new Institute of Professors in Berlin was set up specifically for the purpose of speeding up the translation of relevant Soviet cultural and scientific material. But even with the photographs of the Moscow productions and the translations, German directors were hesitant. They did not have the appropriate Russian national costumes; sheet music was lacking; and at times they simply did not like the plays.

Nevertheless the Soviets were relentless. Not only did they set the guidelines for the repertoires of German theaters but they also often directly intervened in the productions. In September 1945 the Propaganda and Censorship Department (soon to be the Propaganda Administration) took over direct control of Berlin's four leading theaters. At the Deutsches Theater, for instance, a contemporary play by the communist intellectual Julius Hay did not meet the Soviets' approval. The officers in charge insisted that the last act of the play be rewritten, and they participated actively in the last two rehearsals. The Russians organized a general review of the play by communist politicans and cultural figures—Ackermann, Pieck, and Becher, among others—to make sure that the play was done correctly. The Soviets even had to approve the program for the play before it was printed.[94] In Thüringen, the cultural officer Babenko bragged that he and his men took a direct part in the preparation and production of every Russian play in the province, whether Soviet or classical Russian. It must have been especially annoying to the German theater personnel to have to perform the plays of Chekhov, Gogol, and Pushkin just as they were done in the Soviet Union.[95]

In Dresden, the cultural officer Kol'shetov had to convince the hesitant local theater troupe to put on Rakhmanov's *Uneasy Old Age,* and then he had to show them how to do it. He conducted all the initial readings himself and explained and interpreted everything in the play that was not clear to the German professionals. At the premiere, Kol'shetov was more nervous, he wrote, than the director. In the end, he was also deeply disappointed. The actors, he concluded, did not really believe that they could communicate the importance of the play, and as a result they performed poorly. But Dymshits praised his efforts, and he kept at it. In early 1948 Kol'shetov had greater success with Vsevolod Vishnevskii's *Optimistic Tragedy.* It played forty times to packed houses, and he continued to pay great attention to all the details of the production, perfectly comfortable with interfering when he felt it was necessary: "Of course, one had to correct the primitive errors that could lead to the misrepresentation of the spirit of the characters. And I always had to hurry to the place where the production of a Soviet or classical Russian play was being planned, not allowing its opening without having seen its dress rehearsal, [without having] argued, convinced, proved."[96]

Nowhere was Soviet interference in German theater more blatant than in the staging of *The Russian Question* by Konstantin Simonov, a play that belonged uniquely to the immediate postwar world of Henry Wallace, Kurt Schumacher, the meetings of the Council of Foreign Ministers, and the first salvoes of the cold war.[97] The play told the story of an American journalist who learned about the evil, monopolistic character of American capitalism when he tried to tell "the real truth" about the peaceful, good life in the Soviet Union. Wolfgang Langhoff's Deutsches Theater was chosen for the premiere of the play in May 1947, and no resources were spared for its production needs. Protests by the Americans that the play was anti-American and therefore violated Allied Control Council regulations were rebuffed by the Soviets. Some of the leading actors in Berlin refused to take part; others let it be known that they participated under protest. Because of the huge publicity campaign on the communist side and the vocal protests from the Americans, the premiere was built up as one of the most important moments in German postwar cultural history.

Predictably perhaps, nearly everyone was disappointed with the play. Even *Neues Deutschland* admitted that the production came off as wooden and declamatory rather than being full of the supposed passion and vigor of the original. There were some public discussions of the nature of American capitalism, but not at all on the level that the Soviets had hoped. Soviet Military Administration cultural officers expressed no disappointment publicly, but they stepped up their efforts to improve the energy of the production by demanding better acting. In any case, *The Russian Question* continued to run in the Eastern zone from May 1947 through the following fall. In preparation for the celebration of the thirtieth anniversary of the Russian Revolution on November 10, 1947, six provincial theaters featured the play. Dymshits wrote to VOKS in Moscow that *The Russian Question* had been a huge success in the zone and that it had effectively demonstrated to the Germans what the "true America" was all about. He was certainly correct to note that the response to the play had been "lively," but it was far from a critical success. In fact, many Germans interviewed on leaving the play thought of it as little more than exaggerated Soviet propaganda. As one woman in Dresden put it: "The [real] 'Russian Question' has to do with dismantling and the shortage of potatoes."[98]

The Soviets controlled theater repertoires, took direct part in production decisions, and insisted that certain highly political plays, like *The Russian Question,* be staged. (Two other anti-American plays were introduced by the Soviets in the Eastern zone: *Deep Roots,* which depicted the exploitation of American blacks, and *Colonel Kuz'min,* a play by the Sheinin brothers, which contained a dialogue between Soviet and American military commandants about the future of Germany.) As in the film industry, the Soviet officers in charge of theater also tried to develop a German cadre of cultural activists who could carry on the work of the "democratization" of German theater without the constant interference of the military government. General Kolesnichenko in Thüringen took special interest in Max Valentin's Weimar Theater Institute, which was dedicated to training a new generation of "loyal" German actors in the Stanislavsky method.[99] In Saxony, Soviet cultural officers held periodic conferences with the leading actors, producers, and directors in the region to talk about the development of theater. "It is interesting to note," wrote one cultural officer, "that after these conferences the theaters took important measures in selecting new contemporary material." He also noted that the Germans gradually internalized the Soviet system of censorship and demonstrated increasing "discipline" in following literally the texts of the Russian plays.[100]

The Soviets also gave strong support to Wolfgang Langhoff's efforts to organize ties between his Deutsches Theater in Berlin and other theaters in the zone. At a conference of eighty representatives of theaters in the zone in July 1948, Langhoff, fresh from a visit to Moscow, sang the praises of cultural policy in the Soviet Union. Herbert Ihering from the Max Reinhardt Theater also spoke on behalf of the contributions of Soviet socialist culture to theatrical life in the zone. German repertoires, he boasted, had at last been purged of "the contentless, idea-barren, escapist, banal, unambitious productions" of the past. Seemingly never tired of praise from German cultural figures, the Soviets were particularly pleased that Ihering, who was not a party member, "especially emphasized [in his speech] the great positive influence of Russian and Soviet dramaturgy on the cause of educating German audiences and raising the artistic level of the theater."[101] For good reason, the Germans also gave the Soviets credit for ensuring the financial well-being of the theaters in a period in which currency reform in the West had forced the closing of a number of theater houses in Berlin.

It is hard to gauge the impact of Soviet attention to German theater on the audiences themselves. Brandenburg cultural officers reported in January 1947 that theatergoers preferred "mindless" operettas to dramatic performances, and attendance was twice as high for performances of these operettas than for serious theater. According to Soviet data, if attendance at comic theater was added to the operettas, then it was clear that theatergoers were attracted to "light, entertaining genres" rather than to serious plays. Costume balls were a particular rage among young people; it was hard to get the youths to go anywhere near dramatic theater. Nevertheless, the Brandenburg officers made it clear to theater directors that they would be removed if, in their repertoire plans for 1947–48, substantially more serious (that is, classical Russian and contemporary Soviet) material were not introduced.[102]

The Soviet cultural officers also tried to get the "masses" involved in theater through what they called "autonomous artistic activity" *(khudozhestvennyi samodeiatel'nost')*. Factory and school theaters were set up, and SED and FDJ members were encouraged to get involved in one form of cultural activity or another. While these theaters suffered from an even more serious shortage of contemporary material and resources than the professional theaters, tens of thousands of Germans participated in the amateur performances.[103] In addition, the Soviets helped the Germans set up "people's theaters," which had permanent homes in some cities and also sent out five- or six-person troupes to perform in villages and factories in the provinces. Supported directly by the central trade union, the FDGB, the people's theaters arranged for cheap tickets to their performances and produced special plays that emphasized political themes.[104]

Music, Literature, and the Fine Arts

Opera, ballet, chamber music, and symphonic music also fell under the aegis of the Performances Department of SVAG's Information Administration and were subject to many of the same pressures as their theatrical cousins. For example, the Soviets insisted that orchestras, chamber music groups, musical soloists, and choral groups play more Russian and especially more Soviet music. However, as in the case of the theater, there were practical as well as political problems with meeting the demands of the cultural officers. There was very little sheet music available for Russian and Soviet music, and Dymshits had to badger VOKS in Moscow to send to the zone the musical scores of various symphonies. He begged for phonograph records and sheet music, and made a special plea for the scores of Russian folk music and popular choral music, which was almost completely unknown to the Germans. In particular, Dymshits wanted to exploit the great success of the Alexandrov Ensemble's August 1948 guest appearances in Berlin to encourage the Germans to perform Russian folk music and dance.[105]

The Soviet Military Administration did manage to set up a music library in Berlin, which from all accounts was extremely successful. The Germans took well to Tchaikovsky and the Soviet composer Shostakovich. But even in the case of symphonic music, Soviet cultural officers pressured German orchestras to follow "democratic" repertoires and to play Russian and Soviet music according to accepted Soviet norms. For the February 17, 1946, Dresden premier of Tchaikovsky's Fifth Symphony, Soviet cultural officers worked with the orchestra to make sure that the piece was played correctly. In fact it had been more than a dozen years since Tchaikovsky had been played by the Dresden orchestra. Still, the Soviets need not have worried so much. The premiere went splendidly, and the German audiences seemed pleased to hear serious Russian music, as well as the music of Mendelssohn and others, which had not been played during Nazi times.[106]

Despite these successes, Soviet cultural officers from all over the zone complained that German musical performances suffered from the absence of great Russian and Soviet composers in their repertoires. Even beyond the question of whether or not German orchestras played Russian music, Soviet cultural officers were ready to adjust German musical repertoires according to norms they had brought with them from home. The Germans were too attached, they felt, to the romantic, escapist music of Schubert and Schumann, and to the classical symphonies of Mozart, Beethoven, and Bach, without paying enough attention to choral music and to the potential of soloists. The Germans did go in for piano sonatas, but the Soviets complained that they played far too little Chopin—études, mazurkas, ballads, and rhapsodies. In fact, the Soviets thought German orchestras all but ignored Eastern European music (not to mention Russian) and played too little Western European music as well. Cultural officers were ready to grant that there were some concrete problems involved, like the absence of sheet music and the fact that German audiences enjoyed hearing familiar pieces and simply could not identify with Russian and Soviet music. But many shared the attitude of Major Mnozhin, a cultural officer from Brandenburg, who insisted that many more Russian and Soviet pieces could have been included in the musical season of some eighty-seven orchestras, which had performed 722 concerts before 233,700 listeners.[107] The Society for the Study of the Culture of the Soviet Union, which sponsored a large number of concerts featuring Russian and Soviet music, took up some of the slack, but cultural officers were insistent that the regular symphony orchestras could do much better in this regard.

Especially in the world of music, the Soviets were so anxious to recruit high-quality cultural leaders that they employed German artists who had been nominal members of the Nazi Party, or who had at least cooperated with the Nazi cultural establishment. The most notable case of this sort was that of Wilhelm Furtwängler, who remained conductor of the Berlin Philharmonic only because of strong Soviet support. Another was Hermann Abendroth, who organized and conducted the Weimar Symphony Orchestra. In Abendroth's case, local KPD activists insisted that the Nazi conductor not be hired, because of his background. But they were overruled by the local Soviet cultural officer, who wanted, under any circumstances, a first-rate symphony in the city.[108]

The Soviets imposed on German musical life the kind of bureaucratization of cultural affairs that characterized all forms of culture in the USSR. In Thüringen, for example, the symphonies and musical groups were ordered to register with the trade union (FDGB), and all conductors had to be licensed through the Education Ministry. Through these registration processes, tighter controls could be placed on repertoires.[109] In Brandenburg, Major Mnozhin criticized the Education Ministry for leaving concerts to the educated public and for not making efforts to draw in the working people. Neither the Kulturbund nor the FDGB took up the Soviets' suggestions to foster the greater public's knowledge about music in general and about Russian and Soviet music in particular. There were only episodic lectures for the working masses, and it was evident, Mnozhin concluded, that German socialists did not understand the importance of musical life to the working class. As a result, the Brandenburg Education Ministry was ordered to take action by setting up a Music Department and registering all musical organizations in the province. Starting in January 1948, the ministry held compulsory meetings for major cultural officials, including all the conductors of orchestras. But even these measures did not satisfy the Soviets. At the end of September 1948, all the conductors in Brandenburg, some eight in all, met to review the accomplishments of the previous season and lay out the tasks of the coming one. They were forced to submit "plans" for their repertoires to the ministry, which were approved only after consultations with the Soviet Cultural Department on November 10. Finally, as a way to control completely the musical repertoires of all public concerts, a Directorship of Concerts was set up in Brandenburg. One goal of the directorship was to cut back on the guest performances from Berlin and the West, which allegedly exerted an "extremely dangerous influence" on the musical public of the region.[110]

German painters and sculptors were subjected to many of the same pushes and pulls of Soviet cultural policy as were writers, philosophers, musicians, and playwrights. The Soviet cultural officers' dedication to "socialist-realist" painting and sculpture was complete. In the case of fine art, as in other areas, they pressured VOKS to send reproductions, posters, and art books so that German painters could experience the glories of Soviet painting. At the same time, they understood that German painters and sculptors faced particularly difficult circumstances after the war. Those art materials that were produced in the zone—paints, canvases, and plaster, among other necessities—were systematically sent off to the Soviet Union as reparations. The artists were also deprived of their patrons, customers, and dealers, and their ateliers were hard to keep heated, given the shortage of coal and wood. Perhaps even more devastating, the artists faced a deep spiritual crisis. Even those who had been opposed to the Hitler regime and were sympathetic to socialist rhetoric nevertheless had a great deal of trouble bringing themselves to create artworks along socialist-realist lines, which they correctly saw as reminiscent of the "naturalism" that had been demanded by the Nazis.

In their spiritual alienation, German artists in the East tended to swing between expressionism and impressionism and to stay away from the themes of rebuilding that were so dear to SVAG and the SED. Their understanding of "liberated" art was that they would be free of government-mandated themes altogether.[111] The Saxon information officer Lieutenant Colonel Vatnik wrote to Tiul'panov in February 1946: "The creative artists stand aside from life. [They see] social themes only as negative."[112] As late as May 1948, Anton Ackermann noted that even Marxist painters could not be counted on to apply "a healthy realism" in their work. The best thing to do, he suggested, was to allow them to continue their work for the time being. He felt that it would be counterproductive to try to bring order to the chaos that contemporary art represented.[113] The public was also in no mood for the official optimism and transparent tendentiousness of socialist-realist painting, at least not yet. The exhibits of Käthe Kollwitz's somber, moving realism, for example, brought critical responses from the German public. Her paintings were simply too depressing for the broad spectrum of Germans. As one viewer at the exhibit in Chemnitz noted, the people needed to take some "joy in life."[114]

No piece of cultural life in eastern Germany was above scrutiny for its relevance to the political transformation taking place under SVAG's guidance. For Soviet cultural officers, the choice of music for a string quartet performance or the kind of poster used to advertise a Soviet film carried serious political implications. The Soviets also tried to control what the Germans read, stocking bookstores and libraries with German and Russian classics as well as Soviet literature. Thüringen's General Kolesnichenko suggested "flooding the German market with Soviet Marxist political, popular, and creative literature," so that the Germans would read more "fine" literature.[115] But the flood was barely more than a trickle, especially at the outset of the occupation, because VOKS could not supply nearly enough Soviet books in German translation to satisfy the German demand.[116] However, much as in the case of film and theater, the literary issues ran far deeper than the unavailability of Soviet books in German or republished versions of the German and Russian classics. In their reading, in their rare moments of privacy and relaxation, Germans looked to escape the difficult conditions in which they lived and tried to forget the Russians. Romances, detective novels, and science fiction far outsold any of the literature the Soviets hoped to purvey. Even SED leaders (not to mention the SED rank and file) were known among SVAG cultural officers to be poorly read. According to Soviet information, when they did read they barely touched Soviet literature in translation and also completely ignored their own German classics.[117]

The Soviets also urged the Germans to become more literate in the classics of scientific socialism, yet they discouraged them from pursuing their own visions of socialist meaning. Fred Oelssner, a loyal and pragmatic SED ideologue, submitted a manuscript for publication entitled "Hegel and Our Times," in which he tried to demonstrate that Marx and even Lenin were students of Hegel's ideas. The Soviet censor lambasted poor Oelssner for "papering over the reactionary ideas and spirit of Hegel's teaching" instead of exposing them for what they were. After all, the censor bitingly noted, Hitler himself had taken ideas from Hegel to defend his terrible deeds. The censor was also unhappy that Oelssner had dared to suggest that Marx and Engels took their ideas about the dialectic from Hegel. If that were not bad enough, Oelssner had had the temerity to suggest that Lenin himself was "one of the greatest pupils and heirs of

Hegel." In short, for this Soviet censor, Oelssner had ignored the most important lessons in Stalin's writing on philosophy and had missed altogether the class essence of Hegel's writing, which would have made it apparent that Marx and Lenin represented a substantially more advanced and qualitatively different understanding of the historical process than the idealist Hegel.[118]

Oelssner's work on Hegel was eventually revised and published, and the scholastic objections of the Soviet censor need detain one no further. What is important here is the superior tone of the Soviet's critique and his assumption—shared by virtually all the cultural and propaganda officers in Germany—that the value of every branch of knowledge and cultural endeavor, every piece of writing or music, could be assessed only in relationship to Soviet norms. Even before the SED proclaimed itself a party of the new type in the summer of 1948 and proclaimed in its ubiquitous slogan that "To Learn from the Soviet Union Is to Learn to be Victorious," SVAG cultural officers measured the success of their work with their German charges by the extent to which the Germans parroted Soviet examples. Even when the SED was encouraged by SVAG to pursue the "German road to socialism" in its social policies and ideological pronouncements, only Soviet interpretations of the development of Marxism, the history of the Russian Revolution, the outbreak of World War II, and even the history of the German Revolution of 1918 were acceptable.

Ceremonies and Rituals

In their art, music, and literature, eastern Germans wanted things light and easy. Like their western German brethren, they enjoyed smoking and dancing, big-band music, chocolate, and nylons. In their world of hunger, cold, and disease, Käthe Kollwitz's pictures of emaciated children were just the kind of artworks they wanted to avoid. Work was hard and rations were short. Eastern Germany was occupied by Soviet troops and ruled by a Soviet military government that removed the Germans' factories and ordered their lives according to principles and values that only a minority of the population shared. The Soviet occupiers were seldom satisfied with anything the Germans did, and they were relentless in their demands for labor and products. Still, it was not enough that the Germans obeyed, worked, and repented. They also had to participate in a Sovietized cultural life that went far beyond simple changes in repertoires or the appearance of new Soviet films in movie houses and Soviet novels in bookstores. The

Soviets also brought with them their ceremonies and their rituals, their slogans, banners, busts of Lenin and Stalin, medals and orders, their style of radio news, and their anniversaries and holidays.

Sometimes the Soviet way of doing things was translated literally and figuratively into German by thoroughly Sovietized communists, like Ulbricht and Pieck. The creation of the "cult of personality" around the communist martyr Ernst Thälmann is a case in point. In proclaiming itself the party of the new type in January 1949—meaning, of course, the Soviet type—the SED erected statues in Thälmann's memory, named factories and schools after him, and urged Pioneer children to recite odes to him. Fred Oelssner wrote a hagiographic article about Thälmann that took the form of a fictitious letter from the Bautzen prison camp written shortly before Thälmann was killed. But, as in the Soviet cults of personality, no chink was allowed in the armor of communist heroes. Ulbricht struck out in red pencil those passages in Oelssner's article indicating that Thälmann might have wavered in his convictions or that some of his enemies, the Nazi guards, might have treated prisoners, Thälmann included, with respect. Ulbricht also vetted the passages that hinted that Thälmann had contemplated committing suicide.[119] In the end, then, Thälmann was a communist without weaknesses, without blemishes, a knight fighting the evil dragon, a hero and a martyr of utterly unreal proportions, whom many East Germans came to despise, in part as a result of the incessant hyperbole.

The Soviets also brought with them to Germany a whole series of holidays that were at once Moscow-oriented *and* "international." May Day was, of course, the most prominent, and it was celebrated with great pomp and care for the first time in postwar Germany in May 1946. Soviet political officers devoted a great deal of attention to all the trappings of the holiday; flags and banners carrying carefully chosen slogans had to be properly displayed on apartment buildings, institutions, and factories in the towns and cities of the zone. The anniversary of the Russian Revolution was also commemorated in ritualized fashion by German institutions and agencies. In conjunction with the thirtieth anniversary (November 7, 1947), the Soviet and German authorities planned a series of carefully coordinated theater openings, conferences, film festivals, and poster exhibitions.[120]

International Women's Day, March 8, was celebrated with special care and lengthy preparations. Reports of the 1948 celebration from Brandenburg reflected the Soviet obsession with the extensive use of flowers for the occasion. A cultural official from the Kalau region insisted that there be plenty of flowers at the meetings, decorating the halls and podiums. Every woman should also receive flowers on the holiday. Most of the Women's Day celebrations in Kalau went off according to Soviet muster, but a number were criticized for the lack of enthusiasm shown by their participants. At the Lautewerke power station, for example, only about a hundred women showed up at the celebration, and they spent most of their time before and after the formal speeches talking about the shortages of bread and potatoes, even though, according to Soviet reporters, they were well fed. Here and elsewhere, the Soviets blamed a combination of poor ideological preparation and inattention to detail for the failures of the celebrations. "In the hall," wrote one official, "there was not a single poster to be seen commemorating the occasion, there were no flowers." Out of thirty women who worked in the office of the Landrat, only fifteen showed up at the Women's Day celebration, and even they were completely uninterested in the prepared speeches. In this case, the Soviet officer in charge was convinced of the political duplicity of the chief German organizer, and he made sure that she was disciplined by the local party organization.[121]

The Germans were also subjected to anniversary celebrations that had even less to do with their own traditions than did the so-called international holidays. For example, the military government treated the one hundred fiftieth anniversary of the birth of Pushkin in 1949 as a holiday of great political significance for Germany, one that was to be marked by a rare visit by Soviet delegates and by commemorative meetings at the German Academy of Sciences and at the Houses of Soviet Culture in the zone. The Soviets also thought that the Pushkin festivities would offer good opportunities to teach the Germans something about progressive literary methodology.[122] By 1949 the attitude of Soviet cultural officers toward the Germans was condescending in the extreme, and this was reflected in part by the fact that the Soviets rejected the idea that one of the themes to be studied during the commemoration should be Pushkin and the Germans. There could be no intimation in the period of the anti-Western and anticosmopolitan campaign that *the* great Russian poet might have have been influenced in any way by foreigners.

In fact, it was simpler under "high Stalinism" to celebrate the accomplishments of classical German cultural heroes, like Goethe and Schiller, and to show the Russian influences on them than to commemorate Russian (or especially Soviet) cultural figures, who required effusive, formulaic praise and embarrassing national self-effacement on the part of the Germans. From late 1947 until the foundation of the GDR (and after), the Soviets never seemed to tire of even the most sycophantic praise from the Germans. The speech of Wolfgang Harich on the occasion of the thirtieth anniversary of the Russian Revolution in November 1947 was a typical example of this genre:

> If we Germans, who during these days of great admiration and love, participate in the revolutionary celebrations of our Russian liberators and friends, we should be honest with ourselves, we should experience a mixed feeling of wounded pride, shame, and envy. It is difficult to endure the tragedy of a situation in which [one] is amazed at the greatest revolutionary upheaval of the epoch, while belonging to the nation that lost all of its revolutions and never climbed out of its pitiful conservatism.[123]

The Soviets liked the Germans best when they were supine and ready to learn.

Even the Germans' own revolutionary holidays were marked by the constant interference of SVAG officials, who wanted to make sure that the locals did everything correctly. The thirtieth anniversary of the November 1918 German revolution was a typical case. Not only did the Soviets characteristically pay careful attention to the externalities of the ceremonies—appropriate flowers, banners, decorations, and the like— but they also made sure that the SED's "Theses on the November Revolution" conformed to Moscow's needs. Initially Grotewohl drafted the theses, after which they were heavily edited by Oelssner. Then Pieck sent them to Vladimir Semenov (political advisor to the commander-in-chief of SVAG) for approval. Semenov's comments on the draft typified the Soviets' unquenchable thirst for praise of their own importance—a need that was psychological but also pointedly political. There was a great deal that Semenov did not like about the theses, but the fundamental issue was that the Germans did not sufficiently emphasize the influence of the "Great October Revolution" on the German events of 1918. Semenov also wanted the SED to give positive attention to the Left in the SPD, so that the theses would appeal both to former SPD members in the zone and to leftist SPD members, whom the Soviets hoped to court in Berlin and in the Western zones: "It would be desirable to say somehow about the left social democrats that after the Revolution of 1918 they made mistakes but gradually became convinced of the necessity for the creation of the unity of the workers' movement on the basis of Marxism-Leninism." Finally, Semenov wanted his German pupils to adjust their claims to having advanced to a stage of socialism that was further on the road to a people's democracy than the Soviets, for their own reasons, were ready to accept. At the same time, he urged them to condemn the notion of the "special German road to socialism" as contradicting "the great historical experience of the USSR, as well as all of the tenets of Marxism-Leninism on the construction of socialism." The special German road to socialism, Semenov emphatically stated, reflected nothing more than the opportunism and crass nationalism characteristic of Western European socialism. At the same time, Semenov insisted that the Germans should not claim too much for socialism in the Eastern zone. They should stick strictly to Stalin's iterations on "the dictatorship of the proletariat" and step back from suggestions that they had already achieved "an eternal unity between the proletariat and working farmers."[124] For the time being, the Germans were left by the Soviets in an ideological twilight zone, unable to advance to the stage of a people's democracy, like the other countries of Eastern Europe, but forbidden to pursue a uniquely German road to socialism, which might have appealed to their conationals in the West.

No single celebration in the zone held quite the significance for SVAG as the two hundredth anniversary of Goethe's birth, which was commemorated in Weimar from March through August 1949. For the Soviets, Goethe was Germany's Pushkin. Soviet cultural officers were determined to demonstrate to the Germans in both the East and the West that the only way to sanctify their national cultural heroes was in the context of revolutionary socialism. The Soviets subsequently transformed Goethe, like Pushkin, into a symbol of progress and democracy, a revolutionary before his time, and a champion of the folk. Just as Pushkin was claimed as a forerunner of Lenin, Goethe became a precursor of Marx, a dialectician, whose purely Central European radical roots dispelled all claims in the capitalist West that he belonged to some kind of "Atlantic culture."[125] The Goethe ceremonies became ever more elaborate in the course of 1949 as the Soviets urged all-German claims on the SED and the politics of the National Front intensified. Plans to award the first National Prizes in the Eastern zone at a huge ceremony at the National Theater in Weimar on August 25 also heightened the SED's expectations and the public's awareness of the Goethe events.

Given the severe shortage of resources in the zone, the preparations for the celebration were really quite remarkable. Dozens of special exhibitions and plays were installed at various Goethe landmarks throughout Thüringen. More than 3,000 lectures and cultural events in association with the anniversary were put on by the Kulturbund alone. Some 1,500 foreign guests, including 15 Germans from the West, were invited to Weimar and regaled in relatively luxurious circumstances. Even Thomas Mann came to the Soviet zone from Santa Monica, California, for the Goethe events— the culmination of months, even years, of interest on the part of the Soviets in attracting the famous bourgeois antifascist to their side of the German divide.[126] Mann did not hide his priorities in coming to Weimar. He was prepared to accept a Goethe Award from the Kulturbund if he could give the same speech that he would give at Frankfurt am Main for the West German celebration. He was determined, in other words, not to become an instrument in the growing East-West struggle. "I recognize no zones," Mann stated. "My visit is to Germany itself, Germany as a whole, and to no occupied zone."[127]

The Soviets and the SED did everything they could to turn Mann's head, and there can be little doubt that he was dazzled a little by all the attention and praise. Johannes R. Becher personally escorted Mann from Frankfurt to Weimar. Anton Ackermann discussed cultural developments with him, and Paul Wandel exchanged views with him about education.[128] Even Major General Tiul'panov came to Weimar with his wife and daughter to meet with the great writer. Mann was obviously charmed by the Soviet propaganda chief, as he later wrote in the *New York Times Magazine:*

> Chief of the information division of the Soviet Military Administration, General Tulpanov also carries the title of professor. He speaks excellent German. We found a rich topic for conversation in the era of the great Russian novel in the nineteenth century—a literature to which I owe so much of my own literary education. Turning to politics, the general expressed satisfaction over the developments in his domain which he described as being on a fairly even course. Little interference on the part of the occupation authorities was necessary any longer. Popular democracy had become well versed. The Germans could be permitted to proceed independently.

As a self-defined noncommunist rather than an anticommunist, Mann found much to admire in the work of the Russians and the SED. He also picked up on early signs of pride in the citizens of a sovereign eastern Germany "that could not be bought" by the West.[129] Some of Mann's critics in the Western anticommunist press insinuated that the great writer had been "duped" by the communists, but this seems hardly to have been the case, given Mann's instinctive revulsion at any kind of totalitarianism, which was reflected in his Weimar speech which ended with a ringing defense of individual freedom.[130]

Mann's unfailing eye for detail also picked up in the Goethe celebrations "the fatal similarities with the Hitleresque." At least on the surface, Mann wrote, the state ceremonies, the marches, the songs in the eastern zone— he might have added the banners, slogans, and prizes—all played a role in a developing totalitarian socialist state that too easily assumed the forms of the Nazi state against which it had sworn eternal enmity. What Mann did not see clearly enough was that his own visit and the whole structure of the Goethe celebration were part and parcel of the Soviet designs for culture in the zone. Mann refused to be suspicious when he was driven "by chance" past Thomas Mann Street in Plauen, and he did not make a formal inquiry into the internment of young Germans in Buchenwald, as he was asked to do by Western anticommunists. As a result, Mann's visit to the Soviet zone cost him dearly on his return to the West. He was so severely criticized in the United States that he expressed the intention of returning to Europe, specifically to Zürich, which he eventually did.

UNIVERSITIES

The Sovietization of German culture in the Eastern zone should not be looked at as a process planned and executed according to preexisting models developed by Soviet functionaries and their German helpmates in Moscow. What went on in the zone was more anarchic, idealistic, and ultimately more nefarious than that. The Soviets saw themselves as carriers of a superior culture that could right the wrongs of the reactionary German cultural heritage, which was responsible for two calamitous world wars. The Moscow KPD veterans shared the secret of this fountain of cultural wisdom: a peculiar combination of conservative dedication to the classics and a blind devotion to the tendentious products of Soviet socialist realism. Part of the belief system that nurtured the conviction of Soviet cultural superiority was a complete willingness on the part of communists to accept as truth any and all directives from the Soviet Central Committee about what was good and bad about current cultural life. This was combined with a perverse articulation of dialectics that manipulated the contents of cultural products by using baldly utilitarian criteria. The most difficult aspect of transforming culture to suit political needs was reaching into the consciousness of the individual artist to get him or her to produce works that were of high quality both subjectively (as art) and objectively (as politics).

The Soviets and the SED felt that higher education was critical to this process of creating a new German culture. The purpose of the universities was to produce a postwar generation in the German intelligentsia for whom the lessons of Soviet dialectical thinking would be completely internalized. The German universities would produce scientists and engineers, historians and jurists, musicians and philosophers who could perform high-quality tasks in the service of the people and its representative, the SED.

In the end, the universities themselves proved both harder and easier to transform than the culture as a whole. As institutions that had long and revered traditions, the universities were able to hold on to a remarkable degree of traditional autonomy in the face of Soviet and SED ambitions to take them over.[131] In the long run, however, they were easier to "Sovietize" than the minds of the cultural elite, because they were institutions that could be manipulated by SVAG and the SED to the point that serious challenges to the form and content of education—to the inculcation and indoctrination of Marxist-Leninist learning and culture—were swiftly repelled.

When the Soviets marched into the town of Greifswald (Mecklenburg) in May 1945, the situation at the university was indicative, if not typical, of the problems they faced in higher education throughout the zone. The university there was untouched by the war; not a pane of glass had been broken nor a house hit by bombs or gunfire. The university library, filled with books from the Hitler times, was open and still operating. Some 150 out of 180 professors and docents, many with Nazi affiliations, were still in place. When the Soviets interviewed the rector, he said there was no need for anything to change. The university, he felt, should continue to function as it was.[132] The Soviets lost no time in closing down the university and getting rid of the rector, replacing him with Ernst Lohmeyer, an antifascist theologian who had been active in the Confessing Church. But before the university was reopened in February 1946, the NKVD arrested Lohmeyer, and he was never heard from again.[133] The Soviets promptly selected a new rector from among those professors who, according to the unofficial SVAG history of higher education in the zone, "to one extent or another were hostile to Nazism and were democratically inclined, though in a bourgeois sense."[134] It was extremely difficult in the fall of 1945 to find academics of a socialist persuasion. (The physicist and later Marxist dissident Robert Havemann was one of the most prominent.) As a result, the Soviets had to make do with "good democrats," who were expected to heed the SVAG's wishes.

In preparing for the new academic year of 1945–46, the Soviets formally respected the universities' traditional autonomy, though they insisted at the same time that all war criminals and formerly active Nazis be immediately released from their professorships. The Education Department of SVAG (ONO) and its German subordinate, the German Education Administration (DVV), worked with the Ministries of Education in the provinces to study lists of the remaining university personnel. At the outset, "nominal" Nazis were allowed to remain in place, so long as they did not belong to the category of those who "stood in the way of the democratization of the universities." But by the beginning of 1946, all nominal Nazis were also formally released from the universities, with the exception of a dozen or so professors who qualified as "exceptional specialists." (Later on, a number of nominal Nazis were returned to the universities' staffs because of their especially desirable "scientific" qualifications.[135]) At the same time, it is clear from Soviet data that qualified German professors and not just those who had been Nazis, fled the Soviet zone in droves (see Table 3).

The brain drain of both former Nazis and non-Nazis to the West was substantial and significant for the future of education in the Soviet zone. The six major universities in the zone lost some 75 percent of their pro-

Table 3. Professors in the Soviet zone

University	Jan. '45	Jan. '46	No. who left	No. Nazis among those who left
Berlin	583	108	475	150
Jena	133	41	92	34
Halle	144	52	92	73
Leipzig	224	59	165	53
Greifswald	96	35	61	19
Rostock	80	34	46	17
Total	1,260	329	931	346

Source: "Sbornik materialov po istorii otdela narodnogo obrazovaniia," vol. 1, GARF, f. 7317, op. 54, d. 1, l. 122.

fessors and 80 percent of their docents. The problem was even more severe, the Soviets acknowledged, when the number of "world class" scientists who had left was taken into account; in Jena, Leipzig, and Halle, the Americans had identified "the most famous scientists," the heads of laboratories and institutes, and taken them with them when they evacuated those territories in late June 1945. Particularly in Berlin, scholars and professors who were fearful of Soviet retribution or simply wary of Soviet control fled to the West. At the former Prussian Academy of Sciences, located in the Soviet sector of Berlin, of the seventeen leading senior scholars and academicians who were there in January 1945, only two remained at the beginning of 1946. Although some twenty professors eventually returned from emigration to work in the universities of the zone, the losses for eastern German scholarship and education were enormous. Attempts to recruit western "progressive" academics could not make up for the deficit.[136]

Although the emigrations did take care of potentially troublesome academics, the Soviets were unhappy with the university faculties that remained. Lieutenant Colonel Vatnik complained in October 1947 that there were far too few true democrats among the Leipzig University professoriat. The professors and docents, he wrote, were for the most part politically inactive; when they belonged to a party at all, it was to one of the bourgeois parties, the CDU or the LDP. The few Marxists on the faculty were a disappointment and were not nearly as well versed philosophically as the "professor-idealists, who appeared to be outright reactionaries."[137] In Greifswald, SVAG officials also lamented the fact that the faculties, especially the medical faculty, appeared to be dominated by reactionaries.[138] Because SVAG formally recognized the traditional principle of faculty autonomy at the universities, "idealistic" professors were able to influence their colleagues, a situation the Soviets considered embarrassing and even humiliating. The opening of the juridical faculty of Humboldt University in Berlin precipitated a series of confrontations over the wording of the faculty's mandate. In this case, SVAG's Justice Administration intervened to convince the Germans to accept a draft that stated that not only professional knowledge would be a criterion for advancement in the faculty, but that the students' ability "to draw conclusions about the important connections between state, economic, and social life" would also be taken into account.[139]

The papers of the Education Department of SVAG are permeated with the Soviet educational officers' frustration at the obstinance of university faculties. First of all, the Soviets had to deal with an inexperienced and understaffed German Educational Administration under Paul Wandel, who—at least in their view—understood even less about the German universities than their own overburdened Soviet compatriots. The ONO inspectors were the ones who had to write the first study plans in the universities and select the first students. But the chief of ONO, P. V. Zolotukhin worried that his office would never be staffed by enough specialists to carry out the numerous and diverse tasks in the educational and cultural arena delegated to him by the commander-in-chief. As a result, there was a frantic quality to ONO's attempts to increase the number of Soviet officials in the department and improve the quantity and quality of German specialists working in the universities.[140] Because the Soviets and the German university professors in the zone differed radically on the purposes of university education, ONO made no attempts in the first two years of the occupation to draft a university statute. German professors, hoping for a better day, also did not push for the promulgation of a statute. Wandel and the DVV were not happy with the situation, especially since the provinces were able to exert primary control over the universities until 1948–49, but they were able to deal with fundamental problems in higher education by calling on SVAG to issue direct orders on their behalf.[141]

Neither the Soviets nor the SED were satisfied with the standoff in the universities. Their strategy for breaking down the students' and professors' resistance to "democratization" included a number of indirect attacks on traditional German patterns of higher education. First of all, they wanted to increase the number of workers and "working farmers" in the student body. It had been a mistake, they felt, to have admitted so many representatives of the bourgeoisie and petit-bourgeoisie into the first group of students. According to the SVAG education specialists, many of these students were "victims of fascism" and were of "non-Aryan background" (in other words, Jews), who "lined up with the bourgeois parties" and eventually even became opponents of a variety of Soviet policies in the universities. They resisted, for example, suggestions of preferential admissions for workers, as well as the introduction of mandatory courses in political economy (Marxism-Leninism). Among the students and professors, it was hard to find supporters for preferential admissions, and proponents of faculty autonomy continued to oppose Soviet interference. But as time went on, it became harder and harder for the faculties to stick to their principles, especially after the summer of 1947, when it became possible for the universities to release professors from their positions for making "reactionary statements."[142] Of course from the very beginning of the occupation, the NKVD/MVD arrested professors and students for their opposition to communist measures in the university.

Even without opposition from the professoriat, Soviet demands for participation in the universities by sons and daughters of workers and farmers were difficult to meet. In the first place, it was hard to find qualified students at all; the numbers of students in what became Soviet-zone universities fell dramatically, from 25,420 in 1928 to 10,890 in 1941 to 8,500 in 1946. Also, with or without higher education, talented and "progressive" young workers were quickly recruited for important positions in the party and state apparatus or in the trade unions and mass organizations. The DVV had also come up short in recruiting young farmers for its education programs. Its failure to penetrate the countryside meant that there were very few potential recruits from the villages for the universities. By January 1, 1949, of the 25,300 students in the universities (back up to the count in the Weimar period), only 7,268 were children of workers and 1,138 children of farmers: 33.6 percent of the combined student body.[143] Even at that, many of these so-called workers and farmers were the sons and daughters of the new SED elite, who claimed (like Pieck and Honecker) that they were members of the working class on the basis of their earlier professions.

From the SVAG's point of view, the critical failing of its education policy was its inability to find a way for the SED to take over the universities. At the outset of the 1946–47 academic year, the situation was serious enough to attract the attention of the Soviet Central Committee in Moscow. In Leipzig, for example, out of 130 professors and docents, only 30 were in the SED. At the Technische Hochschule in Dresden, out of 42 faculty members, only 8 were in the SED. At the Freiberg Mining Academy there was only 1 SED member out of a total of 17 on the faculty.[144] The situation was equally bad among students. Communist students were sometimes attacked and beaten up. In Halle and in Leipzig, noncommunist student groups met clandestinely and, in the case of the Halle group, engaged in active opposition to Soviet programs among the students.[145] During the 1947–48 academic year, SED candidates again failed to make any headway in student elections.

Like his Soviet "friends," Anton Ackermann was extremely upset about the weak position of the SED among students. Despite all of the SED's efforts, Ackermann lamented, "Our position in the universities has not substantially improved." A major part of the problem, he concluded, was that the SED students simply made no efforts to influence their fellow students, cutting themselves off from the rest in "a sectarian way."[146] Insufficient stipends also threatened to force SED students, especially those from the real working class, out of the universities.[147] For Ackermann and the Soviets, Berlin University was a particularly difficult problem, given the four-power status of the city. According to one SVAG report, the situation was "completely unacceptable." Students and teachers alike "provide very little resistance to the small group of American agents in their attempt to destroy the university."[148] So long as the student body was dominated by students from the "bourgeoisie," the Soviets refused to allow any political organizations of students to function in the universities. In typically cynical fashion, though, as soon as the strength and dominance of the SED was assured, the Soviets permitted student organizations to operate freely.

The Soviets and the SED soon found out, though, that increasing the number of SED students did not necessarily improve the political climate of the university. As a result, SVAG insisted that the SED's Personnel Department check out each of the applicants to the university. Simple possession of a party card, the Soviets warned, did not ensure political reliability and activism. By the winter semester of 1948, the situation—from the point of view of the Soviets—began to improve. In December 1948 ONO gave the orders to restructure the work of the SED in the universities "on a new basis," to influence "masses" of students who still held reactionary, "even hostile," views.[149] The first moves toward establishing the Free University in West Berlin in the spring of 1948, and its formal opening the following November, particularly intensified ONO's efforts to bring Berlin University under SED control.

The process of turning the universities in the Soviet zone into instruments of the party entailed curricular changes as well as changes in the faculties and student bodies. The earliest faculties to be rebuilt were the science and medical faculties; then in the fall of 1946 the faculties of history and psychology were reopened. New faculties were given specific charges to participate in the "democratization" of the zone. In July 1946 Sokolovskii ordered the reopening (and in some cases, the creation) of the pedagogical faculties, for the express purpose of implementing democratic school reform by training progressive teachers.[150] The introduction of new faculties in the social sciences in 1947 had the specific purpose of training cadres for service in the German administration or for teaching the older classes of the schools. These students were exposed to large doses of Marxism-Leninism, and only those students who "had demonstrated positive attributes in the practical restructuring of Germany were admitted."[151]

Faculties of Slavic languages were also introduced in a number of universities, and the two previously existing faculties were substantially expanded. By the 1948–49 academic year, there were some 516 students in these faculties. The idea was to train large numbers of Russian teachers for the secondary schools, which required the study of the language. But more important from the Soviet point of view, university students of Russian could also work as translators in the German state apparatus. In a very practical sense, the study of Russian was promoted to improve the frequently problematic communications between Soviet and German apparatuses.[152] The mandatory study of Marxism-Leninism was also introduced during the 1948–49 academic year. The Soviets encouraged the SED to set up a special advanced training program for teachers of Marxism-Leninism, and the Higher Party School of the SED created courses for this purpose in the summer of 1948. Ackermann, Oelssner, and Kuczynski lectured in these courses, as did Wolfgang Leonhard, who fled the zone for Yugoslavia in March 1949.

While the Higher Party School and the universities became the chief centers for teaching Marxism-Leninism, the SED also set up a Scientific Research Institute of the Party Executive (later known as the Institute for the Social Sciences) to provide proper materials for the teachers. The institute's mandate was to spread the ideas of Marx, Engels, Lenin, and Stalin; to keep them isolated from all "falsifications"; and to apply them to the contemporary situation in Germany. In December 1947, at the outset of the institute's work, its most important task was to develop a "scientific basis" for overcoming "reactionary, Trotskyist, and social revisionistic tendencies" in the ideological makeup of the party.[153] The institute quickly became a center for translating Soviet experience into German reality and for providing up-to-date Soviet models for German institutions. The institute also became an elite party university, whose students were to serve as a shock group for ideological innovation.

Especially once the notion of the German road to socialism was buried and its chief author, Anton Ackermann, had recanted, the institute grew in size and took on a series of projects to bring German learning "up to" Soviet standards. In January 1949, for example, the institute produced a thorough program of lectures on Marxism-Leninism for the universities and higher schools of the zone. Essentially the program was nothing more than a comprehensive exegesis on the history of Marxism-Leninism as seen through Soviet eyes. The institute also produced a paper on the German Two-Year Plan of 1949 and 1950, emphasizing that the plan was "the main instrument of revolutionary transformation and advanced development of society." The entire thrust of the paper was to expand on the proposition that the Soviet Union was "the great master teacher of the planned economy" and that there was no other reasonable or progressive way to think about developing an economic system.[154] The philosophical section of the institute also produced an important paper on the design of courses on dialectical materialism and modern biology; "From Darwin to Lysenko," it was called. To get German universities to overcome their much criticized "backwardness" when it came to understanding modern (that is, Soviet) biology and genetics, the Germans were urged to denounce reactionary teachings of the German followers of Mendel and Morgan, and to trumpet the accomplishments of Lysenko in modernizing the science of Darwin.[155]

The Problems of Sovietization

Despite the active involvement of ONO, SVAG, and the German Education Administration in the transformation of the universities, Soviet political figures in the zone were shocked by the extent to which the universities remained impervious to change. The party committee of ONO sent back to Moscow highly critical reports about the situation in the universities that were confirmed by the SVAG party bureau as a whole. Despite the obvious successes in denazifying the universities, SVAG's party bureau wrote to the Central Committee secretary A. A. Kuznetsov in October 1947, "in the pedagogical and scientific work of the universities there still exists to this day the strong influence of idealistic, that is, essentially reactionary ideologies." According to the party bureau's letter, Marxists and materialists were badly outnumbered in the faculties and found themselves on the defensive. The Education Department itself simply did not have the resources to take on the task of the universities; there were no real specialists on its staff for socioeconomic, philosophical, historical, or natural sciences. The letter concluded with a plea for a systematic program of direct Soviet help. It asked Moscow to send skilled personnel and specialized books and curricula. Otherwise, the party bureau worried, Western military authorities would be even more successful in undermining the progressive forces in Eastern zone universities, not to mention those in the West. Because of "the lack of activity of our organs," the bureau said, the situation in the universities had become intolerable.[156]

As was typical in such cases, the Central Committee appointed a commission to investigate the complaints raised by SVAG's party organization. The subsequent report, however, did little more than reiterate the suggestions made by SVAG. Above all, the report stated, German universities required the involvement of many more qualified Soviet scientists and educators, who should be attached to ONO. The report pointed out that the educational enterprise in the Soviet zone, which included some twenty institutions, 22,000 students, and 1,500 faculty members, was supervised by only six people altogether, two of whom had doctoral degrees *(Kandidat nauk)* and one of whom had been a docent; ONO had no professors and no natural scientists. The commission fully backed up the party bureau's demand for greater involvement on the part of Soviet institutions—especially the Ministry of Higher Education and the Soviet Academy of Sciences—in the development of German institutions of higher learning.[157] Documents from the Soviet Central Committee archives indicate that the Cadres Department drafted a resolution on the improvement of Soviet control of higher education institutions in Germany. Though the draft was approved by representatives of a variety of institutions, no concrete measures were taken.[158] Kuznetsov wrote to A. A. Zhdanov in April 1948 that there was no need for the Central Committee to take special action, since the appropriate Soviet ministries and academic institutions would take care of matters in good order.[159]

But neither the Academy of Sciences nor the Ministry of Education was in the least interested in helping its German colleagues. Without direct Central Committee intervention, it was unlikely that terribly much would change. In fact, a year after the SVAG party bureau had tried to elicit action from Moscow, the Central Committee had to deal with even more sharply worded warnings, this time from Colonel Tiul'panov, about "the activization of reactionary, profascist elements among students and bourgeois professors in the Soviet zone's universities."[160] And Tiul'panov was not alone in his complaints. From all over the zone, the Central Committee received reports that "reactionary" students were gaining the upper hand because there was an absence of appropriate textbooks and curricula. Decent materials were lacking even for courses in Slavic studies.[161] As a result of these reports, Suslov ordered that a meeting be arranged between representatives from the Ministry of Higher Education, Moscow University, the Main Political Administration of the Red Army, the Academy of Sciences, and the Timiriazev Agricultural Academy, for the purpose of putting together a comprehensive program of concrete measures to help education in the zone. The committee was to arrange for sending lecturers to eastern Germany and for translating Soviet textbooks into German and publishing them. It was also assigned the task of developing new curricula and organizational plans for the German universities. The committee members were also supposed to set up exchanges of student and professional delegations and to prepare exhibits about Soviet educational life for display in the zone.[162] The results of these recommendations were, however, relatively paltry. Meanwhile, complaints mounted about the eastern German academics' isolation from Soviet science and about the increasing number of British and American scientists visiting universities in the Western zones.[163]

A smattering of Soviet academics did finally show up in the zone, but neither in the quantity nor of the prominence suggested by Tiul'panov and the Central Committee. In January 1948, for example, Professor Vyshinskii from the Academy of Science's Institute of Philosophy visited Jena University's new Institute of Dialectical Materialism, set up in 1946 by Professor Wolf. For nearly two years the institute had been ignored by Moscow, despite its repeated requests for Soviet materials.[164] When Professor Vyshinskii finally came to town, the members of Wolf's institute were thrilled, and they handed over to their honored guest copies of their recent works, for comment from colleagues in Moscow. When they received their papers back, they were shocked and humiliated by the Soviets' severe criticism of their work, so much so that Wolf, who had authored a paper on Hegel's dialectics, and Professor Winkel, who had written a critique of Nazi racial theories, left the academic pursuit of philosophy altogether.[165] While dismayed by the insensitivity of the criticisms, the local Soviet education officer was even more disturbed by the fact that Vyshinskii did not bother returning to the zone at all.

Some Slavicists also came to eastern Germany, most notably the dean of the philological faculty of Moscow University, Professor Chemodanov, as well as Professor Anisimov, the editor of the journal *Sovetskaia Literatura* (Soviet Literature). A great fuss was made over the fact that they attended the opening of the Saxon Academy of Sciences in December 1948 and subsequently visited a number of Slavic faculties, all with apparent success.[166] Nevertheless it was extremely difficult to convince the vast majority of Soviet academics to travel to Germany. As proud as the Soviets claimed to be of their achievements, they seemed hesitant to expose their science to the scrutiny of the West. Even scientific journals and special publications rarely made it to the zone. Officials in SVAG's Education Department wrote, "We very weakly popularized Soviet science. Scholarly circles in the universities of the Soviet zone had almost no chance to familiarize themselves with the achievements of Soviet science, [nor] with the works of individual Soviet scholars, because of the fact that special scientific publications of the Soviet Union (Academy of Sciences and universities) with rare exceptions are not sent to Germany."[167]

The lack of commitment in Moscow to making over the Soviet zone's universities meant the job was left to SVAG. In Soviet terms, it did its job well. It transformed the old Prussian Academy of Sciences into an organization modeled on the Soviet Academy of Sciences. It eliminated private medical and nursing schools and introduced Soviet practices in medical education. It introduced into German academic life the institution of *aspirantura* (doctoral candidacy), which conformed in almost all its details to the Soviet original. The innovation failed in the end, however, because the Germans simply could not comprehend its supposedly "obvious advantages."[168] Similarly, SVAG education officers had a hard time getting German professors to submit "teaching plans," as was common in the Soviet universities. Given the German university's focus on developing subject-matter expertise, which was eventually tested in state examinations, the kind of teaching plan demanded by the Soviets simply could not be met, and the education officials realized they had to withdraw their demands.[169] Finally, in December 1948, after a number of similar successes and failures in the effort to modernize (Sovietize) the German education system, the Soviets encouraged the German Education Administration to adopt university regulations that would centralize German universities and nail into place the Soviet-style changes that had been introduced over the previous three years. The German regulations, taken almost word for word from the university regulations in the Soviet Union, permanently altered the forms and hierarchies of the traditional German universities in the East.[170]

It was easier for SVAG education officers to introduce Soviet forms of university life into the Eastern zone than it was to recreate the Stalinist content of Soviet higher education in zonal institutions. The Russians complained incessantly that German academics looked to the West for intellectual leadership and tried to revive "outmoded" traditions of the Weimar period. The provincial Ministries of Education were also far too cautious for the Soviets' tastes in applying the principles of Marxism-Leninism to pedagogical problems. "Timidity and empiricism" characterized their approach, noted the ONO history of education in the zone. These provincial officials always wanted to study problems, instead of attacking them in Bolshevik fashion.[171] The Soviets also had to endure repeated failures in trying to get the Germans to take seriously "the progressive science of the Soviet Union," especially the new linguistic theories of Marr and Lysenko's supposed contributions to agronomy and biological sciences. The ONO plan for 1949 focused on the task of spreading Soviet science and pedagogy in the zone, but education officers ran up against the problem of Soviet specialists' lack of interest in coming to the zone, despite repeated pleas from a variety of Soviet and German organizations.[172]

Moscow's attacks on scholars who were accused of supposedly prostrating themselves before foreign "scientific colonizers," for no other reason than that they had cited their work, made it even less attractive for Soviet scientists to visit Berlin.[173] The result was that SVAG education officers had to do the job of spreading the glories of Soviet science on their own, by making sure that German scientific journal editors evaluated articles on the basis of "the accomplishments of progressive science."[174] The education officers also worked with the party organizations in the universities to keep tabs on the lectures of professors and discussions among students. However, as late as January and February 1949, the party organizations themselves had made only minor inroads into the student bodies of the universities.[175] Still, through persuasion, intimidation, and constant attention, the Soviets accomplished their basic goal; the German university in the East was transformed from a historical source of German intellectual autonomy into a socialist institution.

NEW TEACHERS, NEW SCHOOLS

The Soviet Military Administration and the German communists had a similar goal in mind with the school system in the East, but the task of reforming the schools was in many ways even more formidable. Roughly 85 percent of the teachers in the schools, at all levels, had been Nazi Party members, and it was simply impossible to remove all of them. There were no new textbooks for the schools in the fall of 1945 and no resources to publish them. When textbooks from the Weimar period could be found, they were usually used. More often than not, the least offensive pages from Nazi textbooks were torn out and pasted together for classroom use.

In mid-July 1945, the Soviets set up the German Education Administration under the leadership of the reliable KPD functionary Paul Wandel, who had also been a member of the CPSU(b) while in Moscow. But Wandel had no experience in pedagogy himself, and in fact he had never finished his own higher education.[176] Wandel had an additional problem in that German traditions of federalism were especially well developed in the education bureaucracy. The provincial Ministries of Education frustrated many of Wandel's attempts to implement zone-wide policies for the schools. Also, these ministries, especially in the first year of the occupation, usually contained large numbers of bureaucrats from the bourgeois parties, while teachers' organizations reflected the influence of the SPD much more than the KPD. The communists' policies were resisted at every turn.

Still, in the summer of 1945 hopes were high in the KPD for a "democratic school reform," which would create a new German school after so many generations based on Prussian models of blind obedience and undemocratic indoctrination. Anton Ackermann set out a series of principles that would guide the reform of German schools in the zone: (1) the content and goals of education would change to encourage progressive thinking and action; (2) a new "unified school" would be introduced that reflected the modern pedagogical thinking in the USSR; (3) the class system of education would be eliminated, to the benefit of workers and farmers; (4) ongoing reform would characterize the entire education system, from the kindergartens to the universities; (5) higher education would be made generally accessible through "people's universities"; and (6) specialized courses in the trade schools would be reconstituted from the ground up.[177] Ackermann's utopian program was echoed in the pronouncements of high SED officials, who talked of the complete transformation of German education in the Soviet zone.[178]

The actual platform for the democratic school reform was much more modest than the communists (and to some extent the social democrats) had hoped. In a joint declaration of October 18, 1945, the KPD and SPD issued a statement on the schools that made no mention of the Soviet Union, though it did emphasize the importance of the unitary school system. The CDU in particular wanted religion to continue to be a part of the curriculum, and a series of meetings about the problem held by the antifascist bloc in the fall of 1945 led to no concrete results. Subsequently the problem of religious instruction was left until the spring of 1946, when a compromise was worked out: the Church would be allowed to teach religion in the same school buildings after classes were over, but not as part of the regular curriculum and not with regular schoolteachers. On April 16, 1946, the CDU finally approved the draft platform on the democratic reform of the schools, and it was confirmed by SVAG and the provincial legislatures in May and June.[179] In addition to a compromise on religious instruction, there was agreement that a twelve-year school system would be established, with an eight-year general school for all children and the possibility of a four-year *Oberschule* for those who were to go on to a university. All the parties of the bloc agreed that schools would be state run, secular, and free.

The battle over the design of the school reform was fought between the parties and was resolved by compromises within the bloc. But on a much more mundane level, the practical problems of keeping the schools open nearly overwhelmed the Germans and the Soviets. The physical condition of the schools was horrendous. Many school buildings had been destroyed during the war; others had been occupied, ransacked, and abandoned by Soviet troops. The best school buildings were still being used as barracks for Soviet occupation troops. A commission investigating the situation of the schools in Brandenburg described dire conditions. Schools had to be closed in January because there was no coal to heat them. For most of the winter, in fact, Brandenburg's school buildings were barely heated and had poor lighting, if any at all. Students were hungry, and they had to share even the few makeshift textbooks they were able to paste together out of acceptable excisions from Nazi books.[180]

Even more depressing was the fact that the physical condition of the schools did not improve markedly during the academic years of 1946–47 and 1947–48. Given reparations demands, the schools sometimes even deteriorated. For example, SED inspectors reported deplorable conditions in Wanzleben region's schools in August 1947. They had no paper, no chalk, no pens or pencils. Old German maps that referred to Soviet cities by their old names—St. Petersburg, Ekaterinburg, Nizhnii Novgorod, and so on—continued to be used. The bathrooms were unsanitary in the extreme; nothing in the school buildings had been repaired since the war. Mice scampered across the floors, and the children were poorly clothed and seldom had proper shoes.[181]

Frightful conditions in Soviet zone schools continued to be reported as late as October 1949, when the GDR was founded. At the outset of the 1949–50 school year, SED officials in Mecklenburg complained about a severe shortage of classroom space, a situation made worse by dilapidated school buildings and filthy bathrooms. There were no blackboards and few lightbulbs. Teachers as well as pupils went without shoes. The SED worried about health conditions in the schools, especially since school doctors were very few and far between, even in the larger cities of the province, like Schwerin, where there was one school doctor for every 17,000 children.[182] The problem with textbooks also did not markedly improve. Soviet and German education officials lamented the shortage of proper books even after the creation of the GDR.

The Soviet authorities left the physical deficiencies of the schools to the German administration. Their biggest concern was the training of antifascist teachers. A major part of the problem was that there was an acute shortage of teachers as a result of the war. The teacher shortage was compounded by the large cohort of children born before the war who were reaching school age, and by the hundreds of thousands of refugee children in the zone who needed schooling. Depending on the region, an overwhelming number of the available pool of teachers had been members of the Nazi Party. On average, the zone's *Volksschule* had been 72 percent Nazi, but in Thüringen, an extreme example, 90 percent had been Nazis.[183] Schools had to rely on former Nazis to fill administrative positions as well, if for no other reason than to have sufficient supervisory personnel. Under these conditions, the Soviets set up courses in August and September 1945 to transform promising workers, farmers, and other "antifascists" into "new teachers." (In fact, only about 3 percent of the new teachers came from the farming population; 55 percent were recruited from the working class, and the remainder came from the population of private and state employees.[184])

At the outset, the course itself lasted only three weeks, and the conditions experienced by the "new teacher" candidates were not much better than those in the schools themselves. It was hard to find enough for the course participants to eat, and they studied in cold, dark classrooms. Many were politically naive, and despite the poor conditions, some showed up only for a bed and a free meal. Most of the candidates were women, and most also belonged either to the KPD or SPD. Under these conditions, it is not surprising that only some 15,000 new teachers were trained in time for the opening of school on October 1, 1945, and that most of them had received only the most minimal preparation. Complaints from parents about the new teachers were rife; they "didn't know the material, [and they] made gross mistakes in grammar and other things."[185] Even the Russians recognized that there were problems with the new teachers, that most lacked experience in the classroom and did not know even the most rudimentary principles of pedagogy. Conditions improved somewhat in 1946 and 1947, as the course for new teachers was lengthened to eight months and the material conditions for their schooling were looked after by the SED. But it was not until after the creation of the GDR that the new teachers assumed the leadership position in the schools that the Soviets had hoped they would realize in the zone.

The new teachers disappointed the Soviets and the SED by not turning out to be the socialist bulwark within the education system that they were supposed to be. In a September 25, 1946, interview with a Soviet commission, Hermann Matern admitted, "It is curious to note that despite the fact that our party chose them, young teachers have a greater affinity for the CDU. The reasons for this phenomenon are still not at all clear to me."[186] Internally, the SED was much more upset than Matern let on about "the shameful fact" that the new teachers regarded the party "as strangers and with a lack of comprehension [*fremd und verständnislos*]."[187]

But the Soviets were in no mood to accept opposition from a group as important as the school teachers. The Soviet Military Administration therefore installed a three-point program to improve the conditions of work for the new teachers and to accelerate "democratic renewal" in the schools. According to Order no. 219 of July 1946, Sokolovskii authorized a series of teachers' conferences to be held all over the zone. The idea was that these conferences would get the local SED organizations much more heavily involved in the schools, as well as in the recruitment and retention of teachers. The conferences were well attended and relatively well provisioned. The Education Department of SVAG treated the conferences as an important agitational weapon in the struggle for the allegiance of Germans, and they therefore used whatever resources they could muster to make them a success. At the same time, Sokolovskii issued a second order (Order no. 220 of July 19) to improve "the material and legal position of the teachers." In addition to improved pay and rations, teachers were given access to rest homes and other special vacation privileges.[188] With these two orders, the Soviets tried to appeal to teachers by endowing their profession with status as well as material benefits.

The final initiative in the Soviet program to improve conditions in the schools came on the heels of the August 1947 Order no. 201 on denazification. Order no. 201 drew a sharp distinction between "active fascists and militarists" and "nominal" Nazi Party members. Both the Soviets and the SED leadership were anxious to see the latter return to a normal working life, especially if they had demonstrated a willingness to get along with the new "democratic order." This order was very important to the schools, which were still desperately short of teachers and overcrowded with children. In fact, in its instructions of September 20, 1947, the Education Department of SVAG interpreted Order no. 201 as authorizing the return of nominal Nazis to German classrooms and school administrations. At the same time, to alleviate the worries of the new teachers (and some members of the SED), who feared that the Nazis would take over the schools again, the Soviets were quite explicit on the issue of promoting the careers of the new teachers. The returning nominal Nazis were to be treated as beginners, and in no circumstances were they to replace or supervise the new teachers.[189]

Much as in the case of the universities, it was one thing for the Soviets and the SED to transform the structure of education and replace old schoolteachers, and it was quite another to create a classroom that produced the socialist values they wished to instill in the Germans. Failures in this regard cost Zolotukhin, the chief of the SVAG's Education Department, his job, and he was replaced in January 1949 by his former deputy, I. D. Artiukhin. The problem with the schools, Artiukhin suggested, was that the teachers and administrators did not understand that they were involved in a life-and-death struggle between reactionary and democratic forces. In choosing sides, school officials, in particular, could not simply be loyal to the democratization process; they would have to develop a "firm belief in the strength of scientific socialism, in the teachings of Marx-Engels-Lenin-Stalin, in the power and greatness of the Soviet Union."[190]

But Artiukhin and the Soviets had a big problem. To try to force teachers to enter the political struggle was to invite defeat. In February 1949 reports poured in to SED headquarters that the new teachers were actually leaving their jobs in "threatening numbers."[191] Many simply went to the West; others, who wished to remain in the East but were averse to the increasing political role they were forced to play, stayed in the schools but left the party. Even "good comrades" sought out better-paying jobs in industry and the administration instead of continuing to face hardships in the classroom. Great hopes were placed on returning POWs from the Soviet Union, who had been trained in Marxism-Leninism and in Soviet pedagogical methods. But the POWs were heavily recruited by the German administrations and the police, and they rarely showed up in the schools.[192]

The SED realized that it had allowed the situation in the schools to stagnate. Teachers and students remained way behind in the "demands of the class struggle."[193] Despite repeated indictments of the schools, the SED offered little concrete guidance about how their weaknesses could be overcome. The old idea of the "unitary" school system still had not been implemented. The SED seemed incapable of doing anything but repeating its suggestions that more workers' children should be promoted in all branches of the system, that Marxist-Leninist pedagogical theory should be broadly applied, and that the practical accomplishments of the school system in the Soviet Union and the people's democracies should be studied. In short, the SED appeared stuck. The party complained that education in the zone did not reflect a "clear distinction" between the antifascist democratic school system on the one hand and "so-called progressive middle-class schooling" on the other. Yet many members of the SED harbored the "illusion" that they were in the process of building a socialist education system.[194]

Part of the problem with school policy had to do with the fact that the Soviets were not ready to allow the SED to claim that the zone had achieved the status of a people's democracy. Ulbricht reminded his comrades that they could not build a socialist school system, because they had not yet established the preconditions for a socialist society.[195] This put school officials in a delicate position: they were accused of "ultraleftism" if they pushed too resolutely for reforms and of ignoring the class struggle if they were too complacent. But more serious for the party leadership was the generally high level of hostility among students and teachers to the Sovietization of the schools. The SED was forced to move very slowly toward the unitary school system, partly because it was seen as being inconsistent with German traditions. Demands that students study Russian at all levels in the school system met with thoroughgoing antagonism. Many students simply refused to do any work in the subject and expressed utter indifference, if not resistance, in the classroom.[196] In some schools the situation became extremely tense, and administrators threatened students with permanent expulsion if they continued to refuse to study Russian. Other students expressed the more pragmatic view, only marginally more acceptable to the Soviets, that one should learn Russian because the Soviets ran everything in the zone anyway.[197]

To overcome some of these difficulties, the German Education Administration set up special schools for studying Russian and established special courses in the regular schools for the sons and daughters of SED loyalists.[198] Beginning in the spring of 1948, there were also some serious efforts on the part of the SED to change the content of education in the zone. The subject of contemporary studies *(Gegenwartskunde)* became a compulsory course in all schools, including the trade schools. Like civics in the American classroom, contemporary studies was decidedly political in its goals, "explaining through *historical, legal and economic observations* the picture of the present."[199] The course also placed a strong emphasis on the individual's role in society, his or her obligation and responsibility for the entire society, and the moral obligation to take an active role in the antifascist democratic transformation. The ultimate goal was transparent, as expressed in the May 1949 directive for the schools: "The German democratic school should educate the youth to be independently thinking and responsibly acting people, who are ready and able to place themselves fully in the service of the community."[200]

The SED recognized that it had not done its job in the school system, and that both teachers and students remained aloof from the concerns of the party. The Free German Youth was of little help in the schools, and the SED's repeated calls for greater FDJ activism remained, on the whole, unheeded.[201] There still remained too few schoolbooks of reasonable quality, instructional films were lacking, and civic education was ignored by all but the few schools where high party members sent their children. Especially after the creation of the party of the new type in the summer of 1948, the schools were instructed to engage in some forms of Stalinist pedagogy, including practices of criticism and self-criticism. Newspapers that praised activists and denounced enemies were to be put up on the walls, providing a common link "between students and teachers, the school and its environment."[202] The activists' movement was supposed to be brought into the schools, as was the Two-Year Plan. The SED also wanted the schools to promulgate its new "national" program by honoring "the people's special holidays and celebrations" in the classroom, in excursions, and in special assemblies.[203] But the tough realities of the school system overwhelmed most of these plans, leaving the major task of converting German schools and schoolchildren to later generations of GDR leaders.

Conquering the Intelligentsia

From the beginning of the occupation, the Soviets and the German communists supported a "star system" for the zone. Prominent writers, artists, and cultural figures were feted and praised, helped financially, and turned into public celebrities as advertisements for the advantages of the "anti-fascist democratic" system in the East. As noted earlier, the Soviets were interested from the start in Thomas Mann, and as early as June 1945 they queried German communists as to whether he might be enticed into coming to the zone. Alexander Dymshits and Johannes R. Becher sought out Gerhard Hauptmann at his home in Silesia, hoping to convince the sick and elderly writer to come to Berlin, but Hauptmann died before he could be moved.[204]

The Soviets also hoped to attract Thomas Mann's brother, Heinrich, to the zone. Heinrich Mann lived in New York and later in Los Angeles under very difficult circumstances. His health was bad, and his financial condition, except for periodic contributions from his brother, was terrible. The case of Heinrich Mann was of such significance to the SED that Pieck informed the Central Committee in Moscow of his desire to attract the writer to Berlin by sending him "honorarium" payments.[205] Pieck and the Soviets apparently worked out a plan for Mann to come to Berlin through Moscow. At the beginning of January 1949, the Central Secretariat of the SED approved the plans for Mann to come to Berlin and resolved to find him an appropriate job and apartment.[206] But in early 1950 Mann died in tragic poverty in Hollywood before the financial and travel arrangements could be completed.

Due in good measure to the persistence of Alexander Dymshits, the Soviets did somewhat better with the communist writers they encouraged to come to the zone, like Bertolt Brecht, who arrived from Hollywood in 1948, and Anna Seghers, who came from Mexico in 1947, although especially in Brecht's case, the transition to life in the Soviet zone was not without its problems.[207] But Dymshits was a resilient and resourceful patron. He had been a student of literature and poetry and had been in the process of writing his dissertation on the poetry of Mayakovsky when the war broke out. His fondness for German literature served him well in his dealings with German writers. He also had good relations with his superior, Colonel Tiul'panov, and this helped him pursue his interest in recruiting German writers to the Soviet cause in Germany. Long after he was removed from the zone, Dymshits wrote to Pieck: "For the four years that I was in Berlin, I learned to love the German people very much, and since that time a part of my heart belongs to Germany."[208] Some of Dymshits's charges made important contributions to the development of culture in the zone. Alexander Abusch, for example, was transported from Mexico through Vladivostok by special rail car to Moscow, before coming to the zone as editor of the important literary journal *Aufbau*. Other leftist writers, like Theodore Plievier, lived on their laurels (and royalities) and accomplished little of substance in the zone. Hans Fallada, the author of the famous "progressive" novel *Kleiner Mann—was nun?* (Little Man, What Now?) was described by Dymshits as a useless drug addict *(morfinist)*, and he lived in miserable conditions in Thüringen.[209]

Given the frequent problems with the star system, it would be hard to judge it a success. Despite their almost complete control over cultural institutions, the Soviets and the SED were unable to win over the intelligentsia as a sympathetic social pillar of the new order. No doubt part of the problem was the fact that many artists and writers lived "a life of misery" *(Elendsleben)*, as one SED report acknowledged, with only occasional help from SVAG and virtually none at all from the SED.[210] Only those writers and artists who worked directly with large cultural institutions had access to extra rations and artistic materials. The constant emphasis in SED propaganda on its worker and farmer constituency also hurt the party's work among the intelligentsia, especially when this was combined with concrete measures, like preferential acceptance of workers' and farmers' children in the universities. Emmi Damerius—a leading SED women's functionary—complained that the party had a "sectarian" attitude toward intellectuals. "Our disgusting arrogance," she added, "makes the intellectuals skeptical toward us."[211] Issues of freedom of the press and speech also struck close to home for intellectuals in eastern Germany. Especially in 1948 and 1949, the reverberations of the cold war and the Berlin blockade could be felt in the form of increasing arrests, suspicion, and intolerance of anti-Soviet or pro-Western opinions.

By the beginning of 1949, it became clear to the Soviets and the SED that they had not made much of an impact on the intelligentsia as a social group. The Two-Year Plan depended on the initiative and cooperation of the technical intelligentsia. Artists, musicians, and playwrights needed to be recruited to the cause of transformation. The SED had to have prominent intellectuals on its side to bolster its growing national claims. The result was a concerted effort on the part of the Soviet occupation authorities and the SED to—paraphrasing Paul Wandel—speak to the material and existential needs of the intelligentsia.[212] The SED drafted a special proposal on the intelligentsia, which, according to Alexander Abusch, the Kulturbund discussed with Semenov in Karlshorst before it was adopted.[213] The SED issued instructions to all its local and provincial organizations "to assume a new and positive" attitude toward the intelligentsia.[214] Similarly, as part of the campaign to realize a number of measures proposed by the German Economic Commission, orders went out to the factory councils to do something about the "extraordinarily bad" relations between the councils and the engineers and scientists on whom improved production depended.[215]

In a speech given in January 1949, Grotewohl suggested that a package of measures to win over the intelligentsia be adopted, including: increased pay and special payoks; higher rations and access to special sanitoriums and rest homes; a building program to provide housing for the intelligentsia; special tax breaks, prizes, and premiums; fellowships for buying books and for traveling to the USSR and the people's democracies; and special help for expanding the Leipzig and Jena universities, as well as the *Kunsthochschulen* (higher schools for the arts).[216] The party also resolved to help the children of the intelligentsia attend the universities, especially the sons and daughters of those members of the intelligentsia "who have concerned themselves with the democratic rebuilding." This category of applicant was to rank right alongside applicants from workers' and farmers' families.[217]

Although supported by the Soviet military government in general and by Major General Tiul'panov and his Information Administration in particular, the combined program to recruit the German intelligentsia to the SED's banner caused as many problems as it solved. Stefan Heymann, the senior SED functionary responsible for implementing the program, claimed that although the new measures helped attract "a stream of intellectuals" from the West, a number of intellectuals were also reported to have left the Soviet zone because of the heightened political tensions of the period.[218] In a June 1949 meeting with the editors-in-chief of the leading newspapers in the zone, Anton Ackermann claimed that the progressive and democratic intelligentsia was pleased by these positive measures, while a small group of "embittered enemies" of the democratic order in the East was unrepentant. But the real target of the program was the large number of intellectuals who had not chosen sides, and they had still not been won over. They remained, according to Ackermann, "in a posture of waiting, of an undecided wavering here and there between yesterday and tomorrow."[219]

The wait-and-see attitude of the intelligentsia partly had to do with the fact that the program itself was haphazardly and unevenly administered. Some artists and intellectuals were showered with extra payoks and privileges, while the vast majority continued to live in poverty. It was one thing to order the construction of apartments for members of the intelligentsia, but it was quite another, especially in 1949, to find the funds in the provincial and state budgets (not to mention the materials and machinery) to undertake major building projects. Virtually all of those parts of Grotewohl's program that required substantial funding fell far short of their goals. In addition, the SED was unhappy both with the choices for the National Prize winners and with the way that they were ignored by the general public and the intelligentsia.[220]

The Soviets were very anxious for the program for the intelligentsia to succeed; after all, from the awarding of National Prizes and special premiums to the use of summer resorts, the program was based on Soviet models. It was also an extremely important thrust of Soviet policy in this period to develop a "national movement." However, it was not at all clear that the German authorities had the wherewithal to direct and finance a program of such magnitude. Soviet inquiries about the fate of their measures turned up dumbfounded answers on the part of local governments, which received little or no guidance (not to mention funding) on how to improve the life of the intelligentsia.[221] Local and provincial SED organizations, reflecting the views of their members, also abstained from leading the way. The problem was that workers in the SED were almost unanimously opposed to the measures, in this case sharing the hostile attitudes of the vast majority of non-party workers toward the intelligentsia. Typical was the remark of an SED typesetter from Saxony by the name of Schubert: "They always said to us workers that we have to produce first before we could receive more to eat. The intelligentsia can eat to its fill before they [even] think about work."[222] Perhaps the most perceptive of the many negative comments from SED workers about the program came from a woman who was originally from East Prussia. She said that the special measures meant only more rewards for the growing *"Bonzokratie"* (oligarchy of bosses) that was living off the labor of the working masses.[223]

The program to convert the intelligentsia was hardly a great success. Workers, even SED workers, remained hostile and suspicious of advantages for "the bosses." In part it was this hostility that broke out in strikes and riots during the June 1953 uprising in East Berlin and throughout the zone. Moreover, despite their new privileges, the members of the intelligentsia remained ambivalent about SED rule and Soviet norms. A new kind of civilization was created in the Eastern zone—a unique meshing of Soviet culture and German leftist traditions inherited from a half century of struggle against imperial, Weimar, and Nazi domination. But it was a civilization frayed at the edges and full of contradictions.

From the very beginning of the occupation, the Soviet Military Administration had placed a high priority on winning over the German intelligentsia. Soviet officers approached the task on a number of planes. One was to build and support organizations, like the Kulturbund and the Society for the Study of the Culture of the Soviet Union, which linked the interests of the intelligentsia to institutions sympathetic to the Soviet Union. Another was to capture the allegiance of future generations of German intellectuals by taking firm control of the universities, schools, and academies. Along with their German SED helpmates, the Soviets also took over the institutions that shaped culture and presented it to the public— the theaters, film studios, symphonies, and opera houses. Ultimately the Soviets controlled censorship and printing, museums, galleries, libraries— in other words, every possible outlet for intellectual production. Sometimes that control was imperfect, as in the case of the universities. Still, it was virtually impossible for an artist, writer, or intellectual to reach his or her intended audience without the active participation of the cultural agencies supervised by the Soviets. In the end, the powerful combination of the carrot, the stick, and the elixir of the SED's "antifascist" ideology created the East German intelligentsia, which has endured even beyond the collapse of the GDR.

Conclusion

THE SOVIETS DID NOT OCCUPY Germany with specific long-range
goals in mind. Instead they looked to accomplish a number of immediate
tasks that reflected the needs of a variety of Soviet institutions in Moscow
and in the Eastern zone. The Council of People's Commissars was desperately interested in restarting the Soviet economy with the aid of
German assets. Reparations were the means to this end, and they were
the constant subject of Allied negotiations in the postwar period. In this
regard, the Ministry of Foreign Affairs, represented in the zone by Vladimir Semenov, was a powerful influence for four-power consensus in the
Allied Control Council. So long as Germany was run successfully by Allied
agreement, the Soviets thought there was a chance that they could get
access to the coal of the Ruhr and the advanced industries of the German
heartland. After the war, Lavrenti Beria was put in charge of the Soviet
atomic bomb project, and his subalterns in the Commissariat (Ministry)
of Internal Affairs dedicated their energies to securing uranium from the
zone. They also "recruited" German nuclear scientists for Moscow's atom
bomb project, while Soviet military and military-industrial ministries put
a very high priority on the acquisition of German rocket and aviation
technology.

Documents from the Soviet Central Committee, Foreign Ministry, and
Military Administration archives indicate that from the onset of the occupation the Soviets thought of themselves as being in a struggle with the
Western Allies for the future of Germany. Increasingly the Soviets viewed
propaganda setbacks, like the SED's electoral defeat in Berlin or the bad
publicity about the deportation of scientists, as defeats for their policy and
victories for the West. Strikes in the Ruhr or revelations of impro-

prieties in Western denazification procedures were similarly viewed as victories for the Soviets. However, the logical alternative long-term goals of Soviet policy—the Sovietization of the Eastern zone, the creation of a unified Germany run by the Socialist Unity Party, or the establishment of a demilitarized, "neutral" Germany in the center of Europe—remained unreconciled during the period of the occupation. The policies of Sergei Tiul'panov and Walter Ulbricht militated toward the first alternative. The development of the SED-dominated German Interior Administration pointed in the direction of the second, as did Soviet dependence on German uranium. The last goal appeared less likely as the occupation continued, just as the first seemed increasingly likely. Under the right conditions, V. M. Molotov, Semenov, and the Ministry of Foreign Affairs might have been willing to push for an all-German settlement even as late as the eve of the creation of the German Democratic Republic. The apparatus of the Soviet Central Committee also demonstrated a great deal of interest in compromise with the West about the future government of Germany. But, for good reason, neither the Western Allies nor the West German political leadership was ready to take a chance on Soviet goodwill. No doubt most SED members and Soviet political figures would have preferred the creation of a communist-dominated Germany over the other alternatives. Yet there was little indication that either the SED or the Soviets were ready to make serious sacrifices toward that goal. By the end of the occupation period, SED rhetoric aside, there seemed little or no chance of uniting Germany behind the communist leadership.

The Soviet military government, like its counterparts in the Western zones, had to accomplish the somewhat contradictory tasks of destroying the remnants of Nazi administration and rebuilding the local and regional governments. The Germans also had to be fed, housed, and put back to work. Bridges had to be rebuilt and power stations restarted. While relying heavily on the German communists who had been in Moscow during the war, Soviet officers were ready and willing to use the talents of Germans of diverse backgrounds, including ex-Nazis. Gradually the Soviets turned over more and more of their administrative duties to the German communists in the KPD and SED.

In some cases, such as in the creation of an "antifascist" police force and paramilitary police units, the Soviets remained in firm control, in every sense a colonial power that used native formations to satisfy internal and external security concerns. But in the cases of economic administration, justice, and education, the Soviets tried to turn over as much authority to the Germans as they felt was possible. One reason to do so was the shortage of Soviet cadres available to run the military administration in the zone. But it was also the case that Ulbricht, Wilhelm Pieck, Otto Grotewohl, Anton Ackermann, and others demonstrated considerable skill in dealing with the Russians. In a fashion, they won the right to govern the zone through their loyalty, dedication, flexibility, and understanding of Soviet sensibilities. The corresponding loss, however, was great: the German communists lost any chance they might have had of exerting popular influence on the development of postwar Germany. They would always be seen as the tools of Moscow. This was especially the case given the German communists' inability to contain Soviet excesses, whether they be violent crimes against German women, removals of factories, the recruitment of forced labor for the uranium mines, or the arrests of young people. Communists—and social democrats—who urged solutions to German problems that diverged from Soviet policy needs were disciplined and branded as "enemies."

The politics of the Soviet occupation were much more complex and varied than they have typically been portrayed in the historiography. There was no overall plan for the political development of the zone, certainly nothing like JCS 1067, the American policy statement on how to conduct the occupation. Instead the Soviets operated on the basis of a number of fundamental principles, such as the responsibility of large landowners and big capitalists for Nazism and the need to carry out the "antifascist democratic transformation" in Germany. The definitions of "antifascist" and "democratic" took on more militantly communist tones over the four and a half years of Soviet rule in Germany. But even at the outset of the occupation, the terms had never conformed to Western parliamentary usages, as has been claimed in a recent book by Wilfried Loth.[1]

The Soviets also went to Germany with commonly shared historical experiences and social instincts that influenced the development of occupation policy as much if not more than articulated principles of ideology. Soviet officers bolshevized the zone not because there was a plan to do so, but because that was the only way they knew to organize society. They drew their models from the New Economic Plan, the First Five-Year Plan, and collectivization. The campaigns against "enemies of the people" and the purges of the 1930s shaped their mentality. Even previous Soviet occupations, like those of Eastern Poland and the Baltic region from 1939 through 1941, gave concrete forms to the Soviets' notions of how the Eastern zone should be organized. The formation of occupation policy was influenced as well by the disintegration of the Grand Alliance and the emergence of the cold war. Because the fate of Germany itself became a critical source of East-West tension, Soviets' actions in their zone of occupation were simultaneously the causes and the results of deteriorating Allied relations.

The Sovietization of culture in occupied Germany, like that of politics, economics, and society, needs to be examined in the context of the predispositions of Soviet officials, as well as in terms of their preconceived ideas about how to organize theater, film, or music. From the point of view of Soviet cultural officers, there were no legitimate alternatives to socialist realism in the realm of the arts. Every other form of artistic expression was bourgeois and decadent, doomed in the end to be overtaken by superior Soviet-style forms and ideas. By the beginning of 1949, tolerance for nonrealist artistic endeavors had faded, and the Soviets led a "Kulturkampf" against the work of "rootless cosmopolitans" and "lackeys of imperialism."

Soviet policies were also determined by events and trends in Germany itself. The communists' dismal prospects in the elections of the fall 1946 and the growing influence of the SPD had a great deal to do with the founding of the Unity Party, the SED. The internal weaknesses of the SED, especially its inability to respond to blatant anti-Soviet sentiments among the party's rank and file, led to purges in the party and the development of "the party of the new type." The real threat of the SPD and "SPD-ism" proved a powerful impetus to the demonization of Kurt Schumacher and his sympathizers in the East. The lingering strength in the KPD and SED of leftist ideals—in Soviet nomenclature, "sectarianism"—fostered the careers of SED bureaucrats like Ulbricht and Grotewohl, as against those who leaned toward more radical politics, like Franz Dahlem and Paul Merker.

Along with events on the ground, the Bolshevik predispositions of the Soviet occupation authorities and the great-power interests of the Soviet Union dictated Soviet policy in Germany. The chief of the Propaganda (Information) Administration of SVAG, Colonel Tiul'panov, craftily negotiated these sometimes conflicting determinants of policy in the zone. He exerted an important influence on the development of eastern Germany, though there can be little question that the thrust of his policies— the Sovietization of the zone—created powerful enemies as well as supporters in Moscow. There is still a great deal we do not know about Stalin's views on the problems of eastern Germany, but it is reasonably certain that he tolerated Tiul'panov's radical mission and deterred those in the Central Committee who would have had him removed. Tiul'panov was not alone in the zone in his ability to influence affairs in the zone. Though Semenov was hardly the gauleiter of Germany that he claimed to be, still he provided a constant source of Soviet "wisdom" for the German parties and translated four-power politics in the Allied Control Council for his Soviet and German comrades. General I. S. Kolesnichenko in Thüringen was another Soviet official whose personal intervention on a number of issues made a difference in the way Soviet policy was carried out in the zone. Though they were in vain, his protests against harsh Soviet anti-fraternization orders and the arrests of German young people by the NKVD reveal a great deal about the way Soviet policy could be challenged by its representatives in the zone.

The situation of the average Soviet officer and enlisted man in the occupation forces tells us much about the postwar social and cultural aspects of the Soviet citizen. The Soviet soldiers' attitudes and interests, and the way they confronted a different and more highly developed material culture in Germany, reveal a great deal about their mentality after having survived and won a conflict of cataclysmic proportions. Soviet soldiers suffered a rude shock when they found that the defeated and destroyed Germany was materially more advanced and had a far higher standard of living than the victorious Soviet Union. Home leaves were traumatic, as conditions in the towns and villages of Russia and Ukraine were indescribably appalling, even in the eyes of soldiers who had seen the worst ravages of war. The Nazis had wrought terrible destruction in their offensive against and occupation of the Soviet Union. With good reason, Soviet soldiers wondered why the Germans had ever attacked.

The inability of the Soviet military government to control the diverse Moscow-based groups in the zone seriously undermined long-term Soviet interests in Germany. By their own actions, the Soviet authorities created enemies out of potential friends. With their indiscriminate repression of young people, NKVD (later MVD) groups in the East evoked deep hostility among Germans of all political stripes. Even Soviet officers understood that the Germans were deeply alienated by "NKVD methods," which included brutal interrogations, denunciations by spies and informants, summary justice, and the maintenance of eleven special "isolation" camps for political internees. In addition the Soviets' determination to extract uranium from eastern Germany led to the drafting of German forced labor for the mines of the Erzgebirge, where the conditions of labor and living were horrendous. Industrial workers in the zone were fearful of being drafted to work in the mines, and they were angry that the SED and the Free German Federation of Unions could do nothing to stop the threat. The insensitive behavior of the Soviet reparations gangs and the deportations of German technical specialists to the Soviet Union also roused the German population in both the West and the East against the Soviet occupation.

Russian-German relations were negatively influenced, as well, by the inherent inability of Soviet officers to allow for diversity within the German Left. In their insistence on control and with their fetish for administration, the Soviets severely curtailed their possibilities for cooperation from sympathetic German intellectuals and technocrats in the political and spiritual rebuilding of the country. The Soviets crushed the independent initiatives of the Left (the so-called sectarians) and the Right (the "antifas").

Finally, for all its attention to detail in the structuring of German political life according to Soviet communist norms, the military government was tragically unable to control the rampages of some of its nearly half a million troops in the zone. The rapes and assaults committed against German civilians continued long into the occupation, and the wanton violence carried out by Soviet soldiers against German men and, especially, German women left a significant segment of the population in the East angry and embittered.

The behavior, actions, and attitudes of the masses of Soviet officers and soldiers in the zone influenced the Germans' response to the new forms of government and society. That influence was, to be sure, not as positive as Soviet and East German authors once asserted. At the same time, it was also not simply a product of plunder, rape, and exploitation, as some Western sources suggest. Consensual fraternization between Soviets and Germans was quite common, especially in the first years of the occupation. Indeed, given the Germans' brutal behavior in their occupation of Soviet territory, it is astonishing that Russian soldiers and German civilians got along as well as they did. Especially in the cultural field, the achievements of Russian officers earned the admiration of German elites and the envy of less effective American and British administrators.

The German Democratic Republic—as a state, as a "nation," and as a society—was created primarily out of the interaction of Russians and Germans in the Soviet occupied zone. Its successes, its failures, and its ultimate collapse derived from the initial institutions and habits of interaction established during the immediate postwar period. The effects of the Soviet occupation still reverberate throughout eastern Germany. Far from being an isolated episode in the flow of German history that can be dispensed with and forgotten now that unification has been accomplished, the history of the Soviet occupation is a key component in understanding the present and future of German society.

Sources
Notes
Index

Sources

The diplomatic and military intelligence files of the National Archives of the United States and of the British Public Records Office (when available) contain rich materials on the history of the Soviet zone of occupation. West German archives, such as the SPD Ostbüro collection of the Friedrich-Ebert-Stiftung in Bonn and the Berlin city archives, hold interesting and important documents. The rich and varied collections of the Hoover Institution in Stanford, California, and of the Harvard Interview Project, located in Cambridge, Massachusetts, provide particularly useful material on Soviet motivations and actions in the zone.

Between 1989 and 1994, former East German and Soviet archives also became available to researchers. The East German case is a relatively straightforward one. The Central Party Archives of the SED were opened for use in the spring of 1990. After they were turned over to the German federal government's Bundesarchiv in 1992, the collections—with rare exceptions—were made fully accessible to researchers. In particular, the Ulbricht, Pieck, and Grotewohl papers provide an unparalleled inside view of German politics and society in the Soviet zone. Access to ministry documents of the former German Democratic Republic, including the papers of their predecessors in the Soviet zone, is slightly more complicated, especially when military, security, and personnel issues are involved. Nevertheless, while there is a huge demand for reading room space in the archives of the German Ministry for State Security (the Staatssicherheit), it is possible to see the papers of the first German policy and security organizations in the zone. But these files have just been opened, and as of this writing, archival guides have not yet been developed.

Despite the passage of a state archive law in 1993, gaining access to the Russian archives for the postwar period is a much more haphazard and uneven undertaking. The archives of the Central Committee of the Soviet Communist Party for the pre-1952 period (the Russian Center for the Preservation and Study of Documents of Contemporary History, or RTsKhIDNI) have been open to researchers for several years, and a great deal of interesting and important work has been carried out there. Some documents relevant to the postwar period have also been found in the post-

1952 Central Committee archives, the Center for Storage of Contemporary Documentation. In RTsKhIDNI, I had full access to the archives of the various iterations of the International Department of the Central Committee (f. 17, op. 128), which was primarily responsible for politics in the zone. I was able to use the archival guides and to see almost all of the documents I requested. However, at other times and in other circumstances, researchers have been denied access to the collection either in part or in total. The same has been true for access to the files of the Department for Agitation and Propaganda (f. 17, op. 125).

The Foreign Policy Archive of the Russian Federation is much more restrictive than are the former party archives. There, I was not allowed to consult any archival guides at all. Material was brought to me as it was deemed appropriate to my topic. The Foreign Ministry's collection on Germany (f. 082) was very useful indeed. However, researchers still do not have access to cable traffic, nor can they explore the ways in which decisions were made by following promising trails with the help of archival aids to finding documents.

The most critical documents for analyzing the day-to-day activities of the Soviets in the zone are held in the archives of the Soviet Military Administration in Germany (SVAG), located in the State Archives of the Russian Federation (GARF). Fortunately, I was able to use these archives before they were officially closed by order of the Yeltsin government in the summer of 1992. However, as in the case of the Foreign Ministry archives, I was not allowed to see archival guides and had to rely on selections of relevant material made by archivists (and censors). The closing of the SVAG archives (and related materials in RTsKhIDNI) was the result of the Russians' nervousness about the final negotiations for the withdrawal of their troops from Germany. The Russians wanted to prevent possible German financial claims deriving from the occupation period. Although this issue is still not fully resolved, the withdrawal of the last of the Russian troops from Germany during the summer of 1994 means that researchers will soon gain access to the rich collections of SVAG. One also remains hopeful about access to the presidential, KGB, general staff, and ministry archives. Only recently, some selected Ministry of Internal Affairs materials have been made available at GARF. There is no shortage of interesting and important work that can and should be done on the Soviet occupation.

The Russian archives are in a state of transition. The gargantuan task of declassifying materials in sensitive collections has impeded the opening of critical archives from the postwar period. Although I was given the opportunity to read documents from some of these collections, unless the documents had been declassified, I was asked not to provide concrete references to their name or location. In these cases, I follow in the notes the Russian practice of simply citing "Russian Archives, Collection." It was also appropriate at times that I not use the names of Soviet officers allegedly involved in illegal activity, or the names of civilian victims of crimes.

Though based primarily on archival sources, this study owes a great deal to the general literature on the Soviet zone of occupation. In particular the *SBZ Handbuch*, edited by Hermann Weber and Martin Broszat, the joint product of Mannheim University's Section on the History and Politics of the GDR and Munich's Institute for

Contemporary History, provides a valuable overview of the institutions and political parties of postwar eastern Germany. For secondary literature on the Soviet zone of occupation, the reader should consult the bibliographical notes concluding the discrete essays in the *SBZ Handbuch,* as well as the notes at the end of this book.

ARCHIVAL SOURCES

The following abbreviations are used in the notes for the archives cited.

AVPRF—Arkhiv Vneshnoi Politiki Rossiiskii Federatsii (Foreign Policy Archives of the Russian Federation)
  fond (f.) 082—German Materials
  f. 48 "Z"—Internal History of Four-Power Occupation
BStU MfSZ—Bundesbeauftragte für die Unterlagen des Staatssicherheitsdienstes der ehemaligen Deutschen Demokratischen Republik ("Gauck Behörde"), Ministerium für Staatssicherheit Zentralarchiv (Central Archives of the Ministry for State Security)
FES—Friedrich-Ebert-Stiftung (Social Democratic Party archives)
  Nachlass (NL) Erich Gniffke
  NL Lübbe
  NL Hermann Brill
  SPD Ostbüro
GARF—Gosudarstvennyi Arkhiv Rossiiskoi Federatsii (State Archives of the Russian Federation)
  f. 5283—VOKS (Vsesoiuznoe Obshchestvo Kulturnoi Sviazei S Zagranitsei—All-Union Society for Cultural Ties with Foreign Countries)
  f. 7077—SVA (Soviet Military Administration) Brandenburg
  f. 7103—SVA Mecklenburg
  f. 7133—SVA Saxony-Anhalt
  f. 7184—SVA Thüringen
  f. 7212—SVA Saxony
  f. 7317—SVAG (Soviet Military Administration in Germany), General Correspondence
  f. 9401—Secretariat of the NKVD/MVD
HIA—Hoover Institution Archives
  Briegleb
  Margarete Gärtner
  GTUAO—Germany (German Territory under Allied Occupation)
  Kurt Grabe
  David Harris
  Howard P. Jones
  Daniel Lerner
  Louis P. Lochner
  Walter J. Muller

Robert D. Murphy
Boris Nicolaevsky
Boris Pash
William Philp
Ellen Gräfin Poninski
William Sander
Max Schnetzer
Elisabeth Selden
U.S. Department of State, Office of External Research
Volkov
HIP—Harvard Interview Project, Russian Research Center Archives
LAB—Landesarchiv Berlin (Berlin State Archive)
NL Otto Suhr
NL Gustav Klingelhöfer
NA—National Archives
Record Group (RG) 59—State Department, Decimal Files, 1945–1949 Control (Germany), 740.00119
RG 84—U.S. Political Advisor to Germany (POLAD)
RG 218—Joint Chiefs of Staff
RG 226—Office of Strategic Services (OSS)
RG 260—OMGUS Office of the Military Government
RG 319—War Department, G-2, Investigative Records Depository, Ft. Meade (XE, ZE)
PRO—Public Records Office (London)
FO—Foreign Office
RTsKhIDNI—Rossiiskii Tsentr Khraneniia i Izucheniia Dokumentov Noveishei Istorii (Russian Center for the Preservation and Study of Documents of Contemporary History)
f. 17—Central Committee
opis (op.) 117—Materialy k protokolam zasedanii Orgbiuro i Sekretariata TsK VKP(b) (1939-1948)
op. 118—Materialy k protokolam zasedanii Orgbiuro i Sektretariata TsK VKP(b) (1948–1950)
op. 121—Tekhsekretariat Orgbiuro TsK VKP(b)
op. 125—Upravlenie propagandy i agitatsii TsK VKP(b)
op. 128—Otdel mezhdunarodnoi informatsii Ts VKP(b) (1944–45); Otdel vneshnei politik TsK VKP(b) (1948–49); Vneshnepoliticheskaia komissiia TsK VKP(b) (1949–50)
op. 132—Otdel propagandy i agitatsii TsK VKP (b)-TsK KPSS (1948–1956)
op. 137—Vneshnepoliticheskaia komissiia TsK VKP(b) (1949–1952)
f. 77—Andrei Zhdanov
SAPMO-BA—Stiftung Archiv der Parteien und Massenorganisationen der DDR im Bundesarchiv (Foundation for the Archives of the GDR's Parties and Mass Organizations in the Bundesarchiv)

DSF—Gesellschaft für Deutsch-Sowjetische Freundschaft (German-Soviet Friendship Society)

ZPA—Zentral Parteiarchiv (Central Party Archive), especially Nachlass (NL) 36 (Wilhelm Pieck), NL 90 (Otto Grotewohl), and NL 182 (Ulbricht)

TsGALI—Tsentral'nyi gosudarstvennyi arkhiv literatura i iskusstva Rossii (Central State Archive of Literature and Art)

    f. 2843—Alexander Dymshits

The following abbreviations are used in the notes for U.S. government materials in the National Archives and the Hoover Institution Archives.

AGTS	Adjutant General Top Secret
CIC	Command Intelligence Center
ECIC	European Command Intelligence Center
FIS	Field Intelligence Summary
ICIS	Information Control Intelligence Summary
I&R	Intelligence and Research (State Department)
ISCS	Information Services Control Section
ISD	Information Services Division
MID	Military Intelligence District
ODDI	Office of the Deputy Director of Intelligence
ODI	Office of the Director of Intelligence
OIR	Office of Intelligence Research
TSGC	Top Secret General Correspondence

INTERVIEWS

M. I. Burtsev, tape, Moscow, Summer 1992 (Courtesy of Daniel Wolf, Barraclough/ Carey Productions)

Il'ia Fradkin, Moscow, Summer 1989

I. N. Golovin, Stanford University, October 1992

S. I. Kondrashev, tape, Moscow, Summer 1992 (Courtesy of Daniel Wolf, Barra-clough/Carey Productions)

Max Rokhlin, Moscow, Summer 1989

Ia. S. Drabkin, Moscow, Summer 1989

NEWSPAPERS

Abendblatt für Mitteldeutschland (Weimar), 1945–1947

Amtliche Mitteilungsblatt (Magdeburg), 1946

Der Demokrat (Mecklenburg), 1945–1949

Deutsche Volkszeitung, 1946–1947

Izvestiia, 1945–1949

Krasnaia armiia (First Belorussian Front), 1945–1949
Krasnaia zvezda, 1945–1949
Krokodil, 1945–1949
Nacht-Express, 1945–1947
Neue Berliner Illustrierte, 1945–1948
Neues Deutschland, 1945–1949
Sovetskoe slovo, 1945–1949
Tägliche Rundschau, 1945–1949
Za chest' rodiny (First Ukrainian Front), 1945–1949
Zeit im Bild, 1945–1947

Notes

INTRODUCTION

1. See Rolf Badstübner, et al., eds., *Die antifaschistisch-demokratische Umwälzung, der Kampf gegen die Spaltung Deutschlands und die Entstehung der DDR von 1945–1949: Deutsche Geschichte,* vol. 9 (Berlin, GDR: VEB Deutscher Verlag der Wissenschaften, 1989).

2. For an example of post-1991 work, see A. M. Filitov, *Germanskii vopros: ot raskola k ob"edineniiu* (Moscow: Mezhdunarodnye otnosheniia, 1993).

3. See the provocative reflections on this subject by Elisabeth Domansky in " 'Kristallnacht,' The Holocaust and German Unity: The Meaning of November 9 as an Anniversary in Germany," *History and Memory,* vol. 4, no. 1 (Spring/Summer 1992): 60–91, and "Die gespaltene Erinnerung," in Manuel Kötten, ed. *Kunst und Literatur nach Auschwitz* (Berlin: Erich Schmidt Verlag, 1993), pp. 178–196.

4. Wolfgang Leonhard, *Child of the Revolution* (Chicago: H. Regnery Co., 1958). Erich Gniffke's *Jahre mit Ulbricht* (Cologne: Verlag Wissenschaft und Politik, 1966), has also had an important influence on the historiography of the Soviet zone.

5. See especially the work of Peter Christian Ludz. Several of his works have been published in English, including *The Changing Party Elite in East Germany* (Cambridge, Mass.: MIT Press, 1972), and *The German Democratic Republic from the Sixties to the Seventies* (Cambridge, Mass.: Center for International Affairs, Harvard University, 1970).

6. Two Mannheim University scholars, Hermann Weber and Dietrich Staritz, produced some of the best of this work. Among their extensive writings, see Hermann Weber, *Geschichte der DDR* (Munich: Deutscher Taschenbuch Verlag, 1985), and Dietrich Staritz, *Die Gründung der DDR: Von der sowjetischen Besatzungsherrschaft zum sozialistischen Staat* (Munich: Deutscher Taschenbuch Verlag, 1984). See also the recent work of Sigrid Meuschel, *Legitimation und Parteiherrschaft in der DDR* (Frankfurt am Main: Suhrkampf, 1992).

7. See Henry Krisch, *German Politics under Soviet Occupation* (New York: Columbia University Press, 1974), and Gregory W. Sandford, *From Hitler to Ulbricht: The Communist Reconstruction of East Germany, 1945–46* (Princeton, N.J.: Princeton

University Press, 1983). For a recent English-language study based on East German archival sources, see David Pike, *The Politics of Culture in Soviet-Occupied Germany* (Stanford, Calif.: Stanford University Press, 1992).

8. Martin Broszat and Hermann Weber, eds., *SBZ Handbuch,* (Munich: R. Oldenbourg Verlag, 1990). See especially Jan Foitzik's contribution, "Sowjetische Militäradministration in Deutschland (SMAD)," pp. 9–69.

9. Helke Sander and Barbara Johr, eds., *Befreier und Befreite* (Munich: Kunstmann, 1992). Atina Grossmann examines the fascinating reception of the Sander and Johr book (and film), especially by German feminists, in "A Question of Silence: The Rape of German Women by Occupation Soldiers," *October* (April 1995), pp. 43–63.

10. One of the few West Germans to have written about the subject over the years is Karl Wilhelm Fricke. See his recent contribution, " 'Kampf dem Klassenfeind': Politische Verfolgung in der SBZ," in Alexander Fischer, ed., *Studien zur Geschichte der SBZ/DDR* (Berlin: Duncker & Humblot, 1993), pp. 195–211.

11. Some of this new research is contained in Jürgen Kocka, ed., *Historische DDR-Forschung: Aufsätze und Studien* (Berlin: Akademie Verlag, 1993); Alexander Fischer, ed., *Studien zur Geschichte der SBZ/DDR* (Berlin: Duncker & Humblot, 1993); and Klaus Schönhoven and Dietrich Staritz, eds., *Sozialismus und Kommunismus im Wandel: Hermann Weber zur 65. Geburtstag* (Cologne: Bund Verlag, 1993). See also Jan Foitzik, "Die Sowjetische Militäradministration in Deutschland," *Das Parlament: Aus Politik und Zeitgeschichte,* B 11/90 (March 9, 1990): 43–62, and his chapter on the Soviet Military Administration in Broszat and Weber, eds., *SBZ Handbuch;* Peter Strunk, "Die Sowjetische Militäradministration in Deutschland (SMAD) und ihr politischer Kontrollapparat," *Historische und Landeskundliche Ostmitteleuropa Studien,* no. 7 (Marburg an der Lahn: Johann-Gottfried-Herder Institut, 1991), pp. 143–176, and his doctoral dissertation, "Pressekontrolle und Propagandapolitik der Sowjetischen Militäradministration in Deutschland (SMAD)," Free University of Berlin, 1989; Stefan Creuzberger, "Innere Organisation und äussere Beziehungen der SMAD: Ein Beitrag zur Geschichte der sowjetischen Besatzungspolitik in Deutschland, 1945–1949," master's thesis, Bonn, n.d., and "Die Sowjetische Militäradministration in Deutschland (SMAD), 1945–1949," *Deutschland Report,* no. 15, Konrad Adenauer Stiftung, 1991; and Jochen Laufer, "Konfrontation oder Kooperation? Zur sowjetischen Politik in Deutschland und im Alliierten Kontrollräte 1945–1948," *Studien zur Geschichte der SBZ/DDR,* pp. 57–80, and "The Soviet Union and the Zonal Division of Germany," unpublished manuscript, 1994.

12. For the views of those once in power, see Dietmar Keller, Hans Modrow, and Herbert Wolf, eds., *Ansichten zur Geschichte der DDR,* vol. 1 (Bonn and Berlin: PDS/Linke Fraktion, 1993). For the views of former GDR historians who felt persecuted by the system, see, for example, the work of Armin Mitter and Stefan Wolle, especially *Untergang auf Raten* (Munich: C. Bertelsmann, 1993).

13. On the interesting if sometimes problematic use of interviews, see Alexander von Plato and Lutz Niethammer, *Die Volkseigene Erfahrung* (Berlin: Rowohlt, 1991),

and Alexander von Plato, *Alte Heimat, Neue Zeit* (Berlin: Verlag-Anstalt Union, 1991).

14. Together with Bernd Bonwetsch and Gennadii Bordiugov, I have just edited and published a volume in Russian containing some of this documentation. See *SVAG—Upravlenie propagandy (informatsii) i S. I. Tiul'panov, 1945–1949: Sbornik dokumentov* (Moscow: "Rossiia Molodaia," 1994).

15. See Josef Foschepoth, *Die Britische Deutschland- und Besatzungspolitik 1945–1949* (Paderborn: F. Schöningh, 1985); John Gimbel, *The American Occupation of Germany* (Stanford, Calif.: Stanford University Press, 1968); and Frank Roy Willis, *The French in Germany, 1945–1949* (Stanford, Calif.: Stanford University Press, 1962). For a general evaluation of the occupations, see Christoph Klessmann, *Die doppelte Staatsgründung: Deutsche Geschichte 1945–1955*, 5th ed. (Bonn: Bundeszentrale für politische Bildung, 1991), pp. 66–120.

16. Alexander Dallin, *German Rule in Russia* (London: Macmillan, 1957).

17. See, for example, Omer Bartov, *Hitler's Army: Soldiers, Nazis, and War in the Third Reich* (New York: Oxford University Press, 1992), pp. 72–105; and Christian Streit, "Partisans—Resistance—Prisoners of War," in Norman Naimark, Alexander Dallin, et al., eds., *Operation Barbarossa: The German Attack on the Soviet Union, June 22, 1941*, special issue of *Soviet Union: Union Sovietique*, vol. 18, nos. 1–3 (1991): 259–276.

1. FROM SOVIET TO GERMAN ADMINISTRATION

1. Vojtech Mastny, *Russia's Road to the Cold War: Diplomacy, Warfare, and the Politics of Communism, 1941–1945* (New York: Columbia University Press, 1979), p. 261.

2. See Wilfried Loth, *Stalin's ungeliebtes Kind: Warum Moskau die DDR nicht wollte* (Berlin: Rowohlt, 1994), pp. 13–20; Alexander Fischer, *Sowjetische Deutschlandpolitik im Zweiten Weltkrieg 1941–1945* (Stuttgart: Deutsche Verlags-Anstalt, 1975), pp. 120–122.

3. See Charles Gati, *Hungary and the Soviet Bloc* (Durham, N.C.: Duke University Press, 1986), pp. 14–15.

4. Horst Laschitza, *Kämpferische Demokratie gegen Faschismus: Die programmatische Vorbereitung auf die antifaschistisch-demokratische Umwälzung in Deutschland durch die Parteiführung der KPD* (Berlin: Deutscher Militärverlag, 1969), pp. 193–209.

5. *Na boevom postu: Kniga o voinakh Gruppy sovetskikh voisk v Germanii* (Moscow: Voennoe Izdatel'stvo, 1975), pp. 10, 59; *Osvoboditel'naia missiia sovetskikh vooruzhennykh sil v evrope vo vtoroi mirovoi voine: Dokumenty i materialy* (Moscow: Voennoe Izdatel'stvo, 1985), pp. 512–517.

6. John Erickson, *The Road to Berlin* (Boulder, Colo.: Westview, 1983), p. 622.

7. Semenov to Vyshinskii, April 30, 1945, AVPRF, f. 082, op. 30, d. 63 (papka 134), ll. 57–61.

8. See his interview with Alexander Werth in the First Belorussian Front newspaper, *Krasnaia armiia*, June 10, 1945.

9. Ackermann to Konrad Wolf and Wolfgang Kohlhaase, April 27, 1967, SAPMO-BA, NL 109/63 (Ackermann), bb. 38–39.

10. Ackermann report, May 11, 1945, RTsKhIDNI, f. 17, op. 128, d. 40, l. 80. Neither Ackermann nor Wolf mentioned the fact that the young Konrad Wolf soon fell out of favor with the Soviets in the zone, was criticized for doing "more harm than good," and was urged to return to German civilian life. Russian Archives, Collection.

11. Report of Lt. Col. Dubrovitskii, First Ukrainian Front, April 23, 1945, AVPRF, f. 1457a, op. 1, d. 13, l. 109.

12. "Za obrazovuiu komendantskuiu sluzhbu v prifrontovykh gorodakh," *Za chest' rodiny*, March 10, 1945.

13. "Informatsiia o soveshchanii komendantov 18 maia sego goda (gorod Shtettine)," AVPRF, op. 27, d. 10 (papka 121), ll. 19–20.

14. OSS, Field Intelligence Study 17, "Recent Information from the Russian Zone of Occupation," August 8, 1945, pp. 7–8, NA, RG 226, entry 16, box 1627.

15. HQ Berlin Command, "Special Intelligence Memorandum 177," May 2, 1947, p. 2, NA, RG 260, box 24.

16. *Intelligence Review*, no. 85, October 2, 1947, pp. 29–30, NA, RG 260, box 24; Z. B. Sholkovich, "Dokumenty o deiatel'nosti sovetskikh voennykh komendatur v Vostochnoi Germanii" (1945–1949 gg.), *Sovetskie arkhivy*, no. 4 (1978): 73–79.

17. K. Gofman to Dimitrov, "Dokladnaia zapiska," August 15, 1945, RTsKhIDNI, f. 17, op. 128, d. 791, ll. 211–214.

18. See *Rote Fahne* (Coswig), May 8, 1945, b. 37; June 21, 1945, report to Ulbricht, b. 31; June 30, 1945, report from Zeesen to Sägebrecht, in SAPMO-BA, ZPA, NL 182/853. See also SAPMO-BA, ZPA, EA 1845/2 (Rudolf Bühring), p. 381.

19. Ulbricht to Zhukov (draft), May 31, 1945, SAPMO-BA, ZPA, NL 182/246 V (Ulbricht), b. 22. For the commandants' use of ex-Nazis, see also Report from Schwarzenberg, August 13, 1945, SAPMO-BA, ZPA, NL 182/855 (Ulbricht), b. 53.

20. Biuro Informatsii SVAG, *Biulleten'*, no. 4 (February 4, 1948), RTsKhIDNI, f. 17, op. 128, d. 577, l. 70.

21. "Prikaz no. 15," August 19, 1945, GARF, f. 7077, op. 2, d. 1, l. 29.

22. Gniffke to Grotewohl, October 31, 1945, SAPMO-BA, ZPA, NL 90/281.

23. RTsKhIDNI, f. 17, op. 128, d. 1094, ll. 218–219.

24. Altuchow, "Zum politisch-ideologischen Kampf der SED und der KPdSU(B)/SMAD um die Herausbildung eines neuen, freundschaftlichen Verhältnisses zwischen dem deutschen und dem sowjetischen Volk (April 1946/November 1947)," Dissertation A, Parteihochschule "Karl Marx" beim ZK der SED (Berlin, 1985), pp. 29–30.

25. RTsKhIDNI, f. 17, op. 128, d. 682, l. 22.

26. I. Kolesnichenko, "Ukrepliat' mestnye nemetskie organy samoupravleniia," *Sovetskoe slovo*, May 15, 1949.

27. Council of Foreign Ministers, Moscow, March–April 1947, "Armed Forces on Foreign Soil in Europe," HIA, Murphy, box 61–6; European Command, "Weekly Intelligence Report," August 5, 1949, p. 5, NA, RG 260, box 82; U.S. War Department, *Intelligence Review*, no. 24, September 25, 1947, NA, RG 260, box 24.

28. On discipline and political education, see *Sovetskoe slovo*, May 23, 1947; June 11, 1947; October 29, 1947; April 18, 1948. See also the front newspapers: *Za chest' rodiny*, October 20, November 27, and December 13, 1945; *Krasnaia armiia*, September 13, 1945; April 2, 1946; and April 5, 1946. On the importance of the external appearance of the soldiers, see *Krasnaia armiia*, May 13, June 1, and June 7, 1945; and January 4, 1946; and *Za chest' rodiny*, January 4, 1947. For extremely negative views of Soviet troops in the zone, see the émigré newspapers *Sotsialisticheskii vestnik, Nezavisimyi golos'*, and *Za svobodu Rossii*. For the views of deserters, see "Materials for the Project on the Soviet Social System" (Soviet Refugee Interview and Questionnaire Data 1950–1953, HIP, Air Force Contract No. 33 [038]-12909). For conditions in the Soviet occupation army, see, for example, HIP, no. 342, no. 346, no. 446, no. 527. See also HIA, State Department Interview Reports, box 1: no. 14 (August 1955), no. 11 (May 1955), no. 10 (1955).

29. SAPMO-BA, ZPA, EA 1843 (G. I. Patent), b. 3.

30. SAPMO-BA, ZPA, EA 1291/4 (Ackermann), bb. 652–653. See also Bodo Scheurig, *Free Germany: The National Committee and the League of Officers* (Middletown, Conn.: Wesleyan University Press, 1969), pp. 52–53.

31. Dimitrov and Paniushkin to Molotov and Malenkov, March 1945, RTsKhIDNI, f. 17, op. 128, d. 723, l. 23.

32. M. Burtsev, "Spravka o politicheskoi rabote sredi naseleniia Germanii," July 1945, RTsKhIDNI, f. 17, op. 128, d. 791, l. 110.

33. Ibid., l. 109.

34. Altuchow, "Zum politisch-ideologischen Kampf," pp. 115, 118.

35. Burtsev, "Spravka o politicheskoi rabote . . . ," July 1945, RTsKhIDNI, f. 17, op. 128, d. 791, l. 107.

36. Ibid., l. 108.

37. The Central Committee's Department on International Information, headed by Dimitrov, grew out of the earlier Comintern apparat and functioned from July 1944 until the end of December 1945, when it was replaced by the Department of Foreign Policy, which existed until 1948. According to a July 10, 1948, resolution of the Politburo, it was renamed the Department of Foreign Relations, which lasted until April 29, 1949. Then its functions were taken over by the Foreign Policy Commission of the Central Committee.

38. SVAG's Military Council, created by the State Defense Committee on June 28, 1945, served as the "collective leadership" of SVAG and the Group of Soviet Occupation Forces. See S. I. Viskov and V. D. Kul'bakin, *Soiuzniki i 'germanskii vopros' 1945–1949* (Moscow: "Nauka," 1990), p. 96, fn. 105. See also Martin Broszat and Hermann Weber, eds., *SBZ Handbuch*, (Munich: R. Oldenbourg Verlag, 1990), p. 19.

39. A. Smirnov (head of 3rd European Section of the Commissariat for Foreign Affairs) to A. Vyshinskii (deputy foreign minister), September 26, 1945, AVPRF, f. 082, op. 27, d. 3 (papka 120), l. 42.

40. "Sovet narodnykh komissarov SSSR: Postanovlenie no. 1326-301 cc," June 6, 1945, AVPRF, f. 082, op. 27, d. 3, l. 10.

41. *Za antifashistskuiu demokraticheskuiu Germaniiu: Sbornik dokumentov 1945–1949 gg.* (Moscow: Politizdat, 1969), p. 67.

42. "Polozhenie o sovetskoi voennoi administratsii po upravleniiu sovetskoi zonoi okkupatsii v Germanii," AVPRF, f. 082, op. 27, d. 3 (papka 120), l. 15.

43. HQ SHAEF, "Special Intelligence Summary," no. 42, November 1, 1948, NA, RG 260, AGTS, box 646, p. A7.

44. HQ Berlin Command, Special Intelligence Report, "Organization of the Soviet Military Government for Germany," September 27, 1947, NA, RG 84, TSGC, box 3.

45. Zhukov, "O neobkhodimosti podgotovki k organizatsii Tsentral'nykh German-skikh Admin. Departmentov," December 21, 1945, AVPRF, f. 082, op. 30, d. 64 (papka 134), l. 2.

46. OMGUS, "Government and Its Administration in the Soviet Zone of Germany," November 1947, NA, RG 59, box 3724, p. 3.

47. AVPRF, f. 082, op. 27, d. 3 (papka 120), l. 11.

48. K. I. Koval, "Na postu zamestitelia Glavnonachal'stvuiushchego SVAG, 1945–1949 gg.," *Novaia i noveishaia istoriia,* no. 3 (1987): 134; V. I. Rudol'f-Krasov, "Sovetskaia Voennaia Administratsiia v Germanii (SVAG)," HIA, Nicolaevsky, Series 193, no. 249–53, p. 2.

49. "Polozhenie o sovetskoi voennoi administratsii . . . ," AVPRF, f. 082, op. 27, d. 3 (papka 120), l. 14.

50. V. Semenov, "Rabota sektora propaganda i tsenzury," July 15–October 15, 1945, RTsKhIDNI, f. 17, op. 125, d. 321, ll. 156–161.

51. Zhukov letter, November 25, 1945, RTsKhIDNI, f. 17, op. 121, d. 391, l. 1.

52. "Prikaz," April 5, 1946, GARF, f. 7184, op. 2, d. 4, l. 7.

53. The Office of the Political Advisor had only sixteen employees at this point, the Political Department only forty-five. RTsKhIDNI, f. 17, op. 128, d. 54, l. 101–102; Russian Archives, Collection.

54. Mironov and Katiushin (Cadres Department) to Kuznetsov, April 4, 1947, and Mironov to Kuznetsov, August 13, 1948, RTsKhIDNI, f. 17, op. 117, d. 758, l. 163; Russian Archives, Collection.

55. See the accusations against Zhukov and his response to the Central Committee in "Kak 'lomali' Marshala G. K. Zhukova," *Voenno-istoricheskii zhurnal,* no. 12 (1992): 84–87.

56. Sokolovskii and Russov to Malenkov, September 2, 1948, RTsKhIDNI, f. 17, op. 121, d. 363, l. 2; Russian Archives, Collection.

57. RTsKhIDNI, f. 17, op. 128, d. 682, l. 2.

58. See Jan T. Gross, *Revolution from Abroad: The Soviet Conquest of Poland's Western*

Ukraine and Western Belorussia (Princeton, N.J.: Princeton University Press, 1988), pp. 125–126, 231–239.

59. *50 let vooruzhennykh sil SSSR* (Moscow: Voenizdat, 1968), p. 477. See also Vladimir Rudolph, "The Agencies of Control," in Robert Slusser, ed., *Soviet Economic Policy in Postwar Germany* (New York: Research Program on the USSR, 1953), p. 30.

60. GARF, f. 7077, op. 1, d. 196, l. 75.

61. F. E. Bokov, *Vesna Pobedy* (Moscow: Voenizdat, 1979), p. 427; Rudolph, "The Agencies of Control," in Slusser, ed., *Soviet Economic Policy,* p. 22, 31; E. Berg, "Dva goda v okkupirovannoi Germanii," *Pamiat': istoricheskii sbornik,* vyp. 5 (Moscow and Paris, 1981–82), pp. 7, 28; Frank Moraw, *Die Parole der "Einheit" und die deutsche Sozialdemokratie* (Bonn: Verlag Neue Gesellschaft, 1973), p. 204.

62. Wolfgang Leonhard, *Child of the Revolution* (Chicago: H. Regnery Co., 1958), p. 436.

63. N. I. Shishkov, "Sovetskaia voennaia administratsiia i pomoshch' SSSR narodam tsentral'noi i iugo-vostochnoi evropy v 1944–45 godakh," *Voprosy istorii,* no. 2 (1979): 19.

64. GARF, f. 7077, op. 1, d. 196, l. 8.

65. Makarov to Kuznetsov, October 14, 1947, RTsKhIDNI, f. 17, op. 128, d. 358, l. 81.

66. Tiul'panov to Zhukov and Bokov, n.d., AVPRF, f. 0457b, op. 1, d. 9, l. 20.

67. "Sbornik materialov po istorii otdel narodnogo obrazovaniia," vol. 1, GARF, f. 7317, op. 54, d. 1, ll. 8–9.

68. Ibid., l. 8.

69. Ibid., l. 12; GARF, f. 7133, op. 1, d. 252, ll. 21–22.

70. "Sbornik materialov," vol. 2, GARF, f. 7317, op. 54, d. 2, ll. 58–59.

71. See the SVAG order of April 8, 1947, and the Mecklenburg SVA order of April 23, 1947, in GARF, f. 7103, op. 2, d. 4, l. 133.

72. "Sbornik Materialov," vol. 1, GARF, f. 7317, op. 54, d. 1, l. 16.

73. Ibid., ll. 15–16, 31.

74. Ol'shanskii manuscript, HIA, Nicolaevsky, Series no. 177, 231-1, folder 1, p. 38.

75. N. Zhukov and Katiushin to A. A. Kuznetsov, November 12, 1946, RTsKhIDNI, f. 17, op. 128, d. 54, ll. 101–103.

76. RTsKhIDNI, f. 17, op. 121, d. 694.

77. Russian Archives, Collection.

78. The Cadres Department was blamed for the fact that so many had to be sent home. Mironov and Katiushin to Kuznetsov, April 4, 1947, RTsKhIDNI, f. 17, op. 117, d. 758, l. 163.

79. RTsKhIDNI, f. 17, op. 121, d. 693, l. 105.

80. Russian Archives, Collection.

81. RTsKhIDNI, f. 17, op. 117, d. 758, l. 163.

82. Mironov and Katiushin to Kuznetsov, April 4, 1947, RTsKhIDNI, f. 17, op. 117, d. 758, l. 168.

83. RTsKhIDNI, f. 17, op. 128, d. 1140, l. 63.

84. See Chapter 6.

85. Russian Archives, Collection.

86. "The Soviet Union as Reported by Former Soviet Citizens," HIA, Interview Report no. 4, August 1, 1952, box 1, p. 10; Interview Report, no. 19, September 1957, box 1, p. 10.

87. RTsKhIDNI, f. 17, op. 128, d. 1094, l. 221.

88. RTsKhIDNI, f. 17, op. 128, d. 317, l. 37.

89. GARF, f. 7077, op. 1, d. 258, l. 16.

90. GARF, f. 7133, op. 2, d. 4, l. 206. It was rumored that the death in a motorcycle accident of the first commandant of Berlin, Gen. N. E. Berzarin, was caused by heavy drinking.

91. GARF, f. 7133, op. 2, d. 18, l. 68.

92. Gen. Sharov, Prikaz no. 71, November 21, 1945, GARF, f. 7077, op. 2, d. 1, l. 14.

93. Russian Archives, Collection.

94. Zhukov was accused of taking from Germany seven freight cars full of furniture, as well as diamonds, gold, and other precious metals. "Kak 'lomali' Marshala G. K. Zhukova," *Voenno-istoricheskii zhurnal,* no. 12 (1992): 84.

95. Sharov, Rescript of January 9, 1946, GARF, f. 7077, op. 1, d. 196, l. 7.

96. RTsKhIDNI, f. 17, op. 128, d. 572, l. 97.

97. Brandenburg, Prikaz no. 37, February 27, 1946, GARF, f. 7184, op. 2, d. 2, l. 84.

98. RTsKhIDNI, f. 17, op. 128, d. 1094, l. 219–221.

99. RTsKhIDNI, f. 17, op. 127, d. 1720, l. 114.

100. Russian Archives, Collection.

101. Mecklenburg, Prikaz no. 8, January 21, 1947, GARF, f. 7103, op. 2, d. 4, l. 15.

102. Russian Archives, Collection.

103. Russian Archives, Collection.

104. Political Department of SVA Saxony-Anhalt, January 20, 1949, GARF, f. 7133, op. 2, d. 18, l. 5.

105. HIA, State Department Interview Report no. 14, August 1955, box 1, p. 2; NA, RG 260, box 24, p. 6; "Dissension in the Soviet Army," September 10, 1947, NA, RG 84, TSGC, box 3; HQ 7707 European Command Intelligence Center, "Purposes and Developments of the Soviet Army Non-Fraternization Policy in Germany," July 22, 1949, NA, RG 59, 7–2249, POLAD.

106. Shikin to Morozov, February 5, 1949, GARF, f. 7133, op. 2, d. 18, l. 11; *Krasnaia armiia,* May 9 and 12, 1947.

107. Maj. Gen. Smirnov, Prikaz no. 165, July 19, 1947, GARF, f. 7184, op. 2, d. 8, ll. 61–62.

108. Gen. Kolesnichenko, Prikaz no. 254, December 12, 1947, in ibid., l. 306.

109. *Krasnaia armiia,* June 12, 1948.

110. Col. Morozov, SVA Saxony-Anhalt Political Department, March 31, 1949, GARF, f. 7133, op. 2, d. 18, l. 32.

111. Shikin to Morozov, SVA Saxony-Anhalt, February 5, 1949, GARF, f. 7133, op. 2, d. 18, l. 11.

112. GARF, f. 7317, op. 8, d. 7, l. 250.

113. GARF, f. 7133, op. 2, d. 18, l. 58.

114. *Sovetskoe slovo,* May 26, 1949.

115. Sokolovskii, Prikaz 294, October 4, 1946, GARF, f. 7317, op. 8, d. 7, l. 231.

116. Ibid; see also *Krasnaia armiia,* July 21, 1946.

117. GARF, f. 7133, op. 2, d. 18, ll. 54–55.

118. See *Sovetskoe slovo,* July 30, 1949.

119. *Krasnaia armiia,* May 16, May 29, and June 25, 1946, and December 28, 1948. The May 16 article praised the military doctor Shapiro for organizing a jazz band, but urged him to rely less on Western music for his repertoire.

120. Brandenburg, Prikaz no. 48, March 13, 1946, GARF, f. 7184, op. 2, d. 2, l. 98.

121. GARF, f. 7133, op. 1, d. 252, l. 103.

122. Lt. Col. Tikhonov, SVA Saxony-Anhalt, to Zolotukhin, September 15, 1947, GARF, f. 7133, op. 1, d. 252, ll. 92–95.

123. *Za chest' rodiny,* December 21, 1945; *Krasnaia armiia,* April 18, 1946, January 8 and January 15, 1947.

124. Russian Archives, Collection.

125. Russian Archives, Collection.

126. GARF, f. 7133, op. 1, d. 254, l. 165.

127. Ulbricht to Pieck (draft), May 17, 1945, SAPMO-BA, ZPA, NL 182/246, b. 5.

128. "Stenogramma soobshchenii t.t. Ackermana, Ul'brikhta i Sobotka o polozhenii v Germanii," June 7, 1945, RTsKhIDNI, f. 17, op. 128, d. 750, l. 177.

129. Ulbricht to Dimitrov, notes, May 17, 1945, SAPMO-BA, ZPA, NL 182/246, b. 12.

130. "Stenogramma," June 7, 1945, RTsKhIDNI, f. 17, op. 128, d. 750, l. 166.

131. SAPMO-BA, ZPA, NL 182/246, b. 14.

132. SAPMO-BA, ZPA, EA 1291/4 (Ackermann), b. 718. Emphasis in the original.

133. Korotkevich to Dimitrov, November 3, 1945, RTsKhIDNI, f. 17, op. 128, d. 787, l. 58.

134. Bruno Köhler to Dimitrov, November 16, 1945, in ibid., l. 66.

135. Suslov and Aleksandrov to Zhdanov, July 4, 1946, RTsKhIDNI, f. 17, op. 128, d. 846, ll. 93–94.

136. SED Report on Antifa students, October 28, 1947, SAPMO-BA, ZPA, IV 2/11/202 (Kaderfragen), p. 1. See also "Soiuz nemetskikh ofitserov: Nemetskie voennoplennye na sovetsko-germanskom fronte 1943–1945," *Istochnik: dokumenty russkoi istorii,* 1993/0, Prilozhenie k . . . zhurnalu *"Rodina,"* pp. 105–106.

137. Zaisser, "Bericht über die Antifa-Schule," February 8, 1947, in SAPMO-BA, ZPA, IV 2/11/202, p. 2; SAPMO-BA, ZPA, EA 1275/1 (Fomferra), b. 150.

138. Justice Administration to SED, April 13, 1948, SAPMO-BA, ZPA, IV 2/11/202 (Kaderfragen), p. 6.

139. SAPMO-BA, ZPA, EA1275/1 (Fomferra), b. 149.

140. Ibid., bb. 149–151.

141. Zhukov, "O neobkhodimosti podgotovki k organizatsii Tsentral'nykh Germanskikh Admin. Departmentov," AVPRF, f. 082, op. 30, d. 64 (papka 134), l. 2.

142. Smirnov to Molotov, June 19, 1947, AVPRF, f. 082, op. 34, d. 150, l. 2.

143. "Bericht O. Grotewohls anhand von 3 Resolutionen: Zwischenbemerkungen," SAPMO-BA, ZPA, NL 36/694 (Pieck), bb. 3–7.

144. OMGUS, "Government and Its Administration in the Soviet Zone of Germany," November 1947, NA, RG 59, box 3724, p. 5.

145. Smirnov to Molotov, "O nemetskikh administrativnykh organov sovetskoi zony okkupatsii Germanii," December 20, 1947, AVPRF, f. 082, op. 34, d. 150, l. 33.

146. "Sbornik materialov," vol. 1, GARF, f. 7317, op. 54, d. 1, ll. 52–53.

147. SAPMO-BA, ZPA, IV 2/2025/8 (Sekretariat Otto Meier), b. 78.

148. Zabashtanskii to Semenov, October 3, 1945, AVPRF, f. 0457b, op. 1, d. 7, l. 3.

149. "Spravka o soveshchanii prezidentov i vitse-prezidentov provintsii i federal'nykh zemel' i nachal'nikov tsentral'nykh nemetskikh upravlenii sovetskoi zony okkupatsii," in ibid., l. 5.

150. Ulbricht to Bokov (for Zhukov), October 28, 1945, AVPRF, f. 0457b, op. 1, d. 8, l. 1.

151. Dahlem and Gniffke, "Antrag an das Zentralsekretariat," September 30, 1947, SAPMO-BA, ZPA, IV 2/2022/121 (Sekretariat Paul Merker), b. 90.

152. Dahlem, "Verbesserungen in der Arbeit und im Aufbau der Personalpolitischen Abteilung des Zentralsekretariat," August 16, 1948, in ibid., b. 270.

153. SAPMO-BA, ZPA, NL 36/695 (Pieck), b. 51.

154. "Schulungstagung... (Land Sachsen), March 2–4, 1949," SAPMO-BA, ZPA, NL 277/4 (Zaisser), bb. 130–132.

155. Telegram, Murphy to Secretary of State, September 11, 1945, NA, RG 59, 740.00119 Control (Germany), 9-1145.

156. HQ Berlin Command, OMGUS, "Special Intelligence Memorandum" 338, September 29, 1947, p. 2, NA, RG 260, box 72.

157. SAPMO-BA, ZPA, NL 182/1084, b. 29.

158. Ibid., bb. 34–35.

159. This, to be sure, was Paul's version of Zhukov's summary statement. Thüringen President Paul to Presidents of the States and Provinces, November 30, 1945, SAPMO-BA, ZPA, NL 182/857 (Ulbricht), b. 46.

160. SED circular, November 21, 1946, SAPMO-BA, ZPA, NL 182/1084, b. 38.

161. Ulbricht to Makarov (copy), n.d., SAPMO-BA, ZPA, NL 90/314, l. 68.

162. Smirnov to Molotov, June 19, 1947, AVPRF, f. 082, op. 34, d. 150, l. 3.

163. Gribanov to Smirnov, August 18, 1947, AVPRF, f. 082, op. 34, d. 150, l. 30.

164. Foreign Office Memorandum, "Division of Powers," December 3, 1947, PRO, FO 371, no. 114, p. 2.

165. SAPMO-BA, ZPA, IV 2/13/4, b. 17.

166. Protocol of consultations of Fechner and Ulbricht with leaders of the Interior Administration, Fischer, Warnke, Bechler, and Siewart, December 20, 1946, SAPMO-BA, ZPA, NL 182/1192, b. 195.

167. Gribanov to Smirnov, June 20, 1947, AVPRF, f. 082, op. 34, d. 150, ll. 6–7.

168. GARF, f. 7212, op. 1, d. 193, ll. 175–177.

169. Report of January 7, 1948, NA, RG 260, box 72.

170. Ulbricht letter (Russian translation), July 16, 1946, RTsKhIDNI, f. 17, op. 128, d. 146, ll. 19–20.

171. G. P. Arkad'ev of the Office of the Political Advisor stated that his office saw and heard of the order only after Sokolovskii's return. Arkad'ev to Smirnov, June 20, 1947, AVPRF, f. 082, op. 34, d. 150, l. 8.

172. Ministerstvo Inostrannykh Del SSSR: Istoriko-diplomaticheskoe upravlenie, *Germanskii Vopros vo Vzaimootnosheniiakh SSSR, SSHA, Anglii i Frantsii v period ot Berlinskoi konferentsii do Obrazovaniia dvukh germanskikh gosudarstv,* ch. 3, in AVPRF, f. 48Z, op. 11zh, d. 14 (papka 69), l. 597. This is an extremely useful, three-part, Ministry of Foreign Affairs history of the German question, 1945–1949, published internally in 1963.

173. Sokolovskii, Order no. 0315, September 9, 1947, AVPRF, f. 082, op. 34, d. 150, l. 30.

174. Brewster Morris, Memorandum no. 345, April 14, 1948, NA, RG 84, CGC, box 226, folder 25, p. 2.

175. HQ European Command, Intelligence Summary no. 10, June 23, 1947, p. A5, NA, RG 59, 740.00119, Control (Germany), 7-347.

176. SAPMO-BA, ZPA, IV 2/1/21, bb. 8–9.

177. RTsKhIDNI, f. 17, op. 128, d. 1186, l. 145.

178. Russian Archives, Collection.

179. *Germanskii Vopros,* AVPRF, f. 48z, op. 11zh, d. 13 (papka 69), ch. 3, l. 598.

180. SAPMO-BA, ZPA, NL 182/1189 (Ulbricht), bb. 38–39.

181. The Soviets were also hard on the provincial apparatuses, where they identified 66,944 former members of the Nazi Party. They were especially critical of the judicial system, which, despite a series of reforms, remained in the hands of "the bourgeois parties" or prewar nonparty elites according to the Soviets. Russkikh to Tereshkin, December 11, 1948, RTsKhIDNI, f. 17, op. 128, d. 567, ll. 160–161, 169.

182. Brewster Morris, Memorandum no. 345, April 14, 1948, p. 2, NA, RG 84, CGC, box 226, folder 25.

183. The DWK's "Anordnung" (September 1, 1948) is reproduced in "German Economic Commission," FES, 0002 SPD Ostbüro. It is also summarized in U.S. Political Adviser for Germany, Memorandum no. 1378, September 20, 1948, NA, RG 59, 740.00119, Control (Germany), 9-2048.

184. "Directive for the Punishment of Offenses against the Secrecy of Classified Matter," Report RP-295-49, Berlin, July 9, 1949, NA, RG 59, 740.00119, Control (Germany), 3-1749.

185. See Jan Foitzik, "Befehls- und Kommunikationsstruktur der Sowjetischen Militäradministration in Deutschland (SMAD)," in Klaus Schönhoven and Dietrich Staritz, eds., *Sozialismus und Kommunismus im Wandel: Hermann Weber zur 65. Geburtstag* (Cologne: Bund Verlag, 1993) p. 351.

186. Ulbricht at the Schulungstagung for government officials in the state of Saxony, March 2–4, 1949, SAPMO-BA, ZPA, NL 277/4 (Zaisser), bb. 6–10.

187. Ulbricht to Bokov, August 10, 1946, SAPMO-BA, ZPA, NL 182/1190 (Ulbricht).

188. N. Ivanov to A. A. Smirnov, August 15, 1946, AVPRF, f. 082, op. 30, d. 52 (papka 132), l. 1, 55–90; A. Smirnov to A. Ia. Vyshinskii, August 20, 1946, d. 64 (papka 134), ll. 2–9.

189. AVPRF, f. 082, op. 30, d. 27 (papka 3), l. 47.

190. "Zur Einleitung der Besprechung," typed notes with handwritten comments in margins, SAPMO-BA, ZPA, NL 36/695 (Pieck), b. 109.

191. SAPMO-BA, ZPA, NL 36/695 (Pieck), b. 91.

192. Speech to the 19th (33rd) Tagung of the Parteivorstand, May 27, 1949, SAPMO-BA, ZPA, NL 90/288 (Grotewohl), b. 172.

193. SAPMO-BA, ZPA, NL 36/695 (Pieck), bb. 87–90.

194. Ibid., bb. 109–110.

195. See Alexander Fischer, "Die Sowjetunion und die 'deutsche Frage' 1945–1949," in Gottfried Zieger, ed., *Recht, Wirtschaft, Politik im geteilten Deutschland* (Cologne: Carl Hermanns Verlag, 1983), p. 376.

196. SAPMO-BA, ZPA, NL 36/695, b. 111. (My emphasis.)

197. Ibid., b. 112.

198. SAPMO-BA, ZPA, IV 2/1/38 (Parteivorstand Protocol, October 9, 1949), b. 80.

199. Dietrich Staritz, *Die Gründung der DDR* (Munich: Deutscher Taschenbuch Verlag, 1984), p. 169.

200. *Germanskii Vopros,* ch. 3, AVPRF, f. 48z, op. 11zh, d. 14 (papka 69), ll. 626–627.

201. Ibid.

202. SAPMO-BA, ZPA, NL 8/8 (Sobottka), bb. 13–18.

203. For the way orders were issued, see Foitzik, "Befehls- und Kommunkationsstruktur," pp. 303–324.

204. GARF, f. 7184, op. 2, d. 2, ll. 3, 5, 40, 59.

205. Ibid., d. 8, ll. 43–341.

206. "Bericht der Sitzung bei der Zentralverwaltung des Verkehrs," September 20, 1945, SAPMO-BA, ZPA, NL 182/1183 (Ulbricht), bb. 21–23.

207. Kühne to Ulbricht, December 11, 1945, in ibid., b. 39; "Telefongespräch mit General Kwaschin," February 6, 1946, in ibid., b. 41. Emphasis in the original.

208. SAPMO-BA, ZPA, NL 182/1184 (Ulbricht), b. 49.

209. "Reisen nach Westen v. Sobottka an Serow," January 23, 1946, and Sobottka to Bokov, March 7, 1946, in ibid., bb. 49–53.

210. HQ Berlin Command, OMGUS, Special Intelligence Report, "Organization of the Soviet Military Government for Germany," September 27, 1947, NA, RG 84, TSGC, box 3, p. 3.

211. SAPMO-BA, ZPA, NL 182/1084 (Ulbricht), bb. 36–37.

212. Sometimes these demands took the form of orders, sometimes they were simply verbal commands. See GARF, f. 7133, op. 2, d. 9, l. 38; f. 7103, op. 2, d. 4, l. 146.

213. Zhukov and Bokov to Antipenko, August 3, 1945, SAPMO-BA, ZPA, NL 182/1191 (Ulbricht), b. 41. In this case, 110 payoks were ordered by the Soviet generals for what they still called "the Ulbricht group."

214. SAPMO-BA, ZPA, EA 0064/1 (Leni Berner), b. 59.

215. Mil'khiker to Tiul'panov, December 29, 1945, GARF, f. 7077, op. 1, d. 176, ll. 1–3.

216. SAPMO-BA, ZPA, IV 2/13/4, p. 17.

217. Karasev to Ulbricht, October 27, 1945, SAPMO-BA, ZPA, NA 182/1185 (Ulbricht), b. 34.

218. GARF, f. 7133, op. 1, d. 254, l. 276.

219. "Sbornik materialov," vol. 1, GARF, f. 7317, op. 54, d. 1, ll. 213–214; Tiul'panov, "O polozhenii v universitetakh sovetskoi zony okkupatsii v Germanii," February 28, 1948, RTsKhIDNI, f. 17, op. 128, d. 566, l. 30.

220. Makarov to Kuznetsov, October 14, 1947, RTsKhIDNI, f. 17, op. 128, d. 358, l. 81.

221. On the beneficial effects of lifting the curfew, see Serov to Tiul'panov and Bokov, January 25, 1946, GARF, F. 7212, op. 1, d. 186, l. 52.

222. Lerner to Mil'khiker, December 17, 1945, GARF, f. 7077, op. 1, d. 174, l. 58.

223. SAPMO-BA, ZPA, EA 1291/4 (Ackermann), b. 720.

224. RTsKhIDNI, f. 17, op. 128, d. 147, l. 53.

225. "The SMA demands that an open critique of their work should be initiated," noted a June 1, 1946, SED protocol of a meeting at Karlshorst. "We were supposed to recommend ways in which the work of the SMA could be improved. But such a critique is not willingly articulated by the states and provinces." SAPMO-BA, ZPA, NL 182/1190 (Ulbricht), b. 4.

226. Altuchow, "Zum politisch-ideologischen Kampf," pp. 29–30.

227. RTsKhIDNI, f. 17, op. 128, d. 682, l. 4.

228. SAPMO-BA, ZPA, NL 36/440 (Pieck), b. 5. (My emphasis.)

2. SOVIET SOLDIERS, GERMAN WOMEN, AND THE PROBLEM OF RAPE

1. Boris Shorin, untitled manuscript, chapter 7, p. 2, HIA, Volkov collection, box 7.

2. J. Glenn Gray, *The Warriors: Reflections on Men in Battle* (New York: Harper and Row, 1970), pp. 66–67.

3. Jörg K. Hoensch, *Sowjetische Osteuropa-Politik 1945–1975* (Düsseldorf: Athenaeum, 1977), p. 39, n. 7.

4. Julius Hay, *Born 1900: Memoirs,* trans. J. A. Underwood (Lasalle, Ill.: Library Press, 1975), p. 273.

5. Lars G: Son Berg, *Boken Som Försvann: Vad hände i Budapest,* 2nd ed. (Arborga, Sweden: Textab, 1983), pp. 161–163. My thanks to Elena Danielson of the Hoover Institution Archives, who informed me of this source and helped with the translation.

6. See ibid., pp. 126–131, which disputes the *Ny Dag* version. For Swedish descriptions of events, see "Office of War Information, Weekly Propaganda Directive," May 25, 1945, p. 3, HIA, Lerner collection, box 50, folder 5.

7. Milovan Djilas, *Conversations with Stalin,* trans. Michael Petrovich (New York: Harcourt Brace, 1962), pp. 88–89.

8. Ibid., pp. 95, 101.

9. NA, RG 226, 88, box 152, October 22, 1945, B 903.

10. Jan Stransky, *East Wind over Prague* (New York: Random House, 1950), p. 38.

11. Wolfgang Leonhard, *Child of the Revolution,* (Chicago: H. Regnery Co., 1958), p. 365.

12. See for example, *Za chest' rodiny,* January 3, January 4, January 7, January 8, and January 18, 1945; *Krasnaia armiia,* April 1 and April 15, 1945.

13. See, for example, Ilya Ehrenburg, *The War: 1941–1945,* trans. Tatiana Shebunina (Cleveland: World Publishing Co., 1967), pp. 26–32. The Ehrenburg passage is cited in Nikolai Tolstoy, *Stalin's Secret War* (New York: Holt, Reinhart and Winston, 1981), pp. 267–268.

14. Alfred de Zayas, *Zeugnisse der Vertreibung* (Krefeld, Germany: Sinus Verlag, 1983), pp. 64–67.

15. P. A. Pirogov, "Vospominanii o sluzhbe v armii i o begstve . . ." manuscript, p. 9, HIA, Nicolaevsky, box 249-9, Series 193.

16. See Tolstoy, *Stalin's Secret War,* p. 269. See also Lew Kopelev, *Aufbewahren für alle Zeit! (Khranit vechno!)* (Hamburg: Hoffmann und Campe, 1976), p. 125.

17. See de Zayas, *Zeugnisse der Vertreibung,* pp. 74–78, especially the testimony of Marie Neumann. See also Kopelew, *Aufbewahren für alle Zeit,* pp. 90–91.

18. Lev Kopelev, *Ease My Sorrows: A Memoir* (New York: Random House, 1983), pp. ix–x.

19. Alexander Solzhenitsyn, *Prussian Nights,* trans. Robert Conquest (New York: Farrar, Strauss and Giroux, 1977), pp. 7, 39.

20. Kopelew, *Aufbewahren für alle Zeit,* p. 90.

21. Tkachenko to Beria, March 17, 1945, GARF, f. 9401, op. 2, d. 94, ll. 86–87.

22. "Bericht über die Zustände und Vorkommnisse in Königsberg/Pr. seit der Einnahme durch die Sowjet-Russen in April 1945," HIA, Sander, box 1, folder 2.

23. *Ogonek,* February 28, 1945, p. 8.

24. See especially HIA, Sander, box 1, folder 3.

25. "Letters from Dresden," Abschrift: Bericht 1, p. 2, HIA, Sander.

26. See the extraordinary "Polish Women Appeal to the World" in HIA, Poland, Ambasada U.S., no. 82, folder 1.

27. "Letters from Dresden," Bericht 2, p. 3, HIA, Sander.

28. HIA, Sander, box 1, folder 3, p. 8.

29. H. Hoffmann, "Bericht über die Arbeit der antifaschistischen Freiheitsbewegung," SAPMO-BA, ZPA, VG 127/1 (1945), b. 123.

30. Robert Bialek, *The Bialek Affair* (London: A. Wingate, 1955), p. 57.

31. See, for example, Władysław Gomułka's speech to the Plenum of the Central Committee of the Polish Workers' Party, May 20–21, 1945, in which he notes: "We must expel all the Germans because countries are built on national lines and not on multi-national ones." Antony Polonsky and Boleslaw Drukier,

eds., *The Beginnings of Communist Rule in Poland* (London: Routledge and Kegan Paul, 1980), p. 425.

32. See the short history of the German expulsion from Silesia, including some striking photographs, in HIA, Sander, box 2, folder 4.

33. Report from Breslau, August 15, 1945, SAPMO-BA, ZPA, IV 2/11/228, p. viii.

34. Biuro Informatsii SVAG, *Biulleten'*, no. 84/88 (November 23, 1946), RTsKhIDNI, f. 17, op. 128, d. 151, l. 81. See also Serov to Beria, March 8, 1945, GARF, f. 9401, op. 2, d. 93, l. 336.

35. *Pravda*, April 14, 1945. (My emphasis.)

36. See Vojtech Mastny's *Russia's Road to the Cold War: Diplomacy, Warfare and the Politics of Communism, 1941–1945* (New York: Columbia University Press, 1979).

37. Cited in Ernst Lemmer, *Manches war doch anders: Erinnerungen eines deutschen Demokraten* (Frankfurt am Main: H. Scheffler, 1968), p. 258. See also *Za chest' rodiny*, March 11, 1945.

38. B. N. Ol'shanskii, "My prikhodili s vostoka," manuscript, p. 35, HIA, Nicolaevsky, Series no. 177, 231-1.

39. Ibid.

40. F. J. Bokov, *Frühjahr des Sieges und der Befreiung* (Berlin, GDR: Militärverlag der DDR, 1979), p. 187.

41. V. I. Chuikov, *Konets tret'ego reikha* (Moscow: Sovetskaia Rossiia, 1973), p. 43.

42. *Krasnaia zvezda*, March 10, 1945.

43. K. F. Telegin, ed., *Poslednii shturm* (Moscow: Izd. polit. literatury, 1965), p. 253.

44. See Alexander Werth, *Russia at War* (New York: Dutton, 1964), pp. 884–899. Long articles on Auschwitz in the military newspapers did not even mention the Jews. See *Za chest' rodiny*, February 28, 1945.

45. Tolstoy, *Stalin's Secret War*, pp. 267–268.

46. Werth, *Russia at War*, p. 983.

47. Dmitrii Shchegolev, "Military Council Representative (An Officer's Notes)," in *How Wars End: Eyewitness Accounts of the Fall of Berlin*, comp. V. Sevruk (Moscow: Progress Publishers, 1974), p. 299.

48. See Telegin, ed., *Poslednii shturm*, p. 255.

49. Ibid.

50. Werth, *Russia at War*, p. 984.

51. K. Gofman to Dimitrov, August 15, 1945, RTsKhIDNI, f. 17, op. 128, d. 791, ll. 210–211.

52. Ibid., ll. 7–8.

53. Berlin Report, July 19, 1945, NA, RG 84, CGC, box 1.

54. "Notes on General Situation in Berlin," HIA, Lerner, box 70, folder 13.

55. HIA, Lerner, Box 70, folder 13, 6871st District, Information Services Control Command, U.S. Army, 13 July 1945 ("Interview with a man from Berlin").

56. "Digest of interview with a German (Walter Killian) who had acted as Burgomeister [sic] of Charlottenburg," NA, RG 59, 740.00119 Control (Germany), 7-1445.

57. "Rathaus Spandau, May 6, 1945," LAB, Zeitg. Sammlung, 2819. At the bottom of the document it is noted that the case was discussed with the commandant and that he promised to help.

58. "Abschrift. Berlin-Reinickendorf," June 28, 1945, LAB, Zeitg. Sammlung, 2015.

59. To Central Committee of the KPD from KPD group Tegel-South, June 29, 1945, SAPMO-BA, ZPA, NL 182/852 (Ulbricht), b. 132.

60. "Enclosure to despatch No. 451, October 15, 1945, from Vatican City to Department of State," NA, RG 59, 740.00119, Control (Germany), 10-1545.

61. HIA, Max Schnetzer, "Tagebuch der Abenteuer: Endkampf um Berlin, Reise durch Russland" (corrected manuscript), pp. 154–157.

62. HIA, Ellen Gräfin Poninski, "Aufzeichnungen nach täglichen Notizen über die Jahre in Potsdam 1945–1949," Ms DD 901, p. 10.

63. Peter Bloch, *Zwischen Hoffnung und Resignation: Als CDU-Politiker in Brandenburg, 1945–1950* (Cologne: Verlag Wissenschaft und Politik, 1986), p. 31. Kleinmachnow had very serious problems with the Russians; see also Lemmer, *Manches war doch anders,* p. 226.

64. ICIS, no. 32, February 23, 1946, pp. 4–5; NA, RG 59, Control (Germany), 740.00119, 13-246. See also Erich Kuby, *Die Russen in Berlin 1945* (Munich: Scherz, 1965), pp. 291–324.

65. Shikin to Aleksandrov, April 30, 1945, RTsKhIDNI, f. 17, op. 128, d. 321, l. 9.

66. Original taped interview with M. I. Burtsev, 1993. "Moscow Connection," C. Barraclough Carey/Pacem Productions.

67. "Bericht über die Ereignisse in Mecklenburg speziell in Rostock, May 1945–November 1946," HIA, Sander, box 1, folder 7.

68. Report of June 12, 1946, pp. 2–3, FES, SPD, "Gniffke."

69. "G-2 Bulletin no. 87, November 7, 1945—HQ Seventh Army Western Military District," p. 4, HIA, Lerner, box 38, folder 7.

70. FES, SPD Ostbüro 0414, Betr. A 204/82, July 19,1949.

71. Dietrich Güstrow, *In jenen Jahren: Aufzeichnungen eines "befreiten" Deutschen* (Berlin: Sewerin und Siedler), p. 110-111.

72. FES, SPD Ostbüro, 0410a, B 90.

73. See, for example, BStU, MfSZ, 229/66 and 238/66.

74. Chaplin to Vatnik, "O faktakh nedostoinogo povedeniia voenno-sluzhashchikh chastei Sovetskoi Armii . . . v r-ne Kaments," May 30, 1947, GARF, f. 7212, op. 1, d. 194, l. 200. This particular incident, which resulted in the shooting of several Germans trying to stop the rape, occurred in Reichenbach, which—according to Soviet reports—was plagued by an outbreak of rapes and murders at the end of May 1947.

75. GARF, f. 7077, op. 1, d. 196, l. 121. See the report "O nekotorykh faktakh raboty operativnykh grupp [NKVD] Okruga Kottbus," in ibid., ll. 122–123.

76. FES, SPD Ostbüro 0414, Betr. 895/6.

77. See FES, SPD Ostbüro, 0414 and 0410b.

78. "Bericht Lemble," p. 25, FES, SPD Ostbüro, 0406, I.

79. Ibid.

80. See *Weissbuch über die "Demokratische Bodenreform" in der Sowjetischen Besatzungszone Deutschlands: Dokumente und Berichte* (Munich: E. Vogel, 1988). The cases of rape in Brandenburg and Vorpommern alone include: no. 6, p. 25; no. 15, p. 29; no. 18, p. 30; no. 19, p. 31; no. 20, p. 31; no. 21, p. 32, no. 23, p. 33; no. 30, p. 37; no. 31, p. 38; no. 34, p. 39; no. 37, p. 41; no. 40, p. 42; no. 41, p. 43.

81. SAPMO-BA, ZPA, NL 90/314 (Grotewohl), bb. 35–37.

82. "HQ 7707 Military Intelligence Service Center, OI Special Report no. 42," p. 4, NA, RG 59, 740.00119 Control (Germany), 6-2647.

83. GARF, f. 7077, op. 1, d. 196, l. 127.

84. See, for example, the police ledger (in German) from Königsbrück (Saxony), June 1–15, 1946, which lists rapes, shootings, and beatings by "people in Russian uniform." GARF, f. 7212, op. 1, d. 187, l. 163.

85. Merzliakov to Rodionov, June 10, 1946, GARF, f. 7077, op. 1, d. 196, ll. 99–100.

86. Office of Military Government for Great Hesse, Information Control Branch, U.S. Army, April 13, 1946, "Letters from the Russian Zone," HIA, Lochner, box 4, no. 5.

87. FES, SPD Ostbüro, 0400, January 22, 1947.

88. Ibid., 0410a.

89. Vatnik to Tiul'panov, Bokov, Serov, "Donesenie: O nastroeniiakh nemetskogo naseleniia po Fed. zemle Saksoniia," January 25, 1946, GARF, f. 7212, op. 1, d. 186, ll. 53–54.

90. Report of Lt. Chigirev, July 22, 1946, RTsKhIDNI, f. 17, op. 128, d. 146, l. 70.

91. VdgB to SED, December 19, 1946, SAPMO-BA, ZPA, NL 36/731, l. 121.

92. Burtsev to Dimitrov, July 20, 1945, RTsKhIDNI, f. 17, op. 128, d. 39, ll. 51–52. This is the same Burtsev who recently denied that extensive rape went on. Taped interview with M. I. Burtsev, Moscow, 1993.

93. SAPMO-BA, ZPA, NL 182/853 (Ulbricht), l. 30.

94. Biuro Informatsii SVAG, *Biulleten'*, no. 4 (February 4, 1948), RTsKhIDNI, f. 17, op. 128, d. 577, l. 60.

95. "Resolution," April 23, 1949, in German, GARF, f. 7077, op. 1, d. 259, l. 103.

96. Serov to Beria, November 29, 1945, GARF, f. 9401, op. 2, d. 102, ll. 33–34.

97. Tugarinov to Dimitrov, "O politicheskom polozhenii v Germanii," November 3, 1945, RTsKhIDNI, f. 17, op. 128, d. 321, l. 169.

98. K. Gofman to Dimitrov, "Dokladnaia zapiska," August 15, 1945, RTsKhIDNI, f. 17, op. 128, d. 791, l. 215.

99. FES, SPD Ostbüro, Bericht no. 745/5; see also SPD Ostbüro, 0410a (August 1947), and SPD Ostbüro, 0406 (August 3, 1948).

100. SAPMO-BA, ZPA, IV 2/1/3 (Parteivorstand Protocol, July 16–17, 1946), b. 115; SAPMO-BA, ZPA, EA 0120/2 (Robert Büchner), b. 35

101. *Na boevom postu: Kniga o voinakh Gruppy sovetskikh voisk v Germanii* (Moscow: Voennoe Izdatel'stvo, 1975), p. 57.

102. K. F. Skorobogatkin, chief ed., *50 let vooruzhennykh sil' SSSR* (Moscow: Voen-izdat, 1968), p. 475.

103. Interview with I. S. Drabkin, Moscow, July 1989. Drabkin, a historian of Germany, was formerly a political officer in the Information Department of SVAG.

104. Stricken (but still readable) from the report, which was sent on from Erich Mielke to Ulbricht, was the sentence in parenthesis. It may have simply been too much for Mielke. Bezirkspolizeipräsident Merseburg, Biesenbruch, to General Gogunov, Merseburg, June 3, 1946, BStU, MfSZ, 400/66, bb. 239–243.

105. Ibid.

106. RTsKhIDNI, f. 17, op. 128, d. 54, l. 156.

107. See Mecklenburg Orders no. 12 (September 4, 1945), and no. 68 (December 17, 1945), GARF, f. 7103, op. 2, d. 1, ll. 18, 130.

108. See Werner Knop, *Prowling Russia's Forbidden Zone: A Secret Journey into Soviet Germany* (New York: Knopf, 1949), p. 38.

109. Telegram, May 28, 1945, NA, RG 59, 740.00119, Control (Germany) 5–2845. Here American officers voice worry that "Russian officers and men openly go about with German women." See also, "SHAEF Political Intelligence Report," June 4, 1945, NA, RG 59, 740.00119 Control (Germany), 6-455, which notes that "relations between Russian soldiers and German civilians are said to be friendly and fraternization is in full swing." Gen. Lucius Clay, an opponent of the American fraternization order, wrote to Secretary of War Henry Stimson with some relief (August 18, 1945): "Association with Germans in public places is now permitted in American and British zones, as it always was in the Soviet zone." Jean Edward Smith, ed., *The Papers of General Lucius D. Clay: Germany, 1945–1949,* vol. 1 (Bloomington: Indiana University Press, 1974), p. 59.

110. Werth, *Russia at War,* p. 989.

111. "Bericht Lemble," p. 36, FES, SPD Ostbüro, 0406, I.

112. There was no little resentment of these German wives felt by the Soviet wives at home. Interview with Dr. and Mrs. Max Rokhlin, Moscow, July 1989. Rokhlin, an chemist at the Academy of Sciences, was in charge of removing chemical industry targets from the Soviet zone.

113. See "Bericht Lemble," p. 36, FES, SPD Ostbüro, 0406, I.

114. See, for example, HIP, no. 342, no. 346, no. 446, no. 527; HIA, State Department Interview Reports, box 1, no. 14 (August 1955), no. 11 (May 1955), no. 10 (1955). It is interesting to note that a large number of those interviewees who had deserted from the Soviet military government and from the Red Army in Germany and Austria did so primarily because of their German girlfriends.

115. Tiul'panov, "Dokladnaia zapiska," August 11, 1947, RTsKhIDNI, f. 17, op. 128, d. 317, l. 36.

116. *Amtliches Mitteilungsblatt,* July 27, 1946.

117. Hannes Adomeit, *Soviet Risk-Taking and Crisis Behavior: A Theoretical and Empirical Analysis* (London: Allen and Unwin, 1982), p. 120.

118. Kolesnichenko to Ponomarev, November 29, 1948, RTsKhIDNI, f. 17, op. 128, d. 572, ll. 101–103.

119. Ibid., l. 98.
120. Makarov to Kuznetsov, "Donesenie: Ob osnovnykh meropriiatiiakh Sovetskoi Voennoi Administratsii v Germanii . . . za sentiabr' 1947 g.," October 14, 1947, RTsKhIDNI, f. 17, op. 128, d. 358, l. 89.
121. *Sopade Informationsdienst,* October 6, 1947, FES, SPD Ostbüro, 400, no. 294.
122. Iu. Korol'kov to Central Committee, September 3, 1947, RTsKhIDNI, f. 17, op. 128, d. 1094, ll. 221–222.
123. Ibid.
124. "Glavnyi shtab tsentral'noi gruppy sil', May 25, 1947, Prikaz no. 009," *Za svobodu Rossii,* no. 10, 1948, pp. 47–49.
125. This message was contained in SVAG Order no. 0318 of September 12, 1947. RTsKhIDNI, f. 17, op. 128, d. 358, l. 81.
126. HIP, no. 342, p. 47.
127. Russov to Suslov, "Protokol sobraniia partiinogo aktiva Sovetskoi Voennoi Administratsii v Germanii," March 9, 1949, RTsKhIDNI, f. 17, op. 128, d. 682, l. 128.
128. *"Über 'die Russen' und über uns": Diskussion über ein brennendes Thema* (Berlin, 1949), December 10 meeting, pp. 56–57.
129. HIA, State Department Interview Report, no. 10 (1955), box 1, p. 2; see also no. 14 (August 1955), p. 2.
130. FES, SPD Ostbüro, 0406 (July 27, 1949).
131. GARF, f. 7133, op. 2, d. 18, l. 33.
132. "Stenogramma soveshchaniia v upravlenii propagandoi SVAG," September 17–18, 1946, RTsKhIDNI, f. 17, op. 128, d. 150, l. 68; "Informatsionnaia svodka . . . ," September 6, 1947, d. 358, l. 18.
133. *Abendblatt für Mitteldeutschland,* October 19 and December 20, 1946.
134. *Tägliche Rundschau,* November 24, 1946.
135. "Penizillin für alle," *Berliner Nacht-Express,* December 10, 1945. According to one SED report, in Thüringen penicillin was first made available only in November 1947. Dr. George Appell, Bericht . . . , February 26, 1948, SAPMO-BA, ZPA, 2/2025/8 (Sekretariat Otto Meier), b. 48.
136. Interview with Dr. Max Rokhlin, Moscow, July 1989.
137. See Romanov in *Im Dienst am Menschen: Erinnerungen an den Aufbau des neuen Gesundheitswesens 1945–1949* (Berlin, GDR: Dietz, 1985), p. 222.
138. HIA, Sander, folder 6, box 1 (Lübeck, 1 May 1946). See also HIA, Philp, box 4, item 34.
139. *Za svobodu Rossii,* no. 10, 1948, p. 44. This report on the condition of Soviet troops comes from a Russian samizdat newspaper published in the Soviet zone, *Nabat.*
140. "Donesenie: Ob amoral'nykh iavleniiakh v raione Lukenval'de," April 27, 1946, and other reports, GARF, f. 7077, op. 1, d. 196, ll. 80–91.
141. K., "Berichte aus der russischen Besatzungszone," HIA, Sander, folder 6, box 1.
142. "Untersuchung von Frauen auf Geschlechtskrankheiten," Rathaus Tempelhof, May 15, 1945, LAB, Zeitg. Sammlung, 2773.

143. "Bekanntmachung," LAB, Zeitg. Sammlung, 2014.

144. Befehl no. 25, 7 August 1945, Berlin (copy), LAB, Zeitg. Sammlung, 7297.

145. Befehl no. 030, February 12, 1946 (copy), in ibid.

146. Prikaz no. 26, February 19, 1946, Brandenburg, GARF, f. 7184, op. 2, d. 2, l. 59. The language of this and other orders is interesting in the extent to which the German population is blamed for the spread of syphillis and the orders seek to protect the innocent soldiers from this plague.

147. Maj. Gen. Fedotov, Deputy Commander of Brandenburg, "O merakh bor'by s venericheskimi zabolevaniiami," March 6, 1946, GARF, f. 7184, op. 2, d. 2, l. 90.

148. "Betr: Bekämpfung der Geschlechtskrankheiten," April 25, 1946, Magistrat der Stadt Berlin, LAB, Zeitg. Sammlung, 7217.

149. *Abendblatt für Mitteldeutschland,* October 19, 1946; Koloss, "Donesenie o deiatel'nosti zhenskikh komitetov v Berlinskom okruge," February 24, 1946, GARF, f. 7077, op. 1, d. 206, l. 27.

150. See LAB, Zeitg. Sammlung, 8501/44, "Magistratssitzung vom 17 April 1946," p. 3.

151. "Internierung geschlechtskranker Frauen und Mädchen in Brandenburg," December 23, 1946, SAPMO-BA, NL 90/298 (Grotewohl), b. 7.

152. On Allied measures to fight venereal disease in Berlin, see SAPMO-BA, ZPA, IV L-2/13/431 (BK/O [46] 288, July 9, 1946; BK/O [46] 375, September 18, 1946; BK/O [46] 414, October 31, 1946), and IV L-2/13/430 (BK/O [46] 257, June 7, 1946).

153. "Combatting Venereal Disease," Allied Control Authority Coordinating Committee, Directive no. 52, May 7, 1947, HIA, GTUAO, 1945, Control Council, box 2.

154. *Krasnaia zvezda,* June 13, 1945. See also the edition for June 8, 1945, which carries an article of almost identical content.

155. Günter Benser, "Der friedliche, demokratische Weg zum Sozialismus in der DDR," *DDR Geschichte in der Übergangsperiode (1945–1961)* (Berlin, GDR: 1987), p. 128. See also Bokow, *Frühjahr des Sieges,* pp. 381–382, 339.

156. There are literally hundreds of articles in *Sovetskoe slovo* (Soviet Word), the Russian-language newspaper of the Soviet occupation administration (1945–1949), on the ties between the German and the Soviet Left. On Thälmann, see, for example, *Sovetskoe slovo,* April 16, 1948; on the German Left in general, see the series of articles by the political officer (later historian) Ia. Drabkin, *Sovetskoe slovo,* June 5–7, 1947; March 18, 1948; and November 14, 1948. See the history of the newspaper in Horst Bednarek, " 'Sovetskoe slovo,' die Tageszeitung der Sowjetischen Militäradministration in Deutschland," in *Die Entwicklung freundschaftlicher Beziehungen zwischen der DDR und der UdSSR: Referate und Diskussionsbeiträge: XXII. Tagung der Kommission der Historiker der DDR und der UdSSR 4./5. June 1974* (Berlin, GDR: 1977).

157. See, for example, the article on the one hundred fiftieth anniversary of the birth of Beethoven, *Za chest' rodiny,* December 18, 1945.

158. *Krasnaia zvezda,* September 9, 1945.

159. See, for example, "S kazhdym dnem vyshe podnimat' uroven' politicheskoi raboty," *Krasnaia zvezda,* July 2, 1947.

160. See, for examples, *Sovetskoe slovo,* May 23, 1947; June 11, 1947; October 29, 1947; April 18, 1948; June 3, 1949.

161. "Aus einem Tagebuch: Erinnerungen eines Magdeburgers," *Tägliche Rundschau,* July 1, 1948. See also the examples in *Tägliche Rundschau,* October 19, November 2, and November 10, 1946.

162. See, for example, Criminal Police (5) Reports from Weimar, Erfurt, and Gotha in Thüringen, January 25 to February 25, 1946, in BStU MfSZ, 400/66.

163. Gordon Schaffer, *Russian Zone* (London: Allen and Unwin, 1947), p. 13.

164. See, for example, *Zeit im Bild,* February 10 and February 25, 1947; *Abendblatt für Mitteldeutschland,* June 11 and June 12, 1946, and March 4, 1947; and *Der Demokrat,* January 12 and February 10, 1946, and April 18, 1947.

165. "Der Prozess in Eberswalde," *Deutsche Volkszeitung,* January 8, 1946.

166. See, for example, *Nacht-Express,* January 7, 1946.

167. See Gregory Klimov, *Berliner Kreml* (Cologne: Roter Weissbücher, 1951), p. 282.

168. GARF, f. 7212, op. 1, d. 186, l. 55.

169. SAPMO-BA, ZPA, EA 1845/3 (Rudolf Bühring), b. 441. See also NA, RG 226, 88, box 152, October 22, 1945, B 903.

170. See, for example, NA, OBWPI, no. 23, May 15, 1947, 740.00119 Control (Germany), 5-1947, p. 16.

171. Bertolt Brecht, *Arbeitsjournal 1938–1955* (Berlin and Weimar: Aufbau Verlag, 1977), p. 454.

172. On the Americans, see, for example, Daily Intelligence Digest, no. 109, May 7, 1945, NA, RG 260, OMGUS, ISD, box 97, folder 18; HQ European Command, Daily Information and Intelligence Summary, no. 9, June 9, 1947, NA, RG 59, 740.00119 Control (Germany), 6-1347; HQ 7th Army, Western Military District, G-2, December 7, 1945, HIA, Lerner, box 39, folder 2. Martin van Creveld writes that during the war "more [U.S.] servicemen were executed for rape than for any other crime, particularly if they were black and particularly if the victim ended up dead as well as violated." Martin van Creveld, *The Transformation of War* (New York: The Free Press, 1991), p. 79. But the number of cases was "not large": Harold Zink, *The United States in Germany 1944–1955* (Princeton, N.J.: Van Nostrand, 1957), p. 137.

173. Hermann Werner, *Tübingen 1945: Eine Chronik* (Stuttgart: Theiss Verlag, 1986), pp. 88–89, 185–188; Manfred Bosch, *Der Neubeginn: Aus deutscher Nachkriegszeit Südbaden 1945–1950* (Constance, Germany: Südkurier Verlag, 1988), p. 35.

174. See Annamarie Tröger, "Between Rape and Prostitution: Survival Strategies and Changes of Emancipation for Berlin Women after World War II," in Judith Friedlander et al., eds. *Women in Culture and Politics: A Century of Change* (Bloomington: Indiana University Press, 1986), pp. 113–114. Tröger does not go as far as Niethammer in claiming—incorrectly, in my view—that the differences between prostitution on the one side and the fear and reality of rape on the other were not all that great. Lutz Niethammer, *"Hinterher merkt man, dass es richtig*

war dass es schiefgegangen ist": Nachkriegserfahrungen im Ruhrgebiet, vol. 2 (Berlin: J. H. W. Dietz Nachf., 1983), pp. 31–32.

175. The case of the rape of a nine-year-old boy by a Russian soldier is reported in BStU MfSZ, 400/66, b. 24.

176. See the studies by Gerda Lerner, *The Creation of Patriarchy* (New York: Oxford University Press, 1986), especially pp. 115–117, and Susan Brownmiller, *Against Our Will: Men, Women and Rape* (New York: Bantam, 1975).

177. On the refutation of rape as a product of pent-up sexuality, see Sylvana Tomaselli and Roy Porter, eds., *Rape: An Historical and Social Enquiry* (Oxford: Basil Blackwell, 1986), pp. 11, 229–230. For a discussion of rape as a crime of violence, see Anna Clark, *Women's Silence, Men's Violence: Sexual Assault in England 1770–1845* (London: Pandora, 1987), p. 6.

178. Gray, *The Warriors*, pp. 62, 66.

179. Brownmiller, *Against Our Will*, p. 64.

180. *Tägliche Rundschau*, May 22, 1945.

181. Iu. Zhukov, *Liudi 40-kh godov: Zapiski voennogo korrespondenta* (Moscow: Sov. Rossiia, 1969), p. 554.

182. *Krokodil*, no. 8, 1945.

183. *Krokodil*, no. 9, 1945.

184. *Pravda*, May 7, 1945.

185. Marshal V. I. Kazakov, *Artilleriia, Ogon'!* (Moscow: DOSAAF, 1972), p. 212.

186. Vsevolod Vishnevskii, "Berlin Surrenders (From a Wartime Diary)," in *How Wars End*, p. 193.

187. S. I. Tulpanow, "Befreiung des Menschen," *Sonntag (Wochenzeitung)*, no. 19 (1965), cited in Artur Kleine, "Die Hilfe der Sowjetunion für die demokratische Erneuerung der deutschen Kultur in der sowjetischen Besatzungszone von 1945–1949," Ph.D. diss., Martin-Luther University (Halle-Wittenberg), 1969, vol. 1, p. 73.

188. See Chuikov's speech in *Za antifashistskuiu demokraticheskuiu Germaniiu*, pp. 169–170. See also Chuikov, *Konets tret'ego reikha*, pp. 143–144.

189. BStU MfSZ, 238/66, 229/66. See also the report of Pätznik, July 21, 1945, in SAPMO-BA, ZPA, NL 157/10 (Fritz Gäbler), b. 1.

190. Lemmer, *Manches war doch anders*, p. 226.

191. Supreme Headquarters Allied Expeditionary Force Psychological War Division, Intelligence Section, March 2, 1945, "Politische Kurznachrichten," no. 6, February 16, 1945 (German extracts), HIA, Lerner, box 2. Similar documents collected by the Psychological War Division demonstrate Nazi attempts to stop the rumors that the "Bolsheviks" had "supposedly" been treating German civilians decently. Ibid., "Mundpropagandaparole," March 14, 1945.

192. Ibid., "Mundpropagandaparole," March 14, 1945; see also ibid., "Politische Kurznachrichten, no. 5, 11 February 1945." Some Wehrmacht documents recommend an "enlightened" policy toward the Russians. "Der deutsche Soldat und seine politischen Aufgaben in Osten," May 21, 1943, in "Document report for PWD," October 18, 1944, pp. 1–4, HIA, Lerner, box 7. See also OSS, Research

and Analysis, "European Political Report," January 26, 1945, vol. 2, no. 4, "The German Attitude toward Russia," pp. 13–15, HIA, Lerner, box 7.

193. SAPMO-BA, ZPA, NL 182/246 (Ulbricht), b. 337.

194. HIA, Max Schnetzer, "Tagebuch" (manuscript), pp. 156–157.

195. HQ, 7th Army Western Military District, G-2 Bulletin no. 87, November 7, 1945, p. 5, HIA, Lerner, box 38, folder 7.

196. Markus Wolf describes a case in which knowing Russian helped some schoolgirls find their way unscathed through the Russian zone to Berlin. Markus Wolf, *Die Troika* (Düsseldorf: Claasen, 1989), 3rd ed., p. 44. See also Ellen Gräfin Poninski's diary for how she was able to deal with the Russian troops in Potsdam. HIA, Poninski, "Aufzeichnungen" (manuscript).

197. The report adds that "once the Russians have signified their intentions, however, most German girls go voluntarily..." OMGUS ICIS, no. 34, March 9, 1946, "Behavior of the Russian Soldiers," p. 8, NA, RG 59, 740.00019 Control (Germany). Another source cites a Russian soldier's comment to the effect that it is better that the German girls know no Russian: "Then one doesn't have to convince them—simply pull out a pistol and command 'lie down!' finish one's business, and go on." De Zayas, *Zeugnisse der Vertreibung*, p. 68.

198. Naval Intelligence Report No. 1100, Oct. 11, 1945, "Notes from a German Source on Conditions in Russia, Poland, and in Russian-Occupied Poland," NA, RG 59, 740.00119 Control (Germany), 10-1145. See also "Bericht Lemble," Soviet Troops in Thüringen, p. 16, FES, SPD Ostbüro, 0406, I.

199. See "Vier Stationen in Rot," HIA, Kurt Grabe, box 1.

200. HIA, Schnetzer, "Tagebuch" (manuscript), p. 157.

201. FES, SPD Ostbüro, 0410a. See especially Bericht no. 745/5.

202. P. A. Pirogov, "Rukopis'—Vospominanii o sluzhbe v armii i o begstve . . .," HIA, Nicolaevsky, Series 193, box 249-9.

203. Vatnik to Dubrovskii, June 27, 1946, GARF, f. 7212, op. 1, d. 187, l. 160.

204. See David E. Powell, "Alcohol Abuse in the Soviet Union," manuscript, Russian Research Center, Harvard University (1983); Vlad Treml, *Alcohol in the USSR: A Statistical Study* (Durham, N.C.: Duke University Press, 1982), pp. 69–70.

205. "Bericht Lemble," FES, SPD Ostbüro, 0406, I, p. 25.

206. Lerner, *The Creation of Patriarchy*, p. 450.

207. Eve Levin, *Sex and Society in the World of Orthodox Slavs* (Ithaca, N.Y.: Cornell University Press, 1989), pp. 227, 245.

208. Laura Engelstein, "Gender and the Juridical Subject: Prostitution and Rape in Nineteenth-Century Russian Criminal Codes," *Journal of Modern History,* no. 60 (September 1988): 469, 471–473.

209. Lerner, *The Creation of Patriarchy*, p. 78.

210. SAPMO-BA, ZPA, NL 17/7 (Martha Arendsee), l. 102.

211. See among the many examples in the Department of State Interview Project, HIA: Department of State Interview Report no. 4, box 1 (August 1, 1952), pp. 6–7; Department of State Interview Report no. 5, box 1 (September 2, 1952), pp. 1–11; Department of State Interview Report, no. 12 (June 1955), p. 1. See also the

many examples in the Harvard Interview Project: for example, nos. 517, p. 6; 521, pp. 70–74; 532, pp. 94–95; and 536, pp. 17–19.

212. *Krasnaia zvezda,* September 9, 1945.

213. One village outside of Lübben suffered serial rapes and murders of this sort. P. A. Pirogov, "Vospominaniia o sluzhbe v armii i o begstve . . . ," HIA, Nicolaevsky. In one of many similar cases in the police archives, three soldiers forceably entered an Erfurt apartment in February of 1946 and raped a woman, Ida "M." According to the police report, "The husband, who was in the apartment, was forced under armed threats to stay very quiet and to watch the act of rape." BStU MfSZ, 400/66, bb. 7–8.

214. See the criminal police files in BStU MfSZ, 400/66.

215. Cited in de Zayas, *Anmerkungen zur Vertreibung,* p. 93.

216. FES, SPD Ostbüro, Betr. 517/4.

217. See the criminal police cases in BStU MfSZ, 400/66.

218. Lemmer, *Manches war doch anders,* p. 33

219. Bloch, *Zwischen Hoffnung und Resignation,* p. 34.

220. Interview with Dr. Gerhard Simon, Bundesinstitut, Cologne, October 6, 1988.

221. The former technique was described to me by at least a dozen people who lived through the occupation. I owe the latter observation to Prof. Regina Casper of Stanford University, who grew up in a small town outside of Berlin. For a variety of strategies, see Erika M. Hörning, "Frauen als Kriegsbeute: Der zwei-Front Krieg. Beispiele aus Berlin," in Lutz Niethammer, ed., *"Wir kriegen jetzt andere Zeiten"* (Berlin: J. H. W. Dietz Nachf., 1985), p. 37.

222. Güstrow, *In jenen Jahren,* p. 115

223. See Kopelew, *Aufbewahren für alle Zeit,* pp. 100–102, 110.

224. U.S. Political Advisor for Germany, "Conditions in Soviet-Occupied Berlin," July 14, 1945, Digest of Interview with Walter Killian, p. 3, NA, RG 59, 740.00119, Control (Germany), 7-1445.

225. Heinz Brandt, *Ein Traum, der nicht entführbar ist: Mein Weg zwischen Ost und West* (Munich: List, 1967), p. 171.

226. BStU MfSZ, 400/66; Report from Berlin, October 8, 1945, RTsKhIDNI, f. 17, op. 128, d. 793, l. 242. Helga "N," the head of the FDJ in Grimma, was raped by two soldiers. Report of Lt. Chigirev, July 22, 1946, RTsKhIDNI, f. 17, op. 128, d. 146, l. 71.

227. Biuro Informatsii SVAG, *Biulleten'* no. 14/113 (February 5, 1947), RTsKhIDNI, f. 17, op. 128, d. 362, l. 184.

228. Bialek, *The Bialek Affair,* pp. 31, 45.

229. Erich W. Gniffke, *Jahre mit Ulbricht* (Cologne: Verlag Wissenschaft und Politik, 1966), p. 16.

230. SAPMO-BA, ZPA, I 2/5/49 (Secretariat Meeting Protocol, July 12, 1945), b. 14.

231. Pieck's article was taken from a speech to Erfurt KPD leaders in October 1945. SAPMO-BA, NL 182/856 (Ulbricht), b. 27.

232. "Bericht über die Schulungsarbeit," August 24, 1945, SAPMO-BA, I 2/2/27, b. 3.

233. Leonhard, *Child of the Revolution,* pp. 417–418.
234. Burtsev to Dimitrov, July 20, 1945, RTsKhIDNI, f. 17, op. 128, d. 39, l. 52.
235. SAPMO-BA, ZPA, NL 182/852 (Ulbricht), b. 32. Sharp protests by KPD members Hirz and Theo prompted Ulbricht to ask that they be disciplined.
236. Erich W. Gniffke, "Erfahrungen vor und nach der Verschmelzung," p. 12, FES, SPD, Gniffke Nachlass, no. 9/3 (27).
237. SAPMO-BA, NL 90/125 (Grotewohl), b. 34.
238. SAPMO-BA, ZPA, IV 2/1/3 (Parteivorstand Protocol, July 16–17, 1946), b. 115.
239. "Vorschlag für ein Antwortsschreiben . . . ," SAPMO-BA, ZPA, IV 2/11/202 (Kaderfragen), p. 7.
240. Burtsev to Dimitrov, July 20, 1945, RTsKhIDNI, f. 17, op. 128, d. 39, l. 51.
241. ISCS, U.S. HQ Berlin, Weekly Political Summary, November 12, 1945, "Opinions of *Berliner Zeitung* Editorial Writer," pp. 5–6, HIA, Lerner, box 42, no. 9.
242. Gabriel A. Almond, "Ein Brief aus der amerikanischen Zone," October 11, 1945, FES, SPD, Gniffke Nachlass, 7/3 (22).
243. U.S. Political Advisor for Germany, "Conditions in Soviet-Occupied Berlin" July 14, 1945, "Digest of Interview," NA, RG 59, 740.00119, Control (Germany), 7-1445.
244. Vatnik to Klepov, April 18, 1946, GARF, f. 7212, op. 1, d. 187, l. 52.
245. SAPMO-BA, ZPA, IV 2/1/5 (Parteivorstand Protocol, October 24–25, 1946), b. 41.
246. Draft note to Semenov in Ulbricht's hand, July 10, 1945, SAPMO-BA, ZPA, b. 134. In the note, which was apparently never sent, Ulbricht states that the SED in no way wants to undermine the prestige of the Red Army, "but we must prevent our political work from being buried by such occurrences [rape and plunder]."
247. Ibid., b. 108.
248. SAPMO-BA, ZPA, NL 90/314 (Grotewohl), l. 59. During April and May 1946 in Wermsdorf (Oschatz), citizens refused to attend local SED meetings because the commandant could not guarantee the citizens' safety in the face of rampaging soldiers from a newly arrived hospital unit. Vatnik to Dubrovskii, June 14, 1946, GARF, f. 7212, op. 1, d. 187, l. 115–116.
249. Hermann Weber, *Geschichte der DDR* (Munich: Deutscher Taschenbuch Verlag, 1985), p. 142.
250. "Bericht über die Mitgliederwerbung . . . ," SAPMO-BA, ZPA, NL 182/856 (Ulbricht), b. 111; "Stenogramma soveshchaniia," RTsKhIDNI, f. 17, op. 128, d. 149, l. 51.
251. SAPMO-BA, ZPA, NL 90/314 (Grotewohl), b. 317.
252. "Inform-Mitteilung," April 17, 1950, SAPMO-BA, ZPA, NL 90/450 (Grotewohl), b. 91.
253. Almond, "Ein Brief aus der amerikanischen Zone," October 11, 1945, FES, SPD, "Gniffke Nachlass," 7/3 (22).
254. *Neue Berliner Illustrierte,* no. 4 (1948).
255. See Hilde Thunwald, *Gegenwartsprobleme Berliner Familien: Eine soziologische*

Untersuchung an 498 Familien (Berlin: Weidmannische Verlagsbuchhandlung, 1948), p. 146.

256. Hörning, "Frauen als Kriegsbeute," p. 343, n. 31; Helke Sander and Barbara Johr, eds., *Befreier und Befreite,* (Munich: Kunstmann, 1992), pp. 36–39. See also Kuby, *Die Russen in Berlin 1945,* p. 317.

257. *Neues Deutschland,* November 30, 1946, in SAPMO-BA, ZPA, IV 2/17/29, b. 14.

258. Leonhard, *Child of the Revolution,* p. 311. See Atina Grossmann, *Reforming Sex: The German Movement for Birth Control and Abortion Reform, 1920–1950* (New York: Oxford University Press, forthcoming), pp. 189–198 (page proofs). Grossmann's rendition of the "revived debate" about paragraph 218 highlights the accomplishments of the reforms in the Soviet zone versus the restrictive policies on abortions in the West.

259. SAPMO-BA, ZPA, NL 182/246 V (Ulbricht), b. 47.

260. "Stenogramma soobshchenii," June 7, 1945, RTsKhIDNI, f. 17, op. 128, d. 750, l. 174.

261. M. Zetkin, "An der Vorstand der SED über Para. 218," SAPMO-BA, ZPA, IV 2/17/28, b. 9.

262. *Die Welt,* August 17, 1948, in SAPMO-BA, ZPA, IV 2/17/29, b. 112.

263. GARF, f. 7212, op. 1, d. 110, l. 193.

264. SAPMO-BA, ZPA, IV 2/17/11, b. 25.

265. SAPMO-BA, IV 2/17/11, b. 103; IV 2/17/28, bb. 69, 138; IV 2/17/29, bb. 14, 20, 26. The latter collection consists of press clippings about the problem of paragraph 218. See Grossmann, *Reforming Sex,* p. 197.

266. See Bloch, *Zwischen Hoffnung und Resignation,* p. 61.

267. Barbara Willenbacher, "Zerrüttung und Bewährung der Nachkriegs-Familie," in Martin Broszat, Klaus-Dietmar Henke, and Hans Woller, eds., *Von Stalingrad zur Währungsreform: Zur Sozialgeschichte des Umbruchs in Deutschland* (Munich: R. Oldenburg Verlag, 1988), p. 600. Despite the better data for the Western zones, Willenbacher notes that there are still no accurate studies of what happened to occupation children (p. 602). See also Sander and Johr, eds., *Befreier und Befreite,* pp. 53–54. Out-of-wedlock births to foreign fathers in the zone (and Berlin) are usually estimated at about 150,000 to 200,000. Klaus-Jörg Ruhl, ed., *Unsere verlorenen Jahre—Frauenalltag in Kriegs- und Nachkriegszeit 1939–1949* (Darmstadt und Neuwied: Luchterband, 1985), p. 155.

268. Many of the observations in this paragraph derive from the work of Barbara Willenbacher; see Willenbacher, "Zerrüttung und Bewährung der Nachkriegs-Familie," p. 599. See also Sibylle Meyer and Eva Schülze, " 'Als wir wieder zusammen waren, ging der Krieg im Kleinen weiter': Frauen, Männer und Familien im Berlin der vierzigen Jahre," in Niethammer, ed., *"Wir kriegen jetzt andere Zeiten,"* vol. 3, pp. 312–314.

269. See Weber, *Geschichte der DDR,* p. 94. Rations were distributed according to categories of work and were therefore "gender-blind."

270. Telegram MC-741, Moscow, July 3, 1948: summary of speech by Mikhail Dolgopolov on "Prostrate Berlin," NA, RG 59, 740.00119 Control (Germany), 7–345.

271. "Bericht Lemble," Soviet Troops in Thüringen, p. 15, FES, SPD Ostbüro, 0406, I.

272. Robert G. Moeller, *Protecting Motherhood: Women and the Family in the Politics of Postwar West Germany* (Berkeley: University of California Press, 1993), pp. 1–75. See also his "Protecting Mother's Work: From Production to Reproduction in Postwar West Germany," *Journal of Social History,* vol. 22, no. 3 (1989): 413–439.

273. "Stenographische Niederschrift über die Reichsberatung," January 8–9, 1946, SAPMO-BA, I 2/2/17, bb. 148–149.

274. "Po voprosam zhenskikh i iunosheskikh organizatsii," GARF, f. 7077, op. 1, d. 206, l. 45.

275. The Bernau region women's antifascist committee insisted, for example, that wives of returning POWs be particularly targeted for treatment. "Po voprosam . . . organizatsii," GARF, f. 7077, op. 1, d. 206, l. 45.

276. "Bericht aus Schlesien," HIA, Sander, box 1, folder 5; Sibylle Meyer and Eva Schülze, *Wie wir das alles geschafft haben: Alleinstehende Frauen berichten über ihr Leben nach 1945* (Munich: Beck, 1984), p. 53; Dr. Georg Appell, "Bericht des Ministeriums für Arbeit und Sozialwesen über das Jahr 1947," SAPMO-BA, ZPA, IV 2/2025/8 (Sekretariat Otto Meier), b. 31.

277. *Nacht-Express,* February 9, 1946.

278. Says one girl in a cartoon to another, "If I knew languages, then maybe I'd have some chances." Her friend responds: "But Inge, with your figure you'd be understood anywhere." *Nacht-Express,* June 8, 1947. The popular *Nacht-Express* was especially filled with similar cartoons; see, for example, those of June 2 and June 4, 1947, which also portray German girls plotting to hook up with Allied soldiers or a German with a heated apartment.

279. Meyer and Schülze, *Wie wir das alles geschafft haben,* p. 63.

280. Finance Directorate, Allied Control Authority, "Principles Involved in the Consideration and Reimbursement of Claims by Germans against Occupation Forces," July 5, 1947, HIA, GTUAO, box 12.

281. Helmut Vögt, "Was wir den Frauen schuldig bleiben," *Aufbau,* 3 Jahrgang, Heft 7 (1947): 40–62.

282. See Maria Rentmeister, "Beratung bei Generalmajor Kotikow," *"Im Zeichen des roten Sterns" Erinnerungen an die Traditionen der deutsch-sowjetischen Freundschaft* (Berlin, DDR: Dietz, 1974), pp. 465–467, and M. M. Volov, "Iz istorii sozdaniia Demokraticheskogo zhenskogo soiuza Germanii (1945–1947 gg.)," *Novaia i noveishaia istoriia,* no. 2 (1974): 32–46.

283. Werner Stern, "Ihr Mütter!" in *Deutsche Volkszeitung,* July 24, 1945.

284. SAPMO-BA, ZPA, NL 36/731, l. 1.

285. Order no. 253, August 9, 1946 (Sokolovskii), GARF, f. 7317, op. 8, d. 7, l. 12a.

286. "Stenogramma besedy s tov. Maternom," September 25, 1946, RTsKhIDNI, f. 17, op. 128, d. 151, l. 131.

287. GARF, f. 7212, op. 1, d. 193, ll. 173, 175.

288. Report from Berlin to Paniushkin, September 1946, RTsKhIDNI, f. 17, op. 128, d. 151, l. 19.

289. "Auszug aus der Diskussion zweier Konferenzen der Berliner Jugendfunktionär," July 28, 1945, SAPMO-BA, ZPA, NL 182/852, b. 43. Emphasis in the original.

290. "Richtlinien für den Aufbau der Betriebsgruppen," September 18–19, 1946, SAPMO, BA, NL 90/287 (Grotewohl), b. 6.

291. SAPMO-BA, ZPA, EA 0120/2, b. 102. In the summer of 1946, the SED agreed to publish a separate women's section in the monthly magazine *Neuer Weg,* under the title "Frauenfunktionärin" (The Woman Functionary), as a way to improve recruitment into the party. "Massnahmen zur Verbesserung der Arbeit der Frauenabteilungen der SED," SAPMO-BA, ZPA, NL 36/731, b. 18. See also ibid., b. 56.

292. Oelssner report at Agitprop meeting, September 28, 1945, RTsKhIDNI, f. 17, op. 128, d. 792, l. 18; Russkikh to Tereshkin, December 11, 1948, RTsKhIDNI, f. 17, op. 128, d. 567, l. 168. See also GARF, f. 7077, op. 1, d. 206, l. 11.

293. Berlin Propaganda Section to Paniushkin, September 1946, RTsKhIDNI, f. 17, op. 128, d. 151, ll. 17–18.

294. SAPMO-BA, ZPA, IV 2/17/11, b. 22.

295. GARF, f. 7212, op. 1, d. 186, ll. 46–47.

296. Berlin to Paniushkin, September 1946, RTsKhIDNI, f. 17, op. 128, d. 151, ll. 61–63.

297. "Stenogramma soveshchaniia," October (September) 17–18, 1946, RTsKhIDNI, f. 17, op. 128, d. 149, ll. 172–173; Women's Section, May 13, 1947, SAPMO-BA, ZPA, NL 90/298 (Grotewohl), b. 19 ff.

298. Vatnik to Tiul'panov, July 18, 1947, GARF, f. 7212, op. 1, d. 192, ll. 82–85.

299. "Ausführbestimmungen zum Befehl 254 vom 11 Nov. 1947," SAPMO-BA, ZPA, IV 2/2.1/147, Protocol of the Central Secretariat, November 24, 1947, p. 17. Later reports indicate that the Frauenreferate had a very hard time establishing any kind of authority in the ministries. SAPMO-BA, ZPA, NL 36/731, b. 47.

300. See especially Barbara Johr, "Die Ereignisse in Zahlen," in *Befreier und Befreite,* p. 59.

301. "Weimar, December 17, 1945," FES, SPD Ostbüro, 1410b.

302. SAPMO-BA, ZPA, IV 2/1/25 (Parteivorstand Protocol, July 28–29, 1948), bb. 13–14; IV 2/1/26 (Parteivorstand Protocol, September 15, 1948), b. 56.

303. Wolfgang Schneider, "Der politisch-ideologische Reifeprozess der Freundschaft zur Sowjetunion," in *Die Grosse Sozialistische Oktoberrevolution und Deutschland* (Berlin, GDR: Dietz, 1967), vol. 2, pp. 261–262.

304. Russkikh to Ponomarev, January 14, 1949, RTsKhIDNI, f. 17, op. 128, d. 573, l. 122.

305. Rudolf Herrnstadt, "Über 'die Russen' und über uns," *Tägliche Rundschau,* November 19, 1948, p. 5.

306. The discussions were published in part in stenographic form by the Society for the Study of the Culture of the Soviet Union. *"Über 'die Russen' und über uns": Diskussion über ein brennendes Thema* (Berlin 1949). A briefer version of the December 10, 1948, meeting was also published in 1948 under the same title. I use here the 1949 version. Both discussions were also summarized in *Tägliche Rundschau,* December 12, 1948, and January 9, 1949.

307. *"Über 'die Russen' und über Uns"* (1949), p. 8.

308. Ibid., pp. 8–10.

309. Ibid., p. 11.

310. Ibid., p. 14.

311. Ibid., p. 16.

312. Ibid., p. 21.

313. Ibid., p. 23.

314. Ibid., p. 23.

315. Ibid., pp. 23–24.

316. Ibid. (This quote is also included in the shorter *Tägliche Rundschau* summary, December 12, 1945.)

317. Ibid., pp. 27–28.

318. Ibid., p. 33.

319. Ibid., pp. 50–51. (See also the summary of Tregubov's remarks in *Tägliche Rundschau*, January 9, 1949.)

320. Ibid., pp. 56–57.

321. Ibid.

322. Martem'ianov to Tiul'panov, March 22, 1949, GARF, f. 7077, op. 1, d. 247, l. 77.

323. See the reports from dozens of cities and towns in the zone, in SAPMO-BA, DSF, A 85.

3. REPARATIONS, REMOVALS, AND THE ECONOMIC TRANSFORMATION OF THE ZONE

1. J. P. Nettl made some insightful observations on this problem more than forty years ago in his *The Eastern Zone and Soviet Policy in Germany, 1945–1950* (London: Oxford University Press, 1951), pp. 295–314. For newer work on the subject, see Rainer Karlsch, *Allein bezahlt? Die Reparationsleistungen der SBZ/DDR 1945–1953* (Berlin: Ch. Links Verlag, 1993), pp. 223–241.

2. See Alexander Gerschenkron, *Bread and Democracy in Germany* (Ithaca, N.Y.: Cornell University Press, 1989), orig. published in 1943, pp. 165–224. Gerschenkron wrote during the war: "Nothing short of a revolutionary upheaval can ever enable a German government to dislodge the Junkers from their entrenched position in German society" (p. 76).

3. Matthias Graf von Schmettow and Ingrid Gräfin von Schmettow, eds., *Gedenkbuch des deutschen Adels: Nachtrag* (Limburg an der Lahn, Germany: C. A. Starke Verlag, 1980), pp. viii, 63–64 (table 1).

4. Ibid.

5. Dimitrov diary entry, June 9, 1945, RTsKhIDNI, f. 146, op. 2, d. 15, l. 62.

6. SAPMO-BA, ZPA, NL 277/4 (Zaisser), b. 214.

7. See Prikaz no. 54, March 20, 1946, "O rezul'tatakh proverki raboty po provedeniiu zemel'noi reformy v raionakh provintsii Brandenburg," GARF, f. 7184, op. 2, d. 2, ll. 111–115, 137; Prikaz no. 2, July 21, 1945, GARF, f. 7077, op. 2, d. 1, l. 2.

8. "Stenogramma soobshchenii Akkermana, Ul'brikhta i Sobotka v Otdele mezh-

dunarodnoi informatsii TsK VKP[b] o polozhenii v Germanii," June 7, 1945, RTsKhIDNI, f. 17, op. 128, d. 750, l. 42.

9. "Agricultural Conditions in the Russian Zone of Occupation: Interview with Professor Woermann," September 20, 1945, p. 1, NA, RG 226, entry 19, box 0330 (X124343); "Agricultural and Political Conditions in the Mark Brandenburg and Magdeburger Börde," September 1945, NA, RG 226, entry 19, box 0336 (XL 24960).

10. "Views of Edward [Edwin] Hoernle," NA, RG 226, entry 19, box 0336 (XL 24958). American intelligence sources indicate even more severe reduction of livestock: "Current Agricultural Conditions in the Russian-Occupied Zone of Germany," October 8, 1945, FIS 27, in ibid., p. 3.

11. SAPMO-BA, ZPA, I 2/5/50 (Protocol no. 24, Secretariat Meeting, September 6, 1945), b. 16.

12. "Stenogramma," June 7, 1945, RTsKhIDNI, f. 17, op. 128, d. 750, l. 42.

13. Von Schmettow and von Schmettow, eds., *Gedenkbuch des deutschen Adels*, p. 63 (table 1).

14. Report of the Political Section of the 4th Tank Army to the chief of the Political Administration of the First Ukrainian Front, "Ob otnoshenii chekhoslovatskogo naseleniia k nemtsam," May 18, 1945, RTsKhIDNI, f. 17, op. 128, d. 320, l. 161. The NKVD complained that the brutal expulsions from Czechoslovakia went on without any interference from local Soviet commandants. Serov to Beria, July 4, 1945, GARF, f. 9401, op. 2, d. 97, ll. 143–144.

15. Antony Polonsky and Boleslaw Drukier, eds., *The Beginnings of Communist Rule in Poland* (London: Routledge and Kegan Paul, 1980), p. 425.

16. See the reports from various towns in Polish-administered German territory, in SAPMO-BA, ZPA, IV 2/11/228 (Kaderfragen).

17. Dekanat of Waldenburg to Bishop of Berlin, Copy to Murphy, January 19, 1946, NA, RG 84, CGC, Box 2, pp. 5, 9.

18. SAPMO-BA, ZPA, VG 127/7 (Antifaschistische Freiheitsbewegung, Breslau, 1945), bb. 4–9.

19. See the August 6, 1945, report from the antifascist committee of Schweidnitz, in SAPMO-BA, ZPA, IV 2/11/228 (Kaderfragen), b. 5.

20. SAPMO-BA, ZPA, VG 127/7 (Antifaschistische Freiheitsbewegung Breslau, 1945), b. 133.

21. Bruno Köhler to Dimitrov, November 16, 1945, RTsKhIDNI, f. 17, op. 128, d. 787, l. 66; SAPMO-BA, ZPA, I 2/5/50, (Protocol no. 25 of the Secretariat Meeting, September 13, 1945), bb. 5–7.

22. The Breslau antifascists continued to have problems with local authorities in Halle. They felt that they were denied decent housing while members of the Nazi party continued to live well. SAPMO-BA, ZPA, VG 127/7 (Antifaschistische Freiheitsbewegung Breslau, 1945), bb. 45–50.

23. "Food Conditions in the Russian Zone of Germany," November 1, 1945, FIS 36, p. 4, HIA, Lerner, box 49, folder 3.

24. Gerhard Ziemer, *Deutscher Exodus: Vertreibung und Eingliederung von 15 Milli-*

onen Ostdeutschen (Stuttgart: Seewald Verlag, 1973), pp. 94, 227. About 4.5 million Germans were resettled in the Soviet zone of occupation, increasing the region's population of 16.5 million by about 25 percent.

25. Report from Görlitz, January 30, 1946, GARF, f. 7212, op. 1, d. 186, l. 148.

26. Hermann Brill, "Die Sozialdemokraten in heutigen Deutschland," September 30, 1945, SAPMO-BA, ZPA, NL 182/857 (Ulbricht), b. 15.

27. Report of S. Lt. A. Chiguev, July 22, 1946, RTsKhIDNI, f. 17, op. 128, d. 146, l. 71.

28. See Alexander von Plato and Wolfgang Meinicke, *Alte Heimat—neue Zeit: Flüchtlinge, Umgesiedelte, Vertriebene in der Sowjetischen Besatzungszone und in der DDR* (Berlin: Verlags-Anstalt Union, 1991), p. 41.

29. SAPMO-BA, ZPA, NA 182/1194, bb. 171, 198.

30. "Referat auf der öffentlichen Versammlung der Umsiedler," Berlin, August 12, 1949, SAPMO-BA, ZPA, NL 36/440 (Pieck), b. 109

31. For the CDU's position and the response by the KPD and SPD, see documents on the land reform in SAPMO-BA, ZPA, NL 36/722 (Pieck), bb. 30, 38–39, 55–57. See also the KPD Central Committee's October 18, 1945, account of the reform in SAPMO-BA, ZPA, IV 2/7/227, bb. 55–68.

32. Cited in Dietrich Staritz, *Die Gründung der DDR* (Frankfurt am Main: Suhrkampf, 1985), p. 110.

33. SAPMO-BA, ZPA, IV 2/7/227, b. 67.

34. Serov to Beria, September 12, 1945, GARF, f. 9401, op. 2, d. 99, ll. 3–5.

35. See the history of the land reform in SAPMO-BA, ZPA, IV 2/7/227, bb. 10–23.

36. Wilhelm Pieck, *Bodenreform: "Junkerland in Bauernhand"* (Berlin: Verlag Neuer Weg GMBH, 1945), pp. 3–16.

37. See, for example, Wilhelm Pieck, "Die Demokratische Bodenreform—Deutschlands Aufbauproblem—Die Kraft der demokratischen Einheit," Berlin speech, September 19, 1945, in *Reden und Aufsätze: Auswahlband* (Berlin: Dietzverlag, 1948), pp. 72–73.

38. Walter Görlitz, *Adel und Bauern im deutschen Osten: Geschichtliche Bilanz von sieben Jahrhunderten* (Glücksburg: Verlag von C. U. Starke, 1956), p. 414.

39. Hermes also objected to the absence of compensation for "innocent" landowners. Tugarinov to Dimitrov, "O politicheskom polozhenii v Germanii," November 3, 1945, RTsKhIDNI, f. 17, op. 125, d. 321, l. 106.

40. SAPMO-BA, ZPA, EA 0059 (Walter Besenbuch), b. 7.

41. Department of State, Research and Analysis, November 5, 1945, no. 3426, OSS/ State Department Intelligence and Research Reports, Postwar Europe, Microfilm (Reel #10), p. 3.

42. Serov to Beria, September 12, 1945, GARF, f. 9401, op. 2, d. 99, l. 5.

43. SAPMO-BA, ZPA, EA 0059 (Walter Besenbuch), b. 7. Prof. Woermann claimed that at least one-third of the owners of large estates had been arrested. NA, RG 226, entry 19, Box 0330 (XL 24343), p. 7.

44. I have been unable to find archival records that document in a serious way the Rügen "operation." But the island figures prominently in the memoirs of those

who escaped. *Weissbuch über die "Demokratische Bodenreform" in der Sowjetischen Besatzungszone Deutschlands: Dokumente und Berichte* (Munich/Stamsried: Verlag Ernst Vögel, 1988).

45. GARF, f. 7212, op. 1, d. 186, l. 236.

46. Meeting of Zhukov and representatives of the provinces, November 13, 1945, SAPMO-BA, ZPA, NL 182/1084, ll. 31–32.

47. SAPMO-BA, ZPA, I 2/5/50 (Protocol of the Secretariat Meeting, September 13, 1945).

48. January 15, 1946, meeting in Karlshorst between SVAG official Plotnikov and Saxon vice president Fischer, SAPMO-BA, ZPA, NL 182/1188 (Ulbricht), bb. 35–36.

49. "Current Agricultural Conditions in the Russian-Occupied Zone of Germany," October 8, 1945, FIS 27, NA, RG 226, entry 19, box 0336 (XL 29958), p. 12.

50. Ulbricht to Bokov and Kovalev, May 20, 1946, SAPMO-BA, ZPA, NL 182/1191 (Ulbricht), b. 37.

51. Report from Kreis Oberbarnim, July 14, 1948, SAPMO-BA, ZPA IV 2/7/231, b. 126.

52. SAPMO-BA, ZPA, EA 1070 (Karl Lawonn), b. 83. SAPMO-BA, ZPA, NL 182/1084, b. 31. The Raffeisen cooperatives were later allowed to organize beyond the confines of their earlier adherents. See the May 24, 1946, rules for their relations with the VdgBs: SAPMO-BA, ZPA, 2/7/634, b. 68.

53. See, for example, "Beschwerde der Siedlergemeinschaft Klessener Zootzen bei Marschall Sokolovskii," December 1, 1946, SAPMO-BA, ZPA, IV 2/7/109, b. 143.

54. Wilhelm Schneider to FDGB Vorstand, May 25, 1946, SAPMO-BA, ZPA, IV 2/7/231, b. 85.

55. SAPMO-BA, ZPA, IV 2/1/12, (Parteivorstand Protocol, August 20–21, 1947), b. 51.

56. Lt. Gen. Makarov to Kuznetsov, "Donesenie," October 14, 1947, RTsKhIDNI, f. 17, op. 128, d. 358, l. 86.

57. Hoernle to Karlshorst, August 29, 1949, SAMPO-BA, ZPA, IV 2/7/231, b. 27. The average for the whole zone was about 10 percent.

58. SAPMO-BA, ZPA, IV 2/1/20 (Parteivorstand Protocol, February 11–12, 1948), b. 37.

59. Makarov to Kuznetsov, October 14, 1947, RTsKhIDNI, f. 17, op. 128, d. 358, l. 87.

60. Transcript of the functionaries' conference of January 6, 1946, SAPMO-BA, ZPA, I 2/5/39, b. 188

61. Hermann Matern, Protocol of the Secretariat Meeting, September 13, 1945, SAPMO-BA, ZPA, I 2/5/50, b. 15.

62. FES, SPD Ostbüro, 0033, p. 35 (Schwarzenberg).

63. SAMPO-BA, ZPA, IV 2/7/231, bb. 101–113.

64. For several similar cases from Saxony-Anhalt, see SAPMO-BA, ZPA, IV 2/7/231, bb. 245–252.

65. The data on land reform is from SAPMO-BA, ZPA, IV 2/7/634, bb. 25–44. According to an American study, 33 percent of the land that was distributed to

individuals went to the expellees and refugees, 26 percent to agricultural workers, 16 percent to landless farmers, 14 percent to small landowning farmers, and the rest to workers. Department of State, OIR, "Land Reform in the Soviet Zone of Germany, May 16, 1949," HIA, Murphy, 67-3, p. 1.

66. Cited in von Plato and Meinicke, *Alte Heimat—neue Zeit,* p. 60.

67. "Views of Edward [Edwin] Hoernle," NA, RG 226, entry 19, box 1236 (XL 24958), p. 2.

68. Interview with Prof. Woermann, September 20, 1948, p. 3, NA, RG 226, entry 19, box 0330 (XL 24343).

69. "Current Agricultural Conditions," October 8, 1945, FIS 27, pp. 8–9, NA, RG 226, entry 19, box 0336 (XL 29958).

70. Report of November 12, 1946, SAPMO-BA, ZPA, NL 182/1063, b. 6.

71. Report of Hanna Sandtner, November 12, 1946, in ibid., b. 4.

72. SAPMO-BA, ZPA, IV 2/7/231, b. 131.

73. From Max Franke *(Neubauer)* in *Der Freie Bauer* (February 14, 1948), SAPMO-BA, ZPA, IV 2/7/240, b. 50.

74. Paul Merker on discussions with Karlshorst, December 5, 1946, SAPMO-BA, ZPA, NL 182/1063, bb. 19–20; Hoernle, December 5, 1946, SAPMO-BA, ZPA, IV 2/7/109, b. 76–77.

75. To the SED from VdgB, December 19, 1946, SAPMO-BA, ZPA, NL 36/731, l. 121. This report added, almost as an afterthought, that farm women were often raped during these raids.

76. Order no. 121, "Ob ukrytii skota ot obiazatel'noi sdachi produktov zhivotno-vodstva . . .," June 11, 1946, GARF, f. 7103, op. 2, d. 1, ll. 286–288.

77. Fediunskii speech in Schwerin, August 21, 1945, SAPMO-BA, ZPA, NL 8/8 (Sobottka), bb. 13–14.

78. SAPMO-BA, ZPA, IV 2/1/4 (Parteivorstand Protocol, September 18–19, 1946), b. 70.

79. Grotewohl to Ulbricht, March 7, 1946, SAPMO-BA, ZPA, NL 182/857 (Ulbricht), b. 46. See also Paul Schultz to E. Hoernle, November 19, 1947, SAPMO-BA, IV 2/7/240, b. 3.

80. SAPMO-BA, ZPA, NL 90/314.

81. SAPMO-BA, ZPA, EA 1734/1 (Erich Filss), b. 226.

82. SAPMO-BA, ZPA, IV 2/7/231, bb. 3–7, 201–202. Some SED officials admitted in November 1948 that in hundreds of cases the land reform measures had been poorly carried out. Since the reform could not be reversed, the only thing to do was to review the cases one by one. SAPMO-BA, ZPA, IV 2/7/236, b. 1.

83. Chapin to Vatnik, April 17, 1947, GARF, f. 7212, op. 1, d. 194, ll. 184–185.

84. Makarov to Kuznetsov, October 14, 1947, RTsKhIDNI, f. 17, op. 128, d. 358, ll. 86–87.

85. Ibid., l. 88.

86. SAPMO-BA, ZPA, IV 2/7/227, b. 64.

87. Department of State, R&A, November 5, 1945, no. 3426, p. 10, OSS/State Department I&R Reports, Postwar Europe, Microfilm (reel 10).

88. Joachim Piskol, Christel Nehrig, and Paul Trixa, *Anti-faschistisch-demokratische*

Umwälzung auf dem Lande (1945–1949) (Berlin: VEB Deutscher Landwirt-schaftsverlag, 1984), p. 125.

89. "Innenminister Konferenz," Rehfeide, Saxony, October 12, 1947, RTsKhIDNI, f. 17, op. 128, d. 354, l. 3.

90. Maj. Ivaniakov, Report on the Hildburghausen region, June 11, 1948, GARF, f. 7184, op. 1, d. 166, ll. 1–6.

91. GARF, f. 7077, op. 1, d. 258 (Brandenburg), l. 77.

92. GARF, f. 7184, no. 1, d. 166, l. 70.

93. The case of *Grossbauer* Puhlmann of Zepernick, August 12, 1948, SAPMO-BA, ZPA, IV 2/7/240, b. 70. (Emphasis in the original.)

94. "Zapiska i.o. nachal'nika Upravleniia sel'skogo khoziaistva SVAG Korbuta politicheskomu sovetniku pri Glavnonachal'stvuiushchem SVAG V. S. Semenovu o rabote v nemetskoi derevne," September 17, 1948, RTsKhIDNI, f. 17, op. 128, d. 572, ll. 107–111.

95. "Dokladnaia zapiska o zonal'noi konferentsii Krest'ianskoi Demokraticheskoi partii v g. Shverin," July 16–17, 1948, RTsKhIDNI, f. 17, op. 128, d. 567, ll. 19–21.

96. Merker to Reutter, Abteilung Landwirtschaft, November 13, 1948, SAPMO-BA, ZPA, IV 2/7/240, b. 70.

97. Ulbricht, "Schulungstagung," Land Saxony, Dresden, March 2–4, 1949, SAPMO-BA, ZPA, NL 277/4 (Zaisser), bb. 13–14, 23.

98. The data on collectivization is taken from Hermann Weber, *Kleine Geschichte der DDR* (Cologne: Edition Deutschland Archive, 1980), pp. 61–66, and Martin McCauley, *The German Democratic Republic since 1945* (New York: St. Martin's Press, 1983), pp. 56, 98.

99. Some of the problems with coordination can be seen in the case of the removal of printing machines. GARF, f. 7077, op. 1, d. 196, ll. 4–6.

100. Ministerstvo Inostrannykh Del SSSR: Istoriko-diplomaticheskoe upravlenie, *Germanskii Vopros vo Vzaimootnosheniiakh SSSR, SSHA, Anglii i Frantsii v period ot Berlinskoi Konferentsii do Obrazovaniia dvukh germanskikh Gosudarstv (1945–1949 gg.)*, part 2 (1963), in AVPRF, f. 48z, op. 11zh, d. 13 (papka 69), l. 274.

101. On the reparations issue at Potsdam, see Melvyn P. Leffler, *A Preponderance of Power: National Security, the Truman Administration, and the Cold War* (Stanford, Calif.: Stanford University Press, 1992), p. 67; John Backer, *The Decision to Divide Germany: American Foreign Policy in Transition* (Durham, N.C.: Duke University Press, 1978), pp. 88–101.

102. "Proekt zaiavleniia po germanskomu voprosu," draft, July 1946, AVPRF, f. 082, op. 30, d. 26 (papka 129), ll. 51–52.

103. On the Clay-Sokolovskii talks, see Iz dnevnika Generala Armii SOKOLOVSKOGO, "Beseda s General-leitenantom KLEI, zamestitelem Glavnokomanduiushchego Okkupatsionnymi Voiskami SSHA v Germanii," November 15, 1945, AVPRF, f. 082, op. 30, d. 7 (papka 127), ll. 5–8. There is a great deal of evidence to suggest that Gen. Clay was more interested in reaching agreement with the Russians about reparations than were his rivals in the State Department.

His proposal for resolving the reparations issue is discussed in Wolfgang Krieger, *General Lucius Clay und die amerikanische Deutschlandpolitik* (Stuttgart: Klett-Cotta, 1987), pp. 188–196. On the 1946 talks between Clay and Sokolovskii, see especially John Backer, *Winds of History: The German Years of Lucius Clay* (New York: Van Nostrand Reinhold Co., 1983), pp. 148–151. I am grateful to Robert Kleiman for his insights (and references) on the Clay-Sokolovskii talks.

104. *Germanskii vopros,* part 2, AVPRF, f. 48z, op. 11zh, d. 13 (papka 69), ll. 231, 262, 265.

105. Ibid., ll. 272–273.

106. The Soviets underestimated the total of removals both by ignoring accounts before August 2, 1945, and by not including certain categories of valuable merchandise in the reparations accounts. According to British estimates, by the end of October 1947, the Soviets had already seized from eastern Germany $5.5 billion worth of capital equipment (in 1938 values) and $2.25 billion in current production. UK Delegation Brief for Council of Foreign Ministers, "Economic Activity in the Eastern Zone of Germany," PRO, FO 371, Germany File no. 114, p. 2. See also Nettl, *The Eastern Zone,* pp. 199–258.

107. *Germanskii vopros,* part 2, AVPRF, f. 48z, op. 11zh, d. 2, ll. 271–272.

108. "Khoziaistvennyi plan na 1948 g." (trans. from German), RTsKhIDNI, f. 17, op. 128, d. 1186, ll. 70–71.

109. See a series of sequestering orders (nos. 215–239) from May 1946 in Thüringen. GARF, f. 7184, op. 2, d. 4, ll. 74–181.

110. Semenov to Vyshinskii, April 30, 1945, AVPRF, f. 082, op. 30, d. 63 (papka 134), l. 57.

111. SAPMO-BA, NL 182/1190 (Ulbricht), l. 54.

112. Report from F. Grosse, September 18, 1946 (Russian trans.), RTsKhIDNI, f. 17, op. 128, d. 147, l. 32.

113. See the order on the sequestering of beach houses on the Baltic Coast. Mecklenburg SVA, order no. 64, April 29, 1947, GARF, f. 7103, op. 2, d. 4, l. 146.

114. RTsKhIDNI, f. 17, op. 128, d. 147, ll. 33–34.

115. SAPMO-BA, ZPA, IV 2/1/1 (Parteivorstand Protocol, May 14–15, 1946), b. 196.

116. Protocol of SED talks with Saxony SVA, June 15, 1946, SAPMO-BA, ZPA, IV 2/602/107 (Wirtschaftspolitik), bb. 68–72.

117. Gärtner Letter, September 13, 1948 (Russian trans. forwarded from Russkikh to Ponomarev), RTsKhIDNI, f. 17, op. 128, d. 565, ll. 3–4.

118. SAPMO-BA, ZPA, IV 2/602/107 (Wirtschaftsfragen), b. 152.

119. SAPMO-BA, ZPA, NL 182/1181 (Ulbricht), bb. 59–60.

120. Politupravlenie SVAG, "Vnutripoliticheskaia obstanovka v Sovetskoi zone okkupatsii," RTsKhIDNI, f. 17, op. 132, d. 8, ll.

121. On the situation of the SED in Thüringen in January 1948, see GARF, f. 7184, op. 1, d. 165, l. 156.

122. "Stenografischer Bericht über die Innenminister-Konferenz," August 11 and 12, 1947, BStU MfSZ, AS 229/66, b. 35.

123. Semenov to Molotov, Suslov, and Vyshinskii, "Kratkii ekonomicheskii obzor po

Sovet. Zone Okk. Germanii," April 1948, RTsKhIDNI, f. 17, op. 128, d. 573, l. 23.

124. Baranov to Suslov, April 27, 1948, "Informatsionnaia zapiska o 9 Plenume Tsentral'nogo Pravleniia SEPG (April 14–15, 1948)," RTsKhIDNI, f. 17, op. 128, d. 1186, l. 159.

125. A. Zverev to Dekanozov, August 28, 1946, AVPRF, f. 082, op. 30, d. 32 (papka 130), l. 157; "O peredache sekvestrirovannykh predpriiatii," Order no. 191, August 28, 1947, GARF, f. 7184, op. 2, d. 8, l. 122.

126. Russian Archives, Collection.

127. Rescript of Maj. Gen. Sharov, Brandenburg, January 9, 1946, GARF, f. 7077, op. 1, d. 196, l. 7.

128. GARF, f. 7077, op. 1, d. 196, l. 110.

129. Beria to Stalin, Molotov, Mikoyan, July 10, 1945, GARF, f. 9401, op. 2, d. 97, l. 323.

130. Russian Archives, Collection.

131. Ibid.

132. Note of Maj. Tikhonov, May 22, 1947, GARF, f. 7133, op. 2, d. 45, l. 70; V. N. Lazarev, Academy of Sciences, to Malenkov, April 13, 1946, AVPRF, f. 082, op. 30, d. 50 (papka 132), l. 3.

133. "Sbornik materialov po istorii otdela narod. obrazovaniia," vol. 3, GARF, f. 7317, op. 54, d. 3, ll. 75–76.

134. Khrapchenko to Molotov, August 22, 1945, RTsKhIDNI, f. 17, op. 125, d. 308, l. 20.

135. Vatnik to Tiul'panov, "O kul'turnoi zhizni FZ Saksoniia," February 26, 1946, GARF, f. 7212, op. 1, d. 186, ll. 162–163; Report from Bitterfeld, June 15, 1946, GARF, f. 7133, op. 1, d. 252, ll. 54, 78.

136. GARF, f. 7212, op. 1, d. 176, ll. 162–163.

137. "Sbornik materialov," vol. 3, GARF, f. 7317, op. 54, d. 3, l. 76.

138. Ibid., l. 78.

139. Semenov to Vyshinskii, June 15, 1945, AVPRF, f. 082, op. 27, d. 3 (papka 120), l. 7. See also Patricia Kennedy Grimstead, "The Fate of Ukrainian Cultural Treasures during World War II: The Plunder of Archives, Libraries and Museums under the Third Reich," *Jahrbücher für Geschichte Osteuropas,* vol. 1, no. 39 (1991): 75–77.

140. RTsKhIDNI, f. 17, op. 125, d. 308, ll. 23–29.

141. Order no. 012, March 9, 1946, GARF, f. 7184, op. 1, d. 148, l. 1.

142. "Sbornik materialov," vol. 3, GARF, f. 7317, op. 54, d. 3, ll. 52–54.

143. See Gregory Sandford, *From Hitler to Ulbricht,* (Princeton, N.J.: Princeton University Press, 1983), pp. 40–42; Rainer Karlsch, " 'Arbeiter schützt Eure Betriebe!'—Widerstand gegen Demontage in der SBZ," unpublished manuscript, 1994.

144. GARF, f. 7212, op. 1, d. 187, ll. 78–79. These are reports from Leipzig, Chemnitz, and Zwickau.

145. Ibid., l. 79.

146. Dubrovskii and Vatnik to Serov, "Donesenie: O nastroeniiakh nemetskogo naseleniia po FZ Saksoniia," April 19, 1946, GARF, f. 7212, op. 1, d. 188, l. 6.

147. Report of F. Grosse from Saxony, September 18, 1946 (in Russian), RTsKhIDNI, f. 17, op. 128, d. 147, ll. 36–37.

148. GARF, f. 7212, op. 1, d. 187, l. 78.

149. GARF, f. 7212, op. 1, d. 186, l. 57.

150. Ibid., d. 187, l. 80.

151. Ibid., l. 79; SED Thüringen to SED in Berlin, January 15, 1947, SAPMO-BA, ZPA, NL 90/314, b. 42.

152. "O nastroeniiakh nemetskogo naseleniia v FZ Saksoniia," GARF, f. 7212, op. 1, d. 188, l. 6.

153. "Stenogramma soobshchenii," June 7, 1945, RTsKhIDNI, f. 17, op. 128, d. 750, l. 32.

154. Seventh Section of the Political Department of the Group of Soviet Forces to Smirnov, "Informatsionnaia svodka no. 89," July 2, 1945, AVPRF, f. 082, op. 27, d. 35 (papka 123), l. 149.

155. SAPMO-BA, ZPA, IV 2/1/12 (Parteivorstand Protocol, August 20–21, 1947), b. 29.

156. Biuro Informatsii SVAG, *Biulleten'* no. 14/113, February 5, 1947 (in Russian), RTsKhIDNI, f. 17, op. 128, d. 362, l. 195.

157. SAPMO-BA, ZPA, IV 2/1/12 (Parteivorstand Protocol, August 20–21, 1947), bb. 168–169.

158. See Ulbricht to Paniushkin, March 11, 1946 (Russian trans.), RTsKhIDNI, f. 17, op. 128, d. 931, l. 220. Here Ulbricht asked Paniushkin what he could say about dismantling at the upcoming party congress.

159. SAPMO-BA, ZPA, NL 90/337 (Grotewohl), folders 1 and 2. See especially "Anruf von Weimar vom 10. January 1947, 11:30 Uhr," in ibid., folder 2, b. 61.

160. Note of July 19, 1946, SAPMO-BA, ZPA, NL 182/1190, b. 56.

161. "Bittschrift der Niederlausnitzer Bergarbeiter an Herrn Marschall Sokolowski," November 7, 1946, SAPMO-BA, ZPA, NL 90/337, folder 2, b. 70.

162. Ibid., folder 1, b. 104–105.

163. There was a fierce scramble within the Soviet Union about who had the rights to which machines. For the case of the valuable German printing industry, see RTsKhIDNI, f. 17, op. 125, d. 444, l. 82.

164. *Germanskii vopros,* part 2, AVPRF, f. 48z, op. 11zh, d. 13 (papki 69), b. 271. Russian Archives, Collection.

165. Order no. 192, July 4, 1946, Sokolovskii, GARF, f. 7317, op. 8, d. 6, ll. 90–91.

166. Order no. 163, March 3, 1947, and Order no. 191, August 28, 1947, Kolesnichenko, GARF, f. 7184, op. 2, d. 8, ll. 58, 122.

167. "Niederschrift über die 15. Sitzung des gemeinsamen Ausschusses der Einheitsfront," May 29, 1946, SAPMO-BA, ZPA, NL 90/500, l. 117.

168. Tiul'panov to Suslov, "Doklad ob itogakh referenduma v federal'noi zemle Saksoniia," July 9, 1946, RTsKhIDNI, f. 17, op. 128, d. 951, l. 86.

169. Ulbricht to Bokov, May 7, 1946, SAPMO-BA, NL 182/1098, b. 21.

170. "Doklad ob itogakh," July 9, 1946, RTsKhIDNI, f. 17, op. 128, d. 951, l. 83.

171. Ibid., ll. 80, 84.

172. Vatnik to Tiul'panov, "O khode podgotovki k referendumu," July 12, 1946, GARF, f. 7212, op. 1, d. 187, l. 113. See also Vatnik to Tiul'panov, "Dokladnaia zapiska: O formakh bor'by vrazheskikh elementov protiv referenduma," June 24, 1946, in ibid., l. 138.

173. Ulbricht letter, July 16, 1946 (Russian trans.), RTsKhIDNI, f. 17, op. 128, d. 146, ll. 15–16.

174. The SED report on the meeting states that two other "gentlemen from SVAG Karlshorst" also attended, no doubt representatives of the MVD/MGB. "Protokoll über die Besprechung mit der S.M.A. Sachsen am Sonnabend, dem 15. Juni 1946," SAPMO-BA, ZPA, IV 2/602/107, b. 67.

175. Ibid., b. 68.

176. "Doklad ob itogakh," RTsKhIDNI, f. 17, op. 128, d. 951, ll. 78–79.

177. Rolf Badstübner et al., eds., *Die antifaschistisch-demokratische Umwälzung der Kampf gegen die Spaltung Deutschlands und die Entstehung der DDR von 1945 bis 1949: Deutsche Geschichte,* vol. 9 (Berlin, GDR: VEB Deutscher Verlag der Wissenschaften), p. 204.

178. "Iz dnevnika V. S. Semenova," Talks with Ulbricht, Pieck, Grotewohl, September 27, 1947, AVPRF, f. 082, op. 34, d. 4, l. 154.

179. Order no. 21, Brandenburg, February 13, 1946, GARF, f. 7184, op. 2, d. 2, l. 40.

180. Order no. 169, July 25, 1947, Saxony-Anhalt, in ibid., l. 70.

181. SAPMO-BA, ZPA, NL 182/1183 (Ulbricht), b. 47.

182. "Economic Activity in the Eastern Zone of Germany," U.K. Delegation Brief for Council of Foreign Ministers, December 1947, PRO, FO 371, Germany File no. 114, p. 12.

183. "Stenogramma soveshchaniia v upravlenii propagandy SVAG," September 1946, RTsKhIDNI, f. 17, op. 128, d. 149, l. 126.

184. Note of Economics Department of the SED, September 18, 1946, SAPMO-BA, ZPA, NL 182/1198 (Ulbricht), b. 19.

185. SAPMO-BA, ZPA, IV 2/1/4 (Parteivorstand Protocol, September 1946), b. 106.

186. "Khoziaistvennyi plan na 1948 g." (Russian trans.), RTsKhIDNI, f. 17, op. 128, d. 1186, ll. 146–147. See also Baranov to Suslov, April 27, 1948, in ibid., l. 159.

187. Sokolovskii and Bokov to Molotov and Mikoyan, April 5, 1946, AVPRF, f. 082, op. 30, d. 37 (papka 131), ll. 1–3.

188. Order no. 167, June 5, 1946, Sokolovskii, GARF, f. 7133, op. 2, d. 4, l. 86. Initially the Soviets had hoped to keep SAG production from being counted as part of reparations payments. Semenov to Smirnov, October 10, 1947, AVPRF, f. 082, op. 34, d. 37 (papka 149), l. 34.

189. Russian Archives, Collection.

190. "Economic Activity in the Eastern Zone of Germany," UK Deleg. Brief for C.F.M., PRO, FO 371, Germany File no. 114, p. 15.

191. Interview with Dr. Max Rokhlin, July 1989. See also his two-part memoir of the

Soviet exploitation of the German chemical industry, written under a pseudonym. L. Ostapov [M. Rokhlin], "V Germanii v 1945 godu," *Khimiia i zhizn'* no. 9 (September 1971): 30–37; no. 10 (October 1971): 55–61.

192. Selbmann to Ulbricht, September 25, 1947, SAPMO-BA, ZPA, NL 182/1189 (Ulbricht), b. 26.

193. Brack to Morenov, July 5, 1947, SAPMO-BA, ZPA, IV 2/2027/5, p. 1.

194. Eckstein to SED Berlin, January 15, 1947, SAPMO-BA, ZPA, NL 90/314, bb. 41–43.

195. Ibid., l. 42.

196. "Besprechungen über den Befehl 201," October 30, 1947, SAPMO-BA, ZPA, IV 2/13/4, b. 7.

197. Orlov-Merkulov correspondence, July–August 1947, AVPRF, f. 082, op. 34, d. 10 (papka 147), ll. 157, 163.

198. AVPRF, f. 082, op. 34, d. 10 (papka 147), l. 190.

199. Abakumov to Molotov, October 26, 1947, AVPRF, f. 082, op. 34, d. 10 (papka 147), ll. 182–184. Abakumov claimed that in its investigations of the SAGs in the first half of 1947, the MGB had arrested ninety-nine people, of whom five were foreign spies, three were diversionaries, and twenty-seven were "wreckers or saboteurs."

200. "Iz dnevnika V. N. Kuznetsova," Discussions with Fischer and Koenen from Saxony, July 14, 1947, AVPRF, f. 082, op. 34, d. 150, l. 18.

201. Eggerath, "Anruf von Weimar," January 10, 1947, SAPMO-BA, ZPA, NL 90/337 (Grotewohl), folder 2, b. 61.

202. "Iz dnevnika Kuznetsova, V. N.," August 18, 1947, AVPRF, f. 082, op. 34, d. 4 (papka 142), l. 134.

203. "Iz dnevnika V. N. Kuznetsova," July 14, 1947, AVPRF, f. 082, op. 34, d. 150, l. 20.

204. On Selbmann, see Karlsch, *Allein bezahlt?*, pp. 104–107.

205. See, for example, the May 8, 1947, law in Saxony: GARF, f. 7212, op. 1, d. 193, l. 172.

206. "Donesenie ob osnovnykh meropriiatiiakh SVAG i partiino-politicheskoi rabote za sentiabr' 1947 g.," October 14, 1947, RTsKhIDNI, f. 17, op. 128, d. 358, l. 85.

207. Makarov to Kuznetsov, "Donesenie ob osnovnykh meropriiatiiakh sovetskoi voennoi administratsii v Germanii," October 14, 1947, RTsKhIDNI, f. 17, op. 128, d. 358, ll. 85–86.

208. "Rekomendatsii SVAG Tsentral'nomu Sekretariatu SEPG po voprosu raboty v profsoiuzakh," August 1948, RTsKhIDNI, f. 17, op. 128, d. 571, ll. 53–55.

209. SAPMO-BA, ZPA, IV 2/1/20 (Parteivorstand Protocol, February 11–12, 1948), bb. 133–136.

210. "Rekomendatsii SVAG," August 1948, RTsKhIDNI, f. 17, op. 128, d. 571, l. 55.

211. Merker, "Entschliessung zur Lohnpolitik des FDGB," April 10, 1948, SAPMO-BA, ZPA, IV 2/2027/27 (Lehmann), p. 1.

212. "Iz dnevnika V. S. Semenova," Discussion with Pieck and Grotewohl, September 27, 1947, AVPRF, f. 082, op. 34, d. 4 (papka 146), ll. 151–152.

213. Biuro Informatsii SVAG, *Biulleten'* no. 4, February 4, 1948, RTsKhIDNI, f. 17, op. 128, d. 577, l. 57.

214. SAPMO-BA, ZPA, IV 2/2.1/135 (Central Secretariat Protocol, October 1, 1947), p. 2.

215. "Beratungen über Durchführung des Befehls 234," Erfurt, October 18, 1947, SAPMO-BA, ZPA, NL 182/1198 (Ulbricht), b. 120.

216. Russian Archives, Collection.

217. Perelivchenko to Rau, December 23, 1948, SAPMO-BA, ZPA, IV 2/2027/27 (Lehmann), p. 1.

218. Brack to Morenov, July 5, 1947, SAPMO-BA, ZPA, IV 2/2027/5, p. 2.

219. Ibid., p. 5.

220. In fact, Stakhanovism was all but dead in the Soviet Union by the end of the war. See Lewis Siegelbaum, *Stakhanovism and the Politics of Productivity in the USSR, 1935–1941* (Cambridge: Cambridge University Press, 1988), pp. 290–293.

221. See, for example, Horst Barthel, *Adolf Hennecke: Beispiel und Vorbild, Illustrierte historische Hefte* series, no. 16 (Berlin, GDR: Deutscher Verlag der Wissenschaften, 1979).

222. SAPMO-BA, ZPA, (Parteivorstand Protocol, October 20–21, 1948), bb. 49–51.

223. Ibid.

224. See various pieces, including a January 1, 1949, letter from Hennecke to Stakhanov, in the Hennecke papers: SAPMO-BA, ZPA, NL 177/7 (Hennecke), bb. 1–12.

225. SAPMO-BA, ZPA, IV 2/1/28 (Parteivorstand Protocol, October 20–21, 1948), b. 49.

226. Badstübner et al., *Deutsche Geschichte*, vol. 9, p. 385.

227. SAPMO-BA, ZPA, NL 177/3 (Hennecke), bb. 1–18.

228. Paul Wandel, August 25, 1949, at the National Theater, Weimar, GARF, f. 7184, op. 1, d. 169, l. 5.

229. SAPMO-BA, ZPA, NL 177/3 (Hennecke), bb. 47–48, 56, 58. The literal translation of the Hruby poem is as follows: "You are a model for us! Through you many first became an activist! Because of you, production and norms only rose! You were the first to give work style and the right form! The whole people thank you for it. You were the savior in distress. The overfulfillment of the Two-Year Plan is our solemn promise and silent commandment. We will also conquer our enemies, without war and without revolution. We see in you the worker hero, like the Soviet Union has, a kind of German Stakhanov."

230. Report of the German Education Administration, November 1947, SAPMO-BA, ZPA, IV 2/905/71 (Volksbildung), b. 213.

231. GARF, f. 7184, op. 1, d. 166, ll. 300–301.

232. A. Hennecke, "Kann der sowjetische Film unserer Aktivistenbewegung helfen?" November 5, 1949, SAPMO-BA, ZPA, NL 177/7 (Hennecke), b. 12.

233. SAPMO-BA, ZPA, IV 2/1/18 (Parteivorstand Protocol, December 8, 1947), b. 87.

234. Actually Stakhanov initiated this effort when he wrote directly to Stalin asking for material aid. The Central Committee offered to help him in exchange for

Stakhanov's word that he would stay out of trouble. RTsKhIDNI, f. 17, op. 125, d. 310, ll. 36–37.

235. FDGB to Hennecke, January 1, 1949, SAPMO-BA, ZPA, NL 177/7, b. 1.

236. SAPMO-BA, ZPA, NL 177/3, Stakhanov to Hennecke, December 29, 1948, b. 36; NL 177/7, Hennecke to Stakhanov, December 19, 1949, b. 17; NL 177/7, Hennecke, "Mein Lehrer Stakhanov," b. 99.

237. SAPMO-BA, ZPA, IV 2/1/28 (Parteivorstand Protocol, October 20–21, 1948), b. 50

238. SAPMO-BA, ZPA, EA 1839 (Mathias Werner Kruse), b. 27. American intelligence sources estimated that 75 percent of the workers were opposed to "the Hennecke principle." HQ, 7707 ECIC, February 8, 1949, NA, RG 260, box 94.

239. Starodubov to Tiul'panov, September 22, 1949, GARF, f. 7184, op. 1, d. 169, l. 25; SAPMO-BA, ZPA, NL 182/363, l. 133.

240. Ulbricht to Hennecke, September 15, 1949, SAPMO-BA, ZPA, NL 177/14 (Hennecke), b. 5.

241. SAPMO-BA, ZPA, NL 177/3 (Hennecke), bb. 63–64.

242. Ulbricht to Bergbauverwaltung Zwickau, June 16, 1949 (?), SAPMO-BA, ZPA, NL 177/1 (Hennecke), b. 4.

243. Ibid., bb. 5–7.

244. This suggestion was turned down with the remark that Hennecke could hardly repeat his record after being out of the mines for a year. Protocol of the Zwickau SED Kreisvorstand meeting, September 26, 1949, SAPMO-BA, ZPA, NL 177/16 (Hennecke), b. 11.

245. Ibid., bb. 9–13. See also ("Plan für die Auswertung der Hennecke-Konferenz in der Staatsoper Berlin," February 7, 1949, SAPMO-BA, NL 182/1166 (Ulbricht), bb. 1–2.

4. THE SOVIET USE OF GERMAN SCIENCE

1. Tom Bower, *The Paperclip Conspiracy: The Hunt for the Nazi Scientists* (Boston: Little, Brown, 1987); Christopher Simpson, *Blowback: America's Recruitment of Nazis and Its Effects on the Cold War* (New York: Weidenfeld and Nicolson, 1988). See also Linda Hunt, "U.S. Coverup of Nazi Scientists," *Bulletin of the Atomic Scientist* (April 1985): 16–24.

2. John Gimbel, *Science, Technology, and Reparations: Exploitation and Plunder in Postwar Germany* (Stanford, Calif.: Stanford University Press, 1990), pp. 134–135.

3. See especially David Holloway, *Stalin and the Bomb: The Soviet Union and Atomic Energy 1939–1956* (New Haven, Conn.: Yale University Press, 1994), pp. 109–112. See also Ulrich Albrecht, Andreas Heinemann-Grüder, and Arend Wellmann, *Die Spezialisten: Deutsche Naturwissenschaftler und Techniker in der Sowjetunion nach 1945* (Berlin: Dietz Verlag, 1992), pp. 31–32, 48–58.

4. Leslie Groves, *Now It Can be Told: The Story of the Manhattan Project* (New York: Harper and Brothers, 1962), pp. 243–244. Emphasis in the original.

5. *Alsos* is a Greek word meaning sacred grove.

6. See Clarence G. Lasby, *Project Paperclip: German Scientists and the Cold War* (New York: Atheneum, 1971), pp. 27–28. See also HIA, Pash, box 1, p. 5; Pash, "History of the Alsos Mission," box 1, p. 27; box 2, "Information obtained by German Intelligence Service Relative to Allied Atomic Research" (Capt. David S. Teeple, Military Intelligence), report of October 23, 1945, p. 7.

7. HIA, Pash, "History of the Alsos Mission," box 1, p. 21. See also Goudsmit's report of May 11, 1945, HQ European Theater of Operations, U.S. Army Alsos Mission, HIA, Pash, box 2.

8. S. A. Goudsmit, "Report of Scientific Chief of Alsos Mission," HIA, Pash, box 1, p. 15

9. British intelligence clandestinely recorded the Germans' conversations. The tapes were especially revealing when the Germans learned of the explosion of the American atomic bomb. See Jeremy Bernstein, "The Farm Hall Transcripts: The German Scientists and the Bomb," *The New York Review of Books,* no. 14 (August 13, 1992): 47–53. *Operation Epsilon: The Farm Hall Transcripts,* introduction by Sir Charles Frank (Berkeley: University of California Press, 1993), pp. 70–94.

10. Informed of Soviet intentions to contact Hahn, the Americans tried to convince him to move to the American zone "until his qualifications and usefulness to American research" could be determined. September 3, 1945, cable, NA, RG 226, 88, box 151. Although the British claimed in December 1945 that "there is no irrefutable evidence of [Soviet] body snatching," they nevertheless developed— under the name of Scrum Half—a surveillance program meant to deter any Soviet contact with German scientists. Report of December 29, 1945, PRO, FO 371, 1946, file no. 293 (55676), pp. 7029–10190. They were especially worried that the Soviets would try to kidnap Heisenberg, whose Göttingen home lay uncomfortably close to the zonal border. Heisenberg refused to move; as a result, the British maintained a high state of readiness called Dinner Party. "Emigration of German Specialists," PRO, FO 371, Germany 1948, file no. 21 (70952). On Soviet contacts with Heisenberg, see Franz Kurowski, *Allierte Jagd auf deutsche Wissenschaftler: Das Unternehmen Paperclip* (Munich: Kristall bei Langer Müller, 1982), p. 154. Periodically, the West German press would report rumors of Heisenberg's disappearance. *Die Neue Zeitung,* October 28, 1945.

11. *Operation Epsilon,* p. 172.

12. See Kaiser Wilhelm Institut für Elektrochemie, "Bericht über Gründung, Aufbau, Organisation . . . der Kaiser Wilhelm-Gesellschaft über den Stand der Dahlemer Institute vor und nach dem Zusammenbruch," p. 4, LAB, 7406.

13. Robert Berry to Ambassador Murphy, "Soviet Recruitment of German Scientists," January 15, 1946, NA, RG 84, CGC, box 68, folder 13. The Soviets were quite willing to forgive the scientists their Nazi background, which the Americans seemed willing to do only when they were brought to the United States. There are any number of cases of German scientists or technicians, unable to work in their field in the American zone because of their Nazi background, who were

then quickly recruited for work in the Soviet zone. See, for example, the case of a Dr. Kunze, Report, February 6, 1947, HIA, Murphy, 61-1.

14. USPOLAD, "Transfer of Scientific and Military Research Institutions from Germany to Russia," July 17, 1945, pp. 1–2, NA, RG 59, 740.00119, Control (Germany), 7-1745.

15. V. L. Sokolov, *Soviet Use of German Science and Technology, 1945–1946* (New York: Research Program on the U.S.S.R., 1955), p. 8.

16. NA, RG 319, XE 152 328, Ref. no. x-1002, September 19, 1946.

17. Heinz Barwich and Elfi Barwich, *Das rote Atom* (Munich: Scheiz Verlag, 1967), p. 39.

18. Central Intelligence Agency, "German Scientists at Sukhumi, USSR," OSI/SR-2/49, October 31, 1949, p. 5.

19. Barwich and Barwich, *Das rote Atom,* p. 20.

20. Max Steenbeck, *Impulse und Wirkungen: Schritte auf meinen Lebensweg* (Berlin, GDR: Verlag der Nation, 1978), pp. 164–168.

21. M. G. Iaroshevskii, *Repressirovannaia nauka* (Leningrad: "Nauka," 1991), p. 361.

22. Manfred von Ardenne, *Ein glückliches Leben für Technik und Forschung: Autobiographie* (Zürich: Kindler Verlag, 1972), p. 185.

23. Interview with I. N. Golovin, Stanford, California, October 19, 1992. Golovin, a leading Soviet atomic physicist, was on the mission to Austria and Germany in the spring and summer of 1945. Golovin stated that the group had initially been in Vienna in mid-April and had found 340 kilograms of enriched uranium in the Auer Company buildings there.

24. Andreas Heinemann-Grüder, "Die sowjetische Atombombe," Arbeitspapiere der Berghof-Stiftung für Konfliktforschung, no. 40 (Berlin, 1990), p. 23; Mark Walker, *German National Socialism and the Quest for Nuclear Power, 1939–1949* (Cambridge: Cambridge University Press, 1989), p. 156.

25. See Nikolaus Riehl, *10 Jahre im goldenen Käfig: Erlebnisse beim Aufbau der sowjetischen Uran-Industrie* (Stuttgart: Riederer, 1988), pp. 5–14. See also Kurowski, *Allierte Jagd,* pp. 175–176.

26. Dan Charles, "In the Beginning There Was Uranium," *The New Scientist,* October 24, 1992, p. 30.

27. See Central Intelligence Agency, Information Report, EG 1802, "The Problem of Uranium Isotope Separation by Means of Ultracentrifuge in the USSR," October 8, 1957.

28. Holloway, *Stalin and the Bomb,* pp. 109–110; Heinemann-Grüder, "Die sowjetische Atombombe," p. 20.

29. "Selections from OSS Intelligence," September 1, 1945, NA, RG 260, AGTS, box 644; HQ 7707 ECIC, "German Scientists in the Employ of the USSR," August 30, 1948, NA, RG 260, box 65.

30. Barwich and Barwich, *Der rote Atom,* p. 40.

31. See David Holloway, "Entering the Nuclear Arms Race: The Soviet Decision to Build the Atomic Bomb," *Social Studies of Science,* no. 11 (1981): 183. See also

Robert Chadwell Williams, *Klaus Fuchs: Atom Spy* (Cambridge, Mass.: Harvard University Press, 1987).

32. S. Leskov, "Lavrentii Beriia sumel by dobit'sia ekonomicheskogo protsvetaniia strany," *Izvestiia*, January 29, 1993, p. 16. On the other hand, Zaveniagin painted a *very* negative picture of Beria's abilities in his testimony associated with Beria's downfall and execution in 1953. See D. M. Stickle, ed., *The Beria Affair: The Secret Transcripts of the Meetings Signalling the End of Stalinism*, trans. Jean Farrow (New York: Nova Science Publishers, 1992), pp. 130–134.

33. See Heinemann-Grüder, "Die sowjetische Atombombe," p. 20, and Holloway, "Entering the Nuclear Arms Race," p. 183.

34. Central Intelligence Agency, Information Report, EG 1802, "The Problem of Uranium Isotope Separation by Means of Ultracentrifuge in the USSR," October 8, 1957, p. 2. According to Dan Charles, none of the Sukhumi scientists had earlier worked on isotope separation, but they had a huge advantage in their access to a secret U.S. government report on the Manhattan Project. Charles, "In the Beginning Was Uranium," p. 31. At Farm Hall, Heisenberg noted that it would not be hard for the Russians to make the bomb, so long as they figured out the method for separating isotopes. *Operation Epsilon*, p. 18.

35. Amy Knight, *Beria: Stalin's First Lieutenant* (Princeton, N.J.: Princeton University Press, 1993), p. 106.

36. Heinemann-Grüder, "Die sowjetische Atombombe," p. 28.

37. Interview with I. N. Golovin, October 19, 1992, Stanford, California.

38. Barwich and Barwich, *Das rote Atom*, p. 47 ; Steenbeck, *Impulse und Wirkungen*, pp. 188–189; CIA, Information Report, EG 1802, "The Problem of Uranium Isotope Separation," pp. 8–10.

39. Holloway, *Stalin and the Bomb*, p. 221.

40. John Gimbel, "U.S. Policy and German Scientists," *Political Science Quarterly*, no. 3 (1986): 433–451. See also Lasby, *Project Paperclip*, pp. 79, 136–137.

41. Sokolov, *Soviet Use of German Science and Technology*, p. 9.

42. Tokaev's defection produced a series of severe reprimands of his superiors. RTsKhIDNI, f. 17, op. 136, d. 8, l. 107. See Grigorii Tokaev's books *Stalin Means War*, trans. Alec Brown (London: George Weidenfeld and Nicolson, 1951), and *Comrade X* (London: The Harvell Press, 1956). Walter McDougall's analysis of the German contribution to the Soviet rocket program draws extensively on Tokaev's memoirs. Walter McDougall, *The Heavens and the Earth* (New York: Basic Books, 1985). But the ever-careful Boris Nicolaevsky took Tokaev to account for a number of inaccuracies and inconsistencies in his work. "Tokaev Correspondence," HIA, Nicolaevsky, Series no. 248, 504/28.

43. G. Tokaev, "K voprosu o likvidatsii voenno-aviatsionnogo potentsiala Germanii," *Sovetskoe slovo*, July 17 and July 19, 1947.

44. On Soviet claims to have destroyed German war potential, see "O demilitarizatsii Germanii," *Sovetskoe slovo*, May 9, 1947.

45. Kurowski, *Allierte Jagd*, p. 160.

46. Frederick I. Ordway III and Mitchell R. Sharpe, *The Rocket Team* (New York:

Thoms Y. Crowell, 1973), pp. 318–319, B. I. Chertok, "U sovetskikh raketnykh triumfov bylo nemetskoe nachalo," *Izvestiia,* no. 54 (March 4, 1992) and no. 55 (March 5, 1992). In German, *Rabe* means raven; this was the code name for the institute.

47. Chertok, "U sovetskikh raketnykh triumfov," in *Izvestiia,* no. 56 (March 6, 1992).
48. "OMGUS Special Intelligence," March 20, 1947, NA, RG 260, box 65.
49. Irmgard Gröttrup, *Die Bessessenen und die Mächtigen: Im Schatten der roten Rakete* (Stuttgart: Steingrüben Verlag, 1958), p. 16.
50. V. S. Varennikov, "Liudi i tekhnika kosmicheskoi ery," *Voprosy istorii,* no. 2 (1988): 70.
51. "Murphy to the Secretary of State," April 5, 1946, NA, RG 59, 740.00119, Control (Germany), 4-546.
52. Chertok, "U sovetskikh raketnykh triumfov," *Izvestiia,* no. 56 (March 6, 1992).
53. Kurowski, *Allierte Jagd,* p. 162; Lasby, *Project Paperclip,* pp. 44–45.
54. Chertok, "U sovetskikh raketnykh triumfov," *Izvestiia,* no. 55 (March 5, 1992).
55. Office of the Political Advisor to the Commander-in-Chief, William Strang, September 6, 1946, Economic Information Section, Control Commission for Germany (British Element), Berlin, PRO no. 33, September 3, 1946.
56. N. Reddaway, October 10, 1946, PRO, file no. 12188, F 371, 1946 Germany (55933); Office of the Political Advisor to the Commander-in-Chief, William Strang, September 6, 1946, Economic Information Section Control Commission for Germany (British Element), Berlin, PRO, no. 33, September 3, 1946.
57. "Employment of German Scientists and Technicians in the U.K.," PRO, FO 371, 1946, file no. 293, 11940–14227 (55678).
58. Tugarinov to Dimitrov, November 3, 1945, RTsKhIDNI, f. 17, op. 125, d. 321, l. 230.
59. For some of the cases of alleged *Verschleppung* (kidnapping), see FES, SPD Ostbüro, 1391.
60. ICIS, no. 32, February 23, 1946, p. 3; NA, RG 260, ODI, box 35, R-645-48-3; NA, RG 59, 740.00119, Control (Germany), 3-246.
61. There are several versions of the meaning of Osoaviakhim. One that appears in an American intelligence report is that it was an acronym for "special mission emigration operation." OMGUS, ICIS, no. 66, November 2, 1946, HIA, Lerner, box 44, folder 2. The full title of the organization for which the operation was code-named was Obshchestvo sodeistvia oborone i aviatsionno-khimicheskomu stroitel'stvu v SSSR (Society for Aiding the Defense of and Chemical-Aviation Construction in the USSR). See Rainer Karlsch, *Allein bezahlt?* (Berlin: Ch. Links, 1993), p. 52, n. 5.
62. "Deportation of Germans from Berlin (Russian sector), October 25, 1946," Report to General McClure, NA, RG 260, box 65. The document, which is a rough translation from the German, is edited here. Emphasis in the original.
63. "Confidential U.S. Civil Censorship (Germany), October 23, 1946," NA, XE 169886.
64. Gröttrup, *Die Besessenen und die Mächtigen,* p. 16.

65. Headquarters, CIC, Region 8, NA, XE 169886; Abschrift gez. Schmidt, HIA, Sander, folder 5, 1946. The fate of the Oberspreewerk executives had already been decided several days earlier; they had been flown to Moscow by military aircraft on October 20. NA, RG 260, box 65, annex no. 1.

66. See Sokolov, *Soviet Use of German Science,* pp. 15, 27.

67. PRO, FO 371, 1946, Germany, file no. 12188, October 10, 1946; HQ CIC, Region 8, October 23, 1946, NA, XE 169886; G-2, Agent's Daily Report, Zehlendorf, November 7, 1946, NA, XE 169886. In some of the smaller groups, the scientists and technicians were told several days ahead of time that they would sign contracts to work in the Soviet Union and depart on October 22.

68. "Deportationen zur Zwangsarbeit in der Sowjetunion," FES, SPD Ostbüro, 0391; Chertok, "U sovetskikh raketnykh triumfov," *Izvestiia,* no. 56, March 6, 1992; *Der Kurier,* October 24, 1947.

69. NA, RG 260, box 65, annex 1.

70. Weekly Intelligence Report, no. 7, February 12, 1947, NA, RG 260, box 65.

71. HQ Berlin District U.S. Army, G-2, October 31, 1946, NA, XE 169886.

72. "Deportation of German Civilians," October 24, 1946, report of Civilian Administration Branch of OMGUS, Berlin District, and 317 Military Intelligence Detachment, October 24, 1946, annex 2, NA, RG 260, box 65.

73. G-2, Agent's Daily Report, DP Camps, November 7, 1946, NA XE 169886. See also "Bericht eines Flüchtlinges aus der Ostzone," HIA, Sander, folder 5.

74. G-2, Agent's Daily Report, Zehlendorf, November 6, 1946, NA, XE 169886.

75. Interview with Max Rokhlin, Moscow, June 1989. See also his memoirs in L. Ostapov [Rokhlin], "V Germanii v 1945 godu . . .," part 1, *Khimiia i zhizn',* no. 9 (September 1971): 30–37; part 2, *Khimiia i zhizn',* no. 10 (October 1971): 55–61.

76. NA, RG 260, box 65, annex 1, p. 5.

77. Robert Schmid to General McClure, "Deportation of Germans from Berlin (Soviet sector) and Soviet Zone," October 25, 1946, NA, RG 260, box 65.

78. HQ CIC, Region 8, October 23, 1946, and HQ CIC, Region 6 (Bamberg), November 15, 1946, NA, XE 169886.

79. See Lasby, *Project Paperclip,* p. 179.

80. Murphy to Secretary of State, October 26, 1946, NA, RG 59, box 3700, Germany (Control) 10-2646.

81. Ibid.

82. For SVAG reaction, see GARF, f. 7212, op. 1, d. 188, ll. 160 ff. In his telegram to the secretary of state of October 24, 1946, Robert Murphy noted that the deportations were "apparently not formally prohibited by any existing agreement." NA, RG 59, box 3700, Germany (Control) 10-2446.

83. Telegram to Department of State from Berlin, October 30, 1946, NA, RG 59, box 700, Control (Germany) 10-3046.

84. Quoted in Lasby, *Project Paperclip,* p. 182.

85. GARF, f. 7212, op. 1, d. 188, ll. 164–165.

86. Zdorov to Paniushkin, December 19, 1946, RTsKhIDNI, f. 17, op. 128, d. 147, l.

191. See reports in *Abendblatt für Mitteldeutschland,* October 29, 1946, and February 20, 1947.

87. Eisenhower to Truman, August 1945, NA, RG 59, 740.00119, Control (Germany), 9-2845.

88. *Tägliche Rundschau,* October 26, 1946, and October 27, 1946.

89. *Abendblatt für Mitteldeutschland,* October 24, 1946.

90. Kurowski, *Allierte Jagd,* p. 174.

91. "Soviet Exploitation of German Science," NA, RG 260, box 65, p. 64.

92. Soviet archives should soon provide us with a more precise number. This is Murphy's estimate, which—given some of the numbers of people we have on the removals from discrete factories—seems to be on the conservative side. Murphy to Secretary of State, October 24, 1946, NA, RG 59, Box 3700, Control (Germany) 10-2446. Zank suggests a total of 8,000 to 10,000. Wolfgang Zank, *Wirtschaft und Arbeit in Ostdeutschland 1945–1949: Probleme des Wiederaufbaus in der Sowjetischen Bezatzungszone Deutschlands* (Munich: R. Oldenbourg Verlag, 1987), p. 65. Sokolov estimates that 40,000 were evacuated, including 2,000 aviation specialists alone. Sokolov, *Soviet Use of German Science,* p. 25. The only Soviet estimate I have seen is for the number of railway cars—341—used to transport "specialists," counted as part of SVAG's plan for the first quarter of 1947. But this number, unlike the others, also takes into account family members. Russian Archives, Collection. Recent estimates based on East German archival data about returning scientists suggest that fewer specialists were involved, perhaps 2,000 to 4,000. See Albrecht, Heinemann-Grüder, and Wellmann, *Die Spezialisten,* pp. 176–178; Burghard Ciesla, "Der Spezialistentransfer in die UdSSR und seine Auswirkungen in der SBZ und DDR," *Aus Politik und Zeitgeschichte: Beilage zur Wochenzeitung, Das Parlament* B 49-50/93 (December 3, 1993), p. 25; Karlsch, *Allein bezahlt?,* pp. 155–165.

93. See "Sowjetische Raketenforschung auf der Insel Gorodomlja (Werk 88)," FES, SPD Ostbüro.

94. Ordway and Sharpe, *The Rocket Team,* p. 333.

95. Gröttrup, *Die Besessenen und die Mächtigen,* pp. 10–11.

96. Chertok, "U sovetskikh raketnykh triumfov," *Izvestiia,* no. 56 (March 7, 1992).

97. McDougall, *The Heavens and the Earth,* p. 54. Chertok noted that this missile was initially designed by the Nazis to strike the North American continent from Portugal. Chertok, "U sovetskikh raketnykh triumfov," *Izvestiia,* no. 56 (March 6, 1992).

98. "Soviet Exploitation of German Scientists and Facilities," NA, RG 260, box 65, pp. 61–65.

99. Tokaev, *Stalin Means War,* p. 116.

100. HIA, Philp, box 1, pp. 4, 9–10.

101. Werner Knop, *Prowling Russia's Forbidden Zone* (New York: Knopf, 1949), p. 36.

102. HQ Berlin Command OMGUS, Special Intelligence Memorandum 44, December 6, 1946, NA, XE 169866.

103. "Abtransport deutscher Spezialisten nach der Sowjetunion," July 18, 1948, NA,

RG 260, box 65; "Deportationen zur Zwangsarbeit in die Sowjetunion," January 5, 1949, FES, SPD Ostbüro, 0391.

104. "German Scientists with Experience in Chemical Warfare," HQ 7707 ECIC, October 8, 1948, NA, RG 260, box 65; "Russian Policy in Germany," October 8, 1945, BFO: Russian Correspondence 1945, Reel #13, Vol. #47917, Doc. #14490, p. 134. See also, Murphy to Secretary of State, February 21, 1946, attached letter from General Edwin L. Sibert to Clay, January 30, 1946, NA, RG 59, 740.00119, Control (Germany), 2-2146.

105. Kruglov to Stalin and Beria, GARF, f. 9401, op. 2, d. 133, l. 240.

106. "Soviet Recruiting of Scientists," Military Intelligence Report, May 27, 1949, NA, ZE 152-328, pp. 1–3 ("Sanitized copy. Sensitive information deleted.") Military intelligence files in the National Archvies also contain falsified documents used by Soviet agents in the West.

107. Cited in Walker, *German National Socialism and the Quest for Nuclear Power,* p. 185.

108. See the case of the MVD group assigned the task of bringing back to Moscow a group of German shipbuilding specialists for the submarine program. Kruglov to Serov and Stalin, December 13, 1947, GARF, f. 9401, op. 2, d. 171.

109. The material included planes, ships, tanks, radio equipment, underground cables, and boats. Russian Archives, Collection.

110. Ibid.

111. Much of the description of the history of the NTOs comes from a lengthy report of the Thüringen scientific and technical administration of July 1946. "Otchet rabote otd. nauki i tekhniki . . . za vtoroi kvartal [aprel'-iiun'] 1946 goda," GARF, f. 7184, op. 1, d. 148, ll. 6–16. See also A. Mikhailov, K. Koval, and G. Bykov (in Berlin) to the Council of Ministers, January, 1949, RTsKhIDNI, f. 17, op. 128, d. 420, l. 97.

112. "Die sowjetische Rüstungsproduktion in der Ostzone," p. 2, FES, SPD Ostbüro, I, 0406.

113. "Otchet o rabote otd. nauki i tekhniki," GARF, f. 7184, op. 1, d. 148, l. 15.

114. ODI, Report of October 18, 1948, NA, RG 260, box 29.

115. HQ 7707 ECIC, September 14, 1948 report, NA, RG 260, box 65.

116. Kazakov, Secretary of the NTO Party Organization, Land Saxony, to Central Committee, November 12, 1948, RTsKhIDNI, f. 17, op. 128, d. 420, l. 91.

117. Economic Information Section, Economic Subcomission, HQ Conrol Commission for Germany (British Element), July 19, 1946, p. 4, PRO, 1946, Germany File no. 8854.

118. RTsKhIDNI, f. 17, op. 128, d. 420, ll. 97–98.

119. Ibid.

120. "Otchet o rabote otd. nauki i tekhniki," GARF, f. 7184, op. 1, d. 148, l. 13.

121. RTsKhIDNI, f. 17, op. 128, d. 420, ll. 92–93.

122. Ibid.

123. Russian Archives, Collection.

124. Interview with Max Rokhlin, Moscow, June 1989.

125. "Sbornik materialov po istorii otdela narodnogo obrazovaniia," vol. 1, GARF, f. 7317, op. 54, d. 1, l. 206; *Abendblatt für Mitteldeutschland,* July 12, 1946.

126. "Sbornik materialov," vol. 1, GARF, f. 7317, op. 54, d. 1, l. 185.

127. "News of Germany," OMGUS, ISD, NA, RG 260, box 50, folder 9.

128. "Sbornik materialov," vol. 3, GARF, f. 7317, op. 54, d. 3, ll. 162–163.

129. See Jonathan E. Helmreich, *Gathering Rare Ores: The Diplomacy of Uranium Acquisition, 1943–1954* (Princeton, N.J.: Princeton University Press, 1986), pp. 42 ff.

130. Ibid., p. 249.

131. HIA, Pash, box 2. Pash talks about the removal of 1,000 tons of uranium ore in his book. Boris T. Pash, *The Alsos Mission* (New York: Award House, 1969), pp. 197–199.

132. Memorandum of S. A. Goudsmit, June 25, 1945, HIA, Pash, box 2. See Samuel A. Goudsmit, *Alsos* (New York: Henry Schuman, 1947).

133. See Walker, *German National Socialism and the Quest for Nuclear Power,* p. 157.

134. Dr. Greber, Frankfurt, Report of May 22, 1945, in HIA, Pash, box 2.

135. Holloway, *Stalin and the Bomb,* p. 111.

136. S-2 branch, Berlin Command, "Uranium Mining in Oberschlema," February 2, 1948, NA, RG 260, box 6.

137. Helmreich, *Gathering Rare Ores,* p. 70.

138. I have searched extensively in the National Archives and interviewed Barton Bernstein for evidence on the American side, and I interviewed David Holloway and the Russian physicist I. N. Golovin for evidence on the Soviet side.

139. HQ 12th Army Group, "News Roundup," April–May 1945, NA, Lerner, box 41, folders 6 and 7.

140. Murphy to Secretary of State, Paris, June 16, 1945, NA, RG 59, 740.00119, Control (Germany), 6-1645.

141. See Helfried Wehner, "Proletarischer Internationalismus und Sozialistische Besatzungspolitik: Ein Beitrag zur Antifaschistisch-Demokratischen Entwicklung im Ehemaligen Land Sachsen unter besonderer Berücksichtigung der Sozialistischen Besatzungspolitik," Habilitation thesis, Martin Luther University (Halle/Wittenburg, 1969), p. 137.

142. See Chapter 5, "Schwarzenberg."

143. "Demontage des Radiumkurbades Oberschlema," HIA, Sander, box 1, folder 7.

144. See Zank, *Wirtschaft und Arbeit,* p. 58.

145. For the opening of the baths, see *Abendblatt für Mitteldeutschland,* July 9, 1946.

146. "Demontage des Radiumkurbades Oberschlema," HIA, Sander, box 1, folder 7.

147. See "Russia's Uranium," *Newsweek,* November 25, 1946; based on a leak of a "secret" report by Robert Murphy. HIA, Murphy, box 55-1.

148. NA, RG 260, R-151-48, p. 2.

149. Lavrent'ev to Hess, August 1, 1947, NA, RG 260, AGTS, box 645. In the same file, see the letters from Hess to Malinin, July 26, 1947, and to Sokolovskii, of August 4, 1947.

150. The Americans were very interested in the Soviet "trickometer," a new device

that could locate radioactive areas to a depth of 50 meters within a surface area of 300 meters. Military intelligence archives contain a number of sketches of the machine, presumably obtained through German refugees. See HQ 7707 ECIC, October 6, 1948, "Ore Production and Processing in Johanngeorgenstadt," NA, RG 260, box 94.

151. "Information on Schneeberg Mines," November 7, 1947, NA, RG 260, box 6, "Uranium Mining in Saxony," April 27, 1947, NA, RG 260, box 94.

152. Wolfgang Zank estimates that "only" five percent of the population was involved in "slave labor," this presumably all in the mines of the Erzgebirge. Zank, *Wirtschaft und Arbeit*, p. 106.

153. S-2 branch, "Uranium Mining in Annaberg and Vicinity," December 17, 1947, NA, RG 260, box 94. Here, American military intelligence reported uranium mining activities in Marienberg County (Marienberg, Schönbrunn-Wolkenstein), Annaberg County (Annaberg, Frohnau, Cunnersdorf, Niederschlag-Bärenstein, Oberwiesenthal), and Schwarzenberg County (Langenberg-Raschau, Schwarzenberg, Niederschlema, Schneeberg, Johanngeorgenstadt).

154. "Uranium Mining in Saxony," NA, RG 260, box 110, RP-186-48, p. 3.

155. "Uranbergbau macht die Menschen zur Ruine," HIA, Sander, box 1, folder 9 [1948].

156. Order no. 180, April 5, 1946, GARF, f. 7184, op. 2, d. 4, l. 918.

157. "Testimony of former secretary of SED Kreis Committee, Leipzig, Ernst Wolf, 1948," NA, RG 260, ODI, box 15, folder 350.09, vol. 2.

158. "Uranium Mining in Saxony," p. 3, NA, RG 260, RP-186-48, box 110.

159. SAPMO-BA, ZPA, IV 2/11/202 (Kaderfragen, July 4, 1949).

160. SAPMO-BA, ZPA, IV 2/1/15 (Parteivorstand Protocol, October 15–16, 1947), b. 60.

161. See Knop, *Prowling Russia's Forbidden Zone*, p. 136.

162. SAPMO-BA, ZPA, IV 2/1/15 (Parteivorstand Protocol, October 15–16, 1947), b. 60; SAPMO-BA, ZPA, NL 182/986, b. 33.

163. SAPMO-BA, ZPA, NL 90/276 (Grotewohl, n.d.), b. 120.

164. SED Obercunnersdorf to Kreisvorstand of the SED Löbau/Saxony, March 18, 1947 (in German), GARF, f. 7212, op. 1, d. 194, l. 84.

165. Lehmann to Grotewohl, August 12, 1947, "Arbeitsverhältnisse im Uranbergbau in Sachsen," SAPMO-BA, NL 90/359 (Grotewohl), bb. 4–10.

166. Copy, Buchwitz from Wildführ, May 27, 1947, in "Vorlage an das Zentralsekretariat: Arbeitsverhältnisse im Uranbergbau in Sachsen," bb. 6–7; from H. Lehmann, August 12, 1947, SAPMO-BA, ZPA, NL 90/359. See also, "Lungenkrankheiten infolge Radioaktivität," HIA, Sander, box 1, folder 9.

167. See "Interrogation of Fugitive Uranium Ore Miner from the Russian Zone," February 15, 1950, and "Uranium Mining Disaster," January 12, 1950 in NA, RG 260, box 35. One report notes that "a large percentage of workers have become victims of the numerous accidents which occur at frequent intervals." "New Developments in the Uranium Mines," December 5, 1947, NA, RG 260, box 6.

168. SAPMO-BA, ZPA, NL 90/359 (Grotewohl), b. 1.

169. SAPMO-BA, ZPA, IV 2/1/15 (Parteivorstand Protocol, October 15–16, 1947), b. 64 (Max Weber, Saxony).

170. SAPMO-BA, ZPA, (Parteivorstand Protocol, October 15–16, 1947), b. 64.

171. FES, SPD Ostbüro, 0362 I; Franz Rupp, *Die Reparationsleistungen der Sowjetischen Besatzungszone* (Bonn: Bundesministerium für Gesamtdeutsche Fragen, 1951), p. 25; Testimony of Paul Schneidenbach, 1948, NA, RG 260, ODI, box 15, folder 350.09, vol. 2; "Information Report," Hesse, April 15, 1948, NA, RG 260, box 15.

172. *Der Demokrat,* October 23, 1947.

173. SAPMO-BA, ZPA, NL 182/986, bb. 152–153.

174. Pieck to Ulbricht, August 22, 1949, SAPMO-BA, NL 182/986, b. 150.

175. Murphy to Department of State, NA, RG 59, 740.00119, Control (Germany), 8-1147, p. 2; USPOLAD to Secretary of State, "Report of Soviet Conscription of Germans and Consequent Illegal Influx in United States Zone," July 2, 1947, NA, RG 59, 740.00119, Control (Germany), 7-247.

176. Vatnik to Tiul'panov, "O vrazheskoi propagande i antidemokraticheskoi deiatel'nosti v f.z. Saksoniia," July 2, 1947, GARF, f. 7212, op. 1, d. 192, ll. 103–104.

177. To Suslov from Tiul'panov, "Dokladnaia zapiska," November 15, 1947, RTs-KhIDNI, f. 17, op. 128, d. 329, l. 210.

178. "Niederschrift über eine Besprechung mit der SMAD, Karlshorst, August 30, 1947," SAPMO-BA, ZPA, IV 2/2.027/25, b. 5.

179. "Aktennotiz. . ." Aue, September 23, 1947, in ibid.

180. "Wer will freiwillig ins Erzgebirge?" *Landes-Zeitung* (Stralsund), April 4, 1948.

181. August 30, 1948, report, SAPMO-BA, ZPA, IV 2/2027/25.

182. "Dienstverpflichtungen zum Uranbergbau reissen nicht ab," pp. 2–3, HIA, Sander, box 1, folder 9.

183. Reports of August 30, 1948, and September 24, 1948, SAPMO-BA, ZPA, IV 2/2027/25; bb. 1–5.

184. Knop, *Prowling Russia's Forbidden Zone,* pp. 158–163.

185. SAPMO-BA, ZPA, IV 2/2027/25.

186. Ibid., b. 5.

187. "Joachimsthal Uranium Ore Processing Plant," May/July 1948, NA, RG 260, box 106; "Intelligence Report"—R-38-48, in NA, RG 260, box 106; HQ 7707 ECIC, "Uranium Mining at Jáchymov," October 11, 1948, p. 2, NA, RG 260, box 46.

188. The rumors were related to border claims by the Czechs at the Council of Foreign Ministers meetings in Moscow (March–April, 1947) and in London (September 1947), claims involving precisely those regions where uranium was being mined. (It is interesting that the American reports on the September meeting show an awareness of the uranium question, unlike the reports on the spring meeting.) See HIA, Murphy, 66-2. Since the Czech communists were members of the Cominform and the fate of Germany was still being decided, the Soviets might have supported Czech claims to the border areas of the Erzgebirge. On the other hand,

the possibility of getting labor from Germany made that solution less acceptable. VIII-9474, Spot Reports, NA, RG 260, box 82.

189. Brack to Lehmann, June 27, 1949, SAPMO-BA, ZPA, 2/2027/25.

190. Betr. B 675/99, July 11, 1949, FES, SPD Ostbüro, 0414.

191. Lehmann, "Werbung für den Erzbergbau," SAPMO-BA, ZPA, IV 2/2027/5; see also SAPMO-BA, ZPA, IV 2/2027/25, b. 5.

192. See the rules about escaped uranium miners: "Richtlinien über Fahndung nach flüchtigen Bergarbeitern der zentralen Bergwerksverwaltung in Aue/S," from the German Interior Ministry of the Soviet Zone, Section K, June 11, 1948, FES, SPD Ostbüro, 0005.

193. "Vermerk," November 29, 1949, SAPMO-BA, ZPA, IV 2/2027/25.

194. "Sitzung der Aue Kommission am 11 Mai 1950," SAPMO-BA, ZPA, IV 2/2027/ 25.

195. SAPMO-BA, ZPA, NL 182/918, b. 14.

196. "Über die SDAG Wismut," SAPMO-BA, ZPA, NL 62/143 (Heinrich Rau).

197. Ibid., b. 3.

198. "A Grisly Archive of Key Cancer Data," *Science,* vol. 259 (January 22, 1993): 448.

199. See the exchange between Lt. Gen. Russkikh and MVD deputy minister Serov, who denied any MVD improprieties. RTsKhIDNI, f. 17, op. 128, d. 94, ll. 18–22.

200. SAPMO-BA, ZPA, IV 2/11/188 (Kaderfragen). This file contains a list of returning specialists (ninety-eight from Junkers-Dessau, sixty-one from BMW Stassfurt, and six from Askania) for whom the SED wanted to find jobs.

201. McDougall, *The Heavens and the Earth,* p. 64.

202. Heinemann-Grüder, *Die Sowjetische Atombombe,* p. 51.

5. THE SOVIETS AND THE GERMAN LEFT

1. Anton Ackermann, "Einführung zum Clubgespräch: Vom schöpferischen Anfang," April 6, 1971, SAPMO-BA, ZPA, NL 109/58 (Anton Ackermann), b. 4.

2. V. Khvostov to Dimitrov, April 28, 1945, RTsKhIDNI, f. 17, op. 128, d. 787, ll. 22–23.

3. SAPMO-BA, ZPA, EA 1291/4 (Ackermann), b. 744.

4. See the collection of German documents: Gerhard Keiderling, ed. *"Gruppe Ulbricht" in Berlin April bis Juni 1945: von den Vorbereitungen im Sommer 1944 bis zur Wiedergründung der KPD im Juni 1945, Eine Dokumentation* (Berlin: Arno Spitz Verlag, 1993).

5. "Spravka o politicheskoi rabote sredi naseleniia Germanii," July 5, 1945, RTsKhIDNI, f. 17, op. 128, d. 791, l. 107.

6. Ibid., l. 107.

7. Günter Benser, *Die KPD im Jahre der Befreiung: Vorbereitung und Aufbau der legalen kommunistische Massenpartei* (Berlin, GDR: Dietz Verlag, 1985), pp. 189–190. Some of the Soviet commandants fell into this category as well. As a result,

they were ordered by the political organs of SVAG to carry out policy strictly through the German administrations (and not through local committees or parties). N. I. Shishkov, "Sovetskaia voennaia administratsiia i pomoshch' SSSR narodam tsentral'noi i iugo-vostochnoi Evropy v 1944–45 godakh," *Voprosy istorii,* no. 2 (1979): 16–29.

8. See, for example, SAPMO-BA, ZPA, EA 1845/2 (Rudolf Bühring), b. 386.

9. "Stenogramma soobshchenii t.t. Akkermana, Ul'brikhta i Sobotka o polozhenii v Germanii," June 7, 1945, RTsKhIDNI, f. 17, op. 128, d. 759, l. 9.

10. "Nekotorye fakty o rabote gruppy tov. Ul'brikhta v Berline," by Sr. Lt. Fogeler, June 8, 1945, forwarded by seventh Section chief, M. Burtsev, to Dimitrov, June 14, 1945, RTsKhIDNI, f. 17, op. 128, d. 39, l. 32.

11. See, for example, SAPMO-BA, ZPA, EA 1845/3 (Rudolf Bühring), b. 438, and RTsKhIDNI, f. 17, op. 125, d. 321, ll. 107–109.

12. "Stenogramma soobshchenii," June 7, 1945, RTsKhIDNI, f. 17, op. 128, d. 750, l. 7.

13. The literal English translation: "Arise, the day is light early / through the daylight to freedom / forward, without being faint-hearted / 'Red Front,' make way, / the road is clear, / the red battalion is advancing. / Now we stand ready to fight, / the way to freedom is no longer far." "Bericht über Provinz Brandenburg," SAPMO-BA, ZPA, NL 182/853, b. 16.

14. *Rote Fahne* no. 1, May 8, 1945, and no. 3, May 16, 1945; SAPMO-BA, ZPA, NL 182/853, bb. 37, 38.

15. "Spravka o politicheskoi rabote sredi naseleniia Germanii," July 5, 1945, RTsKhIDNI, f. 17, op. 128, d. 791, l. 109.

16. "Kurzer Bericht über die Arbeit der Berliner Parteiorganisation der KPD," n.d., SAPMO-BA, ZPA, NL 182/852 (Ulbricht), b. 7.

17. Horst Laschitza, *Kämpferische Demokratie gegen Faschismus: Die programmatische Vorbereitung auf die antifaschistisch-demokratische Umwälzung in Deutschland durch die Parteiführung der KPD* (Berlin, GDR: Deutscher Militärverlag, 1969), p. 199.

18. "Aufruf: Genossen und Genossinnen von Haselhorst!" SAPMO-BA, ZPA, VG 125/1, b. 44.

19. "Vertraulicher Bericht über die Bezirkskonferenz der Provinz Sachsen," July 20, 1945, SAPMO-BA, ZPA, NL 182/855 (Ulbricht), b. 33.

20. SAPMO-BA, ZPA, EA 0012 (Fritz Koehn), bb. 2–3.

21. SAPMO-BA, ZPA, NL 36/629 (W. Pieck), b. 62. These notes have been published in the *Frankfurter Allgemeine Zeitung,* March 30, 1990, with commentary by Manfred Wilke, and in *Utopie: Kreativ,* no. 7 (March 1991): 103–105, with commentary by Rolf Badstübner.

22. "Stenogramma soobshchenii," June 7, 1945, RTsKhIDNI, f. 17, op. 128, d. 750, l. 177. (Emphasis in the original.)

23. Dietrich Staritz makes this point as well, in "Die SED, Stalin und die Gründung der DDR," *Aus Politik und Zeitgeschichte: Beilage zur Wochenzeitung Das Parlament* B5/91 (January 25, 1991): 4.

24. "Stenogramma soobshchenii," June 7, 1945, RTsKhIDNI, f. 17, op. 128, d. 750, l. 166.

25. Ibid., ll. 181, 185.

26. Ibid., ll. 178, 183–184.

27. See Benser, *Die KPD im Jahre der Befreiung,* p. 87; Wallrab von Buttlar, *Ziele und Zielkonflikte der sowjetischen Deutschlandpolitik 1945–1947* (Stuttgart: Klett-Cotta, 1980), pp. 40–41.

28. "Stenogramma soobshchenii," June 7, 1945, RTsKhIDNI, f. 17, op. 128, d. 750, l. 175; SAPMO-BA, ZPA, EA 0082 (Curt Böhme), bb. 59–63.

29. "Entschliessung der Delegiertenkonferenz des Parteiaktivs der KP Buchenwalds," April 22, 1945, SAPMO-BA, ZPA, NL 128/30 (Georg Handke), bb. 1–2.

30. SAPMO-BA, ZPA, EA 0082 (Curt Böhme), b. 59.

31. SAPMO-BA, ZPA, EA 1365/1 (Heinrich Hoffmann), b. 143.

32. Benser, *Die KPD im Jahre der Befreiung,* pp. 80–81.

33. Ibid., p. 78. Heinrich Hoffmann remembers that Brill was absolutely serious about nationalization of all large industry. SAPMO-BA, ZPA, EA 1365/1 (Hoffmann), b. 144.

34. See Gregory Sandford, *From Hitler to Ulbricht: The Communist Reconstruction of East Germany 1945–46* (Princeton, N.J.: Princeton University Press, 1983), p. 73.

35. Sandford notes that Col. Tiul'panov, in particular, wanted to remove Brill from the beginning, while Semenov—no doubt impressed by Brill's stature among the Allies—was one of his supporters. Sandford, *From Hitler to Ulbricht,* pp. 75–76.

36. Frank Moraw, *Die Parole der "Einheit" und die deutsche Sozialdemokratie* (Bonn: Verlag Neue Gesellschaft, 1973), pp. 113–117.

37. SAPMO-BA, ZPA, EA 1365/1 (Hoffmann), b. 151.

38. For Brill's biography, see Manfred Overesch, *Hermann Brill in Thüringen 1895–1946: Ein Kämpfer gegen Hitler und Ulbricht* (Bonn: Verlag J. H. W. Dietz Nachf., 1992).

39. Manfred Wille, "Studien zur Zusammenarbeit der von der KPD geführten deutschen Antifaschisten mit der Sowjetischen Besatzungsmacht in der Provinz Sachsen (April bis Dezember 1945)," doctoral dissertation, Central Institute for History, Academy of Sciences (Berlin, GDR), 1978, p. 201.

40. Actually, both workers and directors conspired to save the statue. "Abschluss-protokoll über Erhaltung und Aufstellung des Lenindenkmals in Eisleben," August 14, 1959, SAPMO-BA, EA 0120/1 (Robert Büchner).

41. SAPMO-BA, ZPA, EA 0120/2 (Büchner), b. 7; Benser, *Die KPD im Jahre der Befreiung,* pp. 68, 87.

42. SAPMO-BA, ZPA, EA 0120/1 (Büchner), b. 65.

43. Ibid., b. 66.

44. Ibid., b. 66.

45. SAPMO-BA, ZPA, EA 0120/2 (Büchner), b. 144.

46. Ibid., b. 104.

47. Benser, *Die KPD im Jahre der Befreiung,* p. 13; Wille, "Studium zur Zusammenarbeit," p. 76.

48. "Stenogramma soobshchenii," June 7, 1945, meeting, RTsKhIDNI, f. 17, op. 128, d. 750, l. 168.

49. Burtsev to Dimitrov, June 1945, RTsKhIDNI, f. 17, op. 128, d. 39, l. 15.

50. See Anton Ackermann, "Über meine Erlebnisse und Erfahrungen in Meissen in Mai 1945," SAPMO-BA, ZPA, EA 1291/4. Here Ackermann describes his first meetings with the "people's commissars," comrades Mücke and Gerhard Ziller.

51. Ibid., b. 678.

52. "Stenogramma soobshchenii," June 7, 1945, RTsKhIDNI, f. 17, op. 138, d. 750, l. 168.

53. Burtsev to Dimitrov, June 1945, RTsKhIDNI, f. 17, op. 128, d. 39, l. 15.

54. Shikin to Aleksandrov, June 1, 1945, RTsKhIDNI, f. 17, op. 128, d. 321, l. 95.

55. The case was made famous by the novel by Stefan Heym, *Schwarzenberg* (Munich: C. Bertelsmann, 1984). Heym's interesting, if highly politicized, account of the Schwarzenberg case appears to be taken, in good measure, from the work of Werner Grosse, *Die ersten Schritte: Der Kampf der Antifaschisten in Schwarzenberg während der unbesetzten Zeit, Mai/Juni 1945* (Berlin, GDR: Rütten and Loening, 1961).

56. See Chapter 4, "Uranium," for American calculations. See also Helfried Wehner, "Proletarischer Internationalismus und Sozialistische Besatzungspolitik: Ein Beitrag zur Antifaschistisch-Demokratischen Entwicklung im Ehemaligen Land Sachsen unter besonderer Berücksichtigung der Sozialistischen Besatzungspolitik," habilitation thesis, Martin Luther University (Halle/Wittenburg, 1969), p. 137.

57. SAPMO-BA, ZPA, EA 1699 (Ruth Stolz, "Erinnerungen"), b. 5.

58. "Stenogramma soobshchenii," June 7, 1945, RTsKhIDNI, f. 17, op. 128, d. 750, l. 189.

59. Wehner, "Proletarischer Internationalismus," p. 146.

60. Ibid., p. 150.

61. Ibid., p. 147.

62. Benser, *Die KPD im Jahre der Befreiung*, p. 106.

63. Wehner, "Proletarischer Internationalismus," pp. 158, 160–162.

64. Grosse, *Die ersten Schritte*, p. 77.

65. "Bericht vom Unterbezirk Schwarzenberg," August 13, 1945, SAPMO-BA, NL 182/855, b. 53.

66. SED "Tätigskeitbericht" for Landkreis Schwarzenberg, 1946, FES, SPD Ostbüro, 0033.

67. Ulbricht to Dimitrov, May 9, 1945 (draft), b. 60; Ulbricht to Pieck, May 17, 1945 (draft), b. 5; Ulbricht to Dimitrov, May 17, 1945 (draft), b. 12, in SAPMO-BA, ZPA, NL 182/246 V (Ulbricht).

68. "Nekotorye fakty o rabote gruppy tov. Ul'brikhta v Berline," June 8, 1945, RTsKhIDNI, f. 17, op. 128, d. 39, l. 32.

69. Siegfried Thomas, "Der Wiederbeginn des politischen Lebens in Berlin und die Aktionseinheit der Arbeiterparteien (Mai–Juli 1945)," *Zeitschrift für Geschichtswissenschaft*, vol. 8, no. 6 (1960): 320, 323–324.

70. Ulbricht to Dimitrov, May 9, 1945, SAPMO-BA, ZPA, NL 182/246 V, bb. 1–2.

71. Wolfgang Leonhard, *Child of the Revolution* (Chicago: H. Regnery Co., 1958), p. 401.

72. Cited in Moraw, *Die Parole der "Einheit,"* p. 93.

73. Ulbricht to Pieck, May 17, 1945, SAPMO-BA, ZPA, NL 182/246 V, b. 6.

74. See Sandford, *From Hitler to Ulbricht,* pp. 157–161.

75. Ulbricht to Dimitrov, May 9, 1945, SAPMO-BA, ZPA, NL 182/246 V, b. 60.

76. "Nekotorye fakty," June 8, 1945, RTsKhIDNI, f. 17, op. 128, d. 39, l. 33. It is interesting that Ulbricht claimed to have the situation with the commandants firmly in hand. They summoned him when they had complicated problems to solve, he said. He routinely used their offices to phone Moscow. Ulbricht to Pieck, May 17, 1945, SAPMO-BA, ZPA, NL 182/246 V, b. 6.

77. See, for example, Bernt von Kügelgen, *Die Nacht der Entscheidung: Autobiografie* (Berlin, GDR: Verlag der Nation, 1978); Leon Nebenzahl, *Mein Leben begann von neuem: Erinnerungen an eine ungewöhnlichen Zeit* (Berlin, GDR: Dietz Verlag, 1985); and Hans Rodenberg, *Protokoll eines Lebens: Erinnerungen und Bekenntnis* (Berlin, GDR: Henschelverlag Kunst und Gesellschaft, 1980). For other similar titles, see Marianne Lange, "Es hat sich gelohnt zu leben: Gedanken zur Memoirenliteratur in der DDR," *Weimarer Beiträge,* vol. 25, no. 9 (1979): 42–87.

78. "Aktennotiz" of May 19, 1945, HIA, Sander, box 1, folder 3.

79. "Vozzvanie TsK SP partii Germanii" (June 15, 1945), in *Za antifashistskuiu demokraticheskuiu Germaniiu: Sbornik dokumentov 1945–1949 gg.* (Moscow: Izd. politicheskaia lit., 1969), pp. 79–80.

80. Hermann Weber, *Geschichte der DDR* (Munich: Deutscher Taschenbuch Verlag, 1985), p. 115.

81. Petition of the Wildau SPD, June 16, 1945, SAPMO-BA, ZPA, NL 182/853, b. 133.

82. Ibid., bb. 28–31.

83. SAPMO-BA, ZPA, NL 182/853 (Brandenburg), b. 138.

84. SAPMO-BA, ZPA, NL 761/112 (Hermann Matern), b. 191.

85. Weber, *Geschichte der DDR,* p. 117; Henry Krisch, *German Politics under Soviet Occupation* (New York: Columbia University Press, 1974), p. 103.

86. Weber, *Geschichte der DDR,* pp. 118–119.

87. See "Report about the Thüringian District," fall 1945, SAPMO-BA, ZPA, NL 182/856 (Ulbricht), b. 111; "Stenographische Niederschrift über die Reichsberatung am 8. und 9. Januar 1946," SAPMO-BA, ZPA, I 2/2/17, b. 35; "Rede des Gen. Matern auf dem Sekretär-Konferenz," January 7, 1946, SAPMO-BA, ZPA, NL 182/876, b. 70.

88. SAPMO-BA, ZPA, VG 127/7, b. 14.

89. SAPMO-BA, ZPA, EA 1213/1 (Maria Rentmeister), b. 107.

90. SAPMO-BA, ZPA, NL 182/856 (Ulbricht), b. 19.

91. "Kurzer Bericht über die Arbeit der Berliner Parteiorganisation der KPD," July 1945, in ibid., b. 22.

92. "Bericht über öffentliche Versammlungen, June 27–July 3, 1945," SAPMO-BA,

ZPA, NL 182/852 (Ulbricht), b. 33; Report by Waldemar Schmidt, in ibid., bb 38–39.

93. SAPMO-BA, ZPA, NL 182/853 (Brandenburg).

94. Burtsev to Dimitrov, August 16, 1945, RTsKhIDNI, f. 17, op. 128, d. 39, l. 66.

95. The best account in English is still to be found in Krisch, *German Politics under Soviet Occupation*, pp. 101–171. See also Dietrich Staritz, *Die Gründung der DDR* (Munich: Deutscher Taschenbuch Verlag, 1984), pp. 112 ff.

96. See SAPMO-BA, ZPA, NL 182/183, report of October 29, 1945, from Frankfurt-Oder; NL 182/853, b. 12, for complaints; and "Sitzung des Sekretariats," October 3, 1945, Anlage 2, b. 67, for records of special rations to the KPD leadership.

97. "Stenogramma soveshchaniia v upravlenii propagandy SVAG," RTsKhIDNI, f. 17, op. 128, d. 149, l. 148.

98. "Protokoll der Funktionärkonferenz," Berlin, January 4, 1946, SAPMO-BA, ZPA, I 2/5/39, b. 4.

99. Weber, *Geschichte der DDR*, p. 119.

100. O. Grotewohl, "Wo stehen wir. Wohin gehen wir? Der historische Auftrag der SPD," (Berlin: Verlag "Das Volk," September 14, 1945), in SAPMO-BA, ZPA, NL 90/125 (Grotewohl), b. 63 (p. 32).

101. "Rede zum 9. November 1945," in ibid., bb. 94–95.

102. "O politicheskom polozhenii v Germanii," Tugarinov to Dimitrov, November 1945, RTsKhIDNI, f. 17, op. 125, d. 321, l. 10.

103. "Stenographische Niederschrift über die Reichsberatung am 8. und 9. Januar 1946," SAPMO-BA, ZPA, I 2/2/17, b. 9.

104. See Grotewohl to Bokov, March 13, 1946, SAPMO-BA, ZPA, NL 90/314 (Grotewohl), b. 30.

105. Grotewohl to Zhukov, December 6, 1945, SAPMO-BA, ZPA, NL 90/314, b. 16.

106. Gniffke, "Vorbereitung einer Organisationseinheit mit der KPD," October 3, 1945, SAPMO-BA, ZPA, NL 90/281, bb. 11–13.

107. Grotewohl cut this section out of his original report to the first Conference of Sixty, held in December 1945. SAPMO-BA, ZPA, NL 90/125 (Grotewohl), b. 103.

108. Weber, *Geschichte der DDR*, pp. 125–126; Erich Gniffke, *Jahre mit Ulbricht* (Cologne: Verlag Wissenschaft und Politik, 1966), pp. 85–87.

109. "Stenographische Niederschrift über die Reichsberatung am 8. und 9. Januar 1946," SAPMO-BA, ZPA, I 2/2/17, b. 11. Pieck speaks here about "a complete change" in the attitude of Grotewohl at the meeting.

110. S. Tiul'panov, "O polozhenii s ob'edineniem dvukh rabochikh partii: KPG i SDPG v gor. Berline," February 26, 1946, RTsKhIDNI, f. 17, op. 128, d. 931, l. 213.

111. Vatnik to Tiul'panov, January 16, 1946, GARF, f. 7212, op. 1, d. 186, ll. 126–127.

112. For Ebert's case, see, Mil'khiker to Tiul'panov, December 29, 1945, GARF, f. 7077, op. 1, d. 182, l. 21; for Brethorst's see GARF, f. 7212, op. 1, d. 186, l. 102.

113. Moraw, *Die Parole der "Einheit,"* p. 143.

114. Cited in ibid., p. 147.

115. "Stenographische Niederschrift über die gemeinsame Konferenz des Zentralausschusses der SPD und des Zentralkomitees der KPD mit den Bezirksvertretern zu Berlin," February 26, 1946, SAPMO-BA, ZPA, I 2/2/20, b. 11.

116. On this point, see especially Staritz, *Die Gründung der DDR*, pp. 121–123.

117. "An die Partei neuen Typus" (October 28, 1948), appendix to Gniffke, *Jahre mit Ulbricht*, p. 365.

118. Moraw, *Die Parole der "Einheit,"* p. 150. Zhukov also promised that the Soviet commandants would stay out of the unity campaign. Grotewohl to Bokov, March 6, 1946, SAPMO-BA, ZPA, NL 90/314 (Grotewohl), b. 28.

119. "Stenogramma soveshchaniia," September 1946, RTsKhIDNI, f. 17, op. 128, d. 149, l. 157.

120. See Gniffke, *Jahre mit Ulbricht*, p. 138. Dietrich Staritz even claims that the Western SPD left its comrades in the East "in the lurch." Staritz, *Die Gründung der DDR*, p. 119.

121. Tiul'panov, "O polozhenii s ob'edineniem dvukh rabochikh partii: KPD i SDPG v gor. Berline," February 25, 1946, RTsKhIDNI, f. 17, op. 128, d. 931, ll. 214–215.

122. Moraw, *Parole der "Einheit,"* p. 152, n. 293.

123. Klingelhöfer manuscript, Feb. 2, 1946, SAPMO-BA, ZPA, NL 90/281 (Grotewohl), b. 80. Here Klingelhöfer wrote, "The idea to have unity in just our zone is simply a montrosity."

124. Gniffke, *Jahre mit Ulbricht*, p. 170.

125. Tiul'panov, "Dokladnaia zapiska o politicheskoi obstanovke v Berline po sostoianiiu na 13 marta 1946 goda," March 14, 1946, RTsKhIDNI, f. 17, op. 128, d. 931, ll. 271–275.

126. Ulbricht to Paniushkin, March 11, 1946, RTsKhIDNI, f. 17, op. 128, d. 931, l. 219.

127. Weber, *Geschichte der DDR*, pp. 129–130.

128. "Beratungen bei J. W. Stalin," *Utopie: kreativ*, no. 7 (March 1991): 105.

129. "Stenogramma besedy s tov. Maternom," September 25, 1946, RTsKhIDNI, f. 17, op. 128, d. 151, l. 129.

130. *Protokoll des Vereinigungsparteitags der SPD und KPD am 21. und 22. April 1946* (Berlin, 1946), p. 172.

131. Report of I. Filippov, Office of the Political Advisor to the Commander-in-Chief of SVAG, October 9, 1946, RTsKhIDNI, f. 17, op. 128, d. 147, l. 116.

132. Ibid., l. 89.

133. "Stenogramma soveshchaniia," September 1946, RTsKhIDNI, f. 17, op. 128, d. 149, ll. 133, 150.

134. Tiul'panov to Suslov, "Dokladnaia zapiska," July 5, 1947, RTsKhIDNI, f. 17, op. 128, d. 323, l. 204.

135. Kotikov and Tiul'panov to Suslov, "Dokladnaia zapiska: meropriiatiia dlia g. Berlina v sviazi s predstoiashchimi vyborami," August 29, 1946, RTsKhIDNI, f. 17, op. 128, d. 146, l. 268.

136. Korotkevich to Suslov and Paniushkin, August 22, 1946, RTsKhIDNI, f. 17, op. 128, d. 132, ll. 1–2.
137. "O politicheskoi obstanovke v g. Berline nakanune vyborov i rabote Berlinskogo otdela propagandy SVAG," RTsKhIDNI, f. 17, op. 128, d. 151, l. 35.
138. "Stenogramma soveshchaniia," September 1946, RTsKhIDNI, f. 17, op. 128, d. 149, ll. 65–66.
139. Ibid., l. 81.
140. SAPMO-BA, ZPA, IV/2/15, (Parteivorstand Protocol, October 24–25, 1946), b. 77.
141. SAPMO-BA, ZPA, IV 2/1/1, bb. 147, 195.
142. Vatnik to Tiul'panov, "O provintsial'nykh profsoiuznykh konferentsiiakh," June 11, 1946, GARF, f. 2122, op. 1, d. 187, l. 95.
143. "O politicheskoi obstanovke," September 1946, RTsKhIDNI, f. 17, op. 128, d. 151, ll. 12–13, 31.
144. SAPMO-BA, ZPA, NL 182/1191 (Ulbricht), b. 83.
145. RTsKhIDNI, f. 17, op. 128, d. 564, l. 72ff. Sometimes the Central Committee answered that the individual had died after having served terms beginning in 1937; sometimes they said simply that the Germans in question could not be located. Generally, however, Pieck's requests were granted.
146. Pieck to Suslov, January 23, 1948, RTsKhIDNI, f. 17, op. 128, d. 423, l. 1.
147. Pieck to Suslov, December 20, 1948, RTsKhIDNI, f. 17, op. 128, d. 565, l. 59. The Central Committee refused in this case to get involved.
148. See Ulbricht to Bokov, July 15, 16, and 18, 1946, SAPMO-BA, ZPA, NL 182/1190 (Ulbricht), bb. 28, 32, 34, 36, 137; Ackermann to Tiul'panov, December 5, 1945, and Ulbricht to Tiul'panov, December 7, 1945 (in Russian), in SAPMO-BA, ZPA, NL 182/1187 (Ulbricht), bb. 3, 5–7.
149. Ulbricht to Tiul'panov, December 14 and 18, 1945, SAPMO-BA, ZPA, NL 182/1187 (Ulbricht), bb. 13–14.
150. Suslov to A. A. Kuznetsov, December 7, 1946, "Spravochnik o rukovoditeliakh Sotsialisticheskoi Edinoi Partii Germanii i krupneishikh organizatsiiakh Kommunisticheskoi partii Germanii," RTsKhIDNI, f. 17, op. 128, d. 62, l. 7. For an example of Ulbricht's explanations to Tiul'panov, see Ulbricht to Tiul'panov, July 26, 1949, SAPMO-BA, NL 182/1135 (Ulbricht).
151. RTsKhIDNI, f. 17, op. 128, d. 150, l. 51.
152. It is interesting to note that before Florin was allowed even to go to Moscow, Pieck had to ask Suslov of the Central Committee for permission. Suslov, in turn, asked for Zhdanov's approval, which was granted. Suslov to Zhdanov, June 13, 1946, RTsKhIDNI, f. 17, op. 128, d. 59, l. 13.
153. Korotkevich to Suslov and Paniushkin, July 22, 1946, RTsKhIDNI, f. 17, op. 128, d. 59, l. 13. For Ulbricht's letter, see the Russian translation of July 16 in ibid., ll. 15–20. Suslov and Paniushkin answered Ulbricht's questions through Florin, who was often used as a trusted intermediary. Ibid., l. 21.
154. See, for example, SAPMO-BA, ZPA, NL 182/1188 (Ulbricht), b. 35. In this Jan-

uary 1946 case, Karlshorst was upset with the work of Vice President Fischer of the Saxon government regarding land reform. "It would be a good idea," a Soviet official suggested, "if Comrade Ulbricht would speak to Fischer personally about this."

155. SAPMO-BA, NL 182/1190 (Ulbricht), b. 42.

156. See Grotewohl's account of Bokov's offers for a new party headquarters in the early summer of 1945. "Vermerk," July 1, 1945, in FES, SPD, Gniffke papers.

157. Grotewohl to Kotikov, December 24, 1945, and Grotewohl to Bokov, n.d., SAPMO-BA, ZPA NL, 90/914, bb. 1–19; Grotewohl to Bokov, March 6 and 13, 1946, SAPMO-BA, ZPA, 90/314 (Grotewohl), bb. 28, 30.

158. Suslov to Kuznetsov, December 7, 1946, RTsKhIDNI, f. 17, op. 128, d. 62, l. 6.

159. SAPMO-BA, ZPA, NL 30/314 (Grotewohl), bb. 79–80.

160. SAPMO-BA, ZPA, IV 2/1/15 (Parteivorstand Protocol, October 15–16, 1947), bb. 145–146.

161. RTsKhIDNI, f. 17, op. 128, d. 90, l. 53.

162. Merker to Grotewohl, July 13, 1947, SAPMO-BA, ZPA, NL 90/314 (Grotewohl), b. 65.

163. Grosse, September 18, 1946 (Russian trans.) RTsKhIDNI, f. 17, op. 128, d. 147, l. 50.

164. RTsKhIDNI, f. 17, op. 128, d. 150, l. 98.

165. "Sbornik materialov po istorii otdela narodnogo obrazovaniia," vol. 1, GARF, f. 7317, op. 54, d. 1, ll. 76, 177.

166. RTsKhIDNI, f. 17, op. 128, d. 150, ll. 57–58.

167. Tiul'panov to Suslov, "Dokladnaia zapiska," December 9, 1947, RTsKhIDNI, f. 17, op. 128, d. 331. l. 95.

168. Ibid., l. 94.

169. RTsKhIDNI, f. 17, op. 128, d. 683, l. 1.

170. See David Pike, *German Writers in Soviet Exile, 1933–1945* (Chapel Hill: University of North Carolina Press, 1982), pp. 306–357.

171. "Stenogramma soveshchaniia," part 2, September 19, 1946, RTsKhIDNI, f. 17, op. 128, d. 150, l. 116. My emphasis.

172. Gyptner to Suslov, March 8, 1948, RTsKhIDNI, f. 17, op. 128, d. 423, l. 15. My emphasis.

173. SAPMO-BA, ZPA, IV 2/905/108, b. 64.

174. See Mann's favorable description of Tiul'panov in "Germany Today," *New York Times Magazine*, September 25, 1949, pp. 14–15. See also the discussion of Mann's visit in Chapter 8, "Ceremonies and Rituals."

175. SAPMO-BA, ZPA, NL 1276/2 (Willy Sägebrecht), b. 693.

176. In the Mecklenburg case, the communists were hesitant to attack the social democrats, for fear of driving all of them out of the SED organization. "K vnutri-politicheskomu polozheniiu v SEPG: Iz biulletenia Biuro informatsii SVAG," no. 14/113, RTsKhIDNI, f. 17, op. 128, d. 362, l. 187.

177. Karl Stock to Paul Löhe, November 29, 1946, Abschrift, HIA, Sander, box 1, folder 1.

178. SAPMO-BA, ZPA, EA 1319/1 (Werner Bruschke), b. 56.

179. SAPMO-BA, ZPA, IV 2/1/9 (Parteivorstand Protocol, March 26–27, 1947), bb. 71–72.

180. "Stenogramma besedy s tov. Maternom," September 25, 1946, RTsKhIDNI, f. 17, op. 128, d. 151, ll. 9–10, 120.

181. Shikin to Zhdanov, August 3, 1946, RTsKhIDNI, f. 17, op. 128, d. 147, ll. 47, 80.

182. Tiul'panov, "Dokladnaia zapiska," August 11, 1947, RTsKhIDNI, f. 17, op. 128, d. 317, l. 33.

183. See, for example, Chaplin to Vatnik, April 28, 1947, "O deiatel'nostiakh 'pravykh' sektantskikh elementov v SEP," GARF, f. 7212, op. 1, d. 194 (Bautzen), l. 185.

184. Tiul'panov, "Dokladnaia zapiska," August 9, 1947, RTsKhIDNI, f. 17, op. 128, d. 317, l. 31.

185. Gustav Klingelhofer to Dr. Otto Friedländer, July 7, 1946, LAB, Rep. 200, ACC 2435, no. 36.

186. Tiul'panov, "Dokladnaia zapiska," August 11, 1947, RTsKhIDNI, f. 17, op. 128, d. 317, l. 32.

187. SAPMO-BA, ZPA, IV 2/1/1 (Parteivorstand Protocol, May 14–15, 1946), b. 25.

188. Tiul'panov, August 11, 1947, RTsKhIDNI, f. 17, op. 128, d. 317, l. 33.

189. See, for example, "Antisovetskie vystupleniia na zaniatiiakh politkruzhka funk- tsionerov SEPG v Galle," May 29, 1947, RTsKhIDNI, f. 17, op. 128, d. 1094, l. 56; Maj. Gen. Dubrovskii, "O nekotorykh nedostatkakh v podgotovke i proved- enii otchetno-vybornoi kampanii SEPG po Zemle Saksonii," Prikaz of July 25, 1947, in RTsKhIDNI, f. 17, op. 128, d. 317, l. 41.

190. "Stenogramma soveshchaniia," September 1946, RTsKhIDNI, f. 17, op. 128, d. 149, l. 153.

191. "Dokladnaia zapiska," November 15, 1947, RTsKhIDNI, f. 17, op. 128, d. 358, l. 208.

192. GARF, f. 7212, op. 1, d. 188, l. 135.

193. Tiul'panov to Baranov, March 12, 1948, RTsKhIDNI, f. 17, op. 128, d. 566, ll. 47–48.

194. The description of the delegation's visit to Moscow is taken mostly from Central Committee documents on the trip, contained in RTsKhIDNI, f. 17, op. 128, d. 1091. See also Bernd Bonwetsch and Gennadii Bordiugov, "Stalin und die SBZ: Ein Besuch der SED-Führung in Moskau vom 30.Januar–7.February 1947," *Vier- teljahresheft für Zeitgeschichte*, no. 2 (1994): 279–303.

195. The following account of the meeting is taken in the main from "Beseda u tovarishcha Stalina, I. V.," January 31, 1947, 9 to 12 P.M., RTsKhIDNI, f. 17, op. 128, d. 1091, ll. 43–53. The account is supplemented by the typed version of Pieck's notes on the meeting in SAPMO-BA, ZPA, NL 36/694 (Pieck), bb. 1–7. These were also published by Rolf Badstübner in *Utopie: Kreativ*, no. 7 (March 1991): 105–107.

196. The transcript does not fill in the name, though it was probably Stalin and maybe Molotov who spoke. Ibid., l. 51.

197. SAPMO-BA, ZPA, NL 36/694 (Pieck), b. 5.

198. SAPMO-BA, ZPA, NL 36/694 (Pieck), b. 7.

199. Ibid., bb. 8–20; RTsKhIDNI, f. 17, op. 128, d. 1091, ll. 65–66.

200. "Aktennotiz, Hannover," April 25, 1947, FES, SPD Ostbüro, 10301-II.

201. Pieck insisted that the conference was nothing more than an attempt at "deceiving the masses." The question then was whether to forbid the attendance at the conference of the minister-presidents from the East, or to send them with the idea that the other minister-presidents would demonstrate their true reactionary colors and the Eastern minister-presidents would withdraw (or be withdrawn, as was the case.) SAPMO-BA, ZPA, IV 2/1/11, (Parteivorstand Protocol, July 1–3, 1947), b. 71.

202. SAPMO-BA, ZPA, IV/2/15, (Parteivortand Protocol, October 24–25, 1946), bb. 136, 199.

203. U.S. intelligence sources place Fechner and Meier in the Ackermann camp as supporters of the "German line" and Gniffke in the Ulbricht camp as a "Moscow adherent." See "Dissension within the German Socialist Unity Party," December 30, 1947, pp. 5–10, in NA, RG 84, TSGC, box 3.

204. SAPMO-BA, ZPA, IV 2/1/10, (Parteivorstand Protocol, May 21–22, 1947), bb. 155–159.

205. Anton Ackermann, "Gibt es einen besonderen deutschen Weg zum Sozialismus?" *Einheit,* no. 1 (1946): 23–42.

206. "Stenogramma soveshchaniia," RTsKhIDNI, f. 17, op. 128, d. 149, l. 133.

207. SAPMO-BA, ZPA, IV 2/1/12 (Parteivorstand Protocol, August 20–21, 1947), b. 223. For conflicts between Pieck and Ackermann on the idea of a German road to socialism, see SAPMO-BA, ZPA, IV 2/1/8 (Parteivorstand Protocol, February 14, 1947), bb. 85–86.

208. SAPMO-BA, ZPA, IV 2/1/11, (Parteivorstand Protocol, July 1–3, 1947), b. 44.

209. *Neues Deutschland,* September 24, 1948.

210. "Prikaz nachal'nika SVA Z. Saksoniia," July 25, 1947: "O nekotorykh nedostatkakh v podgotovke i provedenii otchetno-vybornoi kampanii SEPG po Zemle Saksonii," RTsKhIDNI, f. 17, op. 128, d. 317, ll. 40–42.

211. Pieck and Grotewohl to Stalin, September 3, 1947 (Russian trans.), RTsKhIDNI, f. 17, op. 128, d. 1094, ll. 94–98.

212. Tiul'panov to Suslov, September 29, 1947, "Itogi II-go S'ezda sotsialisticheskoi edinoi partii Germanii," RTsKhIDNI, f. 17, f. 128, d. 317, l. 44.

213. Ibid., l. 47.

214. Grotewohl thought the meeting had taken place in Warsaw rather than in Szklarska Poręba. Grotewohl, "Zu der Konferenz der Kommunistischen Partei in Warschau," October 7, 1947, SAPMO-BA, ZPA, IV 2/2022/121, (Sekretariat Paul Merker), b. 95.

215. PRO, FO 371, Germany 1948, 70478.

216. Korotkevich, "Informatsionnaia zapiska o prebyvanii v Moskve delegatsii Sotsialisticheskoi Edinoi Partii Germanii," April 10, 1948, RTsKhIDNI, f. 17, op. 128, d. 1166, l. 155.

217. SAPMO-BA, ZPA, NL 36/695 (Pieck), b. 16.

218. RTsKhIDNI, f. 17, op. 128, d. 1166, l. 157.

219. "Kratkaia zapis' besedy sekretaria TsK BKP(b) tov. Suslova M.A. s rukovoditel-iami Sotsialisticheskoi edinoi partii Germanii t.t. Pikom, Grotevolem i El'snerom, sostoiavsheisia 29 marta 1948 goda," in ibid., l. 149.

220. Korotkevich, "Informatsionnaia zapiska," in ibid., l. 156.

221. Tiul'panov to Baranov, "Dokladnaia zapiska o vnutripartiinom polozhenii v SEPG," March 12, 1948, RTsKhIDNI, f. 17, op. 128, d. 71, l. 56.

222. Blestkin to Tiul'panov, Feb. 10, 1948, GARF, f. 7184, op. 1, d. 165, l. 159.

223. Kolesnichenko to Ponomarev, on the Thüringen parties, November 29, 1948, RTsKhIDNI, f. 17, op. 128, d. 572, l. 47.

224. Blestkin to Tiul'panov, February 10, 1948, GARF, f. 7184, op. 1, d. 165, ll. 160–161.

225. Ibid., l. 163.

226. Dahlem, "Schaffung eines Instrukteurstabes beim Z.S.," June 7, 1948, SAPMO-BA, ZPA, IV 2/2022/121 (Sekretariat Paul Merker), b. 241.

227. Cited in Fred Oelssner, "Wie die SED begann, sich zu einer Partei neuen Typus zu entwickeln," manuscript, SAPMO-BA, ZPA, NL 215/84 (Oelssner), b. 46.

228. Report of Lt. Col. Kirillov, Weimar, February 3, 1948, in GARF, f. 7184, op. 1, d. 165, l. 64.

229. SAPMO-BA, ZPA, NL 182/927 (Ulbricht), bb. 125–126.

230. See, for example, Maj. Starodubov to Tiul'panov, September 16, 1949, GARF, f. 7184, op. 1, d. 169, l. 25.

231. "Die Partei neuen Typus," Speech of Walter Ulbricht at the Höheren Polizei-schule Berlin, August 27, 1948, Abschrift, HIA, Briegleb, box 1, no. 46.

232. *Neues Deutschland*, August 22, 1948.

233. In a special session of the Party Executive, called within six hours of their finding out about Gniffke's "betrayal," the SED leaders announced that they had already checked with the Soviets and decided that the right tactic in the Gniffke case was to attack. Indeed, the SED leaders came up with all kinds of nasty personal slander regarding Gniffke's morals, but this hardly concealed their shock at his desertion. See SAPMO-BA, ZPA, IV 2/1/29 (Ausserordentliche Tagung, October 30, 1948), bb. 3–10; IV 2/1/30 (Parteivorstand Protocol, January 24, 1949), b. 18.

234. "An die Partei neuen Typus," October 28, 1948, in Gniffke, *Jahre mit Ulbricht*, pp. 364–369.

235. "Aus der Entschliessung der 13. Tagung des Parteivorstandes vom 15./16. Sept. 1948," SAPMO-BA, ZPA, 2/4/8, bb. 1–2.

236. SAPMO-BA, ZPA, NL 36/695, bb. 43, 53, 71.

237. Cited in Staritz, "Die SED, Stalin und die Gründung der DDR," p. 7, n. 20.

238. SAPMO-BA, ZPA, NL 36/695 (Pieck), bb. 36, 57, 69–70.

239. Hermann Weber writes that by March 1949, the Central Secretariat, which had never had full parity in any case, nevertheless reduced the number of former SPD members to 10 percent. Weber, *Geschichte der DDR*, p. 178.

240. "Organization der Arbeit auf dem Gebiete der Personalpolitik," Beschluss des Politbüros, March 8, 1949, SAPMO-BA, ZPA, IV 2/4/5 (ZPKK), b. 9.

241. "An die Partei neuen Typus," October 28, 1948, in Gniffke, *Jahre mit Ulbricht*, p. 369.

242. Bureau of Information SVAG, *Biulleten'*, no. 4, February 4, 1948, RTsKhIDNI, f. 17, op. 128, d. 577, l. 64.

243. "Zur Lage in der Partei," August 18, 1949, SAPMO-BA, IV 2/4/29 (ZPKK), b. 5.

244. SAPMO-BA, ZPA, IV 2/1/35, (Parteivorstand Protocol, August 23–24, 1949), bb. 13–14.

245. SAPMO-BA, ZPA, IV 2/4/1 (ZPKK), b. 14.

246. SAPMO-BA, ZPA, IV 2/1/36 (Parteivorstand Protocol, October 4, 1949), b. 51.

247. Tiul'panov to Ponomarev, "Dokladnaia zapiska," September 17, 1948, RTsKh-IDNI, f. 17, op. 128, d. 71, ll. 88–94; Lt. Khabalov, Mühlhausen, "Donesenie," GARF, f. 7184, op. 1, d. 166, l. 18.

248. Maj. Shtykin, Gotha, to Lt. Col. Makarushin, October 27, 1948, GARF, f. 7184, op. 1, d. 166, l. 152.

249. Lt. Col. Makarushin to Tiul'panov, "O zemel'noi konferentsii SEPG v Tiuringii," December 11, 1948, GARF, f. 7184, op. 1, d. 166, l. 290. Major Bessonov, "Plan raboty otdeleniia informatsii," Kalau, GARF, f. 7077, op. 1, d. 241, l. 66.

250. Tiul'panov to Pieck and Grotewohl, July 1949, "Perepiska po Soiuzu svobodnoi nemetskoi molodezhi," GARF, f. 7077, op. 1, d. 260, ll. 30–31.

251. "Donesenie o vstreche nemetskikh pionerov s sovetskimi," Brandenburg, July 18, 1949, in ibid., l. 32.

252. Wolfgang Leonhard to Hermann Möhring, January 6, 1965, copy, HIA, Grabe, box 1.

253. SAPMO-BA, ZPA, NL 36/695 (Pieck), b. 85.

254. SAPMO-BA, ZPA, IV 2/4/1 (ZPKK), b. 21. The Party Control Commission questioned the reliability of 4 percent of those investigated, or 344 SED members.

255. See Staritz, "Die SED, Stalin und die Gründung der DDR," p. 8, and SAPMO-BA, ZPA, NL 36/695 (Pieck), bb. 90–91.

256. European Command, ODI, "Weekly Intelligence Report," July 22, 1949, NA, RG 260, box 52.

257. SED Politburo to the Central Committee of the CPSU(b), October 1949, "Ob idiologicheskom ukreplenii kompartii Germanii pri provedenii natsional'noi politiki," RTsKhIDNI, f. 17, op. 128, d. 98, l. 115; Tiul'panov to Smirnov, "Obsuzhdenie itogov vyborov v zapadno-germanskii parlament," August 23, 1949, RTsKhIDNI, f. 17, op. 137, d. 93, ll. 34–35.

258. SAPMO-BA, ZPA, NL 36/695 (Pieck), b. 111.

259. Ibid., bb. 111, 115.

6. THE TIUL'PANOV QUESTION AND SOVIET POLICY-MAKING IN THE ZONE

1. Some of the best examples of this kind of work include: William Taubman, *Stalin's American Policy: From Entente to Détente to Cold War* (New York: Norton, 1982); Vojtech Mastny, *Russia's Road to the Cold War* (New York: Columbia

University Press, 1979); and Boris Meissner, *Russland, die Westmächte und Deutschland: Die sowjetische Deutschlandpolitik, 1943–1953* (Hamburg: H. H. Nölke, 1953).

2. Walrab von Buttlar, *Ziele und Zielkonflikte in der sowjetischen Deutschlandpolitik, 1945–1947* (Stuttgart: Klett-Cotta, 1980); Wolfgang Pfeiler, *Deutschlandpolitische Optionen der Sowjetunion* (Melle: Verlag Ernst Knoth, 1968); Alexander Fischer, "Die Sowjetunion und die 'deutsche Frage' 1945–1949," in Gottfried Zieger, ed., *Recht, Wirtschaft, Politik im geteilten Deutschland* (Cologne: Carl Hermanns Verlag, 1983), pp. 361–376; and Wilfried Loth, "Ziele sowjetischer Deutschlandpolitik nach dem Zweiten Weltkrieg," in Klaus Schönhoven and Dietrich Staritz, eds., *Sozialismus und Kommunismus im Wandel: Hermann Weber zum 65. Geburtstag* (Cologne: Bund-Verlag, 1993), pp. 303–324.

3. See William O. McCagg, Jr., *Stalin Embattled 1943–1948* (Detroit: Wayne State University Press, 1978); Jerry Hough, "Debates about the Postwar World," in Susan Linz, ed., *The Impact of World War II on the Soviet Union* (Totowa, N.J.: Barnes & Noble, 1985), pp. 266–274; and Werner Hahn, *Postwar Soviet Politics: The Fall of Zhdanov and the Defeat of Moderation 1946–1953* (Ithaca, N.Y.: Cornell University Press, 1983).

4. Bernd Bonwetsch, "Deutschlandpolitische Alternativen der Sowjetunion, 1949–1955," *Deutsche Studien*, no. 24 (1986): 320–339.

5. Gavriel D. Ra'anan, *International Policy Formation in the USSR* (Hamden, Conn.: Archon, 1983).

6. See the most recent version of a similar interpretation in Amy Knight, *Beria: Stalin's First Lieutenant* (Princeton, N.J.: Princeton University Press, 1993), pp. 143–146. Stalin's role is explored in R. Raack, "Stalin Plans his Post-war Germany," *Journal of Contemporary History*, vol. 28 (1993): 53–73.

7. The phrase is used repeatedly in Semenov's draft memoirs, a few selections of which are in my possession.

8. Jan Foitzik, "Die Sowjetische Militäradministration in Deutschland," *Das Parlament: Aus Politik und Zeitgeschichte* B 11/90 (March 9, 1990): 43–62, and his chapter on the Soviet Military Administration in Martin Broszat and Hermann Weber, eds., *SBZ Handbuch* (Munich: R. Oldenbourg Verlag, 1990); Peter Strunk, "Die Sowjetische Militäradministration in Deutschland (SMAD) und ihr politischer Kontrollapparat," *Historische und Landeskundliche Ostmitteleuropa Studien*, no. 7 (Marburg an der Lahn: Johann-Gottfried-Herder Institut, 1991): 143–176, and his doctoral dissertation, "Pressekontrolle und Propagandapolitik der Sowjetischen Militäradministration in Deutschland (SMAD)," Free University of Berlin (Berlin, 1989); Stefan Creuzberger, "Innere Organisation und äussere Beziehungen der SMAD: Ein Beitrag zur Geschichte der sowjetischen Besatzungspolitik in Deutschland, 1945–1949," master's thesis, Bonn, n.d., and "Die Sowjetische Militäradministration in Deutschland (SMAD), 1945–1949," *Deutschland Report*, no. 15, Konrad Adenauer Stiftung, 1991; Jochen Laufer, "Konfrontation oder Kooperation? Zur sowjetischen Politik in Deutschland und im Allierten Kontrollrat 1945–1948," in Alexander Fischer, ed., *Studien zur Geschichte der SBZ/DDR* (Berlin: Duncker and Humblot, 1993), pp. 57–80.

9. For only one of many examples, see Ann L. Phillips, *Soviet Policy toward East Germany Reconsidered: The Postwar Decade* (Westport, Conn.: Greenwood Press, 1986), p. 34.

10. In fact, U.S. political advisor Robert Murphy's letter to the secretary of state, August 7, 1946, clearly states that "Colonel Serge Tulpanoff . . . remains a most influential figure with apparently great powers of decision." NA, RG 59, box 3694B, Control (Germany), 8-746.

11. RTsKhIDNI, f. 17, op. 128, t. 1 and 2. Documents especially relevant to the Tiul'panov question have been published in a recent collection; see Bernd Bonwetsch, Gennadii Bordiugov, and Norman Naimark, eds., *SVAG—Upravlenie propagandy i S. I. Tiul'panov, 1945–1949: Sbornik dokumentov* (Moscow: "Rossiia Molodaia," 1994). These documents are edited and abridged; therefore I refer to the originals in the text. The exceptions are documents from the Tiul'panov family archives.

12. AVPRF, f. 082. (Materials on Germany.)

13. There are enough scattered citations in Dmitrii Volkogonov's biography of Stalin to make one think that the presidential archives may contain detailed notes and memoranda from Stalin on the German question. See especially book 2, part 2 in Dmitrii Volkogonov, *Triumf i tragediia: I. V. Stalin, politicheskii portret* (Moscow: Agenstva pechati Novosti, 1989).

14. RTsKhIDNI, f. 17, op. 125, d. 475, l. 8.

15. RTsKhIDNI, f. 17, op. 128, d. 572, l. 95.

16. For biographical data on Tiul'panov, see especially G. Handel, "Zum internationalistischen Wirken von S. I. Tjulpanow als Politoffizier der Sowjetarmee," *Wissenschaftliche Zeitschrift, Karl-Marx-Univ. Leipzig, Ges.-u. Sprachwiss. R.,* no. 4 (1976): 351–367; Manfred Koch, "Zum Tode von Sergej I. Tjulpanov," *Deutschland Archiv,* no. 17 (1984): 341–342; and Sergej Tjulpanow, *Deutschland nach dem Kriege (1945–1949): Erinnerungen* (Berlin, GDR: Dietz Verlag, 1987).

17. Robert Murphy writes, for example: "He [Tiul'panov] is a well-educated Russian, who studied for a time in Germany and who accordingly speaks fluent German and shows himself to be thoroughly conversant with German mentality, history and literature." Murphy to Secretary of State, August 7, 1946, NA, RG 59, box 3694B, Control (Germany), 8-746.

18. Vyshinskii to Malenkov, June 26, 1945, AVPRF, f. 082, op. 27, d. 3, l. 21.

19. Cited in Harold Hurwitz, *Die Eintracht der Siegermächte und die Orientierungsnot der Deutschen 1945–1946* (Cologne: Verlag Wissenschaft und Politik, 1984), p. 224.

20. Otto Meier to Grotewohl, October 30, 1945, SAPMO-BA, ZPA, NL 90/276, b. 60.

21. See SAPMO-BA, ZPA: Ulbricht to Bokov, May 6, 1946, NL 182/1191, b. 7; Ulbricht to Bokov, May 7, 1946, b. 21; Ulbricht to Bokov and Kovalev, May 20, 1946, b. 37; Antipenko to Zhukov and Bokov, August 3, 1945, bb. 41, 64, 83; Kern and Schmidt to Bokov, October 2, 1946, b. 63; Ulbricht to Bokov and Tiul'panov, October 28, 1946, b. 95; Pieck to Bokov, November 14, 1946, b. 183.

22. Shikin to Aleksandrov, March 30, 1946, RTsKhIDNI, f. 17, op. 125, d. 321, l. 37.

23. Ibid.

24. Ibid., l. 28.

25. Ibid., l. 42.

26. Ibid., l. 40.

27. Deputy Head of the Political Department of the Office of the Political Advisor in Germany, I. Filippov, to the Deputy Minister of the Ministry of Foreign Affairs, S. A. Lozovskii, May 25, 1946, RTsKhIDNI, f. 17, op. 128, d. 153, l. 3.

28. Ibid., l. 62.

29. I. Shikin to Zhdanov, August 3, 1946, RTsKhIDNI, f. 17, op. 128, d. 147, l. 1.

30. Ibid., l. 2.

31. Ibid., l. 5.

32. Lt. Col. Konstantinovskii on the preparation for the Berlin local elections; sent from Burtsev to Suslov, September 2, 1946, in ibid., ll. 11–15.

33. Ibid., l. 15.

34. Hermann Weber, *Geschichte der DDR* (Munich: Deutscher Taschenbuch Verlag, 1985), pp. 138–140.

35. Ibid., p. 140.

36. Ibid., p. 143.

37. "Stenogramma Soveshchaniia v Upravlenii Propagandy SVAG," September 17–18, 1946, RTsKhIDNI, f. 17, op. 128, d. 149, l. 2.

38. Ibid., l. 125.

39. Ibid., l. 111.

40. Tiul'panov himself sometimes used hints about Soviet withdrawal "in some German circles" for his own purposes. Steele to the Secretary of State, October 13, 1947, NA, RG 59, 740.00119, Control (Germany), 10-1347.

41. "Stenogramma Soveshchaniia," September 17–18, 1946, RTsKhIDNI, f. 17, op. 128, d. 149, l. 127.

42. Ibid., l. 148.

43. Ibid., l. 156.

44. Ibid., l. 156.

45. Ibid., l. 157.

46. Ibid., l. 128.

47. Ibid., l. 131.

48. Ibid., l. 146.

49. Ibid., l. 166.

50. Ibid., l. 166. Tokaev recalled a meeting at which Tiul'panov supposedly bragged about having accumulated a large stock of potatoes that would be used for electoral purposes. "These vegetables will win the day for the SED," he said. Grigorii Tokaev, *Stalin Means War* (London: Weidenfeld and Nicolson, 1951), p. 84.

51. RTsKhIDNI, f. 17, op. 128, d. 149, l. 166.

52. Ibid., l. 179. Vladimir Semenov investigated the Becher case in some detail and concluded that, for the moment at least, it would be unwise to remove him as head of the Kulturbund. In the process of the investigation, Semenov turned up

a great deal of negative information on both Becher and the Propaganda Administration officer Grigorii Patent, who was charged with supervising the Kulturbund. Notebook of V. S. Semenov, November 13, 1946, RTsKhIDNI, op. 128, d. 147, ll. 155–158. See also Chapter 8, "Kulturbund."

53. RTsKhIDNI, f. 17, op. 128, d. 149, l. 185.

54. RTsKhIDNI, f. 17, op. 128, d. 150, l. 53.

55. Ibid., ll. 54–56.

56. Ibid., l. 62.

57. Stenographic report of discussion with Matern, September 25, 1946, RTsKhIDNI, f. 17, op. 128, d. 151, ll. 135–136.

58. A. Paniushkin, K. Kuzakov, and M. Burtsev to A. A. Kuznetsov, October 11, 1946, RTsKhIDNI, f. 17, op. 128, d. 54, l. 82.

59. Ibid., ll. 92–95.

60. Ibid., l. 100.

61. Ibid., l. 99.

62. Ibid., l. 99.

63. Ibid., l. 82.

64. Bokov, "Results of the Local Elections in Berlin," November 18, 1946, RTsKhIDNI, f. 17, op. 128, d. 147, l. 165.

65. Ibid., l. 179.

66. Ibid., l. 167.

67. Grotewohl drew very similar conclusions from the Berlin elections. "Under no circumstances," he stated, "must it appear that we are something like Quislings. (Absolutely correct!)" SAPMO-BA, ZPA, IV 2/1/15 (Parteivorstand Protocol, October 24–25, 1946), b. 540. This was also the view of Semenov's Office of the Political Advisor. I. Filippov, Office of the Political Advisor, October 9, 1946, RTsKhIDNI, f. 17, op. 128, d. 147, l. 144.

68. The last order he countersigned was Order no. 318 of November 14, 1946. Strunk, "Die Sowjetische Militäradministration in Deutschland," p. 156. The first order countersigned by I. V. Makarov, his replacement as head of the Military Council, was dated November 27, 1946.

69. Zhukov and Katiushkin of the Cadres Administration to Kuznetsov, November 11, 1946, RtsKhIDNI, f. 17, op. 128, d. 54, ll. 101–102.

70. RTsKhIDNI, f. 17, op. 128, d. 54, l. 99.

71. Ibid., l. 104.

72. Tovarishchu STALIN, I. V., and Tovarishchu STALINU, January 3, 1947 (?), RTsKhIDNI, f. 17, op. 125, d. 475, ll. 8–13, 27–28. The draft letters to Stalin were apparently prepared by G. Aleksandrov, M. Suslov, and I. Shikin "in accordance with the exchange of opinions in the Secretariat" of the Central Committee. See the letter from these three to A. A. Kuznetsov, in ibid., l. 20. It is not apparent that they were actually sent; without access to the Presidential Archives, it is difficult to determine what Stalin received and how he reacted.

73. Ibid., l. 12.

74. Ibid., l. 13.

75. Resolution of the Central Committee: "On the Work of the Propaganda Administration of SVAG," draft, in ibid., ll. 21–25. That Tiul'panov was to be kept on as deputy was inserted in this document at Shikin's insistence. See his note to Kuzakov of December 25, 1946, in ibid., l. 17. In the same letter, Shikin is careful to refer to the Information Administration as a joint operation of the Main Political Administration of the Armed Forces (GlavPU) and the Central Committee of the party. The draft resolution was forwarded to the Central Committee secretaries Kuznetsov, Patolichev, and Popov by Aleksandrov, Shikin, Lozovskii, Malik, Paniushkin, Kuzakov, Makarov, Burtsev, and Strunnikov on January 2, 1947. See ibid., l. 16.

76. Ibid., l. 2.

77. Resolution of the TsK: "On the Organization of a Military-political Council in SVAG," n.d., in ibid., l. 14. In a January 17, 1947, document, Sokolovskii and Makarov recommended that D. T. Shepilov be appointed to head the new Information Administration, with Tiul'panov retained as his deputy. But Shepilov had recently been made chief editor of *Pravda,* and the Central Committee turned the issue back over to Shikin. M. Iovchuk and V. Grigor'ian to A. A. Kuznetsov, January 17, 1947, in ibid., l. 19.

78. Ibid., l. 7. GlavPU and the Propaganda Administration of the Central Committee were to "prepare questions" for the Secretariat's review.

79. At the end of a September 1947 report by General Makarov to A. A. Kuznetsov describing the "party-political" work of SVAG, G. Korotkevich, a Central Committee functionary, appended a note to Kuznetsov, saying that Suslov had been in Berlin himself and was fully apprised of the situation. Korotkevich to Kuznetsov, December 24, 1947, RTsKhIDNI, f. 17, op. 128, d. 358, l. 50.

80. Serge Petroff, *The Red Emininence: A Biography of Mikhail A. Suslov* (Clifton, N.J.: Kingston Press, 1988), pp. 56–57. In this critical period of Soviet German policy, Suslov was probably the link between the Central Committee and Stalin.

81. McClure and Tiul'panov letters, March 3 and March 7, 1947, in NA, RG 260, OMGUS ISD, box 15, folder 4; Textor, McClure, and Tiul'panov letters dating from Jan. 29, 1947, to May 19, 1946, in NA, RG 260, ISD, box 120.

82. Allied Control Authority, Control Council Minutes, September 30 and October 20, 1947, in HIA, GTUAO, box 4.

83. A. Sobolev, V. Poliakov, V. Fedoseev, V. Nemchinov, and G. Konstantinovskii to A. A. Zhdanov, "On the Results of the Review of the Work of the Information Administration of SVAG," RTsKhIDNI, f. 17, op. 128, d. 572, l. 27.

84. Ibid., l. 20.

85. Ibid., l. 21.

86. Ibid., l. 22.

87. Ibid., l. 23.

88. Ibid., l. 24.

89. Ibid., l. 29.

90. Ibid., l. 27.

91. Resolution of the Central Committee, draft, RTsKhIDNI, f. 17, op. 128, d. 572, ll. 12–13.

92. Strunk, "Die Sowjetische Militäradministration in Deutschland," p. 158.

93. This is the same Konstantinovskii who reported on the Propaganda Administration's work to Shikin in December 1946.

94. Konstantinovskii to Shikin, August 17, 1948, RTsKhIDNI, f. 17, op. 128, d. 572, l. 2.

95. Ibid., l. 3.

96. Despite the fact that Tiul'panov used much harsher rhetoric when talking about the West than did Semenov—in fact, Tiul'panov's language was periodically the subject of Western complaints in the Allied Control Council—there is evidence that, at least during the spring and summer of 1948, Semenov and Tiul'panov worked well together. See RTsKhIDNI, f. 17, op. 128, d. 573, l. 63.

97. RTsKhIDNI, f. 17, op. 128, d. 572, ll. 3–4.

98. Ibid., l. 6.

99. Ibid., l. 7.

100. Ibid., l. 8.

101. Ibid., l. 9.

102. Wolfgang Leonhard, *Die Revolution entlässt ihre Kinder* (Cologne: Kiepenheuer und Witsch, 1955), pp. 495–496.

103. Shatilov to Suslov, September 11, 1948, in ibid., l. 1.

104. This information was supplied by Colonel Viktor Mukhin, director of the Russian Army General Staff's Historical-Archival Department, January 1993.

105. S. I. Tiul'panov to the Chief Prosecutor of the Soviet Union, June 27, 1955, in Bonwetsch, Bordiugov, and Naimark, eds., *SVAG: Sbornik dokumentov*, pp. 234–235.

106. See, for example, a February 15, 1949, report from Tiul'panov to the Central Committee on Church affairs, in RTsKhIDNI, f. 17, op. 128, d. 683, l. 22.

107. Foitzik, "Sowjetische Militäradministration in Deutschland (SMAD)," *SBZ Handbuch*, p. 24.

108. Semenov's proposed promotion in September 1948 was held up due to the Central Committee's objections that Semenov was inattentive to the wishes of the commander-in-chief and the SVAG collective as a whole. Baranenkov to Suslov, August 13, 1948, RTsKhIDNI, f. 17, op. 128, d. 1140, ll. 63–64. See also Strunk, "Pressekontrolle und Propagandapolitik der Sowjetischen Militäradministration in Deutschland (SMAD)," p. 71.

109. Makariushin to Tiul'panov, December 15, 1948, GARF, f. 7184, op. 1, d. 166, l. 259.

110. Maj. Roger Welles, "Speech of Col. Tulpanov on Occasion of SED Conference, 25 January 1949," Report no. RP-28–49, pp. 1–4, February 2, 1949, NA, RG 260, box 110. David Pike has made the interesting argument that breaking off Tiul'-panov's speech may have been a piece of artful disinformation. Personal communication, July 16, 1994.

111. Shatilov to Malenkov, September 17, 1949, RTsKhIDNI, f. 17, op. 128, d. 567, l. 182.

112. Ibid., l. 182.

113. V. Dobrokhotov (Cadres Department, Central Committee) to Malenkov, September 30, 1949, in ibid., l. 180.

114. Abakumov to Malenkov, August 9, 1949, in ibid., ll. 183–185.

115. Shatilov to Malenkov, September 17, 1947, in ibid., l. 181.

116. "O t. Tiul'panove, S. I.," RTsKhIDNI, f. 17, op. 118, d. 567, l. 179.

117. Tiul'panov to Suslov, June 1960, in Bonwetsch, Bordiugov, and Naimark, eds., *SVAG: Sbornik dokumentov,* pp. 236–238.

118. Tiul'panov to Andropov, October 8, 1963, in ibid., pp. 238–239, n. 1.

119. Top Secret ODDI report, Enclosure to Dispatch 648, December 30, 1947, Frankfurt, NA, RG 59, 740.00119, Control (Germany), 12-3047, p. 2.

120. See Chapter 5, "The Soviets and the SED."

121. A detailed American intelligence report does indicate that Tiul'panov was the chief of the "party-active" of SVAG. See Weekly Intelligence Report, no. 124, OMGUS, ODI, September 15, 1948, NA, RG 319, box 1625. In his memoirs, Tiul'panov also notes that "I spoke before the party activists of SVAG about our style of work, the successes and mistakes of our activities" and then cites from the speech: "Under this circumstance we must as party activists pay attention to the ways in which our collective, in common work with thousands and tens of thousands of Soviet people in Germany, helps with the carrying through of the democratization and denazification of Germany." See Sergej Tjulpanow, *Deutschland nach dem Kriege: Erinnerungen* (Berlin, GDR: Dietz Verlag, 1966), p. 29. For the protocol of the party meeting, see, "Protokol sobraniia partiinogo aktiva SVAG," March 9, 1949, RTsKhIDNI, f. 17, op. 128, d. 682, l. 2.

122. See Lev Sidorovskii, "Neskol'ko stranits iz 'Leningradskogo dela,'" *Avrora,* no. 4 (1989): 23–24.

7. BUILDING THE EAST GERMAN POLICE STATE

1. The commission conducted hearings about the nature of the East German system. Some of the most interesting testimony was published in a number of issues of *Deutschland Archiv* in 1994, under the title "Anhörung der Enquete-Kommission."

2. The commission's full name is Bundesbeauftragte für die Unterlagen des Staatssicherheitsdienstes der ehemaligen Deutschen Demokratischen Republik. The former East German pastor and human rights activist Joachim Gauck is in charge of the operation.

3. See Norman M. Naimark, "Is It True What They're Saying about East Germany?" *ORBIS,* vol. 23, no. 3 (1979): 549–577.

4. See the work of Karl Wilhelm Fricke, especially his *Die DDR-Staatssicherheit: Entwicklung, Strukturen, Aktionsfelder,* 2nd ed. (Cologne: Verlag Wissenschaft und Politik, 1984).

5. See Klaus-Dietmar Henke, ed., *Wann bricht schon mal ein Staat zusammen: Die Debatte über die Stasi-Akten auf dem 39. Historikertage 1992* (Munich: Deutscher Taschenbuch Verlag, 1993).

6. New opportunities for research on selected NKVD/MVD papers have just been made available at GARF. See *Archive of Contemporary Russian History,* vol. 1, *"Special Files" for I. V. Stalin: Materials of the Secretariat of the NKVD-MVD of the USSR, 1944–1953,* ed. by V. A. Kozlov and S. V. Mironenko (Moscow: Blagovest, Ltd., 1994). Similar volumes should soon be available for the files of Beria and Molotov.

7. See "Zur Herausbildung und Organisation des Systems von Speziallagern des NKVD der UdSSR in der sowjetischen Besatzungszone Deutschlands im Jahre 1945," *Deutschland Archiv,* no. 6 (June 1993): 723–735; "On the Russian Archives: An Interview with Sergei V. Mironenko," *Slavic Review,* vol. 52, no. 4 (Winter 1993): 841.

8. "Ob ustranenii nedostatkov v rabote politsii," Order no. 112, May 23, 1946, GARF, f. 7184, op. 2, d. 2, l. 249.

9. In January 1946, Mielke held the post of "ZK Mitarbeiter [Central Committee functionary] for Police and Justice." In the same source, Mickinn is referred to as "Trade Union Secretary of the Police Union group in Berlin and Chairman of the Police Section of the Berlin Union." "Protokoll über die Sitzung der Genossen der Berliner Justiz und der ZVfI," January 19, 1946, BStU MfSZ, 230/66, b. 4.

10. "Rechenschaftsbericht über die bisher geleistete gewerkschaftliche Arbeit in der Berliner Polizei," BStU MfSZ, 230/66, b. 71.

11. Serov to Beria, June 4, 1945, GARF, f. 9401, op. 2, d. 96, l. 202.

12. B. Levitskii, "Unter sowjetischem Befehl," manuscript, HIA, Nicolaevsky, Series 236 (411-13), p. 1.

13. "Ob ustranenii nedostatkov v rabote politsii," Order no. 112, May 23, 1946, GARF, f. 7184, op. 2, d. 2, l. 250.

14. Baumann, "Aufbau des Informationsdienstes der Provincialregierung Brandenburgs," Abschrift, HIA, Sander, box 2, folder 5, p. 3.

15. SAPMO-BA, ZPA, EA 0890/2 (Robert Siewert), b. 259.

16. In many of these cases, the German police were not even allowed to take down the names of the criminals. BStU MfSZ, 400/66, b. 31.

17. "Protokoll über die Sitzung der Genossen von der Berliner Polizei beim Gen. Ulbricht," January 18, 1946, BStU MfSZ, 230/66, b. 112.

18. BStU MfSZ, 238/66, b. 349

19. Some units already armed for special missions in the fall of 1945. Serov to Kruglov, June 26, 1945, GARF, f. 9401, op. 2, d. 138, l. 53. See also Alexander Fischer, "Die Entmilitärisierung und Wiederaufrüstung in der sowjetischen Besatzungszone Deutschlands und in der Deutschen Demokratischen Republik (1945–1956)," in *Vorträge zur Militärgeschichte: Entmilitärisierung und Aufrüstung in Mitteleuropa* (Herford: E. S. Mitter und Sohn), p. 46.

20. "Protokoll," January 18, 1946, BStU, MfSZ, 230/66, b. 112.

21. Report of January 14, 1946, BStU, MfSZ, 238/66, b. 440.

22. SAPMO-BA, ZPA, EA 0059 (Walter Besenbuch), bb. 5–6.

23. GARF, f. 7184, op. 2, d. 2, ll. 249–250.

24. On the issue of secrecy, see Dieter Marc Schneider, "Innere Verwaltung/Deutsche Verwaltung des Innern (DVdI)," in Martin Broszat and Hermann Weber, eds., *SBZ Handbuch* (Munich: R. Oldenbourg Verlag, 1990), p. 211.

25. Serov to Kruglov, June 26, 1946, GARF, f. 9401, op. 2, d. 138, l. 57.

26. Protocol of December 20, 1946, meeting, SAPMO-BA, ZPA, NL 182/1192 (Ulbricht), bb. 191–192.

27. Serov to Kruglov, June 26, 1946, GARF, f. 9401, op. 2, d. 138, ll. 55–56.

28. Secretariat d. Ministers, BStU MfSZ, 333, b. 10; see also BStU MfSZ, 238/66, b. 215.

29. "Rededisposition zur Frage der Kultur-massenarbeit und der kommender Aufgaben der Polizei," September 1948, BStU MfSZ, Sekretariat d. Ministers, AS 323, p. 29.

30. "Bericht über die Länderkonferenz in der Deutschen Justizverwaltung," March 12, 1948, BStU MfSZ, AS 230/66, b. 53.

31. "1947 Jahresbericht Dezernat K 5 im Lande Sachsen," BStU MfSZ, AS 229/66, b. 364.

32. 7707 ECIC, RT-359-48, October 7, 1948, NA, RG 260, box 24.

33. "Protokoll der Tagung über den Befehl 201 am 22 Dez. 1947," SAPMO-BA, ZPA, IV 2/13/2, b. 5.

34. BStU MfSZ, 400/66, bb. 124–125.

35. FES, SPD Ostbüro, 0046 A-G, May 27, 1949.

36. "Jahresbericht: Deutsche Verwaltung des Innern in der Sowjetischen Besatzungszone, 1946–1947," BStU MfSZ, AS 99/58, b. 27.

37. CIC, "Organization of the Political Police in the Soviet Zone," Report RP-174-48, NA, RG 260, box 24, p. 2.

38. BStU MfSZ, AS 229/66, b. 470; "Jahresbericht Dezernat K 5," in ibid., b. 346.

39. Ibid., b. 605.

40. "Protokoll über die Sitzung der Genossen von der Berliner Polizei beim Gen. Ulbricht," January 18, 1946, BStU MfSZ, AS 230/66, b. 112.

41. "Aufgabengebiet und Struktur der Einheiten K 5 für das Land Sachsen ab 1.1.1948," BStU MfSZ, AS 229/66, b. 372.

42. "Die Kommissariat K 5," July 13, 1949, FES, SPD Ostbüro, 0046 A-G.

43. "Allgemeines über die Aufgaben und den Arbeitsbereich des Kommissariats 5," BStU MfSZ, AS 238/66, b. 343.

44. Report of May 27, 1949, FES, SPD Ostbüro, 0046 A-G.

45. CIC, Report R-579-48, October 11, 1948, NA, RG 260, box 24, p. 2.

46. DVdI, Abteilung K, Communication with Saxony-Anhalt, April 13, 1948, BStU MfSZ, AS 282/67, b. 12.

47. BStU MfSZ, AS 229/66, bb. 477–479, 556–558.

48. Report, May 27, 1949, FES, SPD Ostbüro, 0046 A-G.

49. K-5 Saxony-Anhalt, "Änderung des Verhältnisses des Sachgebietes K 5 innerhalb der Polizeibehörde," May 13, 1949, BStU MfSZ, AS 364/66, b. 151.

50. "Jahresbericht Dezernat K 5 im Lande Sachsen," 1948, BStU MfSZ, AS 229/66, b. 599.

51. Ibid., bb. 596–597.

52. Dübow to Mielke, July 29, 1947, BStU MfSZ, Sekretariat d. Ministers, AS 324, b. 23.

53. BStU MfSZ, 400/66, b. 126.

54. "Innenminister Konferenz am 12. Oktober 1947 in Rehfelde/Sachsen," RTs-KhIDNI, f. 17, op. 128, d. 354, l. 13.

55. "Aufbau einer Abteilung *Nachrichten und Information* [N/I] in der D.V.d.I.," November 11, 1947, BStU MfSZ, AS 229/66, bb. 266–267.

56. Ibid., bb. 252–261. Emphasis in the original.

57. "Geschäftsverteilungsplan der Landesnachrichtenämter [H.Abt.N.] in den Innenministerien der Länder," BStU MfSZ, AS 230/66, vol. 2, bb. 42, 124.

58. E. M. (Mielke), "Polizei und Bevölkerung," manuscript, BStU MfSZ, AS 238/66, bb. 204–205.

59. "Rededisposition zur Frage der Kultur-massenarbeit . . .," August–September 1948, BStU MfSZ, Sekretariat d. Ministers, AS 323 b. 26; "Die Aufgaben der Volkspolizei," October 15, 1948, ibid., b. 8.

60. "Instruktion," June 28, 1948 (also in Russian), BStU MfSZ, Sekretariat d. Ministers, AS 331, b. 1.

61. POLAD Secret Intelligence Report no. 495, "Police Developments in the Russian Zone," September 10, 1948, NA, RG 59, 740.00119, Control (Germany), 9-1048, p. 1.

62. "Instruktion," June 28, 1948, BStU MfSZ, Sekretariat d. Ministers, AS 331, b. 1.

63. "Richtlinie zur weiteren Festigung der Volkspolizei," June 27, 1949, BStU MfSZ, Sekretariat d. Ministers, AS 323, b. 22.

64. "Vorläufiges Statut: der Leiter der Kultur-Massenarbeit in der deutschen Polizei der SBZ und Gross-Berlin" (fall 1948?), BStU MfSZ, Sekretariat d. Ministers, AS 323, bb. 1–4.

65. "Die Aufgaben der Volkspolizei," October 15, 1948, BStU MfSZ, Secretariat d. Ministers, AS 323, b. 8.

66. BStU MfSZ, Sekretariat d. Ministers, AS 323, bb. 48, 52, 59.

67. "Besprechung zwischen General Kotikow und Vizepräsident Mielke," March 30, 1947, BStU MfSZ, Secretariat d. Ministers, AS 322, bb. 1, 17. For 1947 budget figures in German and in Russian, see ibid., bb. 74–111.

68. "Antwort auf die Frage zur Besprechung am 18 Dez. 1948," SAPMO-BA, ZPA, NL 36/695 (Wilhelm Pieck), b. 56.

69. Schneider, "Innere Verwaltung," in Broszat and Weber, eds., *SBZ Handbuch*, p. 215.

70. SAPMO-BA, ZPA, EA 1275/1 (Heinrich Fonferra), bb. 149–150.

71. "Antwort auf die Frage zur Besprechung am 18 Dez. 1948," SAPMO-BA, ZPA, NL 36/695 (Wilhelm Pieck), b. 56.

72. "Die Aufgaben der Volkspolizei," October 15, 1948, BStU MfSZ, Sekretariat d. Ministers, AS 323, b. 8.

73. Military Intelligence, Report R-430-48, p. 2, NA, RG 260, box 24. See also B. Levitskii, "Unter sowjetischem Befehl," HIA, Nicolaevsky, Series no. 236/411-13.

74. "Jahresbericht: Deutsche Verwaltung des Innern in der sowjetischen Besatzungs- zone, 1946–1947," BStU MfSZ, AS 99/58, b. 35. See also Levitskii, "Unter sowje- tischem Befehl," p. 5.

75. During the blockade, the number of officers in the Border Police grew from 7,500 to 10,000. Many of the additional police officers were brought into Berlin from Saxony. HQ ECIC, "Border Police Garrison Battalions," October 26, 1948, NA, RG 260, box 24, OIR, Department of State, "The Militarization of the German Police in Eastern Germany," Report 4798, NA, RG 59, p. 1. See also Brewster Morris, Memo no. 347, April 21, 1948, NA, RG 260, ODI, box 27, p. 2; "Formation of Paramilitary Police," U.S. Political Advisor for Germany to Sec- retary of State, September 17, 1948, NA, RG 59, 740.00119 Control (Germany), 9-1748.

76. Markgraf and Gyptner, "Richtlinie zur weiteren Festigung der Volkspolizei," BStU MfSZ, Sekretariat d. Ministers 323, b. 15.

77. Reschke was demoted to commandant of the Bautzen prison camp. Apparently he was at one point caught selling favors to the prisoners in Bautzen. Levitskii, "Unter sowjetischem Befehl," p. 2.

78. Military Intelligence Report R-579-48, October 11, 1948, NA, RG 260, box 24, p. 2.

79. "Recruitment and Preliminary Training of Alert Police," Report RP-231-48, NA, RG 260, box 24, p. 2.

80. Müller was described by American military intelligence as an "energetic pro- Communist; opportunist, who would defect . . .; former commanding officer German XII Corps; acting commander of German Fourth Army; former member of the NKFD." HQ 7707 ECIC, Report RT-771-48, December 21, 1948, NA, RG 260, box 94, p. 7.

81. HQ 7707 ECIC, "Reorganization of the German Ministry of the Interior," Report RP-263-48, December 16, 1948, NA, RG 260, box 110, p. 10.

82. "Deutsche Generale für die Ostpolizei," *Der Kurier* (Berlin), November 3, 1945, in FES, SPD Ostbüro, 0043 01/IM.

83. SAPMO-BA, ZPA, EA 0890/2 (Robert Siewert), b. 260. Riddleberger to the Sec- retary of State, October 19, 1948, NA, RG 59, 740.00119 Control (Germany), 10- 1948.

84. See, for example, 7854th MID, Report R-424-48, October 1948, NA, RG 260, box 24, pp. 1–3; "Training of German Police," RP-249-49, NA, RG 260, box 110; HQ 7707 ECIC, RT-329-49, March 18, 1949, NA, RG 260, box 94.

85. CIC Report RP-221-49, p. 2, NA, RG 59, 740.00119 Control (Germany), 8-2349. The oath ("Eidesstattliche Verpflichtung") signed by the People's Police stated

only that the police were bound "to defend the interests of the German working people from fascist, reactionary, and other enemy and criminal elements" and to serve as "a dependable bulwark of the democratic development in the Eastern zone, as well as also in the struggle for a unified Germany." FES, SPD Ostbüro, 0005 (Police).

86. OIR, Department of State, Report no. 4798.3, NA, RG 59, p. 3; U.S. Political Advisor for Germany to the Secretary of State, August 2, 1949, NA, RG 59, 740.00119 Control (Germany), 8-149; CIC Report RP 220-49, NA, RG 59, 740.00119 Control (Germany), 8-2349. See also Levitskii, "Unter sowjetischem Befehl," p. 14.

87. "Reorg. der Polizei in der SBZ," p. 1, FES, SPD Ostbüro, 0043.

88. OIR, Department of State, Report 4798.3, p. 4, NA, RG 59.

89. External Survey Detachment no. MGB-7483, October 28, 1948, p. 3, NA, RG 84, CGC, box 226, folder 24.

90. See ACC Law no. 31, *Official Gazette of the Control Council for Germany*, no. 8 (July 1, 1946): 54, in HIA, GTUAO, box 30.

91. Russov to Suslov, "Protokol sobraniia," March 9, 1949, RTsKhIDNI, f. 17, op. 128, d. 682, l. 123.

92. BStU MfSZ, Sekretariat d. Ministers, AS 327, b. 93.

93. "Anmerkung zur Vorbereitung und Durchführung des 1. Mai," April 9, 1949, and "Mai-Aufmarsch der Volkspolizei," April 14, 1949, BStU MfSZ, Sekretariat d. Ministers, AS 337, bb. 37–42, 47.

94. FES, SPD Ostbüro, 0046 A-G, May 27, 1949.

95. *Frankfurter Allgemeine Zeitung*, September 24, 1992. Discoveries of mass graves reported in the Berlin newspaper *Der Morgen* and first hand descriptions of the camps are contained in the collection by Michael Klonovsky and Jan von Flocken, eds., *Stalins Lager in Deutschland: Dokumentation, Zeugenberichte 1945–1950* (Munich: Deutscher Taschenbuch Verlag, 1993).

96. *Frankfurter Allgemeine Zeitung*, November 16, 1992.

97. *Kölner Stadt-Anzeiger*, October 2, 1992.

98. *Frankfurter Allgemeine Zeitung*, September 24, 1992.

99. *Kölner Stadt-Anzeiger*, October 2, 1992; Achim Kilian, *Einzuweisen zur völligen Isolierung: NKWD Speziallager Mühlberg/Elbe 1945–1948*, introduction by Hermann Weber (Leipzig: Forum Verlag, 1992), p. 26. According to one official German government report, roughly 60,000 people were interned in Sachsenhausen (which matches the SPD figures), but only 12,500 died, a number that is more in line with the Soviet figures and is unusual in its departure from the general death rate of one in three. *The Week in Germany*, October 9, 1992, p. 3. Given the fact that Sachsenhausen was known for its particularly high death rate (over 50 percent in 1945 and 1946), these government figures appear to be inaccurate. HQ ECIC, Intelligence Summary 61, June 7, 1949, NA, RG 59, Control (Germany) 6-1049.

100. Serov, "Vorläufige Anordnung über die Spezlager des NKVD," July 27, 1945, in Bodo Ritscher "Zur Herausbildung und Organization des Systems von Spezial-

lagern des NKVD der UdSSR in der sowjetischen Besatzungszone Deutschlands im Jahre 1945," *Deutschland Archiv*, no. 6 (June 1993): 732. On the camps, see also "Provisorische Ordnung der Internierungslager in der SBZ/DDR," *Beiträge zur Geschichte der Arbeiterbewegung*, no. 4 (1991): 530–535.

101. "Digest for Germany and Austria," no. 743, March 20, 1948, NA, RG 260, box 75; Karl Wilhelm Fricke, *Politik und Justiz in der DDR: Zur Geschichte der politischen Verfolgung 1945–1968* (Cologne: Verlag Wissenschaft und Politik, 1979), doc. 30, p. 83.

102. See Sopade Informationsdienst, Denkschriften 55, "Die Straflager und Zuchthäuser der Sowjetzone: Gesundheitszustand und Lebensbedingungen politischen Gefangenen," p. 15, in HIA, Grabe, box 1; and Report R-672-49, p. 3, in NA, RG 59, 740.00119, Control (Germany), 6-1449.

103. Milovan Djilas, *Conversations with Stalin*, trans. Michael B. Petrovich (New York: Harcourt Brace Jovanovich, 1962), p. 114.

104. Merkulov and Kruglov to Stalin, January 31, 1946, GARF, f. 9401, op. 2, d. 134, l. 231.

105. A number of such cases are cited in the GARF. See, for example, GARF, f. 7077, op. 1, d. 196, l. 66; Director of the Operations Group of Saxony-Anhalt to the director of Internal Affairs of the Saxony-Anhalt SVA, March 13, 1947, f. 7133, op. 1, d. 253, l. 107; Vatnik to Trufanov, Aug. 9, 1946, f. 7212, op. 1, l. 234.

106. SAPMO-BA, ZPA, EA 1845/3 (Rudolf Bühring), bb. 578–579.

107. Letter of Capt. Potemko, February 1, 1949, RTsKhIDNI, f. 17, op. 128, d. 100, l. 28.

108. HQ SHAEF, "Special Intelligence Summary," no. 37, 1948, NA, RG 260, AGTS, box 646, p. B4.

109. "Breakdown of the Soviet Kommandantura," NA, RG 260, AGTS, box 645; A. Veresov [A. V. Iatsevich], "Rabota 'Smersh' v Sovetskoi Armii," p. 7, in HIA, Nicolaevsky, 411-17.

110. HQ SHAEF, "Special Intelligence Summary," no. 37, 1948, pp. B5–B7, NA, RG 260, AGTS, box 646. See also Christopher Andrew and Oleg Gordievsky, *KGB: The Inside Story* (New York: Harper Collins, 1990), pp. 352–353. For a short history of the NKVD, see Amy Knight, *Beria: Stalin's First Lieutenant* (Princeton, N.J.: Princeton University Press, 1993), p. 106.

111. "Organizations and Activities of the Directorate of Internal Affairs, SMA," NA, RG 260, box 24, p. 21.

112. Sopade Informationsdienst #55, "Straflager und Zuchthäuser der Sowjetzone," p. 15.

113. The suffering in these camps was particularly extreme. Fearful of major scandals, SED Interior Ministry members urged the Mecklenburg government to improve conditions on Rügen. See the letter of K. Fischer, the first vice president of Saxony, February 11, 1946, in GARF, f. 7212, op. 1, d. 186, l. 236.

114. SAPMO-BA, ZPA, NL 182/ 852 (Ulbricht), b. 146.

115. "O politicheskikh nastroeniiakh studentov Gall'skogo universiteta," November 23, 1946, RTsKhIDNI, f. 17, op. 128, d. 151.

116. See Hans Lehmann, "Bericht über Verhaftung, Voruntersuchung und Strafvoll-
zug durch Organe der MGB/UdSSR" and "Der Vernehmungsstab der MGB in
Berlin-Hohenschönhausen zur Untersuchung der verhafteten Sozialdemokraten," both in FES, SPD Ostbüro, 10352, B1.

117. Mielke to "Leiter der Bezirksverwaltungen einschl. 'W' und Gross-Berlin," December 16, 1955, BStU MfSZ, AS 2/59, bb. 489–490.

118. Taped interview with Sergei Kondrashev, Moscow, 1993. Barraclough Carey Productions.

119. Mielke to "Leiter der Bezirksverwaltungen," BStU MfSZ, AS 2/59, b. 490.

120. Copy of report from Düsseldorf, February 7, 1948, BStU MfSZ, AS 282/67, b. 6.

121. On the arrests of more than 600 members of Werewolf groups, see Serov to
Beria, June 22, 1945, GARF, f. 9401, op. 2, d. 97, l. 28. A report from Serov to
Beria of October 3, 1946, refers to having eliminated 359 Werewolf groups with
3,336 members. Ibid., d. 100, l. 92. Extensive documentation on Werewolf arrests
is also contained in Serov to Kruglov, July 25, 1946, in ibid., d. 138, l. 340. Local
political officers in the zone worried that the Free German Youth organizations
would also be infiltrated and taken over by the Werewolves. GARF, f. 7077, op.
1, d. 206, ll. 10–11, 17.

122. Among the numerous examples of this kind of activity cited in the reports of
local Soviet political officers to their superiors in Berlin, see GARF, f. 7184, op.
1, d. 166, l. 112; f. 7212, op. 1, d. 186, l. 61; f. 7212, op. 1, d. 187, ll. 63–67.

123. Three were arrested carrying pistols, and one, a young baker, was accused of
trying to poison the bread intended for the Soviet military. BStU MfSZ, 229/66,
b. 512.

124. "Jahresbericht Dezernat K 5 im Lande Sachsen, 1947," BStU MfSZ, 229/66, b.
383.

125. SAPMO-BA, ZPA, IV 2/1/25 (Parteivorstand Protocol, July 28–29, 1948), b. 257.

126. SED Kreis Leipzig, Stadtteil VII, 1947?, HIA, Sander, box 2, folder 5.

127. The military commandant of the city and district of Nordhausen, Col. Krav-
chenko, complained about frequent attacks on Russian soldiers. HIA, Sander,
folder 5, box 1. SED officials, especially town mayors, were also attacked and
beaten up. For such incidences in Mecklenburg, see RTsKhIDNI, f. 17, op. 128,
d. 572, l. 34.

128. For cases of sabotage, see SAPMO-BA, ZPA, NL 182/1189 (Ulbricht), bb. 46–
47. For outbreaks of Nazi activity, see PRO, FO 371, 1947, File 114, Germany
64310. For German police reports, see "Jahresbericht Dezernat K 5 im Lande
Sachsen, 1948," BStU MfSZ, 229/66, bb. 592, 601, 614–616, 760.

129. The police were particularly upset that the graffiti was put up on the Day of the
New Teachers. BStU MfSZ, 229/66, b. 454.

130. Control commission of Germany, British Element, report on kidnapping of children, February 11, 1947, PRO, Germany, File 1009 (1947), 64472; Curt Riess to
Mr. Dulles, August 3, 1945, NA, RG 84, CGC, box 1.

131. RTsKhIDNI, f. 17, op. 128, d. 564, ll. 79–81. The letter, dated December 12,
1947, was taken very seriously by the Central Committee and was turned over

to a commission investigating the work of SVAG's Information Administration.

132. "About May 1 Demonstrations in the Federal Land of Saxony," Vatnik to Tiul'-panov, May 6, 1947, GARF, f. 7212, op. 1, d. 192.

133. HQ 7707 ECIC, October 19, 1948, NA, RG 260, box 24, p. 2.

134. On the widespread problem of rumors in the Soviet zone, see HQ British Troops Berlin, Intelligence Summary no. 26, January 7, 1946, in PRO, FO 1012/97, "Intelligence Summaries."

135. Russian Archives, Collection.

136. Report of May 8, 1948, BStU MfSZ, 229/66, b. 558. The police reported that the situation with food improved dramatically during the winter of 1948.

137. GARF, f. 7184, op. 1, d. 169, d. 100. The same report admitted that "anti-Soviet feelings are present among the German workers."

138. "Rearrest in the Soviet Zone of German Prisoners of War Released by the Western Powers," December 1947, PRO, Germany (1947), file 1009, 64472.

139. Mielke insisted that new prison space be found and that prisons double up inmates in isolation cells instead of releasing the medically incapacitated. ("The half-dead can run away to the West too," he warned.) He was also distinctly unsympathetic to calls for more food for the interned: "We all have to live on rations." "Protokoll der Tagung über den Befehl 201 am 22 Dezember 1947 mit den stellvertret: Innenministern und den Leitern der Landesuntersuchungsorgane [K-5]," SAPMO-BA, ZPA, IV 2/13/4, b. 16.

140. Ibid., bb. 3–6.

141. Major General Dubrovskii (Saxony) to Serov, April 19, 1946, "Donesenie: O nastroeniiakh nemetskogo naseleniia po FZ Saksoniia," GARF, f. 7212, op. 1, d. 188, l. 30. In one such case, the SED leader and policeman Robert Bialek turned over to the local operations group the names of a number of CDU activists who were tied to the Church. They were all promptly arrested.

142. In 1946 and 1947, the so-called KPO (Communist Party, Opposition) was considered the most serious challenge on the sectarian Left. The group was particularly strong among labor groups in Erfurt, Weimar, and Jena. Several hundred alleged KPO members were arrested by the MVD. As one 1948 report put it, "At the present, they [the KPO] represent less of a danger than the Schumacherites [SPD]." Lt. Col. Blestkin (Thüringen) to Tiul'panov, August 28, 1948, GARF, f. 7184, op. 1, d. 166, l. 70.

143. SAPMO-BA, ZPA, NL 90/125 (Grotewohl), bb. 33–34.

144. "Digest for Germany and Austria," no. 743, March 20, 1948, NA, RG 260, box 75. The Ostbüro was initially set up by Schumacher to take care of refugees from the East. Wolfgang Buschfort, *Das Ostbüro der SPD: Von der Gründung bis zur Berlin-Krise* (Munich: R. Oldenbourg Verlag, 1991), pp. 18–21.

145. Vatnik to Tiul'panov, January 16, 1946, GARF, f. 7212, op. 1, d. 186, l. 50.

146. In February 1946, it was already reported that 83 social democratic leaders were interned in Sachsenhausen. Fricke has recently estimated that around 5,000 SPD functionaries were arrested and imprisoned, of whom some 400 died. Karl Wilhelm Fricke, " 'Kampf dem Klassenfeind': Politische Verfolgung in der SBZ," in

Alexander Fischer, ed., *Studien zur Geschichte der SBZ/DDR* (Berlin: Duncker & Humblot, 1993), pp. 186–187.

147. "O provokatsionnom vystuplenii sekretaria Leiptsigskogo okruzhnogo komiteta sotsial-demokraticheskoi partii Bretkhorsta protiv Okkupatsionnykh vlastei Krasnoi Armii," GARF, f. 7212, op. 1, d. 186, l. 102.

148. "Denkschrift über politische Verfolgungen in der Ostzone," NA, RG 260, box 94.

149. "Supplement to 'German Weekly Background Notes, No. 109,'" September 25, 1947, NA, RG 260, box 75, p. 5.

150. BStU MfSZ, 229/66, b. 479.

151. "O bor'be SEPG protiv shumakherovskikh elementov i sektantskikh nastroenii v partii," August 31, 1948, GARF, f. 7184, op. 1, d. 166, l. 67.

152. Report of May 8, 1948, BStU MfSZ, 229/66, b. 556.

153. "Jahresbericht Dezernat K 5 im Lande Sachsen, 1947," BStU MfSZ, 229/66, b. 385. For some of the illegal leaflets, see FES, SPD Ostbüro, 10330-I.

154. For a good introduction, see Buschfort, *Das Ostbüro der SPD*.

155. The translation: "Germany, Germany without everything, without butter, without fat, and the little bit of jam is eaten up by the administration. Fold your hands, bow your head, and think always about unity [of the SPD and KPD]. The prices are high, the stores shut closed, misery is on the march at a silent, firm pace. Only the small-time comrades are hungry, the big-time ones are hungry with [them] in spirit. Come, Wilhelm Pieck, be our guest, and give us what you promised. Not just turnips, leaves, and cabbage, but what you and Herr Grotewohl eat. It was fine in the Kaiser's time, then we had our pig. When we had the old Hindenburg, now and again we had roasts. With Hitler and Göring at least we had an occasional herring, but with the present leadership, everything is just in the newspaper." SAPMO-BA, ZPA, NL 90/641 (Grotewohl), b. 12. Other illegal leaflets from The Opposition Group of the SPD for the Occupied Zones and the SPD East Zone illegal section, Province of Saxony are also contained in this folder. See also BStU MfSZ, 229/66, b. 460.

156. "Protokoll der Innenminister-Konferenz," January 31–February 1, 1948, Altenstein, Thüringen, BStU MfSZ, 230/66, b. 24.

157. RP-196-48, September 7, 1948, NA, RG 260, box 110, pp. 1–2.

158. SAPMO-BA, ZPA, IV 2/1/12 (Parteivorstand Protocol, August 20–21, 1947), b. 193.

159. SAPMO-BA, ZPA, IV 2/1/1 (Parteivorstand Protocol, May 14–15, 1946), b. 70. At the same meeting, Friedrich Ebert, another former SPD leader, complained that a group of boys was arrested simply for wearing white carnations at a demonstration. Ibid., b. 72.

160. Hoffmann to Pieck and Grotewohl, May 20, 1947, SAPMO-BA, ZPA, NL 90/314, bb. 55–56.

161. SAPMO-BA, ZPA, NL 36/695 (Wilhelm Pieck), b. 3.

162. SAPMO-BA, ZPA, IV 2/1/22 (Parteivorstand Protocol, April 14–15, 1948), b. 15.

163. "O nekotorykh faktakh raboty operativnykh grupp [NKVD] Okruga Kottbus," GARF, f. 7077, op. 1, d. 196, l. 122.

164. Rodionov to Paradov, September 9, 1946, GARF, f. 7177, op. 1, d. 185, l. 133.

165. Tiul'panov to Suslov, August 31, 1946, "Ob usilenii antisovetskoi propagandy pered obshchinymi vyborami," RTsKhIDNI, f. 17, op. 128, d. 146, ll. 271–279.

166. RTsKhIDNI, f. 17, op. 128, d. 94, ll. 15–18. The deputy minister of internal affairs, General Serov, denied that there were any shortcomings in the MVD's handling of returning German prisoners. Ibid., l. 22.

167. The following account is taken from an exhaustive report: Kolesnichenko to Ponomarev, deputy director of the Propaganda and Agitation Administration of the CC, November 29, 1948, RTsKhIDNI, f. 17, op. 128, d. 572, ll. 45–104. In his report, Kolesnichenko quotes extensively from a letter he had written to the "leadership of SVAG" (presumably SVAG's Military Council) in the previous year, in all likelihood at the end of November or early December 1947. Ibid., ll. 91–95.

168. One catches only glimpses of Kolesnichenko's personality in his memoirs: I. S. Kolesnichenko, *Bitva posle voiny* (Moscow: Voennoe izdatel'stvo, 1987). There is no mention of his concerns about NKVD/MVD activity in the zone.

169. Although Kolesnichenko was eventually removed from the zone for political reasons, there was never any indication that his critique of the NKVD got him in trouble. On the other hand, Dmitrii Volkogonov cites archival evidence that General Serov successfully unseated Lieutenant General K. F. Telegin, a member of SVAG's Military Council, for collecting negative material on NKVD activity in the zone. Telegin was eventually arrested and interned for his alleged "animosity to the NKVD." Dmitrii Volkogonov, *Triumf i tragediia: I. V. Stalin, Politicheskii portret*, book 2, part 2 (Moscow: Izd. Agenstva pechati Novosti, 1989), pp. 214–215.

170. "Order No. 43, March 18, 1948, Concerning the Amnesty on [the] Occasion of the 100th Anniversary of the 1848 Revolution, for the Soviet zone of Germany," in "Germany: Fortnightly Background Notes," no. 134, April 15, 1948, NA, RG 260, box 74. p. 62c.

171. SAPMO-BA, ZPA, IV 2/1/22 (Parteivorstand Protocol, April 14, 1948), bb. 15–16.

172. *Tägliche Rundschau*, April 9, 1948.

173. Ibid., February 13, 1950; Jan Foitzik, "Sowjetische Militäradministration in Deutschland (SMAD)," in Broszat and Weber, eds., *SBZ Handbuch*, p. 30.

174. Kilian, *Einzuweisen zur völligen Isolierung*, pp. 175–176.

175. The SPD reports that 20,000 prisoners were deported to the Soviet Union from Buchenwald alone. "Germany: Fortnightly Background Notes," report no. 134, April 15, 1948, NA, RG 260, box 175.

176. A. N. Dugin, "Neizvestnyi Gulag: Dokumenty i fakty," unpublished manuscript, p. 51.

177. SAPMO-BA, ZPA, NL 36/694 (Wilhelm Pieck), bb. 111, 120–121.

178. SAPMO-BA, ZPA, IV 2/1/36 (Parteivorstand Protocol, October 4, 1949), b. 35.

179. Sopade Informationsdienst #55, "Die Straflager und Zuchthäuser der Sowjet-zone," p. 21; Fricke, Politik und Justiz in der DDR, p. 74.

180. Sopade Informationsdienst #55, "Die Straflager und Zuchthäuser der Sowjet-zone," pp. 23–24.

181. Benjamin, Mielke, and Maron to Politburo, SED, August 13, 1952, BStU MfSZ, AS 14/59, b. 32.

182. "Sachstandsberichte," BStU MfSZ, AS 13/59, bb. 10–13, 204–205.

183. "Überprüfung der in Waldheim verurteilten Kriegs- und Naziverbrecher anhand der Akten zwecks Entlassung aus der Haft oder Verminderung der Strafe für einzelne Kategorien der Verurteilten," BStU MfSZ, AS 14/59, b. 30.

8. THE POLITICS OF CULTURE AND EDUCATION

1. "Vortrag von J. R. Becher," spring 1945, SAPMO-BA, ZPA, IV 2/11/199, p. 19.

2. Kolesnichenko to Ponomarev, November 29, 1948, RTsKhIDNI, f. 17, op. 128, d. 572, l. 85.

3. "Some Political Implications of Present Cultural Developments in E. Germany," May 3, 1946, PRO, FO 371, 1946, Germany, file no. 5688, 55876.

4. K. Gofman to Dimitrov, "Dokladnaia zapiska," August 15, 1945, RTsKhIDNI, f. 17, op. 128, d. 791, l. 4.

5. Ibid., l. 6.

6. Biuro Informatsii SVAG, Biulleten', no. 79/83, November 5, 1946, RTsKhIDNI, f. 17, op. 128, d. 151, l. 9.

7. Martem'ianov to Tiul'panov, January 20, 1949; Dymshits to Martem'ianov, January 26, 1949; Martem'ianov to Tiul'panov, March 22, 1949, GARF, f. 7077, op. 1, d. 247, ll. 23–26, 39, 41–53.

8. Sobolev, Poliakov, et al. to Zhdanov, "O rezul'tatakh proverki raboty Upravleniia informatsii Sovetskoi voennoi administratsii v Germanii," 1948, RTsKhIDNI, f. 17, op. 128, d. 1166, l. 24.

9. Some of these problems are analyzed from a somewhat different perspective in a massive study by David Pike, The Politics of Culture in Soviet-Occupied Germany, 1945–1949 (Stanford, Calif.: Stanford University Press, 1993), which is based on East German sources.

10. Ulbricht to Dimitrov, February 13, 1945, RTsKhIDNI, f. 17, op. 128, d. 787, l. 9.

11. Pike, The Politics of Culture, pp. 331–332.

12. SAPMO-BA, ZPA, IV 2/906/140, b. 10. (Emphasis in the original.)

13. Pike, The Politics of Culture, pp. 82–83, 85–86.

14. Kulturbund Conference, Berlin, May 20, 1947, in "Supplement to 'Germany: Weekly Background Notes' no. 115, Cultural Policy in the Soviet Zone of Germany," November 6, 1947, NA, RG 260, box 24, p. 5.

15. SAPMO-BA, ZPA, IV 2/1/18 (Parteivorstand Protocol, December 8, 1947), bb. 36–37.

16. Gofman to Dimitrov, "Dokladnaia zapiska," August 15, 1945, RTsKhIDNI, f. 17, op. 128, d. 791, l. 208.

17. SAPMO-BA, ZPA, EA 1084/1 (Abusch), b. 83.

18. "Stenogramma soveshchaniia v upravlenii propagandy SVAG," September 17–18, 1946, RTsKhIDNI, f. 17, op. 128, d. 149, l. 182.

19. GARF, f. 7077, op. 1, d. 189, l. 2.

20. "Doklad o kul'turnoi rabote v Brandenburgskom okruge v ianv. 1947 g.," GARF, f. 7077, op. 1, d. 216, l. 11–12.

21. Vatnik to Tiul'panov, "O rabote Kul'turbunda fed. zem. Saksoniia," January 14, 1946, GARF, f. 7212, op. 1, d. 186, l. 29.

22. "Stenogramma soveshchaniia," RTsKhIDNI, f. 17, op. 128, d. 149, ll. 180–181.

23. "Stenogramma besedy s tov. Maternom," September 25, 1946, RTsKhIDNI, f. 17, op. 128, d. 151, l. 132.

24. See the documents about the banning, including Allied Coordinating Committee, "Letter from the Kulturbund to the Allied Kommandantura," February 2, 1948, in HIA, GTUAO, box 3.

25. "Beschluss des Sekretariats," January 18, 1946, SAPMO-BA, ZPA, IV 2/1/19 (Parteivorstand Protocol, December 27, 1945), b. 38.

26. "Stenogramma soveshchaniia," September 17–18, 1946, RTsKhIDNI, f. 17, op. 128, d. 149, l. 179.

27. SAPMO-BA, ZPA, 2/906/140, b. 5.

28. SAPMO-BA, ZPA, EA 1084/1 (Abusch), b. 81.

29. SAPMO-BA, ZPA, IV 2/1/18 (Parteivorstand Protocol, December 8, 1947), bb. 30, 36–37.

30. Ibid. Gniffke to Pieck, Grotewohl, Ackermann, and Meier, July 9, 1948, SAPMO-BA, ZPA, NL 36/762 (Pieck), b. 153.

31. "Dokladnaia zapiska ob ocherednom plenume Tsentral'nogo Pravleniia SEPG," December 8, 1947, RTsKhIDNI, f. 17, op. 128, d. 331, l. 92.

32. For the details of the delegation's stay in Moscow and for self-satisfied Soviet renditions of the Germans' laudatory speeches back in the Eastern zone, see RTsKhIDNI, f. 17, op. 128, d. 574.

33. "Vorlage an das kleine Sekretariat," April 19, 1949, SAPMO-BA, ZPA, IV 2/906/140, b. 42.

34. SAPMO-BA, ZPA, IV 2/2.025/2 (Sekretariat O. Meier), b. 256.

35. Heymann to Abusch, June 30, 1949, SAPMO-BA, ZPA, IV 2/906/140, b. 55.

36. Becher to Ulbricht, December 24, 1949, b. 20, SAPMO-BA, ZPA, NL 182/1385 (Ulbricht), b. 20.

37. "Germany: Weekly Background Notes," no. 97, June 26, 1947, NA, RG 260, box 24. The house was a beautiful eighteenth-century palace. "Die Geschichte dieses Hauses," February 28, 1947, SAPMO-BA, DSF, ZM 195, p. 2.

38. The German official was an SPD loyalist who reported to Hannover. HIA, Sander, box 2, folder M (Abschrift), May 29, 1947.

39. SAPMO-BA, ZPA, EA 1367/1 (Hoffmann), bb. 435–437.

40. Martem'ianov [Brandenburg] to Tiul'panov, March 22, 1949, GARF, f. 7077, op. 1, d. 247, l. 46.

41. "Sitzungsprotokoll der Gesellschaft zum Studium der Kultur der Sowjetunion am 30. June 1947 im Haus der Kultur der Sowjetunion," SAPMO-BA, DSF, A1, pp. 1–4 (quote from Kuczynski's speech on p. 2).

42. "Protokoll: Entwurf des Briefes an die Landesgesellschaften," July 25, 1947, in ibid., p. 1.

43. SAPMO-BA, ZPA, NL 182/1135 (Ulbricht), b. 1.

44. Guest book, SAPMO-BA, DSF, ZH 108.

45. Martem'ianov to Tiul'panov, March 22, 1949, GARF, f. 7077, op. 1, d. 247, ll. 41–42.

46. "Vystuplenie polkovnika Tiul'panova S. I. na torzhestvennom sobranii po sluchaiu godovshchiny Obshchestva po izucheniiu kul'tury Sovetskogo Soiuza, Berlin 22 Maia 1948 g.," Upravlenie Informatsii SVAG, *Sbornik statei i materialov*, no. 18 (July 1948): 64.

47. GARF, f. 5283, op. 16, d. 133, l. 153.

48. Kislova to Tiul'panov, January 12, 1946, GARF, f. 5283, op. 16, d. 133, l. 145.

49. GARF, f. 5283, op. 16, d. 137, l. 33. The conference itself was an important signpost in the escalation of the cold war in the area of culture. " 'Lasky und andere,' " *Der Tagesspiegel*, October 11, 1947. See also Pike, *The Politics of Culture*, pp. 375–384.

50. GARF, f. 5283, op. 16, d. 137, ll. 47–123.

51. Poltavtsev to VOKS, March 11, 1948, and May 8, 1948, GARF, f. 5283, op. 16, d. 138, ll. 68, 87.

52. GARF, f. 5283, op. 16, d. 141, l. 68.

53. Kuczynski's note to Kislova, dated July 6, 1948, was written in English, and is cited here in only slightly corrected form. GARF, f. 5283, op. 16, d. 139, l. 106.

54. GARF, f. 5283, op. 16, d. 139, ll. 4–5.

55. Telegram, Tiul'panov to Kemenov (VOKS), April 21, 1948, GARF, f. 5283, op. 16, d. 137, l. ll.

56. GARF, f. 5283, op. 16, d. 140, l. 15.

57. Altogether, 7,524 POWs graduated from these antifascist schools between the end of the war and December 1949, and the graduates played a pivotal role in the development of the GDSF. They also worked in the party, the mass organizations, the economy, the administration, and, especially, the police. "Antifa-Schüler Transport aus Krassnogorsk, der im Juli dieses Jahres erwartet wird," pp. 1–3, SAPMO-BA, ZPA, IV 2/11/202 (Kaderfragen).

58. "Statut der Gesellschaft für Deutsch-Sowjetische Freundschaft," SAPMO-BA, DSF, A1 (Statuten).

59. Ulbricht to Tiul'panov, July 26, 1949, and Heymann to Ulbricht, August 5, 1949, SAPMO-BA, ZPA, NL 182/1135 (Ulbricht), bb. 3–4.

60. Maj. Starodubov (Thüringen) to Tiul'panov, September 19, 1949, GARF, f. 7184, op. 1, d. 169, ll. 15–18; Report of Sharov and Mel'nikov (Brandenburg), July 27, 1949, GARF, f. 7077, op. 1, d. 247, l. 119.

61. Liudomirskii to Dymshits, February 25, 1949, and March 2, 1949, GARF, f. 5283, op. 16, d. 142, ll. 118, 128.

62. GARF, f. 5283, op. 16, d. 142, l. 57. See the cover letter to the Belyi "review" from the secretary of the Union of Soviet Composers, M. Chulaki, September 5, 1949, in ibid., l. 56.

63. Denisov to Tiul'panov, September 26, 1949, GARF, f. 5283, op. 16, d. 142, l. 50.

64. See SAPMO-BA, DSF, ZM 65, ZH 64. These contain protocols of lectures and the question and answer sessions at the House of Soviet Culture from December 2, 1948, to September 9, 1949. For crowds at lectures, see also GARF, f. 7077, op. 1, d. 231, ll. 31–32.

65. As Gertrud Bobek put it, "We didn't understand the difference then between just and unjust wars." SAPMO-BA, ZPA, EA 1622/1 (Bobek), b. 141.

66. Ackermann to Tiul'panov, January 26, 1946, SAPMO-BA, ZPA, NL 182/1187 (Ulbricht), b. 25.

67. "Perepiska po kul'ture i zrelishcham," 1948, GARF, f. 7077, op. 1, d. 231, ll. 37–38.

68. GARF, f. 7212, op. 1, d. 186, l. 82.

69. Report from Weimar, January 5, 1946, GARF, f. 7184, op. 1, d. 159, l. 4.

70. GARF, f. 7077, op. 1, d. 216, l. 11.

71. "Stenogramma soveshchaniia," part 2, September 1946, RTsKhIDNI, f. 17, op. 128, d. 150, ll. 129–130.

72. Report from the Gotha region, January 29, 1946, GARF, f. 7184, op. 1, d. 159, l. 8.

73. Report from Cottbus, December 23, 1945, GARF, f. 7077, op. 2, d. 172, l. 15.

74. "Perepiska po kul'ture i zrelishcham," 1948, GARF, f. 7077, op. 1, d. 231, ll. 37–40.

75. Report from Potsdam, February 26, 1946, GARF, f. 7077, op. 1, d. 231.

76. Report from Cottbus, December 23, 1945, GARF, f. 7077, op. 1, d. 172, l. 14.

77. Dymshits to Maj. Vinokurov (Brandenburg), December 13, 1945, GARF, f. 7077, op. 1, d. 172, ll. 12–13.

78. On film and culture in Saxony (February 1946), see GARF, f. 7212, op. 1, d. 176, ll. 166–167.

79. "Rabota sektora propagandy i tsenzury," October 31, 1945, RTsKhIDNI, f. 17, op. 128, d. 791, l. 161.

80. Poluektov (Brandenburg) to Dymshits, March 20, 1947, GARF, f. 7077, op. 1, d. 216, l. 18.

81. "Cultural Policy in the Soviet Zone of Germany," November 6, 1947, NA, RG 260, box 24, p. 4.

82. "O politicheskoi obstanovke v Berline," September 1946, RTsKhIDNI, f. 17, op. 128, d. 151, l. 70; GARF, f. 7077, op. 1, d. 231, l. 31.

83. Biuro Informatsii SVAG, *Biulleten'*, no. 42, September 25, 1948, RTsKhIDNI, f. 17, op. 128, d. 581, ll. 38–39.

84. But even the first postwar DEFA film, *Die Mörder sind unter uns* (1946), was too harshly realistic for the German public. SAPMO-BA, ZPA, IV 2/906/202, b. 217.

85. On the SED and DEFA (Deutsche Film Aktien Gesellschaft), see SAPMO-BA, ZPA, IV 2/906/202, and "Cultural Policy in the Soviet Zone of Germany," November 6, 1947, NA, RG 260, box 24.

86. SAPMO-BA, ZPA, NL 182/1187 (Ulbricht), b. 28.

87. Interview with Il'ia Fradkin, June 1989, Moscow.

88. "Theaters in the State of Saxony," GARF, f. 7212, op. 1, d. 186, l. 155.

89. See Wolfgang Emmerich, *Kleinere Literaturgeschichte der DDR 1945–1988,* expanded ed. (Frankfurt am Main: Luchterhand Literaturverband, 1989), pp. 71–72.

90. "Theaters in the State of Saxony," GARF, f. 7212, op. 1, d. 186, l. 154–155.

91. "Perepiska po kul'ture i zrelishcham," 1948, GARF, f. 7077, op. 1, d. 231, l. 89.

92. Vatnik to Tiul'panov, February 26, 1946, GARF, f. 7212, op. 1, d. 186, l. 155.

93. Dymshits to Mil'khiker, July 19, 1947, GARF, f. 7077, op. 1, d. 216, l. 72.

94. "Rabota sektora propagandy i tsenzury," October 31, 1945, RTsKhIDNI, f. 17, op. 128, d. 791, l. 161.

95. GARF, f. 7184, op. 1, d. 159, l. 24.

96. "Theaters in the State of Saxony," GARF, f. 7212, op. 1, d. 186, 11.

97. Most of the following treatment of the play comes from reviews and articles in the German press: *Tribune, Tägliche Rundschau, Der Tagesspiegel, Neue Zeit, Neues Deutschland,* and *Der Sozialdemokrat,* from May 6 to 8, 1947. Collected in NA, RG 260, ISD, box 120.

98. Dymshits to Kemerov (VOKS), Reviews of Simonov's "Russkii Vopros," GARF, f. 5283, op. 16, d. 137, ll. 3–8.

99. Kolesnichenko to Kemerov (VOKS), June 22, 1948, GARF, f. 5283, op. 16, d. 136, l. 54.

100. "Theaters in the State of Saxony," GARF, f. 7212, op. 1, d. 186, ll. 156–157.

101. Abramov to Baranov, "O soveshchanii khudozhestvennykh rukovoditelei nemetskikh teatrov," July 30, 1948, RTsKhIDNI, op. 128, d. 567, ll. 29–30.

102. GARF, f. 7077, op. 1, d. 231, l. 90.

103. "Perepiska po kul'ture i zrelishcham," 1948, GARF, f. 7077, op. 1, d. 231, ll. 27–29.

104. "Germany: Weekly Background Notes No. 115, Cultural Policy in the Soviet Zone of Germany," November 6, 1947, NA, RG 260, box 24.

105. Dymshits to Liudomirskii (VOKS), November 22, 1948, GARF, f. 5283, op. 16, d. 136, l. 32.

106. GARF, f. 7212, op. 1, d. 186, l. 158.

107. Mnozhin to Dymshits, "Ob itogakh muzykal'nogo sezona 1947–1948 goda v Zemle Brandenburg," October 23, 1948, GARF, f. 7077, op. 1, d. 231, ll. 93–94.

108. SAPMO-BA, ZPA, EA 0390 (Stefan Heymann), b. 45.

109. "Germany: Weekly Background Notes No. 115, Cultural Policy in the Soviet Zone of Germany," November 6, 1947, NA, RG 260, box 24, pp. 5–6.

110. GARF, f. 7077, op. 1, d. 231, l. 94.

111. GARF, f. 7212, op. 1, d. 186, l. 162.

112. "O kul'turnoi zhizni FZ Saksoniia," February 26, 1946, GARF, f. 7212, op. 1, d. 186, l. 160.

113. SAPMO-BA, ZPA, IV 2/1/23 (Parteivorstand Protocol, May 12–13, 1948), b. 41. SED and Soviet policy changed within a few months, culminating in Dymshits's November 1948 articles in *Tägliche Rundschau* condemning formalism and decadence. See Pike, *The Politics of Culture,* pp. 531–536.

114. GARF, f. 7212, op. 1, d. 186, l. 161.

115. Kolesnichenko to Ponomarev, November 29, 1948, RTsKhIDNI, f. 17, op. 128, d. 572, ll. 85–86.

116. Liudomirskii to Dymshits, October 6, 1948, GARF, f. 5283, op. 16, d. 136, l. 40.

117. GARF, f. 7077, op. 1, d. 247, l. 6.

118. SAPMO-BA, ZPA, NL 215/18 (Oelssner), bb. 153–159 (in Russian).

119. "Eine Antwort auf die Briefe eines Kerkergenossen in Bautzen Januar 1944," manuscript, SAPMO-BA, ZPA, NL 215/102 (Oelssner).

120. Vatnik to Tiul'panov, November 10, 1947, GARF, f. 7212, op. 1, d. 193, l. 111.

121. Reports of Sr. Lt. Geborkian, Beeskov, March 9, 1948; Maj. Bessonov, Kalau region, March 11, 1948; Maj. Stroilov, Potsdam, March 11, 1948; and Maj. Ivchenko, Eberswalde, March 10, 1948, in GARF, f. 7077, op. 1, d. 241, ll. 59–73.

122. Kabanov to Suslov, January 14, 1949, RTsKhIDNI, f. 17, op. 128, d. 683, l. 92.

123. Dymshits to Kemenov, November 1947, GARF, f. 5273, op. 16, d. 134, l. 69.

124. SAPMO-BA, ZPA, NL 215/106 (Oelssner), bb. 157–162.

125. SAPMO-BA, ZPA, EA 1084/1 (Abusch), b. 48.

126. "Stenogramma soobshchenii," June 7, 1945, RTsKhIDNI, f. 17, op. 128, d. 750, l. 188.

127. "Ansprache im Goethe Jahr," *Neue Zeitung* (Munich), July 26, 1949, in Hans Bürgin and Hans-Otto Mayer, *Thomas Mann, a Chronicle of His Life,* (Birmingham: University of Alabama Press, 1965), p. 227.

128. Tiul'panov to Smirnov, August 23, 1949, RTsKhIDNI, f. 17, op. 137, d. 93, l. 26.

129. Thomas Mann, "Germany Today," *New York Times Magazine,* September 25, 1949, pp. 14–28.

130. See Thomas Mann, "To Paul Olberg," August 27, 1949, in *Letters of Thomas Mann, Briefe, 1889–1955,* ed. and trans. Richard and Clara Winston (New York: A. A. Knopf, 1971), pp. 581–584. See also "Reisebericht," in *Thomas Mann, Reden und Aufsätze,* vol. 1 (Frankfurt am Main: S. Fischer Verlag, 1965), pp. 693–704.

131. Although the East German universities resisted Soviet inroads, they were not able to maintain as much autonomy in the postwar period as the Czech and, especially, the Polish universities. See John Francis Connelly, "Creating the Socialist Elite: Communist Higher Education Policies in the Czech Lands, East Germany, and Poland: 1945–1954," Ph.D. dissertation, Harvard University, August 1994.

132. "Stenogramma soobshchenii," June 7, 1945, RTsKhIDNI, f. 17, op. 128, d. 750, ll. 42–44.

133. The mysterious case of Lohmeyer is elucidated in John Connelly, "Creating the Socialist Elite," pp. 72–74.

134. "Sbornik materialov po istorii otdela narodnogo obrazovaniia," vol. 1, GARF, f. 7317, op. 54, d. 1, l. 120.

135. Ibid., l. 121.

136. Ibid., l. 133.

137. Vatnik to Dubrovskii, October 16, 1947, GARF, f. 7212, op. 1, d. 193, l. 60.

138. SAPMO-BA, ZPA, IV 2/1/20 (Parteivorstand Protocol, February 11–12, 1948), b. 91.

139. SAPMO-BA, ZPA, IV 2/904/460, bb. 55–56.

140. "Sbornik materialov," vol. 1, GARF, f. 7317, op. 54, d. 1, ll. 210–214.

141. Ibid., l. 145.

142. Ibid., l. 134.

143. Ibid., ll. 123, 131–132.

144. SAPMO-BA, ZPA, IV 2/1/20 (Parteivorstand Protocol, February 11–12, 1948), b. 246.

145. RTsKhIDNI, f. 17, op. 128, d. 253, l. 121; GARF, f. 7133, op. 1, d. 253, l. 107.

146. Anton Ackermann, "Entwurf einer Resolution über Hochschulfragen," February 2, 1948, SAPMO-BA, ZPA, IV 2/2.025/2 (Sekretariat Otto Meier), b. 178.

147. SAPMO-BA, ZPA, IV 2/2022/121 (Sekretariat Merker), b. 21.

148. "Sbornik materialov," vol. 1, GARF, f. 7317, op. 54, d. 1, l. 193.

149. Ibid., l. 197.

150. Order no. 205, July 12, 1946: "Ob uchrezhdenii pedagogicheskikh fakul'tetov," GARF, f.7317, op. 8, d. 6, l. 149.

151. "Sbornik materialov," vol. 1, GARF, f. 7317, op. 54, d. 1, l. 146. See also Hans-Uwe Feige, "Die Gesellschaftswissenschaftlichte Fakultät an der Universität Leipzig (1947–1951)," *Deutschland Archiv*, no. 5 (May 1993): 572.

152. "Sbornik materialov," vol. 1, GARF, f. 7317, op. 54, d. 1, l. 156.

153. SAPMO-BA, ZPA, IV 2/2.025/2 (Sekretariat Otto Meier), b. 156.

154. "Programm der Grundlagen des Marxismus-Leninismus für die fakultativen Vorlesungen an den Universitäten und Hochschulen der sowjetischen Besatzungszone Deutschlands," January 14, 1949, pp. 1–11; and "Der Zweijahreplan 1949–1950 in der sowjetischen Besatzungszone Deutschlands," p. 1, in SAPMO-BA, ZPA, IV 2/9.07/7 (Volksbildung).

155. "Von Darwin bis Lysenko," August 6, 1949, in ibid., pp. 1–2.

156. Partbiuro to A. A. Kuznetsov, October 22, 1947, RTsKhIDNI, f. 17, op. 117, d. 958, ll. 120–123.

157. Commission (Balezin, Kaftanov, Kalashnikov, Zolotukhin, Korotkevich) to A. A. Kuznetsov, November 24, 1947, in ibid, ll. 124–126.

158. "Postanovlenie TsK VKP[B]," in ibid., ll. 127–129.

159. Kuznetsov to Zhdanov, April 19, 1948, in ibid., l. 131.

160. Biuro Informatsii SVAG, *Biulleten'*, no. 42, September 25, 1948, RTsKhIDNI, f. 17, op. 128, d. 586, l. 82. See also Sobolev, Poliakov, et al. to Zhdanov, "O rezul'tatakh proverki raboty Upravleniia informatsii SVAG," fall 1948, RTsKh-

IDNI, f. 17, op. 128, d. 572, l. 26. Here, Tiul'panov stated: "The universities do not even have a single Soviet higher education program for their orientation. Up to this point, not a single Soviet textbook has been translated into German."

161. Baranov to Suslov, April 1, 1948, RTsKhIDNI, f. 17, op. 128, d. 567, l. 84.

162. Kuznetsov and Zhdanov to Suslov, November 22, 1948, RTsKhIDNI, f. 17, op. 128, d. 567, ll. 82–83.

163. Kabanov to Shepilov, November 17, 1948, RTsKhIDNI, f. 17, op. 128, d. 566, ll. 41–42.

164. Dymshits to VOKS, February 14, 1948, GARF, f. 5283, op. 16, d. 137, l. 74.

165. Wolf went into pedagogy. Kolesnichenko to Ponomarev, November 29, 1948, RTsKhIDNI, f. 17, op. 128, d. 572, ll. 87–88.

166. "Sbornik materialov," vol. 1, GARF, f. 7317, op. 54, d. 1, l. 208.

167. "Sbornik materialov," vol. 3, GARF, f. 7317, op. 54, d. 3, l. 163.

168. "Sbornik materialov," vol. 1, GARF, f. 7317, op. 54, d. 1, l. 134.

169. Ibid., l. 120.

170. Ibid., l. 138.

171. Ibid., l. 107.

172. Ibid., l. 202; "Osnovnye zadachi: o rabote Otdela Narodnogo Obrazovania SVAG na 1949 g.," GARF, f. 7133, op. 1, d. 254, l. 17.

173. The case of the Soviet Physical-chemistry Institute is described in an extraordinary sixty-two page November 6, 1948 report from Professor S. S. Vasil'ev to A. A. Kuznetsov in the Central Committee. RTsKhIDNI, f. 17, op. 125, d. 618.

174. "Sbornik materialov," vol. 1, GARF, f. 7317, op. 54, d. 1, l. 210.

175. "Sbornik materialov," vol. 3, GARF, f. 7317, op. 54, d. 3, l. 163.

176. Soviet officials were very critical of Wandel's competence as a leader of the education system. "Sbornik materialov," vol. 1, GARF, f. 7317, op. 54, d. 1, ll. 41, 73–76.

177. A. Ackermann, "Vom schöpferischen Anfang," manuscript, SAPMO-BA, ZPA, NL 109/58 (Ackermann), p. 7.

178. "Protokoll über die Tagung der kommun. Lehrer Sachsens," August 18–20, 1945, SAPMO-BA, ZPA, IV 2/905/48, b. 6.

179. M. M. Volov, "Bor'ba demokraticheskikh sil Vostochnoi Germanii za shkol'nuiu reformu (1945–1946 gg)," *Novaia i noveishaia istoriia,* no. 5 (1979): 29–31.

180. Lt. Col. Merzliakov, "O massovoi proverke po rabote shkol Brandenburgskogo Okruga," GARF, f. 7077, op. 1, d. 196, l. 41.

181. Report of Lt. Kulichenko, August 31, 1947, RTsKhIDNI, f. 17, op. 128, d. 253, l. 83.

182. SAPMO-BA, ZPA, NL 182/927 (Ulbricht), b. 170.

183. Lothar Mertens, "Die Neulehrer: Die 'grundlegende Demokratisierung der deutschen Schule' in der SBZ und die Veränderungen in der Lehrerschaft," *Deutsche Studien,* vol. 26 (1988): 196.

184. Ibid., p. 199.

185. Vatnik to Tiul'panov, Bokov, and Serov, January 5, 1946, GARF, f. 7212, op. 1, d. 186, l. 6.

186. "Stenogramma besedy s tov. Maternom 25 sentiabria 1946 g.," RTsKhIDNI, f. 17, op. 128, d. 151, l. 132.

187. SED report of December 1946, SAPMO-BA, ZPA, NL 182/927 (Ulbricht), b. 63.

188. Order no. 219, July 19, 1946, and Order no. 220, July 19, 1946, in GARF, f. 7317, op. 8, d. 6, ll. 218–224.

189. I. Artiukhin, "Instruktsiia," September 20, 1947, GARF, f. 7133, op. 1, d. 253, ll. 102–104. SAPMO-BA, ZPA, IV 2/905/77, b. 102.

190. GARF, f. 7133, op. 1, d. 254, l. 23.

191. "Vorlage an das Sekretariat des Pol. Büros," February 5, 1949, SAPMO-BA, ZPA, IV 2/905/73, b. 8.

192. Walther Dreher, "Parteiaustritt eines Lehrers," n.d.; "Bemerkungen für Gen. Wandel," May 12, 1948; and "Bericht über die schulpolitische Tagung in Rathenow," May 9, 1948, in SAPMO-BA, ZPA, IV 2/905/77, bb. 45, 65, 103.

193. "Entwurf: Beschluss des Politbüros zur Verbesserung des Schulwesens," August 13, 1949, SAPMO-BA, ZPA, IV 2/905/73, b. 36.

194. "Grundzüge der Schulpolitik der Partei in der gegenwärtigen politischen Situation in Deutschland," August 23, 1949, SAPMO-BA, ZPA, IV 2/905/73, b. 281.

195. SAPMO-BA, ZPA, NL 182/927 (Ulbricht), b. 125.

196. SAPMO-BA, ZPA, IV 2/905/77, b. 58.

197. Ibid., b. 72.

198. For the special problems of the German-Russian schools, see SAPMO-BA, ZPA, IV 2/905/108.

199. "Gegenwartskunde—Letzte Fassung," Halle, April 15, 1948, SAPMO-BA, ZPA, IV 2/905/79, b. 4. Emphasis in the original.

200. "Richtlinien für die Didaktik und Methodik der deutschen demokratischen Schule," May 18, 1949, SAPMO-BA, ZPA, IV 2/905/79, b. 17.

201. SAPMO-BA, ZPA, IV 2/905/79 (Volksbildung), b. 5.

202. "Richtlinien," May 18, 1949, SAPMO-BA, ZPA, IV 2/905/79 (Volksbildung), b. 26.

203. Ibid.

204. The courting of Hauptmann was not without its opponents among German leftist intellectuals, who felt that Hauptmann's "naturalism" conformed excessively to Nazi patterns of culture. See Pike, *The Politics of Culture,* pp. 186–189.

205. Pieck to Suslov, June 28, 1948, RTsKhIDNI, f. 17, op. 128, d. 564, l. 125.

206. Protocol 142, January 10, 1949, SAPMO-BA, ZPA, IV 2/2.025/2 (Sekretariat Otto Meier), b. 331

207. Pike, *The Politics of Culture,* pp. 620–621.

208. Dymshits to Pieck, December 26, 1955, TsGALI, f. 2843, op. 1, d. 451.

209. "Stenogramma soveshchaniia apparata Upravl. prop. SVAG . . . ," part 2, September 19, 1946, RTsKhIDNI, f. 17, op. 128, d. 150, l. 136.

210. SAPMO-BA, ZPA, IV 2/1/20 (Parteivorstand Protocol, February 11–12, 1948), b. 248. See also the very gloomy report on the mood of the intelligentsia in Cottbus, February 24, 1947, GARF, f. 7077, op. 1, d. 216, l. 16.

211. SAPMO-BA, ZPA, IV 2/1/20 (Parteivorstand Protocol, February 11–12, 1948), b. 245.

212. Paul Wandel, "Die Intellektuellen und die Partei," SAPMO-BA, ZPA, IV 2/1/20 (Parteivorstand Protocol, February 11–12, 1948), b. 86.

213. SAPMO-BA, ZPA, EA 1084/1 (Abusch), b. 78.

214. SAPMO-BA, ZPA, IV 906/109, b. 26.

215. Ibid., b. 31.

216. Heymann, "Vorschläge des Genossen Grotewohl zur Unterstützung der Intellektuellen," March 19, 1949, in ibid., b. 3.

217. Ibid., b 41.

218. Stefan Heymann, "Stellungnahme zur Durchführung der Kulturverordnung der DWK," in ibid., b. 73. On intellectuals leaving the zone, see ibid., b. 148.

219. "Tagung der Chefredakteure am 9. Juni 1949," SAPMO-BA, ZPA, IV 906/109 (Kultur), bb. 35–36.

220. Heymann, "Stellungnahme," in ibid., bb. 73–75.

221. Ibid., b. 56.

222. "Stand der Arbeitern bei der Durchführung der DWK-Verordnung zur Entwicklung der Kultur," May 17, 1949, Saxony, in ibid., b. 322.

223. Ibid., b. 324.

CONCLUSION

1. Wilfried Loth, *Stalin's ungeliebtes Kind* (Berlin: Rowohlt, 1994), p. 24.

Index

Abakumov, Viktor, 192–193, 348

Abendroth, Hermann, 431

Abortion, 121–125; and Catholic Church, 122; Nazi attitude to, 122; and rape victims, 122

Abramov, Colonel A., 340

Abusch, Alexander, 137, 402, 460, 461

Academy of Sciences (Berlin), 233, 234, 235, 436

Academy of Sciences (Moscow), 175, 178, 210, 235, 449, 450, 451

Ackermann, Anton, 10, 12, 18, 41, 42, 59, 60, 67, 131, 357, 439; on artists, 432; and collectivization, 162; and dismantling, 181–182; on division of Germany, 302; and intelligentsia, 462; and Junkers, 143; in Meissen, 266; and occupation of Germany, 257, 258, 259, 260, 265, 268, 291; and political parties, 277, 280, 303; and propaganda, 420, 423; and Red Army, 253; and reform of schools, 453; and Russians, 467; and theater, 426; and universities, 445–446, 447; visits to Moscow, 298

Administration for Soviet Property Abroad (Moscow), 192, 233

Administration for the Study of Science and Technology in Germany, 230, 231, 234

Akhmatova, Anna, 415, 425

Aleksandrov, G. F., 76, 77, 267, 324

All-German Writers' Congress, 412

Allied Control Council, 9, 21, 101, 340, 357, 375, 427; four-power consensus in, 465, 469; policy on abortion, 124; policy on rape victims, 127; and Soviet positions, 22, 51, 225, 306, 319

All-Union Society for Cultural Ties with Foreign Countries (VOKS), 411–416, 417, 418, 425, 427, 429, 432, 433

Almond, Gabriel, 120, 121–122

Alsos Mission, 207, 208, 236

American Combined Intelligence Objectives Subcommittee (CIOS), 215

Americans: compared with Russians, 103, 173, 175

Anticosmopolitan campaign, 32, 37, 40, 416

Antifascism, 75, 76, 77, 80, 89, 117, 132, 148; commandants and, 13, 15; definition of, 467; and expropriation, 183; and German occupation, 10, 41, 55, 94, 252, 253, 256, 257, 352, 470; and German workers, 67, 135–136; and intelligentsia, 464; and land reform, 154, 156, 157; and propaganda, 322, 324, 366; records of, 177. *See also* POW camps

Antifascist committees, 258, 259–260, 261, 262, 263, 264, 268, 270, 272

Antifascist Work Group of Central Germany (AAM), 263, 264–265

Ardenne, Manfred von, 210–211, 212, 213, 249

Art, 10, 37, 39, 432–434, 468; recapturing of Soviet, 175, 177; seizing of German, 175–178

Artiukhin, I. D., 457

Artsimovich, L. A., 210, 211, 212, 213

Association for Farmers' Mutual Help (VdgB), 52, 154–155, 162–163, 164, 165